THE WINSTON COMMENTARY
ON THE GOSPELS

Michael Fallon

Winston Press

By the same author:
At Home With God
Paul's Letters: An Introductory Commentary

Cover: "Supper at Emmaus" by Rembrandt van Rijn, by permission of
Scala/Editorial Photocolor Archives Inc., New York.

Quotations taken from the *Jerusalem Bible,* published and © 1966, 1967, and 1968
by Darton, Longman & Todd Ltd. and Doubleday & Co. Inc., are used by
permission of the publishers.

Library of Congress Catalog Card Number: 82-50295
ISBN: 0-86683-680-2 (previously ISBN: 0-909246-73-4)

Printed in the United States of America
5 4 3 2 1

Winston Press, Inc.
430 Oak Grove
Minneapolis, MN 55403

Introduction to the American Edition

At last we have a commentary on all four Gospels in one volume which is nontechnical, interesting to read, and based on sound, ecumenical biblical scholarship. It is a book that can be recommended to lay persons for enjoyment and educational enrichment. But clergy will also find it useful as a resource for preaching and teaching.

I am not aware of any other book quite like this one. There are introductory commentaries for individual Gospels, but this commentary treats all four comprehensively at an introductory level. The author provides the actual texts from the Gospels within the book. The reader is able to see both similarities and differences among the Gospels. The author goes on to comment on such matters and often explains why the differences exist. While he uses modern scholarly methods and results, he does not allow scholarship to be his focus. Attention is always on the biblical texts—just as it should be.

The attempt to do a commentary on all four Gospels simultaneously runs the risk of flattening out the distinctiveness of each Gospel. But Fallon has avoided harmonization and has succeeded in showing that each Gospel has its own special portrait of Jesus to present.

A particularly fine feature is the author's accent on the Old Testament background of motifs and scenes recorded in the Gospels, showing how this background has influenced the creation of the Gospels. This is in touch with some of the most lively and provocative work being done in Gospel research. Fallon brings this new emphasis into his work in a convincing manner.

Finally, the book contains an appendix for finding concise commentary on texts assigned in the three-year lectionary. Parish clergy of various denominations will discover that the book is a helpful resource, for both individual and group study, in preparation for preaching on Sundays and festivals of the church year. Occasionally the author adds points of reflection to aid individual study or group discussion.

This ecumenical, scholarly, and highly readable commentary is a fine companion for a fresh reading of the Gospels.

Arland J. Hultgren
Associate Professor of New Testament
Luther-Northwestern Theological Seminary
St. Paul, Minnesota

Contents

Page

PREFACE

BOOK 1: INTRODUCING JESUS
Chapter 1:   The beginning   9
Chapter 2:   The Gospel prologues
          I: Matthew's prologue   19
          II: Luke's prologue   30
          III: John's prologue   46
Chapter 3:   Jesus is the Son of God and our brother   57

BOOK 2: THE GOOD NEWS
          Ministry prior to Caesarea Philippi

Part One: God's healing and liberating word
Chapter 1:   Jesus' healing (life-giving) word   71
Chapter 2:   Matthew's presentation of Jesus' word:
          the 'Sermon on the Mount'   85
Chapter 3:   Jesus' liberating word   101
Chapter 4:   Matthew's presentation of Jesus as the alternative
          to the Law   113
Chapter 5:   John's reflections on the nature and implications of
          the new covenant   125
Note: Miracles in the Gospels   146

Part Two: God's powerful word
Chapter 1:   God's word is for all men   151
Chapter 2:   Luke's presentation of Jesus' word and his statement on
          the essence of Jesus' ministry   155
Chapter 3:   The power of God's word as illustrated in parables   169
Chapter 4:   No circumstances can withstand the powerful word of God 181

Part Three: Hearing and perceiving the word
Chapter 1:   The word of God continues to spread in spite of
          growing opposition   187
Chapter 2:   Only a miracle of grace can bring us to hear and
          understand the word of God   191
Chapter 3:   Only a miracle of grace can bring us to see and
          understand the word of God   201

BOOK 3: WHO IS JESUS?
          John's reflections on the question:
          "Who do you say I am?"
Chapter 1:   Jesus is the 'holy one of God' who gives the 'living bread'   209
Chapter 2:   Jesus, the 'Son' supersedes the Law   219

Chapter 3:   Jesus is 'one with the Father'. Man is judged by the stand
             he takes towards Jesus, who gives 'light' and 'life'   235
Chapter 4:   Jesus gives 'eternal life'   249

BOOK 4: THE JOURNEY OF THE DISCIPLE
            Journey to Jerusalem
Chapter 1:   The disciple is to follow Jesus on the road to the cross
             and the resurrection   257
Chapter 2:   Instructions for disciples
             I: Instructions for disciples in Mark and Matthew   265
             II: Instructions for disciples in Luke   268
             III: Further instructions for disciples   296
Chapter 3:   Discipleship is possible only because of a miracle of grace   309

BOOK 5: CONFRONTATION AND DECISION
            Ministry in Jerusalem
Chapter 1:   The final confrontation between Jesus and his opponents
             I: The synoptics   315
             II: John   336
Chapter 2:   The eschatological discourse   341
Chapter 3:   Jesus' last days   363

BOOK 6: FIDELITY TO LOVE
            *John's reflections on the meaning of Jesus' death
            and resurrection*
Chapter 1:   The last supper
             I: The last supper   377
             II: The first supper discourse   381
             III: The second supper discourse   389
             IV: The prayer of Jesus   400

BOOK 7: THE DEATH AND RESURRECTION OF JESUS
Chapter 1:   Jesus' passion and death   407
Chapter 2:   The empty tomb   431
Chapter 3:   The resurrection appearances   441

APPENDIX
A. The structure of the Gospel according to Mark   455
B. The structure of the Gospel according to Matthew   457
C. The structure of the Gospel according to Luke   460
D. The structure of the Gospel according to John   462
E. The Gospels used on Sundays and weekdays throughout the year   463

(After each chapter the reader will find some 'points for reflection'. They are not intended as comprehension questions, but rather as helps to meditation).

Preface

Our story is about a man called Jesus. He came from Nazareth, an out-of-the-way town in Galilee, and he was in his early thirties when he entered public life. His 'career' lasted only two or three years. In that short time he stirred something in people's hearts that they just could not forget. He sensed with intense accuracy the brooding dissatisfaction of his contemporaries, and he challenged them to stop living in fear — whether of man or of God. He urged them to stop hiding behind empty forms and to celebrate life through the wonder of simple prayer and love expressed in mutual service. His fearless preaching and his refusal to compromise brought him into conflict with those who exercised power in the land, both political and religious. After no more than two or three years of public life he was crucified just outside Jerusalem.

His death seemed to show him up as a dreamer, one in a long line of revolutionary idealists. His friends had been fools to listen to him. A beautiful dream it had been, but it was buried with him in the garden. Stunned, his followers dispersed, some back to their jobs in places like Emmaus, others back to fishing on the lake of Tiberias.

He had said that love was more powerful than hatred, than fear, than death. His own death seemed to prove him wrong.

But then something happened. Individuals among his followers, and groups of them together, had experiences that they could explain only as signs to them of his renewed presence among them. From a state of shock, they became convinced that he was still alive. And if he was still alive, then what he had said to them was indeed true after all; the hopes he had stirred in them were not vain. He, Jesus, had been right after all: man can be free; we do not need to act from fear; each of us can have a spring of living water welling up inside him; it is love that is all-important; life, whatever its mystery, does have a meaning; God is a Father; it is possible to live in such a way as to find peace and freedom and wisdom. A wave of excitement ran through that small group of friends. They re-grouped, and there began the amazing story of the Christian Church.

* * * * * * * *

The word spread. The quality of the lives led by these disciples of Jesus was very convincing. Many Jews joined the movement, and many non-Jews. Communities sprang up throughout the Eastern Empire and as far west as Rome and beyond. These very disparate groups were united by a way of life based on the memory of Jesus and sustained by faith in his active presence among them.

One of the foremost missionaries of that early period was Paul of Tarsus. We are fortunate to have a number of letters written by him in the 50's and early 60's. His ministry covered a period of some thirty years, so we cannot expect his few extant letters to give us a complete picture of his preaching, or of the ideas circulating during that period. But they give us some insight into the central ideas that inspired those early communities. Paul did not know Jesus personally, so his letters tell us very little about what Jesus said or did. They concentrate on the central facts of the crucifixion and resurrection, and on their meaning. The Cross stands as a complete statement of the kind of love that Jesus epitomised: a love given unto death, a commitment never taken back, an absolute trust. The Resurrection stands as a vindication of all that Jesus stood for and a proof of his continued active presence, challenging and sustaining his disciples.

If we want to learn something of the life of Jesus before the crucifixion, we have to look beyond Paul to the Gospels wherein we find the memories of those who knew Jesus during the time of his public ministry.

Memories have a life of their own. It is interesting that often, with the passage of time, happenings which may have gone practically unnoticed take on more and more significance for us, while others gradually fade into insignificance. We remember certain things because they somehow capture a special feeling, or symbolise certain central characteristics in a person we loved. Our experiences of a person, moreover, are coloured by our feelings, our expectations, and the whole cultural framework within which we live. When we come to communicate these experiences with others it is natural that we choose a language that will most effectively share with them what has moved us deeply. Similar processes were at work as the disciples of Jesus meditated on their memories of Jesus and tried to find words to express them.

Even a very cursory glance at the Gospels shows how thoroughly Jewish the language and outlook are. Jesus was seen by his contemporaries in the light of the hopes and aspirations expressed in the sacred literature of the Hebrews. When they came to express what Jesus had done, it was natural for them to use Biblical language to do so, and to use all the verve and imagination that attach themselves to a person who is a living legend.

It seems that the account of Jesus' death and resurrection found written form fairly early, no doubt as an aid to catechesis. The account of Jesus' death is surprisingly stark and matter-of-fact, but even here the story is illuminated by references to the prophetic writings. In this way the author shares the meditations of his community on the inner meaning of this death as a revelation of the fidelity of the God who had promised to manifest his love. The accounts of the resurrection, as we shall see, give expression to the wonder and surprise and mystery and excitement of that event, and form a magnificent tapestry, woven with exquisite art. The language is again the language of the Bible.

It is the same for the accounts of Jesus' ministry in Galilee and Judaea. If we read them hoping to find a simple straightforward empirical account of what Jesus said and did we are in for a disappointment. The accounts are highly ornate, for they aim to communicate the profound significance of what externally may have appeared very ordinary events, and they do this in the classical imagery of the sacred writings. The Gospels, in other words, are documents that express faith. They are carefully composed works of art that aim to communicate in the richest way possible the faith of those who knew Jesus personally and were deeply affected by his life.

In an age hungry for the miraculous, there was a danger in the use of such highly dramatic language. It was all right while there were disciples alive who remembered Jesus and knew the simplicity and 'ordinariness' of his life. But as these began to die it became obvious that a careful record would have to be written, placing the sayings of Jesus in the context of his life, and his actions in the context of his teaching. Otherwise both could easily be distorted. It was to meet this need that the Gospels were written.

The earliest of these — at least in the form we now have it — is associated with the name of Mark. He was a disciple of Peter and of Paul, both of whom possibly played a significant role in the work. Tradition has it that his Gospel reached its final form in Rome, probably sometime in the 60's.

Mark's task can be likened to that of an artist creating a mosaic from pieces of coloured glass. Before him lay hundreds of individual pieces: short sayings attributed to Jesus; various traditions of things he was remembered as doing during his life. Mark had to assemble them and arrange them in such a way as to draw out their inner meaning, and convey something of the wonder of the person who had captured the imagination and inspired the lives of so many. Mark's biography covers the last two or three years of Jesus' life culminating in his crucifixion. Mark does not concentrate, as a camera might, on the surface of things, but penetrates into the heart of the events of that time, drawing out their meaning for those who knew Jesus, by imaginative use of classical scriptural imagery. The fact that Matthew and Luke both based their Gospels on the work of Mark is indication of the esteem in which his Gospel was held.

There is a tradition that the first Gospel was written by Matthew, in Aramaic. The Gospel which we have, and which is associated with Matthew's name, was written in Greek. It basically follows Mark's pattern, but incorporates a lot of extra material, mainly sayings of Jesus. It may be that this extra material is drawn from an earlier Aramaic work by Matthew, thus accounting for its title. The Gospel associated with Matthew's name seems to have arisen in Jesus' own country or perhaps Antioch, the capital of Syria. It is addressed to a community that is largely Jewish-Christian, but has Gentile-Christian members. We will observe that the author demonstrates a special interest in the Law and in the Christian community as the fulfilment of the chosen people.

A third Gospel, relying heavily on Mark and drawing also on source material used by Matthew, is associated with Luke. Luke was not a Jew. He was a Gentile physician, probably from Antioch. He worked closely with Paul. It seems that he composed his Gospel, sometime in the seventies, for communities similar to those founded by Paul.

We have no way of knowing whether Luke wrote it himself, or whether it is the work of a later editor who used Luke's travelling diaries and notes. The structure of Luke's Gospel is quite different from that of Mark or Matthew. He also, in the second part of his work, known by us as the Acts of the Apostles, attempts for the first time a history of the first thirty years of the Church. This is in accordance with his explicit aim to establish some historical perspective both for Jesus himself, and for the Christian community.

The Gospels of Mark and Matthew and Luke, differing in approach and perspective, have very obvious similarities, even to having many identical sections. It is for this reason that they are often linked under the title of 'Synoptic Gospels'.

A cursory glance at the fourth Gospel — that associated with the name of John — shows that here we are dealing with a very different kind of work. John presumes the existence of the other Gospels and takes a small number of events from Jesus' public life and draws out their significance in lengthy and poetic meditations. These are composed as discourses of Jesus. They are possibly taken from John's homilies and are his attempt to penetrate into the heart of the Jesus he knew. The Gospel, then, is made up largely of John's reflections on the thoughts and attitudes of the man he loved. Tradition has it that this Gospel grew out of the experiences of the communities around Ephesus where John spent most of his life.

* * * * * * * *

These four documents are about Jesus; especially about what he has to say about God. The very word, 'God', expresses something of the mystery at the heart of man's religious search. It means 'the called one' (Sanskrit 'ghu-to'), God is the one we call. We do not see his face; we do not hear his voice; yet we sense his presence at the heart of our lives, calling us. And we call on him. Men have always wanted to name him. Those who knew Jesus heard him name him 'Father'. They sensed at the heart of Jesus' actions and words a very intimate union with God and a special insight into the meaning of life. He led them along a way to the Father. He became for them the key to the mystery of life and they chose to follow him in their journey to God.

They were constrained to share their experience with others. Paul wrote once to his friends in Corinth:

'It is the same God that said, "Let there be light shining out of darkness" who has shone in our minds to radiate the light of the knowledge of God's glory, the glory on the face of Christ.'

(2 Corinthians 4:6)

When those who knew Jesus looked on his face, they saw there the glory of God. When they listened to his words, they heard the voice of God. When they were encouraged by his love, they knew that it was God who was drawing them.

It is this religious experience that is at the centre of the Gospels. Our aim in this book is to study these documents carefully, the better to share the experience that they express. It is our hope that we, too, by seeing the face of Jesus, might come to experience the glory of God. Without this desire, any knowledge we might gain would simply clutter our minds. The Gospels are religious documents and can be read only by one willing to undertake a sacred journey. Perhaps you and I may be able to give God a name, from ourselves. Perhaps we too will learn to call him 'Father'. Perhaps we too will learn to be disciples of Jesus and so live lives that will manifest God's wisdom and love. We, too, may learn that it is possible, as men, to live as the 'Son of Man' lived: a life of freedom and loving service, born of an intimate union with God.

* * * * * * * *

From what we have said, the reader must be careful not to read the Gospels with the same expectations he might have of a carefully documented and historically accurate modern biography. The Gospels are historically accurate in that they are based on a real person, Jesus of Nazareth, and relate what he actually said and actually did and the actual impression he made on his contemporaries. But they are written according to the manner of writing of the time. Their aim — and they have this in common with historical writings of all ages — was to communicate the significance of their subject. But they were not aiming to write as unbiased observers to unbiased observers. They were written by communities for whom Jesus was of central importance and they were written to share this faith and this enthusiasm. They were written to inspire and uplift. They were written with conscious reference to the central themes and imagery of the Bible. Moreover — and this is central to the way we are to read these documents — they were written not to have accurate archives, accurate memories of a dead leader; they were written within communites that believed that Jesus was alive, in the glory of the Father, and actively present in their midst through his spirit. Thus, while the Gospels were written to give an accurate picture of Jesus of Nazareth, and while they are based on real events of his public life, they were written primarily with the glorified Jesus in mind. They were written to aid the communities in their prayer by bringing them into living contact with the risen Jesus. There is a link, therefore, between the language of the liturgical prayer of the church and the language used in the narratives of the Gospel.

When Matthew tells us of the blind men of Jericho who were cured by Jesus, he is, no doubt basing his narrative on some event from Jesus' life (Matthew 20:29-34, compare Mark 10:46-52 and Luke 18:35-43). But when he has them use three times the expression 'Kyrie' of Jesus, and twice has them plead 'Kyrie eleison' — the language is the language of the liturgy of Matthew's community. Each time the community met and prayed 'Kyrie eleison': 'Lord, have mercy', they would have thought of this scene and of their own blindness and would have pleaded with the living Jesus present among them to give them sight as he gave it once to the men of Jericho. The same could be said of every scene of the Gospel. The language is living language written within a living community and about a living Jesus. Its primary aim is to bring the reader, via the medium of memory, into living contact with the risen Jesus.

If we keep this in mind the Gospels may be for us too the medium through which we are touched by the living word of God. Seen in the reflection of the light of the Gospel, our lives too may be seen to be touched by him; we, too, may have the Good News preached to us as we read. My task is to help you read the words as they were read by those who first used them; your task is to bring to the reading your whole life and be prepared for a journey of faith.

The church has always believed these documents to be inspired: The Spirit of God breathed through the writers, providentially directing them in their composition; the same Spirit breathes through the documents, guaranteeing to bring the open-hearted and humble reader into contact with the risen Jesus as he reflects upon these words from within the praying communion of the community of Jesus' followers. May the same God inspire us as we journey together in this study.

A warning

Some of us may have been in the habit of reading the Gospels superficially. For example, we have read in Mark's account of the death of Jesus that, when Jesus breathed his last, 'the veil of the Temple was torn in two from top to bottom' (Mark 15:38). At most we probably thought of this as some miraculous happening that occurred when Jesus died, but we saw no relationship between the veil and the death. Mark, as we understood it, was simply relating another fact for posterity.

With some study, prayer and reflection, we can come to understand the significance of the veil for the Jewish mind. It demonstrates the fact that no man can see God and live (Exodus 33:30). The veil was an architectural symbol, reflecting the faith of the people that the face of God was veiled. With this knowledge we can come to see that there is an intimate connection between the tearing of the veil and the death of Jesus. In fact, the tearing of the veil is a physical statement and reflection of the fact that now, at last, God's face has been revealed. We, like the centurion, can, in looking upon the face of Jesus, see the face of God. We, in contemplating Jesus' love and fidelity unto death, can see, at last, that God, the hidden God, is love. What has happened is that we have come to see the tearing of the veil as a symbol. Just as Jesus himself is a symbol of God, revealing God in everything he said and did, so all the events of his life as recorded in the sacred words of the Gospels are manifestations of the mystery of God.

So far, so good. Discoveries like the above are exciting and beautiful and open up the Gospels to deeper prayer and a fuller penetration into the mystery of God. But, almost automatically, a question rises in our mind: did the veil actually tear, or is that Mark's way of telling us that we can see God's face in Jesus' death? In other words, are Mark's words simply descriptive of what happened, (and what happened is a symbol), or are Mark's words themselves creative and symbolic? This is a fair question.

Man can create symbols. Made in the likeness of God, man is able to create, through art, things which reflect and manifest the divine. The Temple and the veil are themselves examples of man's creative and religious genius. He can use words, too, for this purpose, and create stories which express God's revelation and link the reader with the divine. This is the essence of all mythology, and we have learned to read, for example, the first eleven chapters of the Book of Genesis in this light. These are Biblical myths, expressing in story form, the profound religious insights of the people of God into matters such as creation, sin, the dignity of man and woman, and the way a man can reach intimacy with God. A myth, as the word denotes, is a veil — a veil in words. But it is a veil which reveals the divine.

We can find simpler examples in the parables of Jesus. When Jesus wished to communicate his experience of God as 'Father' he created the story of the prodigal son (Luke 15:11-32). The father is a creation of Jesus' artistic mind and heart; he is a symbol of God.

Let us return to the example of the veil of the Temple. Our question concerns the way Mark is using words. Is he using words descriptively? If so, he is simply telling us that the veil was torn from top to bottom, and the tearing of the veil is a symbol of God revealing his face. Or is Mark using words symbolically? If so, he is not stating that, as a fact the veil was torn (any more than the author of Genesis is telling us that, as a fact, Eve comes from Adam's rib). Rather, Mark is using a powerful, traditional symbol to tell us that the face of God was revealed when Jesus died.

The question seems to me to be a good one. It also seems to me that it is not possible, from the evidence we have, to give a certain answer. To say that the veil was torn because Mark said it was torn, is, it seems to me, to ignore the poetry, and the creative use of language that we use in our ordinary daily lives to express anything that is wonderful and mysterious and beautiful. The Bible is full of symbolic language. On the other hand to say that the veil was not torn is to go beyond the evidence we have and to limit the possibilities of God's miraculous action in our world.

In either case — and this is the main point of these remarks — we should not stay on the surface; and once we go beneath the surface, the problem falls into perspective and becomes scarcely significant. It is like the story of the finger pointing to the moon. We need the finger, but our attention should go to the moon. If the veil was torn (=the finger), Mark is recording the fact so that we may see God's face revealed in the face of Jesus (=the moon). If Mark is using words symbolically (=the finger), he is doing so in order that we may see God's face revealed in the face of Jesus (=the moon). The reader will see that the moon is the same in either case. To argue about the finger is, perhaps, to be distracted from what Mark is saying.

Ultimately, our faith rests on fact: the fact of Jesus and the fact of what he said and did and what happened to him. But in the telling of that fact, the Gospel authors express years of prayerful reflection, and use the powerful symbolic language of the Bible. There will be times when we are not sure whether the writer is using words descriptively or symbolically. But it is my conviction that, if we approach the sacred text in a prayerful and honest way, we will come to share the faith of the author and his vision of the person who inspired that faith. We will also come to 'the light of the knowledge of God's glory, the glory on the face of Christ' (2 Corinthians 4:6).

* * * * * * * *

Guide to the Typographical Treatment of the Gospel Texts

Let us look at a typical example (from page 177)

MARK 4:30-32 *(Compare Matthew 13:31-32)*

> He also said, 'What can we say the kingdom of God is like? What parable can we find for it? It is like a mustard seed which at the time of its sowing in the soil is the smallest of all the seeds on earth; yet once it is sown it grows into the biggest shrub of them all and puts out big branches so that the birds of the air can shelter in its shade'.
>
> *(Compare Luke 13:18-19 page 283)*

The following are to be noted:

1: **MARK 4:30-32**
   The text actually quoted is indicated by the large bold type.

2: *(Compare Matthew 13:31-32)*
   The bracketed reference above the text indicates:

   a: That Matthew has a statement sufficiently similar both in content and in context to make the commentary on Mark cover also the Matthew text.

   b: The Matthew text, in this case, is not quoted (otherwise this book would be too bulky for its purpose).

   c: If I have judged that there is a difference in the texts that merits attention, I have drawn this to the reader's notice in the commentary.

   d: On the rare occasions where the text referred to is quoted elsewhere in the book, the page reference is given (cf page 86: Luke 6:20-26 page 156).

3: *(Compare Luke 13:18-19 page 283)*
   The bracketed reference below the text indicates:

   a: That Luke has a statement similar in content to Mark, but in another context.

   b: Luke's text is quoted in Luke's context on the page indicated and has its own commentary there.

4: Sometimes (not in the example used) the quoted text refers to the Old Testament. When this occurs (e.g. page 9 Malachi 3:1 and Isaiah 40:3) the references are placed in brackets at the foot of the quoted text.

BOOK 1

Introducing Jesus

FOREWORD

The Gospel-writers set out to communicate to their readers knowledge of the life and teachings of Jesus, and the significance of these for the Christian communities. Recognising the importance of creating perspective for their readers, they chose to set the stage carefully.

As early as 48 A.D., at the Assembly in Jerusalem (cf Acts 15 and Galatians 2), the Church acknowledged officially that Christianity was not a branch of Judaism. It was not necessary to be a Jew to be a follower of Jesus. It was one of Paul's central tasks to convince his hearers, who were largely non-Jews, that the Jesus he spoke of could have meaning for their lives, their history, their culture. At the same time the fact is that Jesus was a Jew. He was part of the history of the Jewish nation. His early followers were Jews and it was by reflection on the sacred literature of the Jews that they found the words to express best their experience of him. Each of the Gospel-writers chose to begin his work by placing Jesus in the context of the religious experience of Judaism. We shall examine this in Chapters One and Two of this Book.

Moreover, each of the Gospel-writers wished his readers to see in what Jesus said and did the words and actions of one in whom God's Spirit was active. To listen to Jesus was to listen to God; to watch Jesus was to watch God. At the same time, the Jesus they knew was not some kind of divine being visiting this earth, though not himself part of it. He was flesh, like us; like us he was born of woman; like us he suffered and was tempted. The wonder of his life was that, unlike us, he did not sin, but was perfectly open to the Spirit of God. We shall examine this in Chapter Three of this Book.

Note: There is a direct sequence from Chapter One (which deals with John the Baptist) and Chapter Three (which deals with Jesus' baptism and temptations). The reader may prefer to follow this sequence and leave Chapter Two (which deals with the Prologues to Matthew's, Luke's and John's Gospels) for later reading. Being introductions, the Prologues are tightly written and differ considerably in style from the rest of the Gospels. Most readers would find it too difficult to read the three Prologues one after the other, and I cannot see any particular merit in trying to do so.

On the other hand, if a reader is interested in following a particular Gospel-writer (e.g. Luke), I suggest he read Luke's Prologue first, as Luke intends it as an Introduction to suggest important themes he wishes to develop and to create the atmosphere in which he wants the reader to proceed.

Chapter 1
The Beginning

John the Baptist heralds the coming of One who is to fulfil the Messianic hopes of Israel.

Mark 1:1-8
Matthew 3:1-12
Luke 1:1-4 and 3:1-20
John 1:6-8, 15, 19-28

MARK 1:1-8 (Compare Matthew 3:1-6 and Luke 3:3-6, 15-18)[1]

1 The beginning of the Good News about Jesus Christ, the Son of God. •It is ½ written in the book of the prophet Isaiah:

> *Look, I am going to send my messenger before you;*
> *he will prepare your way.*
> *A voice cries in the wilderness:* 3
> *Prepare a way for the Lord,*
> *make his paths straight,*[a]

and so it was that John the Baptist appeared in the wilderness, proclaiming 4 a baptism of repentance for the forgiveness of sins. •All Judaea and all the people 5 of Jerusalem made their way to him, and as they were baptised by him in the river Jordan they confessed their sins. •John wore a garment of camel-skin, and 6 he lived on locusts and wild honey. •In the course of his preaching he said, 7 'Someone is following me, someone who is more powerful than I am, and I am not fit to kneel down and undo the strap of his sandals. •I have baptised you 8 with water. but he will baptise you with the Holy Spirit.'

(a: Malachi 3:1 and Isaiah 40:3)

Mark's opening sentence constitutes a powerful beginning to his Gospel. The 'beginning' reminds us of the first words of the Book of Genesis:

'In the beginning God created the heavens and earth'

(Genesis 1:1)

Mark is preparing us for a new beginning, a new creation. Mark's news is 'Good News' and it centres on a person called 'Jesus'. Immediately, Mark attributes to Jesus two titles, 'Christ' and 'Son of God'. Both titles carried immense weight for anyone familiar with Jewish history.

---

1. The reader is referred to the important note concerning the set-out of the texts in this book (page 8).

Chrism was used as a refreshing unguent. It was the base of various perfumes, including myrrh and nard. It was used to make a person's face shine, and was associated with joy and festive celebrations. It had a special cultic use in the coronation of the king. The Spirit of God was seen as anointing the king as the chrism flowed over his head and beard. The anointed king radiated the glory of God throughout the kingdom. He was a 'Christ' — an anointed one.

We read of David:

'Yahweh said: Come, anoint him, for this is the one. At this, Samuel took the horn of oil, and anointed him where he stood with his brothers; and the Spirit of Yahweh seized on David and stayed with him from that day on.'

(1 Samuel 16:12-13)

In different ways, chrism was associated also with the consecration of the High Priest and the prophets. These sacred men were instruments of God. Through them, God permeated the land, like a perfume, with the glory of his presence.

The kings, priests and prophets were, however, imperfect men, and the people hoped that one day the Spirit of God would come down on a man and fill him with God's glory. This man would be *the* Christ. He would be the one to bring about the final fulfilment of God's promises. Through him, the Spirit of God would permeate the nation and the whole world. In his day the kingdom of God would be achieved. Mark is claiming that the Jesus of whom he is about to write is 'the Christ'.

The title 'Son of God' was also used, especially, of the descendants of the royal line of David (cf 1 Chronicles 17:10-14). The title took on a deeper significance for the disciples of Jesus after his resurrection as they meditated on the special relationship that existed between Jesus and God, his Father. As the title is used here at the beginning of the Gospel, it is a claim that Jesus is the royal Messiah, inheritor of the promises made to David.

*   *   *   *   *   *   *   *

Mark goes on to introduce John the Baptist. But before doing so he establishes the perspective from which he wishes the reader to look at John. He does this by combining two texts from the Bible. The first is from the prophecy of Malachi (3:1):

'Look, I am going to send my messenger to prepare a way before me.'

The messenger, as is clear from a later statement of Malachi (3:23) is the prophet Elijah. According to the legends of 2 Kings 2:1-18, Elijah, the greatest of the prophets, had been taken alive to God in a fiery chariot. Malachi's prophecy witnesses to an expectation among the people that one day Elijah would return and would usher in the Messianic Age. Mark wants his readers to see John as the fulfilment of this expectation, for he is the herald proclaiming the coming of Jesus, the Messiah. Mark reinforces this by referring to John's dress (1:6) in words that remind the reader of the dress of Elijah (cf 2 Kings 1:8).

The second text is from the Book of Consolation (Isaiah 40-55), written by disciples of Isaiah on the occasion of the return of the Jews from the exile in Babylon (587-537 B.C.).

'A voice cries, Prepare in the wilderness a way for Yahweh.
Make a straight highway for God across the desert.'

(Isaiah 40:3)

The language is the language of the Exodus (Exodus 14-15), recalling the great act of liberation when God, through Moses, led his people from slavery in Egypt, across the desert to the Promised Land. The event referred to in the text, however, occurred seven centuries later. Jerusalem had been destroyed by the Babylonians and the people of God found themselves, once again, in exile. Then Cyrus of Persia conquered Babylon and issued an edict allowing the Jews to return to their homeland and rebuild their city. As they prepared to make the journey across the desert, back to the Promised Land, they thought naturally of their forefathers and the first Exodus. Once again, Yahweh was liberating his people.

Mark wants his readers to remember that liberation, and that journey, for he wants to present John the Baptist as the herald of the one who is to be the new Moses, leading his people through the desert to their final home. This seems to have been one of the earliest ways of looking at Jesus (compare Hebrews 2:10).

John the Baptist, then, is introduced by Mark as the herald of the Messiah, preparing the people for a journey through the desert, by:

'proclaiming a baptism of repentance for the forgiveness of sins.'

(Mark 1:4)

The word 'baptism' means 'drowning'. The image is of being overwhelmed by water. The Jews were a land people and water was seen, primarily, as a symbol of chaos and destruction. This is clear from the accounts of creation and the flood in the Book of Genesis. The Bible frequently refers to suffering and death in terms of being overwhelmed by the waters. The Baptist asked the people to go down into the river and experience physically what it was like to be overwhelmed ('baptised') and then to come out of the waters to a new life. The imagery of crossing the Red Sea is also part of the symbolism of the act, as is the symbolism of water as a cleansing agent (compare Leviticus 14-15 for ritual acts of purification). It was customary to baptise proselytes (Gentile converts). What is special to John is that he is baptising Jews, asserting, thereby, that being a Jew is not enough, but that they need complete purification.

The Baptist called them to 'repentance'. The word used by Mark is the Greek word 'metanoia' and it denotes a 'change of mind', or a 'change of heart' (cf English word 'nous'). Established religious groups were calling the people in all kinds of directions. The Sadducees (cf page 12) called them to cultic exactitude and fidelity to tradition. The Pharisees (cf page 12) called them to a meticulous observance of the Law. The Zealots (cf page 40) called for violent overthrow of the Roman occupation. The Essenes called for a withdrawal from the darkness of the world. The Baptist, on the contrary, called for a new way of looking at life, a new vision (cf Proverbs 29:18). We are reminded of the call given by the prophet Ezekiel, who, looking forward to God's new covenant with men, wrote:

'I shall pour clean water over you and you shall be cleansed . . .
I shall give you a new heart and put a new spirit in you'.

(Ezekiel 36:25)

All of this was in view of 'forgiveness' (that is 'release', 'liberation') from 'sin'. The Greek word is 'hamartia', and it means 'missing the mark'. One might think of archery, and imagine someone continually missing the target. John the Baptist could see that his contemporaries were 'missing the mark'. They were overwhelmed by all kinds of oppression and were slaves to hypocrisy and mere external religious practice. John wanted them to recognise their need for a journey, and for someone to lead them on this journey to freedom.

John knew that it was not his part to lead them. He was the herald, dramatising their needs through the action of baptising them in water. He told them of 'someone' (1:7), the 'powerful one' who would follow him, and who would:

'baptise you with the Holy Spirit'

(Mark 1:8)

This one, the anointed one, the 'Christ', would be their leader (cf Hebrews 2:10). He would take them on a journey away from 'sin' and towards the holy God. He would anoint them with God's own Spirit.

*   *   *   *   *   *   *   *

Matthew, after a lengthy Prologue which will be the subject of the first part of Chapter Two of this book, opens his Gospel with the same scene. With slight variations, he quotes Mark and then adds the following:

MATTHEW 3:7-12 (Compare Luke 3:7-9)

•But when he saw a 7 number of Pharisees and Sadducees coming for baptism he said to them, 'Brood of vipers, who warned you to fly from the retribution that is coming? 8 But if you are repentant, produce the appropriate fruit, •and do not presume to 9 tell yourselves, "We have Abraham for our father", because, I tell you, God can raise children for Abraham from these stones. •Even now the axe is laid to the roots 10 of the trees, so that any tree which fails to produce good fruit will be cut down and thrown on the fire. •I baptise you in water for repentance, but the one who 11 follows me is more powerful than I am, and I am not fit to carry his sandals; he will baptise you with the Holy Spirit and fire.   •His winnowing-fan is in his hand; 12 he will clear his threshing-floor and gather his wheat into the barn; but the chaff he will burn in a fire that will never go out.'

The Sadducees were members of the leading high-priestly families. They were the aristocracy of their time and saw themselves as upholders of the ancient tradition. Their importance can be traced to the period following the exile (that is, about 500 B.C.). At this time there was no king in Judah and the Persian overlords took to dealing directly with the High Priest. For the Jews there was no real distinction between civil matters and religious matters, and it comes as no surprise that the priestly aristocrats gradually assumed power. In the time of Jesus the Sadducees were a very influential group in the supreme Jewish Council (the 'Sanhedrin') set up by the Romans to administer Jewish affairs in Judaea.

The Pharisees were also represented in the Sanhedrin. They were laymen, and traced their origins to the 'Hasidim' — a group of national purists who strenuously withstood the cultural oppression of the Hellenist overlords and led a successful war of independence from 186 to 183 B.C. (cf the Books of the Maccabees).

Matthew mentions both groups here, for they are to play central roles in his drama. The Sadducees, in the name of tradition, had gone a long way towards using religion as a tool to support their own power in the community. The Pharisees, in the name of religious purity, had trapped themselves and their disciples in the external minutiae of the Law. Both groups had largely lost what was at the heart of their religious tradition and Matthew portrays them as the ones primarily responsible for the rejection of Jesus.

The Baptist was a prophet. He stood out against both these groups. He could see the approach of God's judgement and speaks of it in terms of a raging forest fire before which the serpents are forced to flee. Perhaps, like Jesus after him, the Baptist could foresee the coming holocaust of the war with Rome. Whatever form he imagined the judgement taking, he saw the solution not in terms of institutionalised power (the Sadducees), nor in term of meticulous fidelity to the Law (the Pharisees), but in terms of each person repenting (Matthew 3:8); that is, he called for a change of **heart** on the part of the people. Like the prophets of old he called for action, for 'appropriate fruit' (3:8). One thinks of Isaiah 58 where the action called for is the action of witnessing to the fidelity and love of God primarily by concern for the poor. The established groups think they will be saved just by being children of Abraham. The Baptist rejects this by a play on words lost in English ('children' in Hebrew is 'banim'; 'stones' is 'abanim', Matthew 3:9). According to John, the only way to avoid the coming judgement is to effectively realise in their lives the covenant they have with God (cf also Matthew 21:43).

* * * * * * * *

Luke opens his Gospel with the following statement:

LUKE 1:1-4
1 Seeing that many others have undertaken to draw up accounts of the events 1
   that have taken place among us, ·exactly as these were handed down to us by 2
those who from the outset were eyewitnesses and ministers of the word, ·I in my 3
turn, after carefully going over the whole story from the beginning, have decided
to write an ordered account for you, Theophilus, ·so that your Excellency may 4
learn how well founded the teaching is that you have received.

Luke's opening paragraph introduces us to a careful historian, determined to be faithful to his sources. His main source seems to be Mark's Gospel. We will see that another source contains material also used by Matthew.

Luke follows this paragraph with his Prologue, which we shall study in the following chapter. He then joins Mark in introducing the Baptist. He reproduces Mark, and also the additions we have just studied in Matthew. As part of his 'ordered account' (Luke 1:3), he places Jesus in his historical setting, in the following section:

1: LUKE 3:1-2
3 In the fifteenth year of Tiberius Caesar's reign, when Pontius Pilate was 1
   governor of Judaea, Herod tetrarch of Galilee, his brother Philip tetrarch
of the lands of Ituraea and Trachonitis, Lysanias tetrarch of Abilene, during 2
the pontificate of Annas and Caiaphas, the word of God came to John son of
Zechariah, in the wilderness.   3

The time is the fifteenth year of the reign of Tiberias Caesar; that is, 782 A.U.C. (from the founding of the city of Rome. By our reckoning, 28-29 A.D.).

The place is Palestine, a region attached to the Roman Province of Syria. For administrative purposes it was divided into four areas, governed by tetrarchs. Lysanias administered the northernmost area, bordering Lebanon. The other three were, on the death of Herod the Great (4 B.C.), administered by his three sons, Archelaus, Herod Antipas and Herod Philip. Archelaus administered the most important area, comprising Judaea, Samaria and Idumaea till he was ousted by the Romans who took direct control in 6 A.D. They appointed their own procurator and had a garrison of soldiers at Caesarea. Internal religious affairs were placed under the authority of the Sanhedrin, under the presidency of the High Priest. While Caiaphas was officially High Priest during the time of Jesus' public ministry, the real power seems to have been still in the hands of his father-in-law, Annas.

To his account of the Baptist, Luke adds the following passage:

LUKE 3:10-14

10
11   When all the people asked him, 'What must we do, then?' •He answered, 'If anyone has two tunics he must share with the man who has none, and the
12   one with something to eat must do the same'. •There were tax collectors too
13   who came for baptism, and these said to him, 'Master, what must we do?' •He
14   said to them, 'Exact no more than your rate'. •Some soldiers asked him in their turn, 'What about us? What must we do?' He said to them, 'No intimidation! No extortion! Be content with your pay!'

These practical admonitions tell us very little about the content of the Baptist's ethical teaching. But they do give us a hint of the direction he took: they are concerned with social justice, and with care for the needy.

We may also have an indication here of why it was that Jesus aligned himself with John and not with other groups of his society. Jesus did this, as we shall see, by being baptised by John. Jesus also was concerned with a change of heart, and his ministry centred on practical and prayerful love, especially in regard to the oppressed groups in society.

Finally, before mentioning the Baptism of Jesus, Luke adds the following detail:

LUKE 3:19-20

19   But Herod the tetrarch, whom he criticised for his relations with his brother's
20   wife Herodias and for all the other crimes Herod had committed, •added a further crime to all the rest by shutting John up in prison.

It is clear from a reading of the other Gospels (e.g. Mark 1:9, 14) that John's imprisonment came somewhat later. Luke, in writing his 'ordered account' is not concerned with chronological accuracy. As a historian he is interested in the development of God's plan of salvation, and he wishes to highlight the distinct roles played in it by the Old Testament prophets, the Baptist, Jesus, the Apostolic community and the early church. He therefore completes his treatment of John before going on to introduce Jesus.

* * * * * * * *

John's Gospel opens with a short Prologue, which we shall study in the following chapter. Woven into this Prologue there are two statements concerning John the Baptist. We shall reproduce them here:

1: **JOHN 1:6-8**
A man came, sent by God.
His name was John.
7 He came as a witness,
as a witness to speak for the light,
so that everyone might believe through him.
8 He was not the light,
only a witness to speak for the light.

2: **JOHN 1:15**
15 John appears as his witness. He proclaims:
'This is the one of whom I said:
He who comes after me
ranks before me
because he existed before me'.

The style is rather more poetic, but the main impression is identical with that given by the Synoptics. The enigmatic statement 'because he existed before me' (1:15) will be commented on when we examine the Prologue (pages 50-55).

John then draws on the synoptic tradition for the following:

JOHN 1:19-28
19   This is how John appeared as a witness. When the Jews sent priests and
20 Levites from Jerusalem to ask him, 'Who are you?' •he not only declared, but
21 he declared quite openly, 'I am not the Christ'. •'Well then,' they asked 'are you
22 Elijah?' 'I am not' he said. 'Are you the Prophet?' He answered, 'No'. •So they
   said to him, 'Who are you? We must take back an answer to those who sent us.
23 What have you to say about yourself?' •So John said, 'I am, as Isaiah prophesied:

   a voice that cries in the wilderness:
   Make a straight way for the Lord' [a]

24/25 Now these men had been sent by the Pharisees, •and they put this further
   question to him, 'Why are you baptising if you are not the Christ, and not Elijah
26 and not the prophet?' •John replied, 'I baptise with water; but there stands
27 among you—unknown to you—•the one who is coming after me; and I am
28 not fit to undo his sandal-strap'. •This happened at Bethany, on the far side of
   the Jordan, where John was baptising.

                                                                (a: Isaiah 40:3)

Throughout John's Gospel we will notice an unusual use of the term 'the Jews'. Here (1:19), John is referring, as he tells us himself, to the 'Pharisees' (1:24); but it is an unexpected way of referring to them, since almost all of the characters in the Gospel are 'Jews'. There is quite a deal of hostility between Jesus and his disciples on the one hand and 'the Jews' òn the other (cf John 5:16-18, 8:44, 48, 15:24). The term cannot simply be a way of speaking of the religious authorities who rejected Jesus. It is more likely that we have here an insight into the history of the community within which the Gospel is being written.

The Gospel itself refers to the fact that the followers of Jesus were expelled by the Jews from the synagogue (John 9:22, 16:2). We know from the Acts of the Apostles that Stephen was stoned by the Jews (Acts 7:58-60), that the Christians were persecuted in Jerusalem by the Jews and that James, the brother of John, was martyred under them (Acts 12:2-3). There is also evidence from early historical sources that Christians were handed over to the secular Roman authorities by Jews who were offended by what they considered blasphemy. As John himself reports in his Gospel:

'the Jews began to persecute Jesus . . . because, not content with breaking the sabbath, he spoke of God as his own Father, and so made himself God's equal.'

(John 5:18)

We will see, when introducing John's Prologue, that the community within which John's Gospel was written stressed the divinity of Jesus, with the consequent danger of neglecting his humanity. It may well be that this brought them into special conflict with the Jews who were faithful to their monotheism and who, perhaps inevitably, were offended by the language being used to describe the founder of the Christians. Perhaps the use of the term 'the Jews' in John's Gospel represents a simplistic generalisation reflecting the experience of the community at the hands of the Jews. Unfortunately, throughout history, the Gospel of John especially has been used as a support for anti-Semitism, reversing the experience of the first two centuries when Christianity was a minority faith and a persecuted one. Statement's made of 'the Jews' in John's Gospel need to be read within the limits of that community's experience, and read carefully at that.

John is careful to have the Baptist reject any claim that he is the Christ (1:20). As we shall see later, it appears that some of the followers of the Baptist were making this claim for their leader. Perhaps the allusions made by both Mark and Matthew to the prophet Elijah had led to some confusion, for John has the Baptist stating explicitly that he is not Elijah (1:21). He also rejects the claim that he is the Prophet (1:22). The reference is to the promise made by Moses:

'Yahweh your God will raise up for you a prophet like myself from among yourselves, from your own brothers; to him you must listen.'

(Deuteronomy 18:15)

The 'Christ', the 'Prophet' is not the Baptist; it is the 'one coming after' (John 1:27). This humility of the Baptist before Jesus is developed by John later in his Gospel (cf John 3:29-36, page 133).

* * * * * * *

After this brief scene focussing on John the Baptist, each of the Gospel-writers immediately introduces Jesus himself. However, as we have already mentioned, three of them, Matthew, Luke and John, have Prologues at the beginning of their Gospels. It is to these that we shall now turn our attention.

* * * * * * *

Points for Reflection:

1: Jesus brought something 'new' to his contemporaries (Mark 1:1). Am I open to the surprise he brings me each time we meet? How is the news he brings me and the people I live with 'Good'?

2: Jesus fulfilled the hopes and aspirations of his people (Mark 1:1). What in my past does he complete? What elements in the lives of my contemporaries does he bring to fulfilment?

3: To be prepared for the coming of Jesus, the Baptist demanded a 'change of mind and heart' (Mark 1:4). What new outlook, what new perspective does Jesus bring to my life? How does being a disciple of Jesus affect the way I look on God, on myself, on my fellow man, on society and its values, on history?

4: Jesus brought the gift of the Holy Spirit (Mark 1:8). How does the Spirit of God manifest his presence and power in the community to which I belong? How have I been overwhelmed (baptised) by God's love?

5: Those with most vested interests in religion did not accept Jesus (Matthew 3:7). What about my religious practices and the practices of my church? Are they expressions of a living faith? Are they constantly open to the new movements of God's living Spirit? Are they barriers, on the other hand, to God's word? May I too be resisting God's love in the name of religion?

6: The Baptist demanded that repentance be sincere and that it manifest itself by people producing the appropriate fruit (Matthew 3:8). Paul lists some of the fruits of the Spirit in his Letter to the Galatians (5:22-24). I too should be able to wonder at the transforming activity of the Holy Spirit in my life and in the life of the community of which I am part. If not, how real is Jesus to me?

7: Jesus is not the preserve of one race or nation or religious heritage (Luke 3:38). How careful am I not to impose 'my' faith on others? How much of our religious practice is truly from the Spirit of God, and how much is simply an expression, however beautiful, of a certain limited culture?

8: How often do I 'listen to him' (Deuteronomy 18:15 cf John 1:21) in prayer?

9: Am I willing to take the risk of journeying with Jesus across the desert? If not, is it wise to read on?

Chapter 2
The Gospel Prologues

We saw that Mark wished to introduce Jesus by setting him against the background of the history of the Jewish people. The other Gospel-writers followed Mark in this, but, as we shall see in this present chapter, they did it in a more elaborate way by writing a Prologue as a kind of backdrop to their Gospel narratives. We will see that in these Prologues they highlight in highly poetic and dramatic language some of the themes that are going to be central to their Gospels. The Prologues result from many years of meditation on the significance of Jesus and demand a special kind of attention from the reader.

I: **MATTHEW'S PROLOGUE** (Chapters 1 — 2)

Before looking at Matthew's text, let us examine a form of writing called 'midrash', because Matthew is going to make extensive use of it in his Prologue. ✓

Prior to the Exile in Babylon (587 B.C.) Jesus' ancestors spoke Hebrew and Hebrew was the language of their sacred texts. In Babylon they learned another Semitic language, called Aramaic. As this remained the lingua franca of the Persian Empire during the fifth and fourth centuries before Christ, the Jews continued to use it on their return from exile and it gradually superseded Hebrew in popular use. Jesus and his contemporaries spoke Aramaic.

As fewer and fewer people were able to read or understand Hebrew, problems arose in the use of the sacred texts. It was considered essential that these texts be retained in their original 'sacred' language, and it was forbidden to translate them. The synagogues developed the practice of reading the texts in Hebrew, then giving a loose translation followed by a homily in Aramaic. The preacher would take some current situation and comment on it by reflecting on themes drawn from the sacred texts, weaving them into the fabric of his homily.

This style of meditation, which was often highly imaginative, was called 'midrash'. Everyone at the time of Jesus was familiar with it, as was the community for which Matthew was writing. It is quite possible that Matthew knew no more about Jesus in the period prior to his public ministry than the few details mentioned in his Gospel: namely, that he was 'the carpenter's son' (Matthew 13:55), that his mother was 'the woman called Mary' (Matthew 13:55), and that his home town (Matthew 13:54) was a town called 'Nazareth' (Matthew 4:13) in Galilee. The aim of the Prologue is not to reveal further biographical details, but to reflect on the meaning of Jesus in the light of certain Biblical texts. We are dealing, in other words, with midrash. ✓

using past to validate present

Matthew's Prologue is like a vast backdrop to his Gospel. He draws, as we shall see, on some of the richest material of the Bible, to prepare his readers for the incredible story he is about to narrate. It may be of value to give here a schematic outline of the contents of the Prologue.

MATTHEW CHAPTER ONE: WHO IS JESUS?
- the 'Christ' (1:1): (cf comments in the previous chapter)
- the 'son of David' (1:1): the one in whom the promises made to David are fulfilled.
- the 'son of Abraham' (1:1): the one in whom all the nations of the earth will be blessed.
- the one 'conceived by the Holy Spirit' (1:20).
- the 'one who is to save his people from their sins' (1:21). 'Jesus' means 'God saves'.
- 'God-is-with-us' (1:23): the one in whom God is present to his people.

MATTHEW CHAPTER TWO: FOR WHAT IS JESUS DESTINED?
- mention of 'Bethlehem' (2:1) reminds his readers that Jesus is the son of David, the 'king of the Jews' (2:2).
- the story of the magi reminds them that Jesus is the 'wisdom of God' (cf allusion in 2:9), and the light of the nations (2:9).
- the reference to 'Egypt' (2:15) prepares the readers for one who is to be the new Israel (2:15) and the new Moses (2:16).
- mention of Jeremiah (2:17) brings to mind the new covenant.
- mention of 'Ramah' (2:18) prepares the readers for one who is to suffer (also 2:11).
- mention of 'Nazareth' (2:23) brings the reader back to the historical Jesus, the son of the carpenter who is to be the central figure in the following Gospel.

Matthew writes these chapters with superb skill. It is our task to read them as the early Jewish-Christian community would have read them; that is, as highly imaginative stories, reaching beyond biography to penetrate the divine meaning of the Jesus who emerged from Nazareth in his early thirties to capture his contemporaries with the wonder of his person and his preaching.

*   *   *   *   *   *   *   *

Jesus is the Christ, the Son of David, the Son of Abraham

MATTHEW 1:1-17 (Compare Luke 3:23-38, page 59)

1   **1** A genealogy of Jesus Christ, son of David, son of Abraham:

2   Abraham was the father of Isaac,
        Isaac the father of Jacob,
        Jacob the father of Judah and his brothers,
3   Judah was the father of Perez and Zerah, Tamar being their mother,
        Perez was the father of Hezron,
        Hezron the father of Ram,

4   Ram was the father of Amminadab,
       Amminadab the father of Nahshon,
       Nahshon the father of Salmon,
5   Salmon was the father of Boaz, Rahab being his mother,
       Boaz was the father of Obed, Ruth being his mother,
       Obed was the father of Jesse;
6   and Jesse was the father of King David.
       David was the father of Solomon, whose mother had been
            Uriah's wife,
7   Solomon was the father of Rehoboam,
       Rehoboam the father of Abijah,
       Abijah the father of Asa,
8   Asa was the father of Jehoshaphat,
       Jehoshaphat the father of Joram,
       Joram the father of Azariah,
9   Azariah was the father of Jotham,
       Jotham the father of Ahaz,
       Ahaz the father of Hezekiah,
10   Hezekiah was the father of Manasseh,
       Manasseh the father of Amon,
       Amon the father of Josiah;
11   and Josiah was the father of Jechoniah and his brothers.
       Then the deportation to Babylon took place.
12   After the deportation to Babylon:
       Jechoniah was the father of Shealtiel,
       Shealtiel the father of Zerubbabel,
13   Zerubbabel was the father of Abiud,
       Abiud the father of Eliakim,
       Eliakim the father of Azor,
14   Azor was the father of Zadok,
       Zadok the father of Achim,
       Achim the father of Eliud,
15   Eliud was the father of Eleazar,
       Eleazar the father of Matthan,
       Matthan the father of Jacob;
16   and Jacob was the father of Joseph the husband of Mary;
       of her was born Jesus who is called Christ.

17   The sum of generations is therefore: fourteen from Abraham to David;
fourteen from David to the Babylonian deportation; and fourteen from the
Babylonian deportation to Christ.

The genealogy begins with Abraham (1:1). Matthew stresses, in this way, the
special ties that link Jesus with the Hebrew people. At the same time, there is a
universal dimension in Matthew's genealogy, as is evident when we recall the
promise made to Abraham:

> 'Yahweh said to Abram: "Leave your country, and your family, and your father's
> house, for the land I will show you. I will make you a great nation; I will bless you and
> make your name so famous that it will be used as a blessing. I will bless those who
> bless you; I will curse those who slight you. All the tribes of the earth shall bless
> themselves by you'." *(Genesis 12:1-3)*

Jesus belongs to the Jews; but he is the one by whom all the tribes of the earth shall bless themselves.

David is mentioned three times in the genealogy (cf Matthew 1:1,6,17). There is probably an allusion to David in the stress Matthew places on the number 'fourteen' (1:17). In Hebrew each letter has a numerical equivalent, and the sum of the letters in the name 'David' is 'fourteen'. Also, Matthew traces the ancestry of Jesus through the ruling line of Solomon (1:6). In this way he stresses the fact that Jesus is the royal Messiah promised to David:

> 'I will make you great; Yahweh will make you a House. And when your days are ended and you must go to your ancestors, I will preserve your offspring after you, a son of your own, and make his sovereignty secure. It is he who will build a house for me and I will make his throne firm forever. I will be a father to him and he a son to me. I will not withdraw my favour for him, as I withdrew it from your predecessor. I will preserve him for ever in my house and in my kingdom; and his throne shall be established for ever.'
>
> *(1 Chronicles 17:10-14)*

It has been suggested by some scholars that Matthew's stressing the three lots of fourteen has a further significance. Seven is the number for perfection. If one divides each of the fourteens in half, one has six lots of seven, with Jesus beginning the seventh seven. Everything is therefore in complete readiness for him, and it is he who inaugurates the perfection of the history of his people.

Matthew's genealogy, from Abraham to Zerubbabel (1:1-12) is taken from the First Book of Chronicles (Chapters 1-3). The rest is from non-Scriptural Jewish sources of the Hellenist period.

Against normal custom, Matthew mentions women in his genealogy. It is interesting to look at the Biblical history of the women, for each one draws attention to an occasion on which God was seen to act outside the normal expectations of men to carry out his will.

The first woman mentioned is 'Tamar' (1:3). Her story can be found in the Book of Genesis (38:1-30). She was the wife of Judah's eldest son who died without leaving an heir. In her desire to ensure the continuance of God's promise, but acting against the laws forbidding incest, she tricked her father-in-law, Judah, into having a child by her. She was praised for her action which was seen as a special act of providence.

Another special act of providence occured when 'Rahab' (1:5), the harlot of Jericho, and an outsider to the Jewish race, was chosen as an instrument of God's will (cf Joshua 2:1-21). So was 'Ruth' (1:5), the Moabitess (cf the Book of Ruth, and especially Ruth 4:12, where Ruth is likened to Tamar).

David's union with Bathsheba, 'Uriah's wife' (1:6) was a sinful one for which David was severely reprimanded (cf 2 Samuel 11-12). Yet, once again, God manifested his special providence by using even this sin for his purposes.

The climax comes with 'Mary' (1:16) of whom 'was born Jesus who is called Christ' (1:16).

Matthew has prepared the setting for his account of the extraordinary way in which God brought about the birth of Jesus.

Jesus is the Son of God, the Saviour, God-with-us

MATTHEW 1:18-25

This is how Jesus Christ came to be born. His mother Mary was betrothed 18 to Joseph; but before they came to live together she was found to be with child through the Holy Spirit. •Her husband Joseph, being a man of honour and 19 wanting to spare her publicity, decided to divorce her informally. •He had 20 made up his mind to do this when the angel of the Lord appeared to him in a dream and said, 'Joseph son of David, do not be afraid to take Mary home as your wife, because she has conceived what is in her by the Holy Spirit. •She 21 will give birth to a son and you must name him Jesus, because he is the one who is to save his people from their sins.' •Now all this took place to fulfil the words 22 spoken by the Lord through the prophet:

> The virgin will conceive and give birth to a son 23
> and they will call him Immanuel,[a]

a name which means 'God-is-with-us'. •When Joseph woke up he did what the 24 angel of the Lord had told him to do: he took his wife to his home •and, though 25 he had not had intercourse with her, she gave birth to a son; and he named him Jesus.

(a: Isaiah 7:14)

This is an example of midrash. The key to the understanding of the story is found in the text taken from Isaiah. At this stage it is important to note that whenever a text from the Bible is quoted in the Gospels, the author expects the reader to understand the text within its context. Often the small section quoted is meant as no more than a trigger to remind the reader of a much longer text with which he was assumed to be familiar. We should always go back to the original text and try to become familiar with the whole context.

Isaiah was writing at the time of the advance of the Assyrian army on Israel, an advance which was to climax in the collapse of Samaria and the end of the northern kingdom (721 B.C.). The southern kingdom, Judah, had already broken away from Israel. Israel and the other neighbouring countries were bringing pressure to bear on Ahaz, the king of Judah, to form an alliance with them against the advancing army. Isaiah was adviser to Ahaz, and warned him against such an alliance. He promised Ahaz that, if he relied on Yahweh and not on military power, God would secure his throne and grant him a son to succeed him:

> 'The Lord himself will give you a sign. It is this: the maiden is with child and will soon give birth to a son and she will call him Immanuel.'

(Isaiah 7:14)

Ahaz had a son, Hezekiah, whom history was to see as the greatest king among David's descendants, renowned for his fidelity to the Covenant and his reform of religion. The Book of Kings has this to say of him. (Note the expression 'Yahweh was with him' means Immanuel):

> 'He put his trust in the God of Israel. No king of Judah after him could be compared with him — nor any of those before him. He was devoted to Yahweh, never turning from him, but keeping the commandments that Yahweh had laid down for Moses. And so Yahweh was with him and he was successful in all he undertook.'

(2 Kings 18:5-7)

In choosing this text, Matthew wishes to highlight the fact that Jesus was the greatest 'king' in the line of David, and that in him God was with his people.

Matthew uses, not the Hebrew original, but the Greek translation of Isaiah. In place of the Hebrew 'maiden', the Greek Bible (the 'Septuagint') had the word 'virgin'. This enabled Matthew to draw attention to the special providence of God at work in the birth of Jesus, and the special relationship that existed between Jesus and God his Father. Jesus' conception by a virgin expresses in the physical order the profound mystery of the intimacy of Jesus and the Father, and the wonderful action of the creative Spirit of God in the life of a woman who was so utterly open to God's love.

The midrash takes the form of a dream in which God reveals to Joseph the fact that he, God, is the Father of Mary's child, while making clear to Joseph the role he is to play in rearing the child. It may appear that Joseph intends divorcing Mary because he is in doubt as to the origin of the child. In this way of reading the text, the purpose of the vision is to inform Joseph of the facts and commission him to take Mary home as his wife.

There is another way of reading the text — a way more consistent with the style of such dreams in Old Testament literature. This is to imagine Joseph as being in doubt, not of the child's origin, but of the role he, Joseph, is to play in God's design. It is precisely because he knows that the child is the fruit of God's love for Mary, and the manifestation of God's glory, that he presumes there is no place for him in this holy intimacy. In this way of reading the text, the purpose of the vision is not to inform Joseph (God confirms what Joseph already knows as a sign to Joseph of the authenticity of the dream), but to commission him to take Mary home as his wife (1:20). This Joseph does immediately.

It was well known that Jesus was 'the carpenter's son' (Matthew 13:55) and that his mother was 'the woman called Mary' (Matthew 13:55). Matthew wants his readers to penetrate beyond these facts to a deeper reality. He wants to prepare them for the special relationship that existed between Jesus and God. In Jesus God was with his people. Through Jesus God saved his people from their sins. Jesus was the Son of God. Rather than make these statements as I have done, Matthew creates an imaginative story, using a text of Scripture to focus on the mystery he wished to contemplate.

Born of the royal House of David, Jesus is destined to bring God's saving power to the whole world

MATTHEW 2:1-12

2 After Jesus had been born at Bethlehem in Judaea during the reign of King 1 Herod, some wise men came to Jerusalem from the east. •'Where is the infant 2 king of the Jews?' they asked. 'We saw his star as it rose and have come to do him homage.' •When King Herod heard this he was perturbed, and so was the whole 3 of Jerusalem. •He called together all the chief priests and the scribes of the people, 4 and enquired of them where the Christ was to be born. •'At Bethlehem in Judaea,' 5 they told him 'for this is what the prophet wrote:

> *And you, Bethlehem, in the land of Judah,* 6
> *you are by no means least among the leaders of Judah,*

for out of you will come a leader
who will shepherd my people Israel'. ᵃ

Then Herod summoned the wise men to see him privately. He asked them the 7
exact date on which the star had appeared, •and sent them on to Bethlehem. 8
'Go and find out all about the child,' he said 'and when you have found him,
let me know, so that I too may go and do him homage.' •Having listened to 9
what the king had to say, they set out. And there in front of them was the star
they had seen rising; it went forward and halted over the place where the child
was. •The sight of the star filled them with delight, •and going into the house ¹⁰ ¹¹
they saw the child with his mother Mary, and falling to their knees they did him
homage. Then, opening their treasures, they offered him gifts of gold and
frankincense and myrrh. •But they were warned in a dream not to go back to 12
Herod, and returned to their own country by a different way.

(a: Micah 5:1)

This, too, is midrash. Matthew is reflecting on the destiny of Jesus, and, for
this purpose, draws on a statement from the prophet Micah (Matthew 2:6 —
Micah 5:1).

Micah was a contemporary of Isaiah. He too encouraged the kings of Judah
to maintain their stand against the enticements of the northern kingdom. In the
above passage the prophet is assuring them that it is the kingdom of David that
will prevail, not the kingdom of the north. David's birthplace, Bethlehem, and so
his dynasty, is extolled.

By placing the birth of Jesus at Bethlehem, Matthew is declaring his faith,
and the faith of his community, in the fact that Jesus is the heir to the promises
made to David.

Matthew's story, written in midrash style, seems to draw on the story of
Balak, the Moabite ruler who tried to destroy Moses (cf Numbers 22-24). In that
story, too, a wise man from the east (Numbers 23:7), by name Balaam, speaks
blessings on God's chosen ones. He speaks of the 'star of Jacob' (Numbers 24:17).

Just as the chosen people were guided in their history towards the Christ, so
too, according to Matthew, were the Gentiles. The story of the magi is the story of
the journey of the Gentiles towards the Messiah, under the guidance of God.

The story of the wise men (2:1) is full of allusions to the sacred Scripture (for
example Psalm 72:10-11, Isaiah 49:7, Numbers 24:17). We will content ourselves
here with referring the reader to the Book of Isaiah:

'Arise, shine out, for your light has come,
the glory of Israel is rising on you,
though night still covers the earth
and darkness the peoples.
Above you Yahweh now rises
and above you his glory appears.
The nations come to your light
and kings to your dawning brightness.
Lift up your eyes and look around,
all are assembling and coming towards you,
your sons from far away
and your daughters being tenderly carried.

At this sight you will grow radiant,
your heart throbbing and full;
since the riches of the sea will flow to you
and the wealth of the nations come to you:
camels in throngs will cover you,
and dromedaries of Midian and Ephah;
everyone in Sheba will come,
bringing gold and incense
and singing the praise of Yahweh.'

(Isaiah 60:1-6)

Mention of Sheba (60:6) reminds us of the visit made by the Queen of Sheba to the king in whom the wisdom of Yahweh dwelt, king Solomon (cf 1 Kings 10:1-13 — also Matthew 12:43). In a similar way, Matthew has these wise men journeying from the lands of darkness into the light, to the source of all wisdom.

Matthew may also intend his readers to dwell on the symbolic meaning of the gifts: gold has reference to royalty; frankincense to the prayer of adoration; myrrh to burial.

Notice that the 'whole of Jerusalem' (2:3) was perturbed. It is the strangers who are 'filled with delight' (2:11). Matthew is alluding to the sad fact that the Jews, for the most part, were to reject their Messiah, while it was the gentiles who opened their minds and hearts to him and 'did him homage' (2:11). Matthew makes this point forcefully later in his Gospel when he has Jesus say:

'I tell you, then, that the kingdom of God will be taken from you (the Jews) and given to a people who will produce its fruit.'

(Matthew 21:43)

Jesus is destined to extend the kingdom of David to the ends of the earth!

**Jesus is destined to fulfil in his own person the history of Israel.
He is to be the new Moses liberating God's people from slavery
and giving them a new covenant and a new law.**

MATTHEW 2:13-18

13   After they had left, the angel of the Lord appeared to Joseph in a dream and said, 'Get up, take the child and his mother with you, and escape into Egypt, and stay there until I tell you, because Herod intends to search for the child and
14   do away with him'. •So Joseph got up and, taking the child and his mother
15   with him, left that night for Egypt, •where he stayed until Herod was dead. This was to fulfil what the Lord had spoken through the prophet:

I called my son out of Egypt. [a]

16   Herod was furious when he realised that he had been outwitted by the wise men, and in Bethlehem and its surrounding district he had all the male children killed who were two years old or under, reckoning by the date he
17   had been careful to ask the wise men. •It was then that the words spoken through the prophet Jeremiah were fulfilled:

18
      A voice was heard in Ramah,
      sobbing and loudly lamenting:
      it was Rachel weeping for her children,
      refusing to be comforted
      because they were no more. [b]   *(a: Hosea 11:1   b: Jeremiah 31:15)*

In this midrash, Matthew reflects on a passage from the prophet Hosea (Matthew 2:15 = Hosea 11:1). In context it reads:

'When Israel was a child I loved him,
and I called my son out of Egypt . . .
I myself taught Ephraim to walk,
I took them in my arms . . .
I was the one looking after them.
I led them with reins of kindness,
with leading strings of love.
I was like someone who lifts an infant close against his cheek;
stooping down to him I gave him his food.'

(Hosea 11:1-4)

Using this homely, very intimate, language, Matthew prepares his readers for the way in which God is to show himself to be the Father of Jesus. Moreover, Jesus is to fulfil in his person the early history of Israel. Just as God took the young nation gently by the hand and led it through the desert from slavery in Egypt to freedom in the Promised Land, so God is going to lead this child from apparent subjection to men like Herod ('out of Egypt' 2:15) to himself. Through him, God is going to lead all men to freedom.

The story of Herod seems to be based on the story of the Pharaoh:

'Pharaoh then gave his subjects this command: "Throw all the boys born to the Hebrews into the river".'

(Exodus 1:22)

The comparison between Jesus and Moses is obvious (also Exodus 2:15.)

Finally, Matthew focuses attention on a text from Jeremiah (Matthew 2:18= Jeremiah 31:15).

Jeremiah was speaking on the occasion of the destruction of Jerusalem (587 B.C.). The inhabitants of the city were mustered into makeshift camps at Ramah, a few kilometres to the north of Jerusalem, and there they awaited transportation to Babylon and exile. The prophet is lamenting the suffering of his people, a suffering which he himself shared. Rachel was the wife of Jacob (nicknamed 'Israel'). It is easy to see how Jeremiah could refer to the people of Israel as the children of Rachel. It is perhaps of interest that Rachel was buried at Bethlehem (cf Genesis 35:19).

Matthew himself and his contemporaries had just lived through an experience very like that of Jeremiah. The Roman army had destroyed Jerusalem in 70 A.D. and those Jews and Jewish Christians who had survived had had to flee into exile. Matthew saw this, as had Jeremiah, as a judgment on the people for their rejection of God.

Jeremiah's lament, however, is not without hope. Earlier in the same chapter, Jeremiah wrote:

'They had left in tears,
I will comfort them as I lead them back;
I will guide them to streams of water,
by a smooth path where they will not stumble.
For I am a Father to Israel,
and Ephraim is my first-born son.'

(Jeremiah 31:9)

And later in the chapter, Jeremiah, in the midst of his suffering, looks forward to a new covenant of love that God will make with his people. For whatever the infidelity of the people, God's love is without end and his fidelity without limit.

> 'This is the covenant I will make with the House of Israel when those days arrive — it is Yahweh who speaks. Deep within them I will plant my Law, writing it on their hearts. Then I will be their God and they shall be my people."
>
> *(Jeremiah 31:33)*

By quoting Jeremiah, Matthew is preparing his readers for a story in which they will find much suffering (they will find the cross), but also a proof of the fidelity of God to his covenant of love with his people (they will find the resurrection).

This is an excellent example of midrash. It should be obvious to the reader that without some knowledge of the original texts in their context it is not possible to grasp the message Matthew is conveying.

Jesus of Nazareth

MATTHEW 2:19-23

¹⁹ After Herod's death, the angel of the Lord appeared in a dream to Joseph in ²⁰ Egypt •and said, 'Get up, take the child and his mother with you and go back to ²¹ the land of Israel, for those who wanted to kill the child are dead'. •So Joseph got up and, taking the child and his mother with him, went back to the land of Israel. ²² But when he learnt that Archelaus had succeeded his father Herod as ruler of Judaea he was afraid to go there, and being warned in a dream he left for the ²³ region of Galilee. •There he settled in a town called Nazareth. In this way the words spoken through the prophets were to be fulfilled:

He will be called a Nazarene.

Matthew concludes his Prologue by placing Jesus firmly in Nazareth, his home town, whence he will set out on his public ministry.

There is no statement in the sacred writings linking the Messiah with Nazareth. There are, however, two words in Hebrew which have sounds that Matthew may be playing upon to create the link. There is the word 'neser' which means 'offshoot', and Jesus is, according to Matthew, the 'offshoot' of David (cf 1 Chronicles 17:11, Isaiah 11:1 and Zechariah 3:8-10). There is also the word 'nazir' meaning one who is holy, consecrated to God by a vow (cf the Nazarite vow, Numbers 6:1-21), and Jesus is, according to Matthew, the 'holy one of God'.

It is perhaps the link between the word 'nazir' and 'holy' that gives the clue to the passage Matthew is quoting. Speaking of the remnant who are faithful to God and remain in Jerusalem, Isaiah writes:

> 'That day, the branch of Yahweh
> shall be beauty and glory,
> and the fruit of the earth
> shall be the pride and adornment
> of Israel's survivors.
> Those who are left of Zion
> and remain of Jerusalem
> shall be called holy.'
>
> *(Isaiah 4:2-3)*

Jesus is the branch of Yahweh, the offshoot of David (neser). He is the beauty and glory of Israel, and he shall be called holy, shall be a 'Nazarite'.

Having placed Jesus in his home town of Nazareth, Matthew brings his Prologue into history and is ready to introduce the Baptist, and Jesus of Nazareth to his readers.

*   *   *   *   *   *   *   *

Points for Reflection:

1: God manifests his presence through the events of history (cf Matthew's genealogy). We belong to God, and he is at home with us. Am I ready to see the hand of God in events that are outside the limits of my expectations, or have I a fixed and comfortable idea of God and his will?

2: The Jews thought they knew where to look for the Messiah (Matthew 2:1-12); his approach perturbed them. It was the strangers who knew they did not know, who simply followed the signs, who discovered him and rejoiced. How ready am I to follow the signs that appear in my life, even when they beckon me into strange territory? Is my God too small? Have I attempted to accommodate God to my temperament, to my needs, to my will? Or am I humbly open to his guidance?

3: There was lamenting in Ramah (Matthew 2:18), but it was followed by the joy of the return from exile. The Cross led to the Resurrection. Am I willing to share his sufferings, to journey in the dark, to leave my father and my father's house in answer to his call?

4: Am I willing, like Joseph (1:24; 2:14, 21) to do the will of God even when it is shrouded in mystery? Do I take time off to pray, to listen to God, and give him the opportunity to call me by name and show me his will?

5: Matthew wants me, as I continue to read his Gospel, to see Jesus as God's son; to see God's fatherly care and love as I watch and listen to Jesus; to see Jesus as exercising God's healing and liberating love; to see him as the Christ, the one anointed by the Spirit of God and offering me this same Spirit.

II: **LUKE'S PROLOGUE** (Luke 1:5 — 2:52)

Luke, like Matthew, wished to 'set the stage' for his Gospel. His Prologue has that function.

He tells us himself that:

'after carefully going over the whole story from the beginning, I have decided to write an ordered account.'

(Luke 1:3)

Before examining the text of Luke's prologue, let us briefly examine the implications of his concern to write an 'ordered account'. Luke was writing history; he was writing history as it was written in the first century A.D.; he was writing to highlight the special place in history of Jesus of Nazareth.

1: **Luke was writing history**

Some think of knowledge as a process whereby a 'subject', standing outside an 'object', looks at the object, ascertains certain 'objective facts' about it, and proceeds to draw conclusions from these 'facts' in a methodical manner. Others — and this seems a richer view and one that is true to experience — think of knowledge as a special union of the knower and the known. According to this view, the knowing subject and the known object are not independent; on the contrary, in the act of knowing, they are intimately related. The object-as-known is not independent of the subject's selective processes, environment and education. One can work towards a kind of 'objectivity' by being imaginatively open to the object, by gradually freeing oneself of prejudices, by a humility that makes one constantly open to surprise and ready to make a different selection should the evidence require it, by not being afraid of what one might see, and by becoming increasingly able to experience the wonder of the unknown. One can, with education, become increasingly attentive and sensitive in one's perceptions, increasingly penetrating in one's understanding, increasingly clear and honest in judging, and increasingly responsible in being committed to the demands that follow on knowledge. But in all this the subject, the knower, is intimately and necessarily involved. Knowledge is a relationship of the knower with the known.

In this view, history is not a matter of compiling more and more 'facts' that are imagined as standing on their own, independent of anyone 'knowing' them; it is a process of being involved in reality, of relating to one's present and one's past, and of placing what one knows in such an order that the significance grasped by the historian is communicated to the reader with whom he is sharing this special knowledge. The historian desires to share his insight. As an artist, therefore, he selects his material and arranges it in order to communicate its meaning in the richest way he can. The raw material for his work consists of events of the past as known by those who observed them, and, ultimately, as perceived by the historian himself. The historian, who is an artist, will not simply compile these events; he will order them according to his artistic intuition. The richer the intuition, the better will be the understanding he imparts.

When we say that Luke is a historian, we are saying that he is concerned with *facts;* more precisely, with Jesus of Nazareth, what he said and did, and the meaning this had for Luke himself and for the community of which he was a part. We are also saying that Luke is an artist who is concerned to communicate to his readers, in the most effective way he can, the significance of a person who has profoundly affected himself and his community. The Gospel is written by a historian who believes in his subject. Luke 'orders' his work the better to share this faith-experience. Love, commitment and conviction need not lead to distortion of the truth. On the contrary, truth is attainable only by one who loves.

2: Luke was writing history as it was written in the first century A.D.

Today we are careful to distinguish the historian from the dramatist. We expect the historian to be imaginative in arranging his material, but to present the 'facts' unadorned. In Luke's day history, as the word implies, was basically the telling of 'stories'; stories based on real events, but stories told with all the verve and imagination the historian could muster to communicate, in the richest way he could, the inner meaning of the events. A good historian was one who could write an engaging story that captured the attention of his readers. Of course, he was not permitted to distort events: he was not a writer of fiction. But, so long as he was faithful to the facts as perceived by those who observed them, he was allowed as much imaginative play as he wished.

When we say that Luke was a first century historian who wrote about Jesus, we are saying that the community who knew Jesus accepted what Luke wrote as having grasped the meaning of Jesus accurately, and as having communicated it through attractive and imaginative stories that expressed this meaning in a rich way.

3: Luke was writing to highlight the special place in history of Jesus of Nazareth.

Luke, and the community for which he wrote, were convinced that, in the process of history, Jesus had an ultimate place. It was Jesus who, in their view, made sense of the past and, in some way, brought its processes to a climax. Because Jesus was a Jew, and because nearly all his immediate followers were Jews, the place of Jesus in history was expressed in terms of the Jewish sacred writings. Luke chose to write his Prologue in a special style called 'Apocalyptic'.

Especially during the time after the Exile (500 B.C. onwards) the Jews were very interested in the coming of the Messiah and in the triumph of God when history would reach its fulfilment. They developed a special style of writing when referring to such ultimate matters, a literary genre called 'Apocalyptic', and it is this style that Luke chose for his Prologue. We shall make a study of Apocalyptic writing later in this book when we are examining the Eschatological Discourse (cf page 341-8). The reader may like to look at that section here. For our present purposes I would like to examine only one of the basic features of this style: the use of visions to dramatise God's providence in history and the ultimate triumph of his enduring love. For it is this use of visions that features very prominently in Luke's Prologue.

The 'father' of Apocalpyptic writing was the prophet Ezekiel. He was writing during the Exile in Babylon (c.570 B.C.). He strove to encourage his fellow exiles by reminding them of God's care for their ancestors, especially by showing them his might in rescuing them from Egypt. Ezekiel revelled in the use of quite fantastic imagery, and, to highlight the mystery and wonder of God's special providence, he gave his teaching in the form of revelations granted to him by God in visions. The special literary style associated with these visionary revelations came to be called 'Apocalyptic', from the Greek word for 'Revelation'.

After the Exile, to bolster the people's hopes, and to keep alive their expectation of the Messiah, Apocalyptic sections were added to many of the older prophetic writings. Current events were written of as though they were foreseen in visions centuries before. It was not the aim of the authors of these Apocalyptic writings to claim that the ancient prophets actually received such visions. They were simply using this as a dramatic technique to remind their readers of their past and of the fact that the whole of history is in the hands of God, that nothing happens outside his providence, and that whatever the sufferings they might be going through, God's enduring love would prevail and he would keep the promises he made to their fathers.

The Book of Daniel is the classical example of this. The Apocalyptic sections were written in the second century B.C. (c.168 B.C.), at a time when the Jews were suffering severe persecution at the hands of the Syrian ruler, Antiochus Epiphanes IV. The author wrote of these events as though they had been foreseen, centuries earlier, in visions granted to the prophet Daniel (an obscure prophet of the Sixth Century B.C.). The style and language of these visions was that of Ezekiel. In highly ornate language the author took his readers back to God's action in Egypt and in Babylon and in this way, buoyed up their courage to remain faithful to God in the face of persecution. The vision itself was a literary device; the content of the vision took the readers to the heart of their faith.

The Book of Daniel is the only place in the Old Testament that speaks of the angel Gabriel. It is this angel that speaks of the 'coming of an anointed Prince' (Daniel 9:25) after a lapse of seventy weeks of years (cf Daniel 9:24). Luke saw himself and his community as living at the close of this period, at the time when God chose to fulfil his promises and send the anointed Prince (the 'Christ'). He wanted his readers to read his Gospel with this in mind. In the style of the Apocalyptic, he had this same Gabriel return, this time to the father of the Baptist and the mother of Jesus and announce to them in visions the coming of the promised one and his herald. The visions are a literary device; the content expresses the faith of the early church in Jesus. From the outset, Luke wanted to highlight the ultimate significance of the one who was to be the subject of his Gospel. In his Prologue, Luke was no more interested in biographical detail than was Matthew. His aim was to introduce his narrative of the life of Jesus by creating a significant perspective for the readers. He was, after all, writing 'history'.

1:5-25   **The coming of the herald is revealed to Zechariah in a vision.**

1:26-38   **The coming of the Saviour is revealed to Mary in a vision.**

1:39-56   **The coming of the Saviour is greeted with exultation.**

1:57-80   **The birth of John is greeted with exultation.**

2:1-20   **The birth of the Saviour.**

2:21-40   **Jesus is manifested to the world in the Temple.**

2:41-52   **From the beginning of his maturity, Jesus was the Son of God.**

* * * * * * * *

The coming of the herald is revealed to Zechariah in a vision

LUKE 1:5-25
In the days of King Herod of Judaea there lived a priest called Zechariah 5
who belonged to the Abijah section of the priesthood, and he had a wife,
Elizabeth by name, who was a descendant of Aaron. •Both were worthy in the 6
sight of God, and scrupulously observed all the commandments and observances
of the Lord. •But they were childless: Elizabeth was barren and they were 7
both getting on in years.

Now it was the turn of Zechariah's section to serve, and he was exercising 8
his priestly office before God •when it fell to him by lot, as the ritual custom 9
was, to enter the Lord's sanctuary and burn incense there. •And at the hour of 10
incense the whole ‘congregation was outside, praying.

Then there appeared to him the angel of the Lord, standing on the right 11
of the altar of incense. •The sight disturbed Zechariah and he was overcome with 12
fear. •But the angel said to him, 'Zechariah, do not be afraid, your prayer 13
has been heard. Your wife Elizabeth is to bear you a son and you must name
him John. •He will be your joy and delight and many will rejoice at his birth, 14
for he will be great in the sight of the Lord; he must drink no wine, no strong 15
drink. Even from his mother's womb he will be filled with the Holy Spirit, •and 16
he will bring back many of the sons of Israel to the Lord their God. •With the 17
spirit and power of Elijah, he will go before him *to turn the hearts of fathers
towards their children* and the disobedient back to the wisdom that the virtuous
have, preparing for the Lord a people fit for him.' •Zechariah said to the angel, 18
'*How can I be sure of this?* I am an old man and my wife is getting on in years.'
The angel replied, 'I am Gabriel who stand in God's presence, and I have been 19
sent to speak to you and bring you this good news. •Listen! Since you have not 20
believed my words, which will come true at their appointed time, you will be
silenced and have no power of speech until this has happened.' •Meanwhile 21
the people were waiting for Zechariah and were surprised that he stayed in the
sanctuary so long. •When he came out he could not speak to them, and they 22
realised that he had received a vision in the sanctuary. But he could only make
signs to them, and remained dumb.

When his time of service came to an end he returned home. •Some time later 23 24
his wife Elizabeth conceived, and for five months she kept to herself. •'The Lord 25
has done this for me' she said 'now that it has pleased him to take away the
humiliation I suffered among men.'

Luke is preparing his readers for the appearance of the Messiah. His
writing is in the style of the Apocalyptic, and so the vision in this passage is a
literary device. The fact that it is the angel Gabriel who appears alerts the reader
to the fact that the end of the time of waiting is at hand.

The vision itself follows a classical pattern found frequently in the Old
Testament for the annunciation of the birth of a famous person (cf Ishmael,

Genesis 16; Isaac, Genesis 17; Samson, Judges 13). We will see that the vision given to Mary follows the same pattern. We should then, in reading this scene, be looking not for biographical details but for Luke's theological intent. Through the medium of the vision, what is Luke saying about Jesus?

The scene takes place in Jerusalem, in the 'Lord's sanctuary' (1:9, 21-22). Jerusalem plays a very important role in Luke's writings. Luke is himself a Gentile, and is writing for a Gentile church. He wishes to underline the fact that he and his community have, in the providence of God, a direct link with the chosen people. As a historian, Luke discerns a continuity in God's providential plan. So it is that here, at the beginning of his Gospel, he has a pious Jewish couple (Luke 1:6), described in terms that remind the reader of Abraham and Sarah (cf Genesis 17:17-19), being the recipients of God's good news. Zechariah, a priest (Luke 1:60), and so representing one of the central institutions of Judaism, is receptive to the coming of the Messiah.

Jerusalem is never far from Luke's mind. He gathers the material on discipleship into a long 'Journey to Jerusalem', a journey to the cross and the resurrection (Luke 9:51 — 19:28). The resurrection appearances in Luke occur in Jerusalem (Luke 24:13-49), and he ends his Gospel where it began, in the Temple of Jerusalem (Luke 24:53). It is from Jerusalem that the mission of the church radiates to the ends of the earth (Acts 1:8).

The atmosphere permeating this opening scene is one of prayer (1:10, 1:13); of holiness. It is this atmosphere that permeates the whole of Luke's work. The scene takes place at the time of the evening sacrifice in the Lord's sanctuary (1:9), with the whole of God's people at prayer (1:10). It is the Holy Spirit (1:16) who is to fill Elizabeth's womb; and her child is to take the Nazarite vow (1:15, cf Numbers 6:1ff and Judges 13:4), thus being consecrated to God from his conception.

The scene is also a scene of 'joy' (1:14), the eschatological joy of the Messianic times: God is about to fulfil all his promises. Joy, too, is a dominant theme of Luke's Gospel.

The Baptist is linked with the prophecy of Malachi (Luke 1:17 = Malachi 3:23-24, cf also Malachi 3:1). Popular expectation thought of Elijah returning to issue in the Messianic fulfilment. John the Baptist is, according to Luke, the realisation of that hope.

One final point. After the sacrifice, Zechariah 'could not speak to them' (1:22). His words should have been words of blessing, taken from the Book of Numbers:

'May Yahweh bless you and keep you.
May Yahweh let his face shine on you and be gracious to you.
May Yahweh uncover his face to you and bring you peace.'

(Numbers 6:24-26)

Zechariah, the priest of the old covenant, can no longer offer this blessing. For the Messianic Times have come and only the Messiah now can offer such a blessing (we will see Jesus doing precisely that in the last scene of Luke's Gospel

Luke 24:50-51). It is as if the whole world is hushed in silent expectation for the fulfilment, now imminent, of God's promise. Yahweh is about to uncover his face for the people who will soon see, in Paul's words:

'God's glory on the face of Christ.'

(2 Corinthians 4:6)

The coming of the saviour is revealed to Mary in a vision

LUKE 1:26-38

26   In the sixth month the angel Gabriel was sent by God to a town in Galilee
27 called Nazareth, •to a virgin betrothed to a man named Joseph, of the House
28 of David; and the virgin's name was Mary. •He went in and said to her, 'Rejoice,
29 so highly favoured! The Lord is with you.' •She was deeply disturbed by these
30 words and asked herself what this greeting could mean, •but the angel said
31 to her, 'Mary, do not be afraid; you have won God's favour. •Listen! You are
32 to conceive and bear a son, and you must name him Jesus. •He will be great and
    will be called Son of the Most High. The Lord God will give him the throne
33 of his ancestor David; •he will rule over the House of Jacob for ever and his reign
34 will have no end.' •Mary said to the angel, 'But how can this come about, since
35 I am a virgin?' •'The Holy Spirit will come upon you' the angel answered 'and
    the power of the Most High will cover you with its shadow. And so the child
36 will be holy and will be called Son of God. •Know this too: your kinswoman
    Elizabeth has, in her old age, herself conceived a son, and she whom people called
37
38 barren is now in her sixth month, *for nothing is impossible to God.*' •'I am the
    handmaid of the Lord,' said Mary 'let what you have said be done to me.'
    And the angel left her.

It is obvious that Luke has followed the same pattern in this vision as he used in the vision to Zechariah. This helps him highlight the superiority of Jesus in comparison to John. Elizabeth, like so many of the Old Testament mothers of famous men, is spoken of as 'barren' (Luke 1:7). Mary, too, cannot have a child; but she (and we shall return to this point) is spoken of as a 'virgin' (Luke 1:27 and 1:34). There is no precedent for this in the Old Testament writings. Luke wants to see, in this child, a new creative act of God. God is not simply answering the prayer of the people; he is doing something completely new. The conception of Jesus is an act of divine, creative initiative, like the act of the first creation when the Spirit of God came down upon the waters (Genesis 1:2).

Both Zechariah and Mary, following the pattern of such annunciation stories, have their objection to the message of the angel (Zechariah 1:12, 1:18; Mary 1:29 and 1:34). But whereas Zechariah is punished for his doubt, Mary is portrayed as utterly open to God's spirit and obedient to God's word (Luke 1:38).

Zechariah's son is to be called 'John' (1:13), which means 'Yahweh is gracious'; and he is to 'prepare for the Lord a people fit for him' (1:17). Mary's son is to be called 'Jesus' (1:31), which means 'Yahweh saves', and is to 'rule over the house of Jacob forever' (1:33). He is to be the 'Son of the Most High' (1:32), the 'Son of God' (1:35).

In this scene, Luke is drawing on the same tradition and expressing the same faith as Matthew in Joseph's dream (Matthew 1:18-25). Luke speaks of Jesus, in words drawn from 2 Samuel 7:9-10 as the Davidic Messiah (Luke 1:27, 32-33). Speaking of Mary as a 'virgin betrothed' (1:27), Luke is able also to express his faith and the faith of his community in the fact that Jesus is also, and in a unique way, the 'Son of God'.

The terms he uses are drawn from the Old Testament. Isaiah speaks of the action of the Spirit in the coming of the Messiah (Isaiah 11:1-2); he speaks of holiness (Isaiah 4:2-3); and the Messiah is spoken of as the Son of God (2 Samuel 7:14 and Psalm 2:7). But while the terms come from the classical Old Testament Messianic texts, the faith expressed through them is the faith of the early church in the person of Jesus.

Primarily, as mentioned in relation to Matthew's text (1:18-25), this faith was related to the risen Christ (cf Acts 13:32-33 and Romans 1:3-4). But on further meditation, the community came to see that Jesus was the Son of God prior to the Resurrection, and terms of sonship are applied to him in the Baptism texts (cf Luke 3:21 and 4:14; also Acts 10:37-38) and in the Transfiguration scene during his public ministry (cf Luke 9:34). The text we are now examining illustrates yet a further realisation, shared by both Matthew's and Luke's community; the realisation that Jesus was, indeed, the Son of God, from the first moment of his conception.

Jesus is to be the Son of God because:

'The Holy Spirit will come upon you and the power of the Most High will cover you with its shadow.'

(Luke 1:35)

Mary is to be drawn into the embrace of God himself, and to be caught up in the glory-cloud. One thinks of Moses praying to see God's glory (cf Exodus 33:12-23), the glory that came down upon the Tabernacle (Exodus 40:34-38), on the city of God (Isaiah 4:5) and on the people (Deuteronomy 33:12 and Psalm 91:4). Now at last, Mary, the virgin daughter of Zion (cf Micah 1:13, 4:8, 10, 13) is, unlike the people of God, completely obedient to God (Luke 1:38) and completely faithful to him (Luke 1:45). Now at last God is able to find a resting place for his glory, and is able to dwell among his people. The child, who is the fruit of the love between God and Mary, is to be the holy one, the Son of God.

We mentioned Luke's interest in prayer. This whole scene illustrates this interest. It is God who takes the initiative. Mary is asked to rejoice in the realisation of how she is graced by God, the Lord who is with her (1:28). When she is over-awed at God's presence, it is God himself who comforts her. He calls her by her name, 'Mary' (1:30), and speaks to her of his special love for her and mission for her. She is to be the sacred place where his Son is to dwell; she is to be embraced by God and drawn into his glory.

The coming of the saviour is greeted with exultation

LUKE 1:39-56
39   Mary set out at that time and went as quickly as she could to a town in the
40 hill country of Judah. •She went into Zechariah's house and greeted Elizabeth.
41 Now as soon as Elizabeth heard Mary's greeting, the child leapt in her womb
42 and Elizabeth was filled with the Holy Spirit. •She gave a loud cry and said,

'Of all women you are the most blessed, and blessed is the fruit of your womb.
43
44 Why should I be honoured with a visit from the mother of my Lord? •For the
moment your greeting reached my ears, the child in my womb leapt for joy.
45 Yes, blessed is she who believed that the promise made her by the Lord would
be fulfilled.'

46   And Mary said:

> 'My soul proclaims the greatness of the Lord   *The Magnificat*
47   and my spirit *exults in God my saviour;*
48   because *he has looked upon his lowly handmaid.*
> Yes, from this day forward all generations will call me blessed,
49   for the Almighty has done great things for me.
> *Holy is his name,*
50   and *his mercy reaches from age to age for those who fear him.*
51   He has shown the power of his arm,
> he has routed the proud of heart.
52   *He has pulled down princes* from their thrones *and exalted the lowly.*
53   *The hungry he has filled with good things*, the rich sent empty away.
54   *He has come to the help of Israel his servant, mindful of his mercy*
55   —according to the promise he made to our ancestors—
> of his mercy to Abraham and to his descendants for ever.'

56   Mary stayed with Elizabeth about three months and then went back home.

The time of fulfilment is fast approaching. Luke increases the tempo as Mary hurries 'as quickly as she could' (1:39) to Elizabeth, and the 'moment' she reaches her, the child in Elizabeth's womb leaps for joy (1:41, 44).

Characterising Elizabeth as Mary's 'kinswoman' (Luke 1:36) and having John so exultant at his approach is yet another way of stressing the consistency between Jesus and the Baptist.

Elizabeth is conscious of being in the presence of God and her cry reminds us of the words of David as the ark of the covenant, symbol of God's presence among his people, came into the holy city:

'However can the ark of Yahweh come to me?'

(2 Samuel 6:9)

Finally, Mary herself, in words reminiscent of the words sung by Hannah at the birth of Samuel (1 Samuel 2:1-10) breaks into exultant praise. The mother of the saviour is speaking for the whole of her race that has laboured to bring forth the child of promise.

It seems very likely that the canticle of praise placed on the lips of Mary (commonly called the 'Magnificat') was found by Luke and included here with slight adaptations. It is very like the canticle of Hannah; it is clearly of Jewish origin, and perhaps came from the circle of Jewish-Christians who saw themselves as the poor ones, the remnant of the ones who were faithful to God's covenant. Luke speaks of such a group in his Acts (cf Acts 2:43-47, 4:32-37). The 'Poor ones' ('Anawim') were those who, against all odds, continued to rely on God and place their trust in his love and in his fidelity (cf Psalm 149:4, Isaiah 49:13,66:2). One of Luke's favourite themes, as we shall see when commenting on

Luke 6:20, is the theme of the poor. Ultimately, Jesus is their representative, and when he placed his trust in God on the cross (Luke 23:46), his trust was vindicated by the Resurrection. This canticle was probably sung in reference to the risen Jesus. Luke saw that it was applicable here at the beginning, for it foretells what the child of Mary is to be.

Once again we are in the presence of the 'Holy One' (1:49 cf 1:35). At last the all-powerful God (1:49 cf 1:35, 38) is about to fulfil his promises (1:55) and manifest his love (1:50, 1:55) and his fidelity (1:55). At last, the hope of all those lowly ones who have placed their hope in God (1:48, 1:52) is about to be vindicated, and God's justice is about to be proclaimed for all to see.

The birth of John is greeted with exultation

LUKE 1:57-80

Meanwhile the time came for Elizabeth to have her child, and she gave birth 57
to a son; •and when her neighbours and relations heard that the Lord had shown 58
her so great a kindness, they shared her joy.

Now on the eighth day they came to circumcise the child; they were going 59
to call him Zechariah after his father, •but his mother spoke up. 'No,' she 60
said 'he is to be called John.' •They said to her, 'But no one in your family has 61
that name', •and made signs to his father to find out what he wanted him called. 62
The father asked for a writing-tablet and wrote, 'His name is John'. And they 63
were all astonished. •At that instant his power of speech returned and he spoke 64
and praised God. •All their neighbours were filled with awe and the whole affair 65
was talked about throughout the hill country of Judaea. •All those who heard 66
of it treasured it in their hearts. 'What will this child turn out to be?'
they wondered. And indeed the hand of the Lord was with him.

His father Zechariah was filled with the Holy Spirit and spoke this prophecy: 67

> '*Blessed be the Lord, the God of Israel*,   68
> for he has visited his people, he has come to their rescue
> and he has raised up for us a power for salvation   69
> in the House of his servant David,
> even as he proclaimed,   70
> by the mouth of his holy prophets from ancient times,
> that he would save us from our enemies   71
> and from the hands of all who hate us.
> Thus he shows mercy to our ancestors,   72
> thus *he remembers* his holy *covenant*,
> the oath he swore   73
> to our father Abraham
> that he would grant us, free from fear,   74
> to be delivered from the hands of our enemies,
> to serve him in holiness and virtue   75
> in his presence, all our days.
> And you, little child,   76
> you shall be called Prophet of the Most High,
> for you will go before the Lord
> to prepare the way for him.

To give his people knowledge of salvation   77
through the forgiveness of their sins;
this by the tender mercy of our God   78
who from on high will bring the rising Sun to visit us,
to give light to *those who live*   79
in darkness and the shadow of death,
and to guide our feet
into the way of peace.'

Meanwhile the child grew up and his spirit matured.   And he lived out in   80
the wilderness until the day he appeared openly to Israel.

The angel Gabriel promised that Zechariah's son would be the cause of 'joy'
(Luke 1:14). This is fulfilled here (Luke 1:58). His naming is greeted with 'awe'
(1:65) and 'wonder' (1:66):

'and indeed the hand of the Lord was with him'
                                                            (Luke 1:66)

The canticle, placed here by Luke on the lips of Zechariah (and called,
commonly, the 'Benedictus') seems to have been added by Luke. It comes from
the same source as the Magnificat.

It is carefully constructed. Verses 73-79 mirror verses 68-72, with verses 72
and 73, which speak of the covenant, forming the hinge. The central themes are
God's loving action in history (verses 68, 72a, 73b and 78-79), his prophetic word
(verses 70 and 76) and his promised salvation (verses 69-71, 74-75 and 77). Luke
seems to have touched up verses 76-77 to make the canticle apply more closely to
its subject, John.

Abraham is remembered (1:73) and so is David (1:69) with all that those
names imply. The canticle is an exultant hymn in praise of God's hesed (i.e.,
mercy 1:72, 1:78) and emet (i.e., fidelity to his promises 1:72). The ideal way of life
for God's chosen people is upheld, to 'serve him in holiness and virtue (i.e.,
justice) in his presence, all our days' (1:75).

Ultimately, it will be Jesus who makes such a life possible. It is he who is 'the
Holy One, the Just One' (Acts 3:14).

John is spoken of in terms that call to mind the promise made by Gabriel
(1:76 cf 1:15 and 17). We are also being prepared for the description of John in the
Gospel proper (cf 3:3, 6, 10-14, 7:27, 16:16).

The canticle comes to a magnificent climax:

'this by the tender mercy (the "heart of mercy") of our God who from on high will
bring the rising Sun to visit us'
                                                            (Luke 1:78)

All is in readiness for the birth of the saviour. At last darkness is to be
dispelled (1:79) and our world is to be filled with 'light' and 'peace' (1:79).

The birth of the saviour

LUKE 2:1-20

2 Now at this time Caesar Augustus issued a decree for a census of the whole   1
world to be taken. •This census—the first —took place while Quirinius was   2
governor of Syria, •and everyone went to his own town to be registered. •So Joseph   3
                                                                           4

5 set out from the town of Nazareth in Galilee and travelled up to Judaea, to the town of David called Bethlehem, since he was of David's House and line, •in order to be registered together with Mary, his betrothed, who was with child.
6
7 While they were there the time came for her to have her child, •and she gave birth to a son, her first-born. She wrapped him in swaddling clothes, and laid him in a
8 manger because there was no room for them at the inn. •In the countryside close by there were shepherds who lived in the fields and took it in turns to watch
9 their flocks during the night. •The angel of the Lord appeared to them and the glory of the Lord shone round them. They were terrified, •but the angel
10 said, 'Do not be afraid. Listen, I bring you news of great joy, a joy to be shared
11 by the whole people. •Today in the town of David a saviour has been born to
12 you; he is Christ the Lord. •And here is a sign for you: you will find a baby
13 wrapped in swaddling clothes and lying in a manger.' •And suddenly with the angel there was a great throng of the heavenly host, praising God and singing:

14
'Glory to God in the highest heaven,
and peace to men who enjoy his favour'.

15 Now when the angels had gone from them into heaven, the shepherds said to one another, 'Let us go to Bethlehem and see this thing that has happened
16 which the Lord has made known to us'. •So they hurried away and found
17 Mary and Joseph, and the baby lying in the manger. •When they saw the child
18 they repeated what they had been told about him, •and everyone who heard
19 it was astonished at what the shepherds had to say. •As for Mary, she treasured
20 all these things and pondered them in her heart. •And the shepherds went back glorifying and praising God for all they had heard and seen; it was exactly as they had been told.

Luke mentions Caesar Augustus (2:1), possibly because Caesar Augustus was hailed throughout the Empire as saviour and as peacemaker. Luke, in a gentle way, wishes to present Jesus, rather, as the true saviour and one who brought true peace. There was a census taken about the time of Jesus birth (in fact it was some ten or more years after, in 6 A.D.). Luke mentions the census here because it provides a way of getting Jesus' parents to Bethlehem. It may also be a part of Luke's apologetics. The census was the cause of the rebellion of Judas the Galilean and the founding of the zealot movement, which led, eventually, to the Jewish-Roman war of 66-73 A.D. Luke wishes to indicate that Jesus was not part of this rebellion, but that it was in obedience to the Roman edict that his parents went to Bethlehem. Luke places Jesus' birth in Bethlehem for the same reasons that Matthew places it there: it highlights the fact that Jesus is the fulfilment of the royal messianic promises made to David.

Luke mentions that the child Mary gave birth to was her 'first-born' (2:7). We need to remember that the first-born son held a special place in a Jewish family and was especially consecrated to God (cf Luke 2:23). This was in memory of God's saving action in delivering his people from Egypt (cf Exodus 13:12). Mary's child is to be the one who will achieve the ultimate deliverance of God's people.

Luke mentions that Mary 'wrapped him in swaddling clothes' (2:7). This seems a very ordinary thing to say till we hear the angels give this to the shepherds as an apocalyptic sign (Luke 2:12). Apocalyptic literature abounds in signs, usually of the most fantastic and breathtaking nature. Is Luke stressing here the 'ordinariness' of the birth of Jesus? Is he stressing the fact that the Messiah is one of us? Does he, perhaps, have in mind, the words placed into the mouth of Solomon by the author of the Book of Wisdom?

> 'Like all the others, I too am a mortal man . . .
> I was nurtured in swaddling clothes with every care;
> No king has known any other beginning or existence;
> For all, there is only one way into life, as out of it.'
>
> *(Wisdom 7:1, 4-6)*

In telling us that Mary 'laid him in a manger' (2:7 and 2:12), Luke is perhaps thinking of the prophecy of Micah:

> 'But you, Bethlehem Ephrathah,
> the least of the clans of Judah,
> out of you will be born for me
> the one who is to rule over Israel;
> his origin goes back to the distant past,
> to the days of old.
> Yahweh is therefore going to abandon them
> till the time when she who is to give birth gives birth.
> Then the remnant of his brothers will come back
> to the sons of Israel.
> He will stand and feed his flock
> with the power of Yahweh.'
>
> *(Micah 5:2-4)*

The time has come. She who is to give birth has given birth. Her son is laid in a manger, in the place where God feeds his flock.

Luke adds that 'there was no room for them at the inn' (2:7). Jeremiah had pleaded with God:

> 'Yahweh, hope of Israel,
> its Saviour in time of distress,
> why are you like a stranger in this land,
> like a traveller who stays only for the night.'
>
> *(Jeremiah 14:8)*

Jesus is God's answer to that plea. He does not stay in the inn, for he is no stranger staying only for the night. He is God's son and has come to stay among us.

The climax comes with the apocalyptic vision granted to the shepherds (Luke 2:8-14). God has already been praised, in the magnificat, for exalting the lowly (Luke 1:52). This is dramatised most powerfully here. The news that the whole world is waiting for is given, first, to the poorest of the poor. The vision is, once again, a literary device; the themes are ones we are now familiar with: 'glory' (2:10) and 'joy' (2:10). Jesus is called 'saviour', 'christ' and 'lord' (2:11), terms associated with the parousia (cf Philippians 3:20), and, as we have seen, with the risen Jesus. Here Luke applies them to the newly born child.

Once again Luke inserts a canticle of praise (2:13-14). This time it is the whole of the created universe that breaks into a hymn of cosmic praise. The stars of heaven cry out as the glory of God's dwelling lights up the earth and men know the harmony intended for them by God.

Like Mary on an earlier occasion (Luke 1:39), the shepherds 'hurry' (2:16) to Bethlehem, where they come to Jesus and glorify and praise God. This is Luke's equivalent of the magi scene in Matthew (cf Matthew 2:1-12).

The only person in this narrative who appears during Jesus' public ministry and is still present in the early church is Mary, Jesus' mother (cf Luke 8:19 and Acts 1:14). She is presented as the perfect disciple:

'she treasured all these things and pondered them in her heart'

(Luke 2:19)

Jesus is manifested to the world in the Temple

LUKE 2:21-40

21   When the eighth day came and the child was to be circumcised, they gave him the name Jesus, the name the angel had given him before his conception.

22   And when the day came for them to be purified as laid down by the Law
23   of Moses, they took him up to Jerusalem to present him to the Lord —•observing what stands written in the Law of the Lord: *Every first-born male must be con-*
24   *secrated to the Lord* —•and also to offer in sacrifice, in accordance with what
25   is said in the Law of the Lord, *a pair of turtledoves or two young pigeons.* •Now in Jerusalem there was a man named Simeon. He was an upright and devout man; he looked forward to Israel's comforting and the Holy Spirit rested on
26   him. •It had been revealed to him by the Holy Spirit that he would not see death
27   until he had set eyes on the Christ of the Lord. •Prompted by the Spirit he came to the Temple; and when the parents brought in the child Jesus to do for
28   him what the Law required, •he took him into his arms and blessed God; and he said:

29   'Now, Master, you can let your servant go in peace,
            just as you promised;
30   because my eyes have seen the salvation
31   which you have prepared for all the nations to see,
32   a light to enlighten the pagans
            and the glory of your people Israel'.

33   As the child's father and mother stood there wondering at the things that
34   were being said about him, •Simeon blessed them and said to Mary his mother, 'You see this child: he is destined for the fall and for the rising of many in Israel,
35   destined to be a sign that is rejected—•and a sword will pierce your own soul too—so that the secret thoughts of many may be laid bare'.

36   There was a prophetess also, Anna the daughter of Phanuel, of the tribe of Asher. She was well on in years. Her days of girlhood over, she had been
37   married for seven years •before becoming a widow. She was now eighty-four years old and never left the Temple, serving God night and day with fasting
38   and prayer. •She came by just at that moment and began to praise God; and she spoke of the child to all who looked forward to the deliverance of Jerusalem.

39   When they had done everything the Law of the Lord required, they went back
40   to Galilee, to their own town of Nazareth. •Meanwhile the child grew to maturity, and he was filled with wisdom; and God's favour was with him.

Luke constructed the vision of Zechariah and the vision of Mary according to the same pattern, the better to bring out the pre-eminence of Jesus. He used the same technique in relation to the two births (compare 1:57-58 with 2:1-20). The passage before us parallels the circumcision of John and his manifestation; the song of Simeon (2:29-32) expresses the fulfilment of the song of Zechariah (1:67-79); and both passages conclude with similar words (compare 2:40 with 1:80). In each case the content demonstrates how greatly Jesus surpasses John.

It is worth quoting Malachi in this context:

'Look I am going to send my messenger to prepare a way before me. And the Lord you are seeking will suddenly enter his Temple.'   *(Malachi 3:1-2)*

The Baptist is the messenger. Jesus is the Lord.

Luke has brought together two ordinances of the Law. It was commanded by the Law to consecrate the first-born son to God. Originally, this was in memory of God's sparing the first-born in Egypt, and the first-born was the one in the family responsible for the carrying out of religious rituals (Exodus 13:2). Later, the Levites were dedicated to God for this purpose (Numbers 3:12-13), and so the custom grew up of dedicating the first-born and then buying him back from God, as it were, by an offering made to the Temple (Numbers 18:15-16). The Law also commanded the mother to undergo a rite of purification one month after the birth of a male child (cf Leviticus 12:1-8). Luke does not concentrate his attention on these rituals, but they do provide him with the way of getting Jesus to the Temple. He is making the point that the Law (the two Laws mentioned) and the Prophets (represented here by Simeon and Anna) are fulfilled in Jesus.

Mary and Joseph are painted in such a way as to recall Elkanah and Hannah, the parents of Samuel. He too was taken by his parents to the sanctuary (of Shiloh, 1 Samuel 1:24-28), and Luke's story parallels theirs (cf 1 Samuel 2:20-28).

It is very likely that the Prologue ended with this scene, and, if so, Simeon and Anna provide a perfect balance for Zechariah and Elizabeth.

Luke's scene, one again, takes place in the Temple (2:27). Once again it is the Holy Spirit (2:26-27) who is directing events. Simeon's hymn of praise expresses the peaceful gratitude of God's people that, at last, God's promises are fulfilled. It is all happening 'now' (2:29), before the eyes of the people. Jesus is the 'glory of your people Israel' (2:32). He is also — and this is a theme close to Luke's heart — 'for all the nations to see' a light to 'enlighten the pagans' (2:31-32). The excitement of the preparation resolves into this peaceful (2:29) conclusion.

There is a jarring note in Simeon's second prophecy, addressed to Mary (Luke 2:34-35). We are reminded of the fact that, for the most part, Jesus was rejected by his own people. The paradox of the stone which is an obstacle causing men to stumble (cf Isaiah 8:14) and yet becomes the corner-stone of the edifice (Isaiah 28:16, Psalm 118:22) is recalled here by Luke (cf also Luke 20:17-18). Simeon's words are addressed to Mary because she, too, has to pass the test (and she does: Luke 8:19-21).

Anna's presence, besides providing a female presence and hence a balance (she is described in terms that are typical of a widow in the Christian community, cf 1 Timothy 5:3-16, Acts 6:1, 9:39-41), enables Luke to conclude his Prologue on a positive note. Whatever rejection Jesus may encounter, however many may fail the test, Jerusalem will be delivered (2:38), and God is praised (2:38) for his fidelity in fulfilling his promise.

Luke's concluding words (2:40) balance the words used of the Baptist (1:80) and follow the pattern of Samuel (cf 1 Samuel 2:26).

From the beginning of his maturity, Jesus was the Son of God

LUKE 2:41-52
Every year his parents used to go to Jerusalem for the feast of the Passover. 41 When he was twelve years old, they went up for the feast as usual. •When they 42 43 were on their way home after the feast, the boy Jesus stayed behind in Jerusalem without his parents knowing it. •They assumed he was with the caravan, and 44 it was only after a day's journey that they went to look for him among their relations and acquaintances. •When they failed to find him they went back to 45 Jerusalem looking for him everywhere.

Three days later, they found him in the Temple, sitting among the doctors, 46 listening to them, and asking them questions; •and all those who heard him 47 were astounded at his intelligence and his replies. •They were overcome 48 when they saw him, and his mother said to him, 'My child, why have you done this to us? See how worried your father and I have been, looking for you.' •'Why were you looking for me?' he replied 'Did you not know that I must 49 be busy with my Father's affairs?' •But they did not understand what he meant. 50

He then went down with them and came to Nazareth and lived under their 51 authority. His mother stored up all these things in her heart. •And Jesus increased 52 in wisdom, in stature, and in favour with God and men.

This seems to be a later addition by Luke, for it upsets the balance of the Prologue, and represents a duplication of Jesus' manifestation in the Temple (compare 2:52 and 2:40). It perhaps represents an independent story aimed at stating the fact that Jesus was the Son of God prior to his Baptism and from the beginning of his maturity. Luke includes it here because it reinforces what he has already presented. Jesus is the Son of God; Jesus does belong in the Temple, and Christianity does come from the Temple. There is a continuity in God's providence.

*   *   *   *   *   *   *   *

Luke has expressed his belief in Jesus as the one in whom history reached its fulfilment and found its meaning. He is the God who saves (1:31), the 'Son of God' (1:32, 1:35), the 'Son of David' (1:32). He is 'Lord' (1:43), the one in whom the promises of God are fulfilled (1:54), the one who brings peace and joy (2:10 and 2:14). He is one with us (2:7, 2:40, 2:51), the one who brings Good News to the poor (2:8). He is the light of the nations (2:32), the glory of Israel (2:32), the judge (2:34). He is the one who does the will of God (2:49). He is Jesus of Nazareth (2:51), and it is from Nazareth that he will set out on his mission of love.

In doing this, Luke develops three of his favourite themes. We will see more of them as we study the Gospel. The first is the primacy of the activity of the Spirit of God in history (cf Luke 1:15, 35, 41; 2:25-27). The second is prayer as the primary response of man to this Spirit (cf Luke 1:10, 13, 46-55, 66, 67-79; 2:19, 29-32, 38, 51). The effect of this prayer is a readiness to do the will of God (cf Luke 1:38; 2:49). The third is the spirit of joy and exultation that permeates the Prologue and is the sign of a freed people (cf Luke 1:14, 28, 44, 47, 58; 2:10, 14).

This is the Apocalyptic joy reserved for the last times when God fulfils his promises and manifests his faithful love. This is the Good News about which Luke is writing.

Points for Reflection:

1: The story of Zechariah is a story of the power of prayer. Zechariah's prayer (1:13) is part of the prayer (1:10) of the assembled community. How conscious am I of the power of the Church's liturgy? Zechariah was carrying out his appointed ministry at the time. Paul tells us that each of us has a special gift of the Spirit to be exercised for the community (cf Ephesians 4:1-16). There is a special power in prayer that is coupled with service and gathered up in the prayer of the Church.

2: Mary is presented by Luke as the model disciple of Jesus. She is completely open to the Spirit of God, and willing to believe in the impossible on God's word (1:38). Her reaction to God's gift is one of wonder and praise and gratitude (1:46-55).

3: One of the fruits of the Incarnation is a deeper awareness of the sacredness of the human body. Mary was caught up in God's glory and became the 'Temple' of the Lord. Jesus treated every person he met as sacred, for he experienced God at the heart of the simple people he encountered in his ministry. How respectful am I of others? Do I approach them with reverence?

4: It is possible, thanks to the faithful love of God, to live in the presence of God all our days (1:75). Is this a dimension of my consciousness? Or am I distracted over many things? Do I take time, in prayer, to explore the depths of experiences of my life and to let the God who is present speak to me?

5: Let us pray that, by his tender mercy (1:78) God may bring his Son to visit us (1:78). Walking with him, our feet will be guided into the way of peace (1:78).

6: How much joy and wonder is there in my life when I contemplate the wonderful things God has done for me, and the power of his presence and his tender mercy in our world? There is much suffering too, but Paul sees even this in a positive light:

> 'From the beginning till now the entire creation as we know has been groaning in one great act of giving birth.'
>
> *(Romans 8:22)*

Mary was chosen to play a part in God's design to bring joy and peace to men. Each of us could be an instrument in this same work.

7: In Jesus God became part of the world he loved so much. God identified himself with man. How closely do I identify with the people I claim to serve? How closely does the Christian community identify with the world it claims to love? Does the church belong to the manger or the inn (2:7)?

8: Do I learn contemplation from Mary? She pondered in her heart the mysteries of God's action in her life (2:19, 2:33, 2:51). Do I?

9: Am I 'busy with my Father's affairs'? (2:49)

III. **JOHN'S PROLOGUE** (John 1:1-18)

The Gospels bring us immediately into contact with the community within which they were written; only indirectly do they tell us about what Jesus of Nazareth actually said and did. In other words, we see Jesus through the eyes and through the faith of the community which wrote the Gospel.

The Gospel according to John seems to have been written about 90 A.D. somewhere around Ephesus in the Roman province of Asia. To understand the Gospel we need to know something of the mental outlook of the people in that area at the time. This means, especially, that we need to know something about Gnosticism.

There are many varieties of Gnosticism, and it is not so much a philosophy, with disciplined categories of thought attempting a systematic understanding of the world, as a conglomeration of ideas attempting to make people feel good about life. The gnostics shied away from reason, and made no demands for a consistent, responsible, moral life in the community. Rather, they saw the goal of life as consisting in intimacy with the divine, an intimacy that was emotional, ecstatic and often orgiastic. The way to this intimacy was through enlightenment. (The greek word is 'gnosis', hence the name 'gnostic'). This enlightenment was given only to the initiated, and by especially gifted teachers, who themselves claimed special esoteric knowledge of divine matters, knowledge granted them in a pre-existence. These special teachers claimed, often, to be sinless, and only they could introduce the initiated into the divine mysteries.

Paul addressed himself to people tainted with gnosticism in his letters to the Ephesians and the Colossians, and the Gospel according to John was written within the same milieu. The Gospel was read by gnostics, and the author speaks in their language, the better to attract them away from the distractions of false mysticism to faith in Jesus. Throughout the Gospel he speaks of intimacy with God, he speaks of enlightenment and of initiation. He speaks of the pre-existence of Jesus, and of Jesus' special knowledge. In other words, he presents his faith and the faith of his community in language that could be grasped by his contemporaries.

The price paid was high, for the Gospel according to John, because of its highly poetic form and because of the special perspective it took on Jesus, was able to be used by the gnostics for their own purposes. In fact, for a century after it appeared it was a text they loved to quote. Christian apologists, like Ignatius of Antioch, Polycarp, and Justin did not use this Gospel in their arguments with the gnostics.

The Letters according to John, written within the same community about 100 A.D., indicate that the Christian community was dangerously divided. The author sets about the task of righting a misuse of the Gospel in the church. Gnostic Christians were using John to make of Jesus just another 'divine' mediator between God and man, and were ignoring completely the fact that Jesus was man like us. The Prologue to the first letter stresses the humanity of Jesus (1 John 1:1). The author stresses the fact that Jesus 'came in the flesh' (1 John 4:2 and 2 John 7). He speaks also about the 'blood' of Jesus (1 John 5:6).

The church accepted the Gospel according to John as an authentic expression of the Christian faith. But we need to realise how easily it was used by heretics, lest we, too, fall into the same trap. The Gospel according to John presents us with a beautiful perspective on Jesus; but we need to keep this perspective within the broader picture presented in the Synoptic Gospels and the Letters of John. As our hearts and minds soar with the eagle, let us not forget that the Gospel is about:

'something that we have heard
that we have seen with our own eyes;
that we have watched
and touched with our hands'

(1 John 1:1)

* * * * * * * *

We are using the Jerusalem Bible translation throughout this book. I shall, therefore, give the JB translation of the Prologue. However, I shall place beside it the translation I would prefer to use in this section. The constant use of the pronoun 'he' in the first 13 verses, tends to make the reader think of Jesus. The author, on the other hand does not introduce Jesus till verse 14; 'he' is simply a translation of the Greek pronoun for the masculine gender word 'logos' (='word'). Rather than use 'it', I have simply kept repeating the noun.

I suggest that the reader go over the text slowly and meditatively a number of times before reading the commentary. John's poetry needs to flow over the reader again and again if he is going to penetrate to the profound depths of John's faith.

* * * * * * * *

For the convenience of the reader, you are asked to turn to the next page.

For easier comparison the Jerusalem Bible's translation of John's prologue is printed opposite the author's own translation.

Verses 6-9 and 15 in the prologue are omitted as they refer to John the Baptist. They will be treated separately.

JOHN 1:1-18

In the beginning was the Word: 1
the Word was with God
and the Word was God.
He was with God in the beginning.   2
Through him all things came to be,   3
not one thing had its being but through him.
All that came to be   had life in him   4
and that life was the light of men,
a light that shines in the dark,   5
a light that darkness could not overpower.

The Word was the true light   9
that enlightens all men;
and he was coming into the world.
He was in the world   10
that had its being through him,
and the world did not know him.
He came to his own domain   11
and his own people did not accept him.

But to all who did accept him   12
he gave power to become children of God,
to all who believe in the name of him
who was   born not out of human stock   13
or urge of the flesh
or will of man
but of God himself.

The Word was made flesh,   14
he lived among us,
and we saw his glory,
the glory that is his as the only Son of the Father,
full of grace and truth.

Indeed, from his fulness we have, all of us, received—   16
yes, grace in return for grace,
since, though the Law was given through Moses,   17
grace and truth have come through Jesus Christ.

No one has ever seen God;   18
it is the only Son, who is nearest to the Father's heart,
who has made him known.

JOHN 1:1—18 (Author's translation)

In the beginning was the Word
and the Word was *towards* God
and the Word was God.
The *Word* was *towards* God in the beginning.
Through the *Word* all things came to be
not one thing had its being but through the *Word*.
That which came to be in the *Word* was life
and that life was the light of men,
a light that shines in the dark
a light that darkness could not overpower.

The Word was the true light
that enlightens all men;
and the *Word* was coming into the world.
The *Word* was in the world
that had its being through the *Word*,
and the world did not know the *Word*.
The *Word* came to *its* own domain,
and *its* own people did not accept the *Word*.

But to all who did accept the *Word*
the *Word* gave power to become children of God;
all who believed in the name of the *Word*
were born not out of human stock
or urge of the flesh
or will of man
but of God himself.

The Word was made flesh
and *pitched his tent* among us,
and we saw his glory
the glory that is his as the only Son of the Father
full of *faithful love.*

Indeed, from his fulness we have, all of us, received
yes, grace *in place of* grace,
since, though the Law was given through Moses
faithful love has come through Jesus, the Messiah.

No one has ever seen God;
it is the only Son, who is nearest to the Father's heart,
who has made him known.

When John writes 'no one has ever seen God' (1:18), he is simply repeating traditional Hebrew thought (for example Exodus 33:23). At the same time, it was traditional Hebrew faith that God did reveal himself through his word: the word spoken through the prophets, the word spoken in creation; but, above all, the word spoken through the history of the chosen people. God spoke his word especially when he delivered them from Egypt:

'I have seen the miserable state of my people in Egypt.
I have heard their appeal to be free of their slave-drivers.
Yes, I am well-aware of their sufferings.
I mean to deliver them out of the hands of the Egyptians.'

(Exodus 3:7-8)

In that mighty deed, God revealed himself as a God of love (Hebrew 'hesed'), and a God who is faithful to his love (Hebrew 'emet').

God reveals his presence among his people when they give expression to his faithful love in the practical wisdom with which they live their lives. Wisdom is God's greatest gift because it is a sharing of his own life.

The prophets kept pleading with the people to act wisely; that is, to manifest in their everyday behaviour the faithful love of God. 'What I want is love', says Hosea (6:6). 'Let justice flow like water and integrity like an unfailing stream' says Amos (5:24). 'This is what Yahweh asks of you' says Micah (6:8), 'only this: to act justly, to love tenderly and to walk humbly with your God.'

The people failed to listen to God's word; they failed to live wisely; and so we hear the prophets promising a new covenant, a new revelation:

'I shall pour clean water over you and you shall be cleansed;
I shall cleanse you of all your defilement and all your idols.
I shall give you a new heart and put a new spirit in you;
I shall remove the heart of stone from your bodies,
and give you a heart of flesh instead.
I shall put my spirit in you and make you keep my laws.'

(Ezekiel 36:25-27, cf Jeremiah 31:33)

In his Prologue, John traces the history of God's word. He begins with God and goes on to creation and then to the gift of the Law and the word spoken to Israel. Finally he reaches a climax in Jesus of Nazareth, for it is John's conviction that it was Jesus who finally revealed God to him and to his contemporaries. It was Jesus who made God's word flesh for them; it was Jesus who showed that God is, indeed, a God of faithful love (1:14, 1:17).

JOHN 1:1-5

'In the beginning was the Word
and the Word was towards God
and the Word was God.
Through the Word all things came to be,
not one thing had its being but through the Word.
That which came to be in the Word was life
and that life was the light of men,
a light that shines in the dark,
a light that darkness could not overpower.'

The Hebrew creation mythology can be found in the early chapters of the Book of Genesis, which opens with the words 'In the beginning' (Genesis 1:1). There we read of the Word summoning creation into being, of the light dispelling the darkness of chaos and manifesting the glory of the unseen God. There, too, we learn of the darkness at the heart of man, his pride and disobedience that issue in suffering and frustration and death.

In the first verses of his Prologue, John is reflecting on these same mysteries. The world made by God is also made for God and there is a cry at the heart of creation calling on God and yearning for closer union with him. It is to this Word that John draws the attention of his readers, the Word that was 'towards God', that 'addressed itself to God' (1:1-2), the Word that cries out from the heart of the created universe and from the heart of man.

Paul speaks of it when he writes:

'From the beginning till now the entire creation, as we know, has been groaning in one great act of giving birth.'

(Romans 8:22)

The Psalms are full of the cry that comes from the heart of man and is addressed to God. We shall take but one example here.

'God, you are my God, I am seeking you,
my soul is thirsting for you,
my flesh is longing for you,
a land, parched, weary and waterless;
I long to gaze on you in the sanctuary,
and to see your power and your glory.

Your love is better than life itself,
my lips will recite your praise;
all my life I will bless you,
in your name lift up my hands;
my soul will feast most richly,
on my lips a song of joy and, in my mouth, praise.'

(Psalm 63:1-5)

This cry, this 'Word' that calls on God is itself an expression of the God who is hidden at the heart of his creatures, but is beyond their sight. It is God himself calling his creation to him. 'The Word was God' (1:1).

The Book of Proverbs speaks of God's Wisdom in similar terms. Wisdom is personified and spoken of as being present in the beginning 'delighting to be with the sons of men' (8:31).

'Yahweh created me when his purpose first unfolded,
before the oldest of his works.
From everlasting I was firmly set,
from the beginning, before earth came into being.
The deep was not when I was born,
there were no springs to gush with water.
Before the mountains were settled,
before the hills, I came to birth;
before he made the earth, the countryside,
or the first grains of the world's dust.
When he fixed the heavens firm, I was there,

when he drew a ring on the surface of the deep,
when he thickened the clouds above,
when he fixed fast the springs of the deep,
when he assigned the sea its boundaries
— and the water will not invade the shore —
when he laid down the foundations of the earth,
I was by his side, a master craftsman,
delighting him day after day,
ever at play in his presence,
at play everywhere in his world,
delighting to be with the sons of men.'

(Proverbs 8:22-31)

According to John, it is this word that is the driving force impelling creation towards its maker. It is responsible for the coming into being of 'all things' (1:3), it expresses its presence in 'life' (1:4), a life that cannot, for all the power exercised by darkness, be mastered (1:5). The author of the Book of Wisdom could write:

'light must yield to night, but over Wisdom evil can never triumph.'

(Wisdom 7:30)

For John, too, the word is present at the heart of creation, in the very darkness itself, calling on God, and summoning creation to life.

JOHN 1:9-10

**'The Word was the true light
that enlightens all men;
and the Word was coming into the world.
The Word was in the world
that had its being through the Word,
and the world did not know the Word.'**

John sees God as calling the whole of the created universe to himself. Wherever there is life, there we find God. God's word was always 'coming into the world' (1:9), through the events of every people's history, through the prophets of every nation, calling men to union with God.

But the tragedy, as John sees it (cf Paul too, Romans 1:18-32) is that 'the world did not know the Word' (1:10). The world did not hear the call; it did not heed the summons. Man, made by love and made for love, preferred darkness to light, slavery to freedom, dissipation and distraction to a wholehearted response to the unseen God calling to him in the depths of his own heart and history; calling him to love.

JOHN 1:11

'The Word came to its own domain and its own people did not accept the Word.'

Here we find, according to John, an even greater tragedy. One might have hoped that the people who experienced the deliverance from Egypt, the people who experienced God as 'Yahweh', the God of enduring love, would have accepted God's word and responded by a life of compassion. They had the Law and the Prophets constantly reminding them of the Covenant. Ben Sirach, for example, places the following words on the lips of Wisdom:

'I came forth from the mouth of the Most High,
and I covered the earth like mist.
I had my tent in the heights
and my throne in a pillar of cloud.
Alone I encircled the vault of the sky,
and I walked on the bottom of the deeps.
Over the waves of the sea and over the whole earth,
and over every people and nation I have held sway.
Among all these I searched for rest,
and I looked to see in whose territory I might pitch camp.
Then the creator of all things instructed me,
and he who created me fixed a place for my tent,
He said, "Pitch your tent in Jacob,
make Israel your inheritance".
From eternity, in the beginning, he created me,
and for eternity I shall remain.
I ministered before him in the holy tabernacle
and thus was I established on Zion.
In the beloved city he has given me rest,
and in Jerusalem I wield my authority.
I have taken root in a privileged people,
in the Lord's property, in his inheritance.'

(Ecclesiasticus 24:3-12)

Yes, the Word did take root in a privileged people, but, says John, this people 'did not accept the Word' (1:11).

JOHN 1:12-13

'But to all who did accept the Word
the Word gave power to become children of God,
all who believed in the name (power) of the Word
were born not out of human stock
or urge of the flesh
or will of man
but of God himself.'

The rejection of God's word was never universal. Throughout history specially the history of God's chosen people, there were those who heard and heeded God's word, and who lived according to the wisdom that comes from God.

The author of the Book of Wisdom, speaking of wisdom, wrote:

'In each generation she passes into holy souls, she makes them friends of God and prophets.'

(Wisdom 7:27)

In his first letter, John speaks, in similar terms, of those who live justly and who love their neighbour.

'You know that God is just — then you must recognise that everyone who does justice has been begotten by God.'

(1 John 2:29)

'Everyone who loves is begotten by God and knows God.'

(1 John 4:7)

JOHN 1:14

'The Word was made flesh,
and pitched its tent among us,
and we saw his glory,
the glory that is his as the only Son of the Father,
full of faithful love (grace and truth; hesed and emet).'

The author of Ecclesiasticus spoke of God's wisdom pitching its tent in Jacob (Ecclesiasticus 24:7). The author of the Book of Wisdom wrote of God's glory being revealed in the wisdom that God gives to men:

'Wisdom is a breath of the power of God,
pure emanation of the glory of the Almighty;
hence nothing impure can find a way into her.
She is a reflection of the eternal light,
untarnished mirror of God's active power,
image of his goodness . . .
With you is Wisdom, she who knows your works,
she who was present when you made the world;
she understands what is pleasing in your eyes
and what agrees with your commandments.
Despatch her from the holy heavens,
send her forth from your throne of glory
to help me and to toil with me
and teach me what is pleasing to you,
since she knows and understands everything.
She will guide me prudently in my undertakings
and protect me by her glory.'

(Wisdom 7:25-26; 8:9-11)

John found this wisdom in Jesus. John heard God's word spoken to him in Jesus. In Jesus he saw the glory of God.

This is the climax of the Prologue, and the essence of Christianity. God spoke his word in the flesh of Jesus. 'The Word was made flesh' (1:14). What a daring thing to say! Jesus, the one who knew weariness, who was misunderstood, who suffered denial and rejection; Jesus who knew our human condition, who died on a cross; it was this Jesus who experienced the word of God in the depths of his being and answered the call with all his heart and soul and mind and strength. Not only that; it was this Jesus who spoke God's word to John and his contemporaries, in the wisdom of his life, and so manifested the glory of God. Jesus was 'born of God' in a unique way such that John can call him the 'only Son of the Father' (1:14). Just as God's glory was revealed by his 'hesed' and 'emet', his faithful love, so Jesus revealed the glory of God because he was full of this divine life and manifested it in his life.

JOHN 1:16-17

'Indeed, from his fulness we have, all of us, received —
yes, grace in place of grace,
since, though the Law was given through Moses,
faithful love has come through Jesus, the Messiah.'

The Law of Moses, enacted to ensure that God's work of liberation would continue to carry on the fight against injustice and the sin that leads to oppression, had, in spite of the eulogies of a man like Ben Sirach (cf Ecclesiasticus 24:22), failed in its purpose. We have already mentioned that the prophets looked forward to a new Law written in men's hearts.

John sees Jesus as the answer to this hope. He kept God's word. He, at last, was full of 'faithful love' (John 1:14). More than that, he shared his spirit with others, including John.' He challenged them to answer God's call, and he made it possible for them, too, to receive of his fullness. He brought faithful love with him and gave it as a grace to others. He made it possible for men to 'act justly, love tenderly and walk humbly with their God' (Micah 6:8). He is the 'Christ' (1:17). He is the answer to all the hopes of the Prophets. He is the one through whom God could keep his promises. He is the one who makes it possible for creation to achieve its purpose.

From the beginning God's word has been calling all men to him. This word has been present in the depths of man's being, indeed at the heart of creation, crying out to God. While the darkness could not block it out, at the same time man could not respond to the call with all his heart for he was wounded and weakened. At last, in Jesus, God's word met a wholehearted 'Yes'. In Jesus the word of God and the word in man crying out to God find identity. Jesus is the word of God.

JOHN 1:18

'No one has ever seen God;
it is the only Son, who is nearest to the Father's heart,
who has made him known.'

John wants his readers to realise, from the start, that he is presenting to them the man Jesus so that they will come to know the true God. The world did not know the true God, did not hear God's word (John 1:10). Even 'the Jews', for all their privileges, did not accept God's word (John 1:11); their God, too, was a false one, as their lives showed. John, therefore, is making an enormous claim: he is claiming that by knowing Jesus men can come to know the true God; in living as Jesus lived, men can find a true response to the call at the depths of their hearts, an answer to the word that has been there from the beginning.

*   *   *   *   *   *   *   *

In this chapter we have studied the Prologues of Matthew, Luke and John. In each case they lead into the scene by the Jordan and introduce John the Baptist. We studied this scene in our opening chapter. In the following chapter we shall complete the Introductory section. Jesus appears for the first time in public as he is baptised in the Jordan by John. It is clear from the outset that it is the Spirit of God that is active in Jesus. At the same time the Synoptics contrast this scene with the scene in the desert which makes it clear that this same Jesus is our brother, tempted like us. The Gospel narrative has to be read against this background of the divinity and humanity of Jesus.

*   *   *   *   *   *   *   *   *   *

Points for Reflection:

1. Teilhard de Chardin (from 'The Divine Milieu', page 153)

'Those of us who are disciples of Christ must not hesitate to harness this force, which needs us and which we need. On the contrary, under pain of allowing it to be lost and of perishing ourselves, we should share these aspirations, in essence religious, which make the men of today feel so strongly the immensity of the world, the greatness of the mind, and the sacred value of every new truth. It is in this way that our Christian generation will learn again to expect.'

It is the Word that summons creation to its maker, that drives the evolutionary forces of the world. This word is among us today calling us from within our darkness. It is up to us to 'test every barrier, try every path, plumb the abyss' (The Divine Milieu page 69).

2: Jesus is the one who expresses the Word of God most clearly. Read Paul:

'It is the same God that said: "Let there be light shining out of the darkness", who has shone in our minds to radiate the light of the knowledge of God's glory, the glory on the face of Christ.'

(2 Corinthians 4:6)

'The Lord is the Spirit and where the Spirit of the Lord is there is *freedom*. And we, with our unveiled faces reflecting like mirrors the brightness of the Lord, all grow brighter and brighter as we are turned into the image that we reflect; this is the work of the Lord who is Spirit.'

(2 Corinthians 3:17-18)

3: The Word is, first and foremost, a practical word, calling each of us to work for the liberation of the poor and oppressed. This was the word addressed to Moses; this was the word that found expression in the Law and that was spoken by the Prophets. This was the Word lived out by Jesus who was full of faithful love, thus manifesting the compassion of his Father. To 'accept the Word' is to make practical decisions. It is, as John tells us, to 'do justice', to 'love'.

4: John sees 'life' (1:4) as the expression of the presence of God's creative action, and the response of creation to God's word. According to John, Jesus came that we might have life and have it to the full (John 10:10). Certainly, life is consistent with an agony in a garden and a death on a cross; it is not something as superficial as 'happiness'. But it is an infallible sign of God's presence and action. We must be patient, we must be willing to walk 'in the darkness' trusting in God. But if we, like Jesus, live a life of faithful love, we will know the peace of God. We, like Jesus, must be about life, about giving our life so that others may live and live to the full. There is no place in Christian living, in Christian morality, for a negative attitude to life.

5: When I am in darkness, do I believe that it is there that the light shines (1:5)?

6: Do I strive for perfection by my own efforts (Philippians 3:9)? Do I imagine that life is measured by my striving (John 1:13). Or do I, like a child, open myself to God's gracious gift of life, and wonder at his love, and allow his life to flow through me and find expression in all I do?

Chapter 3
Jesus is the Son of God and our Brother

Mark 1:9-13
Matthew 3:13 — 4:11
Luke 3:21 — 4:13
John 1:29-34

With this chapter we conclude the introductory section of the Gospels. In the Baptism scene, the Gospel-writers present Jesus as the one in whom the Spirit of God comes with power into our world. In the desert scene, Jesus is shown to be our brother, tempted like us, having to work out his mission, like us, in a struggle with the powers of evil.

1: The Baptism of Jesus

MARK 1:9-11 (Compare Matthew 3:13, 16-17 and Luke 3:21-22)
It was at this time that Jesus came from Nazareth in Galilee and was baptised 9 in the Jordan by John. •No sooner had he come up out of the water than he 10 saw the heavens torn apart and the Spirit, like a dove, descending on him. And a voice came from heaven, 'You are my Son, the Beloved; my favour rests 11 on you'.

Jesus' public life began at the Jordan River. Jesus came, like many others, to be baptised by John. The event proved critical in his life, for after this he was moved by the Spirit of God to begin his public preaching and his ministry of love and healing. It was here, in his Baptism, that Jesus received his mission from God.

This was the beginning of the new heaven and the new earth to which the prophets had looked forward. Remembering the waters of chaos over which hovered the Spirit of God, and the creation that emerged from those waters as God spoke his word (cf Genesis 1:2), the Gospel-writers speak of God's Spirit hovering, once again, over the waters (1:10). Without knowing it, the world is experiencing a new beginning.

For a long time the Jews had been troubled by the lack of prophets in their midst (cf Daniel 3:28 and Isaiah 64:12) and had sent up to God a constant cry:

'lower your heavens, Yahweh, and come down to us'

(Psalm 144:5 cf also Isaiah 64:1)

The Gospel-writers see Jesus as God's answer to that plea. The heavens, at last, are 'torn apart' (1:10) and God breaks the long silence, introducing his 'beloved Son' (1:11).

A gentle touch is provided by the mention of the 'dove' (Mark 1:10). We are reminded of the passage from the Song of Songs:

'My Beloved lifts up his voice,
he says to me,
Come then, my love,
my lovely one, come.
For see, winter is past,
the rains are over and gone.
The flowers appear on the earth.
The season of glad songs has come,
the cooing of the turtledove is heard
in our land.
The fig tree is forming its first figs
and the blossoming vines give out their fragrance.
Come then, my love,
my lovely one, come.
My dove, hiding in the clefts of the rock,
in the coverts of the cliff,
show me your face,
let me hear your voice.'

(2:10-14)

The voice that breaks the silence is the voice of the Beloved. It is the God of love who is coming to woo his people.

The Jews believed that the anointed one, the 'Christ' would be of the kingly house of David. At each coronation ceremony when the king was consecrated to God, the words 'You are my Son' (Psalm 2:7) were spoken over him. They are spoken over Jesus at his consecration in the Jordan.

Mark also reminds his readers of the opening words of the first song of the servant of Yahweh:

'Here is my servant whom I uphold, my chosen one in whom my soul delights.'

(Isaiah 42:1)

The Jesus who is about to begin his public ministry is, indeed, the Messiah, the 'Son of God' (1:11). It is God's Spirit that will be working in him (1:10). But, he is not the kind of Messiah many expect and we are going to have to watch him closely if we wish to know what God's Spirit is really like. Mark wants to be sure that his readers look at Jesus in the light of the songs of the Servant of Yahweh, for these songs express best the way in which Jesus is the Christ. The reader would do well to meditate on them before going further. (Isaiah 42:1-9; 49:1-6; 50:4-11; 52:13 — 53:12).

* * * * * * * *

Matthew adds the following passage:

MATTHEW 3:14-15

•John tried to dissuade him. 'It is I who need baptism from you' he said ₁₄ 'and yet you come to me!' •But Jesus replied, 'Leave it like this for the time being; ₁₅ it is fitting that we should, in this way, do all that righteousness demands'. At this, John gave in to him.

The fact that Jesus was baptised by John posed something of a problem for the early Christian community. The followers of the Baptist claimed that this demonstrated John's superiority over Jesus. The above dialogue is part of Matthew's polemic against this group. John baptised Jesus because this was part of the providential will of God (1:15).

＊　＊　＊　＊　＊　＊　＊

In **Luke's** account, note that there is no mention of John: the attention of the reader is centred on Jesus. And Jesus — as one would expect from Luke — is 'at prayer' (Luke 3:21).

Luke immediately inserts the following genealogy. Having established the fact that Jesus is the Son of God, he wishes to remind the reader that he is also the 'Son of Man', born, like us all, of flesh. He is our brother.

Luke follows his account of the Baptism with the genealogy of Jesus. Jesus who is the Son of God is also son of man.

LUKE 3:23-38
When he started to teach, Jesus was about thirty years old, being the son, 23
as it was thought, of Joseph son of Heli, •son of Matthat, son of Levi, son 24
of Melchi, son of Jannai, son of Joseph, •son of Mattathias, son of Amos, son 25
of Nahum, son of Esli, son of Naggai, •son of Maath, son of Mattathias, son 26
of Semein, son of Josech, son of Joda, •son of Joanan, son of Rhesa, son of 27
Zerubbabel, son of Shealtiel, son of Neri, •son of Melchi, son of Addi, son of 28
Cosam, son of Elmadam, son of Er, son of Joshua, •son of Joshua, son of Eliezer, 29
son of Jorim, son of Matthat, son of Levi, •son of Symeon, son of Judah, son 30
of Joseph, son of Jonam, son of Eliakim, •son of Melea, son of Menna, son of 31
Mattatha, son of Nathan, son of David, •son of Jesse, son of Obed, son of Boaz, 32
son of Sala, son of Nahshon, •son of Amminadab, son of Admin, son of Arni, 33
son of Hezron, son of Perez, son of Judah, •son of Jacob, son of Isaac, son 34
of Abraham, son of Terah, son of Nahor, •son of Serug, son of Reu, son of 35
Peleg, son of Eber, son of Shelah, •son of Cainan, son of Arphaxad, son of 36
Shem, son of Noah, son of Lamech, •son of Methuselah, son of Enoch, son of 37
Jared, son of Mahalaleel, son of Cainan, •son of Enos, son of Seth, son of Adam, 38
son of God.

It is interesting to compare this genealogy with the one provided by Matthew (1:1-17, page 20).

Matthew traces the line back only as far as Abraham, thus betraying his peculiarly Jewish interest. Luke, on the other hand, who was himself a non-Jew and was writing for a largely non-Jewish community, goes back to Adam, wishing thereby to underline the universal significance of Jesus.

The genealogy can be divided into three sections. The first traces the ancestry of David (3:32-38). Matthew and Luke draw their material from the same source, the First Book of Chronicles (1:1 — 2:15). The second section traces the line from David to the exile in Babylon (3:27-32). The only names that Matthew and Luke have in common are the last two, Zerubbabel and Shealtiel. Matthew wishes to underline the kingly messiahship of Jesus and he traces the line through the ruling family of Solomon. Luke, on the other hand, traces the line through another of David's sons, Nathan (3:32). The third section runs from the exile to Jesus. Apart from the name of Joseph, the two genealogies have nothing in common, and we have no way of tracing the accuracy of either. There was a great interest in genealogies during the period under consideration, and lists proliferated. Neither writer is guaranteeing complete accuracy. Their aim is to demonstrate that Jesus belonged to the history of his people.

John does not describe the baptism of Jesus directly. He has the Baptist reflect on it later:

JOHN 1:29-34

29   The next day, seeing Jesus coming towards him, John said, 'Look, there is
30   the lamb of God that takes away the sin of the world. •This is the one I spoke
of when I said: A man is coming after me who ranks before me because he
31   existed before me. •I did not know him myself, and yet it was to reveal him to
32   Israel that I came baptising with water.' •John also declared, 'I saw the Spirit
33   coming down on him from heaven like a dove and resting on him. •I did not
know him myself, but he who sent me to baptise with water had said to me,
"The man on whom you see the Spirit come down and rest is the one who is
34   going to baptise with the Holy Spirit". •Yes, I have seen and I am the witness
that he is the Chosen One of God.'

The basic message is the same as that of the Synoptics: the Spirit of God rests on Jesus (1:32, 33), who is described, in words taken from the first Servant song (Isaiah 42:1) as the 'Chosen one of God' (1:34). It is worth reading the whole of the first Servant song, here, as the accent on justice is central to John's understanding of the mission of Jesus:

'Here is my servant whom I uphold,
my chosen one in whom my soul delights.
I have endowed him with my spirit
that he may bring true justice to the nations.

He does not cry out or shout aloud,
or make his voice heard in the streets.
He does not break the crushed reed,
nor quench the wavering flame.

Faithfully he brings true justice;
he will neither waver nor be crushed
until true justice is established on earth,
for the islands are awaiting his law.'

(Isaiah 42:1-4)

John develops two other themes. The Baptist says of Jesus 'he existed before me' (1:30), repeating a statement made in the Prologue (1:15), and reminding the reader that this Jesus is the Word of God, the same word that was present 'in the beginning' (1:1). He also speaks of Jesus as 'the lamb of God who takes away the sins of the world' (1:29). We are reminded again of the Servant of Yahweh who is described as a lamb going to the slaughter (Isaiah 53:7). It is worth reading here the whole of the fourth Servant song (Isaiah 52:13 — 53:12) with its central theme of redemptive suffering leading to final glorification; for this, as we shall see, is a favourite theme of John's. In each episode of his Gospel, John reminds his readers of the cross, and this scene is no exception. For the 'lamb of God' calls to mind also the Passover lamb whose blood was sprinkled over the doorposts of the Hebrews' houses, thus saving them from the wrath of God's avenging angel (cf Exodus 12:1-14). The blood of this lamb is to 'take away the sins of the world' (John 1:29); this servant of God is to 'offer his life in atonement' (Isaiah 53:10).

2: Jesus Undergoes Trial in the Desert

MARK 1:12-13
Immediately afterwards the Spirit drove him out into the wilderness •and he 12 13
remained there for forty days, and was tempted by Satan. He was with the wild beasts, and the angels looked after him.

This scene acts as a balance to the previous one. Jesus is 'divine': he is the one on whom the Spirit of God rests. He is also 'human', he is our brother. As the author of the Letter to the Hebrews wrote:

'It is not as if we had a high priest who was incapable of feeling our weaknesses with us; but we have one who has been tempted in every way that we are, though he is without sin.'

(Hebrews 4:15)

Moses had promised:

'Yahweh your God will raise up for you a prophet like myself, from among yourselves, from your own brothers; to him you must listen.'

(Deuteronomy 18:15)

It is the humanity of Jesus that **Mark** wishes to underline in this scene. The 'forty days' (1:13) is meant to be taken symbolically: it reminds us of the forty years during which the Hebrews were tried in the desert (cf Numbers 14:34). They were tempted to turn back, tempted to abandon God, tempted to stop their journey to freedom. This is the experience of every man, and the literature dealing with the Exodus and desert journey is a classical account of the journey of every man and every nation. The Jesus the disciples knew was no different from us in this. He knew our sufferings; like us he was tried by adversity. He was under constant pressure from his enemies right up to his death. Jesus was not some kind of 'divine being' passing through our world untouched by the evils that assail us. Driven by the Spirit (1:12 — the expression conveys a sense of power!), cared for by God (1:13), he was still, like us, 'in the wilderness' (1:12); he was still like us, 'tempted by Satan' (1:13).

The 'forty days' (1:13) reminds us, too, of the time spent by Moses on the mountain with God (Exodus 24:18 and 34:28) and of the journey of Elijah across the desert to the mountain of God (1 Kings 19:8).

In saying that Jesus was 'with the wild beasts' (1:13), Mark is reminding his readers of the harmony experienced by Adam before the Fall (Genesis 2:19), a harmony the Messiah was to restore:

'The wolf lives with the lamb,
the panther lies down with the kid,
calf and lion-cub feed together.'

(Isaiah 11:6)

Paul wrote to the Corinthians:

'God in Christ was reconciling the world to himself.'

(2 Corinthians 5:19)

The people of God passed through the Red Sea and into the desert. They were tempted and they failed. At the same time the period in the desert was seen by the prophets as a special time of love between God and his people, a kind of courting time. The prophet Hosea, for example, writes:

'I am going to lure her
and lead her out into the wilderness
and speak to her heart.
I am going to give her back her vineyards,
and make the Valley of Achor a gateway of hope.
There she will respond to me as she did when she was young,
as she did when she came out of the land of Egypt . . .

When that day comes I will make a treaty on her behalf with the wild animals,
with the birds of heaven and the creeping things of the earth;
I will break bow, sword and battle in the country,
and make her sleep secure.
I will betroth you to myself forever,
betroth you with integrity and justice,
with tenderness and love;
I will betroth you to myself with faithfulness,
and you will come to know Yahweh.'

(Hosea 2:14-15, 18-20)

Jesus, the leader of the new people of God, passes through the water and into the desert under the powerful impulse of the Spirit of God. He is tempted there, and there he experiences the enduring love of God and consequent harmony.

* * * * * * * *

Mark speaks of 'Satan' (1:13) and of 'angels' (1:13). These words express a way of looking at life that was common at the time of Jesus. It is perhaps of value here to examine the genesis of these ideas, for only then will we be able to grasp the meaning underlying them.

Faced with good fortune and adversity, man seems to fall spontaneously into seeking a 'good' source of his good fortune and a 'bad' source for his adversity. Most ancient religions have good and bad supernatural beings that exercise power over man.

The Hebrews stood out from their neighbours because of their jealously maintained monotheism. In the beginning there was only God (cf Genesis 1:1). God alone is the source of everything that exists. In the ultimate analysis, according to the Hebrew view, there exists no power that can act independently of God, and both good fortune and adversity come from his hand.

There are some stories which speak in the most intimate terms of Yahweh communicating with men (cf, for example, the story of Yahweh appearing to Abraham by the oak of Mamre, Genesis 18:1-15). Generally, however, rather than speak of the transcendent Yahweh dealing directly with men, the Scriptures preferred to speak of the 'Angel of Yahweh' (cf Judges 6:11). They were not referring to some spirit, good or evil, that ministered to God; they were speaking of Yahweh himself in terms that kept his transcendence intact.

The Book of Job sets out to examine the problem of good and evil. Against the ancient superstitions which attributed ill-fortune to man's sin and ultimately to evil spirits ('demons'), the author asserts the basic Hebrew belief that it is God himself who allows adversity to test man. Man should not question God's wisdom in allowing this, but should accept whatever fortune he has as coming from the hand of God and hold on to an upright way of living. If, like Job, he refuses to do evil, he will — so runs the moral — be rewarded ultimately with prosperity. The book is written in dramatic style and introduces a character called the 'Satan', that is, the 'accuser' or 'adversary'. His task was to be God's instrument in testing the authenticity of Job's virtue, much as a barrister in a court of law tests the innocence of the accused. The 'Satan' is not an evil character; certainly not a spirit that is in opposition to God.

Gradually, in post-exilic Judaism, and under the influence of Mesopotamian mythology, ancient superstitions re-asserted themselves in the imagination of the people. Especially in later apocryphal (that is, non-scriptural) Jewish literature, angels (that is, 'good' spirits) and 'devils' or 'demons' (that is 'bad' spirits) abound. Satan (translated into Greek as 'diabolos', whence our 'devil') became the leader of the fallen angels, or evil spirits. These evil spirits, in orthodox Jewish theology, were always under God's power, but in the common understanding were probably misrepresented as being independent of God and the cause of evil. In the New Testament there is evidence that people thought that sickness came from evil spirits and that a person in ill-health was, of necessity, guilty of sin (cf John 9:2).

Even a cursory reading of the New Testament reveals that 'angels' and 'demons' were part of the ordinary people's way of looking at life and interpreting their world. Underneath such expressions lies a way of looking at good and evil and the powers of the supernatural. Our task is to penetrate the mythology, and reach the insights being expressed.

In the case in point (Mark 1:12-13) we are being told that Jesus, like us, and always under the providence of God, was being tried and tempted by evil.

*   *   *   *   *   *   *   *

Matthew chose to dramatise the temptations of Jesus, and he chose the classical temptations experienced by the Hebrews in their forty year sojourn in the desert.

The First Test

MATTHEW 4:1-4 (Compare Luke 4:1-4)

4 Then Jesus was led by the Spirit out into the wilderness to be tempted by the 1 devil. •He fasted for forty days and forty nights, after which he was very 2 hungry, •and the tempter came and said to him, 'If you are the Son of God, tell 3 these stones to turn into loaves'. •But he replied, 'Scripture says: 4

Man does not live on bread alone
but on every word that comes from the mouth of God'.[a]

(a: Deuteronomy 8:3)

Where Mark has 'Satan', Matthew has the 'devil'. We are dealing with the same character. Jesus is being tested, under the direction of the 'Spirit' of God (4:1). Matthew introduces the idea of hunger. We are reminded of the first test that the Hebrews underwent just after they had crossed the sea of Reeds into the wilderness (Exodus 16). They were hungry and were tempted to go back to the flesh-pots of Egypt. They complained against God, who, in his faithful love, fed them himself, sending them manna from heaven.

Commenting on this scene the editors of the Book of Deuteronomy drew the following moral:

'Man does not live on bread alone, but on every word that comes from the mouth of God.'

(Deuteronomy 8:3)

Matthew places Jesus in the same situation, but Jesus, in contrast to the Hebrews, trusted in his Father. He passed the test. Later in the Gospel Jesus says:

'Set your hearts on the kingdom of God first, and on his righteousness, and all these other things will be given you as well.'

(Matthew 6:33)

At the Baptism, God had said: 'This is my Son' (Matthew 3:17). The first temptation begins with the words: 'If you are the Son of God' (4:3). The temptation is to see 'sonship' as 'power'. For Jesus, on the other hand, sonship means obedience. The same temptation recurs while Jesus is on the cross:

'Save yourself! If you are God's Son, come down from the cross.'

(Matthew 27:40)

There, too, Jesus showed his true sonship by obedience to his Father's will. We are reminded of the words from John's Gospel:

'My food is to do the will of the one who sent me, and to complete his work.'

(John 4:34)

The Second Test

MATTHEW 4:5-7 (Compare Luke 4:9-12)

The devil then took him to the holy city and made him stand on the parapet of 5 the Temple. •'If you are the Son of God' he said 'throw yourself down; for 6 scripture says:

> He will put you in his angels' charge,
> and they will support you on their hands
> in case you hurt your foot against a stone'.[a]

Jesus said to him, 'Scripture also says: 7

> You must not put the Lord your God to the test'.[b]
>
> (a: Psalm 91:11-12   b: Deuteronomy 6:16)

The second test flows from the first. The Israelites in the desert had been given manna by God. They proceeded to complain and demand that he give them water (cf Exodus 17:2). They were 'sons' of God, so they assumed they had the right to make demands of him. As they saw it, God should prove his care for them by passing the test and meeting their needs. In fact God did answer their call, for when Moses, in a symbolic gesture, struck the rock (a symbol of God), water flowed from it for the people to drink (Exodus 17:6). However, the account in the Book of Exodus concludes with the words:

'The place was named Massa (= 'trial') and Meribah (= 'contention'), because of the grumblings of the sons of Israel and because they put Yahweh to the test by saying, "Is Yahweh with us or not?"'

(Exodus 17:7)

The same editors of the Book of Deuteronomy drew from this event the following moral:

'You must not put the Lord your God to the test.'

(Deuteronomy 6:16 cf also Wisdom 1:2)

It is obvious that Matthew follows the development closely. Jesus had claimed that he lived on every word that came from the mouth of God (4:4). The devil then gives him such a word (4:6 = Psalm 91:11-12) and tempts him to put God to the test. Unlike the ancient Israelites, Jesus does not try to manipulate God. Sonship, for Jesus, is not a matter of attempting to manipulate God to fit into his needs: it is a matter of true dependence and of doing the will of God.

The Third Test

MATTHEW 4:8-11 (Compare Luke 4:5-8)

Next, taking him to a very high mountain, the devil showed him all the kingdoms 8 of the world and their splendour. •'I will give you all these' he said, 'if you fall at 9 my feet and worship me.' •Then Jesus replied, 'Be off, Satan! For scripture says: 10

You must worship the Lord your God,
and serve him alone.' ᵃ

Then the devil left him, and angels appeared and looked after him.   11

(a: Deuteronomy 6:13)

It was part of the mythology of the day that Satan was the 'prince of this world' (cf John 14:30), permitted by God to exercise power till God himself chose to effect the Day of the Lord and establish his kingdom. Here, in the final test, the devil offers his power to Jesus. Jesus' response is taken, like the earlier responses, from the Book of Deuteronomy (Matthew 4:10 = Deuteronomy 6:13). It is taken from the section in which Moses is describing the essence of the Law:

'Listen, Israel: Yahweh your God is the one Yahweh.
You shall love Yahweh your God with all your heart,
with all your soul, with all your strength.
Let these words I urge on you today be written on your heart.
You shall repeat them to your children
and say them over to them
whether at rest in your house or walking abroad,
at your lying down or at your rising;
you shall fasten them on your hand as a sign
and on your forehead as a circlet;
you shall write them on the doorposts of your house
and on your gates.'

(Deuteronomy 6:4-9)

Moses then speaks of the goal of the desert journey and concludes with the words quoted by Jesus:

'When Yahweh has brought you into the land which he swore
to your fathers Abraham, Isaac and Jacob that he would give you.
with great and prosperous cities not of your building,
houses full of good things not furnished by you,
wells you did not dig,
vineyards and olives you did not plant,
when you have eaten these and had your fill,
then take care that you do not forget Yahweh
who brought you out of the land of Egypt,
out of the house of slavery.
You must fear Yahweh your God, you must serve him,
by his name you must swear.'

(Deuteronomy 6:10-13)

The people of God 'worshipped' Satan (cf Numbers 25: also Ezekiel 20:18-26). Jesus trusted his Father, not on his own terms, but on his Father's. Matthew keeps the final result of the temptations till the very last scene of his Gospel where he has Jesus once again on a mountain. This time, the Father whom Jesus trusted in true sonship has given Jesus more than Satan could ever have promised:

'All authority in heaven and on earth is given to me.'

(Matthew 28:17)

It is interesting to see the parallels between this scene and a later scene in Matthew. At Caesarea Philippi, Peter acknowledges that Jesus is the 'Son of the living God' (Matthew 16:16). But when Jesus speaks of the necessity of suffering, Peter, like Satan, tempts Jesus with the thought that sonship should not involve suffering (Matthew 16:22). Jesus rebukes Peter with words that are reminiscent of his rebuke of Satan in the desert:

'Get behind me, Satan! You are an obstacle in my path, because the way you think is not God's way but man's.'

(Matthew 16:23)

The temptations, besides reminding us that Jesus is our brother, are an exploration of what it means to be the 'Son of God'. It is a matter of trusting obedience to God who is Father.

*   *   *   *   *   *   *   *

Luke uses the same three scenes. His order is different. Because of the central place of the Temple in Luke's theology, he chose to build up to the scene on the Temple parapet.

Luke concludes his account of the temptations with the following statement:

LUKE 4:13
Having exhausted all these ways of tempting him, the devil left him, to return 13
at the appointed time.

In typical apocalyptic style, Luke is preparing his readers for the final clash between the powers of evil and Jesus. Satan will return at the hour of darkness when Jesus is betrayed and killed (cf Luke 22:3).

* * * * * * * *

John's Gospel has as one of its main themes the clash between light and darkness. Jesus is constantly tested and tried by the forces of evil. John does not choose to dramatise this, as the others do, with reference to the desert journey of the Israelites.

* * * * * * * *

Points for Reflection:

1: When we were baptised, we stood with Jesus. For some, this came as a result of a personal commitment resulting from a journey of faith. For others it happened because of the love of parents and the welcome of the church. In every case it resulted, not from what we did, but from the love of God graciously taking us to himself. Baptism is something God does. It is his act of overwhelming us with his love, pouring out his Spirit, making us his sons and pledging to us his enduring love. Adult baptism highlights the necessity of our personal acceptance in faith of his gift. Infant baptism highlights the fact that it is God's gift and is not the result of anything we do. True, at some time, whether gradually or suddenly, we all need to make this gift our own, and respond to God in personal gratitude and wonder. But we must never forget that it is his favour that rests on us (Mark 1:11).

2: Read Romans 6:1-11, where Paul associates baptism with the death and resurrection of Jesus.

3: 'Lamb of God who takes away the sin of the world, have mercy on us.' (from the Mass. cf John 1:29).

4: God's plea in Isaiah is relevant to the study of the temptations:

'Oh, come to the water all you who are thirsty;
though you have no money, come!
Buy corn without money, and eat,
and, at no cost, wine and milk.
Why spend money on what is not bread,
your wages on what fails to satisfy?
Listen, listen to me, and you will have good things to eat and rich food to enjoy.
Pay attention, come to me;
listen and your soul will live.
With you I will make an everlasting covenant.'

(Isaiah 55:1-3)

5: 'My food is to do the will of the one who sent me' (John 4:34).

'He who sent me is with me, and has not left me to myself, for I always do what pleases him.'
(John 8:29)

6: Am I willing to pay the price of liberation? Am I willing to undertake the journey to freedom? Do I attempt to manipulate God, or, am I learning from Jesus to trust God and be open to his will?

7: It may be that God will lead me into the wilderness to speak to my heart. It may be that I am led by God into a prayer that is dry and desert-like, in order that I will learn to rely, not on my own experiences, but on the God whom I do not see, but in whom I have learned to believe.

Schematic Summary of, and Conclusion to, the First Book:

MATTHEW 1-2

Jesus is:

- Son of Abraham (1:1)
- Son of David (1:1)
- The Christ (1:1)
- Son of God (1:18)
- God-who-saves (1:21)
- God-with-us (1:23)
- King of the Jews (2:2)
- The Wisdom of God (2:9)
- The light of the nations (2:9)
- The New Israel (2:15)
- The New Moses (2:16)
- Destined to suffer (2:11, 18)
- The New Covenant (2:18)
- From Nazareth (2:23)

LUKE 1-2

Jesus is:

- The One in whom history reaches its fulfilment and finds its meaning.
- God-who-saves (1:31)
- Son of God (1:32, 35)
- Son of David (1:32)
- Lord (1:43)
- The One in whom the promises of God are fulfilled (1:54)
- Bringer of peace and joy (2:10, 14)
- One with us (2:7, 40, 51)
- Bringer of Good News to the Poor (2:8)
- Light of the nations (2:32)
- Judge (2:34)
- Destined to Suffer (2:34)
- The One who does God's will (2:49)
- From Nazareth (2:51)

JOHN 1:1-18

Jesus is:

The Wisdom of God
- The Word of God (1:14)
- The life of God (1:4)
- The light of God (1:4)
- The glory of God (1:14)
- The gracious love of God (1:14)
- The One who lives among us (1:14)
- The fidelity of God (1:14)
- The One in whom the promises of God are fulfilled (1:15)
- The One who is nearest his Father's heart and who reveals God in the flesh (1:18)

Matthew 3:1-12
Mark 1:1-8
Luke 3:1-20
John 1:19-28

Jesus is the One who will fulfil all the hopes of Israel. He is the One through whom the Holy Spirit is to be poured forth over the people.

Matthew 3:13-17
Mark 1:9-11
Luke 3:21-22   **Matthew 4:1-11**
John 1:29-34   **Mark 1:12-13**
                                    Luke 3:23 — 4:13

Jesus is 'divine':   **Jesus is 'human':**

God's favour rests on him.   He is our brother, tested like us
God's Spirit is active in him.   by evil, but faithful to God his
He is the beginning of new   Father who cares for him in his
creation.   trials.
He is the lamb of God (John).

There are two kinds of information contained in this introductory section, now completed.

There is some biographical material: a record of the first time Jesus was noticed in public, the fact that he was from Nazareth in Galilee, and the names of his mother and father. And that is all. This was what early friends found out when they first met him by the Jordan. The rest of his first thirty years is shrouded in silence.

There is a good deal of profound theology: the fruit of years of reflection on the significance of the life of this man they had grown to love and follow. At first his look and manner and words spoke to them simply of a man of extraordinary perception and love. Gradually they grew to realise something of the mystery of his person, and the special relationship he had with the God he called, familiarly, 'Father'. His words became, for his followers, God's words; his love revealed the love of God. They recognised him as the one who fulfilled the hopes of their people. Before beginning their narrative of his life and words, the Gospel-writers, in this introductory section, present the fruit of those years of meditation, in the hope that their readers will read the Gospel with some awareness of the kind of person they are going to meet. In setting the stage, as it were, they use a variety of highly dramatic and poetic styles. We will notice, in Book Two, a much simpler style as the story of Jesus unfolds. It is, on the surface, a simple story. But it is a story that had profound significance for those who learned to believe in Jesus. The Gospel-writers present it in its simplicity, but they also attempt, in a number of ways, to draw out the inner meaning of his words and actions. For they are not concerned with the surface. They are communicating what Jesus meant to them; they are concerned with his heart.

BOOK 2

The Good News

FOREWORD

Caesarea Philippi is a turning point in Jesus' ministry for Mark, Matthew and Luke. It was there that a disciple, Peter, for the first time, acknowledged Jesus as the Messiah, and committed himself to follow him.

Prior to that acknowledgement and that commitment, our attention is concentrated on the healing and liberating effect of God's powerful love in the life and ministry of someone as open and faithful as Jesus. We are listening to Jesus speak of his Father, and we are watching him live out the Good News, in the hope that we, like Peter, will be attracted to want to follow him.

Book 2 is entitled 'The Good News' and covers the period of Jesus' ministry up to an including Caesarea Philippi.

We have divided the Book into three Parts, following Mark's clear division.

1: Part One (Mark 1:14-3:6) begins with a summary of Jesus' teaching and the call of the first disciples (1:14-20), and ends with the religious leaders rejecting Jesus (3:1-6). Mark concentrates on Jesus' healing and liberating word. We cover these aspects in Chapters 1 and 3. Matthew has two long inserts in this Part, one giving examples of Jesus' word ('The Sermon on the Mount') and the other showing how Jesus in the alternative to the Law. We cover these inserts in Chapters 2 and 4. Chapter 5 is devoted to John's equivalent material. Finally, in a note, we take a look at miracles and what they mean in Gospel literature.

2: Part Two (Mark 3:7-6:6) also begins with a summary of Jesus' teaching and the call of the Twelve (3:7-19). It ends with the people of Nazareth rejecting s (6:1-6). Mark concentrates on the power of God's word and shows Jesus living it in his ministry. We cover this insert in Chapter 2.

3: Part Three (Mark 6:6-8:30) also begins with a summary of Jesus' teaching and the first mission of the Twelve (6:6-13), and ends, this time not with a rejection, but Peter's acceptance of Jesus as the Messiah at Caesarea Philippi (8:27-30). Mark looks at the problem of our hearing and perceiving what Jesus is saying and doing. He shows us the powerful spread of the kingdom of God's love in spite of rejection. We look at this in Chapter 1. He then presents us with the miracle of the loaves and a series of scenes in which people fail to 'hear' what Jesus is saying, culminating in a miraculous healing of a deaf man. We cover this in Chapter 2. Mark then repeats the miracle of the loaves, presents us with scenes in which people fail to 'see' what Jesus is saying, and culminates with a miraculous healing of a blind man and Peter's confession. At last someone hears and sees. We cover this in Chapter 3.

PART 1
The Good News:
God's Healing and Liberating
Word

Chapter 1
Jesus' Healing (Life-Giving) Word

Mark 1:14-45
Matthew 4:12-25 and 7:28 — 8:17
Luke 4:14 — 5:16
John 1:35-51

1. Summary of the Good News

MARK 1:14-15
    After John had been arrested, Jesus went into Galilee. There he proclaimed 14
the Good News from God. •'The time has come' he said 'and the kingdom of 15
God is close at hand. Repent, and believe the Good News.'

    The Baptist has just spoken of one who was 'following him' (Mark 1:7).
Immediately Jesus stands before us telling us that the 'time has come' (1:15): the
time to which the prophets had looked forward with such desire; the time that
had filled the dreams and sustained the lives of a whole people; the time when
God would visit his people and establish his peace and justice and the reign of his
love in this world.

    To appreciate the startling nature of what Jesus is preaching here, one needs
to appreciate the enthusiasm of the Messianic expectation that was central to
Judaism. Against the background of that expectation there is no avoiding the
absoluteness of the challenge offered by Jesus. The time for repentance, the time
for a new outlook, the time for a change of heart, is *now!* Not tomorrow, not in
the distant future. Here and now! Jesus is claiming that God is acting powerfully
now to establish his kingdom, to fulfil his promises, to bring healing and
liberation to his people. They must repent: they must adopt a new way of looking
at life. The new way is the subject of the rest of the Gospel. Here Mark tells us
simply that it requires an attitude of 'believing' (1:15); it is also 'Good' News
(1:15).

    It is typical of Mark to go straight to the heart of Jesus' preaching and
immediately demand of his readers full attention and readiness for commitment.
If we are to read on, we, too, must be ready to 'believe'. Mark insists that the
Good News is 'from God' (1:14) and that it is the 'kingdom of God' (1:15) that is
being established in the world. It was for this that Jesus was anointed king by the
Spirit of God (Mark 1:11).

*   *   *   *   *   *   *   *

Matthew copies Mark's opening statement. However, in accordance with his desire to demonstrate to his fellow-Jews the consistency of God's action in history as well as the fact that Jesus is the fulfilment of their Messianic hopes, he takes the occasion to link Jesus with an Old Testament prophecy which speaks of Galilee.

MATTHEW 4:12-17

Hearing that John had been arrested he went back to Galilee, •and leaving 12
13
Nazareth he went and settled in Capernaum, a lakeside town on the borders of Zebulun and Naphtali. •In this way the prophecy of Isaiah was to be fulfilled: 14

> *Land of Zebulun! Land of Naphtali!*   15
> *Way of the sea on the far side of Jordan,*
> *Galilee of the nations!*
> *The people that lived in darkness*   16
> *has seen a great light;*
> *on those who dwell in the land and shadow of death*
> *a light has dawned.[a]*

From that moment Jesus began his preaching with the message, 'Repent, for 17
the kingdom of heaven is close at hand'.

(a: Isaiah 9:1)

*   *   *   *   *   *   *   *

Luke begins his account of Jesus' Galilean ministry with a short, summary statement (4:14-15) followed immediately by a scene from Jesus' ministry in Nazareth (4:16-30). The scene occurs later in Mark (6:1-6) and Matthew (13:53-58). Luke places it here because it expresses, in words that are dear to Luke, the essence of Jesus' preaching (4:18-19); and also because it is a scene in which Jesus is rejected. One of Luke's central themes is that suffering is the way to glorification; rejection, far from thwarting God's will, is God's providential means of ensuring the spread of the Good News. Luke divides the ministry of Jesus into three sections:

a: The Galilean Ministry 4:12 — 9:50
b: The Journey to Jerusalem 9:51 — 19:40
c: The Jerusalem Ministry 19:41 — 21:38

Each section begins with a rejection scene, and in each the word of God spreads and is victorious. These are followed by the rejection of the crucifixion and the victory of the Resurrection. Luke carries this theme over to his second book, the Acts of the Apostles. There we see that it is the rejection of the Christian community in Jerusalem by the Sanhedrin that leads to the spread of the Church through Judaea and Samaria (cf Acts 8:1 and 8:4), to Antioch (cf Acts 11:18) and finally, to the ends of the earth (cf Acts 8:1 and 28:31).

Jesus announces the Good News, and is rejected by his own people

LUKE 4:14-30

Jesus, with the power of the Spirit in him, returned to Galilee; and his 14
reputation spread throughout the countryside. •He taught in their synagogues 15
and everyone praised him.

16   He came to Nazara, where he had been brought up, and went into the
17   synagogue on the sabbath day as he usually did. He stood up to read, •and they
handed him the scroll of the prophet Isaiah. Unrolling the scroll he found the
place where it is written:

18   *The spirit of the Lord has been given to me,*
                    for he has anointed me.
                    He has sent me to bring the good news to the poor,
                    to proclaim liberty to captives
                    and to the blind new sight,
                    to set the downtrodden free,
19   *to proclaim the Lord's year of favour.* [a]

20   He then rolled up the scroll, gave it back to the assistant and sat down. And all
21   eyes in the synagogue were fixed on him. •Then he began to speak to them, 'This
22   text is being fulfilled today even as you listen'. •And he won the approval of all,
and they were astonished by the gracious words that came from his lips.
23   They said, 'This is Joseph's son, surely?' •But he replied, 'No doubt you will
quote me the saying, "Physician, heal yourself" and tell me, "We have heard all
that happened in Capernaum, do the same here in your own countryside" '.
24   And he went on, 'I tell you solemnly, no prophet is ever accepted in his own
country.
25   'There were many widows in Israel, I can assure you, in Elijah's day, when
heaven remained shut for three years and six months and a great famine raged
26   throughout the land, •but Elijah was not sent to any one of these: he was sent
27   *to a widow at Zarephath, a Sidonian town.* •And in the prophet Elisha's time
there were many lepers in Israel, but none of these was cured, except the Syrian,
Naaman.'
28   When they heard this everyone in the synagogue was enraged. •They sprang
29   to their feet and hustled him out of the town; and they took him up to the brow
30   of the hill their town was built on, intending to throw him down the cliff, •but
he slipped through the crowd and walked away.

(a: Isaiah 61:1-2)
(Compare Mark 6:1-6 and Matthew 13:53-58, page 185)

Luke keeps before the minds of his readers the fact that it is the 'Spirit' (4:14)
that is directing Jesus in his ministry. The essence of this ministry is expressed, for
Luke, in the quotation from Isaiah. The gospel of Jesus is the Good News that, in
Jesus, God has come to liberate the oppressed, to hear the cry of the
downtrodden, to raise up the poor. This was the message of the Magnificat (Luke
1:46-55) and is a central theme throughout Luke's Gospel (cf pages 156-9).

The people reject Jesus, partly, it seems, because he is 'Joseph's son' (Luke
4:23). The Messiah could not, in their estimation, be as 'ordinary' and 'common-
place' as Jesus. The other reason for their rejection is the universal nature of his
saving action: it is for the Gentile world, and not for the narrow interests of Jesus'
own people. There are parallels in the life of Elijah (Luke 4:25-26, 1 Kings 17:7-
16), and in the life of Elisha (Luke 4:27, cf 2 Kings 5:1-9).

Luke chooses to open Jesus' ministry with the scene at Nazareth. Jesus meets
with rejection, but his mission opens up, till it culminates, after his death, in the
mission of the church to the Gentiles — a mission very dear to the heart of Luke,
the Gentile.

2: Jesus invites others to spread the Good News with Him

MARK 1:16-20 (Compare Matthew 4:18-22)

16   As he was walking along by the Sea of Galilee he saw Simon and his brother
17   Andrew casting a net in the lake — for they were fishermen. •And Jesus said to
18   them, 'Follow me and I will make you into fishers of men'. •And at once they
left their nets and followed him.
19   Going on a little further, he saw James son of Zebedee and his brother John;
20   they too were in their boat, mending their nets. He called them at once •and,
leaving their father Zebedee in the boat with the men he employed, they went
after him.

In this simple account, Mark and Matthew record the occasion on which
Jesus' first disciples, who were fishermen, left their trade to follow him. The
reader's attention is directed to the divine initiative — it is Jesus who calls and
who promises to train them for their mission — and to the completeness of the
response asked of these four men.

The Gospel writers are also making the point that Jesus' mission is not one
that he is to carry out alone. It involves building community; it is a mission
shared by others.

*   *   *   *   *   *   *   *

Luke records the same occasion. He, however, dramatises it to bring out its
significance. Luke has the scene after he has introduced us to Jesus the worker of
miracles (Luke 4:31-44). We shall study it here for convenience.

LUKE 5:1-11

1   5 Now he was standing one day by the Lake of Gennesaret, with the crowd
2   pressing round him listening to the word of God, •when he caught sight of two
boats close to the bank. The fishermen had gone out of them and were washing
3   their nets. •He got into one of the boats—it was Simon's —and asked him to put
out a little from the shore. Then he sat down and taught the crowds from the boat.
4   When he had finished speaking he said to Simon, 'Put out into deep water
5   and pay out your nets for a catch'. •'Master,' Simon replied 'we worked hard all
6   night long and caught nothing, but if you say so, I will pay out the nets.' •And
when they had done this they netted such a huge number of fish that their nets
7   began to tear, •so they signalled to their companions in the other boat to come
and help them; when these came, they filled the two boats to sinking point.
8   When Simon Peter saw this he fell at the knees of Jesus saying, 'Leave me,
9   Lord; I am a sinful man'. •For he and all his companions were completely
10   overcome by the catch they had made; •so also were James and John, sons of
Zebedee, who were Simon's partners. But Jesus said to Simon, 'Do not be afraid;
11   from now on it is men you will catch'. •Then, bringing their boats back to land,
they left everything and followed him.

The appendix to the Gospel according to John tells of a wonderful haul made
by the fishermen on the lake. There, however, the anecdote is associated with the
risen Jesus (John 21:4-6). Luke, perhaps, inserts the story here, because it brings
out so well the meaning of this first call. It illustrates the power of Jesus' call and

the amazing effect the decision to follow Jesus was to have on the lives of these fishermen. The call may have appeared 'ordinary' at the time (as ordinary as Mark's and Matthew's account), but time would show that the occasion by the lake was to be the beginning of a 'miraculous' career for these men. Writing history in the richest tradition, Luke creates a story to bring out the true meaning of the event with powerful, dramatic impact. Men who, up to this point, had been drawing fish into their nets, are, from this time on, to be drawing men into the kingdom of God (Luke 5:10).

Luke writes with superb skill and sensitivity. In a very simple way he identifies the preaching of Jesus with the 'word of God' (5:1). The crowd is pressing around listening to Jesus. Jesus cannot cope on his own: he needs the help of others and asks for it. They comply — with wonderful results. The 'catch of fish' cannot be attributed to their own talent: 'We worked hard all night long and caught nothing' (5:5). It came as a result of the word of Jesus and their response to his call. Luke is thinking of the results of the preaching of Jesus' first disciples. By the time he was writing his Gospel, the church was flourishing in the Eastern Empire and west as far as Rome and beyond.

Simon Peter's reaction is the reaction of a man faced with the presence of God. Wonder begets humility. The holiness of God highlights the sinfulness of man (5:8). The response of Jesus is gentle and reassuring. He tells them not to be afraid and invites them to join him in spreading the Good News of the kingdom.

The scene balances the scene at Nazareth. At Nazareth, Jesus is rejected by his own people and is forced to 'walk away' (Luke 4:30). Here, by the lake, he is accepted by strangers who choose to walk with him (Luke 5:11).

* * * * * * * *

John's account of the calling of the first disciples goes back to the period before Jesus began his ministry in Galilee. John the Baptist had not yet been imprisoned and Jesus was still in Judaea.

JOHN 1:35-51
35 On the following day as John stood there again with two of his disciples,
36 Jesus passed, and John stared hard at him and said, 'Look, there is the lamb of
37 God'. •Hearing this, the two disciples followed Jesus. •Jesus turned round, saw
38 them following and said, 'What do you want?' They answered, 'Rabbi,'—which
39 means Teacher—'where do you live?' •'Come and see' he replied; so they went and saw where he lived, and stayed with him the rest of that day. It was about the tenth hour.
40 One of these two who became followers of Jesus after hearing what John had
41 said was Andrew, the brother of Simon Peter. •Early next morning, Andrew met his brother and said to him, 'We have found the Messiah'—which means
42 the Christ—•and he took Simon to Jesus. Jesus looked hard at him and said, 'You are Simon son of John; you are to be called Cephas'—meaning Rock.
43 The next day, after Jesus had decided to leave for Galilee, he met Philip and
44 said, 'Follow me'. •Philip came from the same town, Bethsaida, as Andrew and
45 Peter. •Philip found Nathanael and said to him, 'We have found the one Moses wrote about in the Law, the one about whom the prophets wrote: he is

Jesus son of Joseph, from Nazareth'. •'From Nazareth?' said Nathanael 'Can 46 anything good come from that place?' 'Come and see' replied Philip. •When 47 Jesus saw Nathanael coming he said of him, 'There is an Israelite who deserves the name, incapable of deceit'. •'How do you know me?' said Nathanael. 48 'Before Philip came to call you,' said Jesus 'I saw you under the fig tree.' •Na- 49 thanael answered, 'Rabbi, you are the Son of God, you are the King of Israel'. Jesus replied, 'You believe that just because I said: I saw you under the fig tree. 50 You will see greater things than that.' •And then he added, 'I tell you most 51 solemnly, you will see heaven laid open and, above the Son of Man, the angels of God ascending and descending'.

Before concentrating on the central point of this passage, let us make three observations.

1. The fact that terms such as 'Rabbi' (1:38), 'Messiah' (1:41) and 'Cephas' (1:42) are translated by the author indicates that the Gospel was written for a public that was not familiar with the Hebrew tongue. This has to be taken into consideration alongside the fact that the Gospel is very Jewish in its language and general approach. Tradition has it that the Gospel was written for the largely Jewish-Christian but Greek-speaking community of Ephesus.

2: Jesus says of Nathanael 'There is an Israelite who deserves the name, incapable of deceit' (John 1:47). The name 'Israel' was given by God to Jacob. The account is found in the Book of Genesis:

> 'And there was one who wrestled with Jacob until daybreak who, seeing that he could not master him, struck him in the socket of his hip, and Jacob's hip was dislocated as he wrestled with him. He said, "Let me go, for day is breaking". But Jacob answered, "I will not let you go unless you bless me". He then asked "What is your name?" "Jacob", he replied. He said, "Your name shall no longer be Jacob but Israel; because you have been strong against God, you shall prevail against men".'
>
> *(Genesis 32:26-29)*

Jacob, however, was capable of deceit: he deceived his brother into handing over the inheritance due to the first-born (cf Genesis 25:29-34); and he deceived his father, Isaac, into giving him his blessing (cf Genesis 27:1-45). The old Israel was unfaithful to the Covenant. Nathanael is representative of the new Israel.

3. John alludes to Jacob once again in the final sentence (1:51). He is referring to Jacob's dream:

> 'Jacob left Beersheba and set out for Haran. When he had reached a certain place he passed the night there, since the sun had set. Taking one of the stones to be found at that place, he made it his pillow and laid down where he was. He had a dream: a ladder was there, standing on the ground, with its top reaching to heaven; and there were angels of God going up it and coming down. And Yahweh was there, standing over him saying, "I am Yahweh, the God of Abraham your father, and the God of Isaac. I will give to you and your descendants the land on which you are lying. Your descendants will be like the specks of dust on the ground; you shall spread to the west and the east, to the north and the south, and all the tribes of the earth shall bless themselves by you and your descendants. Be sure that I am with you; I will keep you safe wherever you go, and bring you back to this land, for I will not desert you before I have done all that I have promised you". Then Jacob awoke from his sleep and said, "Truly, Yahweh is in this place and I never knew it!" He was afraid and said, "How awe-inspiring this place is! This is nothing less than a house of God; this is the gate of heaven!"'
>
> *(Genesis 28:10-17)*

The 'house of God' is now Jesus, the Son of Man. He is the sacred place where God touches the earth. He is the one in whom we can be sure that Yahweh is with us. In reminding his readers of Jacob's ladder, John perhaps has in mind the cross, thrown against the sky — the cross on which Jesus was to manifest the enduring love of God, his Father.

With these clarifications, we can now turn our attention to the central thrust of the passage. It is John's account of the call of the first disciples. He dramatises the different ways in which men are called to discipleship. Some, like Andrew and his companion are called directly by Jesus himself (1:39). It is the same with Phillip (1:43). Others, like Simon Peter (1:41) and Nathanael (1:45) are called indirectly, via other disciples. In both situations, the accent is on personal encounter, 'Come and see' (1:39 and 1:46).

More importantly, John takes the occasion to give a compendium of the faith of the early Church in Jesus. Jesus is, first of all, the 'Teacher' (1:38). Then comes John's equivalent of the statement by Mark that 'the time has come' (Mark 1:15). Andrew says to Peter: 'We have found the Messiah' (1:41). Jesus, in other words, is the One who brings to fulfilment the Law and the Prophets (1:45); he is the 'Son of God' (1:49), the 'King of Israel' (1:49).

These last two titles stress the royal aspect of the Messianic promise, and the kingdom that the Christ is to establish. At a deeper level, the title 'Son of God' has mysterious overtones for John as it expresses something of the special, intimate relationship between Jesus and God. John's Gospel is devoted largely to exploring the wonder and mystery of this relationship and its implications for the life of the disciple (cf John 20:31).

The final title used by John — a title that Jesus himself seems to have preferred — is the title 'Son of Man' (1:51). The prophet Ezekiel frequently referred to himself as a 'Son of Man'. It was his way of identifying himself with his hearers in such a way as to stress the simplicity and the ordinary human suffering that is involved in the life of a prophet. The prophet Daniel veiled the title in mystery and gave it a new dimension when he used it of the people of God. He was writing at a time of persecution when it appeared that Judah might be crushed by the Syrian overlords (the persecution under Antiochus 186-183 B.C.). To encourage the Jews to persevere, Daniel wrote:

'I gazed into the visions of the night.
And I saw, coming on the clouds of heaven
one like a son of man.
He came to the one of great age
and was led into his presence.
On him was conferred sovereignty
glory and kingship,
and men of all peoples, nations and languages
became his servants.
His sovereignty is an eternal sovereignty
which shall never pass away
nor will his empire ever be destroyed.'   *(Daniel 7:13-14)*

Daniel was telling his contemporaries that God would lift his humble, persecuted people to himself in glory. Ultimately, it is they, the oppressed, who would be the judges of their oppressors (compare Daniel 7:27).

As used of Jesus, the title 'Son of Man' stresses the fact that Jesus is one who is our brother; one who identified himself with the poor. It carries with it also a reference to his death and his consequent resurrection and exaltation by God.

* * * * * * * *

3: Jesus' Healing Word

(a): The healing effect of Jesus' teachings.

MARK 1:21-28 (Compare Luke 4:31-37)

21   They went as far as Capernaum, and as soon as the sabbath came he went
22 to the synagogue and began to teach. •And his teaching made a deep impression on them because, unlike the scribes, he taught them with authority.
23   In their synagogue just then there was a man possessed by an unclean spirit,
24 and it shouted, •'What do you want with us, Jesus of Nazareth? Have you come
25 to destroy us? I know who you are: the Holy One of God.' •But Jesus said
26 sharply, 'Be quiet! Come out of him!' •And the unclean spirit threw the man into
27 convulsions and with a loud cry went out of him. •The people were so astonished that they started asking each other what it all meant. 'Here is a teaching that is new' they said 'and with authority behind it: he gives orders even to unclean
28 spirits and they obey him.' •And his reputation rapidly spread everywhere, through all the surrounding Galilean countryside.

Mark's primary accent is on Jesus' teachings: 'He began to teach' (1:21); 'his teaching made a deep impression' (1:22); 'he taught them with authority' (1:22). Even the anecdote about the man suffering from convulsions is recorded to illustrate the healing power of Jesus' teaching. This is brought out by the reaction of the people:

'Here is a teaching that is new and with authority behind it' (1:27).

With regard to the 'unclean spirit' (1:23), we refer the reader to our discussion of the place angels and devils played in the mythology of Jesus' contemporaries (cf Mark 1:12-13). In such a world it is not surprising that the meaningless jabbering of a man experiencing convulsions was interpreted as the voice of the evil spirit that brought about his disease. At a more profound level, however, Mark is making a significant claim: Jesus' healing activity is a sign of the coming of the kingdom (cf Mark 1:15). God is manifesting his power over all that would limit man's life, even the spiritual powers of evil that man is wont to fear. Not even they can hold out against the liberating love and powerful word of Jesus:

'He gives orders even to unclean spirits and they obey him' (1:28).

The statement 'Be quiet!' (1:25) is the first of many occasions on which Jesus enjoined secrecy on those who acclaimed him as the Messiah (cf Mark 1:34, 3:12, 7:36, 8:30, 9:30). Two reasons are suggested for the 'Messianic Secret' as it is often called. One reason for secrecy was the fact that Jesus was interested in people really coming to know him so that they could come to know his Father. The only way to do this was to 'Come and see' (John 1:39). Hearsay was not enough, especially as many of the prevailing ideas of the Messiah were false, and people would have only misinterpreted Jesus. It was vital that they come to know the

wanted people to believe through Him not in Him.

way in which he was the Messiah. Another reason for secrecy was the fact that it was actions like the healing of this possessed man that were to bring Jesus into conflict with the authorities and eventually bring about his death. Jesus' actions were life-giving actions that revealed God as a God of 'tenderness and compassion' (Hosea 2:22). They were to prove a powerful challenge to those whose authority was based on the Law, and who, at the same time:

'neglected the weighter matters of the Law — justice, mercy, good faith!'

(Matthew 23:23)

Jesus wished to heal; he did not wish, before he was ready, to bring on a confrontation with the authorities.

A casual observer in the synagogue of Capernaum that day may, perhaps, have witnessed a simple, but very moving scene. Jesus of Nazareth was teaching. His words were about God's love and the desire in the heart of God to liberate and to heal. Jesus' words, and especially his peace and conviction made a powerful impression on all who were listening. One man, a man who suffered from a disease that manifested itself in physical convulsions, was so deeply moved that a deep healing flowed through his spirit and manifested itself in bodily healing. All 'were astonished' (Mark 1:27).

* * * * * * * *

Matthew's equivalent to this one narrative in Mark covers three whole chapters of his Gospel (Matthew 4:23 — 7:29). He begins by giving a longer account of Jesus' teaching and healing activities, and Jesus' spreading reputation:

MATTHEW 4:23-25 (Compare Mark 1:21 and 1:28)

23 He went round the whole of Galilee teaching in their synagogues, proclaiming the Good News of the kingdom and curing all kinds of diseases and sickness
24 among the people. •His fame spread throughout Syria, and those who were suffering from diseases and painful complaints of one kind or another, the possessed, epileptics, the paralysed, were all brought to him, and he cured them.
25 Large crowds followed him, coming from Galilee, the Decapolis, Jerusalem, Judaea and Transjordania.

He concludes with a statement taken from Mark:

MATTHEW 7:28-29 (Compare Mark 1:22)

28 Jesus had now finished what ne wanted to say, and his teaching made a deep
29 impression on the people •because he taught them with authority, and not like their own scribes.

Matthew does not record the incident with the possessed man. Rather than illustrate Jesus' teaching with a miraculous healing, Matthew chose to gather together some of Jesus' basic teaching into what is often called the 'Sermon on the Mount' (Matthew 5:1 — 7:27). We shall examine this Sermon in the following chapter.

* * * * * * * *

(b): **Healing is in view of service**

MARK 1:29-31 (Compare Matthew 8:14-15 and Luke 4:38-39)

29   On leaving the synagogue, he went with James and John straight to the house
30 of Simon and Andrew. •Now Simon's mother-in-law had gone to bed with fever,
31 and they told him about her straightaway. •He went to her, took her by the hand
and helped her up. And the fever left her and she began to wait on them.

The kind of love preached and lived by Jesus was the love of 'service'. The
Greek word is 'diakonia' (whence our word 'deacon'), and it was a technical term
in New Testament writings for the humble, thoughtful, other-centred love that
characterised Jesus (cf Mark 10:41-45). The word translated 'wait on' in the
above passage (Mark 1:31) is the word 'diakonia'. The anecdote is included here
because Mark wants to emphasise the fact that Jesus' healing is in view of a
person experiencing a full life; and fulness of life is realised in service of others,
the kind of service given to Jesus and his friends by Peter's mother-in-law.

(c): **Healing is a demonstration of the activity of God**

MARK 1:32-39 (Compare Luke 4:40-44 and Matthew 8:16)

32   That evening, after sunset, they brought to him all who were sick and those
33 who were possessed by devils. •The whole town came crowding round the door,
34 and he cured many who were suffering from diseases of one kind or another;
he also cast out many devils, but he would not allow them to speak, because they
knew who he was.

35   In the morning, long before dawn, he got up and left the house, and went
36 off to a lonely place and prayed there. •Simon and his companions set out in
37 search of him, •and when they found him they said, 'Everybody is looking for
38 you'. •He answered, 'Let us go elsewhere, to the neighbouring country towns,
39 so that I can preach there too, because that is why I came'. •And he went all
through Galilee, preaching in their synagogues and casting out devils.

Once again Jesus enjoins silence on the devils (1:34 compare commentary on
Mark 1:25, page 78).

For the first time, Mark mentions Jesus' prayer (Mark 1:35). He wishes to
remind his readers that the kingdom being preached by Jesus is God's kingdom.
Jesus is carrying out the will of God. The fact that everybody is looking for him
(Mark 1:37) is not sufficient reason for him to stay. Jesus' mission is not simply a
mission of love; it is a mission of God's love. It is in prayer that Jesus discerns that
it is God's will that he 'go elsewhere' (Mark 1:38). Jesus is not doing his own will,
no matter how loving and caring his will is; he is doing the will of God.

*   *   *   *   *   *   *   *

Matthew omits this scene, apart from a brief statement of Jesus' healing
activity (Matthew 8:16).

*   *   *   *   *   *   *   *

(d) Jesus heals because He shares the condition of the sick

MARK 1:40-45 (Compare Matthew 8:1-4 and Luke 5:12-14)

40   A leper came to him and pleaded on his knees: 'If you want to' he said 'you
41 can cure me'. •Feeling sorry for him, Jesus stretched out his hand and touched
42 him. 'Of course I want to!' he said. 'Be cured!' •And the leprosy left him at once
43 and he was cured. •Jesus immediately sent him away and sternly ordered him,
44 'Mind you say nothing to anyone, but go and show yourself to the priest, and
    make the offering for your healing prescribed by Moses as evidence of your
45 recovery'. •The man went away, but then started talking about it freely and
telling the story everywhere, so that Jesus could no longer go openly into any town,
but had to stay outside in places where nobody lived. Even so, people from
all around would come to him.

In this deeply moving scene, Mark captures something of the heart and
character of Jesus.

A leper comes up to him. That itself tells us a lot about Jesus. Leprosy made a
man an outcast, depriving him of any contact with his fellow men. A leper was
forbidden to approach anyone, and, in turn, had to give warning to passers-by of
his presence. Anyone who touched a leper was, automatically, unclean and had
to go through a process of purification before being able to enter public life. This
leper sensed that Jesus would not reject him.

Mark indicates a double emotional response in Jesus. Jesus is deeply
distressed and disturbed both by the man's condition and by the way the man is
treated by a society that has failed to believe in the compassion of God. He
reaches out to the man and touches him (1:41 — the word can mean 'embrace',
'cling to' cf John 20:17). The man has pleaded with Jesus, 'If you want to you can
cure me'; and from the heart of Jesus burst the words: 'Of course I want to!'
(1:42). Thinking of the Law (cf Leviticus 14:1-32), Jesus tells him to go and carry
out the requirements of the Law so that he can once again enter into social life.

The other response is less easy to grasp. Where our translation says, 'Feeling
sorry for him' (1:41) the New English Bible, for example, prefers the text that
reads, 'Indignant'. This fits in with the fact that Jesus did not simply tell the man
to go to see the priests; he 'sternly ordered him' (1:43). Jesus also experiences, it
seems, a deep anger. This may be explained partly by the harshness of a faithless
people who, rather than show compassion to this sick man have, to preserve
themselves, banished him from society and separated him by Law from anyone
who could love him and heal him (and this in God's name, Leviticus 13:45-46). It
may also be explained as a reaction to the knowledge of how the authorities will
react if they find out about the healing (compare Mark 1:25 and 1:34).

In fact the man cannot remain silent with the result that:

'Jesus could no longer go openly into any town, but had to stay outside in places
where nobody lived.'   *(Mark 1:45)*

Jesus has healed the social outcast, but only by himself becoming an
outsider.

We are reminded of the words of the fourth song of the servant of Yahweh:

'Without beauty, without majesty (we saw him),
no looks to attract our eyes;

a thing despised and rejected by men,
a man of sorrows and familiar with suffering,
a man to make people screen their faces;
he was despised and we took no account of him.
And yet ours were the sufferings he bore,
ours the sorrows he carried.'

(Isaiah 53:2-4)

The price Jesus paid for healing the leper was to take on his condition!

* * * * * * * *

Matthew actually quotes this text from Isaiah as a summary of this whole section:

MATTHEW 8:17
He took our sicknesses away and carried our diseases for us.[a]

(a: Isaiah 53:4)

Matthew alters Mark's order. He has three scenes. The first is the healing of the leper (Matthew 8:1-4), the second is the healing of the centurion's servant (Matthew 8:5-13), and the third is the healing of Peter's mother-in-law (Matthew 8:14-15). He alters the order because he wants to establish Jesus' fidelity to the Law (Matthew 8:4) before adding the following scene in which the servant of a Gentile is healed and in which the Gentiles are praised at the expense of the Jews.

Jesus' healing is in response to faith and extends to the Gentiles

MATTHEW 8:5-13
When he went into Capernaum a centurion came up and pleaded with him. 5 'Sir,' he said 'my servant is lying at home paralysed, and in great pain.' •'I will 6 7 come myself and cure him' said Jesus. •The centurion replied, 'Sir, I am not 8 worthy to have you under my roof; just give the word and my servant will be cured. •For I am under authority myself, and have soldiers under me; and I say 9 to one man: Go, and he goes; to another: Come here, and he comes; to my servant: Do this, and he does it.' •When Jesus heard this he was astonished and 10 said to those following him, 'I tell you solemnly, nowhere in Israel have I found faith like this. •And I tell you that many will come from east and west 11 to take their places with Abraham and Isaac and Jacob at the feast in the kingdom of heaven; •but the subjects of the kingdom will be turned out into the dark, 12 where there will be weeping and grinding of teeth.' •And to the centurion Jesus 13 said, 'Go back, then; you have believed, so let this be done for you'. And the servant was cured at that moment.

(Compare Luke 7:1-10, page 162 and John 4:46-53, page 139)

One of the central features of this anecdote is that it deals with a non-Jew. Matthew must have written verses 10-12 with a deep sadness in his heart, as he reflected on the fact that his own people had, for the most part, rejected Jesus. The church of Matthew's time was largely a Gentile church. At the same time this incident was remembered and recorded because it formed a precedent for the mission of the church to the Gentiles. Jesus' own ministry was, by force of circumstances, confined almost entirely to the Jews of Galilee and Judaea, as was the ministry of his immediate disciples (cf Matthew 10:5-6). Matthew has already developed the theme of the universal significance of the Good News (cf especially the story of the magi, Matthew 2:1-12). The present anecdote is the first indication of the realisation of this divine purpose.

Another central theme in the story is the fact that Jesus does not go in person to heal the boy. He is willing to go; in fact offers even before he is asked (8:7). The man, however, does not need to see in order to believe and he insists:

'just give the word and my servant (boy) will be healed' (8:8).

A frequent prayer of the early Christian community was that the risen Jesus would 'Come' (cf Revelations 22:20). But they also believed that, in the meantime, Jesus was truly present with them, present through his Spirit and his word:

'Know that I am with you always; yes, to the end of time.'

(Matthew 28:20)

Incidents such as the one we are studying supported this faith.

* * * * * * * *

It is interesting to compare Matthew's account of this incident with that recorded by Luke and that recorded by John. It provides a good example of the different ways in which such anecdotes were handed down in the oral tradition that preceded the writing of the Gospels. The differences are slight but they are there nonetheless. Where Matthew speaks of the centurion's 'servant' (Matthew 8:6, the Greek word is 'pais' and it can mean 'boy' or 'servant'), Luke speaks of a 'slave' (Luke 7:2, the Greek word is 'doulos'), and John speaks of a 'son' (John 4:46, the Greek word is 'uios'). In John's account the man is not a centurion but a 'court official' (John 4:47). While John mentions Capernaum (John 4:46), the incident is recorded as having taken place not at Capernaum as in Mark, Matthew (8:5) and Luke (7:1), but in 'Cana' (John 4:46).

* * * * * * * *

Luke is content to follow Mark closely in this section. Because he intended highlighting the miraculous nature of Jesus' call of the first disciples, he transferred it, as we saw, to the centre of this section. He wanted to introduce Jesus as the miracle-worker first. He also added his own conclusion drawing the attention of the reader once again to Jesus' prayer. Jesus' healing activity is an expression of the Spirit that Jesus shares in prayer with his Father:

LUKE 5:15-16
His reputation continued to grow, and large crowds would gather to hear him 15 and to have their sickness cured, •but he would always go off to some place where 16 he could be alone and pray.

* * * * * * * *

Points for Reflection:

1: 'The time has come. Repent' (Mark 1:15). 'If only you would listen to him today' (Psalm 95:7). It is possible *now* to listen and follow, whatever I may have done or not done in the past. Do I believe that? Have I the courage to begin a journey, even now? Even if I can say that I have heard his voice in the past and, in some way, have responded, I must still keep listening *now,* for he keeps calling me on new journeys. A disciple of Jesus must be always ready to 'repent', always remain open to the surprise of his word calling him in new directions, calling him to deeper intimacy, challenging him to love and to work for justice in new ways.

2: God is in the ordinary things of life; He is in 'Joseph's son' (Luke 5:4). There is a danger that I will look for God's will in the big things and in the distant prophets. There is a danger that I, like the people of Nazareth, will not hear God when he speaks to me in my neighbour, in the prophet by my side, in the small things.

3: If Jesus came to 'proclaim liberty to captives' and to 'set the down-trodden free' (Luke 4:18), the same kind of involvement must be expected of anyone who would want to be Jesus' disciple.

4: To follow Jesus is to 'put out into deep water' (Luke 5:4). But we are not to be afraid (Luke 5:10). We are taking a risk, we are going out of our depth, but we are answering the call of someone who lived to the full and who calls us to go with him. History is full of examples of men and women who have lived inspiring and fulfilling lives as his disciples. Why not me?

5: Peter felt humble when faced with the wonder of God's action in him (Luke 5:8). True humility does not come from reflection on one's own sinfulness. True humility comes with a sense of wonder — wonder that takes a person outside himself to a contemplation of God's enduring love.

6: Healing is always for service (Mark 1:31). This goes for all the gifts of the Spirit: they are all in view of service of others (Read Ephesians 4:1-16). Any talent I may have, any time I may have, any sensitivity, or wisdom, or strength, or weakness can be used for the service of my neighbour. It is perhaps surprising how often the serving itself provides the healing! (cf Isaiah 58 especially 58:8-11).

7: Jesus asked us to love. But how do I love? God wills to use me as a channel of his love. This makes it imperative for me to listen to his divine Spirit in the depths of my being if I am going to be able to discern in the circumstances of my life the direction of God's will. Do I follow Jesus' example of prayer? (Mark 1:35).

8: Yahweh is a 'God of tenderness and compassion' (Exodus 34:6), of 'tenderness and love' (Hosea 2:22). Jesus expressed this compassion to the leper (Mark 1:41). The disciple of Jesus is asked to 'be compassionate as your Father is compassionate' (Luke 6:36). He is asked to suffer with the sufferer, to share in man's poverty and isolation and loneliness and pain. There is no other way to heal.

Chapter 2
Jesus' Teaching:
The 'Sermon on the Mount'

Matthew 5:1 — 7:27

This whole section, as we mentioned in the previous chapter, is an insertion by **Matthew** replacing the healing scene in the synagogue at Capernaum (Mark 1:23-27 page 79).

One of Matthew's aims is to demonstrate that Jesus is the Messiah who fulfils the hopes and history of the Jewish nation. Mindful of Moses on the mountain receiving and promulgating the Old Law, Matthew gathers here the sayings of Jesus (or perhaps simply incorporates here a collection already made in Aramaic by the original Matthew), and offers them to his readers in the form of a promulgation made by Jesus, the new Moses, from the mountain. Jesus is giving his disciples the new Law, the new Covenant between God and man.

Ezekiel had looked forward to this Covenant:

'The Lord Yahweh says this:... "I shall give you a new heart, and put a new spirit in you; I shall remove the heart of stone from your bodies and give you a heart of flesh instead. I shall put my spirit in you and make you keep my laws".'

(Ezekiel 36:26-27)

So had Jeremiah:

'This is the covenant I will make with the House of Israel when those days arrive — it is Yahweh who speaks. Deep within them I will plant my Law, writing it on their hearts'.

(Jeremiah 31:33)

The Law promulgated by Jesus is a Law 'of the heart', bringing the Old Law to completion.

As explained in the Preface, one of the reasons for the development of the Gospel form was the desire to avoid the pitfalls inherent in long lists of the sayings of Jesus, divorced from the context of his life. Christianity is not an ethical system; it is not a set of abstract ideals or a philosophy of life. It is a practical wisdom based on the way of life lived by Jesus of Nazareth and learned from him by his disciples.

For the most part, Matthew follows Mark in interweaving action and word. At times, however, as in the present 'sermon', he gives us a list of sayings. It is left to the reader to interpret these sayings in the light of the way Jesus lived. The best commentary on any saying is the life of Jesus. If academic study, based on the meaning of words and even on the themes common in Biblical literature, leads to a meaning that is not in accordance with the actual way Jesus lived, we can be confident that the interpretation is false.

Before examining the 'Sermon on the Mount' we shall divide it into its various parts and refer the reader to the equivalent sections in Luke. It will be apparent that Luke's 'Sermon on the Plain' (Luke 6:20-49) follows a pattern similar to Matthew's sermon. It will also be apparent that large sections of Matthew's sermon are included by Luke in other parts of his Gospel. Luke tends to be more faithful to his sources than Matthew, so it is more probable that Matthew has combined a number of separate sources into one 'sermon'.

MATTHEW'S SERMON ON THE MOUNT	LUKE'S SERMON	LUKE: ELSEWHERE
1: The 'Beatitudes': 5:1-12	6:20-26	
2: Proverbs for disciples: the importance of their living according to the new 'Law': 5:13-16		14:34 8:16, 11:33
3: **Jesus perfects the 'Law'**		
General statement: 5:17-20		16:17
Example a) Anger: 5:21-26		12:57-59
Example b) Adultery: 5:27-32		16:18
Example c) Oaths: 5:33-37		
Example d) Revenge: 5:38-48	6:27-36	
4: **The spirit in which a disciple is to fulfil the practices of the Law**		
Example a) Almsgiving: 6:1-4		
Example b) Praying: 6:5-15		11:2-4
Example c) Fasting: 6:16-18		
5: The disciple's heart must be free: 6:19-34		12:22-34
6: Care in judging others: 7:1-6	6:37-42	
7: Trust in God's care: 7:7-11		11:9-13
8: The essence of the Law: 7:12	6:31	
9: The necessity of whole-hearted commitment: 7:13-14		13:24
10: Doing the will of God: 7:15-23	6:43-46	
11: Conclusion: 7:24-27	6:47-49	

* * * * * * * *

1: The 'Beatitudes'

MATTHEW 5:1-12 (Compare Luke 6:20-26 page 156)

1
2   **5** Seeing the crowds, he went up the hill. There he sat down and was joined by his disciples. •Then he began to speak. This is what he taught them:

3   'How happy are the poor in spirit;
        theirs is the kingdom of heaven.
4   Happy *the gentle:*
        they shall have the earth for their heritage.
5   Happy those who mourn:

they shall be comforted.
6   Happy those who hunger and thirst for what is right:
they shall be satisfied.
7   Happy the merciful:
they shall have mercy shown them.
8   Happy the pure in heart:
they shall see God.
9   Happy the peacemakers:
they shall be called sons of God.
10   Happy those who are persecuted in the cause of right:
theirs is the kingdom of heaven.
11 'Happy are you when people abuse you and persecute you and speak all kinds
12 of calumny against you on my account. •Rejoice and be glad, for your reward will
be great in heaven; this is how they persecuted the prophets before you.

Matthew takes his readers into the heart of Jesus, and into the heart of Jesus'
teaching.

The word 'happy', connoting as it does in English a chance mood and a
haphazard feeling, is not a good translation of the expression used by Jesus. A
better one would be 'Oh, the blessedness of...'. Jesus is speaking of 'bliss'. He is
describing, for his disciples, the kinds of people who share in the bliss of God.
They experience a profound joy, however 'sad' their circumstances may be,
whatever 'sorrow' they may bear.

The first group described as 'blessed' are the 'poor in spirit' (5:3). Ezekiel had
spoken of the new covenant as resulting from a new 'spirit' that God would give
his people (cf Ezekiel 36:26-27). The first beatitude describes a quality of the
Spirit of Jesus, a spirit he shared with his disciples. Jesus knew in his spirit that he
owed everything to God his Father. He placed his life confidently in his Father's
hands. He was constantly open to receive life from his Father and knew the bliss
of being loved by God.

While the beatitude speaks of a quality of man's spirit, there is a necessary
connection between this quality and a man's social and economic position. The
Bible constantly describes Yahweh as the God who has a special concern for the
materially poor, the oppressed, the lonely and the needy (cf Exodus 3:7,
Deuteronomy 10:17-18; Psalm 82). Moreover, as Matthew records later in his
Gospel, Jesus saw how difficult it was for the materially rich to be 'poor in spirit'
(cf Matthew 19:23-26). Of course, material poverty does not lead automatically
to the spirit Jesus extols in this beatitude. But those who know need are more
likely to open their hearts and their hands to God and recognise God in their life,
and so come to know, in their spirit, his graciousness and fidelity. Jesus
experienced this even while dying on the cross. It is a grace that no circumstances,
however dire, can take from a man.

Perhaps the best way to reach an understanding of what the expression 'poor
in spirit' meant to one trained in Jewish spirituality is to read and re-read the
Psalms, and especially the songs of the Servant of Yahweh found in the writings
of the disciples of Isaiah (cf Isaiah 42:1-4, 49:1-6, 50:4-9, 52:13 — 53:12).

The 'kingdom of heaven' (Matthew 5:3) is already present in the hearts and
lives of those who are 'poor in spirit'. God's love is already reigning there.

The second group described as 'blessed' are the 'gentle' (Matthew 5:4). Jesus was a gentle person (cf Matthew 11:29). He was a person who sensed the sacred at the heart of reality. He did not dominate or manipulate or control. He did not exercise power to gain 'all the kingdoms of the world and their splendour' (Matthew 4:8). He was humble and sensitive and open to others, because he knew what it was to wonder, to marvel at the presence of his Father at the heart of the world. Jesus knew that the whole world belonged to someone with this attitude of heart. He promises his disciples that if they learn to be gentle, 'they shall have the earth for their heritage' (5:4).

The third group described as 'blessed' are 'those who mourn' (5:5). Jesus knew the experience of being comforted by his Father when his heart was broken at the lack of justice and the lack of love and the lack of prayer among his contemporaries. He longed to see men free, to see men living to the full (cf John 10:10), to see men living the life of God. His heart was broken by the sickness, the suffering, the sin that surrounded him. (Note the symbolism of the breaking of the heart of Jesus on the cross: John 19:34.) Jesus asks his disciples to open their hearts to the poor and oppressed; he asks them to empty their hearts as he did (cf Philippians 2:7). He promises them the same comfort that he himself experienced: the comfort of God. Matthew was no doubt thinking of those of his contemporaries who mourned the loss of the bridegroom (cf Matthew 9:15); those, that is, who missed Jesus and longed for him to reveal his presence among them. They are promised the comfort of Jesus' Spirit. We are reminded of the promise made in the prophecy of Zechariah to those who mourn the death of God's anointed one. 'A fountain will be opened up' for them (cf Zechariah 12:9 — 13:1).

The fourth group described as 'blessed' are 'those who hunger and thirst for what is right' (Matthew 5:6). 'What is right' means 'the justice that is in accordance with the will of God'. Jesus listened to his Father and responded with all his heart to the call of his Father to work for justice, for the liberation of man, for the new heaven and the new earth that God wanted to build through men. Jesus knew what it was to set his heart first on God's kingdom and on God's justice (cf Matthew 6:33). He had already promised his disciples that the 'kingdom of God is close at hand' (Matthew 4:17). Here he promises that if they cling to God and work to do God's will they will see the accomplishment of that will; if they work for justice they will see justice. The measure of the fulfilment of this promise is the measure of man's faith in it. Peter expresses his faith in this promise when he writes:

'What we are waiting for is what he promised: the new heavens and new earth, the place where righteousness will be at home.'

(2 Peter 3:13)

The final blessedness of those who hunger and thirst for God's justice will be to hear Jesus say:

'Come, you whom my Father has blessed, take for your heritage the kingdom prepared for you.'

(Matthew 25:34)

The fifth group described as 'blessed' are the 'merciful' (Matthew 5:7). The word translates the Hebrew word 'hesed', a word used to describe the 'compassion' or 'merciful kindness' of Yahweh. Jesus criticised the Pharisees primarily because they lacked this virtue (cf Matthew 9:13, 12:7, 23:23, also Matthew 18:33). Jesus' heart was in touch with the heart of God. He knew God's compassion. When his heart went out to the needy, he experienced what the heart of God felt towards them and towards himself. He promises his followers that they too will know the mercy of God if they open themselves to others and have compassion on them.

The sixth group described as 'blessed' are the 'pure in heart' (5:8). Ezekiel promised that God would give his people 'a new heart' (Ezekiel 36:26). Jesus' teaching is not just concerned with externals; he calls for a purification of the heart (cf Matthew 23:26). For, as he says later, 'a man's words flow out of what fills his heart' (Matthew 12:34). So do his actions (cf Matthew 15:19). Jesus knew what happened when the heart of a nation grew coarse (cf Matthew 15:19); so he asks his disciples here to purify their hearts. A pure heart knows the 'spring inside, welling up to eternal life' (John 4:14); a pure heart sees clearly, and knows the bliss of seeing the heart of others because it is in touch with the heart of God (cf 1 John 3:2). The pure in heart 'shall see God' (Matthew 5:8).

The seventh group described as 'blessed' are the 'peacemakers' (5:9). The word translates the Hebrew word 'shalom'. A good image to convey the meaning of 'shalom' is the sound of an orchestra. When each instrument is playing to perfection, and in perfect harmony with all the others, the resultant sound is 'peaceful'. A maker of peace is a person who, like Jesus, works so that each person may live to the full (John 10:10), so that each person's divinely given initiative will be expressed in its fulness, and all in harmony with the will of God. Such a man is an instrument of God's peace. He shares God's action and 'shall be called' a 'son of God' (Matthew 5:9).

Finally, Jesus knew the pain of working for justice. He knew the envy and opposition of those whose vested interests he threatened. His own life was to lead him to the cross; but it would also lead him to the resurrection. He asks his followers not to be deterred by persecution. For all their apparent powerlessness, the kingdom of heaven belongs to them. They, not their persecutors, are the ones who are in touch with the heart of life and the heart of history. It will be their actions that bear fruit. Let them rejoice and be glad.

2: Proverbs for disciples: the importance of their living according to the new 'Law'

MATTHEW 5:13-16

'You are the salt of the earth. But if salt becomes tasteless, what can make it 13 salty again? It is good for nothing, and can only be thrown out to be trampled underfoot by men.

'You are the light of the world. A city built on a hill-top cannot be hidden. 14 No one lights a lamp to put it under a tub; they put it on the lamp-stand where 15 it shines for everyone in the house. •In the same way your light must shine in the 16 sight of men, so that, seeing your good works, they may give the praise to your Father in heaven.

(Similar proverbs can be found in Mark and Luke, but in different contexts. For the proverb on salt cf Mark 9:50 and Luke 14:34; for the proverb on light cf Mark 4:21 and Luke 8:16 and 11:33.)

Proverbs are, of their nature, elusive to the conceptualising mind. They concentrate on images and work at different levels. As Matthew places them here, he seems to intend to stress the need for the disciples to be like their master. For the world needs them, as it needs salt and light. They are of no use if they are like a tasteless herb (Aramaic malluha; 'salt' is 'milha'), or a light hidden under a cover. At the same time the life they are to give, and the light, is not their own; everything they do must be for the glory of God — to make his glory manifest.

3: Jesus perfects the Law

General statement

MATTHEW 5:17-20

'Do not imagine that I have come to abolish the Law or the Prophets. I have 17 come not to abolish but to complete them. •I tell you solemnly, till heaven 18 and earth disappear, not one dot, not one little stroke, shall disappear from the Law until its purpose is achieved. •Therefore, the man who infringes even 19 one of the least of these commandments and teaches others to do the same will be considered the least in the kingdom of heaven; but the man who keeps them and teaches them will be considered great in the kingdom of heaven.

'For I tell you, if your virtue goes no deeper than that of the scribes and 20 Pharisees, you will never get into the kingdom of heaven.

(Matthew 5:18, compare Luke 16:17 page 290)

As a Jewish-Christian writing within a largely Jewish-Christian community, Matthew was interested in the relationship between what Paul called the 'Law of Christ' (Galatians 6:2) and the Law of Moses.

Paul found himself working more and more among non-Jews. He also was constantly hounded by the Judaisers who were determined to impose the 'Law' on Gentile Christians. Paul tended, therefore, to be firm in stating the relative nature of the 'Law'. He worked hard to liberate Jesus' message from the Jewish culture in which it first took root. He could write to the Roman Church:

'The Law has come to an end with Christ.' *(Romans 10:4)*

Matthew's situation was very different. He belonged to a community that had been brought up under the guidance of the Law. They saw it as still relevant to their lives and they respected it. Matthew is encouraging them in this attitude. They are to follow Jesus because he is the one who expressed perfectly, in his words and in his deeds, the essential message and spirit of the Law and the Prophets. They are to study the Law and follow it in the light of Jesus' life.

Matthew rejects the legalism, the pettiness and the hypocrisy associated with the interpretation of the Law current among the scribes and Pharisees. But he upholds the essential wisdom of the Law as a sacred expression of God's covenant love for his people. According to Matthew it was Jesus who made this clear, and Matthew wanted the community to which he belonged to be faithful to the Law as interpreted in the light of Jesus' life. (cf especially Matthew 9:13, 12:7 and 25:31-46)

In this and the following section (Matthew 5:17 — 6:18), Matthew contrasts two ways of interpreting the Law: the way of the scribes and Pharisees, and the way of Jesus.

Example A — Anger and Reconciliation

MATTHEW 5:21-26

'You have learnt how it was said to our ancestors: *You must not kill;* [a] and if 21 anyone does kill he must answer for it before the court. •But I say this to you: 22 anyone who is angry with his brother will answer for it before the court; if a man calls his brother "Fool" he will answer for it before the Sanhedrin; and if a man calls him "Renegade" he will answer for it in hell fire. •So then, if you are bringing 23 your offering to the altar and there remember that your brother has something against you, •leave your offering there before the altar, go and be reconciled with 24 your brother first, and then come back and present your offering. •Come to terms 25 with your opponent in good time while you are still on the way to the court with him, or he may hand you over to the judge and the judge to the officer, and you will be thrown into prison. •I tell you solemnly, you will not get out till you have 26 paid the last penny.

(a: Exodus 20:13,
(Matthew 5:25-26, compare Luke 12:58-59 page 282)

The Law forbade murder (Exodus 20:13). Jesus goes to the heart of the matter and warns his disciples against the spirit and heart that results in murder. He wants the virtue of his disciples to go 'deeper' (5:20) than that of the Pharisees. A purified heart will not harbour vengeful anger, and so will not act murderously. A disciple of Jesus will learn not just to keep his behaviour within the limits imposed by law; he will learn to love his brother (compare Romans 13:8-10 and 1 John 3:15).

A person concerned only with following the Law is likely to present his offering to God, while at the same time failing to have the dispositions without which the offering is useless (Matthew 5:23-24). Such a person's vision is too narrow. The Greek uses the word 'hypocrite' to describe him — a word which means, in its original meaning, 'narrow-minded', 'small-minded'. The Pharisees of Jesus' day were guilty of hypocrisy, and of encouraging hypocrisy in others, because they were more concerned with appearances than with reality; they did not attempt to get to the heart or spirit of the Law (cf John 5:44 and 12:43).

To stress the vital importance of this new way of looking at things, Jesus speaks of 'hell fire' (5:22) as the ultimate punishment for anger.

The word translated 'hell' (5:22) is actually 'gehenna' (see also Matthew 5:29, 30). Jesus is referring to the valley of Ge-Ben-Hinnom, to the south of Jerusalem. At the time of the destruction of Jerusalem (587 B.C.), Jeremiah cursed the valley:

'The sons of Judah have done what displeases me — it is Yahweh who speaks. They have put their abominations in the Temple that bears my name, to defile it; they have built the high place of Topheth in the valley of Ben-Hinnom, to burn their sons and daughters; a thing I never commanded, a thing that never entered my thoughts. So now the days are coming — it is Yahweh who speaks — when people will no longer talk of Topheth, or of the valley of Ben-Hinnom, but of the valley of slaughter. Topheth will become a burial ground, for lack of other space; the corpses of this people will feed the birds of heaven and the beasts of the earth and there shall be no one to drive them away.'   (Jeremiah 7:30-33, see also 19:1-15 and 32:35,

Many Jews were slaughtered in the valley of Ben-Hinnom, that is, in 'gehenna'. The fires in which innocent children were burned in sacrifice at the shrine of the god, Molech, gave way to fires where the bodies of the dead were burned.

The author of the final chapters of Isaiah, writing after the return from exile (538 B.C.), kept the words of Jeremiah before the minds of his readers. In an apocalyptic vision, speaking of the end of history and the final judgment of God, he wrote:

'For, as the new heavens and the new earth I shall make will endure before me — it is Yahweh who speaks — so will your face and name endure. From new moon to new moon, from sabbath to sabbath, all mankind will come to bow down in my presence, says Yahweh. And on their way out they will see the corpses of men who have rebelled against me. Their worm will not die nor their fire go out; they will be loathsome to all mankind.'

(Isaiah 66:22-24)

Gehenna became the classical symbol of the punishment that comes upon those who are not faithful to the covenant. Jesus could see another 'gehenna' coming. It was because his warning against anger and violence was not heeded that Jerusalem suffered destruction in 70 A.D. and the valley, once again, flowed with blood (see page 325).

Anger brings with it its own punishment (Matthew 5:25-26). Jesus warns his disciples that if they do not rid their heart of anger they will find themselves imprisoned by it.

Example B — Adultery and fidelity in loving

MATTHEW 5:27-32

'You have learnt how it was said: *You must not commit adultery.* •But I say 27 this to you: if a man looks at a woman lustfully, he has already committed 28 adultery with her in his heart. •If your right eye should cause you to sin, tear it out 29 and throw it away; for it will do you less harm to lose one part of you than to have your whole body thrown into hell. •And if your right hand should cause 30 you to sin, cut it off and throw it away; for it will do you less harm to lose one part of you than to have your whole body go to hell.

'It has also been said: *Anyone who divorces his wife must give her a writ of* 31 *dismissal.*[b] •But I say this to you: everyone who divorces his wife, except for the 32 case of fornication, makes her an adulteress; and anyone who marries a divorced woman commits adultery.

(a: Exodus 20:14   b: Deuteronomy 24:1)
(Matthew 5:31-32, compare Luke 16:18 page 291)

Jesus uses a stark analogy taken from primitive legal practice to highlight the importance of purity of heart, and the necessity of avoiding sin as being destructive of life itself. We shall leave the discussion of divorce until Matthew himself develops the subject later in his Gospel (19:3-9 pages 296-302).

By including this brief saying here Matthew highlights the infidelity to love that divorce often involves.

Example C — Breaking oaths and respect for the truth

MATTHEW 5:33-37

'Again, you have learnt how it was said to our ancestors: *You must not break* 33 *your oath, but must fulfil your oaths to the Lord.*[a] •But I say this to you: do not 34 swear at all, either by *heaven*, since that is God's throne; •or by *the earth*, since 35

that is *his footstool;* or by Jerusalem, since that is *the city of the great king.* •Do not 36
swear by your own head either, since you cannot turn a single hair white or black.
All you need say is "Yes" if you mean yes, "No" if you mean no; anything more 37
than this comes from the evil one.

(a: Exodus 20:7)

If a man obeys the Law simply because it is a law, he is in danger of speaking
the truth only when the Law enjoins it; only, that is, when he is under oath. Jesus
wants his disciples to love truth for its own sake: then they will not need oaths.

Example D — Revenge and unconditional love

MATTHEW 5:38-48 (Compare Luke 6:27-36 page 159-160)
'You have learnt how it was said: *Eye for eye and tooth for tooth.*ᵃ •But I say 38, 39
this to you: offer the wicked man no resistance. On the contrary, if anyone hits
you on the right cheek, offer him the other as well; •if a man takes you to law 40
and would have your tunic, let him have your cloak as well. •And if anyone 41
orders you to go one mile, go two miles with him. •Give to anyone who asks, 42
and if anyone wants to borrow, do not turn away.

'You have learnt how it was said: *You must love your neighbour* and hate your 43
enemy.ᵇ •But I say this to you: love your enemies and pray for those who 44
persecute you; •in this way you will be sons of your Father in heaven, for he 45
causes his sun to rise on bad men as well as good, and his rain to fall on honest
and dishonest men alike. •For if you love those who love you, what right have 46
you to claim any credit? Even the tax collectors do as much, do they not? •And 47
if you save your greetings for your brothers, are you doing anything exceptional?
Even the pagans do as much, do they not? •You must therefore be perfect just as 48
your heavenly Father is perfect.

(a: Exodus 21:24-25   b: Leviticus 19:18)

'Eye for eye and tooth for tooth' (5:38) is a summary of the lex talionis (cf
Exodus 21:24). In its day it marked an advance in penal practice as it prevented
excessive revenge by laying down a punishment equal to the crime. Jesus goes far
beyond this and his 'law' differs, not in degree but in kind. The spirit is different.

God does not change his attitude to man when man fails to love or obey him.
God is love, faithful enduring love. His actions flow, not from reaction to man,
but from his own inner being. This was the way Jesus lived and he is here asking
his disciples to let their behaviour flow from the life of God in them, rather than
as a reaction against the evil surrounding them. When he tells his disciples to
'offer the wicked man no resistance' (5:39), he seems to be telling them not to meet
evil on its own terms. Paul has the same message when he writes to the Romans:

'Resist evil and conquer it *with good.'*

(Romans 12:21)

This is how God acts, and Jesus exhorts his disciples to 'be perfect as your
heavenly Father is perfect' (5:48).

* * * * * * * *

4: The spirit in which the disciple is to fulfil the practices of the Law

MATTHEW 6:1-18

Example A — Almsgiving

MATTHEW 6:1-4

1 **6** 'Be careful not to parade your good deeds before men to attract their notice;
2 by doing this you will lose all reward from your Father in heaven. •So when
you give alms, do not have it trumpeted before you; this is what the hypocrites do
in the synagogues and in the streets to win men's admiration. I tell you
3 solemnly, they have had their reward. •But when you give alms, your left hand
4 must not know what your right is doing; •your almsgiving must be secret, and
your Father who sees all that is done in secret will reward you.

The only reward worth having is the reward (='regard') of God: being looked
after by God. God sees the heart, the intention.

Example B — Praying

MATTHEW 6:5-15

5   'And when you pray, do not imitate the hypocrites: they love to say their
prayers standing up in the synagogues and at the street corners for people to see
6 them. I tell you solemnly, they have had their reward. •But when you
pray, *go to your private room and, when you have shut your door, pray* to your
Father who is in that secret place, and your Father who sees all that is done in
secret will reward you.
7   'In your prayers do not babble as the pagans do, for they think that by using
8 many words they will make themselves heard. •Do not be like them; your Father
9 knows what you need before you ask him. •So you should pray like this:

'Our Father in heaven,
may your name be held holy,
10   your kingdom come,
your will be done,
on earth as in heaven.
11   Give us today our daily bread.
12   And forgive us our debts,
as we have forgiven those who are in debt to us.
13   And do not put us to the test,
but save us from the evil one.

14 Yes, if you forgive others their failings, your heavenly Father will forgive you
15 yours; •but if you do not forgive others, your Father will not forgive your
failings either.   *(Matthew 6:9-13, compare Luke 11:2-4 page 275)*

We are invited here into Jesus' own 'private room' (6:6), into that 'secret
place' (6:6) where he communed with his Father. He shares the intimacy of his
own prayer with his disciples. He tells them not to babble, not to 'say prayers', but
to pray. Prayer is the experience of being with God. God is constantly speaking
his word to men. It is not up to us to establish the contact. It is up to us to
withdraw from distractions to get in touch with our heart, and there to let God
speak to us. It is sometimes said that prayer is more a matter of listening than
speaking; it is a matter of taking time to listen to the responses arising in our heart
as it expresses its faith in God's presence.

In the first part of Jesus' prayer, we see him completely caught up in his
Father. He wants the glory of his Father which he himself has witnessed (='your

name') to penetrate the world. He wants men to know his Father; he wants the face of the earth to be renewed by the powerful action of God's spirit, so that the world will be a sacred place. What a world it would be if the Father's love was manifest everywhere. Jesus' prayer is primarily a prayer of adoration. There is a lesson for his disciples in this.

Thought of his Father leads Jesus to think of himself and his needs. Jesus, the poor man, conscious of his total dependence on his Father, prays, simply, for the bread that he really needs today. He trusts that his Father knows what his real needs are (cf 6:8). He also asks for forgiveness. His disciples saw Jesus as being sinless: he was so filled with the spirit of God that he completely responded to grace at every moment of his existence. But Jesus himself knew the need to ask his Father to keep giving himself for Jesus (='for-give'). Jesus knew temptation and here asks his Father to keep loving him in his weakness, to keep saving him from evil.

The 'Our Father' is a simple prayer arising from a humble heart. In it we get some glimpse of the trust that Jesus, the Son of God, had in the one he called 'my Father'. Jesus invites his disciples to share in this spirit.

Example C — Fasting

MATTHEW 6:16-18

'When you fast do not put on a gloomy look as the hypocrites do: they pull 16 long faces to let men know they are fasting. I tell you solemnly, they have had their reward. •But when you fast, put oil on your head and wash your face, 17 so that no one will know you are fasting except your Father who sees all that is 18 done in secret; and your Father who sees all that is done in secret will reward you.

The pious Jew was expected to give alms, to pray and to fast (cf Tobit 12:8). No doubt the Christian Jews in Matthew's community continued these practices. Matthew wants to illustrate the spirit in which these practices are to be carried out. The disciple of Jesus must not do them to be acclaimed by others. If he does continue these practices they must come from a pure heart concerned only to manifest the glory of God.

*   *   *   *   *   *   *   *

5: The disciple's heart must be free

MATTHEW 6:19-34

'Do not store up treasures for yourselves on earth, where moths and 19 woodworms destroy them and thieves can break in and steal. •But store up 20 treasures for yourselves in heaven, where neither moth nor woodworms destroy them and thieves cannot break in and steal. •For where your treasure is, there 21 will your heart be also.

'The lamp of the body is the eye. It follows that if your eye is sound, your 22 whole body will be filled with light. •But if your eye is diseased, your whole body 23 will be all darkness. If then, the light inside you is darkness, what darkness that will be!

'No one can be the slave of two masters: he will either hate the first and love 24
the second, or treat the first with respect and the second with scorn. You cannot
be the slave both of God and of money.

'That is why I am telling you not to worry about your life and what you are to 25
eat, nor about your body and how you are to clothe it. Surely life means more than
food, and the body more than clothing! •Look at the birds in the sky. They do not 26
sow or reap or gather into barns; yet your heavenly Father feeds them. Are you
not worth much more than they are? •Can any of you, for all his worrying, add 27
one single cubit to his span of life? •And why worry about clothing? Think of the 28
flowers growing in the fields; they never have to work or spin; •yet I assure you 29
that not even Solomon in all his regalia was robed like one of these. •Now if that 30
is how God clothes the grass in the field which is there today and thrown into the
furnace tomorrow, will he not much more look after you, you men of little faith?
So do not worry; do not say, "What are we to eat? What are we to drink? How 31
are we to be clothed?" •It is the pagans who set their hearts on all these things. 32
Your heavenly Father knows you need them all. •Set your hearts on his kingdom 33
first, and on his righteousness, and all these other things will be given you as well.
So do not worry about tomorrow: tomorrow will take care of itself. Each day 34
has enough trouble of its own.

(Compare Luke 12:22-34 page 279)

Jesus is warning his disciples against 'worry'(6:25,27,28,31,34). He is telling
them where to 'set your hearts'(6:33). The whole of the 'sermon' is about the 'heart'.
Jesus is not giving us a new Law etched on stone. He recognised the vital necessity
to follow our hearts, and so to ensure that our hearts are pure. The author of the
Book of Ecclesiastes (Qoheleth) has the same advice:

'Follow the promptings of your heart and the desires of your eyes.
But this you must know: for all these things God will bring you to judgment.'

(Ecclesiastes 11:9)

The Book of Proverbs tells us:

'More than all else keep watch over your heart, since here are the wellsprings of life'
(Proverbs 4:23)

Jesus warns his disciples that if their eye is caught up in desire for money, their
heart, indeed their whole body will be enclosed in darkness. Worry over
possessions of any kind has the same effect.

It is easy to be possessed by something, to let one's heart be caught up in
material things and superficial worries. Things matter; they have their
importance. But they are to be enjoyed as gifts of a Father who loves us and
knows our needs (6:32); they are to inspire wonder in us and lift our heart to the
God they manifest; they are to be vehicles of our love for one another, expressing
our personality and our love. When things possess us, and capture our heart
(6:21), they darken it (6:23) and distract us from the kingdom of God (6:33).

6: Care in judging others

MATTHEW 7:1-6 (Compare Luke 6:37-42 page 161)

7 'Do not judge, and you will not be judged; •because the judgements you give 1
are the judgements you will get, and the amount you measure out is the 2
amount you will be given. •Why do you observe the splinter in your brother's 3
eye and never notice the plank in your own? •How dare you say to your brother, 4
"Let me take the splinter out of your eye", when all the time there is a plank in

5 your own? •Hypocrite! Take the plank out of your own eye first, and then you
will see clearly enough to take the splinter out of your brother's eye.
6 'Do not give dogs what is holy; and do not throw your pearls in front of pigs,
or they may trample them and then turn on you and tear you to pieces.

Paul tells the community at Rome to 'worship God in a way that is worthy of
thinking beings' (Romans 12:1). Of course we are required to make judgments in
regard to our own actions and in regard to those of others. This seems to be the
point of the proverb in verse six: there is no point in attempting to help people if
they are not open to receive our help. There will be times when we are obliged to
point out to others their faults, and to oppose them. But all this has to be done
humbly and out of love. It is to be done without condemnation. Jesus is warning
his disciples against presuming that they have the wisdom to impute guilt and
measure responsibility. If we set about the task of loving, if we are willing to
suffer through the purification process necessary to become instruments of God's
judgment (a judgment that is concerned to save, not to condemn: John 3:17),
then, and only then, may we attempt to take the splinter out of our brother's eye.

7: Trust in God's care

MATTHEW 7:7-11 (Compare Luke 11:9-13 page 275)
7 'Ask, and it will be given to you; search, and you will find; knock, and the
8 door will be opened to you. •For the one who asks always receives; the one who
searches always finds; the one who knocks will always have the door opened to
9 him. •Is there a man among you who would hand his son a stone when he asked
10 for bread? •Or would hand him a snake when he asked for a fish? •If you, then,
11 who are evil, know how to give your children what is good, how much more will
your Father in heaven give good things to those who ask him!

Jesus speaks with complete assurance of his Father's desire to answer prayer
('it will be given', 'you will find', the door 'will be opened to you', 'always receives',
'always finds', 'always have the door opened'). At the same time he reminds his
disciples of their lack of wisdom. Like children, they often ask for something that
could harm them ('stone', 'snake'). God does not meet their request. He sees more
deeply and answers their real need ('bread', 'fish').

8: The essence of the Law

MATTHEW 7:12 (Compare Luke 6:31 page 160)
12 'So always treat others as you would like them to treat you; that is the
meaning of the Law and the Prophets.

The 'Law and the Prophets' (7:12) meant a lot to Matthew and his
community. If the injunction to 'treat others as you would like them to treat you'
seems too simple to carry such a weight, we should not be deceived. Because of its
simplicity, it is an excellent criterion by which to measure our behaviour, and it
shows up the many subtle ways in which we fail to love and serve our neighbour.

9: The necessity of whole-hearted commitment

MATTHEW 7:13-14 (Compare Luke 13:24 page 283)
13 'Enter by the narrow gate, since the road that leads to perdition is wide and
14 spacious, and many take it; •but it is a narrow gate and a hard road that leads
to life, and only a few find it.

As with all the sayings in this 'sermon', this one must be interpreted in the light of the way Jesus acted.

Part of its meaning is found in another saying of Jesus:

'None of you can be my disciple unless he gives up all his possessions.'

(Luke 14:33)

The 'law of Christ' is not about something extra, something we can take or leave as we will. It is about the very meaning of our life. If we choose to follow him, we must be ready for the demand to leave all and to give all.

Perhaps Jesus is also reflecting his own sadness about the many who did not accept him.

Let us not forget that Jesus is himself the way (John 14:6); he is himself the gate (John 10:9). So the way must be as wide as the arms of Jesus nailed to the cross and extended to the four corners of the earth. Jesus will say later in Matthew:

'It is never the will of your Father in heaven that one of these little ones should be lost.'

(Matthew 18:14)

The present saying warns us against a false reliance on God's love that would neglect the radical demands of love.

10: Doing the will of God

MATTHEW 7:15-23 (Compare Luke 6:43-46 page 161)

15   'Beware of false prophets who come to you disguised as sheep but underneath
16   are ravenous wolves. •You will be able to tell them by their fruits. Can people
17   pick grapes from thorns, or figs from thistles? •In the same way, a sound tree
18   produces good fruit but a rotten tree bad fruit. •A sound tree cannot bear bad
19   fruit, nor a rotten tree bear good fruit. •Any tree that does not produce good
20   fruit is cut down and thrown on the fire. •I repeat, you will be able to tell them by
      their fruits.
21   'It is not those who say to me, "Lord, Lord", who will enter the kingdom of
22   heaven, but the person who does the will of my Father in heaven. •When the day
      comes many will say to me, "Lord, Lord, did we not prophesy in your name,
23   cast out demons in your name, work many miracles in your name?" •Then
      I shall tell them to their faces: I have never known you; *away from me, you evil
      men!*[a]

(a: Psalm 6:8)
(Matthew 7:22-23 compare Luke 13:25-30 page 283-284)

John, too, speaks of fruit (John 15:1 and 15:16); and the fruit is love: 'Love one another as I have loved you' (John 15:12). Matthew makes the same point in his account of the Last Judgment (Matthew 25:31:46). The disciple is the one who loves as Jesus loved; this is the will of God (Matthew 7:21). Love is to be the sign of the true disciple:

'By this love you have for one another, everyone will know that you are my disciples.'

(John 13:35)

The 'false prophets' (Matthew 7:15) were, no doubt, of various kinds. There were those who rejected the Law to live a life free from restraint; there were those who used the excuse of waiting for the appearance of the glorified Jesus to be idle and neglect the task of building the world; there were those who excelled in cult-worship (Matthew 7:21) but who did not work for justice.

We are reminded of the words of Amos:

'Let me have no more of the din of your chanting,
no more of your strumming on harps.
But let justice flow like water,
and integrity like an unfailing stream.'

(Amos 5:23-24)

This is the fruit expected of a disciple of Jesus. It is the fruit of compassionate love that characterises the true prophet.

Jesus' final words in the above passage make abundantly clear the importance of doing the will of God. Nothing can substitute for it. We are reminded of Paul's equally strong words in his First Letter to the Corinthians (1 Corinthians 13:1-3). Matthew will develop this theme of judgment later in his Gospel (Matthew 25:31-46). Always the central theme is the will of God; and the will of God is that man share in God's own compassionate love.

11: Conclusion

MATTHEW 7:24-27 (Compare Luke 6:47-49 page 161)
'Therefore, everyone who listens to these words of mine and acts on them
25 will be like a sensible man who built his house on rock. •Rain came down, floods rose, gales blew and hurled themselves against that house, and it did not fall:
26 it was founded on rock. •But everyone who listens to these words of mine and does
27 not act on them will be like a stupid man who built his house on sand. •Rain came down, floods rose, gales blew and struck that house, and it fell; and what a fall it had!'

We are reminded of the final words of the last discourse of Moses:

'See, today I set before you life and prosperity, death and disaster. If you obey the commandments of Yahweh your God that I enjoin on you today, if you love Yahweh your God and follow his ways, if you keep his commandments, his laws, his customs, you will live and increase, and Yahweh your God will bless you in the land you are entering to make your own. But if your heart strays, if you refuse to listen, if you let yourself to be drawn into worshipping other gods, and serving them, I tell you today, you will most certainly perish; you will not live long in the land you are crossing the Jordan to enter and possess. I call heaven and earth to witness against you today: I set before you life or death, blessing or curse. Choose life then, so that you and your descendants may live, in the love of Yahweh your God, obeying his voice, clinging to him; for in this your life consists, and on this depends your long stay in the land which Yahweh swore to your fathers Abraham, Isaac and Jacob he would give them.'

(Deuteronomy 30:15-20)

* * * * * * * *

Already, here in the 'sermon', a new way of looking at law is beginning to emerge. It will be expressed very clearly later when Jesus says:

"Come to me all you who labour and are overburdened (by the Law) and I will give you rest. Shoulder my yoke (rather than the yoke of the Law) and learn from me, for I am gentle and humble in heart, and you will find rest for your souls. Yes, my yoke is easy and my burden light'.

(Matthew 11:28-30)

Striving for the perfection that comes from the Law (cf Philippians 3:6-16), man labours in vain and is overburdened. Learning from Jesus, man is lifted into the heart of God, and transcends all that the Law ever hoped to achieve.

In this context it is worth reading Paul's words addressed to the churches of Galatia (Galatians 2:15-21).

We will return to this subject in the following chapter (pages 107-109).

Chapter 3
Jesus' Liberating Word

Mark 2:1 — 3:6
Matthew 8:18 — 9:17 and 12:1-4
Luke 5:17 — 6:11

A: **Matthew's introductory insert** — MATTHEW 8:18-34

Mark and Luke begin this section with a scene demonstrating Jesus' power to liberate from sin. Matthew inserts the following section first.

1: **Jesus' challenging word: The demands of discipleship**

MATTHEW 8:18-22 (Compare Luke 9:57-62 page 272)
When Jesus saw the great crowds all about him he gave orders to leave for the 18 other side. •One of the scribes then came up and said to him, 'Master, I will 19 follow you wherever you go'. •Jesus replied, 'Foxes have holes and the birds 20 of the air have nests, but the Son of Man has nowhere to lay his head'.
Another man, one of his disciples, said to him, 'Sir, let me go and bury my 21 father first'. •But Jesus replied, 'Follow me, and leave the dead to bury their dead'. 22

These sayings stress the demands placed upon anyone who would want to be a disciple of Jesus. The community for whom Matthew was writing was a community that had been excommunicated from the synagogue. It had also been recently uprooted by the Roman army and forced to flee. These Jewish-Christians knew what it was to have 'nowhere to lay their head' (8:20). They knew the experience of being outcasts, of having, like Abraham, to leave their father and their father's house to follow the will of God. Their 'father' (the religion of the scribes and Pharisees) is dead. They must have the courage to leave him, and follow Jesus to make a new family and a new home. This comes 'first' (8:21; cf Matthew 6:33). For commentary on 'Son of Man', the reader is referred to page 77.

2: **Jesus' liberating word** — MATTHEW 8:23-34

a: **Jesus liberates from fear of a hostile environment**

MATTHEW 8:23-27 (Compare Mark 4:35-41 and Luke 8:22-25 page 181)
Then he got into the boat followed by his disciples. •Without warning 23 24 a storm broke over the lake, so violent that the waves were breaking right over

the boat. But he was asleep. •So they went to him and woke him saying, 'Save us, 25
Lord, we are going down!' •And he said to them, 'Why are you so frightened, you 26
men of little faith?' And with that he stood up and rebuked the winds and the
sea; and all was calm again. •The men were astounded and said, 'Whatever kind 27
of man is this? Even the winds and the sea obey him.'

Jesus has just insisted on the demands of being his disciple. He has asked the
disciple to follow him. Immediately we see what this involves: the disciples follow
Jesus into the boat (Matthew 8:23) and find themselves in a hostile and
threatening environment. We shall study this scene when we meet it in Mark
(Mark 4:35-41). Matthew uses it to illustrate the fact that if the disciple has faith
(Matthew 8:26), he need not fear the powers of chaos that rise against him.

b: Jesus liberates from fear of hostile spiritual powers

MATTHEW 8:28-34 (Compare Mark 5:1-20 and Luke 8:26-39 page 182)
When he reached the country of the Gadarenes on the other side, two 28
demoniacs came towards him out of the tombs—creatures so fierce that no one
could pass that way. •They stood there shouting, 'What do you want with us, 29
Son of God? Have you come here to torture us before the time?' •Now some 30
distance away there was a large herd of pigs feeding, •and the devils pleaded 31
with Jesus, 'If you cast us out, send us into the herd of pigs'. •And he said to them, 32
'Go then', and they came out and made for the pigs; and at that the whole herd
charged down the cliff into the lake and perished in the water. •The swineherds 33
ran off and made for the town, where they told the whole story, including what
had happened to the demoniacs. •At this the whole town set out to meet Jesus; 34
and as soon as they saw him they implored him to leave the neighbourhood.

This anecdote is linked to the former one also in Mark and Luke. We shall
leave commentary till we study the passage in their context. Matthew inserts it
here, in an abbreviated form, to illustrate the power of the word of Jesus and the
fact that a disciple need have no fear of hostile spiritual powers.

A disciple should not fear the waters as they rise around him and threaten his
life, nor should he fear the strange derangements that are effected in man's psyche
by the mysterious forces of evil. In Jesus the kingdom of God is coming into the
world with power and nothing can resist his powerful word.

We are reminded of Paul:

'I am certain of this: neither death nor life, no angel, no prince, nothing that exists,
nothing still to come, nor any power or height or depth, nor any created thing, can
ever come between us and the love of God made visible in Christ Jesus our Lord.'
                                                                    (Romans 8:38-39)

*   *   *   *   *   *   *   *

B: Jesus liberates his followers from sin, from conformity to religious ritual and from the Law

1: Jesus liberates from sin — MARK 2:1-17

a: **MARK 2:1-12** (Compare Matthew 9:1-8 and Luke 5:17-26)
2 When he returned to Capernaum some time later, word went round that he 1
was back; •and so many people collected that there was no room left, even 2

THE LIBERATING WORD   103

in front of the door. He was preaching the word to them •when some people 3
came bringing him a paralytic carried by four men, •but as the crowd made 4
it impossible to get the man to him, they stripped the roof over the place where
Jesus was; and when they had made an opening, they lowered the stretcher on
which the paralytic lay. •Seeing their faith, Jesus said to the paralytic, 'My child, 5
your sins are forgiven'. •Now some scribes were sitting there, and they thought 6
to themselves, •'How can this man talk like that? He is blaspheming. Who can 7
forgive sins but God?' •Jesus, inwardly aware that this was what they were 8
thinking, said to them, 'Why do you have these thoughts in your hearts?
Which of these is easier: to say to the paralytic, "Your sins are forgiven" or to 9
say, "Get up, pick up your stretcher and walk"? •But to prove to you that the 10
Son of Man has authority on earth to forgive sins,'—•he said to the paralytic— 11
'I order you: get up, pick up your stretcher, and go off home.' •And the man 12
got up, picked up his stretcher at once and walked out in front of everyone, so
that they were all astounded and praised God saying, 'We have never seen
anything like this'.

The Baptist has spoken of 'repentance for the forgiveness of sins' (Mark 1:4)
and of one who would follow him and 'baptise them with the Holy Spirit' (Mark
1:8). This healing of the paralysed man forms a climax to the earlier healing
scenes, for in it Jesus heals the ultimate sickness — the sickness of sin. Sin is a
paralysis of the spirit. 'Sin' is a general word which embraces such things as fear,
conformity, insecurity, failure, ignorance, and lack of freedom: characteristics of
our human condition. We are not wholly responsible for the sin that is in our
lives, any more than the man in the Gospel story is responsible for being
paralysed; our sinful condition is largely due to our heredity and environment.
But at times we do say 'yes' to sin; at times we fail to love others and serve them; at
times we treat people as objects and not as persons; at times we add to the sin that
permeates our social lives. Whatever the measure of our personal responsibility,
the fact is that we are sinners (on 'hamartia' see page 12).

Jesus came preaching repentance. He tried to liberate people from the
domination of sin, to show that it is possible not to give in to fear, that it is
possible to trust and to be faithful to love. In his own life he demonstrated that
one could be a man and not sin. Again and again the Gospels emphasise that
Jesus knew our fears and our insecurities; and he did not give in to them. He knew
what it was to feel the absence of God; and he continued to pray. He knew what it
was to be ignored and denied and betrayed and abandoned by friends; and he
continued to love.

Jesus taught us to 'forgive'. The word means to 'give-for'. You forgive
someone when, in spite of hurt received, you continue to give yourself for him.
The only way to convince an outcast that he is not entirely abandoned is to stay
with him. The only way to heal a person who has betrayed trust is to find ways of
continuing to trust him. The Gospels show us a Jesus that understood men and
was capable of the most incisive criticism. But he was always a loving man; he did
not give up on people. He showed us that if we believe in God we must continue to
believe in people. He himself continued to give himself, his time, his energy, his
love and finally his life.

In the present scene, Jesus cures a man of physical paralysis as a sign of his
power to liberate him from the deeper, underlying paralysis of sin. It is important

to note that Jesus heals in response to faith; in this instance it is not the faith of the man himself but the faith of his friends (Mark 2:5). Just as a paralysed man needs his friends to enable him to move, so we need a community to take us to Jesus.

The scribes, introduced here for the first time in Mark (2:6), are scandalised by Jesus' action: only God can forgive sin and so Jesus is blaspheming in claiming this divine power (Mark 2:6). Jesus is determined to show them how wrong they are in their conception of God.

For Jesus, God is at the heart of the human condition. God is love; therefore, wherever there is God, there we find love. Conversely, wherever we find love we can be sure that God is present. God is the source of forgiveness, and wherever God is, there we find forgiveness. But God is at the heart of people and so he forgives us through each other. It is true, as the scribes say, that only God can forgive sin (2:7). Jesus showed that God does this through men. A man, united to God, can be a channel to others of God's forgiveness and peace (compare John 10:34-38).

Jesus even used the title 'Son of Man' (2:10) to highlight the fact that, in forgiving sin, he is acting as one of us (see page 77).

When the risen Jesus gave his disciples a share in his Spirit, we are told by John:

'He breathed on them and said:
"Receive the Holy Spirit.
For those whose sins you forgive,
they are forgiven".'

(John 20:22)

It is this sharing by men in God's power to forgive that is stressed by Matthew who concludes his account with the words:

'They praised God for giving such power *to men.*'

(Matthew 9:8)

b: **MARK 2:13-17** (Compare Matthew 9:9-12 and Luke 5:27-32)
He went out again to the shore of the lake; and all the people came to him, 13 and he taught them. •As he was walking on he saw Levi the son of Alphaeus, 14 sitting by the customs house, and he said to him, 'Follow me'. And he got up and followed him.

When Jesus was at dinner in his house, a number of tax collectors and sinners 15 were also sitting at the table with Jesus and his disciples; for there were many of them among his followers. •When the scribes of the Pharisee party saw him eating 16 with sinners and tax collectors, they said to his disciples, 'Why does he eat with tax collectors and sinners?' •When Jesus heard this he said to them, 'It is not the 17 healthy who need the doctor, but the sick. I did not come to call the virtuous, but sinners.'

In the Gospel according to Matthew, the Levi mentioned here is identified with Matthew (9:9). 'Matthew' means 'gift of Yahweh' and was possibly the name given to Levi by Jesus.

The tax referred to (2:15) was that introduced by the Roman occupation forces in 6 A.D. It was rejected by the Zealots as a symbol of Roman authority and the paying of it was a humiliation to the Jews who saw themselves as subject to Yahweh alone. The tax collectors were Jews who took on the task of collecting the money. They had to hand over to the Roman authorities a fixed sum determined by the census. They were free to extort as much as they could from the people and to retain for themselves whatever they could get over and above the fixed sum. They were despised as turn-coats, and were refused the synagogue.

Mark could not have chosen a more powerful scene to dramatise the profound difference between the religious attitude of Jesus and that of the lawyers. These people are 'sick' (2:17); Jesus does not deny that. He is concerned to bring them health and he will not do this by condemning and ostracising them, but by loving them, even to the extent of sharing with them the homely intimacy of a meal.

* * * * * * * *

Matthew adds the following statement to his account:

MATTHEW 9:13

•Go and learn the meaning of the words:
What I want is mercy, not sacrifice.[a] And indeed I did not come to call the virtuous, but sinners.'

(a: Hosea 6:6)

Matthew quotes the same passage from Hosea later, in similar circumstances (Matthew 12:7 page 108). The point he is making is that the scribes, even though students of the Law, were missing the whole point of the Law. Their meticulous concern for external observance was causing them to forget that the Law was actually about love — about God's faithful love for man and the liberation this brings to him.

The scribes are accusing Jesus of breaking the Law. On the contrary, it is he who is obeying the Law by carrying out its spirit and intention (cf Matthew 5:7).

2: Jesus liberates from conformity to religious ritual

MARK 2:18-22 (Compare Matthew 9:14-17 and Luke 5:33-39)

One day when John's disciples and the Pharisees were fasting, some people 18 came and said to him, 'Why is it that John's disciples and the disciples of the Pharisees fast, but your disciples do not?' •Jesus replied, 'Surely the bridegroom's 19 attendants would never think of fasting while the bridegroom is still with them? As long as they would have the bridegroom with them, they could not think of fasting. But the time will come for the bridegroom to be taken away from them, and then, 20 on that day, they will fast. •No one sews a piece of unshrunken cloth on an old 21 cloak; if he does, the patch pulls away from it, the new from the old, and the tear gets worse. •And nobody puts new wine into old wineskins; if he does, the wine 22 will burst the skins, and the wine is lost and the skins too. No! New wine, fresh skins!'

In the 'Sermon on the Mount' Matthew has retained certain sayings of Jesus that stress the importance of interior attitude, and the importance of avoiding hypocrisy in the matter of fasting (cf Matthew 6:16-18). It is obvious from the above anecdote that Jesus and his disciples felt free to go even further and ignore

our expectation ultimately prevent us from enjoying our rewards.

the ritual requirements of fasting. Later in his Gospel, Matthew actually has Jesus contrasting himself with John the Baptist precisely in this area:

complain no matter what

> 'John came neither eating nor drinking, and they say, "He is possessed". The Son of Man came, eating and drinking, and they say, "Look, a glutton and a drunkard, a friend of tax collectors and sinners".'
> *(Matthew 11:18-19)*

We know that the early Christians practised fasting — this is indicated in our present text (Mark 2:20). Jesus is not saying anything against fasting. But he is making a point by refusing to submit to the expectations of the people.

Jesus came, as John tells us:

> 'that they may have life and have it to the full'
> *(John 10:10)*

Life is something to be celebrated with joy. There is a place for fasting; but celebration of life must take precedence over fasting. And Jesus believed that he and his disciples had something to celebrate.

The prophets often referred to God as the bridegroom of Israel (cf especially, the prophecy of Hosea). The bridegroom, in the person of Jesus, is visiting his bride. Such 'Good News' is to be received with joy. The Messianic Age has dawned, and it is faith that opens a man to receive God's gift of life, not the meticulous observance of the Law (cf Romans 5:1-11 and Philippians 3:9). This is part of the new outlook that Jesus gave his contemporaries; it is part of the 'repentance' without which forgiveness of sin is not possible.

Jesus makes his point via two powerful metaphors. The Law is the old cloak; Jesus' message is a piece of new cloth. One cannot just fit Jesus into the patterns of the Old Law; a whole new fabric must be woven. The Law is the old wineskin; Jesus' message is new wine. One cannot just pour his 'Good News' into the old containers. The laws of fasting grew out of meditation on the demands of the Old Law. Jesus is bringing a new approach; it will be necessary to find new ways of expressing it.

Surely, this is a lesson each generation has to learn again! There is always something new as well as something old in the wonder and surprise of God's loving approach to man. We cannot contain God, and each generation, each culture, each person, has to find ways of expressing living faith. Otherwise there is a danger that practices become encrusted and inflexible and too dry to take the new wine. 'New wine, fresh skins' (2:22).

*   *   *   *   *   *   *   *

Mark follows that scene with one in which he demonstrates the fact that Jesus liberates his followers from the Law. Luke is content to follow Mark. For Matthew the matter was not so easy. He was writing for a community which respected and, for the most part, continued to follow the Law. Matthew recognised the need to preface this scene with a rather lengthy introduction (Matthew 9:18 — 11:30). It will be the subject of the following chapter.

In this introduction, Matthew establishes the alternative to the Law before removing it. He concentrates the attention of the reader on Jesus and on the community in which Jesus lives (the church). He shows how Jesus incorporates and transcends the Law. He also illustrates the central place of faith in the life of the disciple. Only when he has done this does Matthew feel free to rejoin Mark in narrating the following scene.

* * * * * * * *

3: Jesus liberates from the Law

MARK 2:23-28 (Compare Matthew 12:1-4 and Luke 6:1-5)

One sabbath day he happened to be taking a walk through the cornfields, and 23 his disciples began to pick ears of corn as they went along. •And the Pharisees 24 said to him, 'Look, why are they doing something on the sabbath day that is forbidden?' •And he replied, 'Did you never read what David did in his time of 25 need when he and his followers were hungry—•how he went into the house of 26 God when Abiathar was high priest, and ate the loaves of offering which only the priests are allowed to eat, and how he also gave some to the men with him?'

And he said to them, 'The sabbath was made for man, not man for the 27 sabbath; •so the Son of Man is master even of the sabbath'. 28

Mark uses this anecdote to illustrate a truth that the church came to understand only very slowly. Christianity had its roots in Judaism, and it is understandable that it took some time to undergo the painful uprooting process necessary for it to become relevant to the Gentile world. Stephen and his followers seem to have been the first to realise the necessity of liberating the church from the culture in which it was born; and Stephen was the first victim of the opposition this aroused (cf Acts chapter 6-7). Many among the early Christians fought to retain the Law as the basis of Christianity. Paul opposed these 'Judaisers' all his life and his writings are full of his arguments against them. At the assembly of the church leaders in Jerusalem in 48 A.D. it was decided, in principle, that a non-Jew convert to Christianity was not bound by the Law (cf Acts chapter 15 and Galatians 2:1-10). But old habits die hard and it was probably only with the collapse of Jerusalem in 70 A.D. that the Judaisers were forced to admit defeat. By the time the Gospels were written, the Christian community was predominantly Gentile.

Mark takes the occasion of the anecdote about the cornfields to make the point that the Law (represented by the sabbath) was made to enlighten and liberate men, not to bind and overburden them (Mark 2:27). When the regulations of the Law did not help men express the compassion of God, Jesus, like David (cf 1 Samuel 21:2-7) felt free to dispense with the Law.

* * * * * * * *

Not only does **Matthew** introduce a whole section before this episode, he also adds the following passage to it, the better to ensure that his readers grasp its essential message.

MATTHEW 12:5-8

Or again, have you not read in the Law that on the sabbath day the Temple 5 priests break the sabbath without being blamed for it? •Now here, I tell you, 6

7 is something greater than the Temple. •And if you had understood the meaning
of the words: *What I want is mercy, not sacrifice,*[a] you would not have condemned
8 the blameless. •For the Son of Man is master of the sabbath.'

(a: Hosea 6:6)

The work of sacred ministry increased on the sabbath (cf Numbers 28:9-10).
One of the central points of Jesus' teaching was that the sacred ministry was not
primarily ministry in the physical Temple: God's chosen dwelling place is the
body of man. Sacrifice in the Temple has value only when men show to each
other the mercy of God. The Pharisees should be concerned with showing mercy
on the sabbath. If they were, they would not have misjudged the disciples.

The radical difference between Jesus' attitude and that of the Pharisees can
be expressed in the following diagrams.

1: a) The way to God according to the Pharisees:

God is love. He is faithful to his
covenant. Men cannot see God, but God
reveals to man the way to live so that
man can, one day, see Him. That way is
the Law. The more perfectly a man
conforms his behaviour to the Law, the
better his life.

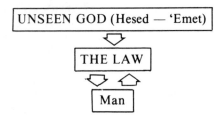

b) The way to God according to Jesus' disciples:

God is Love. He is faithful to his
covenant. Men cannot see God, but God
reveals to man the way to live so that
man can, one day, see Him. That way is
the way Jesus lived. The Law is there as
a guide. But the disciple conforms his
behaviour not to the Law but to Jesus.

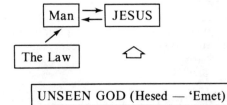

2: a) The way to act according to the Pharisees:

> In order to act responsibly, men should know the Law and conform their behaviour to it.

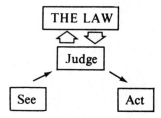

b) The way to act according to Jesus' disciples:

> In order to act responsibly, men should look at Jesus and learn from him how to be compassionate with the compassion of God. The Law, as an expression of human wisdom, is there as a guide; but in the ultimate analysis, it is compassion that must be the deciding factor.

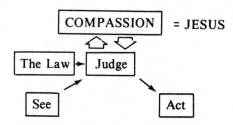

5: The upholders of the Law conspire to destroy Jesus

MARK 3:1-6 (Compare Matthew 12:9-14 and Luke 6:6-11)

1 3 He went again into a synagogue, and there was a man there who had a withered
2 hand. •And they were watching him to see if he would cure him on the sabbath
3 day, hoping for something to use against him. •He said to the man with the
4 withered hand, 'Stand up out in the middle!' •Then he said to them, 'Is it
against the law on the sabbath day to do good, or to do evil; to save life, or to
5 kill?' But they said nothing. •Then, grieved to find them so obstinate, he looked
angrily round at them, and said to the man, 'Stretch out your hand'. He stretched
6 it out and his hand was better. •The Pharisees went out and at once began to
plot with the Herodians against him, discussing how to destroy him.

With this tragic scene, the Synoptics conclude the first section of Jesus'
Galilean ministry. Jesus, by his healing and liberating action, has demonstrated

the powerful presence of God. In doing so he has come up against those with vested interests in power, whether religious (the Pharisees) or political (the Herodians). Jesus has been trying to shake them from their hypocrisy. In this scene he is forced to confront them in a most dramatic way. They are determined not to change, determined not to see, and in the end, they discuss 'how to destroy him' (3:6).

The first part of the Gospel has been concentrating on the new spirit that Jesus introduced into the interpretation of the Law. This scene illustrates this spirit perfectly. The Law is about life, about healing, about God's enduring care for his people. Jesus knows what he must do, and is determined that the people understand. He summons the sick man to 'stand up out in the middle' (3:3). He challenges the Pharisees to face the consequences of their negative attitudes:

'Is it against the Law on the sabbath day to do good or to do evil; to save life, or to kill?' (3:4)

They are not used to arguing on this level. Their concern is for the letter of the law, a letter over which they have power, because they are the learned ones. To accept Jesus' question is to deny the basis of their power. So 'they said nothing' (3:4). Jesus is grieved to find them so obstinate and his act of healing is a demonstration to them of the justice of God. Jesus takes sides, deliberately and obviously, and in so doing takes upon himself the consequences of their opposition.

* * * * * * * *

Points for Reflection:

1: Do I wish to be a follower of Jesus, wherever he might go? (Matthew 8:19). Is the church of which I am a member a pilgrim church? Or, in God's name, do we spend more time and energy making sure we have somewhere to lay our head, than in following Jesus and preaching the Good News?

2: What comes 'first' (Matthew 8:21) in my life?

3: Do I blame a hostile environment for my failure to believe? (Matthew 8:23-27) Or do I risk the rising waters with him? How much of my life is affected by fear (Matthew 8:26)?

4: Meditate on Romans 8:38-39 (cf Matthew 8:28-34).

5: In those areas in my life where I am paralysed have I the courage to come before Jesus and hear him say: 'walk!' (Mark 2:9)? Am I willing to spend my time taking others to him, and encouraging them by my loving service (Mark 2:3)? If there are people whom I have not forgiven, I should reflect on the scene at Capernaum (Mark 2:1-12) to see how powerful forgiveness can be when it is offered as Jesus offered it.

6: The church will always, like Jesus, be seen 'eating with sinners' (Mark 2:16). If there was no room in the church for sinners, there would be no room for us. This should not make us complacent about sin, but it should restrain us from the criticism levelled at Jesus by the scribes (Mark 2:16). The church will always be a church of sinners, and we should not be surprised at the sin we find in her midst. The important thing is that the Risen Lord is there drawing men away from sin and calling sinners to repentance.

7:   There is new wine (Mark 2:22) to be tasted every time a child is born. There is new wine to bottle with every new generation and every new movement within a culture. Our challenge is to taste the new wine, and to finds ways of containing it without destroying it or wasting it. There will always be new ways of expressing faith and prayer. Each person has something creative to offer the community of the church; that is, if the church is a living body.

8:   A law is, at best, an expression of wisdom. We cannot reject all law without dismissing, as fools, those who went before us. It is by obeying a law that we come to learn the value enshrined in it. At the same time, no law can comprehensively express truth, and so we cannot, as the Pharisees did (Mark 2:24), follow law as the ultimate criterion of truth without perpetrating injustices and failing to be open to the spirit of God and the creativity of the human person. There will be times when, to live the spirit of a law, we must break the letter. This is a delicate matter. The ultimate criterion is 'mercy' (Matthew 12:7). There is no substitute (not even law) for constant contact with the enduring love of God and the guidance of his Spirit.

Chapter 4
Matthew's presentation of Jesus as the alternative to the Law

Matthew 9:18 — 11:30

Before examining this insert, let us place it in its context in Matthew. The section is dealing with the liberating effect of Jesus' word. Matthew introduced the section with a statement on the demands of discipleship (Matthew 8:18-22). He followed this with two incidents, taken from a later section in Mark, which illustrate the fact that the word of Jesus liberates the disciple from fear of the environment, whether 'physical' (Matthew 8:23-27) or 'spiritual' (Matthew 8:28-34).

After this introduction, Matthew joined Mark and narrated incidents that illustrated the fact that the word of Jesus liberates the disciple from sin (Matthew 9:1-13) and from conformity to the demands of religious ritual (Matthew 9:14-17).

Mark went straight on to illustrate Jesus' liberation of the disciple from the Law. It is at this stage that Matthew inserted the present section. Matthew judged it was necessary to establish an alternative before removing the Law as the basis of the life of the community.

In this insert, Matthew establishes, first of all, that faith is the foundation of the new covenant established by Jesus (Matthew 9:18-34). He then goes on to introduce the community of his followers as the place in which this covenant is lived out. In the Apostolic Discourse (Matthew 9:35 — 11:1) he gathers together various sayings of Jesus that establish the authority and mission of the community. Finally he develops the theme of the messiahship of Jesus, and examines the essence of his 'law'.

It is only when Matthew has established this foundation that he rejoins Mark with the anecdote concerning eating corn on the sabbath and its consequences (Matthew 12:1-14).

* * * * * * * *

i) Faith is the foundation of the new covenant.

MATTHEW 9:18-26 (Compare Mark 5:21-43 and Luke 8:40-56 page 184)

While he was speaking to them, up came one of the officials, who bowed low 18 in front of him and said, 'My daughter has just died, but come and lay your hand on her and her life will be saved'. •Jesus rose and, with his disciples, followed him. 19

Then from behind him came a woman, who had suffered from a haemorrhage 20 for twelve years, and she touched the fringe of his cloak, •for she said to herself, 21 'If I can only touch his cloak I shall be well again'. •Jesus turned round and saw 22 her; and he said to her, 'Courage, my daughter, your faith has restored you to health'. And from that moment the woman was well again.

When Jesus reached the official's house and saw the flute-players, with the 23 crowd making a commotion he said, •'Get out of here; the little girl is not dead, 24 she is asleep'. And they laughed at him. •But when the people had been turned 25 out he went inside and took the little girl by the hand; and she stood up. •And the 26 news spread all round the countryside.

This is an abbreviated account of the anecdote recorded later by Mark (cf commentary on Mark 5:21-43). For our present purpose it is sufficient to observe the stress Matthew places on faith, both the faith of the official (Matthew 9:18) and the faith of the woman (Matthew 9:22). The healing power of God touched these people's lives, not because they followed a ritual prescription, but because they had faith.

MATTHEW 9:27-31

As Jesus went on his way two blind men followed him shouting, 'Take pity 27 on us, Son of David'. •And when Jesus reached the house the blind men came 28 up with him and he said to them, 'Do you believe I can do this?' They said, 'Sir, we do'. •Then he touched their eyes saying, 'Your faith deserves it, so let this 29 be done for you'. •And their sight returned. Then Jesus sternly warned them, 30 'Take care that no one learns about this'. •But when they had gone, they talked 31 about him all over the countryside.

This incident (which may well be another version of an incident recorded by Matthew later in the Gospel, 20:29-34, page 310) reinforces the message of the last two. The blind men are healed because of their faith (Matthew 9:28-29).

MATTHEW 9:32-34

They had only just left when a man was brought to him, a dumb demoniac. 32 And when the devil was cast out, the dumb man spoke and the people were 33 amazed. 'Nothing like this has ever been seen in Israel' they said. •But the 34 Pharisees said, 'It is through the prince of devils that he casts out devils'.

This incident, too, is mentioned by Matthew in a later context (12:22-24, page 170). He inserts it here because of the contrast it illustrates. On the one hand there is the amazement and openness to faith of the ordinary people; on the other there is the complete lack of faith of the Pharisees.

*   *   *   *   *   *   *

What Jesus responds to is faith, not observance of the Law. And faith involves an awareness of need and that the need can be met only by God. It involves also a freedom of mind and heart to recognise God's presence in Jesus. The official, the sick woman, the blind man and the people who brought the dumb man to Jesus, all placed their trust in him to be a channel to them of God's healing presence. They had faith.

ii) **Faith is experienced in the 'Church' (**= The community of the New Covenant)

1: **Introduction**

MATTHEW 9:35-37

Jesus made a tour through all the towns and villages, teaching in their 35 synagogues, proclaiming the Good News of the kingdom and curing all kinds of diseases and sickness.

And when he saw the crowds he felt sorry for them because they were harassed 36 and dejected, like sheep without a shepherd. •Then he said to his disciples, 37 'The harvest is rich but the labourers are few, so ask the Lord of the harvest to send labourers to his harvest'.

(9:36, cf Mark 6:34. page 191)

Matthew introduced his first 'Sermon' with almost identical words (Matthew 9:35 = Matthew 4:23).

The harassed sheep are looking for guidance. The religious leaders have failed to provide it (compare John 10:1-21), so Jesus is about to commission his own disciples to carry on his work.

2: **Jesus summons Twelve Apostles**

MATTHEW 10:1-4

10 He summoned his twelve disciples, and gave them authority over unclean 1 spirits with power to cast them out and to cure all kinds of diseases and sickness.

These are the names of the twelve apostles: first, Simon who is called Peter, 2 and his brother Andrew; James the son of Zebedee, and his brother John; •Philip 3 and Bartholomew; Thomas, and Matthew the tax collector; James the son of Alphaeus, and Thaddaeus; •Simon the Zealot and Judas Iscariot, the one who 4 was to betray him.

(Compare Mark 3:13-19 and Luke 6:12-16 page 152-153)

We shall defer commentary on this passage till we study Mark's account.

3: **The new covenant community shares in Jesus' mission**

MATTHEW 10:5-8

•These twelve Jesus sent out, instructing them as follows: 5 'Do not turn your steps to pagan territory, and do not enter any Samaritan town; •go rather to the lost sheep of the House of Israel. •And as you go, $\frac{6}{7}$ proclaim that the kingdom of heaven is close at hand. •Cure the sick, raise the 8 dead, cleanse the lepers, cast out devils. You received without charge, give without charge.

Jesus' short ministry was spent among his own people. Later Matthew records a remark attributed to Jesus:

'I was sent only to the lost sheep of the House of Israel.'

(Matthew 15:24)

There were times when Jesus ministered to non-Jews, but these were rare.

It seems that Jesus' immediate followers, understandably, began their ministry among the Jews. The mission 'to pagan territory' (Matthew 10:5) began only after the death of Jesus. Even then it took some time for the implications of the Gospel to be grasped by his followers, especially as regards the place of the Jewish Law in Christian practice. The mission to the Gentiles was spearheaded by a group of Greek-speaking Jewish Christians led by Stephen (cf Acts 8:1, 11:18 and 11:26).

In the discourse upon which we are commenting, Jesus instructs his apostles to carry on the same mission in which he himself is involved. Like him they are to proclaim that the kingdom of heaven is close at hand (Matthew 10:7 = Matthew 4:17). Like him they are to cure the sick, raise the dead, cleanse the lepers, cast our devils (Matthew 10:8, cf many anecdotes about Jesus already studied).

The community of his followers is carrying on the work of Jesus.

MATTHEW 10:9-16

•Provide yourselves with no gold or silver, not even with a few coppers 9 for your purses, •with no haversack for the journey or spare tunic or footwear 10 or a staff, for the workman deserves his keep.

'Whatever town or village you go into, ask for someone trustworthy and stay 11 with him until you leave. •As you enter his house, salute it, •and if the house ¹²₁₃ deserves it, let your peace descend upon it; if it does not, let your peace come back to you. •And if anyone does not welcome you or listen to what you have to say, 14 as you walk out of the house or town shake the dust from your feet. •I tell you 15 solemnly, on the day of Judgement it will not go as hard with the land of Sodom and Gomorrah as with that town. •Remember, I am sending you out 16 like sheep among wolves; so be cunning as serpents and yet as harmless as doves.

(Compare Mark 6:8-11 and Luke 9:3-5 page 187)

We shall leave a detailed commentary on this passage till we study the parallel passage of Mark (Mark 6:7-13). Matthew adds two details. Firstly he adds the statement about Sodom and Gomorrah (Matthew 10:15). These cities were punished because of grave breaches of the laws of hospitality (cf Genesis 19:1-29). Secondly, Matthew makes it explicit that the gift the apostles are offering is the special gift of the messianic age, the gift of 'peace' (Matthew 10:13). If the gift is rejected, the apostles are to take it elsewhere (Matthew 10:13-14).

4: The mission will bring suffering

MATTHEW 10:17-23

'Beware of men: they will hand you over to sanhedrins and scourge you in 17 their synagogues. •You will be dragged before governors and kings for my sake, 18 to bear witness before them and the pagans. •But when they hand you over, do 19 not worry about how to speak or what to say; what you are to say will be given to you when the time comes; •because it is not you who will be speaking; the Spirit 20 of your Father will be speaking in you.

'Brother will betray brother to death, and the father his child; children will 21 rise against their parents and have them put to death. •You will be hated by all 22 men on account of my name; but the man who stands firm to the end will be saved. If they persecute you in one town, take refuge in the next; and if they persecute 23 you in that, take refuge in another. I tell you solemnly, you will not have gone the round of the towns of Israel before the Son of Man comes.

(Compare Mark 13:9-13 and Luke 21:12-19 page 353)

We shall leave detailed commentary on this passage till we study the parallel passage in Mark, where it forms part of the Eschatological discourse.

The mission must lead to persecution, but the missionaries are not to lose heart. The same Spirit that sustained Jesus will sustain them (Matthew 10:20). His father is our father (10:20). God's justice (=the coming of the Son of Man, Matthew 10:23) will prevail, and soon. The apostle must not lose courage, but persevere.

As we shall see when studying the Eschatological Discourse, the Synoptics saw the destruction of Jerusalem in 70 A.D. as a sign of the presence of the Eschaton (the 'last day') and of God's judgment.

5: There is no need to be afraid

MATTHEW 10:24-33

24
25   'The disciple is not superior to his teacher, nor the slave to his master. •It is enough for the disciple that he should grow to be like his teacher, and the slave like his master. If they have called the master of the house Beelzebul, what will they not say of his household?

26   'Do not be afraid of them therefore. For everything that is now covered will
27   be uncovered, and everything now hidden will be made clear. •What I say to you in the dark, tell in the daylight; what you hear in whispers, proclaim from the housetops.

28   'Do not be afraid of those who kill the body but cannot kill the soul; fear him
29   rather who can destroy both body and soul in hell. •Can you not buy two sparrows for a penny? And yet not one falls to the ground without your Father
30
31   knowing. •Why, every hair on your head has been counted. •So there is no need to be afraid; you are worth more than hundreds of sparrows.

32   'So if anyone declares himself for me in the presence of men, I will declare my-
33   self for him in the presence of my Father in heaven. •But the one who disowns me in the presence of men, I will disown in the presence of my Father in heaven.

(Compare Luke 12:2-9 page 278)

Jesus was accused of blasphemy (Matthew 10:25 compare Matthew 9:3) because his mission of love challenged the position of those who used religion for their own power and prestige. Jesus was 'persecuted in the cause of right' (Matthew 5:10). There is no doubt that his disciples will come up against the same treatment (Matthew 10:24-25). Jesus encourages them to carry on with the mission of love and healing that he is sharing with them.

He tells them not to fear men. In the strongest terms possible, he makes the point that the only one worth being afraid of is God:

'who can destroy both body and soul in hell'

(Matthew 10:28,

Compared to this, what man can do pales into insignificance (on the subject of hell, 'gehenna', the reader is referred to page 91). Immediately, lest his hearers misunderstand him, Jesus demonstrates that 'there is no need to be afraid' of God (10:31). In a most gentle way he illustrates the fatherly care of God. His whole gospel is about the love of God. False religion plays on man's fear of the unknown; God himself becomes an object of fear. There was a good deal of this in the religion supported by the Pharisees, and Jesus constantly opposed it. In this present statement, Jesus tries to remove all fear from our relationships with God, our father. True, the Bible speaks of 'fear of the Lord'. It is speaking of reverence before the wonder of God's sacred presence and a profound desire to do God's will. Religion is not about being afraid; it is about wonder and joy and peace and liberation of the human spirit. It is about living to the full and being an instrument of God's creative love to others.

'Do not be afraid for I have redeemed you;
I have called you by your name, you are mine . . .
Do not be afraid, for I am with you.'

(Isaiah 43:1,5)

The only thing that a person should fear is his own ability to throw away his life. Jesus' final remark (Matthew 10:32-33) alerts the reader to this (cf also 2 Timothy 2:12-13). Yet, in reading this statement, we should remember how compassionately Jesus treated Peter when Peter disowned him (cf Matthew 28:10 and John 21:15-19).

6: We are judged by the word

MATTHEW 10:34-36
34 'Do not suppose that I have come to bring peace to the earth: it is not peace I
35 have come to bring, but a sword. •For I have come to set *a man against his father,*
   a daughter against her mother, a daughter-in-law against her mother-in-law.
36 *A man's enemies will be those of his own household.* [a]

(Compare Luke 12:51-53 page 282)
(a: Micah 7:6)

Of course Jesus came to bring peace (cf Matthew 5:9). But there is a false peace, in which nothing matters, nothing happens; there is no disturbance because there is no life and no decisions are being made. Jesus did not come to bring that kind of 'peace'. For the word of God:

'is something alive and active: it cuts like any double-edged sword but more finely; it can slip through the place where the soul is divided from the spirit, or joints from the marrow; it can judge the secret emotions and thoughts. No created thing can hide from the word of God; everything is uncovered and open to the eyes of the one to whom we must give an account of ourselves.'

(Hebrews 4:12-13)

Jesus is warning his missionaries to expect persecution. If they set their heart first on the kingdom of God (cf Matthew 6:33), they will be certain to suffer persecution (cf Matthew 5:10-12), even from their own household (Matthew 10:35-36).

7: Jesus identifies with his followers

MATTHEW 10:37 — 11:1
37 'Anyone who prefers father or mother to me is not worthy of me. Anyone
38 who prefers son or daughter to me is not worthy of me. •Anyone who does not
39 take his cross and follow in my footsteps is not worthy of me. •Anyone who
   finds his life will lose it; anyone who loses his life for my sake will find it.
40   'Anyone who welcomes you welcomes me; and those who welcome me
   welcome the one who sent me.
41   'Anyone who welcomes a prophet because he is a prophet will have
   a prophet's reward; and anyone who welcomes a holy man because he is a holy
   man will have a holy man's reward.

'If anyone gives so much as a cup of cold water to one of these little ones **42** because he is a disciple, then I tell you solemnly, he will most certainly not lose his reward.'

11 When Jesus had finished instructing his twelve disciples he moved on from **1** there to teach and preach in their towns.

(Matthew 10:39 cf Mark 8:35 page 258
Matthew 10:40 cf Mark 9:37 page 263
Matthew 10:42 cf Mark 9:41 page 265)

Jesus stresses the demands of discipleship. The climax is the paradox that recurs again and again in the Gospels:

'Anyone who finds his life will lose it; anyone who loses his life for my sake will find it.'

We will comment further on this when studying Mark 8:35 (page 258).

Matthew concludes this discourse with words that remind his readers that the risen Christ is present in the community of the church, a church characterised by welcome and care.

iii) **Jesus fulfils the law: The nature of his Messiahship** –– MATTHEW 11:2-30

1: **Jesus' actions are signs of his Messiahship**

MATTHEW 11:2-6 (Compare Luke 7:18-23 page 164)
Now John in his prison had heard what Christ was doing and he sent his **2** disciples to ask him, •'Are you the one who is to come, or have we got to wait for **3** someone else?' •Jesus answered, 'Go back and tell John what you hear and see; **4** the blind see again, and the lame walk, lepers are cleansed, and the deaf hear, **5** and the dead are raised to life and the Good News is proclaimed to the poor; and happy is the man who does not lose faith in me'. **6**

Matthew has already referred his readers to the statement of the prophet Hosea:

'What I want is mercy not sacrifice'
(Hosea 6:6 cf Matthew 9:13)

He will repeat the statement towards the end of this section (cf Matthew 12:7).

The essence of Jesus' ministry is found in his mercy. Jesus demonstrates the compassion of God, the 'God of tenderness and compassion' (Exodus 34:6), the God of 'integrity and justice, tenderness and love' (Hosea 2:22).

Luke highlights these same qualities in Jesus in his opening scene in Nazareth:

'The Spirit of the Lord has been given to me,
for he has anointed me.
He has sent me to bring the Good News to the poor,
to proclaim liberty to captives
and to the blind new sight,
to set the downtrodden free,
to proclaim the Lord's year of favour'
(Luke 4:18-19, quoting Isaiah 8:23 — 9:1)

John the Evangelist, too, appeals to Jesus' actions when he wishes to claim that Jesus is the Messiah (cf John 10:34-38, page 246)

This kind of life also constitutes the essence of being a disciple of Jesus (Matthew 25:31-46). John expresses this truth very succinctly:

'By this love you have for one another,
everyone will know that you are my disciples.'

(John 13:35)

The new law is really the old law, the law of love (cf 1 John 2:7-8). Jesus is the Messiah who is taking the people back to the heart and spirit of the Law, and living it to perfection (cf Matthew 5:17).

2. John, the promised herald: a further sign of Jesus' messiahship

MATTHEW 11:7-15 (Compare Luke 7:24-28 page 164)

As the messengers were leaving, Jesus began to talk to the people about John: 7 'What did you go out into the wilderness to see? A reed swaying in the breeze? No? •Then what did you go out to see? A man wearing fine clothes? Oh no, those 8 who wear fine clothes are to be found in palaces. •Then what did you go out for? 9 To see a prophet? Yes, I tell you, and much more than a prophet: •he is the one 10 of whom scripture says:

> *Look, I am going to send my messenger before you;*
> *he will prepare your way before you.* ª

'I tell you solemnly, of all the children born of women, a greater than John 11 the Baptist has never been seen; yet the least in the kingdom of heaven is greater than he is. •Since John the Baptist came, up to this present time, the 12 kingdom of heaven has been subjected to violence and the violent are taking it by storm. •Because it was towards John that all the prophecies of the prophets 13 and of the Law were leading; •and he, if you will believe me, is the Elijah who 14 was to return. •If anyone has ears to hear, let him listen!   15

(a: Malachi 3:1)

Matthew's intention is to highlight the essential nature of Jesus' ministry and Messiahship. For the most part this involves contrasting Jesus with the religious authority of his day — the authority claimed by the scribes and Pharisees. However, it also requires of him that he show how Jesus relates to the great and popular prophet of the time, John the Baptist; especially as the Baptist still had a following at the time Matthew was writing.

In this passage the Baptist is spoken of in terms of the highest praise. At the same time it is said that:

'the least in the kingdom of heaven is greater than he is'.

(11:11)

John belonged to the earlier covenant, to the religion of the 'prophets and of the Law' (11:13). The prophecy of Malachi is quoted (Matthew 11:10 = Malachi 3:1) in which Malachi is speaking of the prophet Elijah. The legends that grew up around this greatest of the prophets can be found in the Books of the Kings (1 Kings 17 — 2 Kings 2). One legend was that, since he was such a great man — too great to die — God had taken him to himself alive, in a fiery chariot (cf 2 Kings 2:11). A popular expectation arose that Elijah would, one day, be sent back to earth by God, to inaugurate the Messianic Age. Malachi concludes his prophecy with the following words:

'Know that I am going to send you Elijah the prophet before my day comes, that great and terrible day. He shall turn the hearts of fathers towards their children and the hearts of children towards their fathers.'

(Malachi 4:4-5,

Jesus points to the Baptist as the one who fulfils the expectation expressed in this legend:

'He, if that is the way you like to see it, is the Elijah who was to return.'

(Matthew 11:14,

Matthew is claiming that Jesus is the one who is bringing about the 'kingdom of heaven' (11:12). Jesus is the Messiah. The prophets and the Law were for the time leading up to the kingdom. They set their own strict limitations on who could and who could not hope for this kingdom of promise. But now, in Jesus, God has set aside all these limitations, allowing sinners and outcasts and strangers to force their way past the defenders of the Law and into the kingdom, making booty of it (Matthew 11:12, compare Luke 16:16).

It is no longer sufficient to listen to the Law and the Prophets. Something new, something final, is being said by Jesus. It is something that fulfils the Law but goes beyond it as well. If a person is to enter the kingdom, he must take John's advice and 'listen' (11:15) to Jesus.

John the Evangelist makes the same contrast when he has the Baptist say:

'The bride is only for the bridegroom;
and yet the bridegroom's friend,
who stands there and listens,
is glad when he hears the bridegroom's voice.
This same joy I feel, and now it is complete.'

(John 3:29,

3: Jesus demands to be judged by his actions

MATTHEW 11:16-19 (Compare Luke 7:31-35 page 165)

16   'What description can I find for this generation? It is like children shouting to each other as they sit in the market place:

17   "We played the pipes for you,
                              and you wouldn't dance;
                              we sang dirges,
                              and you wouldn't be mourners".

18 'For John came, neither eating nor drinking, and they say, "He is possessed".
19 The Son of Man came, eating and drinking, and they say, "Look, a glutton and a drunkard, a friend of tax collectors and sinners". Yet wisdom has been proved right by her actions.'

Jesus exposes the hypocrisy and prejudice of those who rejected John and now reject him. He appeals to his 'actions' (11:9, compare John 10:38) — the actions mentioned earlier (Matthew 11:5-6, see also Commentary page 164-5).

4: Jesus laments the hard-heartedness of his own people

MATTHEW 11:20-24

20   Then he began to reproach the towns in which most of his miracles had been worked, because they refused to repent.

21   'Alas for you, Chorazin! Alas for you, Bethsaida! For if the miracles done in
you had been done in Tyre and Sidon, they would have repented long ago in
22 sackcloth and ashes. •And still, I tell you that it will not go as hard on Judgement
23 day with Tyre and Sidon as with you. •And as for you, Capernaum, did you
want to be exalted as high as heaven? *You shall be thrown down to hell.* For if the
miracles done in you had been done in Sodom, it would have been standing yet.
24 And still, I tell you that it will not go as hard with the land of Sodom on Judgement
day as with you.'
(Compare Luke 10:13-15 page 273)

The language of this passage is borrowed from the oracles against Tyre and
Sidon found in the Book of Isaiah (Chapter 23). Jesus' words about Capernaum
recall the king of Babylon who fancied himself as one to 'rival the Most High'
(Isaiah 14:14). Isaiah says of him what Jesus says here of Capernaum:

'Now you have fallen to Sheol, to the very bottom of the Abyss'
(Isaiah 14:15 = Matthew 11:23)

Jesus is lamenting the hard-heartedness of his own contemporaries.

5: 'O the blessedness of the poor in spirit' (Matthew 5:1)

MATTHEW 11:25-27
25   At that time Jesus exclaimed, 'I bless you, Father, Lord of heaven and of
earth, for hiding these things from the learned and the clever and revealing them
26
27 to mere children. •Yes, Father, for that is what it pleased you to do. •Everything
has been entrusted to me by my Father; and no one knows the Son except the
Father, just as no one knows the Father except the Son and those to whom the
Son chooses to reveal him.
(Compare Luke 10:21-22 page 273)

Faced with the blindness and hypocrisy and apathy of so many, Jesus turns
to his Father in wonder and gratitude for the simple, open-minded, poor people
who see. These are the ones he extolled in the Beatitudes. These are the poor in
spirit, these are the pure in heart, these are the ones who can open their hearts and
minds to God as to a Father. They are blessed because when Jesus offers to lift the
veil and 'reveal' (Matthew 11:27) his Father, they are happy for it to happen.
They are happy to see what Jesus does and judge accordingly.

6: An appeal to let go the burden of the Law and 'Come to me'

MATTHEW 11:28-30
28   'Come to me, all you who labour and are overburdened, and I will give you
29 rest. •Shoulder my yoke and learn from me, for I am gentle and humble in heart,
30 *and you will find rest for your souls.*[a] •Yes, my yoke is easy and my burden light.'
(a: Jeremiah 6:16)

Jeremiah appealed to his contemporaries:

'Yahweh says this:
Put yourselves on the ways of long ago
enquire about the ancient paths:
which was the good way? Take it then,
and you shall find rest.'
(Jeremiah 6:16)

Jesus has all the more reason to ask his contemporaries to 'find rest' with
him. The Law was too heavy a burden, too heavy a 'yoke', especially as

interpreted by the religious leaders. Jesus' heart bled for the people who were enslaved by it. The Law had its purpose, up to the time of the Baptist. Now this purpose has been achieved (Matthew 5:18). There is no need to go back to the ancient paths any more. Something new has come into the world. God's love, unveiled, is present with power, lifting burdens from people's shoulders and inviting them to 'live and live to the full' (John 10:10).

Jeremiah had looked forward to this day:

'The days are coming — it is Yahweh who speaks — when I will make a new covenant with the House of Israel (and the House of Judah), but not a covenant like the one I made with their ancestors on the day I took them by the hand to bring them out of the land of Egypt. They broke that covenant of mine, so I had to show them who was master. It is Yahweh who speaks. No, this is the covenant I will make with the House of Israel when those days arrive — it is Yahweh who speaks. Deep within them I will plant my Law, writing it on their hearts. Then I will be their God and they shall be my people. There will be no further need for neighbour to try to teach neighbour, or brother to say to brother, "Learn to know Yahweh!" No, they will all know me, the least no less than the greatest — it is Yahweh who speaks — since I will forgive their iniquity and never call their sin to mind.'

(Jereremiah 31:31-44)

* * * * * * * *

Matthew is now ready to rejoin Mark with the scene in the cornfields (page 107). He trusts that his Jewish-Christian readers can see now that there is an alternative to the Law, and so can relinquish it peacefully, and accept the challenge to follow the 'Law of Christ' and take his 'yoke' upon their shoulders.

* * * * * * * *

Chapter 5
John's reflections on the nature and implications of the new covenant

John chapters 2-5

In this first part of their Gospels (which we have just concluded), the Synoptics (Mark, Matthew and Luke) concentrated on scenes which demonstrated the life-giving and liberating effect of Jesus' word. What Jesus had to say was indeed Good News. In effect it meant liberation from the Law, and it was this aspect that brought Jesus into conflict with the religious authorities. The conflict came to a head in the final scene where they resolve to kill Jesus (cf Mark 3:6).

It is on this radical challenge inherent in Jesus' message and on his radically new approach to religion that John chose to concentrate in the first part of his Gospel.

The Synoptics had spoken of Jesus' word as 'new wine' (cf Mark 2:22). John begins with a scene at a wedding feast at Cana. The anecdote is chosen for its highly symbolic character and demonstrates the new beginning effected by Jesus. Immediately there follows the clearing of the Temple, illustrating the clash between the Good News and the religious traditions of the Jews as interpreted by the Pharisees. John then draws out the implications of this, firstly for the Jews (John 3:1-21), then for the followers of the Baptist (John 3:22-36) and finally for non-Jews (John 4:1-42). The life-giving power of the word of Jesus, and the fact that it is meant for all men, is dramatised in an anecdote we have already met in Matthew: the anecdote about the son of the court official (John 4:43-54 , cf Matthew 8:5-13). John, like the Synoptics, concludes this section with the clash between Jesus and the Pharisees. He begins with the anecdote about the curing of a man at the pool of Bethzatha (John 5:1-9), and then analyses the issues involved in the clash (John 5:10-47).

In each of the scenes Jesus is centre-stage, and John's reflections take the form of long speeches placed in the mouth of Jesus as he converses with Nicodemus, the woman of Samaria, his disciples and finally the Pharisees. Some scholars suggest that the speeches are actually material taken from John's own sermons preached at Ephesus, incorporating traditional sayings of Jesus and weaving them into a pattern that enables John to comment on the various themes outlined above. These discourses bring us immediately into contact with the faith of the early Christian community; they also give us John's personal insights into the heart of Jesus whom he knew so well.

*   *   *   *   *   *   *

1: **Jesus inaugurates a new covenant** — JOHN 2:1-25

a: **Cana**

JOHN 2:1-12

2 Three days later   there was a wedding at Cana in Galilee. The mother of 1 Jesus was there,   •and Jesus and his disciples had also been invited. •When 2 3 they ran out of wine, since the wine provided for the wedding was all finished, the mother of Jesus said to him, 'They have no wine'. •Jesus said, 'Woman, why 4 turn to me? My hour has not come yet.' •His mother said to the servants, 5 '*Do whatever he tells you*'. •There were six stone water jars standing there, meant 6 for the ablutions that are customary among the Jews: each could hold twenty or thirty gallons. •Jesus said to the servants, 'Fill the jars with water', and they 7 filled them to the brim. •'Draw some out now' he told them 'and take it to the 8 steward.' •They did this; the steward tasted the water, and it had turned into 9 wine. Having no idea where it came from—only the servants who had drawn the water knew—the steward called the bridegroom •and said, 'People generally 10 serve the best wine first, and keep the cheaper sort till the guests have had plenty to drink; but you have kept the best wine till now'.

This was the first of the signs given by Jesus: it was given at Cana in Galilee. 11 He let his glory be seen, and his disciples believed in him. •After this he went 12 down to Capernaum with his mother and the brothers, but they stayed there only a few days.

John has chosen to begin his account of the public ministry of Jesus with a scene at a wedding feast. In the Bible God is frequently likened to a bridegroom wooing Israel his bride; and the infidelity of the chosen people to the Covenant is frequently described by the Prophets as adultery: infidelity to Yahweh's enduring love. Hosea looks forward to a time when God's people will respond to Him, and he has Yahweh say:

'She will respond to me as she did when she was young . . .
I will betroth you to myself for ever,
betroth you with integrity and justice,
with tenderness and love;
I will betroth you to myself with faithfulness
and you will come to know Yahweh.'   (*Hosea 2:17, 21-22*)

We have already listened to Jesus describing himself as a bridegroom (cf Mark 2:19). God, through Jesus, is once again wooing his people. In the scene before us Jesus is invited as a guest. But, as the scene unfolds, it becomes apparent that he is the bridegroom bringing the new wine of the Spirit, the new wine of the covenant of love between God and man. In this way he 'let his glory be seen' (2:11), manifesting the fidelity of God to his marriage with his people.

But, while Jesus let his glory be seen at Cana, this was only

'the first of the signs given by Jesus'. (2:11)

This was because his hour had 'not come yet' (2:4), and the full wine of the Spirit could not be given till that hour — the hour when Jesus would be glorified (cf John 7:37-39). John describes the outpouring of the Spirit from the cross when the heart of Jesus is pierced (cf John 19:30-37). Then the new covenant was sealed with the blood of the Lamb.

An important element of the Cana story as described by John is the presence of Mary. She will be present again when Jesus' hour comes. On both occasions she is addressed as 'Woman' (John 4:4 and 19:26), reminding the reader of Eve. She is present here at the beginning of Jesus ministry as the mother representing the people of the old covenant — the covenant symbolised by the water-jars which are filled to the brim (2:7), but lack wine (2:3). The old covenant-people are waiting for the word from Jesus to effect the fulfilment of the promises in a new covenant of love — the covenant of the Spirit. At the Cross, Mary will be Eve again, this time the mother of the people of the new covenant.

The words of Mary anticipate one of the main themes in John's Gospel: that of obedience to the word of God:

'Do whatever he tells you.' (2:5)

It is also characteristic of John's Gospel that Jesus himself does not perform the miracle. It is his power that makes it possible, but others — in this case the servants (2:7) — actually produce the water-made-wine.

Finally, it is characteristic of John's style for a scene to bring one section to a climax, and, at the same time, introduce the following section. The Cana scene comes as a climax to Chapter One. Jesus anticipates the baptism of the Holy Spirit announced by the Baptist (1:33); he also reveals his glory (2:11). John has so arranged Chapter One that Cana occurs on the seventh day (cf John 1:29, 1:35, 1:43 and 2:1), reminding the reader of God's revelation of his glory in creation (cf Genesis 1). At the same time Cana introduces the next scene. The 'new wine' demands 'fresh skins'. The Temple, symbol of the Old Law is now empty, and a new temple (the Temple of his body) must replace it as the sign of God's new presence among his people.

b: **It is Jesus who is the New Temple, symbol of God's life-giving presence among his people**

JOHN 2:13-25

Just before the Jewish Passover Jesus went up to Jerusalem, •and in the $^{13}_{14}$ Temple he found people selling cattle and sheep and pigeons, and the money changers sitting at their counters there. •Making a whip out of some cord, he 15 drove them all out of the Temple, cattle and sheep as well, scattered the money changers' coins, knocked their tables over •and said to the pigeon-sellers, 'Take 16 all this out of here and stop turning my Father's house into a market'. •Then his 17 disciples remembered the words of scripture: *Zeal for your house will devour me.*[a] The Jews intervened and said, 'What sign can you show us to justify what you 18 have done?' •Jesus answered, 'Destroy this sanctuary, and in three days I will 19 raise it up'. •The Jews replied, 'It has taken forty-six years to build this 20 sanctuary: are you going to raise it up in three days?' •But he was speaking of 21 the sanctuary that was his body, •and when Jesus rose from the dead, his disciples 22 remembered that he had said this, and they believed the scripture and the words he had said.

During his stay in Jerusalem for the Passover many believed in his name 23
when they saw the signs that he gave, •but Jesus knew them all and did not trust 24
himself to them; •he never needed evidence about any man; he could tell what 25
a man had in him.

(Compare Mark 11:15-17, Matthew 21:12-16 and Luke 19:45-46 page 317)

(a: Psalm 69:9)

The 'Passover' referred to here is the Passover of Jesus' death. This is obvious
from a comparison with the Synoptics where this episode occurs at the close of
Jesus' ministry (cf Mark 11:15-19). Time-sequence is of little importance to the
Gospel-writers. John has simply taken this episode from its position in the
Synoptics and placed it here because he wishes to highlight, from the outset, the
revolutionary nature of the Good News: (on 'Passover' see page 210).

Jesus 'drove them all out of the Temple' (2:15). His words (2:16) are an
allusion to the final words of the prophecy of Zechariah:

'There will be no more traders in the Temple of Yahweh Sabaoth when that day
comes.'

(Zechariah 14:21)

In a powerful prophetic gesture Jesus declares that 'that day' has come!

Reflecting on this action, John refers to Psalm 69:9:

'Zeal for your house devours me'

(John 2:17)

Johns seems to be working on two levels. Jesus was devoured with desire to
purify God's house; to empty out those attitudes and practices that obscured the
glory of God and made of God an idol. On another level altogether John is
reminding his readers of the fact that Jesus was devoured, that is, condemned to
death and murdered, because of the religious leaders' rejection of his attitude to
the Law and the Temple. (cf Mark 14:58 for the trial before the Sanhedrin, and
Mark 15:29-30 for the abuse hurled at Jesus while he was dying on the cross.)

John refers again to the coming death and glorification of Jesus (2:22). His
main aim in placing this episode here at the beginning of his Gospel is to
demonstrate, from the beginning, the revolutionary nature of the Good News.
The old Temple has been replaced by the new Temple, and the 'sanctuary that
was his body' (2:21). The Old Law has come to an end. It has been found wanting
and has been judged by God. The sacred place where God dwells among men,
where the glory of God is manifest and where men come to see the face of God, is
no longer the Temple in Jerusalem. It is the body of Jesus (cf John 1:14).

We must continually remind ourselves that John is writing his Gospel for the
Christian community of his day. When they read the expression 'his body' (2:21)
they would have thought of Jesus himself; they would also have thought of the
church of which they were members. John immediately refers to the 'many who
believed in his name' (2:23) — almost a technical term for those who were
Christians. And, lest the community read his account of the clearing of the
Temple and think it applied to Judaism and not to themselves, John goes on to
say, speaking of those who 'believed in his name':

'but Jesus knew them all and did not trust himself to them'. (2:24)

There were idolaters in John's community, too; those who thought they
knew Jesus and his Father, but whose lives belied their belief. John is writing to

tell them what happened to the Jews and their Temple. But he is much more interested in educating his own community to the implications of true belief in Jesus.

One of these men who 'believed in his name', was a leading Jew called Nicodemus. John takes the occasion to draw out the implications of the new covenant for the Jews.

2: The implications for a Jew of the inauguration of the new covenant — JOHN 3:1-21

a: JOHN 3:1-8

2 **3** There was one of the Pharisees called Nicodemus, a leading Jew, •who came to Jesus by night and said, 'Rabbi, we know that you are a teacher who comes from God; for no one could perform the signs that you do unless God were with 3 him'. •Jesus answered:

'I tell you most solemnly,
unless a man is born from above,
he cannot see the kingdom of God'.

4 Nicodemus said, 'How can a grown man be born? Can he go back into his 5 mother's womb and be born again?' •Jesus replied:

'I tell you most solemnly,
unless a man is born through water and the Spirit,
he cannot enter the kingdom of God:
6 what is born of the flesh is flesh;
what is born of the Spirit is spirit.
7 Do not be surprised when I say:
You must be born from above.
8 The wind blows wherever it pleases;
you hear its sound,
but you cannot tell where it comes from or where it is going.
That is how it is with all who are born of the Spirit.'

If the Old Law is bereft of wine (John 2:3), and the Temple is empty (John 2:15), what must a man do who has relied on them? How does a Jew find life? Nicodemus, a leading Jew (3:1) is 'in the dark' (3:2). He comes to Jesus, to the light, to ask this very question.

Jesus' answer opens with the expression 'I tell you most solemnly' (3:3,5). This expression occurs frequently in the Gospels in sayings attributed to Jesus. John uses it twenty five times, Matthew thirty one times, Mark thirteen times and Luke six times. Scholars suggest that it is a way of speaking that was typical of Jesus and tells us something of the confident authority with which he preached. Scholars also suggest that when we find a saying of Jesus introduced by this phrase we can be especially confident that we are in touch with the very words used by Jesus and remembered by those who heard him.

It seems that John has taken certain sayings of Jesus handed down in the tradition and has woven them into a discourse with his own reflections. This is a method John uses throughout his Gospel.

Jesus points out to Nicodemus his need for a radically new orientation (what Mark has called 'repentance'). Life does not come from man's self-inspired efforts. 'What is born of flesh is flesh' (3:6). It does not come from following a law, from belonging to a certain chosen race, from the performance of a certain religious action. Man cannot control life, nor can he predict it, any more than he can predict the wind and its action (3:8). If a man is to 'see' (3:3) and 'enter' (3:5) the kingdom of God, he must be 'born from above' (3:3 and 3:7).

John has already made this point in his Prologue. Speaking of those who truly 'believe in his name' (John 1:12), John tells his readers that they are those who are:

'born not out of human stock
or urge of the flesh
or will of man.
but of God himself.'

(John 1:13)

A Jew therefore must begin by putting aside his expectations and opening himself to the surprise of the movement of the Spirit of God.

At the same time the expression 'born of God' (= being a 'child' of God) has quite definite implications as used by John.

'You know that God is righteous (Greek 'dikaios' = 'just') — then you must recognise that everyone whose life is righteous has been begotten by God.'

(1 John 2:29)

Being born of God means living God's life. God reveals himself as the liberator ('redeemer') who works to effect justice (cf Exodus 3:7-10; Deuteronomy 10:14-20; Psalm 82; Hosea 2:20-22; Isaiah 54:7-8, 56:3-7, 58:1-12; Jeremiah 9:24, 21:12, 22:3). Being born of God means being an instrument of God's liberating of the oppressed. The kingdom of God can only be seen (John 3:3) when men work for justice and thus bring about God's kingdom.

'My dear people,
let us love one another
since love comes from God
and everyone who loves is begotten by God and knows God.'

(1 John 4:7)

This truth is central to John's theology (as it is to the theology of Mark and Matthew and Luke and Paul).

John alludes to the Christian practice of baptism (3:5), a practice taken over from the Baptist, but no longer simply a dramatic action encouraging repentance. Christian baptism, being 'born through water and the Spirit' (3:5) is a celebration of the cleansing and life-giving action of the Holy Spirit (cf John 1:33).

b: JOHN 3:9-15

9
10   'How can that be possible?' asked Nicodemus. •'You, a teacher in Israel, and you do not know these things!' replied Jesus.

11   'I tell you most solemnly,
            we speak only about what we know
            and witness only to what we have seen

and yet you people reject our evidence.
12   If you do not believe me
when I speak about things in this world,
how are you going to believe me
when I speak to you about heavenly things?
13   No one has gone up to heaven
except the one who came down from heaven,
the Son of Man who is in heaven;
and the Son of Man must be lifted up
14   as Moses lifted up the serpent in the desert,
15   so that everyone who believes may have eternal life in him.

Christianity has always been based ultimately on facts. John indicates this in the opening words of his first letter:

'Something that has existed since the beginning,
that we have heard,
and we have seen with our own eyes;
that we have watched
and touched with our hands:
the word who is life
this is our subject.'

(1 John 1:1)

In the scene before us Jesus is stating that the Jews, represented by Nicodemus, reject evidence (3:11). He states that unless they cease to be guided by prejudice; unless they are willing to forego their preconceived theories in face of the facts; they will never be able to penetrate to the heart of reality, to 'heavenly things' (3:12).

The author of the Book of Wisdom prays:

'It is hard enough for us to work out what is on earth,
laborious to know what lies within our reach;
who, then, can discover what is in the heavens?
As for your intention, who could have learnt it,
had you not granted wisdom
and sent your holy Spirit from above?
Thus have the paths of those on earth been straightened
and men been taught what pleases you,
and saved, by Wisdom.'

(Wisdom 9:16-18)

Jesus is God's wisdom made flesh (John 1:14). He is 'in heaven' (3:13). He is with God. He has that special vision of God, that special relationship with him that enables him to speak God's word 'from heaven' (3:13).

This is the statement with which John ended his Prologue:

'No one has ever seen God;
it is the only Son, who is nearest to the Father's heart,
who has made him known.'

(John 1:18; cf also 6:46, 14:7-9)

Mention of the Son of Man coming down from heaven leads John to complete the cycle and speak of him being 'lifted up' (3:13) to heaven. He refers to an incident recorded in the Book of Numbers (21:4-9). The Cross is in his mind, but the cross seen as a glorification of Jesus, a 'lifting up' to the Father (cf also John 8:28 and 12:32-34). We are reminded of the Servant of Yahweh:

'See, my servant will prosper,
he shall be lifted up, exalted, rise to great heights.'

(Isaiah 52:13)

'Eternal life' (3:15), enduring life, does not come from the Law, but from the gracious and enduring love of God, a love convincingly manifested in the gift Jesus gave to us of his life. If a man is to live, he must base his life on this love.

c: JOHN 3:16-21

Yes, God loved the world so much 16
that he gave his only Son,
so that everyone who believes in him may not be lost
but may have eternal life.
For God sent his Son into the world 17
not to condemn the world,
but so that through him the world might be saved.
No one who believes in him will be condemned; 18
but whoever refuses to believe is condemned already,
because he has refused to believe
in the name of God's only Son.
On these grounds is sentence pronounced: 19
that though the light has come into the world
men have shown they prefer
darkness to the light
because their deeds were evil.
And indeed, everybody who does wrong 20
hates the light and avoids it,
for fear his actions should be exposed;
but the man who lives by the truth 21
comes out into the light,
so that it may be plainly seen that what he does is done in God.'

John has just said that:

'everyone who believes may have eternal life in him (=Jesus).'

(John 3:15)

In the concluding section of the discourse (3:16-21) John spells out what he means by 'believing'.

He begins by focusing attention on God, on the God of mercy who wants 'everyone' (3:16) to have eternal life, who wants 'the world' (3:17) to be saved, who loves the world so much.

Against this background, John tells his readers why Jesus was rejected. It was 'because their deeds were evil' (3:19). To believe is to do good works — works of mercy, such as Jesus did. Those who do not believe are those who refuse to do good works. They are judged already (compare Matthew 25:31-46 where the same point is made).

Nicodemus, the Jew, came to Jesus 'by night' (3:2). He is invited by Jesus to 'come out into the light' (3:21). He is invited to look at Jesus' life, to see there the works of a merciful God working as he has always worked for the liberation of his people. He is invited to put his faith in what he sees and to express this faith in a life of discipleship, a life of good works. When 'what he does is done in God' (3:21) it will be obvious that he is 'born from above' (John 3:3). Then, and only then, will he 'see the kingdom of God' (3:3).

3: The implications for the followers of the Baptist of the inauguration of the new covenant

JOHN 3:22-36

After this, Jesus went with his disciples into the Judaean countryside and 22 stayed with them there and baptised. •At the same time John was baptising at 23 Aenon near Salim, where there was plenty of water, and people were going there to be baptised. •This was before John had been put in prison. 24

Now some of John's disciples had opened a discussion with a Jew about 25 purification, •so they went to John and said, 'Rabbi, the man who was with 26 you on the far side of the Jordan, the man to whom you bore witness, is baptising now; and everyone is going to him'. •John replied: 27

'A man can lay claim
only to what is given him from heaven.

'You yourselves can bear me out: I said: I myself am not the Christ; I am 28
the one who has been sent in front of him.

'The bride is only for the bridegroom; 29
and yet the bridegroom's friend,
who stands there and listens,
is glad when he hears the bridegroom's voice.
This same joy I feel, and now it is complete.
He must grow greater, 30
I must grow smaller.
He who comes from above 31
is above all others;
he who is born of the earth
is earthly himself and speaks in an earthly way.
He who comes from heaven
bears witness to the things he has seen and heard, 32
even if his testimony is not accepted;
though all who do accept his testimony 33
are attesting the truthfulness of God,
since he whom God has sent 34
speaks God's own words:
God gives him the Spirit without reserve.
The Father loves the Son 35
and has entrusted everything to him.
Anyone who believes in the Son has eternal life, 36
but anyone who refuses to believe in the Son will never see life:
the anger of God stays on him.'

John takes his readers back to the period before John's arrest when Jesus was still in Judaea (3:22-24). The setting provides the occasion for his reflections on the relationship between Jesus and the Baptist. We know from the Acts of the

Apostles that when Paul arrived in Ephesus he found there some disciples of the Baptist (cf Acts 19:1-7). It seems that such a community was still in existence when John came to write his Gospel. The monologue placed by John on the lips of the Baptist represents the mature thinking of the Christian community on the place the Baptist held in God's saving plan (John 3:27).

Jesus is seen as the bridegroom (3:29, cf Cana, 2:1-10). He is the entering into a covenant of love with God's people. The Baptist claims only to be the 'bridegroom's friend' (3:29), caring for the bride till her husband arrives. John is filled with 'joy' (3:29), now that Jesus has come. His work is done, and he humbly and gladly gives way before Jesus. John has done his best, but his work and words have been limited to preparing the way. Jesus is 'from heaven' (3:31), and 'bears witness to what he has seen and heard' (3:32); he 'speaks God's own words' (3:34). 'God gives him the Spirit without reserve' (3:34). 'The Father loves the Son and has entrusted everything to him' (3:35).

In these words John the Evangelist gives his readers some insight into the effect Jesus had on those who knew him. When he came to them, he came 'from' somewhere; when he spoke to them, he spoke 'from' somewhere. They sensed his peace; they sensed his purity of heart; they sensed the depth of his awareness and compassion. Gradually they came to realise that the secret of his love and insight was his special union with the one he called 'my Father'. Jesus lived in that silent place of intimate prayer with God (='heaven'). From that sacred place ('the sanctuary that was his body' John 2:21) he spoke 'God's own words' (3:34) to them, making God's word flesh in his every word and action.

The Baptist's words also express the attitude we each should have to each other. One senses a deep respect and reverence and humility in the Baptist's attitude to his own disciples. He loves them, not for himself, not to build disciples for himself, but to lead them to truth, to be God's instrument in bringing them into contact with the bridegroom. The Baptist is present caring for them; but all the time he is 'listening' (3:29) for the word of God, ready to obey with gladness, and to leave his disciples with the God who loves them.

John the Evangelist is urging those who continue to follow the Baptist, to go a step further and 'believe in the Son' (3:36).

If they accept the testimony of Jesus (3:33), they will be disciples of Jesus, doing the same works that Jesus did. In this way they will make it possible for God to carry out his promises, they will show forth and realise the action of a merciful God. If they 'refuse to believe in the Son' (3:36), if they refuse to do the works of love that Jesus did, they will not 'see the kingdom' (John 3:3). The 'anger of God' (man's condition when not liberated by God's love) will 'stay with them' (3:36).

4: The implications for the non-Jew of the inauguration of the new covenant — JOHN 4:1-42

a: JOHN 4:1-9
1 4 When Jesus heard that the Pharisees had found out that he was making
2 and baptising more disciples than John—•though in fact it was his disciples
3 who baptised, not Jesus himself—•he left Judaea and went back to Galilee.
4 This meant that he had to cross Samaria.

5   On the way he came to the Samaritan town called Sychar, near the land
6 that Jacob gave to his son Joseph. •Jacob's well is there and Jesus, tired by the
7 journey, sat straight down by the well. It was about the sixth hour. •When
  a Samaritan woman came to draw water, Jesus said to her, 'Give me a drink'.
⁸₉ His disciples had gone into the town to buy food. •The Samaritan woman said
  to him, 'What? You are a Jew and you ask me, a Samaritan, for a drink?'—Jews,
  in fact, do not associate with Samaritans.

The scene is a simple one which draws on one of the richest themes of Biblical
literature: man's thirst for God. The psalmist speaks of himself as:

'thirsting for God, the God of my life'.

(Psalm 42:2)

God himself is spoken of as the:

'fountain of life'.

(Psalm 36:9)

Isaiah promises the people:

'You will draw water joyfully from the springs of salvation.'

(Isaiah 12:3)

And God invites his people:

'Oh, come to the water all you who are thirsty.'

(Isaiah 55:1)

In the scene before us a woman is coming to the water. In fact, she is
approaching Jesus.

The woman is not one of the 'chosen race'; she is a non-Jew, a Samaritan.
The Jewish account of the origin of the Samaritans can be found in the Second
Book of Kings (17:24-41). When the Assyrians conquered Samaria (721 B.C.)
they deported the Israelites to Assyria and:

'The king of Assyria brought people from Babylon, Cuthah, Avva, Hamath and
Sepharvaim, and settled them in the towns of Samaria to replace the Israelites; they
took possession of Samaria and lived in its towns.'

(2 Kings 17:24)

These foreigners inter-married with the Israelites and followed the
Pentateuch according to their own style. The Jewish hatred for the Samaritans
seems to stem especially from the period after the exile when the Samaritans tried
to prevent the Jews rebuilding the Temple (about 500 B.C. cf Ezra Chapter 4).
Ben Sirach gives us some indication of the anti-Samaritan feeling at the
beginning of the Second Century B.C. (cf Ecclesiasticus 50:25-26). There are
frequent testimonies to it in the New Testament (cf, for example, John 8:48 and the
parable of the Good Samaritan, Luke 10:29-37).

In the scene described by John, Jesus ignores social taboos (Jews do not
associate with Samaritans) and speaks to the woman, to her surprise (4:9). He
initiates the conversation with a simple, human request: 'Give me a drink' (4:7).

It is obvious from the time of the woman's coming to the well ('about the
sixth hour' = noon: John 4:6), that she is also an outcast among her own people.
The women normally came to draw water in the cool of the evening; it was a
social gathering as well. This woman comes in the heat of the day; and on her
own. The reasons for this become apparent as the story unfolds.

Jesus has already been approached by a Jew (John 3:1-21); now a non-Jew, and an outcast, comes to draw water from the well. Jesus told Nicodemus that he had to learn that:

'the wind blows wherever it pleases'

(John 3:8)

and that he had come so that:

'everyone who believes may have eternal life.'

(John 3:15)

In this scene John wants us to watch Jesus dealing with a non-Jew, and so come to understand more deeply the implications of Jesus' revolutionary new covenant.

b: JOHN 4:10-15
10 •Jesus replied:

'If you only knew what God is offering
and who it is that is saying to you:
Give me a drink,
you would have been the one to ask,
and he would have given you living water'.

11   'You have no bucket, sir,' she answered 'and the well is deep: how could
12 you get this living water? •Are you a greater man than our father Jacob who
13 gave us this well and drank from it himself with his sons and his cattle?' •Jesus
replied:

'Whoever drinks this water
will get thirsty again;
14   but anyone who drinks the water that I shall give
will never be thirsty again:
the water that I shall give
will turn into a spring inside him, welling up to eternal life'.

15   'Sir,' said the woman 'give me some of that water, so that I may never get
thirsty and never have to come here again to draw water.'

Like Nicodemus in the earlier dialogue, the woman here represents the reader. Her 'misunderstandings' enable Jesus, the protagonist, to clarify his teaching. And his teaching is simple:

'God is offering' her, a non-Jew, 'living water' (4:10). She has only to ask and he will give her:

'a spring inside her, welling up to eternal life'. (4:14)

To all appearances it is the woman who has the water and it is Jesus who is thirsty. But he sees her heart and responds to the deep thirst inside her. He offers her 'living water', that is, running water, fresh and life-giving. He offers her freedom: a source of life that does not come from external law or observance, but from a spring inside her: from the love of her Father who draws her, a non-Jew, an outsider and an outcast, to himself.

c: JOHN 4:16-26
•'Go and call your
17 husband' said Jesus to her 'and come back here.' •The woman answered, 'I have
18 no husband'. He said to her, 'You are right to say, "I have no husband"; •for

although you have had five, the one you have now is not your husband. You
spoke the truth there.' •'I see you are a prophet, sir' said the woman. •'Our
fathers worshipped on this mountain, while you say that Jerusalem is the place
21 where one ought to worship.' •Jesus said:

> 'Believe me, woman, the hour is coming
> when you will worship the Father
> neither on this mountain nor in Jerusalem.
>
> 22   You worship what you do not know;
> we worship what we do know;
> for salvation comes from the Jews.
>
> 23   But the hour will come—in fact it is here already—
> when true worshippers will worship the Father in spirit and truth:
> that is the kind of worshipper
> the Father wants.
>
> 24   God is spirit,
> and those who worship
> must worship in spirit and truth.'

25   The woman said to him, 'I know that Messiah—that is, Christ—is coming;
26 and when he comes he will tell us everything'. •'I who am speaking to you,'
said Jesus 'I am he.'

The personal encounter of the woman and Jesus is enlarged here into an
encounter of the Gentile world with the Christian community. The woman
becomes Samaria itself; the 'five husbands' stand for the five pagan tribes that
inter-married with the Israelites to form the Samaritan people (cf 2 Kings 17:24).
The Jews held that:

'Jerusalem is the place where one ought to worship.' (4:20)

Just as Jesus earlier cleared the Temple (John 2:13-22), so here he transcends the
limits placed on God's saving power by the Jews. True, the Jews have a special
place in the providence of God. They have a special knowledge of God (John
4:22). The Jews, responding in faith to God's special love for them, came to see
that the true God is a living God who transcends all man's conceptions of him and
all man's attempts to define him. The true God cannot be seen. In fact, he cannot
be 'known', if by 'know' we mean 'comprehend'. He cannot be adequately
expressed in word or symbol. It is God who knows man. Any knowledge man has
of God is a knowledge of the heart, born of a response in faith, an obedient
response of a heart and mind open to God's word and to God's will. This the Jews
knew (John 4:22).

In fact salvation came from the Jews in that Christianity was a flowering and
fulfilment of Judaism. But John is also making the point that salvation had to
come 'from' the Jews. It did not stay with them. The time has come (John 4:23)
when Abraham is to be truly the father of many nations; when:

'All the tribes of the earth shall bless themselves by you.'   (Genesis 12:3)

Jesus is inaugurating a new Covenant; the word is spreading from Jerusalem.
Now God is offering living water to a Samaritan woman. There is no longer any
need to go to Jerusalem to worship (John 4:21):

'True worshippers will worship the Father in spirit and truth.'   (John 4:23)

True worship, true religion, is the worship that wells up in a man's heart in response to the gift of God's spirit 'inside him' (4:14). True worship is a response in faith to God's enduring (='true') love. True worship is man's thirst meeting the 'water that I shall give' (4:14).

The dialogue concludes on an intimate personal note. The woman is listening and searching. Jesus tells her:

'I am he.' (4:26)

A similar dialogue will occur later between Jesus and the man born blind. This man too is searching for truth:

'Sir, tell me who he is so that I may believe in him.' (9:36)

Jesus reveals himself to the man as he does in our scene to the Samaritan woman:

'You are looking at him; he is speaking to you.' (9:37)

At the same time, the expression 'I am he' has mysterious overtones.

The author of the Book of Exodus examines the origin of the divine name 'Yahweh', and relates it to the Hebrew expression for 'I am he' ('Ehwah'). By the burning bush Moses asks God:

'If they ask me what his name is what am I to tell them?'

and God's reply was:

'I am who I am (I am he)'.

(Exodus 3:14,

When Jesus uses the same expression (cf John 6:35, 8:12, 8:58 and 11:25) there is present the mystery of the divinity, of the special relationship between Jesus and the one he called 'My Father'. What Jesus is offering, 'God is offering' (4:10).

d: JOHN 4:27-42

At this point his disciples returned, and were surprised to find him speaking 27 to a woman, though none of them asked, 'What do you want from her?' or, 'Why are you talking to her?' •The woman put down her water jar and hurried 28 back to the town to tell the people, •'Come and see a man who has told me 29 everything I ever did; I wonder if he is the Christ?' •This brought people out of 30 the town and they started walking towards him.

Meanwhile, the disciples were urging him, 'Rabbi, do have something to 31 eat'; •but he said, 'I have food to eat that you do not know about'. •So the 32/33 disciples asked one another, 'Has someone been bringing him food?' •But Jesus 34 said:

'My food
is to do the will of the one who sent me,
and to complete his work.
Have you not got a saying: 35
Four months and then the harvest?
Well, I tell you:
Look around you, look at the fields;
already they are white, ready for harvest!
Already •the reaper is being paid his wages,   36
already he is bringing in the grain for eternal life,

and thus sower and reaper rejoice together.
For here the proverb holds good: 37
one sows, another reaps;
I sent you to reap 38
a harvest you had not worked for.
Others worked for it;
and you have come into the rewards of their trouble.'

Many Samaritans of that town had believed in him on the strength of the 39
woman's testimony when she said, 'He told me all I have ever done', •so, when 40
the Samaritans came up to him, they begged him to stay with them. He stayed
for two days, and •when he spoke to them many more came to believe; •and ⁴¹₄₂
they said to the woman, 'Now we no longer believe because of what you told us;
we have heard him ourselves and we know that he really is the saviour of the
world'.

While the woman is not sure who Jesus is ('I wonder if he is the Christ' 4:29),
she is so affected by him that she hurries back to the town and invites the people
of the town to 'come and see' (4:29). Many of them, John tells us, are open
enough to go up to him and beg him to stay with them (4:40). He does so, at their
request, and they grow from a trust based on the women's testimony, to a trust
based on their own personal experience of Jesus (4:42).

In this scene John illustrates the true scope of the Messianic event.

'Already the fields are white, ready for harvest!
Already the reaper is being paid his wages,
already he is bringing in the grain for eternal life.'

(John 4:35-36)

It is the will of God (3:34) that the gift of faith be offered 'to the world' (4:42).
Jesus is offering, now (4:23), eternal life to all men, under the direction and
impulse of God's Spirit. This is the time of the eschaton; the time for the harvest;
the time of justice and peace. God is making a new covenant with all men, and
Jesus is 'the Saviour of the world' (4:42).

5: The new, life-giving, covenant is offered to all men

JOHN 4:43-54 (Compare Matthew 8:5-13, page 82, and Luke 7:1-10, page 162)

When the two days were over Jesus left for Galilee. •He himself had declared ⁴³₄₄
that there is no respect for a prophet in his own country, •but on his arrival the 45
Galileans received him well, having seen all that he had done at Jerusalem
during the festival which they too had attended.

He went again to Cana in Galilee, where he had changed the water into wine. 46
Now there was a court official there whose son was ill at Capernaum •and, 47
hearing that Jesus had arrived in Galilee from Judaea, he went and asked him
to come and cure his son as he was at the point of death. •Jesus said, 'So you will 48
not believe unless you see signs and portents!' •'Sir,' answered the official 'come 49
down before my child dies.' •'Go home,' said Jesus 'your son will live.' The man 50
believed what Jesus had said and started on his way; •and while he was still on 51
the journey back his servants met him with the news that his boy was alive. •He 52
asked them when the boy had begun to recover. 'The fever left him yesterday'
they said 'at the seventh hour.' •The father realised that this was exactly the time 53

when Jesus had said, 'Your son will live'; and he and all his household believed.
54   This was the second sign given by Jesus, on his return from Judaea to Galilee.

We refer the reader to Matthew for the commentary on this scene.

John inserts it here because it illustrates the main theme of this section: Jesus gives life to anyone who believes. Here, in John's account it is the man's faith that is tested by Jesus. He begins, it seems, with a faith based on 'signs and portents' (4:48, cf 2:23). When challenged by Jesus it is his desire for his boy's health that prevails and he grows to 'believe what Jesus had said' (4:50). Finally, he and his household simply 'believe' (4:53). On the strength of this one man's faith, the life-giving covenant is given to him 'and all his household' (4:53).

6: The new covenant is rejected by the religious leaders — JOHN 5:1-47

a: JOHN 5:1-18
1   5 Some time after this there was a Jewish festival, and Jesus went up to Jeru-
2   salem. •Now at the Sheep Pool in Jerusalem there is a building, called Beth-
3   zatha in Hebrew, consisting of five porticos; •and under these were crowds of
4   sick people—blind, lame, paralysed—waiting for the water to move; •for at
     intervals the angel of the Lord came down into the pool, and the water was
     disturbed, and the first person to enter the water after this disturbance was cured
5   of any ailment he suffered from. •One man there had an illness which had lasted
6   thirty-eight years, •and when Jesus saw him lying there and knew he had been in
7   this condition for a long time, he said, 'Do you want to be well again?' •'Sir,'
     replied the sick man 'I have no one to put me into the pool when the water is
     disturbed; and while I am still on the way, someone else gets there before me.'
8
9   Jesus said, 'Get up, pick up your sleeping-mat and walk'. •The man was cured
     at once, and he picked up his mat and walked away.
10   Now that day happened to be the sabbath, •so the Jews said to the man who
     had been cured, 'It is the sabbath; you are not allowed to carry your sleeping-
11   mat'. •He replied, 'But the man who cured me told me, "Pick up your mat and
12   walk" '. •They asked, 'Who is the man who said to you, "Pick up your mat and
13   walk"?' •The man had no idea who it was, since Jesus had disappeared into the
14   crowd that filled the place. •After a while Jesus met him in the Temple and said,
     'Now you are well again, be sure not to sin any more, or something worse may
15   happen to you'. •The man went back and told the Jews that it was Jesus who
16   had cured him. •It was because he did things like this on the sabbath that the
17   Jews began to persecute Jesus. •His answer to them was, 'My Father goes on
18   working, and so do I'. •But that only made the Jews even more intent on killing
     him, because, not content with breaking the sabbath, he spoke of God as his own
     Father, and so made himself God's equal.

There are obvious parallels between this anecdote and the one chosen by the Synoptics as a conclusion to the first period of Jesus' Galilean ministry. The man with the withered hand was healed on a sabbath day (Mark 3:2) and the healing led to the Pharisees 'discussing how to destroy Jesus' (Mark 3:6). Similarly, here in John, a sick man is healed on the sabbath and:

'It was because he did things like this on the sabbath that the Jews began to persecute Jesus.'

(John 5:16)

The justification given by Jesus in the Synoptics for his healing on the sabbath is that:

'The sabbath was made for man, not man for the sabbath;
so the Son of Man is master even on the sabbath.'   *(Mark 2:27-28)*

John's reflections penetrate more deeply into the question. The sabbath was a sacred institution of the Law. It brought the week to an end with a day of rest and rejoicing and reunion in worship. In his six days of work man carried on the work of the Creator, and like the Creator, man rested on the seventh day (Genesis 2:3). In essence the sabbath was observed as a sign of man's special consecration to God. In John, Jesus' answer to the Pharisees is:

'My Father goes on working, and so do I.' (5:17)

In this way he by-passes all the negative restrictive measures that cluttered the Law and led to the hypocrisy we associate with the Pharisees. The sabbath is a day of special consecration to God. Therefore it is a day when man consecrates his time in a special way to being God's instrument in carrying on the work of His creative love and healing. This is the spirit and true meaning of the sabbath.

The sick man seems rather half-hearted about being healed at all, and when Jesus asks him, 'Do you want to be well again?' (5:6), he does not eagerly request a healing, but puts the blame for his condition on to others:

'I have no one to put me into the pool.' (5:7)

Jesus' compassion is such that he accepts the man as he is, and heals him (5:9). However, when the man is challenged by the religious authorities he shows that he has not really changed. He begins by evading responsibility again (5:10-12) and then, when he finds out that it was Jesus who cured him, he goes to the authorities and reports Jesus to them (5:15). John uses the dramatic phrase, 'The man went back and told the Jews' (5:15).

A close comparison of this anecdote with that of the man who was born blind (John 9:1-38), suggests that John writes the story in this way because he wishes to illustrate what happens when a man 'goes back'. John is concerned about those Christians who responded to Jesus' call, who enjoyed the healing and freedom that comes from being his disciple, and then, in the face of persecution, reverted to Judaism. He might have in mind also those who pestered Paul all through his ministry. Nominally they were followers of Jesus, but in fact they were still slaves to the Law. John is stressing the need for inner healing, and the need for commitment to Jesus — a commitment and a healing that the man in this anecdote lacked.

More important is the connection John makes between Jesus' statement that he is doing the same works as his Father (5:17) and the accusation of blasphemy levelled at him by the Jews (5:18).

It is central to John's theology that it is Jesus' works that reveal the true nature of God. Speaking of the man born blind, Jesus says:

'he was born blind so that the works of God might be displayed in him.'   *(John 9:3)*

Later Jesus asks the Jews:

'Even if you refuse to believe in me,
at least believe in the work I do;

then you will know for sure
that the Father is in me and I am in the Father.'

(John 10:38)

It is basic to Jewish theology that the true God is revealed by his works — primarily by his works of justice:

'God stands in the divine assembly,
among the gods he dispenses justice:
"No more mockery of justice,
no more favouring the wicked!
Let the weak and the orphan have justice,
be fair to the wretched and destitute;
rescue the weak and needy,
save them from the clutches of the wicked!"
Ignorant and senseless, they carry on blindly,
undermining the very basis of earthly society.
I once said, "You too are gods,
sons of the Most High, all of you",
but all the same you shall die like other men;
as one man, princes, you shall fall.
Rise, God, dispense justice throughout the world,
since no nation is excluded from your ownership.'

(Psalm 82)

John actually quotes this psalm later (10:34), when, once again, the Jews are accusing Jesus of blasphemy:

'We are not stoning you for doing a good work,
but for blasphemy: you are only a man and you claim to be God.'

(John 10:33)

Jesus himself says to them:

'you want to kill me because nothing I say has penetrated into you.'

(John 8:37)

Jesus has just done a 'good work'; he has just healed a man; he has just been an instrument of the mercy of God. By doing this he has demonstrated that he is 'born from above', that he is a son of God. It is this action that is a threat to the religious leaders. They have to accuse him of blasphemy or they themselves will have to admit that their claimed religious authority is false. Their claim to power is based on the Law according to which healing breaks the sabbath; his claim is based on an act of mercy in which he identifies himself with God his Father.

b: JOHN 5:19-30

19   To this accusation Jesus replied:

'I tell you most solemnly,
the Son can do nothing by himself;
he can do only what he sees the Father doing:
and whatever the Father does the Son does too.
20   For the Father loves the Son
and shows him everything he does himself,
and he will show him even greater things than these,
works that will astonish you.
21   Thus, as the Father raises the dead and gives them life,

22
23
24
25
26
27
28
29
30

so the Son gives life to anyone he chooses;
for the Father judges no one;
he has entrusted all judgement to the Son,
so that all may honour the Son
as they honour the Father.
Whoever refuses honour to the Son
refuses honour to the Father who sent him.
I tell you most solemnly,
whoever listens to my words,
and believes in the one who sent me,
has eternal life;
without being brought to judgement
he has passed from death to life.
I tell you most solemnly,
the hour will come—in fact it is here already—
when the dead will hear the voice of the Son of God,
and all who hear it will live.
For the Father, who is the source of life,
has made the Son the source of life;
and, because he is the Son of Man,
has appointed him supreme judge.
Do not be surprised at this,
for the hour is coming
when the dead will leave their graves
at the sound of his voice:
those who did good
will rise again to life;
and those who did evil, to condemnation.
I can do nothing by myself;
I can only judge as I am told to judge,
and my judging is just,
because my aim is to do not my own will,
but the will of him who sent me.

The Jewish leaders have judged Jesus by their interpretation of the Law and their own misguided view of God. Here Jesus is speaking of true judgment.

In healing the man at the pool of Bethzatha, Jesus was acting as an instrument of God his Father, the source of life and of life-giving works (cf John 5:26, 5:21, 5:24, 5:29). Jesus claims that he sees the divine, creative Spirit of his Father moving to heal and liberate (John 5:19), and that his own actions flow from that contemplation:

'The Son can do only what he sees the Father doing'. (5:19)
'My aim is to do not my own will, but the will of him who sent me.' (5:30)

In this way, Jesus' actions must be life-giving:

'For the Father who is the source of life has made the Son the source of life.' (5:26)

God's life-giving activity is not something reserved for the Last Day; it is something that is happening now, in their midst (5:21, 5:24-25). The cure of the man is but an example of it. It is possible now for the 'dead' (5:25), that is, those separated from the life of God, to:

'hear the voice of the Son of God,
and all who hear it will live.' (5:25)

John uses irony to stress the revolutionary nature of Jesus' revelation. On the surface it appears that the religious leaders are judging Jesus, and rejecting him. In fact, Jesus is judging them, in the sense that their lives are measured by the standards of his. Men will rise to life or to condemnation according to the standards set by Jesus: the standards of obedience to God, of love and of life-giving activity. If a man believes in Jesus he will not need to pass through judgment; he will not be condemned for his sins; he will pass from death to life, now (5:24).

John returns to this theme later. In fact he concludes the first section of his Gospel with the words:

'If anyone hears my words and does not keep them faithfully,
it is not I who shall condemn him,
since I have come not to condemn the world,
but to save the world:
he who rejects me and refuses my words
has his judge already:
the word itself that I have spoken
will be his judge on the last day.
For what I have spoken does not come from myself;
no, what I was to say, what I had to speak,
was commanded by the Father who sent me,
and I know that his commands mean eternal life.'

(John 12:47-50)

It is in this sense that:

'He has entrusted all judgment to the Son.' (5:22)

c: **JOHN 5:31-47**

'Were I to testify on my own behalf,   31
my testimony would not be valid;
but there is another witness who can speak on my behalf,   32
and I know that his testimony is valid.
You sent messengers to John,   33
and he gave his testimony to the truth:
not that I depend on human testimony;   34
no, it is for your salvation that I speak of this.
John was a lamp alight and shining   35
and for a time you were content to enjoy the light that he gave.
But my testimony is greater than John's: 36
the works my Father has given me to carry out,
these same works of mine
testify that the Father has sent me.
Besides, the Father who sent me   37
bears witness to me himself.
You have never heard his voice,
you have never seen his shape,

and his word finds no home in you   38
because you do not believe
in the one he has sent.

'You study the scriptures,   39
believing that in them you have eternal life;
now these same scriptures testify to me,
and yet you refuse to come to me for life!   40
As for human approval, this means nothing to me.   41
Besides, I know you too well: 42
you have no love of God in you.
I have come in the name of my Father   43
and you refuse to accept me;
if someone else comes in his own name
you will accept him.

How can you believe,   44
since you look to one another for approval
and are not concerned
with the approval that comes from the one God?
Do not imagine that I am going to accuse you before the Father: 45
you place your hopes on Moses,
and Moses will be your accuser.
If you really believed him   46
you would believe me too,
since it was I that he was writing about;
but if you refuse to believe what he wrote,   47
how can you believe what I say?'

Jesus reminds the religious leaders that John the Baptist testified to him (5:31-35, cf John 1:5-8, 1:15, 1:19-34 and especially 3:27-30). At the same time he disclaims any dependence on human testimony (5:34, 5:41).

Jesus' claim to be from the Father is based on his actions:

'The works my Father has given me to carry out,
these same works of mine testify that the Father has sent me.' (5:36)

They do not recognise God in Jesus' works:

'because you do not believe in the one he has sent.' (5:38)

The religious leaders stand condemned because they do not do works of mercy — the word of God finds no home in them (5:38). The very Scriptures themselves, which they claim to study, witness, again and again, to the fact that God, the true and living God, is a God of compassion and mercy, a God of justice, a God who gives life and who works to liberate the oppressed. If they read the Scriptures, not for man's approval, not to bolster up their own position of power in the community, but to hear wisdom from God, they would recognise that God is in Jesus:

'these same scriptures testify to me.' (5:39)

'It was I that Moses was writing about.' (5:46)

Like the Synoptics, John has concentrated in the first part of his Gospel, on the liberating nature of Jesus' words and works. Like them, too, he concludes by sharply contrasting the Good News preached by Jesus with the religious bigotry of the upholders of the Law.

NOTE: MIRACLES IN THE GOSPELS

The central thrust of the part of the Gospels which we have just completed, is that Jesus, the carpenter from Nazareth, was a man who, 'taught with authority' (Mark 1:22). His teaching brought healing and liberation to many. While some followed him closely as disciples, the religious and political leaders of his day reacted strongly against him. The Gospel-writers illustrate the power of Jesus by recording certain events from his ministry that are commonly referred to as 'miracles': events such as the wonderful catch of fish (Luke 5:1-11), the curing of the possessed man in the synagogue at Capernaum (Mark 1:21-28), the healing of Simon's mother-in-law (Mark 1:29-31), the healing of the leper (Mark 1:40-45), the healing of the centurion's servant (Matthew 8:5-13), the healing of the paralytic (Mark 2:1-12), the healing of the man with the withered hand (Mark 3:1-6), the changing of water into wine (John 2:1-12) and the healing of the sick man at Bethzatha (John 5:1-18). The Gospel writers give us the impression that these particular events are recorded because of their typical nature, and they indicate that such happenings were common-place in the ministry of Jesus (cf Matthew 4:23-25, Mark 1:32-39, Luke 5:15-16, Matthew 9:35). Even the disciples of Jesus shared his ability to 'work miracles' (cf Matthew 10:1). Matthew understands these 'miracles' to be part of the essence of the ministry of Jesus. In answer to John's question, Jesus replies.

'Go back and tell John what you hear and see:
the blind see again, and the lame walk, lepers are cleansed,
and the deaf hear; and the dead are raised to life and the Good News
is proclaimed to the poor.'

(Matthew 11:2-6)

We will find many more miracles as we continue our study of the Gospels. It seems important at this stage to examine what miracles are, and how we are to understand the way the Gospel-writers report them.

A 'miracle' can be defined as an event which produces wonder and acts as a sign of the presence and action of God. It is sometimes assumed that for an event to be a miracle it must be outside the laws of nature and beyond any possible scientific explanation. This is completely beside the point. For a miracle it is required that the event be such as to produce amazement or wonder in those witnessing it. A cure, for example, may be explicable in terms of psychotherapy, and yet still be a miracle. When the paralytic picked up his mat and walked the people standing around were 'astounded' (Mark 2:12), not because there exists no medical explanation possible, but because:

'we have never seen anything like this.'

(Mark 2:12)

A miracle requires more than wonder: it must also be a sign of God's activity. Later in Mark's Gospel we read:

'He could work no miracle there, though he cured a few sick people by laying hands on them. He was amazed at their lack of faith.'

(Mark 6:6)

Apparently, the people of his own town, Nazareth, were not open enough to see in the wonderful things Jesus said and did a sign of the loving presence of God working among them. His cures lacked sign value for them; they were not, on that account, miracles. His curing of the dumb demoniac was not a miracle for the Pharisees who said:

'It is through the prince of devils that he casts out devils.'

(Matthew 9:34)

Later we will find Jesus refusing to give signs to the Pharisees (cf Matthew 12:38-40, Mark 8:12 and John 4:48) or to Herod (cf Luke 22:8-12). Herod was seeking distraction; the Pharisees were 'hoping for something to be used against him' (Mark 3:2).

In nearly all the miracle stories, the Gospel writers are at pains to stress the importance of faith as a necessary condition for the release of the miraculous power of Jesus' healing and liberating love.

In these terms, the ultimate 'miracle' is the person of Jesus himself and the love he manifested towards all. It was his compassion and understanding and gentleness that aroused wonder in those who met him; and this was, for them, a revelation of the presence and activity of God. John saw the glory of God's enduring love manifested in everything Jesus said and did. In that sense Jesus' whole person was 'miraculous'. He was a 'wonderful' person and he was a sign of God's presence. John opens his first letter with the words:

'Something which has existed since the beginning,
that we have heard,
and we have seen with our eyes;
that we have watched,
and touched with our hands the Word who is life — that is our subject.'

(1 John 1:1)

This is the subject, too, of all the Gospels.

Our interest in this appendix is, however, not so much in the wonder of Jesus' love as in the wonderful effects this love is reported to have had. We are interested in what are commonly called his 'miracles'. Did Jesus actually heal? Did he actually change water into wine?

Before we can reach more precise knowledge of the actual event that is the basis of any particular account we must consider three important facts.

The first fact is that events are described as they are seen by those who witness them. Our mental framework, our way of looking at life, our expectations, all play a part in our observations. This is mostly an unconscious phenomenon. Our environment leads us to interpret what we see and to report accordingly. We analysed one example of this when we studied the scene in which Jesus healed the man 'possessed by an unclean spirit' (Mark 1:23). Because of their way of looking at their world, those who witnessed the event saw, not an epileptic, but a possessed man; they heard, not the meaningless utterances of a man experiencing an epileptic fit, but the cries of an unclean spirit resisting Jesus. Mark is not inventing the incident; he is recording it truthfully as it was reported to him. One day in the synagogue at Capernaum Jesus was teaching and a man was healed. We who read the account need to know something of the mental outlook of the people of the time if we are to distinguish unconscious interpretation from 'objective fact' or 'actual event'.

The second fact is that the Gospel-writers recorded events according to the manner of their time. They were quite consciously writing stories that were pleasant to read and that captured the essential meaning of the event. They were expected to compose their stories in a dramatic style, and they did so. This, too, makes it difficult for us to get to the actual unadorned event.

The third fact is that the interest of the Evangelist was not precisely in the past. He was interested in recording events from Jesus' life, not as the record of a dead man, but as a way of helping his readers achieve a genuine contact with the living, glorified Jesus. The core of the account was an event in Jesus' life; the language was geared more to facilitating prayer. Hence, among other factors, the constant use of imagery drawn from the Old Testament.

With these three facts in mind, we conclude that it is generally not possible to get to the actual unadorned event. Did Luke, for example, create the story of the haul of fish to express truthfully, in story form, the wonderful nature of the call and its miraculous effect in the lives of the disciples; or did something extraordinary happen one day on the lake which was seen as symbolic of the nature of their vocation? It seems to me that this question cannot confidently be answered either way.

While this makes it difficult for us to satisfy our curiosity as to the exact occurrence, we can be sure, in either case, that we are in touch with Jesus and the remarkable effect he had on people's lives. If the event itself is not able to be grasped in precise detail, the meaning of the event for those who knew Jesus is clear; and, after all, that is the main thing.

Another example is the marriage feast of Cana as described by John (John 2:1-12). The central fact of the anecdote is not that water was changed into wine, but that Jesus, in beginning his public ministry, was initiating the new covenant, sealing the new marriage of God to man, pouring out the new wine of the Spirit upon men. Presumably something wonderful happened at the marriage-feast. John's interest is in the significance of the whole situation as expressing symbolically basic truths about Jesus. Questions such as: how many water jars were actually there? Did Jesus actually change some water into wine? What did Mary actually say to the servants? — such questions cannot be answered. We have to let the whole anecdote speak to us. The truth of the account is not found by verifying these details; it rests on whether or not Jesus did communicate to men the new marriage-love of God, the new wine of the Spirit.

The accounts of the miracles in the Gospels witness to the extraordinary effect Jesus had on his contemporaries. But we must take care lest concern for details distracts us from the truly 'wonderful' thing about him, namely, the extraordinary way he communicated God's love, and the faith in God which he engendered. It is important when reading the Gospels, and especially perhaps when reading the accounts of the miracles, to remember that they are written to communicate the faith-experience shared by a community of people who had known Jesus. We have the guarantee of the community within which the Gospels were written that they do convey an accurate impression of Jesus. Therein lies their essential value. We can be grateful that they communicate this faith in the richest way they know and with all the dramatic power of their creative skill. It is this that helps us appreciate the 'wonder' of his life and the 'sign' he was of the powerful activity of God drawing people to fulness of life.

The Good News:
God's Powerful Word

Chapter 1
God's word is for all men

Mark 3:7-19
Matthew 12:15-21
Luke 6:12-19

MARK 3:7-12 (Compare Luke 6:17-19)

7 Jesus withdrew with his disciples to the lakeside, and great crowds from
8 Galilee followed him. From Judaea, •Jerusalem, Idumaea, Transjordania and
the region of Tyre and Sidon, great numbers who had heard of all he was doing
9 came to him. •And he asked his disciples to have a boat ready for him because
10 of the crowd, to keep him from being crushed. •For he had cured so many that all
11 who were afflicted in any way were crowding forward to touch him. •And the
unclean spirits, whenever they saw him, would fall down before him and shout,
12 'You are the Son of God!' •But he warned them strongly not to make him known.

The Pharisees and Herodians may plot against Jesus (Mark 3:6), but nothing
can contain God's powerful word. People come to him from the whole of
Palestine. The spiritual powers of evil are being subdued by the activity of God,
powerfully present in Jesus. The cry of the unclean spirits reminds us of the scene
in the synagogue of Capernaum (Mark 1:25), as does Jesus' injunction not to
make him known (Mark 1:34).

* * * * * * * *

MATTHEW 12:15-21

15 Jesus knew this and withdrew from the district. Many followed him and he
16
17 cured them all, •but warned them not to make him known. •This was to fulfil
the prophecy of Isaiah:

18 *Here is my servant whom I have chosen,*
my beloved, the favourite of my soul.
I will endow him with my spirit,
and he will proclaim the true faith to the nations.

19 *He will not brawl or shout,*
nor will anyone hear his voice in the streets.

20 *He will not break the crushed reed,*
nor put out the smouldering wick
till he has led the truth to victory:

21 *in his name the nations will put their hope.*[a]   (a: Isaiah 42:1-4)

The quotation from Isaiah is taken from the first song of the Servant of Yahweh. Matthew has already quoted the opening words in the scene of the Baptism of Jesus in the Jordan (cf Matthew 3:17), when the Father endowed Jesus with his spirit.

Matthew wants to contrast the spirit of Jesus with the Spirit of the Pharisees who have just been 'discussing how to destroy' Jesus (cf Matthew 12:14). At the same time Jesus' words and actions are such that the Pharisees stand condemned. (This is the theme of the following section: Matthew 12:22-45.) The word translated 'true faith' (12:18) and 'truth' (12:20) in the quotation from Isaiah is the Greek word 'krisis': 'judgment'/'justice'. Jesus, through his gentleness will proclaim God's judgment to the nations (12:18); he will lead justice to victory (12.20).

Matthew wishes to highlight the spirit of Jesus. He wishes also to underline the universal dimension of his mission: 'in his name the nations will put their hope' (12:21).

* * * * * * * *

MARK 3:13-19

13 He now went up into the hills and summoned those he wanted. So they came
14 to him •and he appointed twelve; they were to be his companions and to be sent
15/16 out to preach, •with power to cast out devils. •And so he appointed the Twelve:
17 Simon to whom he gave the name Peter, •James the son of Zebedee and John the brother of James, to whom he gave the name Boanerges or 'Sons of Thunder';
18 then Andrew, Philip, Bartholomew, Matthew, Thomas, James the son of
19 Alphaeus, Thaddaeus, Simon the Zealot •and Judas Iscariot, the man who was to betray him.   *(Compare Matthew 10:1-4 page 115)*

Mark has already introduced us to four of the twelve: Simon, James, John and Andrew (cf Mark 1:16-20). He has already mentioned a certain 'Levi, son of Alphaeus' (Mark 2:14 = 'Matthew', cf Matthew 9:9). The other seven are mentioned here by Mark for the first time. (For Philip cf John 1:44).

The number twelve (3:14) is symbolic of the twelve tribes of Israel. These men are to be the founders of a new covenant-people, a new Israel, an Israel that is to gather in all the nations of the earth.

The twelve are called, first of all, to be companions of Jesus. They are also called to be apostles sharing in the mission of Jesus to bring about the reign of God's love in the world, thereby destroying the power of evil (Mark 3:14-15). Mark, in placing this scene just after Mark 3:1-6, is reinforcing the idea that the opposition of the religious and political leaders led to an expansion of Jesus' activity.

* * * * * * * *

LUKE 6:12-16

12 Now it was about this time that he went out into the hills to pray; and he spent
13 the whole night in prayer to God. •When day came he summoned his disciples

and picked out twelve of them; he called them 'apostles': •Simon whom he 14
called Peter, and his brother Andrew; James, John, Philip, Bartholomew,
Matthew, Thomas, James son of Alphaeus, Simon called the Zealot, •Judas son $^{15}_{16}$
of James,   and Judas Iscariot who became a traitor.

Luke omits the name 'Thaddaeus' and includes 'Judas, son of James' (6:16, cf
also Acts 1:13). This is perhaps the Judas mentioned later by John (cf John
14:22). Luke also explicitly calls the twelve 'apostles' (6:13, cf also Matthew 10:2).
This is a term that Luke uses of those special people who knew Jesus in his public
ministry and were witnesses of Jesus' resurrection. When Judas Iscariot was
being replaced, Luke has Peter say:

'We must choose someone who has been with us the whole time that the Lord Jesus
was travelling round with us, someone who was with us right from the time when
John was baptising until the day when he was taken up from us — and he can act with
us as a witness to his resurrection.'

(Acts 1:21-22, cf John 15:27,

Chapter 2
Luke's presentation of Jesus' word and his statement on the essence of Jesus' ministry

Luke 6:17 — 8:3

Most of this insert consists of material we have already met in Matthew. For the sake of maintaining the continuity of Luke's Gospel we shall give his text here, and, immediately after the text, refer the reader to the parallel passage in Matthew. Much of the commentary on Matthew can be applied to Luke as well. However, Luke does have his own perspective, and so we shall give here some supplementary commentary.

1: **The 'Sermon on the Plain'** — LUKE 6:17-49

Introduction

LUKE 6:17-19
He then came down with them and stopped at a piece of level ground where 17
there was a large gathering of his disciples with a great crowd of people from all
parts of Judaea and from Jerusalem and from the coastal region of Tyre and Sidon
who had come to hear him and to be cured of their diseases. People tormented 18
by unclean spirits were also cured, •and everyone in the crowd was trying to touch 19
him because power came out of him that cured them all.

Jesus, like Moses (cf Exodus 33:12 — 34:28), has just been on the mountain in prayer with his Father (cf Luke 6:12). Moses was commanded not to take anyone with him (Exodus 34:3); Jesus, on the contrary, summoned the Twelve to join him on the mountain, and he called them 'apostles' (Luke 6:13), for they were to share his mission. Now, with the Twelve, he comes down from the mountain to the world, which is eagerly awaiting his healing word. Jesus brings to the world the law of the new covenant (compare Exodus 34:29).

Luke places the Sermon here, after the election of the Twelve, because he wishes to highlight the universal nature of the new law, and associate it closely with the living Christian community.

The Beatitudes and Woes

LUKE 6:20-26

Then fixing his eyes on his disciples he said: 20

> 'How happy are you who are poor: yours is the kingdom of God.
> Happy you who are hungry now: you shall be satisfied.   21
> Happy you who weep now: you shall laugh.

'Happy are you when people hate you, drive you out, abuse you, denounce 22
your name as criminal, on account of the Son of Man. •Rejoice when that day 23
comes and dance for joy, for then your reward will be great in heaven. This was the
way their ancestors treated the prophets.

> 'But alas for you who are rich: you are having your consolation now.   24
> Alas for you who have your fill now: you shall go hungry.   25
> Alas for you who laugh now: you shall mourn and weep.

'Alas for you when the world speaks well of you! This was the way their 26
ancestors treated the false prophets.

(6:20-23, compare Matthew 5:1, 3, 5, 6, 11-12 page 86-87)

We shall limit our comments here to the first and basic beatitude ('How
happy are you who are poor'), and the contrasting woe ('Alas for you who are
rich'). We shall do this for two reasons. Firstly, because they express a central
theme in Luke's Gospel; and secondly, because in each case they include the other
categories mentioned. The 'poor' are 'hungry now', they 'weep now', they are the
ones who are hated, driven out, abused and denounced. The rich, on the other
hand, have their fill now, laugh now, and the world speaks well of them now.

Rather than attempting a definition of 'poor' and 'rich' as used by Luke, let
us examine his Gospel with these categories in mind and see how he demonstrates
the blessedness of the poor and the unhappiness of the rich.

Elizabeth and Zachary are poor. She is barren (Luke 1:7) and suffers
humiliation among men (Luke 1:25). They pray to God (Luke 1:13) and he
answers their prayer. They come to know the joy of this beatitude:

'John will be your joy and delight and many will rejoice at his birth.'

(Luke 1:14)

Mary is poor. She is completely open to the will of God (Luke 1:38). She is
willing to believe that nothing is impossible to God (Luke 1:37). She, too, is told
to 'Rejoice' (Luke 1:28), and her song of joy echoes this first beatitude (read Luke
1:46-55).

The shepherds are poor. It is they who received the 'news of great joy, a joy to
be shared by the whole people' (Luke 2:10). It is the lowly shepherds who witness
the glory of God and see God's saving presence 'lying in the manger' (Luke 2:16).

Simeon is a poor man; a man who longs to 'set eyes on the Christ' (Luke
2:26). He knows the truth of this beatitude when he takes the child into his arms
and praises God (Luke 2:28-32). Anna, too, is poor: she 'never left the Temple,
serving God night and day with fasting and prayer' (Luke 2:37). She, too, is
moved to praise God when she sees the child.

John the Baptist is a poor man, living in the wilderness (Luke 3:3) and
longing for all mankind to see the 'salvation of God' •(Luke 3:6).

The climax of the introductory chapters comes with the appearance of Jesus, the poor man, the man of prayer (Luke 3:21), the humble man, seeking with the crowd, the baptism of repentance for the forgiveness of sins. He knew then the blessedness of this beatitude: the heavens opened and the Holy Spirit came down upon him and God spoke to him of sonship, of love, of grace. Jesus knew hunger, but he looked to God to be satisfied (Luke 6:20 and 4:3-4). He knew powerlessness, but he looked to God his Father to protect him (Luke 4:5-8). He is a poor man who places all his trust in God (Luke 4:9-12).

The poor man is blessed because he is open to God. He has nothing of his own to rely on, nor does he desire worthless things (Psalm 24:4). It is the poor who listen to Jesus. Four times Luke lists those who are open to Jesus' ministrations and in each case the poor are mentioned either at the beginning or end of the list as inclusive of the others:

1: 'He has sent me to bring the good news to the poor,
to proclaim liberty to captives
and to the blind new sight,
to set the downtrodden free.' (Luke 4:18)

2: The Beatitudes (6:20-23)

3: 'The blind see again,
the lame walk,
lepers are cleansed,
the deaf hear,
the dead are raised to life,
the Good News is proclaimed to the poor
and happy is the man who does not lose faith in me.' (Luke 7:22-25)

4: 'Bring in the poor,
the crippled,
the blind
and the lame.' (Luke 14:21)

The widow of Zarephath is a poor woman, spiritually dispossessed (Luke 4:26); so is Naaman, the Syrian (Luke 4:27). It is they who are blessed by God.

Who would have thought that God would bring healing to the demoniac of Capernaum (Luke 4:33-37)? Who would have thought the poor fisherman, Peter, and his friends, would have been chosen to preach the Good News? Who would have expected Jesus to call a tax-collector (Luke 5:27-28)?

The concern of God for the poor is a basic theme of the whole of the Old Testament.

When God first reveals his name to Moses, he reveals himself as the one who is concerned for the oppressed (Exodus 3:7-8). Psalm 82 speaks of God as the one who is concerned for the weak, the orphan, the wretched and the destitute. Psalm 9-10 contrasts the rich and the poor and makes excellent commentary on Luke's beatitudes. So does Psalm 107. The Psalmist speaks of the hungry (107:4-9), the prisoners (107:10-16), the sinners (107:17-22) and those who are lost (107:23-32). They are the poor. They:

'called to God in their trouble and he rescued them from their sufferings.'

(Psalm 107:6, 13, 19. 28,)

It is this same compassion that Jesus shows to the poor. It is they who eat at God's table (cf Psalm 22:26). Three times Jesus is accused of eating with sinners (Luke 5:30, 7:39, 15:3). Each time Jesus speaks of the compassion of God (Luke 5:31-32, 7:47-50, 15:4-32). Those who are invited to share the intimacy of God's table in the messianic banquet are, as we have seen, the:

'poor, the crippled, the blind and the lame.'

(Luke 14:22)

Again and again, Luke concentrates on Jesus' concern for the poor. Apart from the many examples of his healing, we find Jesus eating with those who are refused the synagogue: those spiritually dispossessed; we find him caring for the servant of the Gentile centurion (Luke 7:1-10); we find him offering peace and deep healing to the woman who was a sinner (Luke 7:36-50). He spoke of a Samaritan as inheriting eternal life (Luke 10:25-37). Likewise, it was a Samaritan leper who came back to Jesus with gratitude and received salvation (Luke 17:16-19). Jesus spoke of the Gentiles coming from the four corners of the earth to 'feast in the kingdom of God' (Luke 13:29), and he told his disciples:

'When you have a party, invite the poor.'

(Luke 14:13)

It is the lost sheep that is sought (Luke 15:4-7); a feast is prepared for the lost son (Luke 15:11-32). It is the humble tax collector who goes home 'at rights with God' (Luke 18:14). Zacchaeus is invited to dine with Jesus, for:

'the Son of Man has come to seek out and save what was lost.'

(Luke 19:10)

Lazarus, the poor man (Luke 16:20, 16:22), is the one who feasts with Abraham; the poor widow is upheld as the perfect disciple (Luke 21:1-4), and it is to a dying thief that Jesus addresses the words:

'I promise you today you will be with me in paradise.'

(Luke 23:43)

Twice Luke records the expression:

'everyone who exalts himself will be humbled,
but the man who humbles himself will be exalted.'

(Luke 14:11, 18:14)

The poor man is the man who relies on God. This is demonstrated in his attitude to material possessions (Luke 14:28-33). It is demonstrated, more importantly, in his attitude to 'his father, mother, wife, children, brothers, sisters, yes, and his own life too' (Luke 14:26). It is demonstrated in his looking to God in adversity, in his faith and openness and humility. All examples we have given from Luke's Gospel are examples of the poor. Is it any wonder that Jesus can say:

'How happy are you who are poor:
yours is the kingdom of heaven . . .
rejoice and dance for joy.'

(Luke 6:20, 6:23)

The rich, by contrast, are the 'proud of heart' (Luke 1:51); they are routed when God comes in his power to execute justice. They are unable to receive him. The rich are the princes who are pulled down from their thrones (1:52). The rich 'are sent empty away' (Luke 1:53). They are the unrepentant (Luke 3:7-9). They are those in Nazareth who would not accept Jesus as a prophet because they did not look to God but were determined to impose their own preconceptions on to Jesus (Luke 4:23-24). Jesus was forced to walk away from them (Luke 4:30). They are the scribes and Pharisees, men of power in Judaism, who refused to listen to Jesus. They accused Jesus of blasphemy (Luke 5:21). How could they find forgiveness (Luke 12:10)? The rich are those who:

'are choked by the worries and riches and pleasures of life and do not reach maturity.'
(Luke 8:14)

The priest was a 'rich' man; so was the Levite. They saw the wounded man, but when they saw him they were not moved with compassion (Luke 10:31-32). They did not know the blessedness of the poor; they did not inherit eternal life (Luke 10:25). Jesus spoke out strongly against the Pharisees and the lawyers (Luke 11:37-54). His indictment makes a good commentary on the woes on which we are reflecting.

Luke alone has the parable about the man who hoarded possessions (Luke 12:13-21, cf also the section on renouncing possessions Luke 14:28-33). Luke alone has a long section on the right use of money (Luke 16:1-15) and the parable of the rich man and Lazarus (Luke 16:19-31), and the parable of the Pharisee and the publican (Luke 18:9-14). In each case the rich man misses out on life. The rich man is the man who relies on himself. He demonstrates this in his desire for individual security in material goods; he also demonstrates it in his use of people for his own power and prestige. He exalts himself and is unable to receive the gracious gift of God's healing and life.

When the rich aristocrat wanted to follow Jesus but could not pay the price, Luke tells us that he was very sad. He adds:

'Jesus looked at him and said, "How hard it is for those who have riches to make their way into the kingdom of God!"'
(Luke 18:24)

Is it any wonder that Jesus can say:

'Alas for you who are rich: you are having your consolation now.'
(Luke 6:24)

Let us conclude this section with words spoken by God to the poor:

'Yahweh consoles his people
and takes pity on those who are afflicted.
For Zion was saying, "Yahweh has abandoned me,
the Lord has forgotten me".
Does a woman forget her baby at the breast,
or fail to cherish the son of her womb?
Yet even if these forget,
I will never forget you.
See I have branded you on the palms of my hands.'
(Isaiah 49:13-15)

The Compassion of God

LUKE 6:27-36

'But I say this to you who are listening: Love your enemies, do good to those 27 who hate you, •bless those who curse you, pray for those who treat you badly. 28 To the man who slaps you on one cheek, present the other cheek too; to the man 29 who takes your cloak from you, do not refuse your tunic. •Give to everyone who 30 asks you, and do not ask for your property back from the man who robs you. Treat others as you would like them to treat you. •If you love those who love $^{31}_{32}$ you, what thanks can you expect? Even sinners love those who love them. •And if 33 you do good to those who do good to you, what thanks can you expect? For even sinners do that much. •And if you lend to those from whom you hope to receive, 34 what thanks can you expect? Even sinners lend to sinners to get back the same amount. •Instead, love your enemies and do good, and lend without any hope 35 of return. You will have a great reward, and you will be sons of the Most High, for he himself is kind to the ungrateful and the wicked.

'Be compassionate as your Father is compassionate.

(Compare Matthew 5:38-48 page 93)

Matthew concludes his section with the words:

'You must be perfect just as your heavenly Father is perfect.'

(Matthew 5:38,

Luke prefers to define God's perfection, and he does it in terms of 'compassion' (Luke 6:36).

In the Book of Leviticus we are told:

'Be holy, for I, Yahweh your God, am holy.'   *(Leviticus 19:2,*

God's holiness is exemplified especially in his compassion:

'I will betroth you to myself for ever,
betroth you with integrity and justice,
with tenderness and love;
I will betroth you to myself with faithfulness,
and you will come to know Yahweh.'

(Hosea 2:22,

'Yahweh, Yahweh, a God of tenderness and compassion, slow to anger, rich in kindness and faithfulness.'

(Exodus 34:6,
(Compare Exodus 3:7-8. Deuteronomy 10:18-19,

In Luke's Prologue, Mary sings a joyful hymn to God's mercy (Luke 1:50,54) as does Zechariah. The Baptist preaches of God's forgiveness (Luke 1:77, 3:3). Luke sees this as central to the whole mission of Jesus. Jesus, in his last instruction, says:

'See how it is written that the Christ would suffer and on the third day rise from the dead, and that, in his name, repentance for the forgiveness of sins would be preached to all the nations.'

(Luke 24:46-47,

Luke shows us Jesus exercising God's compassion in forgiving the paralysed man (Luke 5:20-24), and the woman who had a bad name in the town (Luke 7:47-49). From the cross Jesus prayed that his crucifiers might be forgiven (Luke 23:34). He taught his disciples both to pray for forgiveness (Luke 11:4) and to forgive (Luke 17:3-4).

When the lepers asked him to show them mercy, he healed them (Luke 17:13); likewise with the blind man (Luke 18:38-39). He taught his disciples to give alms in mercy to those in need (Luke 11:41 and 12:33).

When Jesus saw the widow whose son was dead, Luke tells us that he 'felt sorry for her' (Luke 7:13). Jesus uses the same expression in his parables of the Good Samaritan (Luke 10:33) and the Prodigal Son (Luke 15:20).

God is the one who sees and is moved with compassion. Jesus learned this compassion in prayer with his Father. In the passage before us, Jesus tells his disciples not to accept the categories of the world; not to react to people the way they expect us to react, but to be 'sons of the Most High' (Luke 6:35): to love as God loves, to be creative of goodness, and not, as so often happens, to add evil to evil. Jesus asks his disciples to see as God sees and to be moved with compassion.

A disciple should not judge his brother

LUKE 6:37-42

•Do not judge, and you $^{36}_{37}$ will not be judged yourselves; do not condemn, and you will not be condemned yourselves; grant pardon, and you will be pardoned. •Give, and there will be 38 gifts for you: a full measure, pressed down, shaken together, and running over, will be poured into your lap; because the amount you measure out is the amount you will be given back.'

He also told a parable to them, 'Can one blind man guide another? Surely 39 both will fall into a pit? •The disciple is not superior to his teacher; the fully 40 trained disciple will always be like his teacher. •Why do you observe the splinter 41 in your brother's eye and never notice the plank in your own? •How can you say 42 to your brother, "Brother, let me take out the splinter that is in your eye", when you cannot see the plank in your own? Hypocrite! Take the plank out of your own eye first, and then you will see clearly enough to take out the splinter that is in your brother's eye.

(Compare Matthew 7:1-5 page 96)

Notice that Luke stresses the superabundance of God's graciousness (Luke 6:38). For this and the following passages the reader is referred to the commentary on Matthew.

On doing the will of God

LUKE 6:43-46

'There is no sound tree that produces rotten fruit, nor again a rotten tree that 43 produces sound fruit. •For every tree can be told by its own fruit: people do not 44 pick figs from thorns, nor gather grapes from brambles. •A good man draws what 45 is good from the store of goodness in his heart; a bad man draws what is bad from the store of badness. For a man's words flow out of what fills his heart.

'Why do you call me, "Lord, Lord" and not do what I say?   46

(Compare Matthew 7:16-21 page 98 and 12:33-35 page 171)

Conclusion

LUKE 6:47-49

'Everyone who comes to me and listens to my words and acts on them—I will show you what he is like. •He is like the man who when he built his house dug, 47 and dug deep, and laid the foundations on rock; when the river was in flood it 48 bore down on that house but could not shake it, it was so well built. •But the one who listens and does nothing is like the man who built his house on soil, with no 49 foundations: as soon as the river bore down on it, it collapsed; and what a ruin that house became!'

(Compare Matthew 7:24-27 page 99)

2: The Essence of Jesus' Mission — LUKE 7:1 — 8:3: Jesus' living of his Word

Jesus heals the slave of the centurion

LUKE 7:1-10
1 7When he had come to the end of all he wanted the people to hear, he went into
2 Capernaum. •A centurion there had a servant, a favourite of his, who was
3 sick and near death. •Having heard about Jesus he sent some Jewish elders
4 to him to ask him to come and heal his servant. •When they came to Jesus they
5 pleaded earnestly with him. 'He deserves this of you' they said •'because he is
friendly towards our people; in fact, he is the one who built the synagogue.'
6 So Jesus went with them, and was not very far from the house when the centurion
sent word to him by some friends: 'Sir,' he said 'do not put yourself to trouble;
7 because I am not worthy to have you under my roof; •and for this same reason
I did not presume to come to you myself; but give the word and let my servant
8 be cured. •For I am under authority myself, and have soldiers under me; and I say
to one man: Go, and he goes; to another: Come here, and he comes; to my
9 servant: Do this, and he does it.' •When Jesus heard these words he was
astonished at him and, turning round, said to the crowd following him, 'I tell
10 you, not even in Israel have I found faith like this'. •And when the messengers
got back to the house they found the servant in perfect health.

(Compare Matthew 8:5-13 page 82)

Jesus is amazed at the Gentile centurion's acceptance of his authority (7:8).
The scribes and Pharisees accuse Jesus of blasphemy (Luke 5:21); they question
his eating and drinking with sinners (Luke 5:30), and his allowing his disciples to
take a walk and pick ears of corn against the sabbath regulations. This centurion,
on the other hand, while not one of the chosen race (Luke 7:9), recognises the fact
that Jesus 'spoke with authority' (Luke 4:32). He loves his slave and places his
trust in the power of Jesus to heal him (see also commentary on Matthew).

Jesus is concerned to heal. But he can only heal where a person is seeking
healing and is seeking it from a God in whom he places his trust. This anecdote
demonstrates the fact that any man can have this faith.

Jesus restores to life the son of the widow of Nain

LUKE 7:11-17
11 Now soon afterwards he went to a town called Nain, accompanied by his
12 disciples and a great number of people. •When he was near the gate of the town
it happened that a dead man was being carried out for burial, the only son of his
mother, and she was a widow. And a considerable number of the townspeople
13 were with her. •When the Lord saw her he felt sorry for her. 'Do not cry' he
14 said. •Then he went up and put his hand on the bier and the bearers stood still,
15 and he said, 'Young man, I tell you to get up'. •And the dead man sat up and
16 began to talk, and Jesus *gave him to his mother* •Everyone was filled with awe
and praised God saying, 'A great prophet has appeared among us; God has
17 visited his people'. •And this opinion of him spread throughout Judaea and all
over the countryside.

There is something ultimate about this miracle of Jesus: not even the gates of
death can withstand the healing and liberating power of God in Jesus. Luke

includes it here to prepare the reader for the remark Jesus is about to make in response to John's disciples:

"the blind see again, the lame walk, lepers are cleansed, and the deaf hear, **the dead are raised to life,** the Good News is proclaimed to the poor and happy is the man who does not lose faith in me."

(Luke 7:22-23 page 164)

We shall study later the development of the Hebrew faith in personal life after death (Luke 20:27-40 pages 326-329). The common understanding was that physical death meant the end of life, and the beginning of a shadowy existence in Sheol. At the same time, they believed that Yahweh possessed ultimate power, even over death:

"Yahweh gives death and life
brings down to Sheol and draws up"

(1 Samuel 2:6)

Presumably this meant that God could save a man from death, bring him back from the brink of Sheol, and was based on the 'miraculous' return to life and health of people who were presumed dead. At a time when a long life was seen as one of God's richest blessings, prayers to God to draw a man's life back from the Pit were frequent (see the canticle of Hezekiah, Isaiah 38:9-20).

Among the legends attached to the names of the great prophets, Elijah and Elisha, we find remarkable stories of people being restored to life (cf 1 Kings 17:17-24 and 2 Kings 4:8-37). In both cases the legend concerns the son of a widow (Compare the text upon which we are commenting, where Luke actually alludes to the Elijah legend. Luke 7:15 = 1 Kings 17:23). One thing is clear: Luke wishes to show Jesus as 'a great prophet' (Luke 7:16), fulfilling in his person all that the prophets did and stood for.

Jesus says 'the dead are raised to life' (Luke 7:22). Yet, in the Gospels, the only examples of the dead being raised back to this life are, besides the one on which we are commenting, the daughter of Jairus (Luke 8:40-56, page 184), and Lazarus (John 11:1-44 pages 249-254). It would seem that Jesus has some other situation primarily in mind. Similarly, Jesus commissions his disciples to carry on this part of his mission:

'Cure the sick, **raise the dead,** cleanse the lepers . . .'

(Matthew 10:8, page 115)

Yet, the only example, in the whole of the New Testament, of someone being brought back from physical death to this life is that of Tabitha (Acts 9:36-42).

It would seem that the kind of death Jesus is referring to is the kind of death spoken of by the father of the prodigal son when, pleading with the elder boy, he says:

"It was only right that we should celebrate and rejoice,
because your brother here was dead and has come to life;
he was lost and is found"

(Luke 15:32, also 15:24, page 288)

For Jesus, physical death does not separate a person from God (cf Luke 20:27-40, pages 326-329); but it is possible for a person, by the way he lives (cf the 'prodigal son'), to separate himself from the love and the life of the Father. It is this 'death' that Jesus wants to heal, especially by showing men the love of the Father, and drawing them back to the One who has compassion on them.

The compassion of Jesus is beautifully portrayed in the scene at Nain:
"When the Lord saw her he felt sorry for her"

(Luke 7:13).

Nothing, not even death, can separate us from the love of God (cf Romans 8:38-39).

Jesus is the Christ who brings about the kingdom of God.

LUKE 7:18-30

The disciples of John gave him all this news, and John, summoning two of his 18 disciples, •sent them to the Lord to ask, 'Are you the one who is to come, or must 19 we wait for someone else?' •When the men reached Jesus they said, 'John the 20 Baptist has sent us to you, to ask, "Are you the one who is to come or have we to wait for someone else?" ' •It was just then that he cured many people of 21 diseases and afflictions and of evil spirits, and gave the gift of sight to many who were blind. •Then he gave the messengers their answer, 'Go back and tell John 22 what you have seen and heard: the blind see again, the lame walk, lepers are cleansed, and the deaf hear, the dead are raised to life, the Good News is proclaimed to the poor •and happy is the man who does not lose faith in me'. 23

When John's messengers had gone he began to talk to the people about John, 24 'What did you go out into the wilderness to see? A reed swaying in the breeze? 25 No? Then what did you go out to see? A man dressed in fine clothes? Oh no, those who go in for fine clothes and live luxuriously are to be found at court! •Then what did you go out to see? A prophet? Yes, I tell you, and much 26 more than a prophet: •he is the one of whom scripture says: 27

> *See, I am going to send my messenger before you;*
> *he will prepare the way before you.* [a]

'I tell you, of all the children born of women, there is no one greater than John; 28 yet the least in the kingdom of God is greater than he is. •All the people who 29 heard him, and the tax collectors too, acknowledged God's plan by accepting baptism from John; •but by refusing baptism from him the Pharisees and the 30 lawyers had thwarted what God had in mind for them.

(a: Malachi 3:1)
(Compare Matthew 11:2-11 page 119-120)

Luke, like Matthew, finds the essence of Jesus' mission in his actions, (see commentary on Matthew pages 119-120). John the Baptist has promised that:

'Someone is coming, someone who is more powerful than I am.'

(Luke 3:16)

That Jesus is this 'someone' is proven by his actions (Luke 7:21-22).

Jesus points to John as a prophet 'and much more than a prophet' (Luke 7:26); and Luke adds a statement (7:29-30) that asserts John's place in the providence of God. It also illustrates the difference between the openness of the ordinary people and the stubbornness of the scribes and Pharisees. These latter 'thwarted what God had in mind for them' (Luke 7:30, compare Jeremiah 18:9-10).

It is clear from Jesus' actions that he is the Christ and that the Messianic kingdom (Luke 7:28) has dawned.

Jesus' mission is to draw the poor into union with God

LUKE 7:31-35

'What description, then, can I find for the men of this generation? What are 31
they like? •They are like children shouting to one another while they sit in the 32
market place:

> "We played the pipes for you,
> and you wouldn't dance;
> we sang dirges,
> and you wouldn't cry".

'For John the Baptist comes, not eating bread, not drinking wine, and you 33
say, "He is possessed". •The Son of Man comes, eating and drinking, and you 34
say, "Look, a glutton and a drunkard, a friend of tax collectors and sinners".
Yet Wisdom has been proved right by all her children.' 35

(Compare Matthew 11:16-19 page 121)

This is the second time that Luke has mentioned the criticism levelled at
Jesus because of his eating and drinking with sinners (compare Luke 5:29-32).
This time he speaks of Jesus as 'Wisdom' (Luke 7:35). We are reminded of the
passage in the Book of Proverbs in which Wisdom invites her children:

> 'And now, my sons, listen to me;
> listen to instruction and learn to be wise,
> do not ignore it.
> Happy those who keep my ways!
> Happy the man who listens to me,
> who day after day watches at my gates
> to guard the portals.
> For the man who finds me finds life,
> he will win favour from Yahweh;
> but he who does injury to me does hurt to his own soul,
> all who hate me are in love with death.
> Wisdom has built herself a house,
> she has erected her seven pillars,
> she has slaughtered her beasts, prepared her wine,
> she has laid her table.
> She has despatched her maidservants
> and proclaimed from the city heights:
> "Who is ignorant? Let him step this way."
> to the fool she says,
> "Come and eat my bread,
> drink the wine I have prepared!
> Leave your folly and you will live,
> walk in the ways of perception". '

(Proverbs 8:32 — 9:6)

Jesus is the expression of God's wisdom. And the fact is that it was the tax
collectors and sinners who knew their ignorance and came to him for instruction.
They were the poor who knew their hunger and came to him to share the
messianic banquet.

In the Old Testament, the intimate union with God that was to characterise
the messianic times was frequently likened to a banquet.

'On this mountain,
Yahweh Sabaoth will prepare for all peoples
a banquet of rich food, a banquet of fine wines,
of food rich and juicy, of fine strained wines.'

(Isaiah 25:6)

The poor eat this banquet, while the rich are sent empty away (Luke 1:53):

'Thus speaks the Lord Yahweh:
You shall see my servants eat
while you go hungry.
You shall see my servants drink
while you go thirsty.
You shall see my servants rejoice
while you are put to shame.
You shall hear my servants sing
for joy of heart,
while you will moan
for sadness of heart;
you will wail for distress of spirit.'

(Isaiah 65:13-14)

The reader would do well to read the whole of Isaiah chapter 55 at this stage. God invites the poor to share his banquet (55:1-3). He promises to make with them 'an everlasting covenant' (Isaiah 55:3). He begs all to seek him 'while he is still to be found' (55:6). His ways, his thoughts are far above those of men (55:9). God will achieve his purposes (55:10-11).

Jesus is making the same plea to his contemporaries (Luke 7:31). They rejected John because he did not fit their expectations. Now they are rejecting Jesus. They cannot see that his mission is proved precisely by the fact that it is the poor who are responding to him. 'Wisdom has been proved right by her children' (Luke 7:35).

Luke is preparing us for the following scene which is the climax of this section. Once again, the scene is a banquet, a Messianic banquet! One of the children of wisdom is there, and it is she who finds salvation.

The Good News is proclaimed to the poor (cf Luke 7:22)

LUKE 7:36-50

One of the Pharisees invited him to a meal. When he arrived at the Pharisee's 36 house and took his place at table, •a woman came in, who had a bad name in 37 the town. She had heard he was dining with the Pharisee and had brought with her an alabaster jar of ointment. •She waited behind him at his feet, weeping, and her 38 tears fell on his feet, and she wiped them away with her hair; then she covered his feet with kisses and anointed them with the ointment.

When the Pharisee who had invited him saw this, he said to himself, 'If this 39 man were a prophet, he would know who this woman is that is touching him and what a bad name she has'. •Then Jesus took him up and said, 'Simon, I have 40 something to say to you'. 'Speak, Master' was the reply. •'There was once a 41 creditor who had two men in his debt; one owed him five hundred denarii, the other fifty. •They were unable to pay, so he pardoned them both. Which of them 42 will love him more?' •'The one who was pardoned more, I suppose' answered 43 Simon. Jesus said, 'You are right'.

Then he turned to the woman. 'Simon,' he said 'you see this woman? I came 44
into your house, and you poured no water over my feet, but she has poured out her
tears over my feet and wiped them away with her hair. •You gave me no kiss, but 45
she has been covering my feet with kisses ever since I came in. •You did not 46
anoint my head with oil, but she has anointed my feet with ointment. •For this 47
reason I tell you that her sins, her many sins, must have been forgiven her, or she
would not have shown such great love. It is the man who is forgiven little who
shows little love.' •Then he said to her, 'Your sins are forgiven'. •Those who 48 49
were with him at table began to say to themselves, 'Who is this man, that he even
forgives sins?' •But he said to the woman, 'Your faith has saved you; go in peace'. 50

This woman is a perfect illustration of the beatitudes (Luke 6:20-23); Simon,
the Pharisee illustrates the woes (Luke 6:24-26). We are present at a meal to
which Simon invited Jesus (7:36). But as soon as Jesus 'took his place at table'
(7:36), a poor woman enters, weeping. She knows her poverty and cries to God
for deliverance. She knows what it is to experience forgiveness (7:43) and her
heart overflows with gratitude to the one who revealed this to her (7:47).

Simon does not know his need. He is the rich man, the centre of his own life.
He is insensitive to Jesus' needs (7:44-46), caught up in his own position and
pride. He sees the woman; but all he sees is her repute (7:39). He does not see her
love. Jesus has to point out to him:

'Her many sins must have been forgiven her or she would not have shown such great
love.'

(Luke 7:47)

In the end it is the woman, not Simon, who enjoys the banquet. She is 'saved'
and offered the messianic gift of 'peace' (7:50).

Once again, Jesus reveals God as a God of compassion. He does not need our
ritual purity. He needs our humility and our openness; he needs our love. It is the
poor who enjoy the feast (compare Luke 13:28-29, 14:16-24, 22:30).

LUKE 8:1-3

8 Now after this he made his way through towns and villages preaching, and 1
proclaiming the Good News of the kingdom of God. With him went the
Twelve, •as well as certain women who had been cured of evil spirits and ailments: 2
Mary surnamed the Magdalene, from whom seven demons had gone out,
Joanna the wife of Herod's steward Chuza, Susanna, and several others who 3
provided for them out of their own resources.

As part of his account of the crucifixion, Luke writes:

'All his friends stood at a distance; so also did the women who had accompanied him
from Galilee, and they saw all this happen.'

(Luke 23:49)

These same women witness the burial of Jesus (Luke 23:55) and are told of
his resurrection when they discover the empty tomb (Luke 24:1-8). Luke names
them:

'The women were Mary of Magdala, Joanna and Mary the mother of James. The
other women with them also told the apostles.'

(Luke 24:10-11)

Luke mentions these women here to reinforce the connection between Jesus' ministry and his resurrection, and to establish these women as authentic witnesses of the latter.

He also mentions them to illustrate the revolutionary nature of Jesus' preaching. No other rabbi had women disciples. This was yet another social expectation that Jesus ignored. Jesus' treatment of women prompted Paul's statement to the Galatians:

> 'There are no more distinctions between Jew and Greek, slave and free, male and female, but all of you are one in Christ Jesus.'
>
> *(Galatians 3:28)*

* * * * * * * *

Points for Reflection:

1: 'Everyone in the crowd was trying to touch him because power came out of him that cured them all. (Luke 6:19).

The servant was 'sick and near death' (Luke 7:2). Jesus' word cured him (Luke 7:7, 7:10). Do I try to touch him? For myself? For those I love? The church uses the words of the centurion in the liturgy just before the reception of communion:

> 'Lord, I am not worthy to receive you,
> but only say the word and I shall be healed.'

Remembering the closeness of his companionship with Jesus, John, in his First Letter, spoke of: 'Something that we have touched with our hands' (1 John 1:1). When I hold out my hand and touch the bread, when the risen Christ places himself in my hands, do I believe in the power that comes out of him; the power that can heal me?

2: 'How happy are you who are poor' (Luke 6:20).

Can I imagine the happiness of the 'woman who had a bad name in the town' (Luke 7:37), when Jesus proclaimed to her the Good News' (Luke 7:22)? She was a sinner; she was unhappy; she could not stop weeping (Luke 7:38). Then Jesus saw her and had compassion on her. He saw her love and he told her of the love of God, her Father. He told her of forgiveness (7:48) and salvation (7:50) and peace (7:50). It is not our reputation that matters; it is our willingness to touch him and be touched by him.

3: 'Happy you who weep now: you shall laugh' (Luke 6:21).

The sinful woman wept for her sins (Luke 7:38). The widow of Nain wept for her son (Luke 7:13). Their tears were turned to joy on contact with Jesus.

4: 'Be compassionate as your Father is compassionate' (Luke 6:36).

Paul reminds his readers of this quality of God when he writes:

> 'Think of God's *mercy*, my brothers, and worship, I beg you, in a way that is worthy of thinking beings, by offering your living bodies as a holy sacrifice, truly pleasing to God.'
>
> *(Romans 12:1)*

He speaks, too, of God as a *'gentle* Father' (2 Corinthians 1:3).

Chapter 3
The power of God's word as illustrated in parables

Mark 3:20 — 4:34
Matthew 12:22 — 13:52
Luke 8:4-21

MARK 3:20-27 (Compare Matthew 12:24-29)

20   He went home again, and once more such a crowd collected that they could
21 not even have a meal. •When his relatives heard of this, they set out to take
    charge of him, convinced he was out of his mind.

22   The scribes who had come down from Jerusalem were saying, 'Beelzebul is
23 in him' and, 'It is through the prince of devils that he casts devils out'. •So he called
    them to him and spoke to them in parables, 'How can Satan cast out Satan?
$^{24}_{25}$ If a kingdom is divided against itself, that kingdom cannot last. •And if
26 a household is divided against itself, that household can never stand. •Now if
    Satan has rebelled against himself and is divided, he cannot stand either—it is
27 the end of him. •But no one can make his way into a strong man's house and
    burgle his property unless he has tied up the strong man first. Only then can he
    burgle his house.

(Compare Luke 11:17-22 page 276)

The setting in which Mark places this first parable seems to imply that Jesus
decided to speak in parables when it became obvious to him that certain groups
of people were not grasping the 'Good News'. In some cases they were determined
not to grasp it, but rather to interpret it in their own prejudiced way; in other
cases they seemed unable to take it in.

'So he called them to him and spoke to them in parables' (3:23)

The Aramaic word for 'parable' can be translated 'riddle' — which is just what the
parables are. A parable does not appeal immediately to the logical mind; it does
not have 'a' meaning that can be clearly worked out and understood. It therefore
cannot easily be 'misunderstood' or made to fit into fixed categories. Its appeal is
directed to the imagination. It aims to startle, usually by use of exaggeration. In
this way it aims to break through the defences of the mind and open the way to
new insight by striking imagery. It aims to fascinate, to puzzle and so to
enlighten. It is important not to treat the parable as though it were an allegory. In
an allegory each element of the story has a definite significance. The task of the

listener is to decipher the hidden code and then everything falls neatly into place and the meaning becomes apparent. The parable has a different purpose and a different thrust. It is a riddle and remains a riddle.

Obviously the scribes from Jerusalem were fixed in their prejudices and, from hearsay, were quite confident that they knew what Jesus was about. He was determined to confront them and, if possible, break through their prejudices. So 'he called them to him' (3:23). He had to find some way of interesting them, almost tricking them into changing their perspective and finding a way out of their carefully constructed mental prison. The parable was his answer.

The scribes were accusing Jesus of working under the power of the prince of demons, Satan or Beelzebul. Beelzebul ('Lord of the House') was a Philistine God. In derision, the Jews often referred to him as 'Beelzebub' (The 'Lord of the Flies' cf 2 Kings 1:2). Jesus speaks of a burglar and a strong man's house (3:27). It is clear that he is claiming to be overpowering Satan rather than to be working for him. But each person listening to Jesus had to answer certain questions for himself. Who is the strong man who is defending my heart? Who is trying to break in and capture my heart? Are there powers defending me against love and truth that must first be 'tied up' (3:27) before love and truth can enter? It should be obvious that there is no single answer to these questions, not even for the same person. The riddle cannot be solved; it must stand as a constant challenge.

* * * * * * * *

Matthew omits the reference to Jesus' relatives. He also places the accusation made by the Pharisees in the context of an act of healing.

MATTHEW 12:22-24
Then they brought to him a blind and dumb demoniac; and he cured him, 22 so that the dumb man could speak and see. •All the people were astounded and 23 said, 'Can this be the Son of David?' •But when the Pharisees heard this they 24 said, 'The man casts out devils only through Beelzebul, the prince of devils'.

(Compare Luke 11:14-16 page 276)

Notice the difference in the reactions of the ordinary people and the Pharisees (compare also Matthew 9:32-34 page 114).

* * * * * * * *

MARK 3:28-30
'I tell you solemnly, all men's sins will be forgiven, and all their 28 blasphemies; •but let anyone blaspheme against the Holy Spirit and he will never 29 have forgiveness: he is guilty of an eternal sin.' •This was because they were 30 saying, 'An unclean spirit is in him'.

With deep feeling, and authority, Jesus tells them that no sin is beyond the healing and forgiving love of God. But they must turn to God, they must open their minds and hearts to his Spirit if they wish to be healed. The Pharisees and scribes cannot be forgiven if they persist in resisting God's Spirit.

Not only are they sinning, they are also rejecting the only healing that can cure them. Their sin will be 'eternal' (3:29).

* * * * * * * *

MATTHEW 12:30-32

'He who is not with me is against me, and he who does not gather with me 30 scatters. •And so I tell you, every one of men's sins and blasphemies will be for- 31 given, but blasphemy against the Spirit will not be forgiven. •And anyone who 32 says a word against the Son of Man will be forgiven; but let anyone speak against the Holy Spirit and he will not be forgiven either in this world or in the next.

(Compare Luke 11:23 page 276 and 12:10 page 278)

Jesus is never the centre of his own world. He is not offended by what they think of him. He is concerned that, in rejecting him, they are rejecting the healing and forgiving Spirit of the one he calls 'My Father'.

MATTHEW 12:33-45

'Make a tree sound and its fruit will be sound; make a tree rotten and its 33 fruit will be rotten. For the tree can be told by its fruit. •Brood of vipers, how 34 can your speech be good when you are evil? For a man's words flow out of what fills his heart. •A good man draws good things from his store of goodness; a bad 35 man draws bad things from his store of badness. •So I tell you this, that for 36 every unfounded word men utter they will answer on Judgement day, •since it 37 is by your words you will be acquitted, and by your words condemned.'

Then some of the scribes and Pharisees spoke up. 'Master,' they said 'we 38 should like to see a sign from you.' •He replied, 'It is an evil and unfaithful 39 generation that asks for a sign! The only sign it will be given is the sign of the prophet Jonah. •For as Jonah *was in the belly of the sea-monster for three* 40 *days and three nights,* so will the Son of Man be in the heart of the earth for three days and three nights. •On Judgement day the men of Nineveh will stand 41 up with this generation and condemn it, because when Jonah preached they repented; and there is something greater than Jonah here. •On Judgement day 42 the Queen of the South will rise up with this generation and condemn it, because she came from the ends of the earth to hear the wisdom of Solomon; and there is something greater than Solomon here.

'When an unclean spirit goes out of a man it wanders through waterless 43 country looking for a place to rest, and cannot find one. •Then it says, "I will 44 return to the home I came from". But on arrival, finding it unoccupied, swept and tidied, •it then goes off and collects seven other spirits more evil than itself, and 45 they go in and set up house there, so that the man ends up by being worse than he was before. That is what will happen to this evil generation.'

(Compare Luke 11:24-26, 29-32 page 276
Matthew 12:33-35: compare Matthew 7:16-20 page 98)

Jesus uses the strongest words in an effort to break through the defences these men have built up against God in the name of a religion that supported their own interests. It is they who have the 'unclean spirit' (12:43). Jesus has cleared the temple, emptied the house. This is a challenge to the religious leaders to 'repent', to open their hearts and religious understanding to the Spirit of God. If they do not welcome the redeeming love of God, their lives will fill again with the unclean spirit and their condition will be worse than if they had never known Jesus. He challenges them to examine their heart (12:34). The only sign he promises them is his death and resurrection (12:40). On God's fidelity, read Jonah 2:2-10.

MARK 3:31-35 (Compare Matthew 12:46-50 and Luke 8:19-21)

His mother and brothers now arrived and, standing outside, sent in a message 31 asking for him. •A crowd was sitting round him at the time the message was passed 32 to him, 'Your mother and brothers and sisters are outside asking for you'. He replied, 'Who are my mother and my brothers?' •And looking round at 33 34 those sitting in a circle about him, he said, 'Here are my mother and my brothers. Anyone who does the will of God, that person is my brother and sister and 35 mother.'

Mark and Matthew have this scene here at the beginning of their section on Jesus' parables. Luke places it immediately after the parables. The effect in each case is the same: to highlight the central message of Jesus' teaching and especially of the parables. The word of God is all-powerful; our task is to listen to this word and carry it out.

Mention of Jesus' 'brothers and sisters' (3:32) may sound inconsistent to those familiar with the very early tradition that Mary had only the one child, Jesus. They are mentioned again in Mark 6:3 where some of the brothers are named: 'James and Joset and Jude and Simon'. The fact is that in Aramaic usage the term 'brother' simply meant a male blood-relation.

Later in his Gospel, when speaking of the women who were watching the crucifixion, Mark speaks of:

'Mary who was the mother of James the younger and Joset.'

(Mark 15:40)

This 'Mary' is obviously not the mother of Jesus or Mark would have identified her as such. The implication is that James and Joset are relations, not blood-brothers of Jesus. This is consistent with early Church tradition.

The central point of the passage lies in the final words: 'Anyone who does the will of God, that person is my brother and sister and mother'. It is this point that will be developed in the parables, centring as they do on the 'kingdom of God' and the wonderful effects of doing his will.

MARK 4:1-9 (compare Matthew 13:1-9 and Luke 8:4-8)

4 Again he began to teach by the lakeside, but such a huge crowd gathered 1 round him that he got into a boat on the lake and sat there. The people were all along the shore, at the water's edge. •He taught them many things in parables, 2 and in the course of his teaching he said to them, •'Listen! Imagine a sower 3 going out to sow. •Now it happened that, as he sowed, some of the seed fell on 4 the edge of the path, and the birds came and ate it up. •Some seed fell on rocky 5 ground where it found little soil and sprang up straightaway, because there was no depth of earth; •and when the sun came up it was scorched and, not having 6 any roots, it withered away. •Some seed fell into thorns, and the thorns 7

grew up and choked it, and it produced no crop. •And some seeds fell into rich 8
soil and, growing tall and strong, produced crop; and yielded thirty, sixty,
even a hundredfold.' •And he said, 'Listen, anyone who has ears to hear!'   9

We are listening to Jesus, the teacher (4:1-2 cf also Mark 1:21-22 and 2:13).
The parable opens with words which direct the response of his hearers: 'Listen!'
'Imagine!' (4:3). Most of the story is quite common-place. The surprise comes at
the end: this seed is capable of producing a harvest of 'thirty, sixty, even a
hundredfold' (4:8). Seven-fold was considered a good harvest at the time! Herein
lies the riddle. What kind of seed is it that, in spite of so many difficulties, can
produce such a miraculous harvest?

MARK 4:10-12 (compare Luke 8:9-10)

When he was alone, the Twelve, together with the others who formed his 10
company, asked what the parables meant. •He told them, 'The secret of the 11
kingdom of God is given to you, but to those who are outside everything comes
in parables, •so that *they may see and see again, but not perceive; may hear and* 12
hear again, but not understand; otherwise they might be converted and be forgiven'.[a]

(a: Isaiah 6:10)

The quotation is from Isaiah. God is encouraging the prophet to accept the
mission to preach and not to be dissuaded by the obstinate refusal of so many to
listen. God promises Isaiah that his mission will succeed in spite of the blindness
and hardness of heart surrounding him. Mark has shown us Jesus facing similar
prejudices and a similar refusal to perceive and understand, especially from the
Pharisees. These are 'those who are outside' (Mark 4:11). Punning on the
nuances of the word 'parable', Mark tells us that everything comes to them in
riddles (4:11).

The consequence of Jesus' use of parables was that the Pharisees did not
perceive and did not understand. This was not Jesus' intention: we have already
seen that he used parables precisely to help his listeners come to a deeper
understanding. They did not perceive because they did not want to perceive. Had
they wanted to they could have been 'converted and forgiven' (4:12).

While for some the parables remain riddles, because of their unwillingness to
'be converted and be forgiven' (4:12), for others they reveal the 'secret of the
kingdom' (4:11). The seed sown by Jesus is producing a harvest; his mission is
succeeding, at least as far as the 'Twelve together with those who formed his
company' (4:10) are concerned.

MATTHEW 13:10-17

Then the disciples went up to him and asked, 'Why do you talk to them in 10
parables?' •'Because' he replied 'the mysteries of the kingdom of heaven are 11
revealed to you, but they are not revealed to them. •For anyone who has will be 12
given more, and he will have more than enough; but from anyone who has not,
even what he has will be taken away. •The reason I talk to them in parables is 13
that they look without seeing and listen without hearing or understanding. •So in 14
their case this prophecy of Isaiah is being fulfilled:

> *You will listen and listen again, but not understand,*
> *see and see again, but not perceive.*

15   *For the heart of this nation has grown coarse,*
        their ears are dull of hearing, and they have shut their eyes,
        for fear they should see with their eyes,
        hear with their ears,
        understand with their heart,
        and be converted
        and be healed by me.^a

16   'But happy are your eyes because they see, your ears because they hear!
17   I tell you solemnly, many prophets and holy men longed to see what you see, and
      never saw it; to hear what you hear, and never heard it.

(a: Isaiah 6:9-10)

The parable is a gentle way of teaching. No one is forced to see, or forced to
reject. A parable penetrates only in so far as the listener is open to receive. Jesus
uses the parable to try to break into the hearts and minds of those who 'look
without seeing and listen without understanding' (Matthew 13:13). The fact is
that if Jesus does not get through to them in this way, their condition can only get
worse (Matthew 13:12). Jesus' teaching makes sense of and brings to completion
the revelation of the Old Covenant. Those who listen to Jesus are growing in their
understanding of life. The Pharisees, on the other hand, by their refusal to listen
to Jesus will find that without his revelation their own Law will fail to achieve its
purpose (cf Matthew 5:18)

Matthew concludes with a beatitude directed to the disciples (13:16-17). It
stands in sharp contrast to the following statement of Mark (Mark 4:13-14).

MARK 4:13-20 (Compare Matthew 13:18-23 and Luke 8:11-15)
13   He said to them, 'Do you not understand this parable? Then how will you
14   understand any of the parables? •What the sower is sowing is the word. •Those
15   on the edge of the path where the word is sown are people who have no sooner
      heard it than Satan comes and carries away the word that was sown in them.
16   Similarly, those who receive the seed on patches of rock are people who, when
17   first they hear the word, welcome it at once with joy. •But they have no root
      in them, they do not last; should some trial come, or some persecution on
18   account of the word, they fall away at once. •Then there are others who receive
19   the seed in thorns. These have heard the word, •but the worries of this world,
      the lure of riches and all the other passions come in to choke the word, and so
20   it produces nothing. •And there are those who have received the seed in rich
      soil: they hear the word and accept it and yield a harvest, thirty and sixty and a
      hundredfold.'

The opening statement is addressed to 'the Twelve, together with the others
who formed his company' (Mark 4:10). It is only in Mark and is very different
from the beatitude we have just read in Matthew (13:16-17). This is not the only
occasion where Matthew alters statements in which Mark stresses the failure of
the disciples to understand Jesus (contrast Mark 8:17-18, 21 with Matthew
16:12). Matthew wishes to focus attention on the fact that a disciple does have
some understanding of Jesus; Mark highlights the fact that this understanding
comes only through a miracle of grace and is not because of any personal merit of
the disciple. A disciple is identified not by his understanding, but by his faith.

This 'explanation' of the parable treats it as though it were an allegory, not a parable. We must be careful that it does not fix, for us, the meaning of the parable. As a parable, it is meant to startle and surprise and puzzle. The above 'explanation' does not take from us the necessity to 'Listen! Imagine!' (Mark 4:3).

MARK 4:21-25 (Compare Luke 8:16-18)

He also said to them, 'Would you bring in a lamp to put it under a tub or 21 under the bed? Surely you will put it on the lamp-stand? •For there is nothing 22 hidden but it must be disclosed, nothing kept secret except to be brought to light. If anyone has ears to hear, let him listen to this.'   23

He also said to them, 'Take notice of what you are hearing. The amount you 24 measure out is the amount you will be given—and more besides; •for the man 25 who has will be given more; from the man who has not, even what he has will be taken away.'

We saw that the purpose of a parable is to break through the defences of the mind, and in this way to enlighten. A proverb — which can be thought of as a short parable — often has the same function, and Mark uses shock tactics here by giving the reader four proverbs in quick succession. There is no logical progression; there is no easy way of fooling ourselves into thinking we understand; so we are forced to stop and listen:

'If anyone has ears to hear, let him listen to this.' (Mark 4:23)

'Take notice of what you are hearing.' (Mark 4:24)

a: The first proverb reads:

'Would you bring in a lamp to put it under a tub or under the bed? Surely you would put it on the lamp-stand?'

(Mark 4:21)

It is the word of Jesus that is the lamp and Jesus is telling his listeners that he is not speaking for nothing. It is meant to give light. We are reminded of John's words:

'I am the light of the world;
anyone who follows me will not be walking in the dark;
he will have the light of life.'

(John 8:12)

It may be of interest to note that the Gospel-writers use this same proverb in quite different contexts. Luke uses it later in his Gospel to bring out the need for the disciple to purify his life so that he will be able to see clearly (Luke 11:33). Matthew reminds the disciple that he, like Jesus, is to be a light to the world (Matthew 5:15).

b: The second proverb reads:

'For there is nothing hidden but it must be disclosed, nothing kept secret except to be brought to light.'

(Mark 4:22)

In this present context Mark and Luke are referring to the word of Jesus. We are reminded of the words of the author of the Letter to the Hebrews:

'The word of God is something alive and active. It cuts like any double-edged sword but more finely: it can slip through the place where the soul is divided from the spirit, or joints from the marrow; it can judge the secret emotions and thoughts. No created thing can hide from him; everything is uncovered and open to the eyes of the one to whom we must give an account of ourselves.'

(Hebrews 4:12-13)

This proverb, too, is used in a different context by Matthew and Luke to encourage the disciple not to be afraid of men (Matthew 10:26 and Luke 12:2).

c: The third proverb (omitted by Luke in this present context) reads:

'The amount you measure out is the amount you will be given — and more besides.'

(Mark 4:24b)

Mark seems to be speaking here of openness: the more space there is for God's word to fill us, the more he will be able to give us of himself. In another context Luke uses this proverb in relation to a disciple being compassionate like God his Father and being generous in forgiving (Luke 6:38). Matthew, on the other hand, uses it in the context of judging (Matthew 7:2).

d: The fourth proverb reads:

'for the man who has will be given more;
from the man who has not, even what he has will be taken away.'

(Mark 4:25)

We are reminded of the fact that the more we listen to the word of Jesus the more we will be attuned to hear it. There is the constant danger that we take it for granted that we are hearing, when in fact we are not really listening. We do it with each other; we do it with God. Or we have listened once, and we keep acting on what we once heard; but we are not listening now. Jesus is warning us that we must keep on listening, we must keep on taking notice of what we hear, or the facade will fall away, the crusted shell will crumble, and we will learn, to our dismay, that we are in fact no longer living the way we thought we were; we are no longer truly disciples of Jesus, following him to the Father.

This is one occasion on which Matthew uses the proverb in the same context (Matthew 13:12). He also, as does Luke, uses it in the context of our use of our God-given talents (cf Matthew 25:29 and Luke 19:26).

*   *   *   *   *   *   *

We note at this point that Luke concludes his rather brief listing of the parables, with the statement about the necessity of the disciple doing the will of God (8:19-21). We examined this earlier in Mark (3:31-35 page 172).

*   *   *   *   *   *   *

MARK 4:26-29

He also said, 'This is what the kingdom of God is like. A man throws seed on
27 the land. •Night and day, while he sleeps, when he is awake, the seed is sprouting
28 and growing; how, he does not know. •Of its own accord the land produces first
29 the shoot, then the ear, then the full grain in the ear. •And when the crop is ready,
he loses no time: he starts to reap because the harvest has come.'

At the beginning of his Gospel Mark told us that the preaching of Jesus concerned 'the kingdom of God' (Mark 1:15). He has just mentioned that the 'secret of the kingdom of God' was given to the disciples (Mark 4:11). In this parable Jesus underscores one of its essential qualities. There is no room either for anxiety, or for pride. There is something happening among us that is much bigger than us. We are to sow the seed. We are to live the Christ-life. But the results are not in proportion to our effort. The seed is good and it will yield a harvest. Jesus is asking his disciples to be willing, like him, to wait on God, free of care, and open to his will.

Matthew does not use this parable (it is one of the very few passages that we find in Mark but not in either Matthew or Luke, see also Mark 8:22-26). Matthew substitutes the following parable:

MATTHEW 13:24-30
He put another parable before them, 'The kingdom of heaven may be 24 compared to a man who sowed good seed in his field. •While everybody was 25 asleep his enemy came, sowed darnel all among the wheat, and made off. •When 26 the new wheat sprouted and ripened, the darnel appeared as well. •The owner's 27 servants went to him and said, "Sir, was it not good seed that you sowed in your field? If so, where does the darnel come from?" •"Some enemy has done this" 28 he answered. And the servants said, "Do you want us to go and weed it out?" But he said, "No, because when you weed out the darnel you might pull up the 29 wheat with it. •Let them both grow till the harvest; and at harvest time I shall 30 say to the reapers: First collect the darnel and tie it in bundles to be burnt, then gather the wheat into my barn." '

The task of the disciple is to sow the right seed, not to judge weed from wheat. The harvest is God's. The disciple must never forget that he is working for God's kingdom, not his own. The disciple does not have the wisdom to discern weed from wheat. If he concerns himself with judging others he may well find himself destroying good seed. Judgment is to be left to God.

MARK 4:30-32 (Compare Matthew 13:31-32)
He also said, 'What can we say the kingdom of God is like? What parable can 30 we find for it? •It is like a mustard seed which at the time of its sowing in the 31 soil is the smallest of all the seeds on earth; •yet once it is sown it grows into the 32 biggest shrub of them all and puts out big branches so that the birds of the air can shelter in its shade.' *(Compare Luke 13:18-19 page 283)*

The startling contrast between the seed and the shrub encourages us not to judge by appearances. Jesus stresses that God is at work; it is his kingdom. The results are in relation to that fact.

*   *   *   *   *   *   *   *

Matthew adds here another parable with a similar thrust:

MATTHEW 13:33
He told them another parable, 'The kingdom of heaven is like the yeast 33 a woman took and mixed in with three measures of flour till it was leavened all through'. *(Compare Luke 13:20-21 page 283)*

MARK 4:33-34

33   Using many parables like these, he spoke the word to them, so far as they were
34 capable of understanding it. •He would not speak to them except in parables,
    but he explained everything to his disciples when they were alone.

While the parables aimed at 'understanding' (4:33), a man could only grasp
the secret of the kingdom by close companionship with Jesus (4:34).

MATTHEW 13:34-35

34   In all this Jesus spoke to the crowds in parables; indeed, he would never speak
35 to them except in parables. •This was to fulfil the prophecy:

> *I will speak to you in parables*
> *and expound things hidden since the foundation of the world.*^a

(a: Psalm 78:2)

* * * * * * * *

Mark's section on Parables ends here. **Matthew** adds the following parables.

1: **An allegorical explanation of the parable of the weeds** (confer Matthew
    13:24-30)

MATTHEW 13:36-43

36   Then, leaving the crowds, he went to the house; and his disciples came to
37 him and said, 'Explain the parable about the darnel in the field to us'. •He said
38 in reply, 'The sower of the good seed is the Son of Man. •The field is the world;
    the good seed is the subjects of the kingdom; the darnel, the subjects of the evil
39 one; •the enemy who sowed them, the devil; the harvest is the end of the world;
40 the reapers are the angels. •Well then, just as the darnel is gathered up and burnt
41 in the fire, so it will be at the end of time. •The Son of Man will send his angels
    and they will gather out of his kingdom all things that provoke offences and all
42 who do evil, •and throw them into the blazing furnace, where there will be
43 weeping and grinding of teeth. •Then the virtuous will shine like the sun in the
    kingdom of their Father. Listen, anyone who has ears!

This is an allegorical explanation (compare Mark 4:13-20), applying the
parable to one specific context. We must remember, however, that no
'explanation' can exhaust the potential of a parable.

2: **The parable of the treasure hidden in a field.**

MATTHEW 13:44

44   'The kingdom of heaven is like treasure hidden in a field which someone has
    found; he hides it again, goes off happy, sells everything he owns and buys the
    field.

The discovery of treasures hidden centuries before by people trying to defend
their property from advancing looters was not an uncommon experience among
Jesus' contemporaries. One can imagine their happiness and their care to make
sure the treasure was theirs. Jesus puts the kingdom of God into that kind of
setting. The reader has to listen to the riddle, imagine it, and let it work on him.

What does it say about the kingdom? Could you be the treasure for which God, in his love, has given everything? He gave his Son to 'redeem' you (= 'buy you back')!

3: The parable of the pearl

MATTHEW 13:45-46
45 'Again, the kingdom of heaven is like a merchant looking for fine pearls;
46 when he finds one of great value he goes and sells everything he owns and buys it.

4: The parable of the dragnet

MATTHEW 13:47-50
47 'Again, the kingdom of heaven is like a dragnet cast into the sea that brings
48 in a haul of all kinds. •When it is full, the fishermen haul it ashore; then, sitting
   down, they collect the good ones in a basket and throw away those that are no
49 use. •This is how it will be at the end of time: the angels will appear and separate
50 the wicked from the just •to throw them into the blazing furnace where there
   will be weeping and grinding of teeth.

The reign of God's love is offered to all. Being drawn by God into the kingdom of his love is no guarantee of ultimate salvation. It is always possible for man to be unfaithful. Man can elect to die. He can — as Jesus has just been saying to the Pharisees — refuse to see, to understand, to let his life be transformed by grace. The consequences of such a refusal are eternal. But this, as Matthew pointed out in an earlier parable (13:24-30) is a matter to be left to God.

5: Conclusion

MATTHEW 13:51-52
51
52 'Have you understood all this?' They said, 'Yes'. •And he said to them,
   'Well then, every scribe who becomes a disciple of the kingdom of heaven is like
   a householder who brings out from his storeroom things both new and old'.

It has been suggested that the image Jesus has in mind is not so much a 'storeroom' as a strong-box, used for coins. One can use the coins of the old currency and the coins of the new currency for exchange. Both are genuine. Matthew is assuring his community that there is value in the Law and the Prophets, in the way of life they once led. One of the main themes of the 'Sermon on the Mount' however was that this old way of life has been fulfilled in Jesus (cf Matthew 5:17).

* * * * * * *

One cannot summarise the message of the parables. One can only 'listen' and 'imagine' while praying to have the courage to open one's heart and mind and accept the risk of seeing things old and new. At the same time there is a consistent theme running through them all. Our attention is fixed on God and on the power of God's word, and we are encouraged in each of the parables to take hold of his word with all our heart and let it direct our lives. If we do that, says Jesus, wonderful things will happen to our lives; things beyond all our expectations.

* * * * * * *

Points for Reflection:

1: 'If a household is divided against itself, that household can never stand' (Mark 3:25).
Read Jesus' prayer for the unity of his disciples (John 17:20-23), and Paul's statement to the Ephesians (4:1-16). What kind of unity is there in my household? Is it a unity of conformity, or a unity arising out of the free and creative contributions of the people in the house?

2: 'All men's sins will be forgiven' (Mark 3:28). Do I believe that in relation to my own sins? In relation to other people's sins? Do I seriously believe in the possibility of forgiveness?

3: It is not sufficient to eradicate faults (Matthew 12:43-45). Far more important is the task of filling our lives with:

'everything that is true, everything that is noble,
everything that is good and pure, everything that we love and honour
and everything that can be thought virtuous and worthy of praise.'

(Philippians 4:8)

4: 'Happy are your eyes because they see, your ears because they hear' (Matthew 13:16).

5: 'The worries of this world, the lure of riches and all the other passions come in to choke the word, and so it produces nothing' (Mark 4:19).

6: 'A man's words flow out of what fills the heart' (Matthew 12:34).

7: 'Anyone who does the will of God, that person is my brother and sister and mother' (Mark 3:35).

Chapter 4
No circumstances can withstand the powerful word of God

Mark 4:35 — 6:6
Matthew 13:53-58
Luke 8:22-56

a: No environment can withstand the powerful word of God

MARK 4:35-41 (Compare Luke 8:22-25)

35 With the coming of evening that same day, he said to them, 'Let us cross over
36 to the other side'. •And leaving the crowd behind they took him, just as he was,
37 in the boat; and there were other boats with him. •Then it began to blow a gale
38 and the waves were breaking into the boat so that it was almost swamped. •But
39 he was in the stern, his head on the cushion, asleep. •They woke him and said
to him, 'Master, do you not care? We are going down!' And he woke up and
rebuked the wind and said to the sea, 'Quiet now! Be calm!' And the wind
40 dropped, and all was calm again. •Then he said to them, 'Why are you so
41 frightened? How is it that you have no faith?' •They were filled with awe and said
to one another, 'Who can this be? Even the wind and the sea obey him.'

(Compare Matthew 8:23-27 page 101-102)

The parables we have just studied speak of the power of God's word. Mark illustrates this power in this and the following two scenes.

Our interest is not in the precise nature of what happened on the lake. It is in why Mark chooses to relate the incident here, and the basic themes it illustrates for him.

Water is a symbol of chaos, and so of resistance to the creative order of God's action in the world. We see this in the creation myth (cf Genesis 1:2, 6-8) and in the flood myth (Genesis chapters 6-9). The latter speaks of the sin of man all but resulting in a collapse of world-order and the return of primitive chaos. It was the virtue of one man, Noah, that saved the world.

Man's fragile existence is under constant threat from the powers of evil. The disciples of Jesus are no exception. The lake symbolises the forces that constantly threaten our life. The disciples cannot rise above the swirling waters by their own power. They cry out in prayer, but Jesus is 'asleep' (4:38). How often God seems silent! The disciples lose heart. But the action of Jesus demonstrates to them that

God is still with them, and his word stills the roaring of the waves. The anecdote expresses the faith of Mark's church in the presence of the Risen Christ in a church suffering persecution.

Notice that Jesus does not contrast faith with doubt, but with fear (4:40). There is a doubt that is compatible with faith; a doubt that rises from a humble mind which recognises the limits of its own perceptions. This kind of doubt is essential, for it is the knife-edge of the mind seeking deeper insight. Such doubt is accompanied by wonder and emerges from a mind that is bravely open to the mystery of life.

There is another kind of doubt, a doubt that feeds on fear. This is the doubt of a small-mind, a self-centred doubt, a doubt that leads to cynicism and despair. It is as though a person expects to be able to understand everything, and the realisation that this is not the case produces insecurity and fear. Again and again in the Gospels we hear Jesus saying: 'Do not be afraid'. It is fear that makes us slaves, whether to the vagaries of our own fickle feelings, or to those who would enslave us. The episode on the lake is telling us not to be afraid, whatever the circumstances, because Jesus, though silent, is in the boat with us. In the words of Paul:

> 'No circumstance can ever come between us and the love of God made visible in Christ Jesus our Lord'.
>
> *(Romans 8:39)*

b: No 'spiritual' powers can withstand the powerful word of God

MARK 5:1-20 (Compare Luke 8:26-39)

$\frac{1}{2}$ 5 They reached the country of the Gerasenes on the other side of the lake, •and no sooner had he left the boat than a man with an unclean spirit came out
3 from the tombs towards him. •The man lived in the tombs and no one could
4 secure him any more, even with a chain; •because he had often been secured with fetters and chains but had snapped the chains and broken the fetters, and no
5 one had the strength to control him. •All night and all day, among the tombs
6 and in the mountains, he would howl and gash himself with stones. •Catching
7 sight of Jesus from a distance, he ran up and fell at his feet •and shouted at the top of his voice, 'What do you want with me, Jesus, son of the Most High God?
8 Swear by God you will not torture me!' •—For Jesus had been saying to him,
9 'Come out of the man, unclean spirit'. •'What is your name?' Jesus asked. 'My
10 name is legion,' he answered 'for there are many of us.' •And he begged him
11 earnestly not to send them out of the district. •Now there was there on the
12 mountainside a great herd of pigs feeding, •and the unclean spirits begged
13 him, 'Send us to the pigs, let us go into them'. •So he gave them leave. With that, the unclean spirits came out and went into the pigs, and the herd of about two thousand pigs charged down the cliff into the lake, and there they were drowned.
14 The swineherds ran off and told their story in the town and in the country round
15 about; and the people came to see what had really happened. •They came to Jesus and saw the demoniac sitting there, clothed and in his full senses—the very
16 man who had had the legion in him before—and they were afraid. •And those who had witnessed it reported what had happened to the demoniac and what had
17 become of the pigs. •Then they began to implore Jesus to leave the neighbourhood.
18 As he was getting into the boat, the man who had been possessed begged to be

allowed to stay with him. •Jesus would not let him but said to him, 'Go home 19 to your people and tell them all that the Lord in his mercy has done for you'. So the man went off and proceeded to spread throughout the Decapolis all that 20 Jesus had done for him. And everyone was amazed.

(Compare Matthew 8:28-34 page 102)

Just as we should not be afraid whatever physical circumstances may appear to threaten our life, so we should not fear the strange, demonic powers that evil seems to have over our mind. Nothing can resist the love of God manifest in the powerful, healing word of Jesus.

This episode occurred by the lake. Gerasa was one of the Greek cities making up the district of the Decapolis. In fact it was fifty kilometres from the lake. Matthew locates the episode at Gadara, a town bordering the lake (cf Matthew 8:28).

The scene takes place among the tombs. Everything speaks of death. Centre-stage is an idiot. The awful meaninglessness of his world has broken his mind. He desperately needs deep healing. His fellow Gerasenes cannot cope with him. They try to bind him and lock him away. But he cannot be contained (5:4-5).

Then Jesus enters his world, and, with him, the power of God. The idiot, sensing the possibility of healing but also the demands this would place upon him, runs up to Jesus, but is afraid of what Jesus might do. He is unable to answer Jesus' direct question: 'What is your name?' (5:9). He is many people; he is a constant prey to the vagaries of his uncontrolled mind. All he can say is: 'My name is legion' (5:9).

Jesus healed the man; healed him by his presence and the peace and security and love that emanated from him. Jesus gave meaning to his meaningless world. Jesus gave the man to himself and the Gerasenes 'saw the demoniac sitting there, clothed and in his full senses' (5:15). The dramatic description of the expulsion of the demons and the flight of the pigs into the lake has elements of popular legend about it, and may, some scholars suggest, be an embellishment from local Jewish legendary material. Behind the embellishments is a simple story of Jesus bringing healing and peace to a broken man. It is another miracle of love, illustrating the words of God through Isaiah:

'Do not be afraid, for I have redeemed you;
I have called you by your name, you are mine.'

(Isaiah 43:1)

The effect on the others is instructive. They came to see what 'really happened' (5:14) but they were 'afraid' (5:15). Jesus has upset their comfortable world. They implore him to go away (5:16). The idiot is the only one to respond truthfully to the presence of God. We are told that he 'begged to be allowed to stay with Jesus' (5:18).

The man wanted to follow Jesus and no doubt Jesus would have responded warmly to his desire. But the truly needy ones in the story are the other Gerasenes. They too were living in a world of tombs; but, unlike the demoniac, they did not realise it. They were sane because they had not even asked the questions that had tormented this man. They did not want to run the risk of having their world disturbed, either by the idiot or by Jesus. Seeing their need,

Jesus asks this man to forego the pleasure of the company of the disciples and to go back to his own people to 'tell them all that the Lord in his mercy has done for you' (5:19), that is, 'what really happened' (5:14).

The episode illustrates powerfully that whatever powers the forces of evil may have, they cannot withstand the word of God. We are reminded of the psalmist:

'God gives the lonely a permanent house;
makes prisoners happy by setting them free;
but rebels must live in an arid land.'

(Psalm 68:6)

c: **Sickness and death cannot withstand the powerful word of God**

MARK 5:21-43 (Compare Luke 8:40-56)
When Jesus had crossed again in the boat to the other side, a large crowd 21 gathered round him and he stayed by the lakeside. •Then one of the synagogue 22 officials came up, Jairus by name, and seeing him, fell at his feet •and pleaded 23 with him earnestly, saying, 'My little daughter is desperately sick. Do come and lay your hands on her to make her better and save her life.' •Jesus went with him 24 and a large crowd followed him; they were pressing all round him.

Now there was a woman who had suffered from a haemorrhage for 25 twelve years; •after long and painful treatment under various doctors, she had 26 spent all she had without being any the better for it, in fact, she was getting worse. •She had heard about Jesus, and she came up behind him through the crowd 27 and touched his cloak. •'If I can touch even his clothes,' she had told herself 28 'I shall be well again.' •And the source of the bleeding dried up instantly, and she 29 felt in herself that she was cured of her complaint. •Immediately aware that 30 power had gone out from him, Jesus turned round in the crowd and said, 'Who touched my clothes?' •His disciples said to him, 'You see how the crowd is 31 pressing round you and yet you say, "Who touched me?" ' •But he continued 32 to look all round to see who had done it. •Then the woman came forward, 33 frightened and trembling because she knew what had happened to her, and she fell at his feet and told him the whole truth. •'My daughter,' he said 'your faith 34 has restored you to health; go in peace and be free from your complaint.'

While he was still speaking some people arrived from the house of the 35 synagogue official to say, 'Your daughter is dead: why put the Master to any further trouble?' •But Jesus had overheard this remark of theirs and he said to 36 the official, 'Do not be afraid; only have faith'. •And he allowed no one to go 37 with him except Peter and James and John the brother of James. •So they came 38 to the official's house and Jesus noticed all the commotion, with people weeping and wailing unrestrainedly. •He went in and said to them, 'Why all this 39 commotion and crying? The child is not dead, but asleep.' •But they laughed 40 at him. So he turned them all out and, taking with him the child's father and mother and his own companions, he went into the place where the child lay. And taking the child by the hand he said to her, 'Talitha, kum!' which means, 41 'Little girl, I tell you to get up'. •The little girl got up at once and began to walk 42 about, for she was twelve years old. At this they were overcome with astonishment, and he ordered them strictly not to let anyone know about it, and told them 43 to give her something to eat.

(Compare Matthew 9:18-26 pages 113-114)

Here we see Jesus face and overcome what was considered the ultimate expression of the power of evil: death. But first the episode with the haemorrhaging woman stresses that the healing power of Jesus is a special power that is effective in response to faith (5:34). The woman's disease made her ritually unclean and she is ashamed. Jesus however senses her yearning for a deeper contact (5:30, 32). His gentleness in seeking her out encourages her to speak about herself in front of the whole crowd (5:33) and she experiences a deeper healing — the healing of 'peace' (5:34).

Jesus' gentleness is evident in the anecdote about Jairus' daughter, in the way he treats her parents (5:40) and in the final simple consideration he pays to the girl's hunger. There is something ultimate about Jesus' action here, and only the chosen three are invited to witness it (5:37 compare Mark 9:2 and 14:33). It is proof that not even death can separate us from the love of God. The raising of this girl is a sign of an even greater power that God will, we believe, exercise for us. When our turn comes to die, no miracle, presumably, will occur to restore us to this life. But we are asked to believe that God has the power to take us through death to eternal life. If death carries no fears for us, we have nothing to fear. (For further commentary the reader is referred to Luke 7:11-17, page 162).

Lack of faith is the only barrier to God's powerful word

MARK 6:1-6 (Compare Matthew 13:53-58)

6 Going from that district, he went to his home town and his disciples accompa- 1 nied him. •With the coming of the sabbath he began teaching in the synagogue 2 and most of them were astonished when they heard him. They said, 'Where did the man get all this? What is this wisdom that has been granted him, and these miracles that are worked through him? •This is the carpenter, surely, the son 3 of Mary, the brother of James and Joset and Jude and Simon? His sisters, too, are they not here with us?' And they would not accept him. •And Jesus said to them, 4 'A prophet is only despised in his own country, among his own relations and in his own house'; •and he could work no miracle there, though he cured a few 5 sick people by laying his hands on them. •He was amazed at their lack of faith. 6

(Compare Luke 4:16-30 page 73)

This scene concludes the second part of the section dealing with the early ministry of Jesus. The first part dealt with the healing and liberating word of Jesus; it concluded with a scene in which the religious leaders rejected his word (Mark 3:1-6). This part has been dealing with the power of God's word. Once again the concluding scene is one of rejection: the ordinary people reject Jesus.

It is important to notice the reason for their rejection. It is not because he is a wonder-worker. It is because he is so 'ordinary'. This is the tragedy. God's love came so close to man; God, in Jesus, entered the human condition intimately. Yet man, afraid of the demands of a religion that enters every sphere of his activity and demands everything of him, was not willing to take the risk and journey with Jesus to the Father.

The parables and the scenes we have just been reading have all illustrated the power of God. Yet God's power cannot effect anything when faced with man's lack of faith (6:5). For God's power is as powerful and as weak as love. He cannot force himself, because of his respect for our freedom.

'He could work no miracle there ...
He was amazed at their lack of faith.' (6:6)

* * * * * * * *

Points for Reflection:

1: When the disciples saw that their boat was almost swamped, they woke Jesus with the question: 'do you not care?'. Rather a strange question to ask Jesus. Those invited to the wedding did not care (cf Matthew 22:5), the religious leaders did not care for their flock (cf John 10:13); Judas did not care for the poor (cf John 12:6). But it must have been obvious from everything Jesus said and did that he cared. No wonder he accuses them of lack of faith (Mark 4:40). Do I believe, even when adverse circumstances threaten me, that God cares for me?

2: Like the man from the country of the Gerasenes, I, too, can find my identity through contact with Jesus (cf Mark 5:9 and 5:15). It is in contemplation of Jesus that I can find my true self, the often 'hidden self' that Paul prays will grow strong (cf Ephesians 3:16).

3: We are called to do the will of God. The demoniac 'begged to be allowed to stay with him' (Mark 5:18). He was, however, instructed to go home to his people: 'Tell them all that the Lord in his mercy has done for you' (Mark 5:19). Our own desires are only to be followed when they have been tested in prayer, and after a deep listening to discover the will of God.

4: God wants us to live to the full. The physical cure (for example, of the woman with the haemorrhage) is part of this; but it is in view of, and often a statement of, a deeper healing. Jesus draws the woman into dialogue with him to share with her this deeper healing and offer her his 'peace' (Mark 5:34).

Part 3
The Good News:
By a Miracle of Grace, we are
able to Hear and Perceive the
'·'ord of God

Chapter 1
The word of God continues to spread, in spite of growing opposition

Mark 6:6-31
Matthew 14:1-12
Luke 9:1-9

a: The mission of the Twelve

MARK 6:6-13 (Compare Luke 9:1-6)

7   He made a tour round the villages, teaching. •Then he summoned the Twelve
     and began to send them out in pairs giving them authority over the unclean spirits.
8   And he instructed them to take nothing for the journey except a staff —no bread,
9   no haversack, no coppers for their purses. •They were to wear sandals but, he
10   added, 'Do not take a spare tunic'. •And he said to them, 'If you enter a house
11   anywhere, stay there until you leave the district. •And if any place does not
     welcome you and people refuse to listen to you, as you walk away shake off
12   the dust from under your feet as a sign to them.' •So they set off to preach
13   repentance; •and they cast out many devils, and anointed many sick people with
     oil and cured them.   *(Compare Matthew 10:1, 9-14 page 115-116, also Luke 10:1-12 page 272)*

Like the beginning of Section One (Mark 1:14-15) and Section Two (Mark
3:7-12), this Section opens with a summary statement of Jesus' teaching (Mark
6:6). Like the beginning of Section Two (Mark 3:13-15) it illustrates the fact that
opposition does not curtail God's word but leads to its spread. Jesus is rejected by
his own townsfolk (6:3), so he spreads his mission to the surrounding villages
(6:6), and sends his disciples even further afield (6:7).

Mention of the staff (Mark 6:8) reminds us of the staff of Moses, the symbol
of the authority of God with which he effected God's will. The staff gave Moses
miraculous powers (cf Exodus 4:2-31). With it he brought about the plagues of
Egypt, confounding the magicians and rulers of Egypt (cf Exodus 7:15, 8:15,
10:13). With the staff Moses divided the Sea of Reeds (cf Exodus 14:16) and
struck the rock in the wilderness (cf Exodus 17:5). The Twelve are to share in the
power of God over evil.

They are to take no bread, no haversack (food pouch). They are to place their
trust in God who will care for them as he cared for the people in the desert when
he fed them with manna from heaven.

They are not to touch money, for they are to be poor as Jesus was poor and rely on the providence of the one who is sending them on their mission. For the same reason they are not to take a spare tunic.

They are to wear sandals, like the people of God who were preparing for a journey (cf Exodus 12:11). For they are to go from village to village, as Jesus was doing (cf Mark 1:38), telling the Good News.

They are to accept nothing from a village that does not listen to their message, and from others they are to accept only what hospitality requires of them. Their mission is an urgent one, so they are to keep on the move.

It is obviously the spirit rather than the details of this instruction that are important. Jesus was not issuing instructions after the manner of the Pharisees. This becomes obvious when we compare Mark's account with Matthew's or Luke's. Both these latter have Jesus instructing the disciples not to take a staff (Matthew 10:10, Luke 9:3) or sandals (Matthew 10:10, Luke 10:4). In the Mishna (a collection of Rabbinical opinions dating from about 200 A.D.), a Jew is forbidden to enter the Temple with a staff, sandals or begging wallet. It is possible that this was the practice at the time Matthew was writing. By excluding the sandals and staff, Matthew may be underlining the fact that the task of a missionary is a sacred one. He should enter people's lives as he would enter the Temple.

b: **The death of the Baptist**

MARK 6:14-29 (compare Matthew 14:1-12 and Luke 9:7-9)

14   Meanwhile King Herod had heard about him, since by now his name was well-known. Some were saying, 'John the Baptist has risen from the dead, and that
15 is why miraculous powers are at work in him'. •Others said, 'He is Elijah';
16 others again, 'He is a prophet, like the prophets we used to have'. •But when Herod heard this he said, 'It is John whose head I cut off; he has risen from the dead'.
17   Now it was this same Herod who had sent to have John arrested, and had him chained up in prison because of Herodias, his brother Philip's wife whom he
18 had married. •For John had told Herod, 'It is against the law for you to have
19 your brother's wife'. •As for Herodias, she was furious with him and wanted to
20 kill him; but she was not able to, •because Herod was afraid of John, knowing him to be a good and holy man, and gave him his protection. When he had heard him speak he was greatly perplexed, and yet he liked to listen to him.
21   An opportunity came on Herod's birthday when he gave a banquet for the nobles of his court, for his army officers and for the leading figures in Galilee.
22 When the daughter of this same Herodias came in and danced, she delighted Herod and his guests; so the king said to the girl, 'Ask me anything you like
23 and I will give it you'. •And he swore her an oath, 'I will give you anything you
24 ask, even half my kingdom'. •She went out and said to her mother, 'What shall
25 I ask for?' She replied, 'The head of John the Baptist'. •The girl hurried straight back to the king and made her request, 'I want you to give me John the Baptist's
26 head, here and now, on a dish'. •The king was deeply distressed but, thinking of the oaths he had sworn and of his guests, he was reluctant to break his word
27 to her. •So the king at once sent one of the bodyguard with orders to bring
28 John's head. •The man went off and beheaded him in prison; then he brought

the head on a dish and gave it to the girl, and the girl gave it to her mother.
29 When John's disciples heard about this, they came and took his body and laid
it in a tomb.

This is a story of intrigue, adultery, evil conscience, and a passion for luxury
that stands out in stark contrast to the life of one of whom Jesus said:

'Of all the children born of woman, a greater than John the Baptist has never been
seen.'   *(Matthew 11:11)*

The murder of the Baptist prepares the reader for the price Jesus will pay for
preaching the 'Good News' in a violent and unscrupulous world (cf Mark 3:6).

The Jewish mind had always conceded that Yahweh had the power to bring
someone back from Sheol (cf 1 Samuel 2:6). John was so close to God that the
popular mind could easily believe that God would avenge his murder in a special
way. Herod's guilty conscience, too, is prey to this fear (6:14-16). We have
already examined the legend that Elijah would return and inaugurate the
Messianic Age (cf commentary on Matthew 11:14).

*   *   *   *   *   *   *   *

Matthew is somewhat harder on Herod than Mark. He omits Mark 6:19-20
and adds the following statement:

'Herod had wanted to kill John, but was afraid of the people who regarded John as a
prophet.'   *(Matthew 14:5)*

Matthew concludes his account by mentioning that John's disciples went off
to tell Jesus about the murder (Matthew 14:12 page 120).

*   *   *   *   *   *   *   *

Luke omits the scene in the banquet hall. He has already made brief mention
of Herodias (Luke 3:19-20). Here he simply mentions Herod and Jesus,
mentioning that Herod was:

'anxious to see him.'   *(Luke 9:9)*

This is to prepare the reader for the meeting at the time of the Passion, a meeting
which Luke alone mentions (cf Luke 23:8-12).

*   *   *   *   *   *   *   *

c: **The return of the Twelve**

MARK 6:30-31
30   The apostles rejoined Jesus and told him all they had done and taught.
31 Then he said to them, 'You must come away to some lonely place all by yourselves
and rest for a while'; for there were so many coming and going that the apostles
32 had no time even to eat.

It may be of interest that this is the one occasion when Mark explicitly relates
the word 'apostle' (6:30) to the 'Twelve' (6:7). Matthew omits this brief section
because he has not mentioned the mission in this context.

*   *   *   *   *   *   *   *

Chapter 2
Only a miracle of grace can bring us to hear and understand the word of God

Mark 6:32 — 7:37
Matthew 14:13 — 15:31
Luke 9:10-17

a: The miracle of the loaves (first account)

MARK 6:32-44 (Compare Matthew 14:13-21, Luke 9:10-17)

•So they went off in a boat to a lonely place where they
33 could be by themselves. •But people saw them going, and many could guess where;
and from every town they all hurried to the place on foot and reached it before
34 them. •So as he stepped ashore he saw a large crowd; and he took pity on them
because they were like sheep without a shepherd, and he set himself to teach them
35 at some length. •By now it was getting very late, and his disciples came up to him
36 and said, 'This is a lonely place and it is getting very late, •so send them away,
and they can go to the farms and villages round about, to buy themselves
37 something to eat'. •He replied, 'Give them something to eat yourselves'. They
answered, 'Are we to go and spend two hundred denarii on bread for them to
38 eat?' •'How many loaves have you?' he asked 'Go and see.' And when they had
39 found out they said, 'Five, and two fish'. •Then he ordered them to get all the
40 people together in groups on the green grass. •and they sat down on the ground
41 in squares of hundreds and fifties. •Then he took the five loaves and the two fish,
raised his eyes to heaven and said the blessing; then he broke the loaves and
handed them to his disciples to distribute among the people. He also shared out
42/43 the two fish among them all. •They all ate as much as they wanted. •They
44 collected twelve basketfuls of scraps of bread and pieces of fish. •Those who had
eaten the loaves numbered five thousand men. *(Compare John 6:1-15 page 209)*

This is one of the most important scenes in Mark's Gospel. It dominates the
rest of this section (Mark 6:32 — 8:26) and illustrates the essence of the Good
News by demonstrating both the power of God's word and the nature of
discipleship.

Before examining Mark's account in detail, let us look at some of the Biblical
themes that are illustrated in the anecdote.

We are reminded of the time that God fed his people with manna in the desert (cf Exodus 16). John develops this theme in his account (cf John 6:22-66).

We are reminded also of the legend concerning the prophet Elijah who was said to have miraculously multiplied the flour and oil belonging to the widow of Zarephath (cf 1 Kings 17:8-16). A similar legend about the prophet Elisha runs as follows:

> 'A man came from Baal-shalishah, bringing the man of God bread from the first-fruits, twenty barley-loaves and fresh grain in the ear. "Give it to the people to eat", Elisha said. But his servant replied, "How can I serve this to a hundred men?". "Give it to the people to eat," he insisted, "for Yahweh says this: 'They will eat and have some left over'." He served them; they ate and had some left over, as Yahweh had said.'
>
> *(2 Kings 4:42-44)*

There is a striking similarity, also, between Mark 6:41 and Mark's account of the Last Supper:

> 'He took some bread
> and when he had said the blessing,
> he broke it
> and gave it to them.'
>
> *(Mark 14:22)*

Mark seems to be consciously alluding to this and wanting his readers to listen to the miracle of the loaves in the light of their experience of the 'Breaking of Bread'. On the first day of each week the early Christians would gather as a community and break bread together. In this way they were re-membering and re-presenting the dying of Jesus and his giving his life to nourish theirs (cf Acts 2:42, 5:46, 20:7, 20:11, 27:35 and 1 Corinthians 11:23-33).

It is against this background that Mark writes his account. Once again it is Jesus the 'teacher' whom we are watching (Mark 6:34). The people are hungry and the disciples suggest that Jesus 'send them away' (6:36) so that they can obtain food. Jesus' teaching always focuses attention on the need for 'repentance' (Mark 1:15), for a new outlook on life, a new attitude to it. This is illustrated here by his rejoinder: 'Give them something to eat yourselves!' (6:36). The disciples do not understand; but Jesus insists: 'How many loaves have you?' (6:37). They had not thought to examine their own resources; they had taken it for granted that they were unable to meet the need of the crowd. When they look around their assumptions seem to be confirmed: they have only five loaves and two fish (6:38). Then Jesus teaches them.

Jesus asks them to place their resources in his hands. Jesus prays to his Father, and, in his hands, the loaves and fish are multiplied, and more than meet the requirements of the hungry crowd. Jesus is telling them that their lives, their gifts, their resources are, by the power of God, transformed in his hands. It is God's power that feeds the people; but the disciples can be instruments of that power, can channel that nourishing grace, if they give themselves to Jesus.

This has been the central message of the parables. The disciple sows God's seed and its power is such that it will achieve results well beyond his expectations. The task of the disciple is simply to do the will of God (Mark 3:35), however impossible it may seem.

The anecdote captures something of the effect Jesus had on his disciples. How often he fed them, just by his presence and his words. He was God's manna for them, nourishing the hunger and thirst of their hearts.

There are close parallels with Luke's account of the miraculous catch of fish (Luke 5:1-11). The disciples did, in fact, work wonders well beyond their own talents. The story of the early Church is proof of this.

Nothing is impossible to God. Our talents, our time, our hands, our hearts, our love, our acts of service can bring sustenance to a hungry world. We do not need to 'send them away'. We do need to unite ourselves to Jesus and be caught up in his prayer to his Father. We need to believe the Good News and be open to what God may choose to do through us.

* * * * * * * *

Note on Luke:

Luke follows this scene immediately with the scene at Caesarea Philippi, thus omitting Mark 6:45-8:26 (the rest of this Section). We shall see that one half of this section (Mark 8:1-26) duplicates the other half. This serves Mark's purpose well, but not Luke's. One of the main themes of the omitted section is the failure of the disciples to understand Jesus; this is not a theme Luke develops. Perhaps the main reason for Luke's omission of this section is the fact that it includes anecdotes relating Jesus' mission to Gentiles (Mark 7:24-37). Luke prefers to keep the mission to the Gentiles for after the death of Jesus.

* * * * * * * *

b: **The disciples fail to grasp the meaning of the miracle of the loaves**

MARK 6:45-52 (Compare Matthew 14:22-27)

Directly after this he made his disciples get into the boat and go on ahead to 45 Bethsaida, while he himself sent the crowd away. •After saying good-bye to 46 them he went off into the hills to pray. •When evening came, the boat was far out 47 on the lake, and he was alone on the land. •He could see they were worn out 48 with rowing, for the wind was against them; and about the fourth watch of the night he came towards them, walking on the lake. He was going to pass them by, but when they saw him walking on the lake they thought it was a ghost and cried 49 out; •for they had all seen him and were terrified. But he at once spoke to them, 50 and said, 'Courage! It is I! Do not be afraid.' •Then he got into the boat with them, 51 and the wind dropped. They were utterly and completely dumbfounded, •because 52 they had not seen what the miracle of the loaves meant; their minds were closed.

(Compare John 6:16-21 page 210)

This is reminiscent of the earlier scene in which the disciples faced the raging of the waters while Jesus was asleep in the boat (cf Mark 4:35-41). This time Jesus is, to all appearances, absent. He is with his Father (Mark 6:46).

Just as the giving of manna in the desert is linked with the crossing of the Sea of Reeds (Exodus 14:15-31), so Mark explicitly (6:52) links the crossing of the water with the miracle of the loaves. If we are to journey to the Promised Land we will have to walk with God upon the waters (Job 9:8, 38:16; Ecclesiasticus 24:6). We can do it, even when Jesus is apparently absent).

Jesus is able to walk on the water because of his union with his Father. He is able, that is, to master the chaos surrounding him. The disciples are gripped by fear and anxiety and near-despair. Jesus can rise above all this by the power of God. This was the message of the miracle of the loaves, a message they had not understood (Mark 6:52). They, too, if they had enough faith in God (if they 'went off to the hills to pray'), could walk on water, could cope with impossible situations. They should not lose 'courage' (6:50), nor 'be afraid' (6:50).

We are reminded of a number of texts from the Old Testament:

'Do not be afraid, for I have redeemed you;
I have called you by your name, you are mine.
Should you pass through the sea, I will be with you.'

(Isaiah 43:1)

'Give thanks to Yahweh, for he is good,
his love is everlasting . . .
Some had lost their way in the wilds and the desert,
not knowing how to reach an inhabited town;
they were hungry and desperately thirsty,
their courage was running low.
Then they called to Yahweh in their trouble
and he rescued them from their sufferings . . .
Let these thank Yahweh for his love,
for his marvels on behalf of men;
satisfying the hungry,
he fills the starving with good things . . .
Others, taking ship and going to sea,
were plying their business across the ocean;
they too saw what Yahweh could do,
what marvels on the deep!
He spoke and raised a gale,
lashing up towering waves.
Flung to the sky, then plunged to the depths,
they lost their nerve in the ordeal,
staggering and reeling like drunkards
with all their seamanship adrift.
Then they called to Yahweh in their trouble
and he rescued them from their sufferings,
reducing the storm to a whisper
until the waves grew quiet,
bringing them, glad at the calm,
safe to the port they were bound for.'

(Psalm 107:1, 4-9, 23-30)

Similar themes are found in a triumphant song from Isaiah:

'Clothe yourself in strength, arm of Yahweh . . .
Did you not dry up the sea,
the waters of the great Abyss,
to make the sea-bed a road
for the redeemed to cross? . . .

The captive is soon to be set free; he will not die in a deep
dungeon nor will his bread run out.
I am Yahweh your God who stirs the sea, making its waves roar.'

(Isaiah 51:9-10, 14-15)

Mark tells us that Jesus 'was going to pass them by' (Mark 6:48) — an
expression used by Luke of Jesus in the Emmaus account (Luke 24:28). We are
reminded of the fact that God does not force himself upon man; he waits on our
invitation.

'Look, I am standing at the door, knocking. If one of you hears me calling and opens
the door, I will come in to share his meal, side by side with him.'

(Revelations 3:20)

The episode of the walking on the water is used by Mark to illustrate the faith
of his community in the presence of the risen Jesus in their midst and the power
this gave them to withstand opposition and carry out the will of God.

*   *   *   *   *   *   *   *

Matthew has a slightly different sequence from Mark. Jesus' desire to be
alone with his disciples follows directly upon his receiving the news of the
Baptist's murder (Matthew 14:13).

But even with a sorrowful, aching heart at the death of his friend and theirs,
he can still go out to those who need him in their hunger (14:14). Only when the
people are fed does Jesus go into the hills by himself to be with his Father (14:23).
It is a beautiful example of living in the present moment.

Matthew adds the following incident:

MATTHEW 14:28-33

•It was Peter 28
who answered. 'Lord,' he said 'if it is you, tell me to come to you across the water.'
'Come' said Jesus. Then Peter got out of the boat and started walking towards 29
Jesus across the water, •but as soon as he felt the force of the wind, he took fright 30
and began to sink. 'Lord! Save me!' he cried. •Jesus put out his hand at once and 31
held him. 'Man of little faith,' he said 'why did you doubt?' •And as they got into 32
the boat the wind dropped. •The men in the boat bowed down before him and 33
said, 'Truly, you are the Son of God'.

This addition reflects clearly the resurrection faith of the early Church, both
in the address 'Lord' (14:28) and in the final gesture of adoration (14:33). This
passage illustrates once again, the two types of doubt (14:28 and 14:30, cf
commentary on Mark 4:40 page 182).

It emphasises the fact that the disciple, too, can walk on the water, so long as
it is in response to the call of Jesus ('Come' 14:28), and so long as the disciple
keeps his eyes on Jesus, and does not doubt in his heart with that doubt that
engenders fear (14:30-31). The enduring love of Jesus is brought out by the fact
that, even when Peter did take fright in his doubt:

'Jesus put out his hand at once and held him.'

(Matthew 14:31)

We recall the Psalms:

'He sends from on high and takes me,
He draws me from the deep waters.'

(Psalm 18:16)

'Save me, God! The water
is already up to my neck!. . .
I have stepped into deep water
and the waves are washing over me.'

(Psalm 69:1, 3)

'Reach down your hand from above,
save me, rescue me from deep waters.'

(Psalm 144:7)

Whatever the trouble, Jesus is there. Matthew concludes his Gospel on this very note:

'Know that I am with you always; yes, to the end of time.'

(Matthew 28:20)

c: The crowds fail to understand Jesus

MARK 6:53-56 (Compare Matthew 14:34-36)

Having made the crossing, they came to land at Gennesaret and tied up. •No ₅₃ sooner had they stepped out of the boat than people recognised him, •and started ₅₅ hurrying all through the countryside and brought the sick on stretchers to wherever they heard he was. •And wherever he went, to village, or town, or farm, they ₅₆ laid down the sick in the open spaces, begging him to let them touch even the fringe of his cloak. And all those who touched him were cured.

It is not easy to discern Mark's intention in placing this here. Perhaps he wishes to contrast the simple faith of the crowds against the failure of the disciples to understand. Or perhaps he wishes to illustrate the fact that the crowds did not understand Jesus either. For, while there are many 'cures' (6:56), there is no mention of a miracle. The crowds flock to Jesus to get what they can from him. His love cannot refuse them. But do they understand? Do they believe in him? Are they seeking true healing and liberation? Do they want to follow him as disciples?

d: The Pharisees fail to understand Jesus

MARK 7:1-23 (Compare Matthew 15:1-11, 15-20)

7 The Pharisees and some of the scribes who had come from Jerusalem gathered ₁ round him, •and they noticed that some of his disciples were eating with ₂ unclean hands, that is, without washing them. •For the Pharisees, and the Jews ₃ in general, follow the tradition of the elders and never eat without washing their arms as far as the elbow; •and on returning from the market place they never ₄ eat without first sprinkling themselves. There are also many other observances which have been handed down to them concerning the washing of cups and pots and bronze dishes. •So these Pharisees and scribes asked him, 'Why do your ₅ disciples not respect the tradition of the elders but eat their food with unclean hands?' •He answered, 'It was of you hypocrites that Isaiah so rightly prophesied ₆ in this passage of scripture:

> *This people honours me only with lip-service,*
> *while their hearts are far from me.*
> 7 *The worship they offer me is worthless,*
> *the doctrines they teach are only human regulations.*[a]

8
9 You put aside the commandment of God to cling to human traditions.' •And
he said to them, 'How ingeniously you get round the commandment of God
10 in order to preserve your own tradition! •For Moses said: *Do your duty to your*
father and your mother, and, *Anyone who curses father or mother must be put to*
11 *death.* •But you say, "If a man says to his father or mother: Anything I have
12 that I might have used to help you is Corban (that is, dedicated to God), •then
he is forbidden from that moment to do anything for his father or mother".
13 In this way you make God's word null and void for the sake of your tradition
which you have handed down. And you do many other things like this.'
14   He called the people to him again and said, 'Listen to me, all of you, and
15 understand. •Nothing that goes into a man from outside can make him unclean;
16 it is the things that come out of a man that make him unclean. •If anyone has
ears to hear, let him listen to this.'
17   When he had gone back into the house, away from the crowd, his disciples
18 questioned him about the parable. •He said to them, 'Do you not understand
either? Can you not see that whatever goes into a man from outside cannot
19 make him unclean, •because it does not go into his heart but through his stomach
20 and passes out into the sewer?' (Thus he pronounced all foods clean.) •And he
21 went on, 'It is what comes out of a man that makes him unclean. •For it is from
within, from men's hearts, that evil intentions emerge: fornication, theft, murder,
22
23 adultery, •avarice, malice, deceit, indecency, envy, slander, pride, folly. •All these
evil things come from within and make a man unclean.'

(a: Isaiah 29:13)

Jesus is taking a very firm stand against the scribes and the Pharisees. The
conflict has been present since the very beginning of Mark's Gospel when the
scribes objected to Jesus when he forgave a man's sins (cf Mark 2:6), when he ate
with sinners (cf Mark 2:16), and when his disciples picked corn on the sabbath (cf
Mark 2:24). When Jesus challenged them publicly by curing a man in the
synagogue on the sabbath, Mark tells us that:

'the Pharisees went out at once and began to plot with the Herodians against him,
discussing how to destroy him.'

(Mark 3:6)

As part of their strategy they set out to discredit him by saying:

'Beelzebul is in him; it is through the prince of devils that he casts devils out.'

(Mark 3:22)

In the scene before us, Jesus confronts them publicly. Mark takes some
trouble to detail, for his largely Gentile audience, the mentality of the Pharisees
(Mark 7:3-4). They adhere strictly to external observance of the Law; they are
determined to preserve its letter, while indicating very little perception of its spirit
or true purpose.

Jesus points out their hypocrisy (Mark 7:9-12) and refers to Isaiah (Mark
7:6-7 = Isaiah 29:13) to underline the fact that the Pharisees are concerned with
their own human traditions rather than with the will of God (Mark 7:6-9).

His own position is the opposite of theirs and he is determined to make it clear. No other statement in Mark's Gospel is underlined as heavily:

'He called the people to him again and said: "Listen to me, all of you, and understand!".' (7:14)

'If anyone has ears to hear let him listen to this!' (7:16)

And Jesus' attitude is expressed in the words:

'Nothing that goes into a man from the outside can make him unclean; it is the things that come out of a man that make him unclean.'

(Mark 7:15)

In fact the disciples do not understand Jesus (7:17-18), so Jesus repeats and clarifies his position. The list of 'sins' (7:21-22) is typical of the lists current in the Stoic moral handbooks of the time (and found occasionally also in Paul, e.g., Colossians 3:5-9). They are used as examples of the evil intentions that emerge from a man's heart. Jesus is concerned with the intentions of a man's heart, rather than with the meticulous observance of external law.

It is not the external environment that takes God from us, for God is at the heart of everything, even a raging storm (Mark 4:35-41), or the howling of an idiot among the tombs (Mark 5:1-20), or a woman whose sickness brands her as unclean (Mark 5:25-34). God is even at the heart of death (Mark 5:35-43). Nothing that affects a man from the outside can make him unclean. Jesus is not saying that we should not be concerned with our circumstances. He himself challenged injustice wherever he found it. But he knew that circumstances are only changed effectively when there is repentance; that is, when the heart of man is changed. We are reminded of the same recurring theme in Matthew's Sermon on the Mount (Matthew chapter 5-7).

As an aside Mark mentions the subject of 'foods' (7:19). This is a good example of the kind of problem that arose in the communities of the early church which were made up of people from different cultures, some of whom were conditioned to be concerned about externals of eating and drinking. We can find reference to the problem and the practical solutions in the Acts (15:29), and in Paul's First Letter to the Corinthians (Chapters 8-10) and in his Letter to the Church in Rome (Chapter 14). Mark sees in Jesus' statement here the basis for the solutions arrived at by the early Christian communities.

*   *   *   *   *   *   *   *

Matthew adds the following:

MATTHEW 15:12-14
12   Then the disciples came to him and said, 'Do you know that the Pharisees
13 were shocked when they heard what you said?' •He replied, 'Any plant my
14 heavenly Father has not planted will be pulled up by the roots. •Leave them alone. They are blind men leading blind men; and if one blind man leads another, both will fall into a pit.'

Matthew, as always, is careful to distinguish between the Law itself (which was planted by the Father) — a Law which he and the community for which he wrote still followed — and the narrow and blind way in which the Pharisees interpreted and enforced it. The Law was inspired by the Spirit of God and we must pray to understand its spirit.

*   *   *   *   *   *   *   *

e: A stranger, a Gentile woman, understands

MARK 7:24-30

24   He left that place and set out for the territory of Tyre. There he went into a house and did not want anyone to know he was there, but he could not pass
25 unrecognised. •A woman whose little daughter had an unclean spirit heard about
26 him straightaway and came and fell at his feet. •Now the woman was a pagan, by birth a Syrophoenician, and she begged him to cast the devil out of her
27 daughter. •And he said to her, 'The children should be fed first, because it is not
28 fair to take the children's food and throw it to the house-dogs'. •But she spoke up: 'Ah yes, sir,' she replied 'but the house-dogs under the table can eat the
29 children's scraps'. •And he said to her, 'For saying this, you may go home happy:
30 the devil has gone out of your daughter'. •So she went off to her home and found the child lying on the bed and the devil gone.

This scene is meant to surprise the reader. The disciples have failed to understand Jesus (Mark 6:45-52); the crowds, perhaps, have failed to understand what he is really saying to them (Mark 6:53-56); the Pharisees stand in direct opposition to the Good News preached by Jesus (Mark 7:1-23). Suddenly, here is an outsider who has complete and simple trust in his power to save. It seems that Jesus himself is surprised. He is not expecting to carry on his mission at Tyre (7:24) and he, at first, tries to dissuade the woman (7:27).

This last point is more obvious in Matthew's account:

MATTHEW 15:21-28

21
22   Jesus left that place and withdrew to the region of Tyre and Sidon. •Then out came a Canaanite woman from that district and started shouting, 'Sir, Son
23 of David, take pity on me. My daughter is tormented by a devil.' •But he answered her not a word. And his disciples went and pleaded with him. 'Give
24 her what she wants,' they said 'because she is shouting after us.' •He said in
25 reply, 'I was sent only to the lost sheep of the House of Israel'. •But the woman
26 had come up and was kneeling at his feet. 'Lord,' she said 'help me.' •He replied,
27 'It is not fair to take the children's food and throw it to the house-dogs'. •She retorted, 'Ah yes, sir; but even house-dogs can eat the scraps that fall from their
28 master's table'. •Then Jesus answered her, 'Woman, you have great faith. Let your wish be granted.' And from that moment her daughter was well again.

Jesus' primary concern was to do his Father's will. Apparently, he interpreted this as being for him to confine his mission to the Jews (Matthew 15:24 compare Matthew 10:6). However, the woman's faith makes it clear to Jesus that, in her case, an exception is to be made; and he heals her daughter.

This is another example of Jesus' capacity to recognise faith in the most unexpected places, and to respond with unconditional love. He gives in response to her simple plea (15:25) and tested faith (15:26); not, as his disciples would have had it (15:23) to save embarrassment.

f: Hearing comes because of a miracle of grace

MARK 7:31-37

31 Returning from the district of Tyre, he went by way of Sidon towards the Sea
32 of Galilee, right through the Decapolis region. •And they brought him a deaf
man who had an impediment in his speech; and they asked him to lay his hand on
33 him. •He took him aside in private, away from the crowd, put his fingers into the
34 man's ears and touched his tongue with spittle. •Then looking up to heaven he
35 sighed; and he said to him, 'Ephphatha', that is, 'Be opened'. •And his ears were
opened, and the ligament of his tongue was loosened and he spoke clearly.
36 And Jesus ordered them to tell no one about it, but the more he insisted, the
37 more widely they published it. •Their admiration was unbounded. 'He has done
all things well,' they said 'he makes the deaf hear and the dumb speak.'

When speaking his parables, Jesus said:

'Listen, anyone who has ears to hear'

(Mark 4:9)

He had a similar thing to say when he was confronting the Pharisees:

'If anyone has ears to hear, let him listen to this'

(Mark 7:16)

For the most part we have been witnessing the failure of people to hear Jesus, even the failure of his own disciples (Mark 4:13 and 6:52). Now, in this scene, a man, at last, hears Jesus. Once again we are dealing with an outsider, a Gentile. And the hearing comes through a miracle of God's gracious and powerful love.

This is the message Mark wants his readers to hear. In case it is still not clear, Mark duplicates this last section in Mark 8:1-26 (cf the following Chapter), hoping, by repetition, to drive home his point.

Note the physical way in which Jesus works this miracle (Mark 7:33). Jesus is God's word made flesh. His body is holy. God's healing Spirit works through the hands and eyes and heart of Jesus, for we are flesh and blood and we need to see and touch and feel (cf 1 John 1:1).

* * * * * * * *

Jesus lives the Good News

MATTHEW 15:29-31

29 Jesus went on from there and reached the shores of the Sea of Galilee, and
30 he went up into the hills. He sat there, •and large crowds came to him bringing
the lame, the crippled, the blind, the dumb and many others; these they put
31 down at his feet, and he cured them. •The crowds were astonished to see the
dumb speaking, the cripples whole again, the lame walking and the blind with
their sight, and they praised the God of Israel.

Matthew has been following Mark's order, but without the same dramatic aim in mind. Here he omits the miracle of the deaf man and gives a general account of Jesus' healing.

* * * * * * * *

Chapter 3
Only a miracle of grace can bring us to see and understand the word of God

Mark 8:1-30
Matthew 15:32 — 16:20
Luke 9:18-21

a: The Miracle of the Loaves (second account)

MARK 8:1-10 (Compare Matthew 15:32-39)
1 **8** And now once again a great crowd had gathered, and they had nothing to eat.
2 So he called his disciples to him and said to them, •'I feel sorry for all these
people; they have been with me for three days now and have nothing to eat.
3 If I send them off home hungry they will collapse on the way; some have come
4 a great distance.' •His disciples replied, 'Where could anyone get bread to feed
5 these people in a deserted place like this?' •He asked them, 'How many loaves
6 have you?' 'Seven' they said. •Then he instructed the crowd to sit down on the
ground, and he took the seven loaves, and after giving thanks he broke them and
handed them to his disciples to distribute; and they distributed them among the
7 crowd. •They had a few small fish as well, and over these he said a blessing and
8 ordered them to be distributed also. •They ate as much as they wanted, and they
9 collected seven basketfuls of the scraps left over. •Now there had been about four
10 thousand people. He sent them away •and immediately, getting into the boat
with his disciples, went to the region of Dalmanutha.

We seem to be dealing here with another tradition of the event narrated in
Mark 6:32-40. At all events Mark repeats it here to reinforce his message, as is
clear from the structure of this section. We are reminded too of the fact that God
constantly nourishes his people, and of the repeated ritualisation of this in the
Church's celebration of the Eucharist.

b: The Pharisees are obstinate in their refusal to 'see' Jesus

MARK 8:11-13 (Compare Matthew 16:1-4)
11 The Pharisees came up and started a discussion with him; they demanded
12 of him a sign from heaven, to test him. •And with a sigh that came straight from
the heart he said, 'Why does this generation demand a sign? I tell you solemnly,
13 no sign shall be given to this generation.' •And leaving them again and re-em-
barking he went away to the opposite shore.

In spite of Jesus' clear teaching to the Pharisees (cf Mark 7:1-23) here they are demanding that he fit into their preconceptions and satisfy their criteria. Jesus is clearly broken-hearted. Apparently Jesus decided it was pointless to continue trying to break through their stubbornness, for he left them and 'went away to the opposite shore' (8:13). They were free to follow him, of course, but he had to get on with his mission.

Matthew speaks, once again, of the 'sign of Jonah' (16:4 cf 12:38-40 page 171).

* * * * * * * *

c: The disciples still fail to understand

MARK 8:14-21 (Compare Matthew 16:5-11)

The disciples had forgotten to take any food and they had only one loaf with 14 them in the boat. •Then he gave them this warning, 'Keep your eyes open; be 15 on your guard against the yeast of the Pharisees and the yeast of Herod'. •And 16 they said to one another, 'It is because we have no bread'. •And Jesus knew it, 17 and he said to them, 'Why are you talking about having no bread? Do you not yet understand? Have you no perception? Are your minds closed? •Have you 18 *eyes that do not see, ears that do not hear?*[a] Or do you not remember? •When 19 I broke the five loaves among the five thousand, how many baskets full of scraps did you collect?' They answered, 'Twelve'. •'And when I broke the seven loaves 20 for the four thousand, how many baskets full of scraps did you collect?' And they answered, 'Seven'. •Then he said to them, 'Are you still without 21 perception?'

(a: Jeremiah 5:21)

We have just seen the 'yeast of the Pharisees' (Mark 8:31-33, and 7:1-23). The 'yeast of Herod' was clearly illustrated in his murder of the Baptist (Mark 6:14-29). The values these men followed, their attitude to religion, their obstinate pride were, indeed, insidious, and Jesus is warning his disciples against letting them infect their lives.

They misunderstand him, and the topic goes back to 'bread' (8:16). In very strong words, Mark heavily underlines the failure, even of the disciples, to understand Jesus. All their faculties are dulled (8:18) — their understanding, perception, sight, hearing, even their memories.

* * * * * * * *

Matthew alters Mark's conclusion and has the disciples coming to understanding:

MATTHEW 16:12

•Then they understood that he was telling them to be 12 on their guard, not against the yeast for making bread, but against the teaching of the Pharisees and Sadducees.

We are reminded of an earlier alteration made by Matthew. Mark was dwelling on the failure of the disciples to understand Jesus' parables (cf Mark 4:13). Matthew had Jesus praising his Father because of the understanding given to the disciples (cf Matthew 13:16-17). In keeping with this, Matthew omits the following scene and concludes his account of the first part of Jesus' ministry with the above statement. The disciples had come to understand the difference between Jesus and the religious leaders; Jesus is now ready to take them more deeply into the mystery of his person and mission.

*   *   *   *   *   *   *   *

d: Perception comes only through a miracle of grace

MARK 8:22-26

They came to Bethsaida, and some people brought to him a blind man whom 22 they begged him to touch. •He took the blind man by the hand and led him outside 23 the village. Then putting spittle on his eyes and laying his hands on him, he asked, 'Can you see anything?' •The man, who was beginning to see, replied, 'I can see 24 people; they look like trees to me, but they are walking about'. •Then he laid 25 his hands on the man's eyes again and he saw clearly; he was cured, and he could see everything plainly and distinctly. •And Jesus sent him home, saying, 'Do 26 not even go into the village'.

The drama is superb. Jesus has just said: 'Are you still without perception?' (8:21), when a man, symbol of the disciple, enters the stage. He is without perception; and Jesus gives it to him. The parallel between this and the earlier scene of the deaf man (Mark 7:31-37) is obvious.

With this scene Mark concludes his account of the first part of Jesus' ministry. Now, at last, the disciples have come to see Jesus and to listen to his words with understanding. Mark has insisted on the fact that this achievement is an achievement of grace.

The repetition of the miracle of the loaves, the repetition of the failure of the opponents and disciples of Jesus to understand, the repetition of the miracles of healing, dramatise the truth that we will constantly come to see, only to realise that we are still blind; we will constantly hear only to realise that we are still deaf. We need the healing of Jesus repeatedly if we are to grow in understanding of his word.

To be a disciple of Jesus is to embark upon a journey, following Jesus; a journey that will take us all our life, and a journey that will demand constant repentance, constant vigilance and constant surprise. The one thing we can be sure of is that God will endure in his love: he will feed us, again and again. He will repeat his call, and he cannot resist our cry for help.

*   *   *   *   *   *   *   *

4: Caesarea Philippi: Jesus is acknowledged as the Messiah

MARK 8:27-30 (Compare Matthew 16:13-16, 20 and Luke 9:18-21)

Jesus and his disciples left for the villages round Caesarea Philippi. On the 27 way he put this question to his disciples, 'Who do people say I am?' •And they 28 told him. 'John the Baptist,' they said 'others Elijah; others again, one of the

prophets.' •'But you,' he asked 'who do you say I am?' Peter spoke up and said 29
to him, 'You are the Christ'. •And he gave them strict orders not to tell anyone 30
about him.

For centuries the Jews had looked forward to the coming of 'the Christ', the
anointed king who would bring about the reign of God's love, the fulfilment of all
God's promises, the conquering of evil and the final manifestation of the glory of
God over the entire world. Jesus was an unlikely candidate: the religious leaders
rejected him as a law-breaker and a blasphemer (Mark 3:1-6); his own relatives
were unconvinced (Mark 3:21 and John 7:2-8); the people from his native town
did not believe in him (Mark 6:1-6); even the Baptist, it seems (Matthew 11:2-3)
had his doubts.

The scene at Caesarea Philippi is the turning point of Jesus' public ministry
in each of the Synoptic Gospels. At last, one man, Peter, accepts Jesus, just as he
is, as 'the Christ' (Mark 8:29). Peter is accepting the Jesus he knew as the
fulfilment of all the hopes and aspirations of his people. The crowds are not ready
to grasp this yet — hence the instruction 'not to tell anyone'; but we will notice a
definite change in Jesus' teaching of his disciples. After Caesarea Philippi he
begins to introduce them to the heart of his mission, and to the central values he
wants them to live by, as his disciples. Peter has accepted the basic fact — that
Jesus is the one sent by God and anointed for the task of effecting the kingdom of
God on earth. Jesus now has to bring home to him and his friends the
implications of this, in his own life and in theirs.

Matthew adds the following:

MATTHEW 16:16-19

•Then Simon Peter spoke
up, 'You are the Christ,' he said 'the Son of the living God'. •Jesus replied, 17
'Simon son of Jonah, you are a happy man! Because it was not flesh and blood
that revealed this to you but my Father in heaven. •So I now say to you: You 18
are Peter and on this rock I will build my Church. And the gates of the underworld can never hold out against it. •I will give you the keys of the kingdom 19
of heaven: whatever you bind on earth shall be considered bound in heaven;
whatever you loose on earth shall be considered loosed in heaven.'

Matthew enlarges Peter's statement with the addition of the words: 'the Son
of the living God' (16:16). Like his earlier addition to the scene of the walking on
the water (Matthew 14:33 compare Mark 6:52), this is an expression of the faith
of the post-resurrection community, which, in the light of the resurrection of
Jesus, penetrated more deeply into the intimate relationship between Jesus and
God, his Father.

Jesus' reply reminds us of an earlier statement in Matthew:

'Jesus exclaimed: I bless you, Father, Lord of heaven and earth, for hiding these
things from the learned and the clever and revealing them to mere children. Yes,
Father, for that is what it pleased you to do. Everything has been entrusted to me by
my Father; and no one knows the Son except the Father, just as no one knows the
Father except the Son and those to whom the Son chooses to reveal him.'

(Matthew 11:25-27)

Jesus recognises in Peter's statement a special grace and revelation from his
Father. He sees Peter as the first in a long line of disciples. In fact, upon the death

of Jesus, it was Peter who took the place of Jesus as the leader of the community, or church (Greek 'ekklesia' 16:18). This is the first time the word 'Church' has appeared in the Gospels. The Greek word 'ekklesia' was used in the Septuagint translation of the Hebrew Bible for the 'People-of-God-assembled-in-response-to-God's-call'. By the time Matthew was writing, the Christians had been expelled from the synagogue and had to assemble independently. They came to see themselves as the new assembly ('church') of God.

Matthew sees in the event at Caesarea Philippi the beginnings of the special place Peter was to hold in the church. Ultimately, of course, the only foundation of the church is Jesus himself. Paul writes:

'For the foundation, nobody can lay any other than the one which has already been laid, that is Jesus Christ.'

(1 Corinthians 3:11)

Peter tells us that Jesus is the 'living stone'; at the same time, he advises the disciples to set themselves close to him:

'so that you too . . . may be living stones making a spiritual house.'

(1 Peter 2:4-5)

Paul tells the church in Ephesus:

'You are part of the building that has the apostles and prophets for its foundations, and Christ Jesus himself for its main corner-stone.'

(Ephesians 2:20)

Peter (Greek 'Petros') is the first disciple, the first stone laid by Jesus in the foundations of the church. He is the rock (Greek 'petra') on which Jesus will build his community.

We have already witnessed the power of God defeating the forces of evil (cf especially Jesus' miracles). Jesus commissions his disciples for the same task (cf Matthew 10:1). They are to storm the city of the world, held by the forces of evil, and break down its gates, bringing life and liberation to the world. Death itself ('the underworld' Matthew 16:18) cannot hold out against the community called together by God and founded on Peter and his friends.

By virtue of their office, the synagogue officials exercised certain legal powers over the synagogue. They could excommunicate or free from excommunication; they could forbid or allow certain practices. The technical term used by the rabbis for this power was 'binding and loosing'. Peter is being invested with the same authority in the new synagogue, the church.

* * * * * * * *

Luke places the scene at Caesarea Philippi in the context of Jesus' prayer:

LUKE 9:18
18 Now one day when he was praying alone in the presence of his disciples he
19 put this question to them, 'Who do the crowds say I am?'

* * * * * * * *

Points for Reflection:

1: The disciple is not meant simply to admire Jesus. If he really believes in what Jesus said and did, he must also share in Jesus' mission (Mark 6:6-13).

2: 'You must come away to some lonely place all by yourselves and rest for a while' (Mark 6:31).

Am I so indispensable that I can never do this? Is there no time in the year when I can arrange it? Is there no time in the day when I can take time and go into that silent place and experience his presence? Or is it a matter of priorities? Is it a matter of false assumptions I have about the importance of what I am doing? If I am not doing the will of God, what I am doing is of no value to anyone, however distracted, however 'busy' (full of 'business') my day may be.

3: There are many examples of the miracle of the loaves in our own day. There is the example of Mother Theresa of Calcutta. She had only 'five loaves and two fish'; she had only one pair of hands, one heart, a little time, a little courage and a little love. But she placed these gifts in the hands of Christ, and she gave them to the dying. Then came the miracle. She 'fed five thousand'. Thousands benefited from her love. Others joined her and a movement of love was born. There is the example of the Cheshire Homes. There is the example of Abbe Pierre. The list is too long to produce. It is true that if I look at my resources and give them in faith, hope and love, I can work miracles too. Jesus said that his disciples would perform even greater works that he performed (cf John 14:12).

4: How do I respond when Jesus tells me to come to him across the waters? (Matthew 14:29). Do I share Peter's courage or do I not get out of the boat? Assuming I start, what do I do when I grow afraid and begin to sink? Do I, like Peter, call out to God? Or do I rationalise my position and try to pretend I am doing quite well?

5: Do I put aside the commandment of God (the commandment of love) to cling to human traditions, church customs, learned responses, other people's expectations, my own security, formed habits? (Mark 7:8)

6: 'Whatever goes into a man from the outside cannot make him unclean' (Mark 7:18). Yet how often I blame my circumstances for the way I am!

7: Be the deaf man with the impediment in his speech (Mark 7:32). Be the blind man (Mark 8:22). Ask Jesus to break open your deafness so that you can hear God's word to you; to loosen your tongue that you may speak his love to others; to heal your blindness so that you can see as God meant you to see.

8: 'You, who do you say I am?' (Mark 8:29). The question is not: what do your parents say? It is not: what are you expected to say? It is not: what would you like to say? The question penetrates deeply into our hearts and tests our commitment. As with any living relationship, we will not be able to give the same answer each time the question is asked. The main thing is that the question cannot be avoided. If, like Peter, I can say that he is the answer to all my dreams, that he is the one who expresses my ideals, that he is the one who teaches me about love and about life and about freedom, and about prayer, and about compassion and gentleness and humility and integrity; if I can say that, I too am a man blessed by God.

BOOK 3

Who is Jesus?

FOREWORD

Book 3 is entirely devoted to John. John does not have the scene at Caesarea Philippi in his Gospel. However, he devotes Chapters 6 to 11 of his Gospel to examining the question asked by Jesus on that occasion: "Who do you say I am?" For this reason we have inserted this Book here before proceeding with the Synoptics to follow Jesus on the road of discipleship.

John builds up his picture of Jesus by going back to the Exodus and the journey of liberation across the desert to the Promised Land. On that occasion God nourished his people with manna. Jesus is the 'living bread' that nourishes us on our journey to freedom.

John then develops the images of water and light, taken from the New Year Jewish celebrations of creation and of the giving of the Covenant and the Temple. Jesus supersedes the Law and it is to him that we must now go for the water and the light of life.

John then proceeds to the whole question of judgment and the very meaning of our life. He gathers up the image of light in the story of the man born blind and he presents Jesus as the true shepherd who guides us to life.

Finally, John brings the first part of his Gospel to a climax in the resurrection of Lazarus, preparing us for the much greater resurrection that will happen after the crucifixion. Jesus is the one through whom 'eternal' life comes.

This powerful presentation of John's Christology is covered in the following four Chapters.

Chapter 1
Jesus is the 'Holy One of God' (6:69)
who gives the 'Living Bread' (6:51)

John 6:1-71

The miracle of the loaves

JOHN 6:1-15

1 6 Some time after this, Jesus went off to the other side of the Sea of Galilee—
2 or of Tiberias—•and a large crowd followed him, impressed by the signs he
3 gave by curing the sick. •Jesus climbed the hillside, and sat down there with his
4 disciples. •It was shortly before the Jewish feast of Passover.
5 Looking up, Jesus saw the crowds approaching and said to Philip, 'Where
6 can we buy some bread for these people to eat?' •He only said this to test Philip;
7 he himself knew exactly what he was going to do. •Philip answered, 'Two hundred
8 denarii would only buy enough to give them a small piece each'. •One of his
9 disciples, Andrew, Simon Peter's brother, said, •'There is a small boy here
10 with five barley loaves and two fish; but what is that between so many?' •Jesus
said to them, 'Make the people sit down'. There was plenty of grass there, and
11 as many as five thousand men sat down. •Then Jesus took the loaves, gave
thanks, and gave them out to all who were sitting ready; he then did the same with
12 the fish, giving out as much as was wanted. •When they had eaten enough he
said to the disciples, 'Pick up the pieces left over, so that nothing gets wasted'.
13 So they picked them up, and filled twelve hampers with scraps left over from the
14 meal of five barley loaves. •The people, seeing this sign that he had given, said,
15 'This really is the prophet who is to come into the world'. •Jesus, who could see
they were about to come and take him by force and make him king, escaped
back to the hills by himself.   *(Compare Mark 6:32-44, Matthew 14:13-21*
and Luke 9:10-17 page 191)

We have already studied this anecdote in Mark, and refer the reader to the
commentary (Mark 6:32-44). John's own commentary follows (John 6:26-66).
Here we wish to note two aspects of John's setting.

John uses this anecdote as an illustration of the claim made by Jesus: 'the
scriptures testify to me' (John 5:39), and 'it was I that Moses was writing about'
(John 5:46). John develops the idea in his commentary that what Moses says of
the manna refers, at a deeper level, to Jesus, the 'living bread' (John 6:51). The
people rea':se this when they exclaim:

'This really is the prophet who is to come into the world.'   *(John 6:14)*

Jesus, in other words, is the new Moses (cf Deuteronomy 18:15 and our commentary on John 1:21) who is to inaugurate the new covenant. Jesus is the Christ (cf John 1:41, 4:25-26, 20:31).

The second thing to notice is that John wants his readers to read the story against the background of the 'Jewish feast of Passover' (John 6:4). This was originally a pastoral celebration, offering the finest lamb in sacrifice to God in thanksgiving for the new flock. Later, it celebrated the birth of the Jewish nation when Yahweh delivered the people from Egypt. They 'passed over' the Red Sea, and 'passed over' from slavery to freedom. The lamb that was slain was the 'Passover' Lamb. Its blood, according to Jewish custom, was poured out as a symbol of the return of its life to God; its body was then eaten. At first the lamb was slain and eaten in anticipation of God's saving act. From then on it was sacrificed as a memorial. We read in the Book of Exodus:

> 'You shall eat it like this: with a girdle round your waist, sandals on your feet, a staff in your hand. You shall eat it hastily: it is a Passover in honour of Yahweh. That night, I will go through the land of Egypt and strike down all the first-born in the land of Egypt, man and beast alike, and I shall deal out punishment to all the gods of Egypt, I am Yahweh! The blood shall serve to mark the houses that you live in. When I see the blood I shall pass over you and you shall escape the destroying plague when I strike the land of Egypt. This day is to be a day of remembrance for you, and you must celebrate it as a feast in Yahweh's honour. For all generations you are to declare it a day of festival, for ever.'
>
> *(Exodus 12:11-14)*

This is the second time John has mentioned the feast of Passover. The first time (John 2:23) was when Jesus cleared the Temple. On that occasion Jesus demonstrated that the old covenant had come to an end. He spoke of a new sanctuary, the sanctuary that was his body (John 2:21). In the scene of the multiplication of the loaves, John wishes to develop the positive side of this theme. By linking the Passover with a meal, he wishes to demonstrate how men can make God's new redemptive act their own. Jesus is the 'lamb of God who takes away the sins of the world' (John 1:29, cf 1:36). By sharing in this meal the people are sharing in the new covenant. The obvious Eucharistic link is made by John in his commentary later. It is worth noting here that the Synoptics explicitly link the Passover with the Last Supper (cf Mark 14:22-25). That meal, too, is held in anticipation of the great redeeming act of God, and is then to be celebrated as a memorial (cf Luke 22:19).

Jesus walks on the water

JOHN 6:16-21

16
17   That evening the disciples went down to the shore of the lake and •got into a boat to make for Capernaum on the other side of the lake. It was getting
18 dark by now and Jesus had still not rejoined them. •The wind was strong, and
19 the sea was getting rough. •They had rowed three or four miles when they saw Jesus walking on the lake and coming towards the boat. This frightened them,
20
21 but he said, 'It is I. Do not be afraid.' •They were for taking him into the boat, but in no time it reached the shore at the place they were making for.

(Compare Mark 6:45-52 and Matthew 14:22-27 page 193)

This scene is linked with the preceding one in Mark also. We refer the reader to Mark (6:45-52) for commentary.

A comparison with Mark's account shows that John does not mention Jesus' calming of the sea, nor does he mention Jesus getting into the boat with his disciples. John concentrates the attention of the reader on the mysterious presence of Jesus who is unexpectedly present to his disciples in their need. The 'it is I. Do not be afraid' (John 6:20) makes of the scene a theophany, reminding us of the mysterious 'I am he' of John 4:26 (page 137-8).

Just as the God of the Exodus, the God of the Passover, was mysteriously with his people through their difficult desert journey, so Jesus is with his disciples in their journey, and is with the church in hers. The disciples will, because of the power of the risen Jesus, reach the Promised Land, 'the place they were making for' (John 6:21).

Jesus is the one sent by God, the one in whom we must believe

JOHN 6:22-31
22   Next day, the crowd that had stayed on the other side saw that only one boat had been there, and that Jesus had not got into the boat with his disciples, but
23 that the disciples had set off by themselves. •Other boats, however, had put in
24 from Tiberias, near the place where the bread had been eaten. •When the
25 people saw that neither Jesus nor his disciples were there, they got into those
26 boats and crossed to Capernaum to look for Jesus. •When they found him on the other side, they said to him, 'Rabbi, when did you come here?' •Jesus answered:

> 'I tell you most solemnly,
> you are not looking for me
> because you have seen the signs
27 > but because you had all the bread you wanted to eat.
> Do not work for food that cannot last,
> but work for food that endures to eternal life,
> the kind of food the Son of Man is offering you,
> for on him the Father, God himself, has set his seal.'
28
29   Then they said to him, 'What must we do if we are to do the works that God
30 wants?' •Jesus gave them this answer, 'This is working for God: you must
31 believe in the one he has sent'. •So they said, 'What sign will you give to show us that we should believe in you? What work will you do? •Our fathers had manna to eat in the desert; as scripture says: *He gave them bread from heaven to eat.'*[a]

(a: Psalm 78:2)

Jesus 'never needed evidence about any man; he could tell what a man had in him' (John 2:25). He knew that the people were seeking him because they were excited by his signs and liked having their needs supplied (6:26). He tried to lead them on to 'work for food that endures to eternal life' (6:27). He, the Son of Man, can offer them this food because:

'on him, the Father, God himself, has set his seal.'   *(John 6:27)*

John is fond of describing the intimacy that existed between Jesus and his Father. We are reminded of earlier expressions:

'we saw his glory
the glory that is his as the only Son of the Father
full of grace and truth' (1:14)

'It is the only Son, who is nearest the Father's heart,
who has made him known' (1:18)

'I saw the Spirit coming down on him from heaven
like a dove, and resting on him' (1:32)

'He is the Chosen One of God' (1:34)

'God gives him the Spirit without reserve.' (3:34)

The crowd ask Jesus what is, perhaps, the fundamental practical religious question:

'What must we do if we are to do the works that God wants?' (6:28)

Paul puts the same question in different words when he asks how a person is justified. Paul's answer is:

'the upright man finds life through faith.'   *(Romans 1:17)*

The answer given by Jesus in John's Gospel is the same:

'you must believe in the one he has sent.' (6:29)

In his letter to the Philippians, Paul distinguishes between two types of 'perfection': the perfection 'that comes from the Law', and 'the perfection that comes through faith in Christ, and is from God and based on faith' (Philippians 3:9).

The question asked by the crowd is a practical question. So, ultimately is the answer. Jesus insists on perspective. They must open their mind and heart to God and to the activity of God's spirit. Then they will discover God's will for them. Theirs must be an activity not flowing from their own controlled decisions, but in response to the initiative of God.

The crowd ask Jesus to prove his credentials. They already have the Law, and it was given them by Moses, the one who gave them the manna:

'What sign will you give to show that we should believe in you? What work will you do?'   *(John 6:30)*

The text quoted by the crowd: 'He gave them bread from heaven to eat' (Psalm 78:2), becomes the basis for the rest of John's discourse. He will use it to show the superiority of Jesus over Moses, and the superiority of the living bread over the manna given in the desert.

I suggest that the reader, before continuing this commentary, read slowly the account of the manna in the desert (Exodus Chapter 16). We see God present with his people on their journey and, like a father, constantly caring for their needs. He is asking them to trust that he will give them their daily bread. It is against this background that John wishes his readers to understand the story of the loaves in the desert.

Jesus is the bread of life, the 'bread from heaven' (6:31)

JOHN 6:32-51

a: **JOHN 6:32-40**

Jesus answered: **32**

'I tell you most solemnly,
it was not Moses who gave you bread from heaven,

it is my Father who gives you the bread from heaven,
the true bread;
for the bread of God   33
is that which comes down from heaven
and gives life to the world'.

'Sir,' they said 'give us that bread always.' •Jesus answered: 34
                                                                   35

'I am the bread of life.
He who comes to me will never be hungry;
he who believes in me will never thirst.
But, as I have told you,   36
you can see me and still you do not believe.
All that the Father gives me will come to me,   37
and whoever comes to me
I shall not turn him away;
because I have come from heaven,   38
not to do my own will,
but to do the will of the one who sent me.
Now the will of him who sent me   39
is that I should lose nothing
of all that he has given to me,
and that I should raise it up on the last day.
Yes, it is my Father's will   40
that whoever sees the Son and believes in him
shall have eternal life,
and that I shall raise him up on the last day.'

Jesus pleads with the people to go beyond Moses to 'my Father' (6:32), and beyond the manna to the 'true bread' (6:32). We recall the words written by the prophet:

'Oh, come to the water, all you who are thirsty;
though you have no money, come!
Buy corn without money, and eat,
and at no cost wine and milk.
Why spend money on what is not bread,
your wages on what fails to satisfy?
Listen, listen to me, and you will have good things to eat
and rich food to enjoy.
Pay attention, come to me;
listen and your soul will live.
With you I will make an everlasting covenant.'

(Isaiah 55:1-3)

The true bread is Jesus himself (John 6:35), a gift given 'to the world' (John 6:33). Everyone is welcome to come to Jesus (compare John 12:32). Jesus will not turn anyone away because he is doing his Father's will, and:

'God loved the world so much
that he gave his only Son
so that everyone who believes in him
may not be lost
but may have eternal life.'

(John 3:16)

Anyone who hears God's word and responds to God's invitation — anyone who believes in Jesus (John 6:36, 6:40) 'shall have eternal life' (John 6:40). The invitation is universal.

b: JOHN 6:41-51

41   Meanwhile the Jews were complaining to each other about him, because he
42 had said, 'I am the bread that came down from heaven'. •'Surely this is Jesus son of Joseph' they said. 'We know his father and mother. How can he now say,
43 "I have come down from heaven"?' •Jesus said in reply, 'Stop complaining to each other.

44   'No one can come to me
            unless he is drawn by the Father who sent me,
            and I will raise him up at the last day.
45   It is written in the prophets:
            They will all be taught by God, [a]
            and to hear the teaching of the Father,
            and learn from it,
            is to come to me.
46   Not that anybody has seen the Father,
            except the one who comes from God:
            he has seen the Father.
47   I tell you most solemnly,
            everybody who believes has eternal life.
48   I am the bread of life.
49   Your fathers ate the manna in the desert
            and they are dead;
50   but this is the bread that comes down from heaven,
            so that a man may eat it and not die.
51   I am the living bread which has come down from heaven.
            Anyone who eats this bread will live for ever;
            and the bread that I shall give
            is my flesh, for the life of the world.'

(a: Isaiah 54:13)

The Jews do not accept Jesus, do not believe in him, because they are caught in their own prejudices and expectations (6:41-42; compare Luke 4:23 and Mark 6:2-4). Jesus asks them to be open to the Father and to allow themselves to be drawn by him. If they allow themselves to be taught by God, they will come to Jesus (6:45). God's word has always been a word of love, a word of compassion:

'I led them with reins of kindness,
with leading-strings of love.'

(Hosea 11:4)

'I have loved you with an everlasting love,
so I am constant in my affection for you.'

(Jeremiah 31:3)

If they let themselves be drawn by God, they would see in Jesus God's word made flesh (John 1:14). They would be nourished by Jesus' love. They would 'live for ever' (John 6:51).

Compared to the manna, Jesus is 'living bread' (John 6:51); he gives 'eternal life' (6:47); and he gives this life to the 'world' (6:51).

The concluding statement 'the bread that I shall give is my flesh for the life of the world' (6:51) is explained in the following section.

Jesus is God's food that we must 'eat': the 'bread from heaven to eat' (John 6:31)

JOHN 6:52-58

52 Then the Jews started arguing with one another: 'How can this man give
53 us his flesh to eat?' they said. •Jesus replied:

> 'I tell you most solemnly,
> if you do not eat the flesh of the Son of Man
> and drink his blood,
> you will not have life in you.

54 Anyone who does eat my flesh and drink my blood
has eternal life,
and I shall raise him up on the last day.

55 For my flesh is real food
and my blood is real drink.

56 He who eats my flesh and drinks my blood
lives in me
and I live in him.

57 As I, who am sent by the living Father,.
myself draw life from the Father,
so whoever eats me will draw life from me.

58 This is the bread come down from heaven;
not like the bread our ancestors ate:
they are dead,
but anyone who eats this bread will live for ever.'

To eat the flesh of the Son of Man and to drink his blood is to listen to Jesus, to make a home for his words in the depths of our mind and heart. It is to undertake to journey with him, to 'drink the cup that I must drink' (Mark 10:38) It is to give our lives, too, in service of others. God gives us food for this journey of discipleship: he gives us his Son, Jesus. Jesus gives his life for us, his words, his heart, his love. He is asking the Jews to open their minds and hearts to receive him.

We are reminded of the 'Breaking of Bread' in which the truths just mentioned are celebrated symbolically in a meal shared by the assembled community of the disciples of Jesus. There bread and wine are taken by the communicants as symbols of Jesus himself who is really present and offering himself as nourishment for the journey of discipleship. Because of the injunction of Jesus at the Last Supper (cf 1 Corinthians 11:23-25), the community to which John belonged used to celebrate this sacred meal in memory of Jesus. They would have grasped, through their own experience, what Jesus meant when he said:

'anyone who eats my flesh and drinks my blood has eternal life.'   *(John 6:54)*

The Eucharist was a ritual celebration of the reality spoken of by John in this passage.

God is the 'living Father' (6:57). He lives in Jesus, and Jesus' works of love flow from this union. Jesus is offering this same life to the people. If they, like

Jesus, listen to God's word; if they allow themselves to be drawn by the Father to become disciples of Jesus and learn from him how to live; if they stop trying for perfection that comes from conformity to the Law; if they learn to draw life from the Father and to give expression in their lives to God's love, they will know what it is to live God' s life (6:56, compare John 15:1-17).

The conclusion to the Discourse

JOHN 6:59-66

59
60   He taught this doctrine at Capernaum, in the synagogue. •After hearing it, many of his followers said, 'This is intolerable language. How could anyone
61 accept it?' •Jesus was aware that his followers were complaining about it and
62 said, 'Does this upset you? •What if you should see the Son of Man ascend to where he was before?

63   'It is the spirit that gives life,
            the flesh has nothing to offer.
            The words I have spoken to you are spirit
            and they are life.

64 'But there are some of you who do not believe.' For Jesus knew from the outset
65 those who did not believe, and who it was that would betray him. •He went on,
66 'This is why I told you that no one could come to me unless the Father allows him'. •After this, many of his disciples left him and stopped going with him.

We are not dealing here with a rejection of Jesus by his enemies. John is speaking of 'his followers' (6:60), 'his disciples' (6:66). His words stood as a warning to John's own Christian community.

'The flesh has nothing to offer' (6:63). They reject the fact that someone as ordinary as the son of Joseph (John 6:42) could be the Christ. But, Jesus, the 'flesh for the life of the world' (6:51) has everything to offer, for his flesh has been given life by the Spirit (6:63). His words are spirit and life because his flesh is the Word made flesh (John 1:14).

To follow Jesus truly is to let his word find a home in you (John 5:37). Those who rejected Jesus in the name of God were worshipping a false God (compare 1 John 5:21).

John's equivalent of Caesarea Philippi

JOHN 6:67-71

67   Then Jesus said to the Twelve, 'What about you, do you want to go away too?'
68 Simon Peter answered, 'Lord, who shall we go to? You have the message of
69 eternal life, • and we believe; we know that you are the Holy One of God.'
70 Jesus replied, 'Have I not chosen you, you Twelve? Yet one of you is a devil.'
71 He meant Judas son of Simon Iscariot, since this was the man, one of the Twelve, who was going to betray him.

As in the Synoptic accounts of Caesarea Philippi, so here, it is Peter who expresses his faith in the fact that Jesus is the Christ, the 'Holy One of God' (6:69).

But the cross is never far from John's thoughts, and even here, in the intimacy of the Twelve, John reminds us of the presence of evil and the betrayal that awaits Jesus. Jesus is to give his flesh for the life of the world (John 6:51) by enduring in his love.

* * * * * * * *

This whole section has been an illustration of the fact that Jesus is the word made flesh (John 1:14). God did speak his word through Moses; he did make his care visible in his gift of manna in the desert. But, in Jesus, this same God showed himself as a 'living Father' (John 6:57), giving his own Son, his 'flesh and blood', to nourish every man on his journey (John 6:56-57). This is the message of the miracle of the loaves.

* * * * * * * *

Points for Reflection:

1: Jesus challenges each of us to 'work for food that endures to eternal life' (John 6:27). 'Why spend money on what is not bread, your wages on what fails to satisfy?' (Isaiah 55:2). Our question is the same as that asked by the crowd: 'What must we do to do the works that God wants?' (John 6:28). There is no ready answer, except that the way to the answer is clear: 'believe in the one he has sent' (John 6:29). We find the answer by contemplating Jesus and putting our trust in what we see. And there is much to see. His 'works' are clear enough. Perhaps the ultimate symbolic work is the washing of the feet of the disciples (John 13:1-20). The way is the way of service, of self-giving love. If our heart is trained by such contemplation, our heart will direct what works we must do. Our actions can only be as big as our heart. If we want to be Jesus' disciples our heart will grow, under his guidance, to be as gentle and humble as his. Then, but not before then, we will be able to do works such as he did, 'even greater works' (John 14:12).

2: To eat the Eucharistic bread is to make a statement of commitment: commitment to the task of giving my flesh, too, for the life of the world (John 6:51). To drink the Eucharistic wine is to commit myself to the journey of pouring out my life, with him, for the life of the world. It is to pledge myself to drink the cup that he had to drink (Mark 10:38). To eat his flesh and to drink his blood (John 6:56) is to make my food and drink, as he did, the will of God (John 6:38). It is to live in Jesus as he lived in his Father (John 6:56). It is to draw my life from him. In the words of Paul:

'The life I now live in this body I live in faith:
faith in the Son of God who loved me and who sacrificed
himself for my sake.'

(Galatians 2:20)

In effect this means that: 'I have been crucified with Christ' (Galatians 2:19). It is this that is ritually expressed in the Eucharist. Jesus promises the experience of eternal life (John 6:58).

3: 'Do you want to go away?' (John 6:67) Do you?

Chapter 2
Jesus, the 'Son' supersedes the Law

John 7:1 — 8:59

A: The setting for the dialogues

JOHN 7:1-13

7 After this Jesus stayed in Galilee; he could not stay in Judaea, because the 1
Jews were out to kill him.
As the Jewish feast of Tabernacles drew near, •his brothers said to him, 2
'Why not leave this place and go to Judaea, and let your disciples see the works 3
you are doing; •if a man wants to be known he does not do things in secret; since 4
you are doing all this, you should let the whole world see'. •Not even his brothers, 5
in fact, had faith in him. •Jesus answered, 'The right time for me has not come yet, 6
but any time is the right time for you, •The world cannot hate you, but it does 7
hate me, because I give evidence that its ways are evil. •Go up to the festival 8
yourselves: I am not going to this festival, because for me the time is not ripe
yet.' • Having said that, he stayed behind in Galilee. 9
However, after his brothers had left for the festival, he went up as well, but 10
quite privately, without drawing attention to himself. •At the festival the Jews 11
were on the look-out for him: 'Where is he?' they said. •People stood in groups 12
whispering about him. Some said, 'He is a good man'; others, 'No, he is leading
the people astray'. •Yet no one spoke about him openly, for fear of the Jews. 13

The main themes of this section are provided by the setting, 'the Jewish feast
of Tabernacles' (7:2).

In pre-exile days the people celebrated an end of year harvest feast when they
were told to 'gather in the fruit of your labours from the fields' (Exodus 23:16). It
was called the feast of Ingathering. After the exile there was a change of calendar,
and the feast of Ingathering seems to have been divided into a number of feasts all
in the seventh month (Tishri), and each focusing on a different aspect of the
earlier celebration.

The first day of Tishri became New Year's Day. This was celebrated as a day
of judgment, and the liturgy included readings like the following:

'Yahweh, Yahweh, a God of tenderness and compassion, slow to anger, rich in
kindness and faithfulness; for thousands he maintains his kindness, forgives faults,
transgression, sin; yet he lets nothing go unchecked, punishing the father's fault in the
sons and in the grandsons to the third and fourth generation.'
(Exodus 34:6-7)

'I will let all my splendour pass in front of you, and I will pronounce before you the name Yahweh. I have compassion on whom I will, and I show pity to whom I please.'

(Exodus 33:19)

'Repent, renounce all your sins, avoid all occasions of sin!
Shake off the sins you have committed against me,
and make yourselves a new heart and a new spirit!'

(Ezekiel 18:30-31)

The liturgical colour was white, remembering the statement of Isaiah:

'Though your sins are as scarlet, they shall be as white as snow.'

(Isaiah 1:18)

The shofar (ram's horn) was sounded, calling the nation to repentance and reminding them that their God, Yahweh was coming in victory (cf Joel 2:1, 15).

New Year's Day, reminding them as it did of the passing of time and summoning them to repentance, was followed by ten days of repentance (teshuvah): days of almsgiving, prayer and fasting. The liturgy included the following readings:

'Seek Yahweh while he is still to be found
call to him while he is still near.'

(Isaiah 55:6)

'Yahweh said: "I forgive them as you ask".'

(Numbers 14:20)

'What God can compare with you: taking fault away, pardoning crime, not cherishing anger for ever but delighting in showing mercy? Once more have pity on us, tread down our faults, to the bottom of the sea throw all our sins. Grant Jacob your faithfulness, and Abraham your mercy, as you swore to our fathers from the days of long ago.'

(Micah 7:18:20)

These ten days ended on the tenth Tishri with the feast of Atonement (Yom Kippur). A twenty-four hour fast was kept (read Isaiah 57:14 — 58:14). The feast celebrated the release of the people from sin (Leviticus 16). The universal salvific will of God was remembered with a reading of the Book of Jonah, and the liturgy ended with the solemn chanting of the Shema:

'Listen, Israel: Yahweh your God is the one Yahweh.'

(Deuteronomy 6:4)

Finally, on the fifteenth Tishri, and the night of the harvest full-moon, began the solemn week-long feast of Tabernacles. This feast celebrated the gathering in of the 'produce of the threshing-floor and the wine press' (Deuteronomy 16:13) and the falling of the first autumn rains, so important for the spring harvest. Coming as a culmination of the New Year celebrations, this feast of Tabernacles (called such because of the temporary dwellings made of boughs which were erected in the fields during the grape and fruit-picking) celebrated the creation motifs of water and light. On the 'last and greatest day of the festival' (John 7:37), that is the seventh day, the day of the 'rejoicing in the Torah', the Law was read (Deuteronomy 31:10-13), and the people celebrated their birth as God's chosen people. Solomon dedicated the Temple on this feast (1 Kings 8:66). Water was brought from the pool of Siloam and poured over the altar, flowing from the Temple as a sign of God's abundance flowing through the land (read Ezekiel 47:1-12, Zechariah 13:1). At the same time, the women's court was lit up in preparation for the dancing and festivities which concluded the feast.

John is going to develop all these themes in this section. The people are being called to repentance ('Metanoia'/'teshuvah'). John's own community is being summoned to decide for Jesus before it is too late. Jesus is presented, in contrast to the Law, as the 'living water' (John 7:38), and as the 'light of the world' (John 8:12). In Jesus, God is making all things new. He is the new creation; in him God is making a new covenant with his people. Jesus is the new Temple, and those who are in him are solemnly dedicated to God.

The scene is one of tension right from the opening words. John has just spoken of the coming betrayal of Jesus by Judas (John 6:71). Here we find that 'the Jews were out to kill him' (John 7:1). Even his family do not believe in him (John 7:5), and the people in Jerusalem are afraid to speak openly about him (John 7:13).

The reason for the tension is given by Jesus:

'the world hates me, because I give evidence that its ways are evil.'

(John 7:7)

We are reminded of an earlier statement:

'though the light has come into the world
men have shown they prefer darkness to light
because their deeds were evil.'

(John 3:19)

Whereas their 'god' was inextricably bound to their narrow interpretation of the Law, Jesus showed unmistakably that God is a God of mercy and faithful love. He summoned them to leave their idolatry and live a life of love; and they hated him for it.

John also makes a play on the words 'go up'. His brothers taunt Jesus to 'go up' to the festival to show the world that he is the Christ. Jesus replies:

'I am not going up to this festival,
because for me the time is not ripe yet.'

(John 7:8)

He does, as we see, go to the festival, but it is not a 'going up'. That will be later, when he goes up to his Father (when he is lifted up on the cross, and glorified; when he ascends to his Father). Then, at the right time (7:6), he will 'let his disciples see the works he is doing' (John 7:3); then, indeed, 'the whole world will see' (John 7:4). The cross and resurrection and glorification of Jesus are never far from John's mind.

B: The seven dialogues (John 7:14 — 8:59)

1: The first dialogue: Jesus and Moses (balances the seventh dialogue)

JOHN 7:14-24

When the festival was half over, Jesus went to the Temple and began to 14 teach. •The Jews were astonished and said, 'How did he learn to read? He has 15 not been taught.' •Jesus answered them: 16

'My teaching is not from myself:
it comes from the one who sent me;
and if anyone is prepared to do his will, 17
he will know whether my teaching is from God

or whether my doctrine is my own.
When a man's doctrine is his own   18
he is hoping to get honour for himself;
but when he is working for the honour of one who sent him,
then he is sincere
and by no means an impostor.
Did not Moses give you the Law?   19
And yet not one of you keeps the Law!

'Why do you want to kill me?' •The crowd replied, 'You are mad! Who wants 20
to kill you?' •Jesus answered, 'One work I did, and you are all surprised by it. 21
Moses ordered you to practise circumcision—not that it began with him, it goes 22
back to the patriarchs—and you circumcise on the sabbath. •Now if a man 23
can be circumcised on the sabbath so that the Law of Moses is not broken,
why are you angry with me for making a man whole and complete on a sabbath?
Do not keep judging according to appearances; let your judgement be according 24
to what is right.'

John presents Jesus, on the feast which celebrated the giving of the Law, as
the new Moses, who sees and reveals God (cf John 3:13, 31; 5:20; 6:46; 7:16).
Jesus refers to his curing of the man at the pool of Bethzatha (John 7:21, cf John
5:1-9). That was the occasion on which the authorities began their persecution of
Jesus, for his breaking of the Law. Jesus defended his action by saying that he
was simply carrying on the work of his Father (5:16-17). Here, he returns to the
debate, accusing them of not keeping the Law (7:19) and of 'judging according to
appearances' (7:24). Circumcision, which they allowed on the sabbath (7:23)
aimed at 'making a man whole and complete' (7:23) by bringing him into contact
with the healing and liberating spirit of God at the heart of the chosen people. If
they were prepared to do God's will (7:17), if they were truly interested in making
a man whole and complete, they would see that Jesus' action, far from breaking
the Law, was expressing the heart and spirit of the Law.

This idea of the Law is expressed in Psalm 146:

'Praise Yahweh, my soul!
I mean to praise Yahweh all my life,
I mean to sing to my God as long as I live.

Do not put your trust in men in power,
or in any mortal man — he cannot save,
he yields his breath and goes back to the earth he came from,
and on that day all his schemes perish.

Happy the man who has the God of Jacob to help him,
whose hope is fixed on Yahweh his God,
maker of heaven and earth,
and the sea and all that these hold!

Yahweh, forever faithful,
gives justice to those denied it,
gives food to the hungry,
gives liberty to prisoners.

Yahweh restores sight to the blind,
Yahweh straightens the bent,
Yahweh protects the stranger,

He keeps the orphan and widow.
Yahweh loves the virtuous,
and frustrates the wicked.
Yahweh reigns for ever,
your God, Zion, from age to age.'

(Psalm 146)

When Jesus did the works of Yahweh, the world hated him, and the religious leaders, in the name of Yahweh himself, opposed him.

2: The second dialogue: the decision is *now* (balances the sixth dialogue)

JOHN 7:25-36

25   Meanwhile some of the people of Jerusalem were saying, 'Isn't this the man
26 they want to kill? •And here he is, speaking freely, and they have nothing to
say to him! Can it be true the authorities have made up their minds that he is
27 the Christ? •Yet we all know where he comes from, but when the Christ appears
no one will know where he comes from.'

28   Then, as Jesus taught in the Temple, he cried out:

> 'Yes, you know me and you know where I came from.
> Yet I have not come of myself:
> no, there is one who sent me and I really come from him,
> and you do not know him,
29 but I know him
> because I have come from him
> and it was he who sent me.'

30   They would have arrested him then, but because his time had not yet come no one laid a hand on him.

31   There were many people in the crowds, however, who believed in him; they were saying, 'When the Christ comes, will he give more signs than this man?'
32 Hearing that rumours like this about him were spreading among the people, the Pharisees sent the Temple police to arrest him.

33   Then Jesus said:

> 'I shall remain with you for only a short time now;
> then I shall go back to the one who sent me.
34 You will look for me and will not find me:
> where I am
> you cannot come.'

35   The Jews then said to one another, 'Where is he going that we shan't be able to find him? Is he going abroad to the people who are dispersed among
36 the Greeks and will he teach the Greeks? •What does he mean when he says:

> "You will look for me and will not find me:
> where I am,
> you cannot come"?'

'When the Christ appears no one will know where he comes from' (7:27), represents one of the opinions concerning the Messiah that was current at the time of Jesus. According to this opinion, the Christ would appear suddenly, like a flash of lightning. He would manifest the glory of God, rout God's foes and set

Israel free. He would inaugurate the time of Messianic peace in which Israel would rule the world and all men would come to worship at Jerusalem.

By these criteria — or so they thought — Jesus could not be the Christ. They knew where he came from (7:27 and 7:28): he was brought up in Nazareth, the son of Joseph and Mary. They failed to recognise the deeper truth: that Jesus came from the Father (7:28).

We should not miss the dramatic impact of Jesus' words. He is in the Temple. It is the feast of Tabernacles, a feast celebrating the glory of the Jewish faith. And Jesus says to the Jews:

'you do not know him.' (7:28)

He will make this accusation twice more in this section (8:19 and 8:55). Jesus is accusing them of idolatry. The God they claim to know and worship is not the God of Moses, the God of the Exodus, the God of compassion. If he were they would recognise God's action in the 'works' of Jesus.

John has told his readers that the teaching of Jesus comes from God (7:17). He has told them that Jesus himself comes from God (7:28). Now we learn that Jesus is going to God (7:33). From now on this motif will be a frequently recurring one, preparing us for the passion, death and glorification of Jesus when his 'hour' comes (cf John 8:21; 12:35; 13:3; 13:33, 13:36; 14:4-5, 14:12, 14:19, 14:28; 16:5, 16:16-19, 16:28).

The 'short time' (7:33) reminds us of the fact that religion is not just a matter of 'eternal truths' that can be meditated on endlessly and accepted at leisure. The religion of Moses and the religion of Jesus is a summons, a call, a word to man from God to be an instrument of God's justice in the world. If the summons is ignored, it can be too late:

'The light will be with you only a little longer now.
Walk while you have the light,
or the dark will overtake you.'   (John 12:35,

3: The third dialogue: the offer of life (balances the fifth dialogue)

JOHN 7:37-44

37   On the last day and greatest day of the festival, Jesus stood there and cried out:
'If any man is thirsty, let him come to me!
38   Let the man come and drink •who believes in me!'

As scripture says, From his breast shall flow fountains of living water.
39   He was speaking of the Spirit which those who believed in him were to receive; for there was no Spirit as yet because Jesus had not yet been glorified.
40   Several people who had been listening said, 'Surely he must be the prophet',
41 and some said, 'He is the Christ', but others said, 'Would the Christ be from
42 Galilee? •Does not scripture say that the Christ must be descended from David
43 and come from the town of Bethlehem?' •So the people could not agree about
44 him. •Some would have liked to arrest him, but no one actually laid hands on him.

As mentioned earlier, the feast of Tabernacles celebrated God's creative activity, especially in the renewal of the harvest. The Temple stood as a visible sign of God's continued presence among his people. On the last day of the feast, water, symbol of the spirit of God, was poured over the altar and flowed freely through the Temple precincts. Among the readings chosen from Scripture to highlight the significance of this act was the following prophecy from Ezekiel:

1 **47** He brought me back to the entrance of the Temple, where a stream came out from under the Temple threshold and flowed eastwards, since the Temple faced east. The water flowed from under the right side of the Temple, 2 south of the altar. •He took me out by the north gate and led me right round outside as far as the outer east gate where the water flowed out on the right-hand 3 side. •The man went to the east holding his measuring line and measured off a thousand cubits; he then made me wade across the stream; the water reached 4 my ankles. •He measured off another thousand and made me wade across the stream again; the water reached my knees. He measured off another thousand 5 and made me wade across again; the water reached my waist. •He measured off another thousand; it was now a river which I could not cross; the stream 6 had swollen and was now deep water, a river impossible to cross. •He then said, 'Do you see, son of man?' He took me further, then brought me back to 7 the bank of the river. •When I got back, there were many trees on each bank 8 of the river. •He said, 'This water flows east down to the Arabah and to the 9 sea; and flowing into the sea it makes its waters wholesome. •Wherever the river flows, all living creatures teeming in it will live. Fish will be very plentiful, for wherever the water goes it brings health, and life teems wherever 10 the river flows. •There will be fishermen on its banks. Fishing nets will be spread from En-gedi to En-eglaim. The fish will be as varied and as 11 plentiful as the fish of the Great Sea. •The marshes and lagoons, however, will 12 not become wholesome, but will remain salt. •Along the river, on either bank, will grow every kind of fruit tree with leaves that never wither and fruit that never fails; they will bear new fruit every month, because this water comes from the sanctuary. And their fruit will be good to eat and the leaves medicinal.

(Ezekiel 47:1-12,

It is against this setting that:

'Jesus stood there and cried out:
If any man is thirsty let him come to me!'

(John 7:37,

The Temple has been cleared. The new Temple is the sanctuary of the body of Jesus (John 2:21). Jesus is the vehicle of the living water from God. We are reminded of his words to the Samaritan woman:

'Anyone who drinks the water that I shall give
will never be thirsty again:
the water that I shall give
will turn into a spring inside him
welling up to eternal life.'

(John 4:14)

The water of life flows now, not from the heart of the Temple, but from the heart of Jesus, God's word made flesh (cf John 19:34). It will also well up in the heart of the disciple who believes in Jesus (7:37).

The water, according to John (7:39), symbolises the Spirit. This spirit was given at the first moment of creation. This Spirit came through the words of the prophets and flowed from the Temple. But the gift of the Spirit for which the prophets had longed, the messianic gift, was to come from the heart of Jesus, and, finally, from the pierced heart of Jesus on the cross (cf John 19:34).

It was on the cross that Jesus was 'glorified' (John 7:39), for it was on the cross that he finally manifested, in his complete gift of self, the love of God. It was from the cross, as John tells us, that:

'he gave up his Spirit.'

(John 19:30, cf John 20:22)

'Christ must come from the town of Bethlehem' (7:42) represents another of the opinions current at the time of Jesus concerning the origin of the Messiah. It was based on the prophecy of Micah:

'But you, (Bethlehem) Ephrathah,
the least of the clans of Judah,
out of you will be born for me
the one who is to rule over Israel;
his origin goes back to the distant past,
to the days of old.'

(Micah 5:1-2)

Once again, they reject Jesus because he does not fit with their expectations. They are being challenged to drop their expectations and believe in what they see and hear.

4: The fourth dialogue: division among the authorities

JOHN 7:45-52
The police went back to the chief priests and Pharisees who said to them, 45 'Why haven't you brought him?' •The police replied, 'There has never been 46 anybody who has spoken like him'. •'So' the Pharisees answered 'you have been 47 led astray as well? •Have any of the authorities believed in him? Any of the 48 Pharisees? •This rabble knows nothing about the Law—they are damned.' 49 One of them, Nicodemus—the same man who had come to Jesus earlier—said to 50 them, •'But surely the Law does not allow us to pass judgement on a man without 51 giving him a hearing and discovering what he is about?' •To this they answered, 52 'Are you a Galilean too? Go into the matter, and see for yourself: prophets do not come out of Galilee.'

The reaction of the police, and the statement by Nicodemus, highlight the stubborn refusal of the religious leaders. They persist in refusing to see Jesus and to accept the consequences both for themselves and for the Law they were claiming to uphold.

5: The fifth dialogue: The offer of light (balances the third dialogue)

JOHN 8:12-20
When Jesus spoke to the people again, he said: 12
    'I am the light of the world;
    anyone who follows me will not be walking in the dark;
    he will have the light of life'.
At this the Pharisees said to him, 'You are testifying on your own behalf; 13 your testimony is not valid'. •Jesus replied: 14
    'It is true that I am testifying on my own behalf,

but my testimony is still valid,
because I know
where I came from and where I am going;
but you do not know
where I come from or where I am going.
You judge by human standards; 15
I judge no one,
but if I judge, 16
my judgement will be sound,
because I am not alone:
the one who sent me is with me;
and in your Law it is written 17
that the testimony of two witnesses is valid.
I may be testifying on my own behalf, 18
but the Father who sent me is my witness too.'

They asked him, 'Where is your Father?' Jesus answered: 19

'You do not know me, nor do you know my Father;
if you did know me, you would know my Father as well'.

He spoke these words in the Treasury, while teaching in the Temple. No one 20
arrested him, because his time had not yet come.

The women's court, as we mentioned earlier, was lit up in preparation for the
celebrations that were to form a climax to the week of festivities. God, who
created light (Genesis 1:3), who went before his people like a pillar of fire (Exodus
13:21; also Wisdom 18:3-4; Isaiah 9:1-2, 42:6, 49:6), was shining from the Temple
— or so they thought. For John and his community, it was Jesus who was the
light of the world (John 1:4-5; 1:9; 3:21; chapter 9). Those who walked by the
Law, without recognising Jesus, were, in fact, 'walking in the dark' (John 8:12).

In an earlier section, John had spoken of the witness given to Jesus (John
5:31-47). Here he speaks of the witness of Jesus' actions (8:14, 18 cf John 13:11, 32
and 5:36), and the witness of the Father (8:18 cf John 3:33; 5:37, 39). The fact that
the Pharisees will not accept this witness is proof that they do not know the living
God (John 8:19).

Jesus also states: 'I judge no one' (8:15). It is perhaps because of this remark,
and as an illustration of the contrast between the Pharisees and Jesus that an
editor of the third or fourth century inserted, just before this dialogue, the
following anecdote. The material is ancient, and non-Johannine, but is a fitting
commentary on the debate we are studying.

Insert: **The adulterous woman**

JOHN 7:53 — 8:11

They all went home, 8 and Jesus went to the Mount of Olives. 53
1

At daybreak he appeared in the Temple again; and as all the people came 2
to him, he sat down and began to teach them.

The scribes and Pharisees brought a woman along who had been caught 3
committing adultery; and making her stand there in full view of everybody,
they said to Jesus, 'Master, this woman was caught in the very act of committing 4
adultery, •and Moses has ordered us in the Law to condemn women like this to 5

death by stoning. What have you to say?' •They asked him this as a test, looking 6
for something to use against him. But Jesus bent down and started writing on
the ground with his finger. •As they persisted with their question, he looked 7
up and said, 'If there is one of you who has not sinned, let him be the first to
throw a stone at her'. •Then he bent down and wrote on the ground again. 8
When they heard this they went away one by one, beginning with the eldest, 9
until Jesus was left alone with the woman, who remained standing there. •He 10
looked up and said, 'Woman, where are they? Has no one condemned you?'
'No one, sir' she replied. 'Neither do I condemn you,' said Jesus 'go away, and 11
don't sin any more.'

This anecdote illustrates the difference between the approach of the
Pharisees and the approach of Jesus. The Pharisees judge, rightly, that adultery
is a sin. They proceed to condemn the woman for her action and insist that the
Law's punishment be inflicted upon her (John 8:5, cf Deuteronomy 22:22-24).
Jesus recognises that she has sinned (John 8:11), but he does not condemn her
(John 8:11). In this sense he does not 'judge' (Greek: 'krino') anyone (cf John
8:15). As John said earlier:

'God sent his Son into the world
not to condemn the world
but so that through him the world might be saved.'

(John 3:17)

Jesus' concern is to demonstrate to the woman the love of God, and thus give her
the confidence to rise above her sin and 'live to the full' (John 10:10).

6: The sixth dialogue: The decision is *now* (balances the second dialogue)

JOHN 8:21-30

Again he said to them: 21

'I am going away; you will look for me
and you will die in your sin.
Where I am going, you cannot come.'

The Jews said to one another, 'Will he kill himself? Is that what he means by 22
saying, "Where I am going, you cannot come"?' •Jesus went on: 23

'You are from below;
I am from above.
You are of this world;
I am not of this world.
I have told you already: You will die in your sins.   24
Yes, if you do not believe that I am He,
you will die in your sins.'

So they said to him, 'Who are you?' Jesus answered: 25

'What I have told you from the outset.
About you I have much to say   26
and much to condemn;
but the one who sent me is truthful,
and what I have learnt from him
I declare to the world.'

27   They failed to understand that he was talking to them about the Father.
28 So Jesus said:

> 'When you have lifted up the Son of Man,
> then you will know that I am He
> and that I do nothing of myself:
> what the Father has taught me
> is what I preach;

29
> he who sent me is with me,
> and has not left me to myself,
> for I always do what pleases him'.

30   As he was saying this, many came to believe in him.

The words 'I am He' (8:24), carry with them an unmistakable reference to the divine name, Yahweh (cf Exodus 3:13-14 where God gives his name as 'I am'). Jesus claims:

> 'if you do not believe that I am He,
> you will die in your sins.'

(John 8:24)

We recall an earlier statement:

> 'whoever refuses to believe is condemned already,
> because he has refused to believe
> in the name of God's only Son.'

(John 3:18)

The contrary statement has also appeared already in John:

> 'I tell you most solemnly,
> whoever listens to my words,
> and believes in the one who sent me,
> has eternal life;
> without being brought to judgment
> he has passed from death to life.'

(John 5:24)

John is making the same point that the Synoptics make when they speak of 'blasphemy against the Holy Spirit' (cf Mark 3:29 and commentary). If a person does not believe that Jesus' words are the words of God; if a person does not see that Jesus' works are the works of God; if he cannot see that 'I always do what pleases him' (8:29); if, on the contrary, a person hates Jesus, opposes him, accuses him of blasphemy, claims that he has an unclean spirit, he cannot but die in his sins. There is no other way out of the fixed and erroneous religious practices of the Law. There is no other way to find forgiveness, for they have to come to see that they do not know God, that the God they worship is an idol, that their religion is false.

Faced with such an accusation, the Jews ask the leading question:

> 'Who are you?' (8:25)

Jesus asks them to answer the question for themselves. The answer can only be found by listening to his words, by believing in him, by accepting the challenge he places before them of living a life of mercy.

> 'When you have lifted up the Son of Man,
> then you will know that I am He.' (8:28)

When they 'look on the one they have pierced' (John 19:37), then they will see God revealed. When that hour comes they will see the glory of God — the ultimate manifestation of the nature of the true and living God who is love.

7: The seventh dialogue: Jesus and Abraham (balances the first dialogue)

7/1: JOHN 8:31-33

31   To the Jews who believed in him Jesus said:

> 'If you make my word your home
> you will indeed be my disciples,
32   you will learn the truth
> and the truth will make you free'.

33   They answered, 'We are descended from Abraham and we have never been the slaves of anyone; what do you mean, "You will be made free"?'

The seventh dialogue is itself divided into seven parts. The debate is reaching its climax. John seems to be addressing this passage to a group of Jewish Christians. They 'believe in' Jesus (8:31), but, as will soon become clear, they do not accept Jesus' word. They think they can believe in Jesus and still remain with their attitudes to the Law and to God. Jesus tells them that the only way they can truly be his disciples is to live in and by his word. The *'truth'* he speaks of is no speculative thing. It is the reality of God's be*troth*ing of them:

> 'with integrity and justice
> with tenderness and love:
> I will betroth you to myself
> with faithfulness,
> and you will come to know Yahweh.'   *(Hosea 2:21-22)*

If they would only truly believe this, the fruit of justice and love would show in their lives, too. They would recognise God in Jesus and rejoice in the works of Jesus: works of love. They would be liberated, not just from sickness and sin, but from the religious attitudes that are binding them and causing them to bind others.

7/2: JOHN 8:34-38

34   Jesus replied:

> 'I tell you most solemnly,
> everyone who commits sin is a slave.
35   Now the slave's place in the house is not assured,
> but the son's place is assured.
36   So if the Son makes you free,
> you will be free indeed.
37   I know that you are descended from Abraham;
> but in spite of that you want to kill me
> because nothing I say has penetrated into you.
38   What I, for my part, speak of
> is what I have seen with my Father;
> but you, you put into action
> the lessons learnt from your father.'

The only way to freedom is to 'put into action the lessons learned from' Jesus (John 8:38). These men claim to believe in Jesus but their actions belie their claim. They are obviously still in slavery; their actions do not flow from God. They have another source. The God who liberated their ancestors from Egypt, the God who offers to liberate them through Jesus, is not, in reality, able to do so because they refuse to move from their religious position. They refuse to give their lives in love. Their lives are sinful (8:34). They are still slaves (8:34).

7/3: JOHN 8:39-41

They repeated, 'Our father is Abraham'. Jesus said to them: 39

'If you were Abraham's children,
you would do as Abraham did.
As it is, you want to kill me   40
when I tell you the truth
as I have learnt it from God;
that is not what Abraham did.
What you are doing is what your father does.'   41

Abraham was a man of faith (Genesis 12:1; also Romans 4, 9:7; Galatians 3; James 2:21). He trusted in God's love and acted accordingly.

7/4: JOHN 8:42-48

'We were not born of prostitution,' they went on 'we have one father: God.' Jesus answered: 42

'If God were your father, you would love me,
since I have come here from God; yes, I have come from him;
not that I came because I chose,
no, I was sent, and by him.
Do you know why you cannot take in what I say?   43
It is because you are unable to understand my language.
The devil is your father,   44
and you prefer to do
what your father wants.

He was a murderer from the start;
he was never grounded in the truth;
there is no truth in him at all:
when he lies
he is drawing on his own store,
because he is a liar, and the father of lies.
But as for me, I speak the truth   45
and for that very reason,
you do not believe me.
Can one of you convict me of sin?   46
If I speak the truth, why do you not believe me?
A child of God   47
listens to the words of God;
if you refuse to listen,
it is because you are not God's children.'

They claim to be children of God. They are not, because they cannot tolerate the fact that God is summoning them (8:43). Jesus is the word of God and they do not 'love' him (8:42); they do not 'believe' him: even though he speaks so clearly of his origins (8:42).

They are children of the devil (8:44. Greek 'diabolos' = slanderer). He is the 'father of lies' (8:44), the 'murderer' (8:44) who through his lies brought death into the world (cf Wisdom 2:24). They refuse to listen to God's word; they listen to lies; they cannot be children of God:

'A child of God
listens to (='obeys') the words of God;
if you refuse to listen
it is because you are not God's children.'

(John 8:47)
(cf John 1:12-13; 3:3-8)

7/5: JOHN 8:49-53

The Jews replied, 'Are we not right in saying that you are a Samaritan and possessed by a devil?' Jesus answered:

'I am not possessed;   49
no, I honour my Father,
but you want to dishonour me.
Not that I care for my own glory,   50
there is someone who takes care of that and is the judge of it.
I tell you most solemnly,   51
whoever keeps my word
will never see death.'

The Jews said, 'Now we know for certain that you are possessed. Abraham 52 is dead, and the prophets are dead, and yet you say, "Whoever keeps my word will never know the taste of death".   53

Already we have seen that Jesus is the 'living bread' (6:51), God's nourishment for his people as they journey on their exodus to freedom. We have seen that Jesus is the 'holy one of God' (6:69), the source of living water (7:38) and the 'light of the world' (8:12). We have seen that it is Jesus who knows God and reveals him to us (1:18); he makes God's word flesh for us (1:14), if we allow the word to 'penetrate into us' (8:37).

Here, Jesus promises, in words that echo an earlier claim (6:58):

'whoever keeps my word will never see death.' (8:51)

This word, as will become abundantly clear later (14:15, 21-24; 15:10; 17:6; 1 John 2:3-5; 3:22-24; 5:3), is the command of love. He is God's faithful love to us. We will know fulness of life and freedom if we become instruments of this same faithful love to others.

We are nearing the climax of the debate, and the Jews explicitly ask him:

'Who are you claiming to be?'

7/6: JOHN 8:54-57

•Are you greater than our father Abraham, 54 who is dead? The prophets are dead too. Who are you claiming to be?' •Jesus answered:

'If I were to seek my own glory
that would be no glory at all;
my glory is conferred by the Father,

by the one of whom you say, "He is our God"
although you do not know him.   55
But I know him,
and if I were to say: I do not know him,
I should be a liar, as you are liars yourselves.
But I do know him, and I faithfully keep his word.
Your father Abraham rejoiced   56
to think that he would see my Day;
he saw it and was glad.'

The Jews then said, 'You are not fifty yet, and you have seen Abraham!' 57

Here, in reply to their question, Jesus claims that they do not know who he is because they do not know God (8:54). He claims to know God (8:55). The proof of this lies in the fact that:

'I faithfully keep his word.' (8:55)

They do not know God because they do not 'keep his word' (8:51).

Abraham rejoiced when he heard he would have a son (Genesis 17:17); he was glad when God's word to him was fulfilled. Jesus is claiming to be that fulfilment (John 8:56). In Jesus, God's word is made flesh (John 1:14).

7/7: JOHN 8:58-59
Jesus replied: 58

'I tell you most solemnly,
before Abraham ever was,
I Am'.

At this they picked up stones to throw at him; but Jesus hid himself and left 59 the Temple.

At the scene in the burning bush (Exodus 3:1-15), God revealed his name to Moses:

'Say to the sons of Israel: *I Am* has sent me to you.'   *(Exodus 3:14)*

We cannot give God a name. God is what God has been for us in our history:

'Yahweh, the God of your Fathers, the God of Abraham, and the God of Isaac, and the God of Jacob, has sent me to you.'   *(Exodus 3:15)*

God reveals himself in history, the history of people and the history of a people. He reveals himself as a God of faithful love.

Those who knew Jesus saw in him the revelation of God. He it was who made God's word flesh (John 1:14). It was Jesus who was God for them. In Jesus' words they heard the words of God; in Jesus' love they saw God's love. Jesus revealed to them the glory of God.

The final line highlights the tragedy. The Temple is left without the 'light of the world' (John 8:12, cf Jeremiah 7:5-7 and Ezekiel 10:18-22). The religious leaders stayed with their theology, their images of God, their securities and power and prestige. They refused to follow Jesus, and so refused to leave their father and their 'father's house and come to a land I will show you' (Genesis 12:1). By this refusal they showed that they were not true children of Abraham, nor obedient to the word obeyed by him.

This scene at the feast of Tabernacles has been a scene of tragic contrasts. On the one side stands the Temple, water flowing from the altar and light streaming from the court; on the other side stands Jesus, calling the people to come to him for water (7:37-38) and light (8:12). John constantly reminds his readers that Jesus' life was in danger (7:1, 13, 19, 25, 30, 32; 8:37, 40, 59). Against this mounting tension, the religious authorities argue against Jesus' Messianic claims, while Jesus publicly exposes their false leadership to the crowds. The dominant theme is the manifestation and rejection of the Word as life and light. The Temple authorities are rejected because they refuse to let this word penetrate into them (John 7:37). They refuse to answer God's summons to live a life of justice.

*   *   *   *   *   *   *   *

Points for Reflection:

1: Jesus was hated because he gave evidence that people's lives were evil (7:7). He showed up the false religion of the Pharisees, especially by manifestly believing, himself, in a God of compassion: the God of the Exodus. If I am not hated by anyone, does that say something of my failure to live a life of 'hungering and thirsting after justice' (Matthew 5:6, cf 5:10-12)?

2: Am I prepared to do God's will (John 7:17)? The Pharisees took it for granted that they were; and they were wrong. The proof is in my willingness to listen to Jesus' teaching and follow it.

'This is my commandment: love one another as I have loved you.'

(John 15:12)

3: God wants us to come to know him (cf John 7:28-29):

'I will betroth you to myself for ever,
betroth you with integrity and justice,
with tenderness and love;
I will betroth you to myself with faithfulness,
and you will come to know Yahweh.'

(Hosea 2:22)

4: 'There has never been anybody who has spoken like him' (John 7:46).

5: Jesus did not condemn the woman caught in adultery (John 8:3-11). He loved her. He faced her sin, admitted it for what it was and for what she knew it to be; but still he loved her and believed in her. His final words to her are words full of trust: 'Don't sin any more' (John 8:11). He, obviously, believed that she did not have to sin, did not have to find substitutes for love. No doubt his compassion, his non-judgmental attitude, and his confidence gave her the courage to rise above her sin and seek true love. The condemnation of the Pharisees brought her nothing but embarrassment.

6: 'The one who sent me is with me, and has not left me to myself, for I always do what pleases him' (John 8:29).
We have here, an insight into Jesus' intimate prayer and union with his Father.

Chapter 3
Jesus is 'one with the Father'.
Man is judged by the stand
he takes towards Jesus,
who gives 'light' and 'life'

John 9:1 — 10:42

JOHN 9:1-7

1/2 **9** As he went along, he saw a man who had been blind from birth. •His disciples asked him, 'Rabbi, who sinned, this man or his parents, for him to have been 3 born blind?' •'Neither he nor his parents sinned,' Jesus answered 'he was born blind so that the works of God might be displayed in him.

4   'As long as the day lasts
           I must carry out the work of the one who sent me;
           the night will soon be here when no one can work.
5   As long as I am in the world
           I am the light of the world.'·

6   Having said this, he spat on the ground, made a paste with the spittle, put 7 this over the eyes of the blind man. •and said to him, 'Go and wash in the Pool of Siloam (a name that means 'sent'). So the blind man went off and washed himself, and came away with his sight restored.

The two central motifs of the last section were those of water and light. They are drawn together in this anecdote. It is in the act of washing (9:7), symbol of Baptism, that the blind man receives sight from the one who calls himself, once again, the:
'light of the world'. (9:5 = 8:12)

In the last section we witnessed the religious leaders doing their best to 'overpower' the light (cf John 1:5). In this scene John demonstrates the fact that Jesus is truly:
'a light that shines in the dark,
a light that darkness could not overpower.'   *(John 1:4-5)*

It is important to note that Jesus is not simply healing a blind man. The man was born blind — a fact stressed by John (cf 9:2 and 3. cf also 9:19, 9:20, 9:32). The act of Jesus is a creative act.

The main point John wants to make is that, in this action of Jesus, we see the 'works of God' (9:3) displayed. In his word and in his works Jesus reveals the living God:

'If I am not doing my Father's work,
there is no need to believe me;
but if I am doing it,
then even if you refuse to believe in me,
at least believe in the work I do.
then you will know for sure
that the Father is in me and I am in the Father.'

(John 10:37-38)

'You must believe me when I say
that I am in the Father and the Father is in me;
believe it on the evidence of this work,
if for no other reason.'

(John 14:11)

John also introduces into the narrative a sense of urgency. It is vitally important to accept the light when it is offered, for:

'the night will soon be here.' (9:4)

JOHN 9:8-41

His neighbours and people who earlier had seen him begging said, 'Isn't 8 this the man who used to sit and beg?' •Some said, 'Yes, it is the same one'. 9 Others said, 'No, he only looks like him'. The man himself said, 'I am the man'. So they said to him, 'Then how do your eyes come to be open?' •'The man called 10 11 Jesus' he answered 'made a paste, daubed my eyes with it and said to me, "Go and wash at Siloam"; so I went, and when I washed I could see.' •They asked, 12 'Where is he?' 'I don't know' he answered.

They brought the man who had been blind to the Pharisees. •It had been a 13 14 sabbath day when Jesus made the paste and opened the man's eyes, •so when 15 the Pharisees asked him how he had come to see, he said, 'He put a paste on my eyes, and I washed, and I can see'. •Then some of the Pharisees said, 'This 16 man cannot be from God: he does not keep the sabbath'. Others said, 'How could a sinner produce signs like this?' And there was disagreement among them. So they spoke to the blind man again, 'What have you to say about him yourself, 17 now that he has opened your eyes?' 'He is a prophet' replied the man.

However, the Jews would not believe that the man had been blind and had 18 gained his sight, without first sending for his parents and •asking them, 'Is this 19 man really your son who you say was born blind? If so, how is it that he is now able to see?' •His parents answered, 'We know he is our son and we know he 20 was born blind, •but we don't know how it is that he can see now, or who 21 opened his eyes. He is old enough: let him speak for himself.' •His parents 22 spoke like this out of fear of the Jews, who had already agreed to expel from the synagogue anyone who should acknowledge Jesus as the Christ. •This was why 23 his parents said, 'He is old enough; ask him'.

So the Jews again sent for the man and said to him, 'Give glory to God! 24 For our part, we know that this man is a sinner.' •The man answered, 'I don't 25 know if he is a sinner; I only know that I was blind and now I can see'. •They 26 said to him, 'What did he do to you? How did he open your eyes?' •He replied, 27 'I have told you once and you wouldn't listen. Why do you want to hear it all

again? Do you want to become his disciples too?' •At this they hurled abuse 28
at him: 'You can be his disciple,' they said 'we are disciples of Moses: •we 29
know that God spoke to Moses, but as for this man, we don't know where he
comes from'. •The man replied, 'Now here is an astonishing thing! He has 30
opened my eyes, and you don't know where he comes from! •We know that God 31
doesn't listen to sinners, but God does listen to men who are devout and do his
will. •Ever since the world began it is unheard of for anyone to open the eyes 32
of a man who was born blind; •if this man were not from God, he couldn't do 33
a thing.' •'Are you trying to teach us,' they replied 'and you a sinner through 34
and through, since you were born!' And they drove him away.

Jesus heard they had driven him away, and when he found him he said to 35
him, 'Do you believe in the Son of Man?' •'Sir,' the man replied 'tell me who 36
he is so that I may believe in him.' •Jesus said, 'You are looking at him; he is 37
speaking to you'. • The man said, 'Lord, I believe', and worshipped him.   38
Jesus said: 39

> 'It is for judgement
> that I have come into this world,
> so that those without sight may see
> and those with sight turn blind'.

Hearing this, some Pharisees who were present said to him, 'We are not blind, 40
surely?' •Jesus replied: 41

> 'Blind? If you were,
> you would not be guilty,
> but since you say, "We see",
> your guilt remains.

This is a trial scene. The follower of Jesus, newly enlightened by God and
welcomed, by baptism, into the Christian community, is threatened and judged
and condemned and cast out of the synagogue. In the final scene the tables are
turned and Jesus emerges as the judge. John seems to have had in mind those
Christians who reverted to Judaism when threatened with expulsion from the
synagogue.

By contrast, the blind beggar has his sight given him by Jesus and he will not
be cajoled into denying the facts (cf John 9:9, 11, 15, 24-34). As a consequence he
is drawn into closer and closer intimacy with Jesus. At first Jesus is the 'man' who
made the paste and daubed his eyes (John 9:11); then Jesus is the 'prophet' (John
9:17). Finally, he sees Jesus for the first time. Jesus seeks him out, speaks to him
and calls him to discipleship (John 9:35-37). We might recall the words of John's
first Letter:

> 'We are already the children of God
> but what we are to be in the future has not yet been revealed;
> all we know is that when it is revealed
> we shall be like him
> because we shall see him as he really is.'

(1 John 3:2)

The man, seeing Jesus for the first time, sees him as he really is, and his response is
simple and complete:

> 'Lord, I believe.'

(John 9:38)

We are reminded of the words of Jesus as recorded by Mark:

'When they lead you away to hand you over, do not worry beforehand about what to say; no, say whatever is given to you when the time comes, because it is not you who will be speaking: it will be the Holy Spirit. Brother will betray brother to death, and the father his child ... You will be hated by all men on account of my name; but the man who stands firm to the end will be saved.'

(Mark 13:11-13)

In the end it is Jesus who is the judge. The man's parents stand accused because they shrugged their shoulders (9:22); the Pharisees, because they obstinately refused to see (9:16). The blind man was given sight; they were left in the dark. John alludes to the statement of Isaiah:

'Go and say to this people
"Hear and hear again, but do not understand;
see and see again, but do not perceive".
Make the heart of this people gross,
its ears dull;
shut its eyes,
so that it will not see with its eyes,
hear with its ears,
understand with its heart,
and be converted and healed.'   *(Isaiah 6:9-10, cf John 9:39, cf also Matthew 13:14-15)*

Up to this stage it has been the powers of darkness that have been on the attack, testing Jesus, accusing him, judging him. But Jesus is the 'light of the world' (8:12 and 9:5), 'a light that darkness could not overpower' (1:5). He gives light to the blind man and exposes the darkness of the authorities.

JOHN 10:1-3a

10 'I tell you most solemnly, anyone who does not enter the sheepfold 1 through the gate, but gets in some other way is a thief and a brigand. The one who enters through the gate is the shepherd of the flock; •the $\frac{2}{3}$ gatekeeper lets him in,

This is still Jesus the judge who is speaking. The religious authorities who coerce God's people are branded as thieves and brigands.

JOHN 10:3b-6

the sheep hear his voice, one by one   he calls his own sheep and leads them out. •When he has brought out his flock, he goes 4 ahead of them, and the sheep follow because they know his voice. •They never 5 follow a stranger but run away from him: they do not recognise the voice of strangers.'

Jesus told them   this parable but they failed to understand what he meant 6 by telling it to them.

We recall Mark's statement:

'His teaching made a deep impression on them because, unlike the scribes, he taught them with authority.'

(Mark 1:22)

Notice that the shepherd calls his sheep and 'leads them out' (10:3). We are dealing here with the God of the Exodus, the liberator, the one who calls his people by name and leads them out of slavery.

JOHN 10:7-9
So Jesus spoke to them again: 7

>'I tell you most solemnly,
> I am the gate of the sheepfold.
> All others who have come   8
> are thieves and brigands;
> but the sheep took no notice of them.
> I am the gate.   9
> Anyone who enters through me will be safe:
> he will go freely in and out
> and be sure of finding pasture.

In this passage, and the ones following, John gives an allegorical interpretation of the two parables just quoted (10:1-6). Jesus is the 'gate' (10:7, 9 cf 10:1). The Pharisees claim to be the way to God. They claim to be the ones who open the way for God to speak to his people through the Law and the Prophets of which they are custodians. Jesus accuses them of using their position for their own advantage. They do not liberate the people; on the contrary, they keep them enslaved. Jesus is the way to freedom and salvation.

The language is drawn from a celebrated passage in the prophet Ezekiel. Since this whole section relies on Ezekiel so heavily, we shall quote it here in full:

34 The word of Yahweh was addressed to me as follows, •'Son of man, $\frac{1}{2}$ prophesy against the shepherds of Israel; prophesy and say to them, "Shepherds, the Lord Yahweh says this: Trouble for the shepherds of Israel who feed themselves! Shepherds ought to feed their flock, •yet you have fed on 3 milk, you have dressed yourselves in wool, you have sacrificed the fattest sheep, but failed to feed the flock. •You have failed to make weak sheep strong, or to 4 care for the sick ones, or bandage the wounded ones. You have failed to bring back strays or look for the lost. On the contrary, you have ruled them cruelly and violently. •For lack of a shepherd they have scattered, to become the prey of any 5 wild animal; they have scattered far. •My flock is straying this way and that, 6 on mountains and on high hills; my flock has been scattered all over the country; no one bothers about them and no one looks for them.

'Well then, shepherds, hear the word of Yahweh. •As I live, I swear it—it is $\frac{7}{8}$ the Lord Yahweh who speaks—since my flock has been looted and for lack of a shepherd is now the prey of any wild animal, since my shepherds have stopped bothering about my flock, since my shepherds feed themselves rather than my flock, •in view of all this, shepherds, hear the word of Yahweh. •The Lord $\frac{9}{10}$ Yahweh says this: I am going to call the shepherds to account. I am going to take my flock back from them and I shall not allow them to feed my flock. In this way the shepherds will stop feeding themselves. I shall rescue my sheep from their mouths; they will not prey on them any more.

For the Lord Yahweh says this: I am going to look after my flock myself 11 and keep all of it in view. •As a shepherd keeps all his flock in view when he 12 stands up in the middle of his scattered sheep, so shall I keep my sheep in view. I shall rescue them from wherever they have been scattered during the mist and darkness. •I shall bring them out of the countries where they are; I shall gather 13 them together from foreign countries and bring them back to their own land. I shall pasture them on the mountains of Israel, in the ravines and in every

14 inhabited place in the land. •I shall feed them in good pasturage; the high mountains of Israel will be their grazing ground. There they will rest in good grazing ground; they will browse in rich pastures on the mountains of Israel.
15 I myself will pasture my sheep, I myself will show them where to rest—it is
16 the Lord Yahweh who speaks. •I shall look for the lost one, bring back the stray, bandage the wounded and make the weak strong. I shall watch over the fat and healthy. I shall be a true shepherd to them.
17 As for you, my sheep, the Lord Yahweh says this: I will judge between
18 sheep and sheep, between rams and he-goats. •Not content to graze in good pastures, you trample down the rest; not content to drink clear water, you
19 muddy the rest with your feet. •And my sheep must graze on what your feet have
20 trampled, drink what your feet have muddied. •Very well then, the Lord Yahweh says this: I myself am now about to judge between fat sheep and lean sheep.
21 Since you have butted all the weak sheep with your rumps and shoulders and
22 horns, until you have chased them away, •I am going to come and rescue my sheep from being cheated; I will judge between sheep and sheep.
23 I mean to raise up one shepherd, my servant David, and to put him in charge of them and he will pasture them; he will pasture them and be their shepherd.
24 I, Yahweh, will be their God, and my servant David shall be their ruler. I, Yahweh,
25 have spoken. •I shall make a covenant of peace with them; I shall rid the country of wild animals. They will be able to live safely in the wilderness and go to sleep
26 in the woods. •I shall settle them round my hill; I shall send rain at the proper
27 time; it will be a fertile rain. •The trees of the countryside will yield their fruit and the earth its produce; they will feel safe on their own farms. And men will learn that I am Yahweh when I break their yokestraps and release them from
28 their captors. •No more will they be a prey to foreign countries, no more will they be eaten by wild animals in this country. They will live without fear and
29 no one will disturb them again. •I shall make splendid vegetation grow for them; no more will they suffer from famine in this land; no more will they have to bear
30 the insults of other nations. •And men will learn that I, their God, am with them and that they, the House of Israel, are my people—it is the Lord Yahweh who
31 speaks. •And you, my sheep, are the flock I shall pasture, and I am your God— it is the Lord Yahweh who speaks." '

(Ezekiel 34:1-31)

JOHN 10:10

10   The thief comes
        only to steal and kill and destroy.
        I have come
        so that they may have life
        and have it to the full.

Those who exercise religious authority are 'thieves' (cf 10:1); they 'feed themselves rather than my flock' (Ezekiel 34:8). Jesus, on the contrary, can claim:

'I have come
so that they may have life
and have it to the full.'

(John 10:10)

The theme of life has been present since the Prologue (John 1:4). In the discourse between Jesus and Nicodemus, we read:

'God loved the world so much
that he gave his only Son,

so that everyone who believes in him may not be lost
but may have eternal life.'

(John 3:16)

John the Baptist, too, said of Jesus:

'Anyone who believes in the Son has eternal life.'

(John 3:36)

Jesus, the source of 'living water' (John 4:10) promised:

'the water that I shall give
will turn into a spring inside him,
welling up to eternal life.'

(John 4:14)

In the debate with the religious authorities, Jesus claimed:

'I tell you most solemnly,
whoever listens to my words,
and believes in the one who sent me,
has eternal life;
without being brought to judgment
he has passed from death to life.'

(John 5:24)

Later he claims to be the 'bread of God':

'which comes down from heaven and gives life to the world.'

(John 6:33)

Life is linked, too, with the image of light:

'I am the light of the world;
anyone who follows me will not be walking in the dark;
he will have the light of life.'

(John 8:12)

This theme will come to a climax in the next chapter in which Jesus restores
Lazarus to life.

JOHN 10:11-13

11   I am the good shepherd:
      the good shepherd is one who lays down his life for his sheep.
12   The hired man, since he is not the shepherd
      and the sheep do not belong to him,
      abandons the sheep and runs away
      as soon as he sees a wolf coming,
      and then the wolf attacks and scatters the sheep;
13   this is because he is only a hired man
      and has no concern for the sheep.

The Pharisees are hired men (10:12 cf the 'strangers' of 10:5). Jesus is the
shepherd of the flock (10:11 cf 10:3). Ezekiel had God saying:

'I am going to look after my flock myself and keep all of it in view.' (34:11)

He spoke also of God saying:

'I mean to raise up one shepherd, my servant David, and to put him in charge of them
and he will pasture them; he will pasture them and be their shepherd.' (34:23)

Jesus is the Son of David, the Christ, the one in whom God cares for his flock
himself.

John enters deeply into the mystery of God's care by telling us that Jesus 'is the one who lays down his life for his sheep' (10:11). This goes well beyond any Old Testament allusion to penetrate to the heart of the life-giving love of God. We are reminded of the Servant of Yahweh:

'We had all gone astray like sheep,
each taking his own way,
and Yahweh burdened him
with the sin of all of us.
Harshly dealt with, he bore it humbly,
he never opened his mouth,
like a lamb that is led to the slaughter-house,
like a sheep that is dumb before its shearers
never opening his mouth.
By force and by law he was taken;
would anyone plead his cause?
Yes, he was torn away from the land of the living;
for our faults struck down in death.'

(Isaiah 53:6-8)

John goes further: he has the shepherd himself giving his life for his sheep. Jesus gives his life that we may live. He gives his:

'flesh for the life of the world.'

(John 6:51)

JOHN 10:14-16

14   I am the good shepherd;
I know my own
and my own know me,
15   just as the Father knows me
and I know the Father;
and I lay down my life for my sheep.
16   And there are other sheep I have
that are not of this fold,
and these I have to lead as well.
They too will listen to my voice,
and there will be only one flock,
and one shepherd.

When the first disciples wanted to know Jesus, he asked them to:

'Come and see.'

(John 1:39)

Jesus did not want them only to know *about* him. He sought to share with them the kind of knowledge that comes from the experience of a personal encounter. In the Old Testament the basic image behind the word 'to know' is the image of intimate sexual union:

'Adam knew his wife Eve and she conceived and gave birth to Cain.'

(Genesis 4:1)

The same imagery is used of the intimacy between God and his people:

'I will betroth you to myself for ever,
betroth you with integrity and justice,

with tenderness and love;
I will betroth you to myself with faithfulness,
and you will come to know Yahweh.'

(Hosea 2:22)

This knowledge is the knowledge of love:

'what I want is love, not sacrifice; knowledge of God, not holocausts.'

(Hosea 6:6)

Jesus claims to have this knowledge of his Father (10:15). He is:

'the only Son who is nearest to the Father's heart.'

(John 1:18)

'The Father loves the Son.'

(John 5:20)

Jesus is spoken of as:

'the one who comes from God:
he has seen the Father.'

(John 6:46)

He claims:

'there is one who sent me and I really come from him,
and you do not know him,
but I know him
because I come from him
and it was he who sent me.'

(John 7:28-29)

'I am not alone:
the one who sent me is with me.'

(John 8:16)

'he who sent me is with me,
and has not left me to myself,
for I always do what pleases him.'

(John 8:29)

'What I, for my part, speak of
is what I have seen with my Father.'

(John 8:38)

'my glory is conferred by the Father,
by the one of whom you say, "He is our God"
although you do not know him.
But I know him,
and if I were to say I do not know him,
I should be a liar as you are liars yourselves.
But I do know him, and I faithfully keep his word.'

(John 8:54-55 cf 8:19)

Jesus' desire is to make his Father known by others (cf John 1:18); that is, to draw them, too, into this intimate union he has with God. Therefore he wants to know men. He is the bridegroom (cf John 3:29-36). He is the one who lays down his life, who gives all he is and has, to share his love and draw others into the embrace of God. Jesus prays:

'Father, may they be one in us,
as you are in me and I am in you,
so that the world may believe that it was you who sent me.

I have given them the glory you gave to me,
that they may be one as we are one.
With me in them and you in me,
may they be so completely one
that the world will realise that it was you who sent me
and that I have loved them as much as you loved me.'

(John 17:21-23)

John, in the text upon which we are meditating, reminds his readers of the fact that Jesus is giving his life 'for the world' (6:51). He speaks, therefore, of the Gentiles, the 'other sheep' (10:16) who are to be drawn into the fold.

JOHN 10:17-18

17   The Father loves me,
        because I lay down my life
        in order to take it up again.
18   No one takes it from me;
        I lay it down of my own free will,
        and as it is in my power to lay it down,
        so it is in my power to take it up again;
        and this is the command I have been given by my Father.'

The parable speaks of the shepherd as one who 'goes ahead of' the sheep (John 10:4). Jesus does this by freely giving his life in obedience to the command of his Father. God himself is self-giving, life-giving love. He has entrusted (='commended' = 'commanded') to his Son the mission of manifesting this to the world. Jesus 'knows' his Father, and from the deep intimacy of his listening to (='obeying') his Father's word, he freely chooses to give his life for the world. In his passion and resurrection Jesus manifests the glory of God and draws the sheep to himself:

'When I am lifted up from the earth,
I shall draw all men to myself.'

(John 12:32)

JOHN 10:19-21

19
20   These words caused disagreement among the Jews. •Many said, 'He is
21 possessed, he is raving; why bother to listen to him?' •Others said, 'These are
   not the words of a man possessed by a devil: could a devil open the eyes of the
   blind?'

Men are judged by their relationship to Jesus. We are reminded of Simeon's prophecy:

'He is destined for the fall and for the rising of many in Israel, destined to be a sign
that is rejected.'

(Luke 2:34)

We may also think of the words of the author of the Letter to the Hebrews:

'The word of God is something alive and active: it cuts like any double-edged sword
but more finely: . . . it can judge the secret emotions and thoughts. No created thing
can hide from him; everything is uncovered and open to the eyes of the one to whom
we must give account of ourselves.'

(Hebrews 4:12-13)

JOHN 10:22-24

It was the time when the feast of Dedication was being celebrated in Jerusalem. 22
It was winter, •and Jesus was in the Temple walking up and down in the Portico 23
of Solomon. •The Jews gathered round him and said, 'How much longer are 24
you going to keep us in suspense? If you are the Christ, tell us plainly.'

The 'Temple' (10:23) dominates the scene. The feast of Dedication was
instituted to celebrate the recovery of the Temple from the Syrians and its
purification by Judas Maccabaeus in 165 B.C. Jesus has been making Messianic
claims, and, for the first time, his opponents ask him outright the question that
has been implicit throughout this and the previous discussions:

'If you are the Christ, tell us plainly.' (10:24)

JOHN 10:25-30

•Jesus replied: 25

'I have told you, but you do not believe.
The works I do in my Father's name are my witness;
but you do not believe,   26
because you are no sheep of mine.
The sheep that belong to me listen to my voice;   27
I know them and they follow me.
I give them eternal life;   28
they will never be lost
and no one will ever steal them from me.
The Father who gave them to me is greater than anyone,   29
and no one can steal from the Father.
The Father and I are one.'   30

The answer to their question has already been given (John 8:42). The
evidence is here in:

'the works I do in my Father's name.'   *(John 10:25)*

God has always been revealed by his works, from the work of Exodus
through the history of his liberating presence among his people. Jesus is the
Christ; not the Christ they expected, not the Christ who would ensure the
dominance of the Jews or the continuance of the power of the religious
leadership. He is the Christ, the anointed one, who makes God's liberation
powerfully present to the world. He is God's word summoning men to the
intimate union with God that shows itself in works of love and justice.

The Jews want to know whether Jesus is the Christ. But they do not really
want to know. They 'do not believe' (10:25). They are unwilling to listen to his
word; they are unwilling to respond to his summons. The religious leaders persist
in their determination to rob God of his glory by attempting to 'steal' the sheep
for themselves. They persist in being 'thieves and brigands' (John 10:1). They will
not, for all their efforts, be able to wrest the sheep from the care of the true
shepherd (10:28).

Jesus, as his works prove, is one with his Father (10:30).

JOHN 10:31-33

The Jews fetched stones to stone him, •so Jesus said to them, 'I have done 31 32
many good works for you to see, works from my Father; for which of these

are you stoning me?' •The Jews answered him, 'We are not stoning you for doing   33
a good work but for blasphemy: you are only a man and you claim to be God'.

We have heard this before:

'His answer to them was, "My Father goes on working and so do I". But that only
made the Jews even more intent on killing him, because, not content with breaking
the sabbath, he spoke of God as his own Father, and so made himself God's equal.'
(John 5:17-18)

The Jews fetch stones to stone him because Jesus identifies God with the works
that he does. They cannot accept this for it demands a repentance that they are
unwilling to undergo. In fact, Jesus' works are an accusation that the God they
are worshipping is an idol. They must accuse him of blasphemy if they are to
maintain their 'religious' stance. Jesus says:

'You must believe me when I say
that I am in the Father and the Father is in me;
believe it on the evidence of this work if for no other reason.'
(John 14:11)

The Jews are unwilling to believe him; they must reject him. And they reject him
in God's name (compare the accusation brought against Jesus in the trial scene
recorded by the Synoptics, Mark 14:64 and Matthew 26:65).

JOHN 10:34-38
Jesus answered: 34

'Is it not written in your Law:
I said, you are gods? [a]

So the Law uses the word gods   35
of those to whom the word of God was addressed,
and scripture cannot be rejected.
Yet you say to someone the Father has consecrated and sent   36
        into the world,
"You are blaspheming",
because he says, "I am the Son of God".
If I am not doing my Father's work,   37
there is no need to believe me;
but if I am doing it,   38
then even if you refuse to believe in me,
at least believe in the work I do;
then you will know for sure
that the Father is in me and I am in the Father.'
(a: Psalm 82:6)

The argument that is meant to clinch the debate with the Jewish leaders is the
argument from Psalm 82. We quoted this psalm earlier (cf commentary on John
5:17). According to this psalm, the true, living God, Yahweh is distinguished
from all other gods, by his concern for justice. The psalm is an indictment of
those who were judges in Israel. Their function was to dispense God's justice and
therefore:

'I once said, "You, too, are gods,
sons of the Most High, all of you".'
(Psalm 82:6)

If these judges could be called sons of the Most High, how much more right has Jesus to be called the 'Son of God' (10:36), when he is doing his Father's work. Jesus is manifesting God's justice to the world. His works prove that:

'the Father is in me and I am in the Father.'

(John 10:38)

JOHN 10:39-42

They wanted to arrest him then, but he eluded them.   39

He went back again to the far side of the Jordan to stay in the district where   40 John had once been baptising. •Many people who came to him there said, 'John   41 gave no signs, but all he said about this man was true'; •and many of them   42 believed in him.

*   *   *   *   *   *   *   *

Points for Reflection:

1: The disciples saw the blind man. They asked the wrong question. They wanted to know why. Jesus, on the other hand, asked the question: What can be made of this sickness? How can God be glorified in it? If we wasted less energy asking why? why? why? and instead concentrated our attention on finding ways of accepting the facts of our life and seeing how to use them to the best advantage, we would probably be happier people. Do I believe with Paul that 'nothing can ever come between us and the love of God' (Romans 8:39)? It may be that I should change the circumstances of my life; it may be that I should accept them.

'Lord, grant me the courage to change what I can
the serenity to accept what cannot be changed
the wisdom to know the difference.'

2: 'You are looking at him. He is speaking to you' (John 5:17). How often we are looking at Jesus and listening to him, but we do not realise it.

3: 'I have come so that they may have life and have it to the full' (John 10:10). This is the basis of all Christian morality. If a way of acting is morally good, it must lead to a fuller life. It may be that much suffering is involved on the way; it may be that much patience is required. There is no easy way to life. But every moral act does lead to life and it must be able to be shown that it does. A negative, small-minded, petty attitude is incompatible with the morality of Christ. He asks all of us; he challenges us to give of our best. But it is always so that we might live to the full.

4: The more we know Jesus (John 10:14), the more we know God, his Father (10:30), the more we, too, will want everyone to know them; the more we will want one flock and one shepherd (John 10:16). This is not a matter of ensuring uniformity in theology, uniformity in ritual expression, uniformity in all aspects of organisation. It is a matter of sharing.

'There is one Body, one Spirit, just as you were all called into one and the same hope when you were called. There is one Lord, one faith, one baptism, and one God who is Father of all, over all, through all and within all.'

(Ephesians 4:4-6)

If each person seeks to know God more and respects the other person's search, then in God's time, and as our hearts are freed by the journey, we shall approach each other. The nearer we come to the centre, the nearer we come to one another.

5: Meditate on Psalm 82 (John 10:34). It gives the essential qualities of the One the Bible presents as the true, living God. Yahweh is recognised by his justice.

Chapter 4
Jesus gives 'Eternal Life' (11:26)

John 11:1-54

JOHN 11:1-4

11 There was a man named Lazarus who lived in the village of Bethany with 1
the two sisters, Mary and Martha, and he was ill.—•It was the same 2
Mary, the sister of the sick man Lazarus, who anointed the Lord with
ointment and wiped his feet with her hair. •The sisters sent this message to 3
Jesus, 'Lord, the man you love is ill'. •On receiving the message, Jesus said, 4
'This sickness will end not in death but in God's glory, and through it the Son
of God will be glorified'.

The anointing mentioned here (11:2) is recorded in John 12:1-11. Jesus'
comment on receiving the news of Lazarus' illness (11:4) reminds us of his words
in reference to the man born blind:

'he was born blind so that the works of God might be displayed in him.'

(John 9:3)

In his every action Jesus' aim was to give glory to his Father (John 7:18); that is,
to reveal God's faithful love. In this he contrasted himself to the religious leaders
who sought their own glory (John 5:44 and 7:18).

Because this was Jesus' basic attitude, God chose to reveal himself through
the works and words of Jesus. In this way Jesus himself was glorified:

'If I were to seek my own glory
that would be no glory at all;
my glory is conferred by the Father.'

(John 8:54)

In the Prologue, John claimed:

'he lived among us
and we saw his glory,
the glory that is his as the only Son of the Father,
full of enduring love.'

(John 1:14)

This glory, according to John (John 7:39) was only finally manifested on the
cross. There Jesus revealed, in a complete way, the enduring love of God and his
own intimate union with his Father in this love. But every word he spoke and
every work he did manifested in some way this glory. This is especially true of

those special actions of Jesus that John calls 'signs'. The first was at Cana (John 2:11). There, Jesus manifested to all the fact that he was the Christ who was bringing in a new covenant between God and men:

> 'This was the first of the signs given by Jesus: it was given at Cana in Galilee. He let his glory be seen, and his disciples believed in him.'
>
> *(John 2:11)*

To Nicodemus, Jesus explained that this new covenant meant 'eternal life' to 'everyone who believes' (John 3:16). To the woman of Samaria, he explained that it meant a 'spring inside a man, welling up to eternal life' (John 4:14). This Messianic gift would set a person free from the powers of darkness and enable him to 'come out into the light' (John 3:21).

The second sign (John 4:54) was a life-giving act: Jesus cured the nobleman's son. Likewise with the third sign, the cure of the palsied man (John 5:1-15). Once again, Jesus spoke of eternal life:

> 'I tell you most solemnly,
> whoever listens to my words,
> and believes in the one who sent me,
> has eternal life;
> without being brought to judgment
> he has passed from death to life.
> I tell you most solemnly,
> the hour will come — in fact it is already here —
> when the dead will hear the voice of the Son of God,
> and all who hear it will live.
> For the Father, who is the source of life,
> has made the Son the source of life;
> and because he is the Son of Man,
> has appointed him supreme judge.
> Do not be surprised at this,
> for the hour is coming
> when the dead will leave their graves
> at the sound of his voice.'
>
> *(John 5:25-28)*

The fourth and fifth signs are linked: the miracle of the loaves (John 6:1-15) and the walking on the water (John 6:16-21). In commenting upon them, Jesus says:

> 'Yes, it is my Father's will
> that whoever sees the Son and believes in him
> shall have eternal life,
> and that I shall raise him up on the last day.'
>
> *(John 6:40)*

The sixth sign was the curing of the man born blind. In the discourse leading up to this sign, Jesus spoke of himself as the 'light of the world' (8:12), leading men from darkness to light. He spoke too of 'freedom' (8:36) and 'eternal life' (8:51).

John, then, has been building up to the seventh sign. It comes as a climax to the other six and gathers up their main themes in a powerful act when Lazarus comes out of the darkness of death (John 11:43), is freed (11:44) and given life

(11:25-26). It is also the climax of Jesus' public ministry. It is, in John's account, the action that finally caused the religious leaders to decide to kill Jesus (John 11:45-54). John will mention it again in relation to Jesus' triumphant entry into Jerusalem (John 12:17-18). We notice a double meaning in the statement that through the sickness of Lazarus: 'the Son of God will be glorified' (John 11:4). John is telling us that Jesus will manifest his life-giving power. He is also telling us that his action will be the direct cause of his death, a death that would finally reveal his glory (cf John 7:39).

JOHN 11:5-17

5
6   Jesus loved Martha and her sister and Lazarus, •yet when he heard that
7 Lazarus was ill he stayed where he was for two more days •before saying to the
8 disciples, 'Let us go to Judaea'. •The disciples said, 'Rabbi, it is not long since
9 the Jews wanted to stone you; are you going back again?' •Jesus replied:

> 'Are there not twelve hours in the day?
> A man can walk in the daytime without stumbling
> because he has the light of this world to see by;
10 > but if he walks at night he stumbles,
> because there is no light to guide him.'

11   He said that and then added, 'Our friend Lazarus is resting, I am going to
12 wake him'. •The disciples said to him, 'Lord, if he is able to rest he is sure to get
13 better'. •The phrase Jesus used referred to the death of Lazarus, but they thought
14
15 that by 'rest' he meant 'sleep', so •Jesus put it plainly, 'Lazarus is dead; •and
for your sake I am glad I was not there because now you will believe. But let
16 us go to him.' •Then Thomas—known as the Twin—said to the other disciples,
'Let us go too, and die with him'.
17   On arriving, Jesus found that Lazarus had been in the tomb for four days
already.

John wants to stress the fact that Lazarus was indeed dead (11:17). This is directly related to Jesus' delay (11:6). The early church experienced the delay in Jesus' coming. The Thessalonian church were troubled by those of their members who died 'before' the coming of Jesus (1 Thessalonians 4:13). The Book of Revelation concludes with the prayer:

> 'Come, Lord Jesus.'
> *(Revelation 22:20)*

John wants to illustrate the truth that:

> 'if anyone believes in me even though he dies he will live.'
> *(John 11:25)*

An early Christian hymn, quoted by Paul, says:

> 'Wake up from your sleep,
> rise from the dead,
> and Christ will shine on you.'
> *(Ephesians 5:14)*

This is something that can happen here, and now. This particular anecdote is a 'sign' of this truth: Jesus is going to wake Lazarus (11:11).

JOHN 11:18-27

18
19   •Bethany is only about two miles from Jerusalem, •and many Jews had
20 come to Martha and Mary to sympathise with them over their brother. •When

Martha heard that Jesus had come she went to meet him. Mary remained sitting
21 in the house. •Martha said to Jesus, 'If you had been here, my brother would
22 not have died, •but I know that, even now, whatever you ask of God, he will
23/24 grant you'. •'Your brother' said Jesus to her 'will rise again.' •Martha said,
25 'I know he will rise again at the resurrection on the last day'. •Jesus said:

> 'I am the resurrection.
> If anyone believes in me, even though he dies he will live,
26 > and whoever lives and believes in me
> will never die.
> Do you believe this?'

27 'Yes, Lord,' she said 'I believe that you are the Christ, the Son of God, the one
who was to come into this world.'

Martha expresses her faith in a resurrection that will take place on the last
day (11:24). Jesus, in the most explicit terms, claims that the last day is present.
The woman of Samaria had spoken of a Christ:

> 'who is coming.'
> *(John 4:25)*

Jesus had corrected her, too:

> 'I who am speaking to you, I am He.'
> *(John 4:26)*

Jesus made a similar claim to the man born blind:

> 'You are looking at the Son of Man; he is speaking to you.'
> *(John 9:37)*

We shall examine this later when studying the Eschatological Discourse (Mark
13:26, page 356). For the moment it is sufficient to point out that John is claiming
that Jesus is the Christ, and that therefore the final judgment and the last day (the
Eschaton) has arrived:

> 'I *am* the Resurrection.' (11:25)

John tells us that he wrote his Gospel:

> 'so that you may believe that Jesus is the Christ,
> the Son of God.'
> *(John 20:31)*

Martha comes to that point of faith (John 11:27).

JOHN 11:28-44
28   When she had said this, she went and called her sister Mary, saying in a low
29 voice, 'The Master is here and wants to see you'. •Hearing this, Mary got up
30 quickly and went to him. •Jesus had not yet come into the village; he was still
31 at the place where Martha had met him. •When the Jews who were in the house
sympathising with Mary saw her get up so quickly and go out, they followed
her, thinking that she was going to the tomb to weep there.
32   Mary went to Jesus, and as soon as she saw him she threw herself at his
33 feet, saying, 'Lord, if you had been here, my brother would not have died'. •At
the sight of her tears, and those of the Jews who followed her, Jesus said in great
34 distress, with a sigh that came straight from the heart, •'Where have you put
35/36 him?' They said, 'Lord, come and see'. •Jesus wept; •and the Jews said, 'See

37 how much he loved him!' •But there were some who remarked, 'He opened the
38 eyes of the blind man, could he not have prevented this man's death?' •Still
   sighing, Jesus reached the tomb: it was a cave with a stone to close the opening.
39 Jesus said, 'Take the stone away'. Martha said to him, 'Lord, by now he will
40 smell; this is the fourth day'. •Jesus replied, 'Have I not told you that if you
41 believe you will see the glory of God?' •So they took away the stone. Then
   Jesus lifted up his eyes and said:

> 'Father, I thank you for hearing my prayer.
42
> I knew indeed that you always hear me,
> but I speak
> for the sake of all these who stand round me,
> so that they may believe it was you who sent me.'

43   When he had said this, he cried in a loud voice, 'Lazarus, here! Come out!'
44 The dead man came out, his feet and hands bound with bands of stuff and a
   cloth round his face. Jesus said to them, 'Unbind him, let him go free'.

Jesus' reaction to the tears of Mary and her friends, is described as being one
of 'great distress' (11:33). We are told that he spoke 'with a sigh that came straight
from the heart' (11:33) and that this sigh persisted (11:38). Mark used the same
expression when describing Jesus reaction to the leper (Mark 1:43. cf also
Matthew's use in relation to the blind men, Matthew 9:30). The word implies a
very deep emotional state, usually a mixture of fear and anger. The reason for
this reaction becomes clear when we remember that it was Jesus' good works that
led to the opposition of the religious authorities and finally to his death. Whenever Jesus healed he knew he was feeding the fires of hatred that would bring
about his own death. The raising of Lazarus, as we have already pointed out, was
to be the final act that led to the decision to kill him. Knowing this, Jesus is in
agony. He is struggling with the powers of death and darkness and sin.

He calls Lazarus forth from the tomb (11:43). He orders the bystanders to
free him (11:44). God has manifested his power and in this ultimate sign shows his
'glory' (11:40). Jesus is the Christ, the source of eternal life.

The signs are complete. The reader is ready to see Jesus caught up in the hour
of the great eschatological battle and, through his trust in God, conquer death
and rise to a new and eternal life (see also commentary on Luke 7:11-17, page 162).

JOHN 11:45-54
45   Many of the Jews who had come to visit Mary and had seen what he did
46 believed in him, •but some of them went to tell the Pharisees what Jesus had
47 done. •Then the chief priests and Pharisees called a meeting. 'Here is this man
48 working all these signs' they said 'and what action are we taking? •If we let
   him go on in this way everybody will believe in him, and the Romans will come
49 and destroy the Holy Place and our nation.' •One of them, Caiaphas, the
   high priest that year, said, 'You don't seem to have grasped the situation at all;
50 you fail to see that it is better for one man to die for the people, than for the
51 whole nation to be destroyed'. •He did not speak in his own person, it was as
   high priest that he made this prophecy that Jesus was to die for the nation—
52 and not for the nation only, but to gather together in unity the scattered children
53
54 of God. •From that day they were determined to kill him. •So Jesus no longer

went about openly among the Jews, but left the district for a town called Ephraim, in the country bordering on the desert, and stayed there with his disciples.

John concludes his account of the raising of Lazarus with a scene packed with dramatic irony. The one who gives life is himself condemned to death. The members of the Sanhedrin, in their efforts to defend God's dwelling place condemn to death the one who is God's sanctuary. They see themselves as doing this so that the whole nation will not be destroyed; and, in an ironic way, they are bringing about an action which will, indeed, save the nation. More than that, it will, as John points out:

'gather together in unity the scattered children of God.' (11:52)

For all their plotting they cannot bind the one who has loosed Lazarus:

'The Father loves me,
because I lay down my life
in order to take it up again.
No one takes it from me;
I lay it down of my own free will,
and as it is in my power to lay it down,
so it is in my power to take it up again.'

(John 10:17-18,

The persistence of Jesus' enemies reminds us of a statement attributed to Jesus by Luke. It is in a parable concerning a man called Lazarus:

'If they will not listen either to Moses or the prophets, they will not be convinced even if someone should rise from the dead.'

(Luke 16:31,

* * * * * * * *

With this scene John concludes the public ministry of Jesus. All that remains is the story of the last week of Jesus' life, including his passion and resurrection.

Let us now return to the Synoptics. After the scene at Caesarea Philippi, in which Peter acknowledges that Jesus is the Christ, the Synoptics have Jesus journeying towards Jerusalem. In the course of the journey they develop ideas on the nature of discipleship. This will be the subject of the following book.

* * * * * * * *

Points for Reflection:

1: Jesus delayed to answer the prayer of the two sisters (John 11:6). Martha did not understand why (John 11:21), but she retained her faith in him (11:22).

2: 'Whoever lives and believes in me will never die' (John 11:26). Do you believe this?

3: 'Come out!' (John 11:43) 'Unbind him, let him go free' (John 11:44).
The word of God is constantly challenging each of us to come out into the light. It is constantly challenging each of us to unbind our brothers and let them go free.

BOOK 4

The Journey of the Disciple

FOREWORD

At Caesarea Philippi, a disciple, Peter, at last acknowledged that Jesus was the Messiah. Moreover, Peter expressed his commitment to Jesus and his desire to follow him.

This commitment is basic to discipleship, and so only now are the Gospel writers ready to show us what it means to follow Jesus. Caesarea Philippi is at the source of the Jordan. Jesus journeys down the Jordan getting closer and closer to his destination, Jerusalem, where he is to die and to be raised to glory by his Father. This is a powerful image for the journey of discipleship: the journey following Jesus to the cross, but through the cross to the glory of the resurrection.

Mark states the essence of discipleship, gives some instructions and then shows that we need a special miracle of love and enlightenment if we are to understand Jesus' teaching. We cover this material in the following three Chapters.

Luke has a very long insert in this section (Luke 9:51 — 18:14). In it he gathers together many anecdotes, sayings and parables of Jesus which illustrate different aspects of the journey of discipleship. We cover this insert in the second sub-section of Chapter 2.

Chapter 1
The Disciple is to follow Jesus
on the road to the Cross and
the Resurrection

Mark 8:31 — 9:40
Matthew 16:21 — 18:5
Luke 9:22-50

a: Jesus speaks for the first time of his suffering, death and resurrection

MARK 8:31-32a (Compare Matthew 16:21, Luke 9:22)

And he began to teach them that the Son of Man was destined to suffer 31 grievously, to be rejected by the elders and the chief priests and the scribes, and to be put to death, and after three days to rise again; •and he said all this quite 32 openly.

The murder of John the Baptist was a warning to Jesus — in fact to anyone who had eyes to see — that the political and religious leaders would tolerate no opposition to their power. They had already determined to 'destroy' Jesus (Mark 3:6). Jesus, on the other hand, was determined to continue to preach the Good News even when this involved him in direct confrontation with the leaders (cf Mark 7:1-13). Jesus could see that this confrontation would lead to his death.

Peter has just stated publicly his belief in Jesus as the Christ (Mark 8:29). At the time ideas of the 'Christ' included ideas of political and military victory over the enemies of God and of God's people. So Jesus immediately makes it clear to Peter and the others that his Messiahship has nothing to do with these expectations that were common among the people. On the contrary, he is going to be 'put to death' (8:31). Yes, he is going to die. At the same time Jesus tries to communicate to them that his death will not be the end. He trusts that his Father will take him to himself; he will 'rise again after three days' (8:31). In Biblical terminology, the third day is God's decisive day (cf Hosea 6:1-3). Whatever men do to Jesus, ultimately, he will be vindicated by his Father.

b: The disciple Peter fails to understand

MARK 8:32b-33 (Compare Matthew 16:22-23)

Then, taking him aside, Peter started to remonstrate with him. •But, 33 turning and seeing his disciples, he rebuked Peter and said to him, 'Get behind me, Satan! Because the way you think is not God's way but man's.'

The failure of the disciple to understand the mystery of suffering is a theme that will recur. In the strongest terms, Jesus makes it clear to Peter that he has a lot to learn about 'God's ways' (8:33).

c: The disciple will find life by following Jesus

MARK 8:34 — 9:1 (Compare Matthew 16:24-28 and Luke 9:23-27)

34 He called the people and his disciples to him and said, 'If anyone wants to be a follower of mine, let him renounce himself and take up his cross and follow
35 me. •For anyone who wants to save his life will lose it; but anyone who loses his
36 life for my sake, and for the sake of the gospel, will save it. •What gain, then, is
37 it for a man to win the whole world and ruin his life? •And indeed what can
38 a man offer in exchange for his life? •For if anyone in this adulterous and sinful generation is ashamed of me and of my words, the Son of Man will also be ashamed of him when he comes in the glory of his Father with the holy angels.'
1 9 And he said to them, 'I tell you solemnly, there are some standing here who will not taste death before they see the kingdom of God come with power'.

This passage expresses the central paradox of the Gospel. It is addressed to everyone (8:34). It is, what Mark called earlier, the 'secret of the kingdom' (4:11). It stands in stark contrast to the ways of the world (Mark 8:33).

Jesus knew his Father as the living God. His whole ministry was intended to liberate men to live to the full (cf John 10:10). He knew that life is so precious that nothing can be offered in exchange for it (cf Mark 8:36-37). At the same time he knew that man's life was in the image of God's (cf Genesis 1:26). He knew that man must be perfect as his heavenly Father is perfect (cf Matthew 5:48). And God *gives* life. Jesus' whole life was a daily giving of his life for others; what Paul calls an 'emptying' of himself (Philippians 2:7). Jesus has just spoken about his coming suffering and death which are to be the final statement of his complete self-giving. Here he tells the people that to seek one's own life is to lose it; to seek love for oneself is to lose it; to seek gratitude is to lose it. It is only when a man seeks these things for others, it is only when a man spends himself for others, empties himself for others in humility and in the wonder of a life spent in prayerful and loving service, that he will find that he is fully alive with God's own creative life.

Death by crucifixion was the death suffered by a convicted slave. Perhaps Jesus used this expression (8:34) to symbolise the complete life of service to which he was calling his followers. On the other hand the expression 'take up his cross and follow me' may have its origins in the period after Jesus' own crucifixion and have been used by the early church as a summary of Jesus' teaching.

The teaching given here is the teaching on which men will be judged (8:38); nor will they have to wait long before they see it vindicated (9:1). The resurrection of Jesus will demonstrate the power of God over the forces of darkness, and God's gift of life to the one who gave his life for others. The destruction of Jerusalem was also seen as the coming of the kingdom of God with power. On that day those who oppressed Jesus stood condemned.

d: God's response to Jesus and his disciples

MARK 9:2-8 (Compare Matthew 17:1-8 and Luke 9:28-36)

2 Six days later, Jesus took with him Peter and James and John and led them up a high mountain where they could be alone by themselves. There in

3 their presence he was transfigured: •his clothes became dazzlingly white, whiter
4 than any earthly bleacher could make them. •Elijah appeared to them with
5 Moses; and they were talking with Jesus. •Then Peter spoke to Jesus: 'Rabbi,'
he said 'it is wonderful for us to be here; so let us make three tents, one for
6 you, one for Moses and one for Elijah'. •He did not know what to say; they were
7 so frightened. •And a cloud came, covering them in shadow; and there came
8 a voice from the cloud, 'This is my Son, the Beloved. Listen to him.' •Then
suddenly, when they looked round, they saw no one with them any more but
only Jesus.

This scene is a preview of the resurrection and is God's response to Jesus'
statement about his coming suffering and death. Jesus is ascending the mountain
'to pray' (Luke 9:28). The special nature of this occasion is indicated by the
selection of 'Peter and James and John' (Mark 9:2), the disciples who witnessed
the raising of Jairus' daughter (Mark 5:37) and are to be with Jesus in his agony
(Mark 14:32).

Mark mentions 'Moses' (9:4) and we are reminded of the occasion when
Moses, too, ascended the mountain to see God. He asked to see God's glory
(Exodus 33:18). God's glory did pass by, but Moses was not able to see the face of
God (Exodus 33:23). Nevertheless, the intimate contact Moses had with God on
the holy mountain had a profound effect upon him:

'When Moses came down from the mountain of Sinai . . . he did not know that the
skin of his face was radiant after speaking with Yahweh. And when Aaron and all the
sons of Israel saw Moses, the skin on his face shone so much that they would not
venture near him.'

(Exodus 34:29-30)

Jesus is the new Moses, the one who gives the new Law from the mountain of
prayer. He, too, is transfigured by the glory of God in a way far surpassing that of
Moses.

Elijah, too, is mentioned (Mark 9:4). We are told in the Book of the Kings
that Elijah, desiring to see the glory of God, travelled to the 'mountain of God' (1
Kings 19:8):

'He was told: Go out and stand on the mountain before Yahweh. Then Yahweh
himself went by. There came a mighty wind, so strong it tore the mountains and
shattered the rocks before Yahweh. But Yahweh was not in the wind. After the wind
came an earthquake. But Yahweh was not in the earthquake. After the earthquake
came a fire. But Yahweh was not in the fire. And after the fire there came the sound of
a gentle breeze. And when Elijah heard this, he covered his face with his cloak
and went out and stood at the entrance of the cave.'

(1 Kings 19:11-13)

Jesus is *the* prophet, fulfilling in his person all that was seen and spoken of by
the ancient prophets of Israel. Jesus is the prophet foretold by Moses:

'Yahweh your God will raise up for you a prophet like myself, from among
yourselves, from your own brothers; to him you must listen!'

(Deuteronomy 18:15)

This, too, is revealed to the chosen disciples on the mountain:

'This is my Son, the beloved, listen to him.'

(Mark 9:7)

Peter wants to keep the Law and the Prophets (Mark 9:5). But there is no need, for Jesus fulfils them in himself. They have all that is necessary; 'only Jesus' (Mark 9:8). They must listen to him.

The scene is rich in symbolism. The glory-cloud (Mark 9:7) reminds the reader of the presence of God leading his people through the desert (cf Exodus 13:21); this is now the task of Jesus. It reminds us, too, of the presence of God in the Temple (cf 1 Kings 8:10); Jesus is now the temple of the living God (cf John 2:21). It takes us back to the baptism of Jesus (Mark 1:10-11); God, who brought order out of original chaos (cf Genesis 1:2) is beginning a new creation with his 'Son' (Mark 9:7) (cf also Luke 1:35: at the Incarnation, Jesus' mother is caught up in the glory-cloud).

These same themes are reinforced by the mention of the 'tents' (Mark 9:5). The Feast of the Tents ('Tabernacles') commemorated God's creative act, his presence in the Temple and his giving of the Covenant. In Jesus, 'only Jesus' (Mark 9:8) this has all come to fulfilment.

Jesus is in intimate contact with his Father. He is 'the beloved' (9:7). The glorification on the mountain prefigures the glorification of which Jesus has just spoken (Mark 8:31, 8:38), and we can look at him with 'unveiled faces' (2 Cor 3:18).

* * * * * * * *

Luke chooses to highlight this glorification in his addition to the scene:

LUKE 9:30-32

•Suddenly 30 there were two men there talking to him; they were Moses and Elijah •appearing 31 in glory, and they were speaking of his passing which he was to accomplish in Jerusalem. •Peter and his companions were heavy with sleep, but they kept awake 32 and saw his glory and the two men standing with him.

'They were speaking of his "passing" (The Greek word is "Exodus") which he was to accomplish in Jerusalem'; they were speaking, that is, of his suffering and death.

Luke will remind us of this scene when he comes to describe the agony Jesus underwent just before his death. On that occasion, too, Jesus goes up a mountain to pray (cf Luke 22:39-40). On that occasion, too, he is transfigured in prayer, though it is the agony, not the ecstasy that is apparent (cf Luke 22:44). The parallels even extend to the fact that on both occasions the disciples are 'heavy with sleep' (cf Luke 22:45).

The second part of Jesus' ministry (i.e., after Caesarea Philippi) begins with clear and reiterated statements of the essential connection between the giving of one's life and glorification by God.

e: The fate of the Baptist is prophetic of the fate of Jesus

MARK 9:9-13 (Compare Matthew 17:9-13)

As they came down from the mountain he warned them to tell no one 9 what they had seen, until after the Son of Man had risen from the dead.

10 They observed the warning faithfully, though among themselves they discussed
11 what 'rising from the dead' could mean. •And they put this question to him,
12 'Why do the scribes say that Elijah has to come first?' •'True,' he said 'Elijah
is to come first and to see that everything is as it should be; yet how is it that the
scriptures say about the Son of Man that he is to suffer grievously and be treated
13 with contempt? •However, I tell you that Elijah has come and they have
treated him as they pleased, just as the scriptures say about him.'

His disciples are still fascinated by the legend concerning the return of Elijah
(cf commentary on Matthew 11:14). Mark has already made a link between
Elijah and the Baptist (cf Mark 1:6 and 6:16). That he is referring to the Baptist
here (9:13) is made explicit by Matthew (17:13). Jezebel sought the life of Elijah
(cf 1 Kings 19:2), and we have already seen Herodias bringing about the murder
of the Baptist (cf Mark 6:17-29). All of this is preparing the disciples and the
reader for the fate of Jesus and for the mysterious connection between suffering
and glory.

Luke omits this scene. In his Prologue he spoke of the Baptist as destined to
preach 'with the spirit and power of Elijah' (Luke 1:17), but elsewhere, in his
gospel, in order to highlight 'God's plan' (Luke 7:29), he prefers to keep the
prophets, the Baptist, and Jesus separate to help clarify their separate roles.
(Compare his omission of any reference to Elijah in Luke 3:1-18.)

f: Jesus' union with his Father's will is the source of his healing power

MARK 9:14-29 (Compare Matthew 17:14-20 and Luke 9:37-43)
14   When they rejoined the disciples they saw a large crowd round them and
15 some scribes arguing with them. •The moment they saw him the whole crowd
16 were struck with amazement and ran to greet him. •'What are you arguing about
17 with them?' he asked. •A man answered him from the crowd, 'Master, I have
18 brought my son to you; there is a spirit of dumbness in him, •and when it
takes hold of him it throws him to the ground, and he foams at the mouth and
grinds his teeth and goes rigid. And I asked your disciples to cast it out and
19 they were unable to.' •'You faithless generation' he said to them in reply. 'How
much longer must I be with you? How much longer must I put up with you?
20 Bring him to me.' •They brought the boy to him, and as soon as the spirit
saw Jesus it threw the boy into convulsions, and he fell to the ground and
21 lay writhing there, foaming at the mouth. •Jesus asked the father, 'How
22 long has this been happening to him?' 'From childhood,' he replied •'and it
has often thrown him into the fire and into the water, in order to destroy him.
23 But if you can do anything, have pity on us and help us.' •'If you can?' retorted
24 Jesus. 'Everything is possible for anyone who has faith.' •Immediately the
25 father of the boy cried out, 'I do have faith. Help the little faith I have!' •And
when Jesus saw how many people were pressing round him, he rebuked the
unclean spirit. 'Deaf and dumb spirit,' he said 'I command you: come out of him
26 and never enter him again.' •Then throwing the boy into violent convulsions it
came out shouting, and the boy lay there so like a corpse that most of them
27 said, 'He is dead'. •But Jesus took him by the hand and helped him up, and he
28 was able to stand. •When he had gone indoors his disciples asked him privately,
29 'Why were we unable to cast it out?' •'This is the kind' he answered 'that can
only be driven out by prayer.'

It is because Jesus himself has been in prayer (Mark 9:2-8) that he is able to channel God's power and love in such a way as to bring about the defeat of the powers of evil and the healing of this boy. His disciples must learn this (Mark 9:29). 'Everything is possible' (9:23) because there is no limit to the power of God. But we must 'pray' (9:29); that is, we must be in union with God. We must believe (9:19; 9:23-24) in God's desire to give us life. The father knows his limitations, but humbly pleads with Jesus to heal his boy (9:24).

The scene illustrates the intimate connection between contemplation and mission, between being a 'companion' of Jesus and being sent out to 'preach with power to cast out devils' (Mark 3:14).

Matthew concludes his scene:

MATTHEW 17:19-20

19 Then the disciples came privately to Jesus. 'Why were we unable to cast it
20 out?' they asked. •He answered, 'Because you have little faith. I tell you
solemnly, if your faith were the size of a mustard seed you could say to this mountain, "Move from here to there", and it would move; nothing would be impossible for you.'

(Compare Mark 11:23 and Matthew 21:21 page 319
                                                        and Luke 17:5-6 page 292)

The power of God works through us if we are open in faith and prayer. The effectiveness of our actions therefore is not measured by anything we have (not even the size of our faith). Matthew repeats the illustration concerning the mountain in a later context (Matthew 21:21. Compare Luke's 'mulberry tree' Luke 17:6).

g: Jesus speaks for the second time of his suffering, death and resurrection

MARK 9:30-32 (Compare Matthew 17:22-23 and Luke 9:44-45)

30 After leaving that place they made their way through Galilee; and he did
31 not want anyone to know, •because he was instructing his disciples; he was telling them, 'The Son of Man will be delivered into the hands of men; they will put him to death; and three days after he has been put to death he will rise again'.
32 But they did not understand what he said and were afraid to ask him.

Jesus is concentrating his attention on the instruction of his disciples (9:31). He speaks for the second time of his coming passion and resurrection. Again Mark mentions that they did not understand (9:32).

*   *   *   *   *   *   *   *

Matthew inserts the following scene:

MATTHEW 17:24-27

24 When they reached Capernaum, the collectors of the half-shekel came to
25 Peter and said, 'Does your master not pay the half-shekel?' •'Oh yes' he replied, and went into the house. But before he could speak, Jesus said, 'Simon, what is your opinion? From whom do the kings of the earth take toll or tribute? From
26 their sons or from foreigners?' •And when he replied, 'From foreigners', Jesus
27 said, 'Well then, the sons are exempt. •However, so as not to offend these

people, go to the lake and cast a hook; take the first fish that bites, open its mouth and there you will find a shekel; take it and give it to them for me and for you.'

The half-shekel represented a personal link between each 'son of Israel' and Yahweh (cf Exodus 30:11-16).

'It will remind Yahweh of the sons of Israel.' *(Exodus 30:16)*

In fact the tax was used for the upkeep of the Temple.

Claiming to be the 'Son', and implying that Peter and the other disciples were also sons (Matthew 17:25), Jesus indicates that he has no interest in paying the tax. He is perhaps also indicating his lack of interest in supporting the Temple. We are not told that Peter ever actually caught the fish, or paid the tax. It has been suggested that Jesus, with some humour, was telling Peter that if he wanted the money he'd have to go and fish for it!

h: His disciples fail to understand

MARK 9:33-37 (Compare Matthew 18:1-5 and Luke 9:46-48)
They came to Capernaum, and when he was in the house he asked them, 33 'What were you arguing about on the road?' •They said nothing because they 34 had been arguing which of them was the greatest. •So he sat down, called the 35 Twelve to him and said, 'If anyone wants to be first, he must make himself last of all and servant of all'. •He then took a little child, set him in front of them, 36 put his arms round him, and said to them, •'Anyone who welcomes one of 37 these little children in my name, welcomes me; and anyone who welcomes me welcomes not me but the one who sent me'.

Peter failed to understand Jesus when he first spoke of his coming passion (cf Mark 8:33). Obviously the disciples are still failing to grasp his teaching (cf 9:32). Jesus has just been speaking of giving his life for others, and his disciples are arguing about which is the greatest. (Note that Matthew does not mention the argument. He must have thought it too unedifying.)

Once again, Jesus speaks to them of service (compare Mark 8:35). He identifies himself with a child (Mark 9:37); so must his disciples. No one would think of a child being the greatest. They are all children of the Father, and in their relationship with God and with each other, they must learn to become like little children (cf Mark 10:15).

MARK 9:38-40 (Compare Luke 9:49-50)
John said to him, 'Master, we saw a man who is not one of us casting out 38 devils in your name; and because he was not one of us we tried to stop him'. But Jesus said, 'You must not stop him: no one who works a miracle in my name 39 is likely to speak evil of me. •Anyone who is not against us is for us. 40

A group of Jewish Christians from Jerusalem tried to stop Paul because he was not one of their group (cf Galatians 2:4 and Acts 15:24-25). The community at Corinth was broken because various groups claimed that others did not belong (cf 1 Corinthians 1:12).

This scene stands as a powerful statement against any kind of group or institutional arrogance. John was wrong to put his own limited measure on the working of the Spirit of God. That was the very fault for which Jesus was constantly castigating the Pharisees. A tree is to be judged by its fruit. If a man is doing wonderful things that draw men to God, we can be sure the Spirit of God is working through him. He must not be stopped.

We are reminded of the following scene from the Book of Numbers:

> Moses went out and told the people what Yahweh had said. Then he gathered seventy elders of the people and brought them round the Tent. Yahweh came down in the Cloud. He spoke with him, but took some of the spirit that was on him and put it on the seventy elders. When the spirit came on them they prophesied, but not again.
>
> Two men had stayed back in the camp; one was called Eldad and the other Medad. The spirit came down on them; though they had not gone to the Tent, their names were enrolled among the rest. These began to prophesy in the camp. The young man ran to tell this to Moses, 'Look,' he said 'Eldad and Medad are prophesying in the camp'. • Then said Joshua the son of Nun, who had served Moses from his youth, 'My Lord Moses, stop them!' • Moses answered him, 'Are you jealous on my account? If only the whole people of Yahweh were prophets, and Yahweh gave his Spirit to them all!' • Then Moses went back to the camp, the elders of Israel with him.
>
> (Numbers 11:24-30)

Points for Reflection:

1: 'The way you think is not God's way but man's' (Mark 8:34).
The only way to learn God's way of thinking is to listen to God (compare Mark 1:35 and commentary).

2: 'This is my Son, the Beloved. Listen to him' (Mark 9:7).

3: 'I do have faith. Help the little faith I have' (Mark 9:24).

4: 'If anyone wants to be first, he must make himself last of all and servant of all' (Mark 9:35).

Chapter 2
Instructions for Disciples

Mark 9:41 — 10:31
Matthew 18:6 — 20:16
Luke 9:51 — 18:30

I: Instructions for disciples in Mark and Matthew

MARK 9:41-50 (Compare Matthew 18:6-9)

'If anyone gives you a cup of water to drink just because you belong to Christ, 41
then I tell you solemnly, he will most certainly not lose his reward.

'But anyone who is an obstacle to bring down one of these little ones who 42
have faith, would be better thrown into the sea with a great millstone round
his neck. •And if your hand should cause you to sin, cut it off; it is better for you 43
to enter into life crippled, than to have two hands and go to hell, into the fire that
cannot be put out. •And if your foot should cause you to sin, cut it off; it is 45
better for you to enter into life lame, than to have two feet and be thrown into
hell. •And if your eye should cause you to sin, tear it out; it is better for you to 47
enter into the kingdom of God with one eye, than to have two eyes and be thrown
into hell •where *their worm does not die nor their fire go out.*[a] •For everyone will ⁴⁸₄₉
be salted with fire. •Salt is a good thing, but if salt has become insipid, how can 50
you season it again? Have salt in yourselves and be at peace with one another.'

(a: Isaiah 66:24)
(Mark 9:41 compare Matthew 10:42 page 118
Mark 9:42 compare Luke 17:1-2 page 292)

Jesus is speaking of his disciples, of those who 'belong to Christ' (9:41), the
'little ones who have faith' (9:42). God will regard with love those who care for his
disciples (9:41). We are reminded of Jesus' use of the word 'reward' in the Sermon
on the Mount (cf commentary on Matthew 6:1-18). It is obvious from Matthew's
account of the Last Judgment (cf Matthew 25:37) that Jesus is not stating that
God's loving regard is restricted to those who act from an explicitly Christ-
centred motive ('because you belong to Christ' Mark 9:41). A cup of water given
to anyone is a cup of water given to Christ (cf Matthew 25:40).

We examined the concept of 'hell' ('Gehenna' Mark 9:43) when examining
Matthew 5:22. It seems that, outside official juridical practice, there existed the
custom of punishing people in accordance with the nature of the crime. Everyone
accepted the fact that it was better to have one's hand cut off for stealing than to
lose one's life for it. Jesus is using the same primitive language here. He is

speaking of the importance of 'life' (Mark 9:43, 45 = the 'kingdom of God' Mark 9:47). It is of such supreme importance that nothing is worth holding on to if it means losing one's life (cf Mark 8:37), like those who died amid raging thirst and fever in the valley of Ge-Ben-Hinnom. These are:

'the corpses of men who have rebelled against me.
Their worm will not die nor their fire go out;
they will be loathsome to all mankind.'

(Isaiah 66:24, cf Mark 9:48)

'Everyone will be salted with fire' (Mark 9:49). Just as meat is salted for sacrifice, so the lives of Jesus' disciples, if they are to be offered in sacrifice, must pass through the ordeal of suffering, the fire of purification. This is the price of being a peacemaker. It is better to go through it, to be crippled, to be lame, to have one eye, than to become insipid (9:50) and go to Gehenna and 'be loathsome to all mankind' (Isaiah 66:34).

* * * * * * * *

Matthew adds the following proverbs and parables:

1: MATTHEW 18:10

'See that you never despise any of these little ones, for I tell you that their 10 angels in heaven are continually in the presence of my Father in heaven.

The 'little ones' (18:10), like the 'little children like this' (Matthew 18:5) or the 'mere children' mentioned earlier in Matthew's Gospel (cf Matthew 11:25), are those who, in their childlike trust of God and simplicity have 'become like little children' (Matthew 18:3). They come under the intimate, personal care of God (cf commentary on Mark 1:13, page 62-3).

MATTHEW 18:12-14 (Compare Luke 15:4-6)

'Tell me. Suppose a man has a hundred sheep and one of them strays; will 12 he not leave the ninety-nine on the hillside and go in search of the stray? •I tell 13 you solemnly, if he finds it, it gives him more joy than do the ninety-nine that did not stray at all. •Similarly, it is never the will of your Father in heaven that 14 one of these little ones should be lost.

(Note: there is no 18:11 in the text accepted by the Jerusalem Bible Edition)

In this parable Jesus takes us to the heart of a compassionate Father and the joy he experiences at the safety of his 'little ones'. The last statement should be a source of profound peace and confidence to those who place their trust in God as Jesus did. It should also provide a powerful incentive to 'become like little children' (Matthew 18:3). We are reminded of Jesus telling us never to be afraid of God (cf Matthew 10:28-31 page 117).

The wonder of the Good News is that everyone is called to be a 'little one'; that it is never the will of God that anyone should be lost. Paul tells us:

'God our saviour wants everyone to be saved and reach full knowledge of the truth.'

(1 Timothy 2:4)

He wrote to Titus:

'God's grace has been revealed, and it has made salvation possible for the whole human race.'

(Titus 2:11)

John has Jesus himself saying:

'When I am lifted up from the earth I shall draw all men to myself.'

(John 12:32)

MATTHEW 18:15-22

'If your brother does something wrong, go and have it out with him alone, 15 between your two selves. If he listens to you, you have won back your brother. If he does not listen, take one or two others along with you: *the evidence of two* 16 *or three witnesses is required to sustain any charge.* •But if he refuses to listen to 17 these, report it to the community; and if he refuses to listen to the community, treat him like a pagan or a tax collector.

'I tell you solemnly, whatever you bind on earth shall be considered bound in 18 heaven; whatever you loose on earth shall be considered loosed in heaven.

'I tell you solemnly once again, if two of you on earth agree to ask anything 19 at all, it will be granted to you by my Father in heaven. •For where two or three 20 meet in my name, I shall be there with them.'

Then Peter went up to him and said, 'Lord, how often must I forgive my 21 brother if he wrongs me? As often as seven times?' •Jesus answered, 'Not seven, 22 I tell you, but seventy-seven times.

(Compare Luke 17:3-4 page 292,

The early Jewish-Christian community, to maintain fidelity to the Gospel, found it necessary to exercise discipline within the community, even to the extent of excommunicating those who publicly defied the community by unrepentantly living lives that were in opposition to the values of Jesus. In exercising this discipline they were simply carrying on the tradition of the synagogue, as indicated by the expressions: 'treat him like a pagan or a tax collector' (18:17) and 'binding' and 'loosing' (18:18 cf Matthew 16:19 page 205).

Matthew places these instructions immediately after the parable of the straying sheep (Matthew 18:12-14). He follows them immediately with two sayings of Jesus: one on prayer (18:19-20) and one on forgiveness (18:21-22). Discipline is necessary, but it is always to be exercised according to the mind and heart of Jesus. (Compare Paul's statement in 2 Thessalonians 3:15 and 2 Corinthians 2:5-11.)

A parable about forgiveness

MATTHEW 18:23-35

'And so the kingdom of heaven may be compared to a king who decided 23 to settle his accounts with his servants. •When the reckoning began, they 24 brought him a man who owed ten thousand talents; •but he had no means of 25 paying, so his master gave orders that he should be sold, together with his wife and children and all his possessions, to meet the debt. •At this, the servant threw 26 himself down at his master's feet. "Give me time" he said "and I will pay the whole sum." •And the servant's master felt so sorry for him that he let him go 27 and cancelled the debt. •Now as this servant went out, he happened to meet a fellow 28 servant who owed him one hundred denarii; and he seized him by the throat and began to throttle him. "Pay what you owe me" he said. •His fellow servant 29 fell at his feet and implored him, saying, "Give me time and I will pay you". But the other would not agree; on the contrary, he had him thrown into prison 30 till he should pay the debt. •His fellow servants were deeply distressed when 31

they saw what had happened, and they went to their master and reported the
32 whole affair to him. •Then the master sent for him. "You wicked servant," he
33 said "I cancelled all that debt of yours when you appealed to me. •Were you not
bound, then, to have pity on your fellow servant just as I had pity on you?"
34 And in his anger the master handed him over to the torturers till he should pay
35 all his debt. •And that is how my heavenly Father will deal with you unless you
each forgive your brother from your heart.'

Those listening to this 'riddle' would have been startled by the extraordinary
discrepancy between the debts. A denarius was a day's wage for a casual labourer
(for example, a fruit-picker). The servant was, therefore, owed one hundred days'
wages by his fellow servant (18:28). This is a considerable sum and one might be
excused for being upset. But — and here lies the shock of the riddle — the servant
had just been let off paying his master 'ten thousand talents' (18:24), the
equivalent of 160,000 years' wages! Whatever someone may owe us, there can be
no comparison with what God has forgiven. We must forgive our brother 'from
our heart' (18:35).

$$* \quad * \quad * \quad * \quad * \quad * \quad * \quad *$$

II: Instructions for Disciples in Luke (Luke 9:51 — 18:14)

1: We entitled the previous chapter 'A disciple is to follow Jesus on the road to
the cross'. Mark, followed by Matthew and Luke, gathered together material
which illustrated the fact that to be a disciple of Jesus a person must be ready to
give his life as Jesus gave his. This is the context chosen by Luke for the present
lengthy insert in which he draws out the implications of a journey of discipleship.

The opening words are:

'Now as the time drew near for him to be taken up into heaven, he resolutely took the
road for Jerusalem.'

(Luke 9:51)

He then dramatises the life of a disciple as a journey with Jesus to Jerusalem, to
the cross and to the consequent glorification.

When Jesus chose his first disciples he demonstrated the power that would be
theirs and said:

'Do not be afraid; from now on it is men you will catch.'

(Luke 5:11)

They accompanied him during the time of his early ministry. Then came the
day when, like Moses, Jesus went up the mountain of prayer (Luke 6:12). Luke
tells us that:

'When day came he summoned his disciples and picked out twelve of them; he called
them "apostles".'

(Luke 6:13)

After further experience and instruction:

'He called the Twelve together and gave them power and authority over all devils and
to cure diseases, and he sent them out to proclaim the kingdom of God and to heal.'

(Luke 9:1-2)

They set out on their first mission, and it soon became obvious that they had a lot to learn. They did not realise that they had the power to feed the multitudes themselves (Luke 9:13). They were unable to cure the epileptic (Luke 9:40). They did not understand that: 'the least among you all, that is the one who is great' (Luke 9:48). They did not realise that they should welcome all who exercised Jesus' authority (Luke 9:49-50). Hence the need for further instruction.

The main lesson they had to learn, it seems, was the lesson of suffering. Immediately on their recognition of him as the Christ, Jesus told them:

'The Son of Man is destined to suffer greviously, to be rejected by the elders and chief priests and scribes and to be put to death, and to be raised up on the third day.'

(Luke 9:22)

He went on to say:

'If anyone wants to be a follower of mine, let him renounce himself and take up his cross every day and follow me.'

(Luke 9:23)

They were given their first vision of the mystery of Jesus, the Transfiguration. In that vision, too, according to Luke:

'they were speaking of his passing that he was to accomplish in Jerusalem.'

(Luke 9:31)

Their second vision will be the resurrection, and only then will they be brought to understand the mystery of suffering (cf Luke 24:6-7, 25-26, 44-46).

In between these two visions stands the journey we are about to study: a journey to Jerusalem, a journey in which the disciples are trained in what it means to follow Jesus to the cross in order to follow him to glory.

2: In fact, the journey, as dramatised in Luke's Gospel, covers the section from Luke 9:51 to Luke 19:40. It is the second stage of Jesus' ministry according to Luke's structure. The first stage, Jesus' Galilean Ministry, opened in Nazareth where Jesus was rejected by his own people (Luke 4:14-30). The third stage, Jesus' Jerusalem Ministry, opens also with a rejection scene (Luke 19:41-44). This second stage, the journey to Jerusalem, also opens, as we shall see, with a scene in which Jesus is rejected by the people of a Samaritan village (Luke 9:51-56). At each stage, rejection does not stifle the power of God but is the occasion for an expansion of Jesus' ministry. The same pattern carries over to the second part of Luke's work, the Acts of the Apostles. Persecution in Jerusalem (Acts 8:1) occasions the spread of the community 'throughout Judaea and Samaria, and indeed to the ends of the earth' (Acts 1:8).

3: While Luke's journey extends from 9:51 to 19:40, we shall study here the section from 9:51 to 18:14. This represents an insert made by Luke. After 18:14 he links up again with Mark. We shall examine 18:15 — 19:40 in the following section.

Half the material of this insert can be found also in Matthew's Gospel, and we have, for the most part, already examined it in Matthew's context. In order to maintain the continuity of Luke's text we shall reproduce the whole of his insert here. After those sections which are also in Matthew we shall refer the reader to the relevant text in Matthew and its accompanying commentary. Here we shall restrict our commentary to the passages that are only in Luke, plus supplementary commentary on the other passages where Luke is making some special observation.

4: The following is an outline of Luke's insert. It is somewhat arbitrary, but may help the reader get some idea of the development of Luke's treatment. Where the material is found also in Matthew we shall give the relevant text. In this way the reader can see at a glance which sections are proper to Luke.

		(parallel passages in Matthew)
I: Introduction		
1: The journey to Jerusalem begins.	9:51-56	
2: The cost of journeying with Jesus.	9:57-62	8:19-22
3: Those who journey with Jesus share his mission and the mission of the Twelve.	(a): 10:1-16 (b): 10:17-24	9:37; 10:7-16; 11:21-23 11:25-57; 13:16-17
II: Basic Aspects of Discipleship		
1: The central place of love in the life of a disciple.	10:25-42	22:34-40
2: The central place of prayer in the life of a disciple.	11:1-13	6:9-13; 7:7-11
3: Opposition in the life of a disciple: (a) A disciple must hear and keep God's word.	11:14-36	12:22-45
(b) The hypocrisy of those who refuse to hear and keep God's word.	11:37-54	23:4, 6-7, 13, 23-36
(c) A disciple must not fear opposition.	12:1-12	10:17-20, 26-33; 12:32
4: A disciple must place his trust in God, not in possessions.	12:13-34	6:19-34
5: Discipleship and the judgment of God. (a) A disciple will be judged on his service.	12:35-48	25:1-13; 24:42-51
(b) Now is the hour of judgment. A disciple must discern the will of God and repent.	12:49 — 13:5	10:34-36; 16:2-3; 5:25-26
(c) God's judgment is compassionate.	13:6-17	
(d) God's victory is inevitable.	13:18-21	13:31-33
(e) Men are judged by their acceptance or rejection of God's word.	13:22-35	7:13-14, 22-23; 8:11-12; 23:37-39; 25:10-12
6: A disciple must be poor. (a) Only the poor accept God's word and experience intimacy with him.	14:1-24	22:1-10
(b) A disciple, therefore, must give up all his possessions.	14:25-35	5:13; 10:37-39
7: Discipleship and the compassion of God.	15:1-32	18:12-14
III: The Implications of Discipleship		
1: What a man must do with his riches to become a disciple.	16:1-15	

2: Men are called to be disciples of Jesus,
   not disciples of the Law.   16:16-17   11:12; 5:18
3: Marriage fidelity: an example of how
   the kingdom of God surpasses the
   Law.   16:18   5:31-32
4: 'Woe for you who are rich'.   16:19-31
5: Care, correction and forgiveness in the
   life of a disciple.   17:1-4   18:6-7, 15, 21-22
6: The power of faith.   17:5-6   17:20; 21:21
7: Humble service in the life of a disciple. 17:7-10
8: An outsider has the faith to be a
   disciple.   17:11-19
9: The kingdom of God is brought about
   by divine intervention.   17:20-37   24:17-18, 26-28, 37-41
10: God will answer the cry of the poor
   man.   18:1-8
11: A disciple must be humble.   18:9-14

Note: Luke's insert ends here. He goes on to speak of the poor and the rich (Luke 18:15 — 19:10). Since this material is found, for the most part, in Mark and Matthew, we shall leave study of it to the next section.

* * * * * * * *

I: Introduction

1: The journey to Jerusalem begins

LUKE 9:51-56

51   Now as the time drew near for him to be taken up to heaven, he resolutely
52 took the road for Jerusalem •and sent messengers ahead of him. These set out,
53 and they went into a Samaritan village to make preparations for him, •but the
54 people would not receive him because he was making for Jerusalem. •Seeing
this, the disciples James and John said, 'Lord, do you want us to call down fire
55
56 from heaven to burn them up?' •But he turned and rebuked them, •and they
went off to another village.

Jesus 'resolutely took the road for Jerusalem' (9:51) because, as Luke records:

'It would not be right for a prophet to die outside Jerusalem.'

(Luke 13:33)

In the Transfiguration scene, Jesus' death was spoken of as:

'his passing which he was to accomplish in Jerusalem.'

(Luke 9:31 compare John 13:1)

Here Luke speaks of it in terms of Jesus being:

'taken up into heaven.'

(Luke 9:51 compare Mark 16:19, Acts 1:2, 10-11)

A similar expression is used of Elijah's death (2 Kings 2:9-11). Just as Elijah had to instruct Elisha before he died, so Jesus, as his death approaches, sets about the task of thoroughly training his disciples to carry on his mission.

They obviously have a lot to learn. In a scene reminiscent of Elijah (cf 2 Kings 1:10-12) James and John want a demonstration of God's power to force the Samaritans into a recognition of the disciples' authority (compare Mark 3:17 where they are called 'sons of thunder'). Jesus rebukes them. A variant text adds:

'You do not know what spirit you are made of. The Son of Man came not to destroy souls but to save them.'

The remainder of the journey will be given over to a training of the disciples in the spirit of Jesus.

2: The cost of journeying with Jesus

LUKE 9:57-62

57 As they travelled along they met a man on the road who said to him, 'I will
58 follow you wherever you go'. •Jesus answered, 'Foxes have holes and the birds of the air have nests, but the Son of Man has nowhere to lay his head'.
59 Another to whom he said, 'Follow me', replied, 'Let me go and bury my
60 father first'. •But he answered, 'Leave the dead to bury their dead; your duty is to go and spread the news of the kingdom of God'.
61 Another said, 'I will follow you, sir, but first let me go and say good-bye
62 to my people at home'. •Jesus said to him, 'Once the hand is laid on the plough, no one who looks back is fit for the kingdom of God'.

(Luke 9:57-60 compare Matthew 8:19-22 page 101)

Luke has already spoken of the price that a disciple must pay if he is to follow Jesus (Luke 9:1-6, 9:23-26). Here he speaks of the urgency and primacy of the mission:

'Your duty is to go and spread the news of the kingdom of God.'

(9:60 and not in Matthew's text)

It may be of interest to note that Elijah called Elisha while he was ploughing (1 Kings 19:19-21, compare Luke 9:62).

3: Those who journey with Jesus share his mission and the mission of the Twelve

(a) LUKE 10:1-16

1 **10** After this the Lord appointed seventy-two others and sent them out ahead of him, in pairs, to all the towns and places he himself was to visit.
2 He said to them, 'The harvest is rich but the labourers are few, so ask the Lord
3 of the harvest to send labourers to his harvest. •Start off now, but remember,
4 I am sending you out like lambs among wolves. •Carry no purse, no haversack,
5 no sandals. Salute no one on the road. •Whatever house you go into, let your
6 first words be, "Peace to this house!" •And if a man of peace lives there, your
7 peace will go and rest on him; if not, it will come back to you. •Stay in the same house, taking what food and drink they have to offer, for the labourer deserves
8 his wages; do not move from house to house. •Whenever you go into a town where
9 they make you welcome, eat what is set before you. •Cure those in it who are
10 sick, and say, "The kingdom of God is very near to you". •But whenever you enter
11 a town and they do not make you welcome, go out into its streets and say, •"We wipe off the very dust of your town that clings to our feet, and leave it with you.
12 Yet be sure of this: the kingdom of God is very near." •I tell you, on that day it will not go as hard with Sodom as with that town.

'Alas for you, Chorazin! Alas for you, Bethsaida! For if the miracles done 13 in you had been done in Tyre and Sidon, they would have repented long ago, sitting in sackcloth and ashes. •And still, it will not go as hard with Tyre and Sidon at the 14 Judgement as with you. •And as for you, Capernaum, did you want to be exalted 15 high as heaven? *You shall be thrown down to hell.ᵃ*

'Anyone who listens to you listens to me; anyone who rejects you rejects me, 16 and those who reject me reject the one who sent me.'

(a: Isaiah 14:15)
(Luke 10:2, compare Matthew 9:37 page 115
Luke 10:3-12, compare Matthew 10:7-16 page 115-116
Luke 10:13-15, compare Matthew 11:21-23 page 121,

It is obvious from a comparison of this passage with the instructions given by Jesus to the Twelve (Luke 9:1-6), that the seventy-two disciples are called to share the mission of the Twelve. In doing so they are sharing the mission of Jesus (Luke 10:16).

The authority they exercise is not an authority of power as the world understands it. It is the authority of the poor who, in relying on God, find that they lack nothing (Luke 22:35).

The disciples will be rejected just as Jesus was rejected (Luke 10:16, compare Luke 9:51-56); but those who reject them are rejecting God and will reap condemnation. This theme will recur throughout this journey (Luke 11:29-32, 11:39-46, 13:35, 17:26-30. Also 19:27, 19:41-44, 20:16, 21:20-24).

(b) LUKE 10:17-24

The seventy-two came back rejoicing. 'Lord,' they said 'even the devils 17 submit to us when we use your name.' •He said to them, 'I watched Satan fall 18 like lightning from heaven. •Yes, I have given you power to tread underfoot 19 serpents and scorpions and the whole strength of the enemy; nothing shall ever hurt you. •Yet do not rejoice that the spirits submit to you; rejoice rather that 20 your names are written in heaven.'

It was then that, filled with joy by the Holy Spirit, he said, 'I bless 21 you, Father, Lord of heaven and of earth, for hiding these things from the learned and the clever and revealing them to mere children. Yes, Father, for that is what it pleased you to do. • Everything has been entrusted to me by my Father; and 22 no one knows who the Son is except the Father, and who the Father is except the Son and those to whom the Son chooses to reveal him.'

Then turning to his disciples he spoke to them in private, 'Happy the eyes 23 that see what you see, •for I tell you that many prophets and kings wanted to see 24 what you see, and never saw it; to hear what you hear, and never heard it'.

(Luke 10:21-22, compare Matthew 11:25-27 page 122
Luke 10:23-24, compare Matthew 13:16-17 page 174,

The disciples rejoice at the power they exercise over evil (10:17). Jesus agrees, and, in words reminiscent of Isaiah (14:12-15), he reveals to them the ultimate significance of their victory: they are part of the eschatological battle and are victorious over Satan himself (10:18).

At the same time Jesus corrects their thinking and alters their perspective. They should rejoice with the joy of the poor (Luke 6:20). As he said to them on an earlier occasion:

'The mysteries of the kingdom are revealed to you.'   *(Luke 8:10).*

They share in the intimacy of Jesus with God, his Father. They are experiencing the eschatological joy of the messianic times. This joy is one of the dominant themes of the journey (Luke 11:27-28, 12:35-38, 14:12-14, 14:15-24, 15:4-32 and 19:1-10).

II: Basic Aspects of Discipleship

1: The central place of love in the life of a disciple

(N.B. The reader is reminded that the following commentaries are only supplementary. In each case the commentary on Matthew is to be read.)

LUKE 10:25-42

There was a lawyer who, to disconcert him, stood up and said to him, 'Master, 25 what must I do to inherit eternal life?' •He said to him, 'What is written in the 26 Law? What do you read there?' •He replied, '*You must love the Lord your God* 27 *with all your heart, with all your soul, with all your strength*, and with all your mind, *and your neighbour as yourself*'.ᶜ •'You have answered right,' said Jesus 28 'do this and life is yours.'

But the man was anxious to justify himself and said to Jesus, 'And who is 29 my neighbour?' •Jesus replied, 'A man was once on his way down from Jerusalem 30 to Jericho and fell into the hands of brigands; they took all he had, beat him and then made off, leaving him half dead. •Now a priest happened to be travelling 31 down the same road, but when he saw the man, he passed by on the other side. In the same way a Levite who came to the place saw him, and passed by on the 32 other side. •But a Samaritan traveller who came upon him was moved with 33 compassion when he saw him. •He went up and bandaged his wounds, pouring 34 oil and wine on them. He then lifted him on to his own mount, carried him to the inn and looked after him. •Next day, he took out two denarii and handed them 35 to the innkeeper. "Look after him," he said "and on my way back I will make good any extra expense you have." •Which of these three, do you think, proved 36 himself a neighbour to the man who fell into the brigands' hands?' •'The one 37 who took pity on him' he replied. Jesus said to him, 'Go, and do the same yourself'.

In the course of their journey he came to a village, and a woman named 38 Martha welcomed him into her house. •She had a sister called Mary, who sat 39 down at the Lord's feet and listened to him speaking. •Now Martha who was 40 distracted with all the serving said, 'Lord, do you not care that my sister is leaving me to do the serving all by myself? Please tell her to help me.' •But the Lord 41 answered: 'Martha, Martha,' he said 'you worry and fret about so many things, and yet few are needed, indeed only one. It is Mary who has chosen the better 42 part; it is not to be taken from her.'   *(a: Deuteronomy 6:5 and Leviticus 19:18)*
(Luke 10:25-28, compare Mark 12:28-34 and Matthew 22:34-40 page 329)

The lawyer knows the answer to his own question (Luke 10:27. In the other Synoptics it is Jesus who gives the answer). Luke wants to highlight the fact that theoretical knowledge is not the solution. If a man wants life he must 'do this' (Luke 10:28).

The parable reinforces this lesson. There is no theoretical answer to the question 'Who is my neighbour?'. The question, once again, is answered by action: 'Go and do the same yourself' (Luke 10:37). It is typical of Luke to choose a parable in which the man who finds life is an alien and an outsider. The Samaritan is another example of a poor man, spiritually dispossessed, but sharing in the compassion of God (Luke 10:33, compare Luke 6:36 page 160).

If a man is going to be able to channel God's compassion to others, he must first be open to God. Without contemplation he will not see. Hence the insertion here of the anecdote concerning Mary and Martha. Martha is doing many things for Jesus, but she is 'distracted' (10:40). She does not see Jesus. She is 'worried' (10:41). We are reminded of the seed (the 'word of God') that fell into thorns and was choked by the 'worries of life' (Luke 10:41). If a man is to learn to love he must learn to listen to God's word, like Mary, and not be distracted like Martha. (Compare Luke 12:1-2, 12:28-29, page 278-9).

2: The central place of prayer in the life of a disciple

LUKE 11:1-13

1   **11** Now once he was in a certain place praying, and when he had finished one of his disciples said, 'Lord, teach us to pray, just as John taught his 2   disciples'. •He said to them, 'Say this when you pray:

> "Father, may your name be held holy,
> your kingdom come;
3   > give us each day our daily bread,
> and forgive us our sins,
4   > for we ourselves forgive each one who is in debt to us.
> And do not put us to the test." '

5   He also said to them, 'Suppose one of you has a friend and goes to him in 6   the middle of the night to say, "My friend, lend me three loaves, •because a friend of mine on his travels has just arrived at my house and I have nothing to offer 7   him"; •and the man answers from inside the house, "Do not bother me. The door is bolted now, and my children and I are in bed; I cannot get up to give 8   it you". •I tell you, if the man does not get up and give it him for friendship's sake, persistence will be enough to make him get up and give his friend all he wants.

9   'So I say to you: Ask, and it will be given to you; search, and you will find; 10   knock, and the door will be opened to you. •For the one who asks always receives; the one who searches always finds; the one who knocks will always have the door 11   opened to him. •What father among you would hand his son a stone when he 12   asked for bread? Or hand him a snake instead of a fish? •Or hand him a 13   scorpion if he asked for an egg? •If you then, who are evil, know how to give your children what is good, how much more will the heavenly Father give the Holy Spirit to those who ask him!'   *(Luke 11:2-4, compare Matthew 6:9-13 page 94*
Luke 11:9-13, compare Matthew 7:7-11 page 107,

Luke's account of the 'Lord's Prayer' is placed in the context of Jesus' own prayer (Luke 11:1). He goes on to stress the need for persistence in prayer (11:5-8). God gives us what we need, because of his love.

We need to persist, for it is in prayer that we accept from God the intimacy which he desires to have with us. At the same time, Luke reminds his readers that God's thoughts are above our thoughts (Luke 11:11-13, cf Isaiah 55:9). We do not have the wisdom to know what we truly need. Our prayer is always to be like the prayer of Jesus in the Agony:

'Let your will be done, not mine.'   *(Luke 22:42)*

God will always give us 'the Holy Spirit' (Luke 11:13, compare John 14:13-16).

3: Opposition in the life of a disciple

(a) A disciple must hear and keep God's word

LUKE 11:14-36

He was casting out a devil and it was dumb; but when the devil had gone 14
out the dumb man spoke, and the people were amazed. •But some of them 15
said, 'It is through Beelzebul, the prince of devils, that he casts out devils'. •Others 16
asked him, as a test, for a sign from heaven; •but, knowing what they were 17
thinking, he said to them, 'Every kingdom divided against itself is heading for
ruin, and a household divided against itself collapses. •So too with Satan: if he is 18
divided against himself, how can his kingdom stand?—Since you assert that
it is through Beelzebul that I cast out devils. •Now if it is through Beelzebul 19
that I cast out devils, through whom do your own experts cast them out? Let
them be your judges, then. •But if it is through the finger of God that I cast 20
out devils, then know that the kingdom of God has overtaken you. •So long as 21
a strong man fully armed guards his own palace, his goods are undisturbed;
but when someone stronger than he is attacks and defeats him, the stronger 22
man takes away all the weapons he relied on and shares out his spoil.

'He who is not with me is against me; and he who does not gather with me 23
scatters.

'When an unclean spirit goes out of a man it wanders through waterless coun- 24
try looking for a place to rest, and not finding one it says, "I will go back to
the home I came from". •But on arrival, finding it swept and tidied, •it then goes $^{25}_{26}$
off and brings seven other spirits more wicked than itself, and they go in and
set up house there, so that the man ends up by being worse than he was before.'

Now as he was speaking, a woman in the crowd raised her voice and said, 27
'Happy the womb that bore you and the breasts you sucked!' •But he replied, 28
'Still happier those who hear the word of God and keep it!'

The crowds got even bigger and he addressed them, 'This is a wicked genera- 29
tion; it is asking for a sign. The only sign it will be given is the sign of Jonah.
For just as Jonah became a sign to the Ninevites, so will the Son of Man be to this 30
generation. •On Judgement day the Queen of the South will rise up with the men 31
of this generation and condemn them, because she came from the ends of the
earth to hear the wisdom of Solomon; and there is something greater than
Solomon here. •On Judgement day the men of Nineveh will stand up with this 32
generation and condemn it, because when Jonah preached they repented; and
there is something greater than Jonah here.

'No one lights a lamp and puts it in some hidden place or under a tub, but 33
on the lamp-stand so that people may see the light when they come in. •The lamp 34
of your body is your eye. When your eye is sound, your whole body too is filled with
light; but when it is diseased your body too will be all darkness. •See to it then that 35
the light inside you is not darkness. •If, therefore, your whole body is filled with 36
light, and no trace of darkness, it will be light entirely, as when the lamp shines
on you with its rays.'   *(Luke 11:14-26 and 29-32, compare Matthew 12:22-45 page 169-171)*

Jesus has just spoken of his being rejected (Luke 10:16) and of the
condemnation of those who reject him (Luke 10:12-15). This is the theme of this
passage. Its key is in the words:

'still happier those who hear the word of God and keep it.'

(Luke 11:27-28)

The reference to Jesus' mother (11:27) takes us back to the Magnificat in which Mary sang of the source of her happiness (Luke 1:46-55). People like Mary are happy; not only are they themselves 'filled with light' (Luke 11:34), but all about them is suffused with light (Luke 11:36). Those, on the other hand, who do not hear the word of God and keep it — such as those who are accusing Jesus of blasphemy — cannot recognise the spirit of God, so they reject the one who comes in God's name. Such people are blind, because the light inside them is darkness (Luke 11:35).

(b) The hypocrisy of those who refuse to hear and keep God's word

LUKE 11:37-54

He had just finished speaking when a Pharisee invited him to dine at his 37 house. He went in and sat down at the table. •The Pharisee saw this and was 38 surprised that he had not first washed before the meal. •But the Lord said to him, 39 'Oh, you Pharisees! You clean the outside of cup and plate, while inside yourselves you are filled with extortion and wickedness. •Fools! Did not he who made the 40 outside make the inside too? •Instead, give alms from what you have and then 41 indeed everything will be clean for you. •But alas for you Pharisees! You who pay 42 your tithe of mint and rue and all sorts of garden herbs and overlook justice and the love of God! These you should have practised, without leaving the others undone. •Alas for you Pharisees who like taking the seats of honour in the 43 synagogues and being greeted obsequiously in the market squares! •Alas for 44 you, because you are like the unmarked tombs that men walk on without knowing it!

A lawyer then spoke up. 'Master,' he said 'when you speak like this you 45 insult us too.' •'Alas for you lawyers also,' he replied 'because you load on men 46 burdens that are unendurable, burdens that you yourselves do not move a finger to lift.

'Alas for you who build the tombs of the prophets, the men your ancestors 47 killed! •In this way you both witness what your ancestors did and approve it; they 48 did the killing, you do the building.

'And that is why the Wisdom of God said, "I will send them prophets and 49 apostles; some they will slaughter and persecute, •so that this generation will have 50 to answer for every prophet's blood that has been shed since the foundation of the world, •from the blood of Abel to the blood of Zechariah, who was 51 murdered between the altar and the sanctuary". Yes, I tell you, this generation will have to answer for it all.

'Alas for you lawyers who have taken away the key of knowledge! You have 52 not gone in yourselves, and have prevented others going in who wanted to.'

When he left the house, the scribes and the Pharisees began a furious attack 53 on him and tried to force answers from him on innumerable questions, •setting 54 traps to catch him out in something he might say.

(Luke 11:39-52, compare Matthew 23:4, 6-7, 13, 23-36 page 331-334)

The setting is a common one in Luke's Gospel: we are present at the messianic banquet. On the surface it appears that Jesus is dining with the Pharisees. It becomes apparent that they are not one with him. As usual, a conflict arises (compare Luke 5:29-32, 7:34-50, 14:1-24, 15:1-32 and, in relation to the disciples themselves, Luke 22:1-32, 24:13-35).

In reading the accusations made by Jesus against the Pharisees and lawyers it is important for us to look at our own lives and to see ourselves in the Pharisees. How much of our 'religion' too is a matter of external observance? Are we concerned primarily with 'justice and the love of God' (Luke 11:42)?

The Zechariah mentioned in the passage (Luke 11:51) is probably the Zechariah who was murdered during the reign of Joash, about 790 B.C. (2 Chronicles 24:20-22).

From the first prophet, Abel (Luke 11:51), to the last, the message of the prophets has been rejected. This is a pattern that repeats itself in the life of Jesus (Luke 4:16-30, 13:33) and the disciple can expect the same fate (Luke 6:23, Acts 7:52).

(c) A disciple must not fear opposition

LUKE 12:1-12

1   12 Meanwhile the people had gathered in their thousands so that they were treading on one another. And he began to speak, first of all to his disciples. 'Be on your guard against the yeast of the Pharisees—that is, their hypocrisy.
2   Everything that is now covered will be uncovered, and everything now hidden
3   will be made clear. •For this reason, whatever you have said in the dark will be heard in the daylight, and what you have whispered in hidden places will be proclaimed on the housetops.
4   'To you my friends I say: Do not be afraid of those who kill the body and
5   after that can do no more. •I will tell you whom to fear: fear him who, after he
6   has killed, has the power to cast into hell. Yes, I tell you, fear him. •Can you not buy five sparrows for two pennies? And yet not one is forgotten in God's
7   sight. •Why, every hair on your head has been counted. There is no need to be afraid: you are worth more than hundreds of sparrows.
8   'I tell you, if anyone openly declares himself for me in the presence of men, the
9   Son of Man will declare himself for him in the presence of God's angels. •But the man who disowns me in the presence of men will be disowned in the presence of God's angels.
10   'Everyone who says a word against the Son of Man will be forgiven, but he who blasphemes against the Holy Spirit will not be forgiven.
11   'When they take you before synagogues and magistrates and authorities,
12   do not worry about how to defend yourselves or what to say, •because when the time comes, the Holy Spirit will teach you what you must say.'

(Luke 12:2-9, compare Matthew 10:26-33 page 117
Luke 12:10, compare Matthew 12:32 page 171
Luke 12:11-12, compare Matthew 10:17-20 page 116)

For all their apparent power, men cannot harm a disciple who has been drawn into the providential care of God (Luke 12:6-7) and is sustained by God's Holy Spirit (Luke 12:12).

It is interesting to note that this is the only occasion when Luke speaks of 'gehenna' (see page 91).

4: A disciple must place his trust in God, not in possessions

LUKE 12:13-34

13 A man in the crowd said to him, 'Master, tell my brother to give me a share
14 of our inheritance'. •'My friend,' he replied-'who appointed me your judge, or
15 the arbitrator of your claims?' •Then he said to them, 'Watch, and be on your
guard against avarice of any kind, for a man's life is not made secure by what he
owns, even when he has more than he needs'.
16 Then he told them a parable: 'There was once a rich man who, having had
17 a good harvest from his land, •thought to himself, "What am I to do? I have
18 not enough room to store my crops." •Then he said, "This is what I will do:
I will pull down my barns and build bigger ones, and store all my grain and my
19 goods in them, •and I will say to my soul: My soul, you have plenty of good
things laid by for many years to come; take things easy, eat, drink, have a good
20 time". •But God said to him, "Fool! This very night the demand will be made
21 for your soul; and this hoard of yours, whose will it be then?" •So it is when
a man stores up treasure for himself in place of making himself rich in the sight
of God.'
22 Then he said to his disciples, 'That is why I am telling you not to worry
about your life and what you are to eat, nor about your body and how you are
23 to clothe it. •For life means more than food, and the body more than clothing.
24 Think of the ravens. They do not sow or reap; they have no storehouses and
no barns; yet God feeds them. And how much more are you worth than the
25 birds! •Can any of you, for all his worrying, add a single cubit to his span of
26 life? •If the smallest things, therefore, are outside your control, why worry
27 about the rest? •Think of the flowers; they never have to spin or weave; yet,
I assure you, not even Solomon in all his regalia was robed like one of these.
28 Now if that is how God clothes the grass in the field which is there today and
thrown into the furnace tomorrow, how much more will he look after you, you
29 men of little faith! •But you, you must not set your hearts on things to eat and
30 things to drink; nor must you worry. •It is the pagans of this world who set their
31 hearts on all these things. Your Father well knows you need them. •No; set your
hearts on his kingdom, and these other things will be given you as well.
32 'There is no need to be afraid, little flock, for it has pleased your Father to
give you the kingdom.
33 'Sell your possessions and give alms. Get yourselves purses that do not wear
out, treasure that will not fail you, in heaven where no thief can reach it and
34 no moth destroy it. •For where your treasure is, there will your heart be also.

(Luke 12:22-31, 33-34 compare Matthew 6:19-34 page 95-96)

This whole passage is a commentary on the beatitude:

'How happy are you who are poor.'

(Luke 6:20)

and on the corresponding woe:

'Alas for you who are rich.'

(Luke 6:24)

This is a favorite theme of Luke's. In her Magnificat, Mary said:

'the rich are sent empty away'

(Luke 1:53)

and constantly throughout the Gospel Luke returns to the danger of riches.

(Luke 1:53, 3:25, 6:24, 8:14, 12:16, 12:21, 14:12, 16:1, 16:19-22, 21:1.) At the end of the journey, Luke contrasts the rich aristocrat (18:15-26) with Zacchaeus, a wealthy man (19:1-10). The reader is referred to commentary pages 156-9.

In the passage we are considering, a man approaches Jesus asking for possessions (Luke 12:13). Jesus warns him:

'A man's life is not made secure by what he owns, even when he has more than he needs.'

(Luke 12:15)

After the parable of the rich fool, he tells the disciples where they should place their trust: in their 'Father' (12:30, 12:32) who has given them 'the kingdom' (12:32). The disciple is blessed with God's merciful love; he should not distract himself, he should not worry:

'It is the pagans of this world that set their hearts on all these things.'

(Luke 12:30)

It is those who:

'as they go on their way are choked by the worries and riches and pleasures of life and do not reach maturity'.

(Luke 8:14)

In conclusion, Jesus tells his disciples that, rather than seek for possessions, they should sell their possessions:

'and give alms.'

(Luke 12:33)

The word for 'alms' is related to the word for 'mercy'. In giving alms, a disciple is sharing in the mercy of God. This, too, is a constantly recurring theme in Luke's Gospel (Luke 3:11, 6:30, 7:5, 11:41, 14:14, 16:9, 18:22, 19:8. See also Acts 9:36, 10:2, 10:4, 10:31).

It is interesting to note how frequently Luke speaks of God as 'Father'. Following Mark, Luke has God address Jesus as 'My Son' in the Transfiguration scene (Luke 9:36), and Jesus address God as 'Father' in the Agony (Luke 22:42). Following Matthew he has Jesus speak of God as a Father (Luke 6:36, 11:13 and in the text we are examining, 12:30), and address him as 'Father' (10:21 and 11:2). But over and above these occasions, and apart from the parable of the Prodigal Son (Luke 15:11-32), Luke has Jesus speak of God as a Father on four occasions (Luke 2:49, 12:32, 22:29, 24:49); and address him as 'Father' twice from the cross (Luke 23:34, 23:46).

Jesus invites his disciples to know his Father and to experience a complete trust in his Father's care. This experience of God's compassion is had precisely in the actions of having compassion on one's neighbour (Luke 12:33). It is in selfless self-giving that we come to know the heart of God who is love. Riches are a danger because they clutter our hearts, they blind us to the needs of our brothers, they deprive us of the experience of knowing that our Father knows our need, and, that even in the most deprived circumstances (circumstances like those of Jesus on the cross), he cares for us. It is in being compassionate as our Father is compassionate (Luke 6:36) that we come to know the compassion of God. Indeed:

'How happy are you who are poor: yours is the kingdom of God.' *(Luke 6:20)*

5: Discipleship and the Judgment of God

(a) A disciple will be judged on his service

LUKE 12:35-48

'See that you are dressed for action and have your lamps lit. •Be like men ³⁵₃₆ waiting for their master to return from the wedding feast, ready to open the door as soon as he comes and knocks. •Happy those servants whom the master 37 finds awake when he comes. I tell you solemnly, he will put on an apron, sit them down at table and wait on them. •It may be in the second watch he comes, 38 or in the third, but happy those servants if he finds them ready. •You may be 39 quite sure of this, that if the householder had known at what hour the burglar would come, he would not have let anyone break through the wall of his house. You too must stand ready, because the Son of Man is coming at an hour you 40 do not expect.'

Peter said, 'Lord, do you mean this parable for us, or for everyone?' •The ⁴¹₄₂ Lord replied, 'What sort of steward, then, is faithful and wise enough for the master to place him over his household to give them their allowance of food at the proper time? •Happy that servant if his master's arrival finds him at this 43 employment. •I tell you truly, he will place him over everything he owns. •But ⁴⁴₄₅ as for the servant who says to himself, "My master is taking his time coming", and sets about beating the menservants and the maids, and eating and drinking and getting drunk, •his master will come on a day he does not expect and at 46 an hour he does not know. The master will cut him off and send him to the same fate as the unfaithful.

'The servant who knows what his master wants, but has not even started to 47 carry out those wishes, will receive very many strokes of the lash. •The one who 48 who did not know, but deserves to be beaten for what he has done, will receive fewer strokes. When a man has had a great deal given him, a great deal will be demanded of him; when a man has had a great deal given him on trust, even more will be expected of him.

(Luke 12:35-38, compare Matthew 25:1-13 page 358-9
Luke 12:39-46, compare Matthew 24:42-51 page 357-8)

The best commentary on this passage is found in words inserted by Luke into the Last Supper account. Jesus says:

'The greatest among you must behave as if he were the youngest, the leader as if he were the one who serves. For who is the greater: the one at table or the one who serves? Yet here am I among you as one who serves!'

(Luke 22:26-27, compare John 13:1-16)

The authority of Jesus was the authority of one who gave his life in service of his brothers' needs. It is to be the same with his disciples. It is on this that they will be judged. Whatever gifts a man has he has 'on trust' (12:48). If a man follows Jesus in a life of service, he will enjoy the intimacy of the messianic banquet with Jesus (12:37) and experience Jesus himself ministering to his needs. This is not something reserved for a select few (Luke 12:41). It is something offered to 'everyone' who follows Jesus faithfully.

(b) Now is the hour of judgment. A disciple must discern the will of God and repent.

LUKE 12:49 — 13:5

49 'I have come to bring fire to the earth, and how I wish it were blazing
50 already! •There is a baptism I must still receive, and how great is my distress till
it is over!
51 'Do you suppose that I am here to bring peace on earth? No, I tell you, but
52 rather division. •For from now on a household of five will be divided: three
53 against two and two against three; •the father divided against the son, son
against father, mother against daughter, daughter against mother, mother-in-law
against daughter-in-law, daughter-in-law against mother-in-law.'
54 He said again to the crowds, 'When you see a cloud looming up in the west
55 you say at once that rain is coming, and so it does. •And when the wind is from
56 the south you say it will be hot, and it is. •Hypocrites! You know how to
interpret the face of the earth and the sky. How is it you do not know how to
interpret these times?
57
58 'Why not judge for yourselves what is right? •For example: when you go
to court with your opponent, try to settle with him on the way, or he may drag
you before the judge and the judge hand you over to the bailiff and the bailiff
59 have you thrown into prison. •I tell you, you will not get out till you have paid
the very last penny.'
1 **13** It was just about this time that some people arrived and told him about
the Galileans whose blood Pilate had mingled with that of their sacrifices.
2 At this he said to them, 'Do you suppose these Galileans who suffered like that
3 were greater sinners than any other Galileans? •They were not, I tell you. No;
4 but unless you repent you will all perish as they did. •Or those eighteen on whom
the tower at Siloam fell and killed them? Do you suppose that they were more
5 guilty than all the other people living in Jerusalem? •They were not, I tell you.
No; but unless you repent you will all perish as they did.'

(Luke 12:51-53, compare Matthew 10:34-36 page 118
Luke 12:54-56, compare Matthew 16:2-3 page 201
Luke 12:57-59, compare Matthew 5:25-26 page 91)

The opening words, found only in Luke, take us into the heart of Jesus. He
longed to spread the kingdom of God; he longed to convince men of God's love;
he longed, in John's words, to 'draw all men to himself' (John 12:32) to
overwhelm (='baptise') them with the love of the Spirit of God (Luke 3:16). But he
faced constant rejection. He warns his disciples that, with his coming, something
final and definitive has happened. Nothing can be the same again (cf 'from now
on' 12:52. Compare Luke 2:11, 3:22, 14:11, 19:5, 19:9 and 23:43). It is necessary
that men listen to Jesus and 'repent' (13:4-5). If they do not they will perish (13:3,
13:5).

(c) God's judgment is compassionate

LUKE 13:6-17

6 He told this parable: 'A man had a fig tree planted in his vineyard, and he
7 came looking for fruit on it but found none. •He said to the man who looked
after the vineyard, "Look here, for three years now I have been coming to look
for fruit on this fig tree and finding none. Cut it down: why should it be taking
8 up the ground?" •"Sir," the man replied "leave it one more year and give me
9 time to dig round it and manure it: •it may bear fruit next year; if not, then
you can cut it down." '
10
11 One sabbath day he was teaching in one of the synagogues, •and a woman
was there who for eighteen years had been possessed by a spirit that left her

12 enfeebled; she was bent double and quite unable to stand upright. •'When Jesus saw her he called her over and said. 'Woman, you are rid of your infirmity'
13 and he laid his hands on her. And at once she straightened up, and she glorified God.
14 But the synagogue official was indignant because Jesus had healed on the sabbath, and he addressed the people present. 'There are six days' he said 'when work is to be done. Come and be healed on one of those days and not on the
15 sabbath.' •But the Lord answered him. 'Hypocrites!' he said 'Is there one of you who does not untie his ox or his donkey from the manger on the sabbath
16 and take it out for watering? •And this woman, a daughter of Abraham whom Satan has held bound these eighteen years—was it not right to untie her bonds
17 on the sabbath day?' •When he said this, all his adversaries were covered with confusion, and all the people were overjoyed at all the wonders he worked.

Jesus has been speaking of God's judgment. Here he reminds his disciples, first by a parable (13:6-9) and then by his healing of the sick woman (13:10-17) that God's judgment is the judgment of a patient and compassionate Father.

It has been suggested that the three years mentioned in the parable (Luke 13:7) may be an allusion to the length of Jesus' ministry. Jesus tried for three years to find fruit on the fig tree of contemporary Judaism as practised by the religious leaders. He found none. Mark (11:12-14, 20-22) and Matthew (21:18-20) both have Jesus cursing the fig tree and causing it to wither. It is interesting that Luke omits this. Is he hoping that it may yet produce fruit?

The anecdote (Luke 13:10-17) reminds the reader that God's judgment flows from his love, not from the Law.

(d) God's victory is inevitable

LUKE 13:18-21
18 He went on to say, 'What is the kingdom of God like? What shall I compare
19 it with? •It is like a mustard seed which a man took and threw into his garden: it grew and became a tree, and the birds of the air sheltered in its branches.'
20 Another thing he said, 'What shall I compare the kingdom of God with?
21 It is like the yeast a woman took and mixed in with three measures of flour till it was leavened all through.'   *(Compare Matthew 13:31-33 page 177,)*

(e) Men are judged by their acceptance or rejection of God's word

LUKE 13:22-35
22 Through towns and villages he went teaching, making his way to Jerusalem.
23 Someone said to him, 'Sir, will there be only a few saved?' He said to them,
24 'Try your best to enter by the narrow door, because, I tell you, many will try to enter and will not succeed.
25 'Once the master of the house has got up and locked the door, you may find yourself knocking on the door, saying, "Lord, open to us" but he will answer,
26 "I do not know where you come from". •Then you will find yourself saying,
27 "We once ate and drank in your company; you taught in our streets" •but he will reply, "I do not know where you come from. *Away from me, all you wicked men!"* [a]
28 'Then there will be weeping and grinding of teeth, when you see Abraham and Isaac and Jacob and all the prophets in the kingdom of God, and yourselves

turned outside. •And men from east and west, from north and south, will come 29
to take their places at the feast in the kingdom of God.

'Yes, there are those now last who will be first, and those now first who will 30
be last.'

Just at this time some Pharisees came up. 'Go away' they said. 'Leave this 31
place, because Herod means to kill you.' •He replied, 'You may go and give 32
that fox this message: Learn that today and tomorrow I cast out devils and on
the third day ^{b} attain my end.   •But for today and tomorrow and the next day 33
I must go on, since it would not be right for a prophet to die outside Jerusalem.

'Jerusalem, Jerusalem, you that kill the prophets and stone those who are 34
sent to you! How often have I longed to gather your children, as a hen gathers
her brood under her wings, and you refused! •So be it! Your house will be left 35
to you. Yes, I promise you, you shall not see me till the time comes when you
say:

Blessings on him who comes in the name of the Lord!'

(a: Psalm 6:8 b: Psalm 118:26)
(Luke 13:23-24, compare Matthew 7:13-14 page 97
Luke 13:25, compare Matthew 25:10-12 page 358
Luke 13:26-27, compare Matthew 7:22-23 page 98
Luke 13:28-29, compare Matthew 8:11-12 page 82
Luke 13:34-35, compare Matthew 23:37-39 page 334)

Questions about the number saved or their relative positions in the kingdom
are foolish questions (Luke 13:23, 13:30). Salvation comes as a gracious gift of
God; but it makes radical demands of anyone who would receive it. This has been
the message of this whole insert. It is not achieved by saying the right words, or by
belonging to the right group. It is open to all 'from east and west, from north and
south' (13:29). It is not achieved even by a close table intimacy with Jesus.

The man who hears and keeps God's word will share the messianic banquet
(13:29). As John says:

'If anyone hears my words and does not keep them faithfully,
it is not I who shall condemn him,
since I have come not to condemn the world,
but to save the world:
he who rejects me and refuses my words
has his judge already:
the word itself that I have spoken
will be his judge on the last day.'

(John 12:47-48)

Jesus is getting closer to Jerusalem (13:22, 13:33). Jesus will leave Herod's
territory. But it is not out of fear of Herod. It is so that he will attain his end
(13:32): an expression that includes the concept of glorification (Luke 9:51) and
death (Luke 13:33).

Jesus laments over the city (13:34-35). Because of its rejection of him, it will
not find the life he so longed to give it (compare Luke 12:49-50). At the same time,
Jesus is confident that the holy city will not be able to withstand the grace of God
for ever, and he looks forward to the time when it will welcome the coming of
God with joy (13:35, compare Romans 11:25-32).

6: A disciple must be poor

(a) Only the poor accept God's word and experience intimacy with him

LUKE 14:1-24

¹ **14** Now on a sabbath day he had gone for a meal to the house of one of the
² leading Pharisees; and they watched him closely. •There in front of him was
³ a man with dropsy, •and Jesus addressed the lawyers and Pharisees. 'Is it
⁴ against the law' he asked 'to cure a man on the sabbath, or not?' •But they
⁵ remained silent, so he took the man and cured him and sent him away. •Then
he said to them, 'Which of you here, if his son falls into a well, or his ox, will
⁶ not pull him out on a sabbath day without hesitation?' •And to this they could
find no answer.
⁷   He then told the guests a parable, because he had noticed how they
⁸ picked the places of honour. He said this, •'When someone invites you to a
wedding feast, do not take your seat in the place of honour. A more distinguished
⁹ person than you may have been invited, •and the person who invited you both
may come and say, "Give up your place to this man". And then, to your em-
¹⁰ barrassment, you would have to go and take the lowest place. •No; when you
are a guest, make your way to the lowest place and sit there, so that, when your
host comes, he may say, "My friend, move up higher". In that way, everyone
¹¹ with you at the table will see you honoured. •For everyone who exalts himself
will be humbled, and the man who humbles himself will be exalted.'
¹²   Then he said to his host, 'When you give a lunch or a dinner, do not ask
your friends, brothers, relations or rich neighbours, for fear they repay your
¹³ courtesy by inviting you in return. •No; when you have a party, invite the poor,
¹⁴ the crippled, the lame, the blind; •that they cannot pay you back means that
you are fortunate, because repayment will be made to you when the virtuous
rise again.'
¹⁵   On hearing this, one of those gathered round the table said to him, 'Happy
¹⁶ the man who will be at the feast in the kingdom of God!' •But he said to him,
'There was a man who gave a great banquet, and he invited a large number of
¹⁷ people. •When the time for the banquet came, he sent his servant to say to those
¹⁸ who had been invited, "Come along: everything is ready now". •But all alike
started to make excuses. The first said, "I have bought a piece of land and must
¹⁹ go and see it. Please accept my apologies." •Another said, "I have bought five
yoke of oxen and am on my way to try them out. Please accept my apologies."
²⁰ Yet another said,"I have just got married and so am unable to come".
²¹   'The servant returned and reported this to his master. Then the householder,
in a rage, said to his servant, "Go out quickly into the streets and alleys of the
²² town and bring in here the poor, the crippled, the blind and the lame". •"Sir,"
said the servant "your orders have been carried out and there is still room."
²³ Then the master said to his servant, "Go to the open roads and the hedgerows
²⁴ and force people to come in to make sure my house is full; •because, I tell you,
not one of those who were invited shall have a taste of my banquet". '

(Luke 14:16-24, compare Matthew 22:1-10 page 322)

The setting is familiar: a meal at which Jesus heals someone and has to
defend himself against criticism.

The parable (14:7-11) is a simple one, geared to the mentality of the leading
Pharisee and his guests who would avoid humiliation at all costs. Its central point
is emphasised by Luke:

'Everyone who exalts himself will be humbled, and the man who humbles himself will be exalted.'

(Luke 14:11)

Jesus then instructs the Pharisee to be compassionate as his Father is compassionate (Luke 6:36):

'When you have a party, invite the poor, the crippled, the lame and the blind.'

(Luke 14:13)

It is these (14:21) who will be 'at the feast in the kingdom of God' (14:15. Compare Luke 4:18 and 7:29).

We are reminded of Isaiah:

'I called and you would not answer,
I spoke and you would not listen.
You did what I consider evil,
you chose to do what displeases me.
Therefore, thus speaks
the Lord Yahweh:
you shall see my servants eat
while you go hungry.
You shall see my servants drink
while you go thirsty.
You shall see my servants rejoice
while you are put to shame.
You shall hear my servants sing
for joy of heart,
while you will moan
for sadness of heart;
you will wail for distress of spirit.'

(Isaiah 65:12-14, compare Isaiah 55:1-2)

The instructions given here by Jesus to the Pharisee and his guests will be given by him later to his own close companions (Luke 22:25-30). The truth contained in the beatitude 'How happy are you who are poor' (6:20) is a truth that is hard to learn.

(b) A disciple, therefore, must give up all his possessions

LUKE 14:25-35

25   Great crowds accompanied him on his way and he turned and spoke to
26   them. •'If any man comes to me without hating his father, mother, wife, children,
27   brothers, sisters, yes and his own life too, he cannot be my disciple. •Anyone who does not carry his cross and come after me cannot be my disciple.

28   'And indeed, which of you here, intending to build a tower, would not first
29   sit down and work out the cost to see if he had enough to complete it? •Otherwise, if he laid the foundation and then found himself unable to finish the work, the
30   onlookers would all start making fun of him and saying, •"Here is a man who
31   started to build and was unable to finish". •Or again, what king marching to war against another king would not first sit down and consider whether with ten thousand men he could stand up to the other who advanced against him with
32   twenty thousand? •If not, then while the other king was still a long way off, he
33   would send envoys to sue for peace. •So in the same way, none of you can be my disciple unless he gives up all his possessions.

'Salt is a useful thing. But if the salt itself loses its taste, how can it be 34
seasoned again? •It is good for neither soil nor manure heap. People throw it 35
out. Listen, anyone who has ears to hear!'

(Luke 14:25-27, compare Matthew 10:37-39 page 118
Luke 14:34-35, compare Matthew 5:13 page 89)

The word 'hate' (14:26) conveys the wrong sense in English. Luke is using the
word according to its Biblical usage where it is frequently contrasted with 'love',
and is a stark way of speaking of the one who is not chosen as distinct from the
one who is chosen. It does not imply any antipathy. It is used, for example, to
distinguish the less favoured from the more favoured wife in a polygamous
marriage (Deuteronomy 21:15). In the Book of Genesis we are told that Jacob
'loved' Rachel and 'hated' Leah (Genesis 29:31), that is, he had set his heart on
Rachel rather than Leah (compare Malachi 1:2-3 and Romans 9:13 re Jacob and
Esau). Jesus is telling his disciples that God and God's kingdom must take
precedence over even such sacred people as one's father, mother, wife, children,
brothers and sisters, as well as over one's own life (Luke 12:31).

Matthew (10:37-38) and Mark (8:34) give similar teaching. Note that Luke
alone mentions 'wife' in the list (14:26, cf also Luke 18:29). Perhaps he was
influenced by Paul's encouragement of celibacy (cf 1 Corinthians 7:25-28).

Jesus goes on to give the basic foundation for discipleship. If a man is going
to build a tower he must first make sure he has enough material to complete the
job. If he is going to wage a war, he should first ascertain his chances of victory. In
the same way, if a man wants to be a disciple, he must know from the start that
this requires of him that he 'give up all his possessions' (14:33). Like Jesus, a
disciple must be open to do God's will. Any possessions that bind a man's heart,
whether they be material possessions, or possessions as intimate as a parent, a
spouse or a child, will prevent him from hearing and keeping God's word. Of
course a man can enjoy things; of course a man can and should love his dear ones.
But he cannot let his heart be so possessed by them that they come first in his
affections. Only if God comes first can his heart be free to truly love these people
in a way that is in accordance with the will of God.

It is this single-mindedness, this 'loving the Lord your God with all your
heart, with all your soul, with all your strength, and with all your mind' (Luke
10:27) that gives taste to the life of a disciple (14:34). If he loses this quality, if he
puts other things before God, he becomes useless.

7: Discipleship and the compassion of God.

LUKE 15:1-32

15 The tax collectors and the sinners, meanwhile, were all seeking his company 1
to hear what he had to say, •and the Pharisees and the scribes complained. 2
'This man' they said 'welcomes sinners and eats with them.' •So he spoke this 3
parable to them:

'What man among you with a hundred sheep, losing one, would not leave 4
the ninety-nine in the wilderness and go after the missing one till he found it?
And when he found it, would he not joyfully take it on his shoulders •and then, 5 6
when he got home, call together his friends and neighbours? "Rejoice with me,"
he would say "I have found my sheep that was lost." •In the same way, I tell you, 7

there will be more rejoicing in heaven over one repentant sinner than over ninety-nine virtuous men who have no need of repentance.

'Or again, what woman with ten drachmas would not, if she lost one, light 8 a lamp and sweep out the house and search thoroughly till she found it? •And 9 then, when she had found it, call together her friends and neighbours? "Rejoice with me," she would say "I have found the drachma I lost." •In the same way, 10 I tell you, there is rejoicing among the angels of God over one repentant sinner.'

He also said, 'A man had two sons. •The younger said to his father, "Father, ¦¦ let me have the share of the estate that would come to me". So the father divided ¹² the property between them. •A few days later, the younger son got together 13 everything he had and left for a distant country where he squandered his money on a life of debauchery.

'When he had spent it all, that country experienced a severe famine, and now 14 he began to feel the pinch, •so he hired himself out to one of the local inhabitants 15 who put him on his farm to feed the pigs. •And he would willingly have filled 16 his belly with the husks the pigs were eating but no one offered him anything. Then he came to his senses and said, "How many of my father's paid servants 17 have more food than they want, and here am I dying of hunger! •I will leave 18 this place and go to my father and say: Father, I have sinned against heaven and against you; •I no longer deserve to be called your son; treat me as one of your 19 paid servants." •So he left the place and went back to his father. 20

'While he was still a long way off, his father saw him and was moved with pity. He ran to the boy, clasped him in his arms and kissed him tenderly. •Then his 21 son said, "Father, I have sinned against heaven and against you. I no longer deserve to be called your son." •But the father said to his servants, "Quick! 22 Bring out the best robe and put it on him; put a ring on his finger and sandals on his feet. •Bring the calf we have been fattening, and kill it; we are going to 23 have a feast, a celebration, •because this son of mine was dead and has come 24 back to life; he was lost and is found." And they began to celebrate.

'Now the elder son was out in the fields, and on his way back, as he drew 25 near the house, he could hear music and dancing. •Calling one of the servants 26 he asked what it was all about. •"Your brother has come" replied the servant 27 "and your father has killed the calf we had fattened because he has got him back safe and sound." •He was angry then and refused to go in, and his father came 28 out to plead with him; •but he answered his father, "Look, all these years 29 I have slaved for you and never once disobeyed your orders, yet you never offered me so much as a kid for me to celebrate with my friends. •But, for this 30 son of yours, when he comes back after swallowing up your property—he and his women—you kill the calf we had been fattening."

'The father said, "My son, you are with me always and all I have is yours. 31 But it was only right we should celebrate and rejoice, because your brother 32 here was dead and has come to life; he was lost and is found." '

(Luke 15:3-7, compare Matthew 18:12-14 page 266)

Those who knew Jesus came to see him as revealing to them the heart of God; they came to listen to his words, knowing they were hearing the words of God. As we read these three parables we should try to believe that we are reading the word of God, that the attitudes portrayed here by Jesus are the attitudes of God himself and that the judgments made by Jesus are the judgments of God.

Jesus is explaining why it is that he:

'welcomes sinners and eats with them'

Luke 15:2, compare Luke 5:30, 7:37 and 14:21)

They are the lost ones. Jesus speaks of God as one who goes out after the lost sheep (15:4), who searches for the lost coin (15:8) who waits patiently, longing for the return of the lost son and who goes out to meet him when he is still a long way off:

'His father saw him and was moved with pity. He ran to the boy, clasped him in his arms and kissed him tenderly.'

(15:20)

God even goes out to the elder son and pleads with him to come to the feast (15:28).

So often we think of religion as our search for God. In these parables Jesus makes it clear that religion is first and foremost God's searching for us. God is love and he longs to share his life with men. He knows no greater joy than that we celebrate our existence in union with him (Luke 15:6, 15:9, 15:20-24).

We 'sinners' (15:2) have wandered off and become lost. We are:

'choked by the worries and riches and pleasures of life and do not reach maturity'.

(Luke 8:14)

We have failed to bear fruit (Luke 13:6). That is the very reason for God's compassionate concern. That is the very reason why Jesus is eating and drinking with us. He longs for us to 'come to life' (15:32). He longs for us to be found by God (15:32) and 'feast in the kingdom of God' (Luke 14:15).

The elder son (15:25 = the Pharisees, 15:2) is sadly mistaken about the Father and about the nature of life itself. But the offering is made to him too if he will only learn to forgive and to become a poor man who can humbly enjoy the graciousness of God.

III: **The Implications of Discipleship**

(N.B. The reader is again reminded that the following commentaries are supplementary only. In each case the commentary on Matthew is to be read.)

1: **What a man must do with his riches to become a disciple**

LUKE 16:1-15

1 **16** He also said to his disciples, 'There was a rich man and he had a steward
2 who was denounced to him for being wasteful with his property. •He called for the man and said, "What is this I hear about you? Draw me up an account of
3 your stewardship because you are not to be my steward any longer." •Then the steward said to himself, "Now that my master is taking the stewardship from me, what am I to do? Dig? I am not strong enough. Go begging? I should be too
4 ashamed. •Ah, I know what I will do to make sure that when I am dismissed from office there will be some to welcome me into their homes."
5 'Then he called his master's debtors one by one. To the first he said, "How
6 much do you owe my master?" •"One hundred measures of oil" was the reply. The steward said, "Here, take your bond; sit down straight away and write fifty".
7 To another he said, "And you, sir, how much do you owe?" "One hundred measures of wheat" was the reply. The steward said, "Here, take your bond and write eighty".

8   'The master praised the dishonest steward for his astuteness. For the children of this world are more astute in dealing with their own kind than are the children of light.'

9   'And so I tell you this: use money, tainted as it is, to win you friends, and thus make sure that when it fails you, they will welcome you into the tents of

10   eternity. •The man who can be trusted in little things can be trusted in great;

11   the man who is dishonest in little things will be dishonest in great. •If then you cannot be trusted with money, that tainted thing, who will trust you with genuine

12   riches? •And if you cannot be trusted with what is not yours, who will give you what is your very own?

13   'No servant can be the slave of two masters: he will either hate the first and love the second, or treat the first with respect and the second with scorn. You cannot be the slave both of God and of money.'

14
15   The Pharisees, who loved money, heard all this and laughed at him. •He said to them, 'You are the very ones who pass yourselves off as virtuous in people's sight, but God knows your hearts. For what is thought highly of by men is loathsome in the sight of God.

(Luke 16:13, compare Matthew 6:24 page 95)

Jesus is trying to touch the hearts of these men. They cannot understand God's love for the sinner, partly because they live on the surface of their lives. They love money (16:14) and 'pass themselves off as virtuous in people's sight' (16:15). They are caught up in externals. He tries to appeal to them through a parable that their crafty minds could easily understand. But they refuse to listen. They 'laughed at him' (16:14). Jesus sees their hearts as God sees them (16:15) and exposes them in an effort to break through their pride and obstinacy.

Riches (= possessions) are a barrier to being a disciple (compare Luke 6:24, 8:14, 12:13-34, 14:33, 18:18-27). The best thing a rich man can do is to sell his possessions and give alms (Luke 12:33, 16:9).

2: Men are called to be disciples of Jesus, not of the Law

LUKE 16:16-17

16   'Up to the time of John it was the Law and the Prophets; since then, the kingdom of God has been preached, and by violence everyone is getting in.

17   'It is easier for heaven and earth to disappear than for one little stroke to drop out of the Law.

(Luke 16:16, compare Matthew 11:12 page 120
Luke 16:17, compare Matthew 5:18 page 90)

The violence spoken of here is the violence of God, spoken of by Jesus in an earlier parable:

'The master said to the servant, "Go to the open roads and the hedgerows and force people to come in to make sure my house is full".'

(Luke 14:23)

There was a time ('up to the time of John' 16:16) when God was seen to be working through the 'Law and the Prophets' (16:16). Jesus was aware that something different was happening in his own time: God's grace was flowing beyond the confines of the Law, was working outside the Temple and the synagogue, was powerfully drawing the outcasts, the sinners, the strangers, 'everyone' (16:16) to a change of heart and a community of love.

Luke seems to be using the second statement (16:17) ironically (compare use of irony in Luke 5:39 and 15:7). Even though the Law had been surpassed and by-passed by God himself, the religious leaders, who used the Law as a power-base, would not let the tiniest stroke go. They were clinging to the Law and in so doing:

'You have not gone in yourselves, and have prevented others going in who wanted to'
(Luke 11:52)

3: Marriage fidelity: an example of how the kingdom of God surpasses the Law

LUKE 16:18
'Everyone who divorces his wife and marries another is guilty of adultery, and 18 the man who marries a woman divorced by her husband commits adultery.

We shall leave a detailed study of the teaching of Jesus on marriage fidelity till we study Mark 10:1-12 in the following Chapter.

Luke's statement here (and it is his only reference to the matter) is revolutionary in relation to Jewish legal practice at the time of Jesus.

In Jewish Law adultery was an offence against the rights of a husband. A woman had no rights in this matter before the Law. A man was guilty of adultery only when he had sexual intercourse with a married woman: his action was against the rights of her husband. There was no question of adultery when a man, although himself married, had intercourse with a single or divorced woman.

Jesus ignores the law and insists on the need for fidelity to love within marriage. In doing so he by-passes the discrimination against women that was taken for granted by his contemporaries. A man has no right to divorce his wife. As a disciple of the kingdom of God he is called to be faithful and to love unto death.

4: 'Alas for you who are rich'

LUKE 16:19-31
'There was a rich man who used to dress in purple and fine linen and feast 19 magnificently every day. •And at his gate there lay a poor man called Lazarus, 20 covered with sores, •who longed to fill himself with the scraps that fell from 21 the rich man's table. Dogs even came and licked his sores. •Now the poor man 22 died and was carried away by the angels to the bosom of Abraham. The rich man also died and was buried.

'In his torment in Hades he looked up and saw Abraham a long way off 23 with Lazarus in his bosom. •So he cried out, "Father Abraham, pity me and 24 send Lazarus to dip the tip of his finger in water and cool my tongue, for I am in agony in these flames". •"My son," Abraham replied "remember that during 25 your life good things came your way, just as bad things came the way of Lazarus. Now he is being comforted here while you are in agony. •But that is not all: 26 between us and you a great gulf has been fixed, to stop anyone, if he wanted to, crossing from our side to yours, and to stop any crossing from your side to ours."

'The rich man replied, "Father, I beg you then to send Lazarus to my father's 27 house, •since I have five brothers, to give them warning so that they do not 28 come to this place of torment too". •"They have Moses and the prophets," 29

said Abraham "let them listen to them." •"Ah no, father Abraham," said the 30
rich man "but if someone comes to them from the dead, they will repent." •Then 31
Abraham said to him, "If they will not listen either to Moses or to the prophets,
they will not be convinced even if someone should rise from the dead". '

This is one more parable on the theme 'How happy are you who are poor . . .
But alas for you who are rich' (Luke 6:20, 6:24). Jesus had said:

'When you have a party, invite the poor, the crippled, the blind and the lame.'

(Luke 14:13)

Here, at the banquet of heaven (the 'bosom of Abraham' 16:22. Compare
Matthew 8:11 and John 13:23), it is the poor man, Lazarus (the name means 'God
helps') who is invited to 'feast in the kingdom of God' (Luke 14:15); the rich man
is in torment in Hades and he cannot join the feast (16:26). He did not invite the
poor man to enjoy his meal. Now the poor man cannot invite him.

The rich man, in not sharing his wealth with the poor, was refusing to listen
'either to Moses or to the prophets' (Luke 16:31). Luke is reflecting on the fact
that those who dressed in 'purple and fine linen and feasted magnificently every
day' (16:19) continued to refuse to listen to Jesus, even when he rose from the
dead (Luke 16:31). No wonder Jesus could say: 'Alas for you who are rich' (Luke
6:24)!

It has been suggested that there is a connection between this parable and the
anecdote concerning the raising of Lazarus (cf John chapter 11).

5: Care, correction and forgiveness in the life of a disciple

LUKE 17:1-4

17 He said to his disciples, 'Obstacles are sure to come, but alas for the one 1
who provides them! •It would be better for him to be thrown into the sea 2
with a millstone put round his neck than that he should lead astray a single
one of these little ones. •Watch yourselves!   3
'If your brother does something wrong, reprove him and, if he is sorry,
forgive him. •And if he wrongs you seven times a day and seven times comes 4
back to you and says, "I am sorry", you must forgive him.'

(Luke 17:1-2, compare Mark 9:42 and Matthew 18:6-7 page 265
Luke 17:3-4, compare Matthew 18:15, 21-22 page 267)

6: The power of faith

LUKE 17:5-6 (Compare Matthew 17:20)

The apostles said to the Lord, 'Increase our faith'. •The Lord replied, 'Were 5/6
your faith the size of a mustard seed you could say to this mulberry tree, "Be
uprooted and planted in the sea", and it would obey you.

(Compare Matthew 17:20 page 262; Matthew 21:21 page 319)

The disciples ask for more faith. Jesus corrects them. It is God who gives life,
and for God nothing is impossible. A disciple must place his trust in God. If he
does, then the tiniest bit of faith, the smallest opening (the size of a mustard seed)
is enough. God can achieve wonders through men if they will only believe.

7: Humble service in the life of a disciple

LUKE 17:7-10

'Which of you, with a servant ploughing or minding sheep, would say to him 7
when he returned from the fields, "Come and have your meal immediately"?
Would he not be more likely to say, "Get my supper laid; make yourself tidy 8
and wait on me while I eat and drink. You can eat and drink yourself afterwards"?
Must he be grateful to the servant for doing what he was told? •So with you: 9, 10
when you have done all you have been told to do, say, "We are merely servants:
we have done no more than our duty".'

We refer the reader back to Luke 12:35-48. The disciple is to be a servant, like
Jesus (Luke 12:38 and 22:24-27). It is not service from above, the 'service' of a
benefactor who hands down to the poor what he has over. It is service from
below, service given by someone who considers it a duty and a privilege to give his
time and talent to another. It is service born of love and prayer: the kind of service
Jesus gave.

8: An outsider has the faith to be a disciple

LUKE 17:11-19

Now on the way to Jerusalem he travelled along the border between Samaria 11
and Galilee. •As he entered one of the villages, ten lepers came to meet him. 12
They stood some way off •and called to him, 'Jesus! Master! Take pity on us.' 13
When he saw them he said, 'Go and show yourselves to the priests'. Now as they 14
were going away they were cleansed. •Finding himself cured, one of them 15
turned back praising God at the top of his voice •and threw himself at the feet 16
of Jesus and thanked him. The man was a Samaritan. •This made Jesus say, 17
'Were not all ten made clean? The other nine, where are they? •It seems that no 18
one has come back to give praise to God, except this foreigner.' •And he said to 19
the man, 'Stand up and go on your way. Your faith has saved you.'

Once again, Luke reminds us of Jerusalem (17:11, cf Luke 9:51, 13:22, 13:33).
Once again, it is an outsider who has faith and finds salvation (17:18-19, cf Luke
10:29-37).

9: The kingdom of God is brought about by divine intervention

LUKE 17:20-37

Asked by the Pharisees when the kingdom of God was to come, he gave them 20
this answer, 'The coming of the kingdom of God does not admit of observation
and there will be no one to say, "Look here! Look there!" For, you must know, 21
the kingdom of God is among you.'

He said to the disciples, 'A time will come when you will long to see one of 22
the days of the Son of Man and will not see it. •They will say to you, "Look 23
there!" or, "Look here!" Make no move; do not set off in pursuit; •for as the 24
lightning flashing from one part of heaven lights up the other, so will be the Son
of Man when his day comes. •But first he must suffer grievously and be rejected 25
by this generation.

'As it was in Noah's day, so will it also be in the days of the Son of Man. 26
People were eating and drinking, marrying wives and husbands, right up to the 27
day Noah went into the ark, and the Flood came and destroyed them all. •It 28

will be the same as it was in Lot's day: people were eating and drinking, buying
29 and selling, planting and building, •but the day Lot left Sodom, God rained fire
30 and brimstone from heaven and it destroyed them all. •It will be the same when
the day comes for the Son of Man to be revealed.
31   'When that day comes, anyone on the housetop, with his possessions in the
house, must not come down to collect them, nor must anyone in the fields turn
32
33 back either. •Remember Lot's wife. •Anyone who tries to preserve his life will lose
34 it; and anyone who loses it will keep it safe. •I tell you, on that night two will be
35 in one bed: one will be taken, the other left; •two women will be grinding corn
37 together: one will be taken, the other left.' •The disciples interrupted. 'Where,
Lord?' they asked. He said, 'Where the body is, there too will the vultures gather'.

(Compare Mark 13:14-15 and Matthew 24:17-18 page 354
compare Matthew 24:26-28 page 355, Matthew 24:37-41 page 357)

The material inserted here by Luke is found in the Eschatological Discourse
in Mark and Matthew and we refer the reader to the commentary there for a
fuller analysis.

Jesus is correcting a false idea of the coming of the kingdom of God. He is
insisting that it is already happening in their midst (17:21). God is already
working in the world like the leaven working in the dough, or a mustard seed
growing in the soil (Luke 13:18-21). One day the kingdom will be manifestly
present and completely victorious, but:

'first the Son of Man must suffer grievously and be rejected by this generation.'
(Luke 17:25)

Once again Jesus returns to the mystery of suffering (cf Luke 9:22-45).

The kingdom of God will not come in such a way as to destroy man's
freedom. As we shall see more clearly when discussing the Eschatological
Discourse, the kingdom of God depends very much on the extent of man's
cooperation with grace. In any case speculation about the time (17:20) and the
place (17:37) of the final manifestation of God's love and power is idle. Suffering
must come, to Jesus (17:25) and to his disciples (17:22). God will seem to be
absent and man's injustice will seem to be triumphing. Jesus is asking his disciples
to believe that ultimately the justice of God will prevail, whatever disasters have
to be suffered (17:31-36). The disciple must remember:

'Anyone who tries to preserve his life will lose it; and anyone who loses it will keep it
safe.'
(Luke 17:33)

Let him follow Jesus in his kind of life and he need not fear anything from the
coming of God's judgment; nor need he be distracted about its timing or place.

10: God will answer the cry of the poor man

LUKE 18:1-8
1 **18** Then he told them a parable about the need to pray continually and never
2   lose heart. •'There was a judge in a certain town' he said 'who had neither
3 fear of God nor respect for man. •In the same town there was a widow who kept
on coming to him and saying, "I want justice from you against my enemy!"
4 For a long time he refused, but at last he said to himself, "Maybe I have neither
5 fear of God nor respect for man, •but since she keeps pestering me I must give
this widow her just rights, or she will persist in coming and worry me to death". '

⁶⁷   And the Lord said, 'You notice what the unjust judge has to say? •Now will
not God see justice done to his chosen who cry to him day and night even when
8 he delays to help them? •I promise you, he will see justice done to them, and
done speedily. But when the Son of Man comes, will he find any faith on earth?'

We are reminded of Psalm 82:

'God stands in the divine assembly,
among the gods he dispenses justice:
No more mockery of justice,
no more favouring the wicked!
Let the weak and the orphan have justice,
be fair to the wretched and destitute;
rescue the weak and needy,
save them from the clutches of the wicked!'

(Psalm 82:1-4)

If an unjust judge can be forced to do justice by the persistence of a widow:

'will not God see justice done to his chosen
who cry to him day and night
even when he delays to help them?' (18:7)

The disciples, and the community for whom Luke was writing, were living in
a time of delay; as we are. Jesus asks his disciples to maintain their faith in God. It
is not the justice and fidelity of God that man should call into question. The real
question is the one asked by Jesus:

'When the Son of Man comes, will he find faith on earth?'

(Luke 18:8)

God is faithful, but will men be so? God wants justice done; but will men hear
God's word and keep it? Will men become disciples of Jesus and be instruments
of the compassion of God and of his justice?

11: A disciple must be humble

LUKE 18:9-14
9   He spoke the following parable to some people who prided themselves on being
10 virtuous and despised everyone else, •'Two men went up to the Temple to pray,
11 one a Pharisee, the other a tax collector. •The Pharisee stood there and said this
prayer to himself, "I thank you, God, that I am not grasping, unjust, adulterous
like the rest of mankind, and particularly that I am not like this tax collector here.
¹²₁₃ I fast twice a week; I pay tithes on all I get." •The tax collector stood some
distance away, not daring even to raise his eyes to heaven; but he beat his breast
14 and said, "God, be merciful to me, a sinner". •This man, I tell you, went home
again at rights with God; the other did not. For everyone who exalts himself will
be humbled, but the man who humbles himself will be exalted.'

The Pharisee is a rich man. He is a man who relies on his own possessions,
priding himself on being rich in virtue. The tax collector is a poor man, conscious
of his need and humbly looking to God for mercy. For all his 'virtue', the Pharisee
is not at rights with God. For all his sin, the tax collector is (18:14).

On this note Luke ends his insert and rejoins Mark and Matthew with an
assertion that reinforces the lesson of this parable:

'Anyone who does not welcome the kingdom of God like a little child will never enter it.'

(Luke 18:17)

* * * * * * * *

III: Further instructions for disciples

1: Marriage, for a disciple of Jesus, involves a special commitment to love

MARK 10:1-12

10 Leaving there, he came to the district of Judaea and the far side of the Jordan. And again crowds gathered round him, and again he taught them, as his custom was. •Some Pharisees approached him and asked, 'Is it against the law for a man to divorce his wife?' They were testing him. •He answered them, 'What did Moses command you?' •'Moses allowed us' they said 'to draw up a writ of dismissal and so to divorce.' •Then Jesus said to them, 'It was because you were so unteachable that he wrote this commandment for you. But from the beginning of creation *God made them male and female.* •*This is why a man must leave father and mother, •and the two become one body.*ª They are no longer two, therefore, but one body. •So then, what God has united, man must not divide.' •Back in the house the disciples questioned him again about this, •and he said to them, 'The man who divorces his wife and marries another is guilty of adultery against her. •And if a woman divorces her husband and marries another she is guilty of adultery too.'

(a: Genesis 1:27 and 2:24)

The command of Moses (10:3) is found in the Book of Deuteronomy:

'Supposing a man has taken a wife and consummated the marriage; but she has not pleased him and he has found some impropriety (Hebrew: "'erwat dabar") of which to accuse her; so he has made out a writ of divorce for her and handed it to her and then dismissed her from his house; she leaves his home and goes away to become the wife of another man. If this other man takes a dislike to her and makes out a writ of divorce for her and hands it to her and dismisses her from his house (or if this other man who took her happens to die), her first husband, who has repudiated her, may not take her back as his wife.'

(Deuteronomy 24:1-4)

The law of Deuteronomy represented a primitive attempt to ensure some rights to a woman in a society in which she could be treated as a possession of a man. At least it made it impossible for a man to divorce his wife and then, at whim, demand her back. As such, the law represented an advance over the even more primitive customs prevailing at the time.

It is typical of Jesus to by-pass the law altogether. He returns to the ideal expressed in the Book of Genesis. Marriage is not about a man's rights; it is about union — an intimate union that has its origins in the will of God (10:9). Jesus' whole preaching was about the enduring love of God. He himself expressed this love in his faithful service of those he met, and he wanted his disciples to follow his example. He saw marriage, too, as one way of two people expressing God's enduring love to one another.

Jesus also considers adultery as infidelity to married love. In doing so he transcended current legal practice which defended the rights of the married man only (cf commentary on Luke 16:18 page 291).

Finally, Mark takes the liberty of applying Jesus' words to the situation in Roman law in which it was possible for a woman to divorce her husband (10:12).

* * * * * * * *

The earliest record of Jesus' teaching on divorce is found in a letter written by Paul some ten to fifteen years before Mark's Gospel: Paul's First Letter to the Corinthians, written, probably, from Ephesus around 54 A.D. It is important to study what Paul wrote because it shows that the question of divorce is not as simple as Mark's statement would lead us to believe.

MARK 7:1-16

1 7 Now for the questions about which you wrote. Yes, it is a good thing for
2 a man not to touch a woman; •but since sex is always a danger, let each
3 man have his own wife and each woman her own husband. •The husband must give his wife what she has the right to expect, and so too the wife to the husband.
4 The wife has no rights over her own body; it is the husband who has them. In the
5 same way, the husband has no rights over his body; the wife has them. •Do not refuse each other except by mutual consent, and then only for an agreed time, to leave yourselves free for prayer; then come together again in case Satan should
6 take advantage of your weakness to tempt you. •This is a suggestion, not a rule:
7 I should like everyone to be like me, but everybody has his own particular gifts from God, one with a gift for one thing and another with a gift for the opposite.
8 There is something I want to add for the sake of widows and those who are
9 not married: it is a good thing for them to stay as they are, like me, •but if they cannot control the sexual urges, they should get married, since it is better to be married than to be tortured.
10 For the married I have something to say, and this is not from me but from
11 the Lord: a wife must not leave her husband — or if she does leave him, she must either remain unmarried or else make it up with her husband—nor must a husband send his wife away.
12 The rest is from me and not from the Lord. If a brother has a wife who is an unbeliever, and she is content to live with him, he must not send her away;
13 and if a woman has an unbeliever for her husband, and he is content to live with
14 her, she must not leave him. •This is because the unbelieving husband is made one with the saints through his wife, and the unbelieving wife is made one with the saints through her husband. If this were not so, your children would be
15 unclean, whereas in fact they are holy. •However, if the unbelieving partner does not consent, they may separate; in these circumstances, the brother or
16 sister is not tied: God has called you to a life of peace. •If you are a wife, it may be your part to save your husband, for all you know; if a husband, for all you know, it may be your part to save your wife.

It is obvious that Paul is not writing an abstract statement of Christian ideals, but an answer to specific questions asked by a community with which he was familiar (7:1). To understand the passage just quoted it is necessary to have some grasp of the situation prevailing in Corinth at the time Paul was writing.

It is evident from Paul's letter that an influential group in Corinth was disrupting the community. The members of the group were claiming special wisdom; and the area of sexuality was one in which they fancied they had special competence to speak. They distinguished between things of the flesh and things of the spirit. According to them a Christian should live in the spirit. This made marriage abhorrent, for it is, by definition, a commitment of man's spirit to things of the flesh. Not that they lived ascetical lives. Far from it. They were quite content to indulge in all kinds of irresponsible sexual behaviour. In their view, what the body did was irrelevant. Sin was something committed in the spirit. The important thing was not to commit one's spirit to such activities. Spiritual release was a matter of keeping the spirit above the activities of the flesh.

They used all kinds of rationalisations to support their behaviour, even attempting to use Paul's own teaching to back them up. Paul had recommended celibacy; they used that as an argument against marriage. Paul had spoken of the importance of sharing faith-values; in a young Christian community in which, quite frequently, one of the partners in the marriage was an unbeliever, they used this argument to try to break up marriages. The situation was a network of rationalisations and hypocrisies to support irresponsible sexual licence.

Paul took them to task. Firstly he admits that he did recommend and continued to recommend celibacy, but a celibacy that was a gift of the Spirit of God (7:7). His recommendation was not meant to break already existing marriages, nor was it meant to place a person in a situation in which he lacked peace and was so consumed with passion that he needed to find an outlet outside the commitment of married love (7:9).

To support his position Paul quotes Jesus as his authority for the following statement:

'a wife must not leave her husband — or if she does leave him, she must either remain unmarried or else make it up with her husband — nor must a husband send his wife away'

(7:10-11)

Like Mark (cf Mark 10:12), Paul is applying Jesus' words to a situation in which a woman could initiate divorce; also, like Mark (10:11) and Luke (16:18), Paul witnesses to a tradition that understood Jesus as being against divorce.

At the same time — and this is the main point of our digression into this Letter of Paul — Paul feels quite free to treat this teaching of Jesus, not as a law admitting of no exceptions and demanding to be applied mindlessly, but as an expression of ideals based on certain values. Conscious that he is not quoting Jesus, but is giving his own ideas (7:12), Paul speaks of a situation in which divorce and remarriage are, in his opinion, possible for a disciple of Jesus.

In view of the teaching of Jesus, Paul tries to encourage couples to stay together even when one of them is an unbeliever:

'If you are a wife, it may be your part to save your husband, for all you know; if a husband, for all you know, it may be your part to save your wife.'

(7:16)

At the same time, he recognises the cardinal principle:

'God has called you to a life of peace.'

(7:15)

He recognises that in situations in which such an important value as the Christian faith was not shared it could well be impossible for the married couple to live together in peace. The unbeliever may make it impossible for the believer to live out his or her Christian life. It is important for us to remember that a 'believer' for Paul was a person who lived by certain values. It should not be confused with a 'baptised person'. A person could quite easily be baptised but be an unbeliever in Paul's terms. When the unbeliever does make it impossible, Paul judges:

'they may separate; in these circumstances, the brother or sister is not tied.'

(7:15)

In other words, while upholding the ideal taught by Jesus, Paul recognises that there are marriages in which the kind of love pledged by the partners is not the kind of love taught by Jesus. He recognises that there are times when upholding the marriage contract would lead to loss of peace and would make it impossible for a person to live as a disciple of Jesus. A believer should try to be faithful to the commitment contracted in marriage, even with a partner who does not share his or her values. But where this proves impossible because of the unwillingness of the unbeliever, separation is called for, and, in Paul's opinion, the believer may marry again.

Paul does not know of any statement of Jesus on the matter, but is confident that his opinion is in accordance with the mind of Jesus (cf 7:40).

Mark quoted Jesus as saying:

'What God has united, man must not divide.'

(Mark 10:9)

One could say that, in the complexities of the Corinthian situation, Paul is judging that there are some couples whose marriage union was not made by God, and whose marriage therefore could be divided by man. Every generation of Christians has this same task before it. Paul stands as a warning against taking Jesus' teaching absolutely and applying it without assessing the values involved.

Matthew's Gospel too indicates that the community for which he was writing had problems in this matter and had to qualify Jesus' words to adapt them to their situation. We shall quote Matthew's text in its entirety as the differences from Mark are most instructive.

MATTHEW 19:1-11

1 **19** Jesus had now finished what he wanted to say, and he left Galilee and
2 came into the part of Judaea which is on the far side of the Jordan. •Large crowds followed him and he healed them there.
3 Some Pharisees approached him, and to test him they said, 'Is it against the
4 Law for a man to divorce his wife on any pretext whatever?' •He answered, 'Have
5 you not read that the creator from the beginning *made them male and female* •and that he said: *This is why a man must leave father and mother, and cling to his wife,*
6 *and the two become one body?* •They are no longer two, therefore, but one body. So then, what God has united, man must not divide.'
7 They said to him, 'Then why did Moses command that a writ of dismissal
8 should be given in cases of divorce?' •'It was because you were so unteachable' he said 'that Moses allowed you to divorce your wives, but it was not like this
9 from the beginning. •Now I say this to you: the man who divorces his wife— I am not speaking of fornication—and marries another, is guilty of adultery.'

The disciples said to him, 'If that is how things are between husband and wife, 10 it is not advisable to marry'. •But he replied, 'It is not everyone who can accept 11 what I have said, but only those to whom it is granted.

Matthew differs from Mark, significantly, in two places. In the question asked by the Pharisees, instead of the simple 'Is it against the Law for a man to divorce his wife?' of Mark (10:2), Matthew has:

'Is it against the Law for a man to divorce his wife on any pretext whatever?'
(Matthew 19:3)

Secondly, to the answer given by Jesus, Matthew adds the statement:

'I am not speaking of fornication (the Greek "porneia" would be better translated by the much vaguer word "uncleanness").'
(Matthew 19:9, compare Matthew 5:32)

Matthew is posing the question in terms of the debate current at the time concerning the interpretation of the expression "'erwat dabar" in Deuteronomy (24:1). There were two schools of thought. One — the more liberal school and the one followed in practice by the Jews — followed the Rabbi Hillel. According to this school 'any impropriety' could give grounds for divorce. In other words a man could divorce his wife 'on any pretext whatever' (Matthew 19:3). Obviously, Jesus does not agree with Hillel.

The stricter school followed Rabbi Shammai. According to this school the impropriety had to be serious. In fact only adultery gave a man the right to divorce his wife. Is Matthew, by his addition of the words 'I am not speaking of fornication' (19:9) interpreting Jesus as siding with Shammai, and allowing divorce in cases of adultery? Paul found that the non-sharing of faith values could make a marriage impossible, and he understood Jesus as allowing divorce in such cases, with the possibility of another marriage. Perhaps Matthew and his community argued to a similar conclusion in cases of serious infidelity leading to complete marriage break-down.

There is, however, one problem with this interpretation of Matthew. Had he wanted to present Jesus as agreeing with Shammai he would have said: 'I am not speaking of adultery' (Greek: moicheia cf Matthew 15:19). Instead he uses a more general word 'porneia', translated here 'fornication'. This word, from the Greek 'porne' meaning harlot, technically means 'harlotry'. It is used to translate the Hebrew 'zenut' (cf Jeremiah 3:2, 9) and is used rather vaguely in the New Testament for 'unlawful sexual intercourse'. Perhaps Matthew and his community were more liberal than Shammai in the grounds they allowed for divorce. On the other hand, there is an interpretation of 'fornication' (= 'porneia') which is more in accordance with Matthew's context and the more absolute statements on divorce found in Mark, Luke and Paul (1 Corinthians 7:10-11 and Romans 7:2-3).

We know from the Dead Sea scrolls that the community at Qumran, at the time of Jesus, did not allow divorce even for adultery. They criticised mainstream Judaism as being infected with 'zenut' (='porneia'). As examples of this they instanced the prevalence of divorce, polygamy, and marriage within the degrees of relationship forbidden in Leviticus 18. As already stated, they were against divorce on any grounds. In this they followed the prophet Malachi, whose statement is perhaps worth quoting here:

'Here is something else you do: you cover the altar of Yahweh with tears, with weeping and wailing, because he now refuses to consider the offering or to accept it from your hands. And you ask, "Why?" It is because Yahweh stands as witness between you and the wife of your youth, the wife with whom you have broken faith, even though she was your partner and your wife by covenant. Did he not create a single being that has flesh and the breath of life? And what is this single being destined for? God-given offspring. Be careful of your own life, therefore, and do not break faith with the wife of your youth. For I hate divorce, says Yahweh the God of Israel, and I hate people to parade their sins on their cloaks, says Yahweh Sabaoth. Respect your own life, therefore, and do not break faith like this.'   *(Malachi 2:13-16)*

The Qumran scrolls use the Hebrew equivalent ('zenut') for illicit marital unions within the degrees of kinship prescribed by Leviticus 18:6-18. This throws light on Matthew's use of 'porneia' (19:9 and 5:32).

We have seen that Matthew is writing largely for a Jewish-Christian community; but it is also a community that includes Gentiles (some scholars suggest the church in Syria). It could be that Matthew's community needed to include the exception in regard to 'porneia' to cover the case of Gentiles entering the Christian community who were involved in marital situations not allowed to the Jewish Christians who followed Leviticus.

This is in accordance with the agreement reached in the Assembly of Jerusalem in 48 A.D. This meeting was called to sort out just what was required of non-Jews entering the Christian community. One school of thought wanted them to follow the Law in its entirety. Paul was the leader of the opposing school. He was determined that the Gentiles be allowed to join the Christian community without having to submit to the Jewish Law. As it turned out Paul won the day. However, in order to establish some order in communities where there were Jews and Gentiles, and in order not to offend the sensibilities of the Christian Jews, the Assembly drafted a letter stating that the Gentile Christians did not have to follow the Law, except in those matters which the Law required of those who were aliens living among Jews. One of these matters concerned regulation of marriages. The Gentile Christians were asked to abstain from 'porneia' (translated 'fornication' Acts 15:20,29). They were asked, that is, to fit in with the regulations covering marriage.

It is most likely that it is to this that Matthew is referring. Like Mark and Luke, he is giving Jesus' statement against divorce. But he includes the exception to indicate that what Jesus said does not apply to those marriage unions that are not in accordance with Leviticus.

What is important for us is that Matthew, like Paul, found it necessary to apply the ideal presented by Jesus within the context of the community. Not all marriages are 'made in heaven'; not all unions are so sacred that they must be retained. Consideration must be given to the values shared by the married persons, and the quality of the love pledged. Matthew feels free to interpret the mind of Jesus in the light of the judgment of the Jerusalem Assembly and the complexities of a mixed community. Paul goes even deeper and looks at the faith-values shared by the married couple. Both uphold the ideal proposed by Jesus, but they indicate the need of the Christian community to continue interpreting Jesus' words in the light of Jesus' heart and mind and the values he lived by.

That Jesus was upholding a high ideal, and asking of his followers a commitment to love that went beyond the expectations of his contemporaries, of whatever school, is made obvious by the remark of the disciples:

'If that is how things are between husband and wife, it is not advisable to marry.' (19:10)

The ideal seems impossible to attain. It is an application of the teaching that Jesus has been reiterating throughout this section:

'If anyone wants to be a follower of mine, let him renounce himself and take up his cross and follow me. For anyone who wants to save his life will lose it; but anyone who loses his life for my sake and for the sake of the gospel, will save it.'
(Mark 8:34-35)

'If anyone wants to be first he must make himself last of all and servant of all.'
(Mark 9:35)

And his disciples react as they have reacted throughout: they see Jesus as asking the impossible. And he is!

'It is not everyone who can accept what I have said, but only those to whom it is granted.'
(Matthew 19:11)

To live as a disciple of Jesus requires a miracle of grace. This applies to the ideals of marriage as to every other area of the Christian life. Jesus admits he is upholding a high ideal, and he admits that not all can attain it. But, as he said earlier:

'What can a man offer in exchange for his life?'
(Mark 8:37)

Jesus is offering life. In the area of marriage, he is offering a life of self-sacrifice, and service, and forgiveness. But he is offering life, and the possibility of a love unto death, and the ideal of a trust, committed for life and held to through the journey of the cross to the glory of the resurrection.

*   *   *   *   *   *   *   *

Matthew takes the occasion to insert another saying of Jesus:

MATTHEW 19:12

•There are eunuchs born 12 that way from their mother's womb, there are eunuchs made so by men and there are eunuchs who have made themselves that way for the sake of the kingdom of heaven. Let anyone accept this who can.'

'There are eunuchs born that way from their mother's womb'. Is Jesus asking for fidelity to one's partner even when that partner cannot have children?

'There are eunuchs made so by men'. Is Jesus asking for fidelity to one's partner even when, through some action of man, having a family is not possible?

'There are eunuchs who have made themselves that way for the sake of the kingdom of heaven'.

According to the Law (cf Deuteronomy 23:1) a eunuch 'was not to be admitted to the assembly of Yahweh'. At the same time Isaiah recognised that God's faithful love extended even to these castrated men:

'For Yahweh says this: To the eunuchs who observe my sabbaths, and resolve to do what pleases me and cling to my covenant, I will give, in my house and within my walls, a monument and a name better than sons and daughters; I will give them an everlasting name that shall never be effaced.'   *(Isaiah 56:4-5, compare Wisdom 3:13-14)*

Is Jesus offering a 'name better than sons and daughters' to those who, like him, choose a celibate life?

A few verses later in the same chapter, Matthew has Jesus say:

'Everyone who has left houses, brothers, sisters, father, mother, children (Luke adds "wife" 18:28) or land for the sake of my name will be repaid a hundred times over, and also inherit eternal life.'   *(Matthew 19:29)*

After upholding the ideal of marriage in which a man consecrates his living body to the loving service of a woman and becomes 'one flesh' with her, Jesus offers his disciples another ideal: they can offer their living bodies to the service of the community 'for the sake of the kingdom of heaven' (Matthew 19:12). We have already seen Paul recommending celibacy. He saw it as enabling a man to 'give undivided attention to the Lord' (1 Corinthians 7:35).

It involves a personal commitment in love to Jesus. It also involves a commitment to serve his body, the church. The celibate performs something of a prophetic role, reminding us that our hearts can be filled only by God. He is a witness, too, to belief in 'eternal life' (Matthew 19:29), and a fulfilment of love that transcends the love of the human family.

According to Paul, celibacy, like marriage fidelity, is a special gift of the spirit of Jesus (1 Corinthians 7:7). At the same time Jesus holds this ideal out to anyone who can 'accept' it (Matthew 19:12). 'Make room for', 'have space for' would be better translations than 'accept'. It is a matter of how big a man's heart is, how free of possessions, how uncluttered, how open to people and to God. If, in response to God's grace, a man can let his heart be free, he will not have sons and daughters, but he will be an instrument for bringing about the reign of God's love on earth (= 'the kingdom').

2: Jesus asks of his followers a childlike faith

MARK 10:13-16 (Compare Matthew 19:13-15 and Luke 18:15-17)

13   People were bringing little children to him, for him to touch them. The
14   disciples turned them away, •but when Jesus saw this he was indignant and said
     to them, 'Let the little children come to me; do not stop them; for it is to such as
15   these that the kingdom of God belongs. •I tell you solemnly, anyone who
     does not welcome the kingdom of God like a little child will never enter it.'
16   Then he put his arms round them, laid his hands on them and gave them his
     blessing.

God's love is a grace — a free gift. There are no pre-conditions. The task of a disciple is simply to 'welcome' this gift 'like a little child' (10:15).

This basic truth is demonstrated in the Church's practice of receiving children into the Christian community through infant baptism. The adult community welcomes the child as Jesus welcomed these children, and undertakes to provide for the child an environment to love, to nourish and support him while he matures to a personal faith in the love with which God has freely graced him.

3: Jesus asks of his followers that they rely on God, not on their possessions

MARK 10:17-27 (Compare Matthew 19:16-26 and Luke 18:18-27)

17   He was setting out on a journey when a man ran up, knelt before him and
put this question to him, 'Good master, what must I do to inherit eternal life?'
18 Jesus said to him, 'Why do you call me good? No one is good but God alone.
19 You know the commandments: *You must not kill; You must not commit adultery;*
You must not steal; You must not bring false witness; You must not defraud;
20 *Honour your father and mother.'* [a] •And he said to him, 'Master, I have kept all
21 these from my earliest days'. •Jesus looked steadily at him and loved him, and
he said, 'There is one thing you lack. Go and sell everything you own and give
the money to the poor, and you will have treasure in heaven; then come, follow
22 me.' •But his face fell at these words and he went away sad, for he was a man
of great wealth.
23   Jesus looked round and said to his disciples, 'How hard it is for those who
24 have riches to enter the kingdom of God!' •The disciples were astounded by
these words, but Jesus insisted, 'My children,' he said to them 'how hard it is to
25 enter the kingdom of God! •It is easier for a camel to pass through the eye of
26 a needle than for a rich man to enter the kingdom of God.' •They were more
astonished than ever. 'In that case' they said to one another 'who can be saved?'
27 Jesus gazed at them. 'For men' he said 'it is impossible, but not for God: because
everything is possible for God.'

(a: Exodus 20:12-16)

Jesus' opening remark referring all goodness to his Father (10:18) comes as a
necessary reminder to us of the central reference point in Jesus' life. The Gospels
were written by disciples of Jesus and, understandably, much of what they say
centres on Jesus as the one who made God's word flesh for them. The disciples
admired Jesus. It is important to remember that Jesus did not admire himself.
There is a danger that Christians place Jesus at the centre of their religious
consciousness. Jesus would want them to place his Father there. He taught us
how to direct our prayer to a God who is a Father. He showed us, by his own life,
the kind of freedom and love that is possible for a man who draws on the
assurance of his Father's love. His whole attention was focused on his Father
who revealed his presence at the heart of every event of Jesus' life and at the heart
of every person. Jesus wanted us to do the same. Therefore when this young man
addresses him as good, Jesus is careful to direct his attention to the source of all
goodness.

There is an early tradition that claims that Mark's Gospel draws on the
experiences of Peter. One can imagine Peter behind such remarks as:

'Jesus looked steadily at him and loved him' (10:21)

and also:

'Jesus gazed at them' (10:27)

Jesus' immediate disciples would, no doubt, have learned much from Jesus'
eyes.

What Jesus asked of the young man caused him to go away sad (10:22); and
what Jesus said about riches 'astonished' the disciples (10:26). Wealth and
prosperity were considered signs of God's favour, but Jesus was speaking of the
grave disadvantages of wealth. He does not contradict them when they recognise

how impossible it is to live the way he was recommending. He simply refers them again to his Father: only complete reliance on God makes the journey possible (10:27).

It is obvious from the Gospel accounts that Jesus was not one to despise created things. He celebrated life, seeing in the world around him signs of the loving care and creative presence of his Father. And he encouraged others to celebrate their existence in gratitude to God. The Baptist was renowned for his asceticism; not so Jesus. Matthew records Jesus as saying:

> 'John came, neither eating nor drinking, and they say, "He is possessed". The Son of Man came, eating and drinking, and they say, "Look! a glutton and a drunkard, a friend of tax collectors and sinners".'
> *(Matthew 11:18-19 and Luke 7:33-34)*

Things exist to be received with thanks, to be enjoyed and to be shared as expressions of love. At the same time Jesus knew how easily things can clutter our hearts and prevent us from seeing people clearly.

As Matthew expresses it in the Sermon on the Mount:

> 'Where your treasure is, there will your heart be.'   *(Matthew 7:21 and Luke 12:34)*

Jesus does not ask people to give up their possessions as pre-requisites to receiving the call. That is impossible. But he does ask his followers to give up their possessions when called to do so, as this young man was.

Material possessions should not be at the centre of a disciple's awareness, whether to acquire them or to be rid of them. He is to seek the kingdom of God first and be ready to accept whatever demands this might have.

It is very difficult for a rich man to hear God's call, for his mind and heart are easily cluttered.

Paul expresses the disposition of a disciple when he writes:

> 'I have learned to manage on whatever I have; I know how to be poor and I know how to be rich too. I have been through my initiation and now I am ready for anything anywhere: full stomach or empty stomach, poverty or plenty. There is nothing I cannot master with the help of the one who gives me strength.'   *(Philippians 4:11-13)*

4: The reward offered by Jesus to his followers:

MARK 10:28-31 (Compare Matthew 19:27-29 and Luke 18:28-30)
28   Peter took this up. 'What about us?' he asked him. 'We have left everything
29   and followed you.' •Jesus said, 'I tell you solemnly, there is no one who has left house, brothers, sisters, father, children or land for my sake and for the sake of
30   the gospel •who will not be repaid a hundred times over, houses, brothers, sisters, mothers, children and land—not without persecutions—now in this present time and, in the world to come, eternal life.
31   'Many who are first will be last, and the last first.'

Without allowing his readers to forget the cross (10:30), Mark is assuring them that the reward offered to a disciple is nothing less than life itself, 'eternal life' (10:30). But there are no comparisons possible here; there are no human criteria by which to determine or weigh reward:

> 'Many who are first will be last, and the last first.' (10:31)

* * * * * * * *

Matthew adds the following remark:

MATTHEW 19:28

•Jesus said to him, 'I tell you 28 solemnly, when all is made new and the Son of Man sits on his throne of glory, you will yourselves sit on twelve thrones to judge the twelve tribes of Israel.

(Compare Luke 22:30 page 370)

Jesus is not suggesting a position of power among his followers. He has already spoken of true greatness in the kingdom (Matthew 18:1-4) and will soon warn them against power-seeking (Matthew 20:20-28).

He is saying that men will be judged by the standards set by Jesus and lived by his followers.

* * * * * * * *

Luke adds 'wife' (18:29) to the list of those a man might give up for the kingdom (cf also Luke 14:26). He is, perhaps, influenced by Paul's teaching on celibacy (cf 1 Corinthians 7).

* * * * * * * *

On the subject of rewards, and by way of commentary on Mark's statement 'Many who are first will be last, and the last first' (Mark 10:31), Matthew adds the following parable:

MATTHEW 20:1-16

20 'Now the kingdom of heaven is like a landowner going out at daybreak 1 to hire workers for his vineyard. •He made an agreement with the workers 2 for one denarius a day, and sent them to his vineyard. •Going out at about the 3 third hour he saw others standing idle in the market place •and said to them, 4 "You go to my vineyard too and I will give you a fair wage". •So they went. At 5 about the sixth hour and again at about the ninth hour, he went out and did the same. •Then at about the eleventh hour he went out and found more men standing 6 round, and he said to them, "Why have you been standing here idle all day?" "Because no one has hired us" they answered. He said to them, "You go into 7 my vineyard too". •In the evening, the owner of the vineyard said to his bailiff, 8 "Call the workers and pay them their wages, starting with the last arrivals and ending with the first". •So those who were hired at about the eleventh hour came 9 forward and received one denarius each. •When the first came, they expected to 10 get more, but they too received one denarius each. •They took it, but grumbled 11 at the landowner. •"The men who came last" they said "have done only one hour, 12 and you have treated them the same as us, though we have done a heavy day's work in all the heat." •He answered one of them and said, "My friend, I am 13 not being unjust to you; did we not agree on one denarius? •Take your earnings 14 and go. I choose to pay the last-comer as much as I pay you. •Have I no right 15 to do what I like with my own? Why be envious because I am generous?" •Thus 16 the last will be first, and the first. last.'

It is true that God will reward the disciples of Jesus. But it is a reward that cannot be measured by our standards. It will be just — and the landowner is not unjust to those who worked all day; but it will be a reward that is measured by

God's gracious and generous love. As first used by Jesus it was perhaps a warning to the religious leaders similar to that which is given later in Matthew:

'tax collectors and prostitutes are making their way into the kingdom of heaven before you.'

(Matthew 21:31)

Matthew would also have in mind the entrance into the church of the Gentiles at the 'eleventh hour' (20:9).

God will not be measured by our narrow competitive standards. We should be grateful for his regard, and wonder at his generosity to all.

Chapter 3
Discipleship is possible only
because of a miracle of grace

Mark 10:32-52
Matthew 20:17-34
Luke 18:31 — 19:27

a: Jesus speaks for the third time of his suffering, death and resurrection

MARK 10:32-34 (Compare Matthew 20:17-19 and Luke 18:31-34)

32   They were on the road, going up to Jerusalem; Jesus was walking on ahead of them; they were in a daze, and those who followed were apprehensive. Once more taking the Twelve aside he began to tell them what was going to happen
33 to him: •'Now we are going up to Jerusalem, and the Son of Man is about to be handed over to the chief priests and the scribes. They will condemn him
34 to death and will hand him over to the pagans, •who will mock him and spit at him and scourge him and put him to death; and after three days he will rise again.'

The three-fold repetition (Mark 8:31, 9:31 and 10:33-34) indicates how persistent Jesus was in trying to make his disciples understand the kind of messiahship that was his. Matthew goes a step further and has Jesus mention that he will be 'crucified' (Matthew 20:19).

Both Mark (10:32) and Luke (18:34) stress the fear and the failure to comprehend that characterised the reaction of the disciples.

b: For the third time the disciples fail to understand Jesus

MARK 10:35-45 (Compare Matthew 20:20-28)

35   James and John, the sons of Zebedee, approached him. 'Master,' they said
36 to him 'we want you to do us a favour.' •He said to them, 'What is it you want
37 me to do for you?' •They said to him, 'Allow us to sit one at your right hand
3᾿ and the other at your left in your glory'. •'You do not know what you are asking' Jesus said to them. 'Can you drink the cup that I must drink, or be baptised
39 with the baptism with which I must be baptised?' •They replied, 'We can'. Jesus said to them, 'The cup that I must drink you shall drink, and with the
40 baptism with which I must be baptised you shall be baptised, •but as for seats at my right hand or my left, these are not mine to grant; they belong to those to whom they have been allotted'.

When the other ten heard this they began to feel indignant with James and 41
John, •so Jesus called them to him and said to them, 'You know that among the 42
pagans their so-called rulers lord it over them, and their great men make their
authority felt. •This is not to happen among you. No; anyone who wants to become 43
great among you must be your servant, •and anyone who wants to be first 44
among you must be slave to all. •For the Son of Man himself did not come to 45
be served but to serve, and to give his life as a ransom for many.'

(Mark 10:42-45, compare Luke 22:24-27 page 369,

The three-fold repetition by Jesus of the fact that he will give his life for men is
immediately followed by a three-fold statement of the failure of Jesus' disciples to
understand him (Mark 8:33, 9:33-37 and here). The disciples persisted in their
blindness. They were still thinking in terms of 'saving' their life, not of 'losing' it
(cf Mark 8:35-36); they were still thinking in terms of power and not of service.
(Matthew has the request being made by 'the mother of Zebedee's sons', Matthew
20:20. Presumably he found Mark's account unedifying! Compare Matthew
18:1.)

Jesus asks them: 'Can you drink the cup that I must drink?' (10:38). The
image is of the bitter dregs left in the bottom of the cup. He asks them: 'Can you
be baptised with the baptism with which I must be baptised?' (10:38). He has told
them that he will be 'overwhelmed' (= 'baptised') with suffering; are they willing
to share this?

They can exercise leadership if they wish. But Jesus does not want them to
take it on without realising the price they will have to pay. Leadership for Jesus is
a matter of self-sacrificing service.

c: Jesus gives sight to a blind man

MARK 10:46-52 (Compare Matthew 20:29-34 and Luke 18:35-43)
They reached Jericho; and as he left Jericho with his disciples and a large 46
crowd, Bartimaeus (that is, the son of Timaeus), a blind beggar, was sitting at the
side of the road. •When he heard that it was Jesus of Nazareth, he began to shout 47
and to say, 'Son of David, Jesus, have pity on me'. •And many of them scolded 48
him and told him to keep quiet, but he only shouted all the louder, 'Son of David,
have pity on me'. •Jesus stopped and said, 'Call him here'. So they called the 49
blind man. 'Courage,' they said 'get up; he is calling you.' •So throwing off his 50
cloak, he jumped up and went to Jesus. •Then Jesus spoke, 'What do you want 51
me to do for you?' 'Rabbuni,' the blind man said to him 'Master, let me see
again.' •Jesus said to him, 'Go; your faith has saved you'. And immediately 52
his sight returned and he followed him along the road.

With this scene, Mark concludes his section on the second part of Jesus'
ministry (Mark 8:27 — 10:52). He concluded the first part of Jesus' ministry
(Mark 1:14 — 8:26) with a similar scene: the cure of the blind man at Bethsaida.
The message is the same. In the first part of his ministry, we find scene after scene
depicting the growing opposition of the religious leaders, the rejection by the
ordinary people and the constant blindness of Jesus' own followers. Then, by a
miracle of grace, sight is given! In the second part of his ministry, Jesus has been
journeying with his disciples to Jerusalem. He has spoken to them again and
again of the mystery of the cross, but again and again they fail to see what he is

saying. They are, as Mark puts it, 'in a daze' (Mark 10:32). Then, a blind man appears — symbol of the disciple. He asks for pity, but is helpless till he receives a call from Jesus. It is always God who takes the initiative. Jesus, through his disciples, that is, through the church, calls the man to him, and gives him sight. With this gift of divine grace, he is able to follow Jesus 'along the road' (Mark 10:51). He is able to journey with him.

* * * * * * * *

Matthew mentions 'two blind men' (20:30). He is particularly interested in the community, and so it is the community here that is portrayed as being blind. Moreover their cry is the cry of the community's liturgical prayer, 'Lord, have mercy on us' ('Kyrie eleison 20:30, 31). Jesus responds mercifully to the cry of the community, and gives them sight so that they can follow him on the road to the cross and the resurrection.

* * * * * * * *

Luke adds the following anecdote and parable.

LUKE 19:1-10

19 He entered Jericho and was going through the town •when a man whose
2   name was Zacchaeus made his appearance; he was one of the senior tax
3 collectors and a wealthy man. •He was anxious to see what kind of man Jesus
4 was, but he was too short and could not see him for the crowd; •so he ran ahead
  and climbed a sycamore tree to catch a glimpse of Jesus who was to pass that
5 way. •When Jesus reached the spot he looked up and spoke to him: 'Zacchaeus,
6 come down. Hurry, because I must stay at your house today.' •And he hurried
7 down and welcomed him joyfully. •They all complained when they saw what
8 was happening. 'He has gone to stay at a sinner's house' they said. •But Zacchaeus
  stood his ground and said to the Lord, 'Look, sir, I am going to give half my
  property to the poor, and if I have cheated anybody I will pay him back four
9 times the amount'. •And Jesus said to him, 'Today salvation has come to this
10 house, because this man too is a son of Abraham; •for the Son of Man has come
  to seek out and save what was lost'.

Perhaps no scene in the Gospel illustrates better the capacity Jesus had to accept a person unconditionally than his treatment here of Zacchaeus. Zacchaeus must have been one of the most hated men in Jericho: not only had he acquired wealth by unjust extortion of his fellow-countrymen, he had done it in the name of the hated foreign overlords, the Romans. What mattered to Jesus, however, was, as always, a man's present dispositions. Zacchaeus was searching, 'he was anxious to see what kind of man Jesus was' (19:3); he was not afraid of looking a fool. Jesus recognised these qualities and responded to Zacchaeus; he presumed on his generosity and invited himself to enjoy Zacchaeus's hospitality. Jesus' love unlocked suppressed desires in this outcast, and he received Jesus with joy and found repentance (contrast Luke 12:16-21 and 18:18-25).

Luke loves to dwell on such scenes, and with it he concludes Jesus' journey to Jerusalem. The final words sum up one of Luke's major themes:

'The Son of Man has come to seek out and save what was lost.'

(Luke 19:10)

LUKE 19:11-27 (Compare Matthew 25:14-30 page 359-60)

11   While the people were listening to this he went on to tell a parable, because he was near Jerusalem and they imagined that the kingdom of God was going
12 to show itself then and there. •Accordingly he said, 'A man of noble birth went
13 to a distant country to be appointed king and afterwards return. •He summoned ten of his servants and gave them ten pounds. "Do business with these" he told
14 them "until I get back." •But his compatriots detested him and sent a delegation to follow him with this message, "We do not want this man to be our king".

15   'Now on his return, having received his appointment as king, he sent for those servants to whom he had given the money, to find out what profit each had made.
16
17 The first came in and said, "Sir, your one pound has brought in ten". •"Well done, my good servant!" he replied "Since you have proved yourself faithful in a very
18 small thing, you shall have the government of ten cities." •Then came the second
19 and said, "Sir, your one pound has made five". •To this one also he said, "And
20 you shall be in charge of five cities". •Next came the other and said, "Sir, here
21 is your pound. I put it away safely in a piece of linen •because I was afraid of you; for you are an exacting man: you pick up what you have not put down and reap
22 what you have not sown." •"You wicked servant!" he said "Out of your own mouth I condemn you. So you knew I was an exacting man, picking up what
23 I have not put down and reaping what I have not sown? •Then why did you not put my money in the bank? On my return I could have drawn it out with
24 interest." •And he said to those standing by, "Take the pound from him and
25 give it to the man who has ten pounds". •And they said to him, "But, sir, he has
26 ten pounds . . ." •"I tell you, to everyone who has will be given more; but from the man who has not, even what he has will be taken away.

27   "But as for my enemies who did not want me for their king, bring them here and execute them in my presence." '

Throughout the long insert that made up Chapter Two of this section, Luke stressed the urgency of discipleship and the need for radical decision on the part of the disciple. As the journey comes to an end and Jesus is about to enter Jerusalem, Luke concludes with this parable which underlines the responsibility inherent in discipleship.

This provides the balance to the story of Zacchaeus. God's love is enduring, indeed; and his offer of life is always open. But our acceptance of life has its cost. If we accept life, we must live it; and that will mean — as Luke has told us again and again in his insert on the nature of discipleship — following Jesus on the road to Jerusalem and using the gifts God has given us in service of our brothers.

If we use these gifts they will grow; if we neglect them we will lose them (19:26 cf also Luke 8:18, Mark 4:25 and Matthew 13:12). Loving expands our capacity to love; listening expands our capacity to listen. On the other hand if we neglect love we become less and less capable of it. Luke sees the necessity of the disciple taking Jesus' offer seriously and setting out now on the road to Jerusalem.

BOOK 5

Confrontation and Decision

FOREWORD

In this Book we cover the final stage of Jesus' ministry: his ministry in Jerusalem. We have seen Jesus liberating people from the many things that oppressed them. The most oppressive thing is religion that does not reveal the living God, and so the bulk of the first section on Jesus' ministry was given over to the conflict between Jesus and the upholders of the Law. It is this theme that the Gospel-writers return in this last section. Jesus enters the Temple and clears it; he looks at the fig-tree and curses it; he confronts the religious authorities again and again. Jesus is concerned with 'metanoia', a new vision. Central to it is a new vision of God and a demonstration of what God is really like. We cover this in Chapter 1, giving the Synoptic version first and then John's.

After this series of confrontations, the Synoptics, include what is called the 'Eschatological Discourse'. It examines Jesus' teaching on the very meaning of history and on judgment. We cover this in Chapter 2.

Finally, all four Gospel writers give an account of the last days (for John, the last week) of Jesus' ministry. We cover this in Chapter 3.

Chapter 1
The final confrontation
between Jesus and his opponents

Mark 11:1 — 12:44
Matthew 21:1 — 23:39
Luke 19:28 — 21:4

1: The Synoptics

a: Jesus enters Jerusalem

MARK 11:1-11a (Compare Matthew 21:1-11 and Luke 19:28-40)

11 When they were approaching Jerusalem, in sight of Bethphage and Bethany, 1 close by the Mount of Olives, he sent two of his disciples •and said to them, 2 'Go off to the village facing you, and as soon as you enter it you will find a tethered colt that no one has yet ridden. Untie it and bring it here. •If anyone says to 3 you, "What are you doing?" say, "The Master needs it and will send it back here directly".' •They went off and found a colt tethered near a door in 4 the open street. As they untied it, •some men standing there said, 'What are you 5 doing, untying that colt?' •They gave the answer Jesus had told them, and the 6 men let them go. •Then they took the colt to Jesus and threw their cloaks on its 7 back, and he sat on it. •Many people spread their cloaks on the road, others green- 8 ery which they had cut in the fields. •And those who went in front and those who 9 followed were all shouting, '*Hosanna! Blessings on him who comes in the name* 10 *of the Lord!*ᵃ•Blessings on the coming kingdom of our father David! *Hosanna* 11 in the highest heavens!' •He entered Jerusalem and went into the Temple.

(a: Psalm 118:25-26)

To appreciate what Mark is saying in this passage, we need to have some understanding of the history of the Temple.

The first Temple, the Temple of Solomon, was destroyed in 587 B.C. Many of the leading Jews were taken into exile by their Babylonian conquerors. The Babylonian Empire, however, was on the verge of collapse at the time and Babylon was over-run by the Persians, under King Cyrus, in 538 B.C. It was his policy to allow subject peoples to return to their home countries, and so, the Jewish exiles were allowed to journey back to Jerusalem. One can imagine the excitement of these returning pilgrims, journeying, like their fathers, across the desert to the Promised Land. They were led by a prince of Judah, Sheshbazzar,

316 CONFRONTATION AND DECISION

but he led them as viceroy of the Persian king and as governor of Judah, not as a king in his own right (cf Ezra 5:14). His successor as governor was Zerubbabel, also a member of the royal family (cf Haggai 1:1).

Upon their return to Jerusalem, the exiles were keen to rebuild the Temple. Some of them were afraid to do this, fearing that their Persian overlords might see it as a sign of national independence, and return with their armies. The local Samaritans, too, did everything to thwart the early attempts to get the Temple started (cf Ezra Chapter 4). The hatred of the Jews for the Samaritans stems mainly from this period. In 520 B.C., however, the Babylonians staged an uprising against the Persians, and the Jewish leaders took the occasion of the ensuing confusion to push ahead with the Temple. In this they were encouraged by two prophets, Haggai and Zechariah. It is to the prophecy of Zechariah that we shall now turn our attention, as Mark has drawn heavily upon it in creating the scene before us.

Zechariah looked on Zerubbabel, the governor, as the instrument chosen by God to restore the fortunes of Judah and the Davidic monarchy. He saw him as the branch of the tree of David that would, at last, bear fruit; and it is under this title that he refers to him in his prophecy.

'Now listen, High Priest Joshua, you and your friends who sit before you — for you are men of good omen. I now mean to raise my servant Branch, and I intend to put aside the iniquity of this land in a single day. On that day — it is Yahweh Sabaoth who speaks — you will entertain each other under your vine and fig tree.'

(Zechariah 3:8-10)

Zechariah continues:

'Yahweh Sabaoth says this: Here is a man whose name is Branch; where he is there will be a branching out (and he will rebuild the sanctuary of Yahweh). It is he who is going to rebuild the sanctuary of Israel.'

(Zechariah 6:12-13)

Zechariah describes the entry of Zerubbabel into the Temple:

'Rejoice, heart and soul, daughter of Zion!
Shout with gladness, daughter of Jerusalem!
See now, your king comes to you;
he is victorious, he is triumphant,
humble and riding on a donkey,
on a colt, the foal of a donkey.'

(Zechariah 9:9)

One final point from the prophecy of Zechariah. The prophet, naturally, was speaking of events of his own time. However, it was customary to conclude one's prophecy with an Apocalypse — a vision in which present events are seen as foreshadowing the final glorious revealing of God in all his power and majesty. The restoration of the Temple under Zerubbabel was seen as a 'day of the Lord': a manifestation of God's justice. But it was only a foreshadowing of the final day of the Lord, the Messianic Day of the Lord, when God would ultimately restore Jerusalem and the Temple and the chosen race, and vindicate his promises against the enemies of Israel. Zechariah spoke of that Day:

'Then Yahweh will take the field; he will fight against these nations as he fights in the day of battle. On that day his feet will rest on the Mount of Olives, which faces Jerusalem from the east. The Mount of Olives will be split in half from the east to the west, forming a huge gorge . . .'

(Zechariah 14:3-4)

Zechariah's final chapter continues in the same vein.

It is obvious that Mark is relying on the imagery of Zechariah in building this and the following scenes. He tells his readers that the scene took place 'close by the Mount of Olives' (11:1 cf Zechariah 14:3-4). This is the Messianic fulfilment of the hopes expressed by the prophet. The prophet Malachi had written:

'The Lord you are seeking will suddenly enter his Temple'   *(Malachi 3:1)*

In Jesus God is entering his city in triumph.

Like Zerubbabel, the branch (Hebrew 'nezer'), Jesus, the 'Nazarene', the Son of God, enters the city on a donkey amid the rejoicing of the people. The 'greenery' (11:8) and the song (11:9-10) belong to the liturgy of the Feast of Tabernacles (read Psalm 118). Mark may be drawing on some incident that occurred in relation to that Feast. Whatever the incident that lies behind this scene, Mark is using highly symbolic language to emphasise the dramatic importance of this entry into Jerusalem. The discussion between Jesus and his disciples about the donkey, and the fulfilment of Jesus' words (11:2-4) remind the reader that Jesus is here in total command of the situation. In witnessing this scene we are witnessing the activity of God.

Mark has drawn on Zechariah to evoke in his readers the feelings and hopes associated with the Messiah. One would expect Jesus to enter the temple and 'rebuild the sanctuary of Yahweh' (Zechariah 6:13). We would expect to find that the fig-tree of Israel would now be covered in fruit (cf Zechariah 3:10). The following scene powerfully reverses these expectations! Jesus' entry over-turns the prophecies. He has come with something new, something entirely revolutionary. The prophetic hopes are fulfilled but in ways that transcend man's expectations.

b: The judgment of God on Israel

MARK 11:11b — 22 (compare Matthew 21:12-20 and Luke 19:45-46)   He
looked all round him, but as it was now late, he went out to Bethany with the Twelve.
12
13   Next day as they were leaving Bethany, he felt hungry. •Seeing a fig tree in leaf some distance away, he went to see if he could find any fruit on it, but when he came up to it he found nothing but leaves; for it was not the season for figs.
14 And he addressed the fig tree. 'May no one ever eat fruit from you again' he said. And his disciples heard him say this.
15   So they reached Jerusalem and he went into the Temple and began driving out those who were selling and buying there; he upset the tables of the money
16 changers and the chairs of those who were selling pigeons. •Nor would he allow
17 anyone to carry anything through the Temple. •And he taught them and said, 'Does not scripture say: *My house will be called a house of prayer for all*
18 *the peoples?* [a] But you have turned it into *a robbers' den.*' [b] •This came to the ears of the chief priests and the scribes, and they tried to find some way of doing away with him; they were afraid of him because the people were carried away
19 by his teaching. •And when evening came he went out of the city.

20   Next morning, as they passed by, they saw the fig tree withered to the roots.
21 Peter remembered. 'Look, Rabbi,' he said to Jesus 'the fig tree you cursed has
22 withered away.'

(a: Isaiah 56:7
b: Jeremiah 7:11
(compare John 2:13-22 page 127)

The fig-tree was to blossom and bear fruit when the Messiah came (cf
Zechariah 3:10, 1 Macabees 14:12). But it is all leaf and show. It has failed to bear
fruit. God's judgment is passed upon it:

'May no one ever eat fruit from you again' (11:14)

The season for bearing fruit has passed (11:13). The Old Covenant is no more!

The Temple was to be rebuilt in all its magnificence when the Messiah came
(Zechariah 6:13). But Jesus condemns it (11:15-17). Nothing is to pass through it
again. It is no longer the way God approaches men. A new Temple is needed, for
this one has failed!

The Messiah was to vindicate Israel before the world. Here Israel is herself
judged. And the reason?

'Does not Scripture say: My house will be called a house of prayer for all the peoples?
But you have turned it into a robbers' den!' (11:17)

There are two quotations here from Scripture. We must look at each in its
context, for in these texts is the key to the understanding of the scene.

The first quotation is from the third part of the Prophecy of Isaiah, the
section (chapters 56-66) written after the exile.

'Let no foreigner who has attached himself to Yahweh say, "Yahweh will surely
exclude me from his people". Let no eunuch say, "And I, I am a dried-up tree". For
Yahweh says this: to the eunuchs who observe my sabbaths, and resolve to do what
pleases me, and cling to my covenant, I will give, in my house and within my walls, a
monument and a name better than sons and daughters; I will give them an everlasting
name that shall never be effaced. Foreigners who have attached themselves to
Yahweh to serve him and to love his name and to be his servants — all who observe
the sabbath, not profaning it, and cling to my covenant — these I will bring to my
holy mountain. I will make them joyful in my house of prayer. Their holocausts and
their sacrifices will be accepted on my altar, for *my house will be called a house of
prayer for all the peoples.* It is the Lord Yahweh who speaks, who gathers the outcasts
of Israel: there are others I will gather besides those who are already gathered.'

(Isaiah 56:3-8)

The prophet is speaking out against those who were trying to confine God to
their own narrow nationalism, who were using religion, and the revelation and
presence of God in their midst for their own benefit, rather than for service of 'all
the peoples' (56:7). Jesus is making the same accusation against the official
religion of his day. Later Stephen will say the same thing and be martyred for it
(cf Acts 7:48-49, 6:13).

The second quotation is from the prophet Jeremiah and dates from the
period just prior to the destruction of the first Temple.

'The word that was addressed to Jeremiah by Yahweh, "Go and stand at the Temple
of Yahweh and there proclaim this message. Say: Listen to the word of Yahweh, all
you men of Judah who come in by these gates to worship Yahweh. Yahweh Sabaoth,
the God of Israel says this:

'Amend your behaviour and your actions and I will stay with you, here in this place.'
'Put no trust in delusive words like these: this is the sanctuary of Yahweh, the sanctuary of Yahweh, the sanctuary of Yahweh!'
'But if you do amend your behaviour and your actions, if you treat each other fairly, if you do not exploit the stranger, the orphan and the widow (if you do not shed innocent blood in this place), and if you do not follow alien gods, to your own ruin, then, here in this place I will stay with you, in the land that long ago I gave to your fathers for ever.'
'Yet, here you are trusting in delusive words to no purpose! Steal, would you, murder, commit adultery, perjure yourselves, burn incense to Baal, follow alien gods that you do not know? — and then come presenting yourselves in this Temple that bears my name, saying: Now we are safe — safe to go on committing all these abominations!'
'Do you take this Temple that bears my name for a robbers' den? I, at any rate, am not blind — it is Yahweh who speaks.'
(Jeremiah 7:1-11)

During the whole of his ministry Jesus had been trying to bring the Pharisees and scribes to see that religion was about prayer, and about love — about God's love manifested through our care especially of the oppressed. But his teaching fell largely on deaf ears. The clearing of the Temple is a powerful symbolic statement of the judgment of God upon a religion that is not concerned with justice.

With the Temple cleared and the fig-tree withered, what is left? Where does man turn? In what is he to place his trust? Jesus gives the reply in his answer to Peter:

c: **The necessity of faith**

MARK 11:23-25 (Compare Matthew 21:21-22)

23   •Jesus answered, 'Have faith in God. •I tell you solemnly, if anyone says to this mountain, "Get up and throw yourself into the sea", with no hesitation in his heart but believing that what he says will happen, it will be done
24   for him. •I tell you therefore: everything you ask and pray for, believe that you
25   have it already, and it will be yours. •And when you stand in prayer, forgive whatever you have against anybody, so that your Father in heaven may forgive your failings too.'
(Mark 11:23, compare Matthew 17:20 page 262 and Luke 17:5-6 page 292,)

Faced with the withering of the fig-tree and the emptiness of the Temple, faced with the withdrawal of all the obvious signs of God's blessing, man is asked by Jesus to 'have faith in God' (Mark 11:23). It is in God that a man must place his trust. He must believe that 'the favours of Yahweh are not all past' (Lamentations 3:22).

The stock of Jesse may wither, but:

'A shoot springs from the stock of Jesse,
a scion thrusts from his roots:
on him the spirit of Yahweh rests,
a spirit of wisdom and insight,
a spirit of counsel and power,
a spirit of knowledge and of the fear of Yahweh.'
(Isaiah 11:13)

Their faith in God will be rewarded. Isaiah continues:

'That day, the root of Jesse will stand as a signal to the Peoples . . . That day, the Lord will raise his hand once more to ransom the remnant of his people . . . He will hoist a signal for the nations . . . That day you will say: I give thanks to you, Yahweh, you were angry with me, but your anger is appeased and you have given me consolation . . . Sing of Yahweh, for he has done marvellous things, let them be made known to the whole world.'

(Isaiah 11 and 12)

The disciples have no need to fear the crumbling of the old forms. God will be faithful to his promises and to his love (read Habakkuk 3:17).

*   *   *   *   *   *   *

Matthew's account follows Mark's, with slight alterations. He mentions Jesus' healing activity (21:14), rather than his teaching (cf Mark 11:17). He builds up to the clearing of the Temple as the climax of the entry into Jerusalem, placing them on the same day, rather than on the following day as in Mark.

*   *   *   *   *   *   *

Luke omits the symbolic withering of the fig-tree, and in its place has the following lament. The effect is the same:

LUKE 19:41-44
As he drew near and came in sight of the city he shed tears over it •and said, 41 42 'If you in your turn had only understood on this day the message of peace! But, alas, it is hidden from your eyes! •Yes, a time is coming when your enemies 43 will raise fortifications all round you, when they will encircle you and hem you in on every side; •they will dash you and the children inside your walls to the 44 ground; they will leave not one stone standing on another within you—and all because you did not recognise your opportunity when God offered it!'

This scene marks the end of the second phase of Jesus' ministry in Luke's structure: the Journey to Jerusalem. As mentioned earlier, Luke begins each of his sections with a rejection scene. With this present scene he begins Jesus' ministry in Jerusalem.

*   *   *   *   *   *   *

Luke has Jesus clear the Temple so that he himself can teach in it.

LUKE 19:47-48
He taught in the Temple every day. The chief priests and the scribes, with 47 the support of the leading citizens, tried to do away with him, •but they did not 48 see how they could carry this out because the people as a whole hung on his words.

d: Where does religious authority lie?

MARK 11:27-33 (Compare Matthew 21:23-27 and Luke 20:1-8)
They came to Jerusalem again, and as Jesus was walking in the Temple, the 27 chief priests and the scribes and the elders came to him, •and they said to him, 28

'What authority have you for acting like this? Or who gave you authority to do
29 these things?' •Jesus said to them, 'I will ask you a question, only one; answer
30 me and I will tell you my authority for acting like this. •John's baptism: did it
31 come from heaven, or from man? Answer me that.' •And they argued it out
this way among themselves: 'If we say from heaven, he will say, "Then why did
32 you refuse to believe him?" •But dare we say from man?'—they had the people
33 to fear, for everyone held that John was a real prophet. •So their reply to Jesus
was, 'We do not know'. And Jesus said to them, 'Nor will I tell you my authority
for acting like this'.

One thing is certain: the religious 'authorities', those responsible for the fig-
tree and the Temple do not have genuine authority from God. Nor will they find
it, for they are not sincerely seeking the truth. As John writes, making the same
point:

'How can you believe, since you look to one another for approval and are not
concerned with the approval that comes from the one God?'   *(John 5:44 cf 12:43)*

If the Pharisees had been willing to listen, they would have recognised Jesus'
authority as the ordinary people did.

'His teaching made a deep impression on them because, unlike the scribes, he taught
them with authority.'   *(Mark 1:22)*

* * * * * * * *

To bring out the meaning of this encounter, Matthew adds the following
scene:

MATTHEW 21:28-32
28   'What is your opinion? A man had two sons. He went and said to the first,
29 "My boy, you go and work in the vineyard today". •He answered, "I will not go",
30 but afterwards thought better of it and went. •The man then went and said the
31 same thing to the second who answered, "Certainly, sir", but did not go. •Which
of the two did the father's will?' 'The first' they said. Jesus said to them, 'I tell
you solemnly, tax collectors and prostitutes are making their way into
32 the kingdom of God before you. •For John came to you, a pattern of true
righteousness, but you did not believe him, and yet the tax collectors and
prostitutes did. Even after seeing that, you refused to think better of it and
believe in him.

The 'authorities' have put Jesus on trial. But he is the judge, and his verdict is
that it is they who are guilty. They are the ones who give the appearance of saying
'yes' to God, but they do not do God's will. They have branded the prostitutes and
tax-collectors as sinners. But it was these who listened to John and who came to
Jesus.

* * * * * * * *

e: **God will sentence the religious authorities. He will vindicate his Son**

MARK 12:1-12 (Compare Matthew 21:33-46 and Luke 20:9-19)
1   **12** He went on to speak to them in parables, 'A man planted a vineyard; he
fenced it round, dug out a trough for the winepress and built a tower; then
2 he leased it to tenants and went abroad. •When the time came, he sent a servant

to the tenants to collect from them his share of the produce from the vineyard
But they seized the man, thrashed him and sent him away empty-handed. •Next ³₄
he sent another servant to them; him they beat about the head and treated
shamefully. •And he sent another and him they killed; then a number of others, 5
and they thrashed some and killed the rest. •He had still someone left: his beloved 6
son. He sent him to them last of all. "They will respect my son" he said. •But 7
those tenants said to each other, "This is the heir. Come on, let us kill him, and the
inheritance will be ours." •So they seized him and killed him and threw him out 8
of the vineyard. •Now what will the owner of the vineyard do? He will come and 9
make an end of the tenants and give the vineyard to others. •Have you not read 10
this text of scripture:

> *It was the stone rejected by the builders*
> *that became the keystone.*
> *This was the Lord's doing* 11
> *and it is wonderful to see?*ᵃ

And they would have liked to arrest him, because they realised that the parable 12
was aimed at them, but they were afraid of the crowds. So they left him alone
and went away.

(a: Psalm 118:22-23)

The basic meaning of the parable is obvious. Mark is also preparing his
readers for the coming death and resurrection of Jesus. It is God himself who will
vindicate his Son against those who refuse to listen to him.

*   *   *   *   *   *   *

Matthew adds the following statement, which he proceeds to clarify with a
parable:

MATTHEW 21:43

I tell you, then, that the kingdom of God will be taken from you and given to 43
a people who will produce its fruit.'

John the Baptist had the same jugment to make:

'If you are repentant produce the appropriate fruit'

(Matthew 3:8)

The religious authorities are rejected because they did not do this.

MATTHEW 22:1-14

¹₂ **22** Jesus began to speak to them in parables once again, •'The kingdom of
heaven may be compared to a king who gave a feast for his son's wedding.
3 He sent his servants to call those who had been invited, but they would not come.
4 Next he sent some more servants. "Tell those who have been invited" he said
"that I have my banquet all prepared, my oxen and fattened cattle have been
5 slaughtered, everything is ready. Come to the wedding." •But they were not
6 interested: one went off to his farm, another to his business, •and the rest seized
7 his servants, maltreated them and killed them. •The king was furious. He
8 despatched his troops, destroyed those murderers and burnt their town. •Then
he said to his servants, "The wedding is ready; but as those who were invited
9 proved to be unworthy, •go to the crossroads in the town and invite everyone

10 you can find to the wedding". •So these servants went out on to the roads and
collected together everyone they could find, bad and good alike; and the wedding
11 hall was filled with guests. •When the king came in to look at the guests he noticed
12 one man who was not wearing a wedding garment, •and said to him, "How did
you get in here, my friend, without a wedding garment?" And the man was silent.
13 Then the king said to the attendants, "Bind him hand and foot and throw him
14 out into the dark, where there will be weeping and grinding of teeth". •For many
are called, but few are chosen.'   *(22:1-11 compare Luke 14:16-24 page 285)*

Matthew seems to have combined two separate parables here. The first (22:1-
10), found also in Luke, refers to the providence of God that, in the life of Jesus,
reached out beyond the synagogue to the sinners and outcasts; and in the life of
the early church reached out beyond the Jews to the Gentile world.

The second parable, found only in Matthew, illustrates the execution of the
sentence passed against those who do not produce the fruit of the kingdom (= the
wedding garment). Matthew will later detail, in his account of the Last
Judgment, just what these fruits are (cf 25:31-46). We might compare a very
similar statement made earlier by Matthew:

'I tell you that many will come from east and west to take their places with Abraham
and Isaac and Jacob at the feast in the kingdom of heaven; but the subjects of the
kingdom will be turned out into the dark, where there will be weeping and grinding of
teeth.'   *(Matthew 8:11-12)*

Indeed 'many are called' (22:14). God's gracious love reaches to the ends of
the earth. 'Invite everyone you can find to the wedding' (22:9). Men might try to
limit God's call. Men might try to confine God within their own national or
religious group. But God will not be so confined. Matthew has already made this
point:

'The Son of Man came to give his life as a ransom for many'
          (Matthew 20:28)

Jesus will use similar words at the Last Supper:

'This is my blood, the blood of the covenant, which is to be poured out for many for
the forgiveness of sins.'
          (Matthew 26:28)

The word 'many' is not to be taken in a restrictive sense (compare Paul's use in
Romans 5:15-19). Quite the contrary. It accents the largesse of God and proclaims
God's mercy, in contradistinction to those who would restrict his love to a 'few'.

But while many are called, 'few are chosen' (Matthew 22:14). In the context
this would seem to be a sad reflection on the fact that the 'chosen people', the
'subjects of the kingdom', the religious authorities and those who followed them,
did not respond to the invitation and so missed out on the feast. It is also a sad
reflection by Matthew the Jew, as he saw the church of his time growing rapidly
among the Gentiles but rejected by many of his fellow Jews.

We should remember that Matthew is making a statement of fact, not an
ultimate judgement. He could well have shared Paul's hope that:

'those who are disobedient now will also enjoy mercy eventually'
          (Romans 11:31)

* * * * * * * *

f: Jesus exposes the hypocrisy of the Pharisees and Herodians

MARK 12:13-17 (compare Matthew 22:15-22 and Luke 20:20-26)

Next they sent to him some Pharisees and some Herodians to catch him out 13 in what he said. •These came and said to him, 'Master, we know you are an honest 14 man, that you are not afraid of anyone, because a man's rank means nothing to you, and that you teach the way of God in all honesty. Is it permissible to pay taxes to Caesar or not? Should we pay, yes or no?' •Seeing through their 15 hypocrisy he said to them, 'Why do you set this trap for me? Hand me a denarius and let me see it.' •They handed him one and he said, 'Whose head 16 is this? Whose name?' 'Caesar's' they told him. •Jesus said to them, 'Give back 17 to Caesar what belongs to Caesar—and to God what belongs to God'. This reply took them completely by surprise.

We recall a scene in the synagogue at Capernaum, very early in Jesus' ministry. He challenged the Pharisees publicly by curing a man with a withered hand on the sabbath. As a result, according to Mark;

'The Pharisees went out and at once began to plot with the Herodians against him, discussing how to destroy him.'

(Mark 3:6)

To understand why their apparently innocent question about taxes was, in fact, part of their attempt to bring Jesus down, and was recognised immediately by Jesus as a 'trap' (12:15), we need to grasp something of the political situation at the time. To do this we must go back to the time of Jesus' birth.

Herod the Great, an Idumean by birth, had won favour with the Roman Emperor, Augustus Caesar, and had been appointed king of Palestine by the Roman Senate. When he died (4.B.C.) three of his sons inherited his kingdom. The largest and most important section, Judaea (including Idumea and Samaria), was ruled by Archelaus (cf Matthew 2:22). Archelaus was very unpopular with the Jews who petitioned Rome in 6 A.D. to have him removed. Rome took the occasion to establish direct rule in Judaea. They appointed a Roman procurator, answerable to the Legate of Syria, and quartered a Roman garrison at Caesarea. The Roman Legate of Syria, Quirinius, ordered a census to be taken with a view to organising taxation, and coins were minted for the purpose. The denarius held out to Jesus was one such coin. On it was engraved the head of the ruling Caesar, and the words: 'Tiberias Caesar, son of the Divine Augustus, High Priest'.

Many Jews resented the Roman occupation, and took the occasion of the census to organise themselves into a movement for national liberation. They were led by a man called Judas and had their headquarters in Galilee (cf Acts 5:37). The extreme wing of this movement was a group called the 'Zealots', of whom Simon, one of the Twelve, was a member (cf Mark 3:18).

The scene we are examining took place just before the Feast of Passover. Jesus and his disciples had come for the feast. So had many other Galileans, and we can imagine that there were many revolutionaries among them, eager to take any opportunity that offered to stage an anti-Roman uprising. To pay tax to Caesar, was, in their opionion, tantamount to selling out to the enemy. The Pharisees, on the other hand, were eager, at all costs, to avoid trouble. This is clear from John's account of the meeting of the Sanhedrin where the decision to kill Jesus was taken (cf John 11:45-53).

The trap, therefore, is clear. If Jesus says to pay the tax, he will lose credit with the Galileans; if he says not to pay the tax, he can be arrested and handed over to the Romans for disturbing the peace and encouraging civil disobedience and revolution.

Jesus avoids their trap and, as usual, goes straight to the heart of the matter. He answers their question with another question:

'Whose head is this?'

(Mark 12:16)

The question is heavy with irony. His questioners had said:

'You are not afraid of anyone, because a man's rank means nothing to you'(12:14).

Jesus shows them just how true this is, even of the man whom they all regarded as the most important man in the world. Jesus indicates that his face and name mean little to him. He goes further. The Pharisees put up a front of being offended by the payment of the tax. Jesus sees through their hypocrisy (12:15). He knows that they are quite happy with the tax, because they benefit from the Roman way of life. The system suited them quite well and was one source of their power. (It was the Romans who set up the Sanhedrin to look after internal Jewish affairs, and the Pharisees held a powerful position in this body.)

Jesus exposes them. The fact that they have the coin indicates that they are not sincere in pretending to be offended by it.

If they are really offended by the tax, then they should rid themselves of the coins and not use them for their own benefit. If they are sincerely concerned for the purity of religion, let them set their hearts on the kingdom of God first, and on his righteousness (cf Matthew 6:33).

Jesus does not directly answer their question, but he does go to the heart of the problem. If they could free themselves from their desire for the benefits of the Roman economy, if they truly sought God's will first, if they acknowledged the fact that everything belongs to God, they would find the answer to their question.

It is sometimes said that Jesus, in the scene before us, by-passes the political arena to make a religious statement. Nothing could be further from the truth. The very distinction between what is 'political' and what is 'religious' would have no meaning for Jesus or for his contemporaries. Politics is the art and science of government. It is concerned with the direction in which a community of people is going. Obviously, Jesus was very concerned about the direction his society was taking; he was very concerned, that is, with politics; and he saw this as a religious question.

From his first public appearance, Jesus' politics are clear. He agreed with the Baptist's assessment of the situation: the Jews were heading towards war with Rome and consequent destruction (they were heading towards another 'gehenna') unless something radically changed. Everywhere Jesus looked he saw oppression, he saw people downtrodden, persecuted, enslaved. Whole groups of people were lost, frustrated, in disgrace, helpless, suffering under guilt, anxiety and superstition. The Sadducees urged fidelity to ancient traditions, traditions that gave them considerable power. The Pharisees urged meticulous fidelity to the Law, the Law of which they were the official interpreters. The Zealots worked for the violent overthrow of the Roman occupying forces, and the tools they used were just as violent and just as oppressive. The Essenes refused to be defiled by the world and chose to live apart in a seclusion reinforced by constant ritual purifications. Jesus chose to stand beside John the Baptist, the only true prophet among them all. Like John, Jesus saw that the only answer was a change of heart. He therefore deliberately chose to identify with the oppressed. He himself believed in God; he believed in the power of love to liberate. With the compassion of God he sought out the poor and they sought him out. He shared with them the Good News that they were loved by God, that they need not submit to the authorities who were keeping them in submission. He spoke to them of compassion, of forgiveness, of the dignity of man as man. He not only spoke to them, he loved this way; and his faith and hope and love were infectious. He brought healing, and not only physical healing, to many.

Jesus also spelled out, in very clear terms, the way society should be ordered if peace was ever to be achieved. He spoke of radical sharing: 'none of you can be my disciple unless he gives up all his possessions' (Luke 14:33). Men would have to learn to use things in the cause of love and justice, and not for self-security or self-aggrandisement. Jesus spoke also, again and again, of service: 'If anyone wants to be first, he must make himself last of all and servant of all' (Mark 9:35). Jesus also spoke of every man as his brother, he called every man by his name, he asked his followers to love every person with the compassion of God (Luke 6:36).

Jesus was concerned to build a peaceful society: he called it the 'kingdom of God'. It was to be a society that realised the creative, patient, forgiving, faithful love of God. When, in the present scene, he debates with the Pharisees and Herodians, it is not because he is not concerned with politics. On the contrary, Jesus is taking a very definite political stance, and in direct opposition to theirs which is based on possessions, prestige and religious and national bigotry. He challenged them to rid themselves and their society of the kind of power represented by the denarius, and to 'give to God what belongs to God'.

As his own death was approaching, Jesus seems to have sensed his own failure to convince people to change their attitudes. Luke has Jesus weeping as he draws near the city (Luke 19:41-44). His clearing of the Temple is almost a last desperate effort to awaken people to what is happening to them, and in the eschatological discourse Jesus spells out what he sees coming upon the city and the people.

But while Jesus may have failed to convince his contemporaries to change their hearts, his words still stand, as does his life and death, as a profound political statement, a statement vindicated by his resurrection and by the community that carried on his Spirit.

g: Jesus exposes the errors of the Sadducees

MARK 12:18-27 (Compare Matthew 22:23-33 and Luke 20:27-40)

Then some Sadducees—who deny that there is a resurrection—came to him and they put this question to him, •'Master, we have it from Moses in writing, if a man's brother dies leaving a wife but no child, the man must

marry the widow to raise up children for his brother. •Now there were seven 20
brothers. The first married a wife and then died leaving no children. •The second 21
married the widow, and he too died leaving no children; with the third it was
the same, •and none of the seven left any children. Last of all the woman herself 22
died. •Now at the resurrection, when they rise again, whose wife will she be, 23
since she had been married to all seven?'

Jesus said to them, 'Is not the reason why you go wrong, that you understand 24
neither the scriptures nor the power of God? •For when they rise from the dead, 25
men and women do not marry; no, they are like the angels in heaven. •Now 26
about the dead rising again, have you never read in the Book of Moses, in the
passage about the Bush, how God spoke to him and said: *I am the God of
Abraham, the God of Isaac and the God of Jacob?*[a] •He is God, not of the dead, 27
but of the living. You are very much mistaken.'

(a: Exodus 3:6)

To understand this passage it is necessary to know a little about the
Sadducees and about the development, in the Old Testament, of ideas about
resurrection from the dead.

The Sadducees were members of the leading priestly families. It has been
suggested that their name derives from Zadoc who was priest during the reign of
David (cf 2 Samuel 15:24). The political importance of the Sadducees dates from
the period after the exile. Initially the Persians appointed a governor who was
independant of the High Priest. We know of Sheshbazzar and Zerubbabel. After
the completion of the Temple we find mention only of the High Priest who seems
to have assumed complete control — a development that is not surprising for a
people for whom there is no distinction between church and state.

At the time of Jesus the power of the Sadducees had been lessened by the rise
of the lay Pharisee movement. They still held an important position on the
Sanhedrin, but it was shared with other leading families and the scribes. All the
same their influence was very strong. They took a conservative position on
religious matters, rejecting new ideas such as the existence of angelic creatures
and the resurrection of the body (cf Acts 23:8). In the scene before us they are
making fun of the latter idea.

It is true that the notion of the resurrection of the body was, at the time of
Jesus, very much a disputed matter, and did develop quite late in Judaism.
Initially, the Jews, like their neighbours, assumed that death was the end of life.
After death a man's shade went to the underworld, Sheol (=Hades), where it eked
out a shadowy existence that was not bodily and could not be called life.
Examples of such a notion can be found in the psalms:

'My soul is troubled,
my life is on the brink of Sheol;
I am numbered among those who go down to the Pit,
a man bereft of strength.
A man alone, down among the dead,
among the slaughtered in their graves,
among those you have forgotten,
those deprived of your protecting hand.'

(Psalm 88:3-5)

'The dead cannot praise Yahweh,
they have gone down to silence;

but we, the living, bless Yahweh
henceforth and evermore.'

(Psalm 115:17)

The canticle of Hezekiah, quoted in Isaiah chapter 38, but possibly a post-exilic psalm, expresses the same consciousness:

'For Sheol does not praise you,
Death does not extol you;
those who go down to the Pit do not go on
trusting in your faithfulness.
The living, the living are the ones who praise you,
as I do today.'

(Isaiah 38:18-19)

While the shades in Hades did not live in any real sense of the word, and were, as the above statements indicate, unable to praise God, God was still present to them, and his power reached into Sheol:

'Where could I go to escape your spirit?
Where could I flee from your presence?
If I climb the heavens, you are there,
there too if I lie in Sheol.'

(Psalm 139:7-8)

It was also taken for granted that God had the power to bring a dead person back to life — to this bodily life:

'Yahweh gives death and life,
brings down to Sheol and draws up.'

(1 Samuel 2:6)

There are examples of the exercise of such power in the legends surrounding the names of Elijah (cf 1 Kings 17:17-24) and Elisha (cf 2 Kings 4:8-37).

A man did live on, but only through his children, or through the nation (cf Ezekiel 37, Isaiah 26:19).

While this was the prevailing mentality, there existed side by side with it a yearning of man to have an unbreakable union with his God:

Even so, I stayed in your presence,
you held my right hand;
now guide me with advice
and in the end receive me into glory.
I look to no one else in heaven,
I delight in nothing else on earth.
My flesh and my heart are pining with love,
my heart's Rock, my own, God for ever!'

(Psalm 73:23-26)

'So my heart exults, my very soul rejoices,
My body too will rest securely,
For you will not abandon my soul to Sheol,
nor allow the one you love to see the Pit;
you will reveal the path of life to me,
give me unbounded joy in your presence,
and at your right hand everlasting pleasures.'

(Psalm 16:9-11)

Reflections such as the above, based on a growing realisation of the fidelity of God, the source of life, led gradually to the belief in God's gift of life in some way going beyond the grave. The first clear statements of belief in a personal bodily resurrection occur in the second century B.C. at the time of the persecution under Antiochus and the Maccabean revolt (168-165 B.C.). This is the central theme of the statements made by those suffering martyrdom (cf 2 Maccabees chapter 7). We also find the following statement in a section of the Book of Daniel that dates from this same period:

'When that time comes, your own people will be spared, all those whose names are found written in the Book. Of those who lie sleeping in the dust of the earth many will awake, some to everlasting life, some to shame and everlasting disgrace.'

(Daniel 12:1-2)

Finally, the Book of Wisdom, written in the century just before Jesus, has a complete section on the resurrection. It is written, however, under the influence of Greek thought. It is concerned, therefore, with the resurrection of the soul, rather than with a bodily resurrection (cf Wisdom 3:1 — 5:16).

At the time of Jesus the matter was hotly disputed. The Pharisees, representing a lay movement that had its origins in the Maccabean revolt, espoused the idea, while the Sadducees rejected it.

Jesus goes to the heart of the matter. Using texts which the Sadducees respected, he concentrates simply on the fidelity of God, and the fact that:

'He is God, not of the dead, but of the living' (12:27)

Abraham and Isaac and Jacob are alive, therefore, because they are united to God. Though dead, they are living. The implication is that whoever is in union with God is, by that fact, living, not only here in this life, but also beyond the grave.

h: **The central place of love**

MARK 12:28-34 (Compare Matthew 22:34-40)

One of the scribes who had listened to them debating and had observed how 28 well Jesus had answered them, now came up and put a question to him, 'Which is the first of all the commandments?' •Jesus replied, 'This is the first: *Listen,* 29 *Israel, the Lord our God is the one Lord,* •*and you must love the Lord your God with* 30 *all your heart, with all your soul,* with all your mind and *with all your strength.* The second is this: *You must love your neighbour as yourself.* There is no com- 31 mandment greater than these.' •The scribe said to him, 'Well spoken, Master; 32 what you have said is true: that he is one and there is no other. •To love him with 33 all your heart, with all your understanding and strength, and to love your neighbour as yourself, this is far more important than any holocaust or sacrifice.' Jesus, seeing how wisely he had spoken, said, 'You are not far from the kingdom 34 of God'. And after that no one dared to question him any more.

(Compare Luke 10:25-42 page 274)

The first commandment is the 'Shema', the profession of faith made morning and night by a devout Jew. The text comes from the Book of Deuteronomy:

'Listen, Israel: Yahweh our God is the one Yahweh. You shall love Yahweh your God with all your heart, with all your soul, with all your strength.'

'Let these words I urge on you today be written on your heart. You shall repeat them
to your children and say them over to them whether at rest in your house or walking
abroad, at your lying down or at your rising; you shall fasten them on your hand as a
sign and on your forehead as a circlet; you shall write them on the doorposts of your
house and on your gates.'

(Deuteronomy 6:4-9)

In fact, based on the above text, certain pious Jews had the practice of
wearing either on their foreheads or on their arm a small parchment capsule
called a phylactery. It contained four texts which were central to the Jewish faith,
one of which was the above. Another practice was to hang tassels from the
corners of their outer-garment as a reminder of the special love they should have
for Yahweh. (This practice follows Numbers 15:37-41. It seems that Jesus
followed it — cf Matthew 9:20 and Luke 8:44.)

The second commandment is from the Book of Leviticus (19:18). Jesus' reply
is significant in that he places the two commandments side by side. Love of God
implies love of neighbour, because God is found at the heart of our neighbour.
For the same reason, love of neighbour means love of God.

This is stressed especially by John. In one of his letters he wrote:

'This is the love I mean:
not our love for God,
but God's love for us when he sent his Son
to be the sacrifice that takes away our sins.'

(1 John 4:10)

God is the source of all love. It is his love for us that enables us to respond in love
to him. And we do this by loving our neighbour: John went on to write:

'Anyone who says "I love God",
and hates his brother, is a liar,
since a man that does not love his brother whom he can see,
cannot love God whom he has never seen.'

(1 John 4:20)

i: Jesus makes a final effort to open the minds of his adversaries:

MARK 12:35-37 (Compare Matthew 22:41-46 and Luke 20:41-44)

35   Later, while teaching in the Temple, Jesus said, 'How can the scribes maintain
36 that the Christ is the son of David? •David himself, moved by the Holy Spirit,
said:

The Lord said to my Lord:
Sit at my right hand
and I will put your enemies
under your feet.[a]

37 David himself calls him Lord, in what way then can he be his son?' And the
great majority of the people heard this with delight.

(a: Psalm 110:1)

The scribes were complacently confident that they knew God and God's will.
They were masters of the Scriptures. Or so they thought. Jesus seems to be trying
to make them see that they did not have all the answers, in the hope that they may
stop seeing themselves as teachers and judges and begin to ask questions. While

the people were pleased that Jesus exposed the scribes, the scribes themselves seemingly learned nothing.

j: Jesus' final judgment on the hypocrisy of the religious leaders:

MARK 12:38-40 (Compare Luke 20:45-47)

38 In his teaching he said, 'Beware of the scribes who like to walk about
39 in long robes, to be greeted obsequiously in the market squares, •to take
40 the front seats in the synagogues and the places of honour at banquets; •these
are the men who swallow the property of widows, while making a show of lengthy prayers. The more severe will be the sentence they receive.'

*   *   *   *   *   *   *

Matthew considerably enlarges this section.

1: Jesus addresses the people and his disciples (Matthew 23:1-12)

a: MATTHEW 23:1-4

1
2   **23** Then addressing the people and his disciples Jesus said, •'The scribes and
3   the Pharisees occupy the chair of Moses. •You must therefore do what they
tell you and listen to what they say; but do not be guided by what they do: since
4   they do not practise what they preach. •They tie up heavy burdens and lay them
on men's shoulders, but will they lift a finger to move them? Not they!

(23:4 compare Luke 11:45-6 page 277)

This seems to be upholding the teaching authority of the scribes and Pharisees, while warning against following their behaviour. We are reminded of an earlier statement of Jesus:

"If your virtue goes no deeper than that of the scribes and Pharisees, you will never get into the kingdom of heaven."

(Matthew 5:20)

But Jesus' warning is not only against 'what they do'; it is also concerned with 'what they tell you' and 'what they say'. This is, firstly, because Jesus has come to complete the Law (Matthew 5:17-19, page 90). It is also because the scribes and Pharisees failed to hand on the official Law unadulterated. On an earlier occasion he castigated them for breaking away from God's commandment for the sake of their own traditions (Matthew 15:3-9, page 196). Jesus not only warned his disciples against their teaching (Matthew 16:12, page 202); he also went so far as to say:

"Leave them alone. They are blind men leading blind men; and if one blind man leads another, both will fall into a pit."

(Matthew 15:14)

Jesus speaks of them 'tying up heavy burdens' (23:4). We refer the reader to an earlier section where Jesus said:

"Come to me, all you who labour and are overburdened."

(Matthew 11:28, page 122)

b: **MATTHEW 23:5-7**

•Everything   5
they do is done to attract attention, like wearing broader phylacteries and longer
tassels,   •like wanting to take the place of honour at banquets and the front   6
seats in the synagogues, •being greeted obsequiously in the market squares and   7
having people call them Rabbi.

(Compare Luke 11:43, page 277)

The wearing of phylacteries (cf Deuteronomy 6:4-9) and tassels (cf
Numbers 15:37-41) was a devotional practice to remind the wearer of God's
covenant with him, especially the covenant of lo·.e. Jesus himself seems to
have worn tassels (Matthew 9:20, Luke 8:44). He is warning the people against
the ostentation of *broader* phylacteries and *longer* tassels.

c: **MATTHEW 23:8-12**

'You, however, must not allow yourselves to be called Rabbi, since you have   8
only one Master, and you are all brothers. •You must call no one on earth your   9
father, since you have only one Father, and he is in heaven. •Nor must you allow   10
yourselves to be called teachers, for you have only one Teacher, the Christ.
The greatest among you must be your servant. •Anyone who exalts himself will   11
be humbled, and anyone who humbles himself will be exalted.   12

Jesus is reminding his disciples that all positions of authority are exercised
only as instruments of God, and must therefore be referred to God, who alone
is great (Hebrew 'Rab'), and who is Father of all. Matthew adds that it was Jesus,
the anointed one ('Christ') who taught them the way to God, not the scribes
and Pharisees.

2: **The sevenfold indictment of the scribes and Pharisees** (Matthew 23:13-32)

a: **MATTHEW 23:13 False religion: they block people's way to God and do it in God's name.**

'Alas for you, scribes and Pharisees, you hypocrites! You who shut up the   13
kingdom of heaven in men's faces, neither going in yourselves nor allowing
others to go in who want to.

(Compare Luke 11:52, page 277)

b: **MATTHEW 23:15 They lead people on the wrong road.**

'Alas for you, scribes and Pharisees, you hypocrites! You who travel over
sea and land to make a single proselyte, and when you have him you make him
twice as fit for hell as you are.

On hell ('gehenna') see Matthew 5:22, page 91.

c: **MATTHEW 23:16-22 Hypocrisy: they are caught up in trivia.**

'Alas for you, blind guides! You who say, "If a man swears by the Temple,   16
it has no force; but if a man swears by the gold of the Temple, he is bound".
Fools and blind! For which is of greater worth, the gold or the Temple that   17
makes the gold sacred? •Or else, "If a man swears by the altar it has no force;   18
but if a man swears by the offering that is on the altar, he is bound". •You blind   19
men! For which is of greater worth, the offering or the altar that makes the
offering sacred? •Therefore, when a man swears by the altar he is swearing by   20
that and by everything on it. •And when a man swears by the Temple he   21

22 is swearing by that and by the One who dwells in it. •And when a man swears by heaven he is swearing by the throne of God and by the One who is seated there.

d: MATTHEW 23:23-24 They neglect the heart of their religion.

23 'Alas for you, scribes and Pharisees, you hypocrites! You who pay your tithe of mint and dill and cummin and have neglected the weightier matters of the Law—justice, mercy, good faith! These you should have practised, without 24 neglecting the others. •You blind guides! Straining out gnats and swallowing camels!

(Compare Luke 11:42, page 277)

They neglected 'justice'; they neglected the judgment of God which is determined to effect justice in our world. (see also Matthew 12:18-20, page 151, and Matthew's account of the Last Judgment, Matthew 25:31-36, page 360).

They neglected 'mercy'; they neglected the compassionate love of God. (See also Matthew 9:13, page 105, and Matthew 12:7, page 108; and Matthew 5:7, page 87).

They neglected 'good faith'; they neglected to place their trust in the fidelity of God, and to teach others to do the same.

e: MATTHEW 23:25-26 They use their position for their own aggrandisement.

25 'Alas for you, scribes and Pharisees, you hypocrites! You who clean the outside of cup and dish and leave the inside full of extortion and intemperance.
26 Blind Pharisee! Clean the inside of cup and dish first so that the outside may become clean as well.

(Compare Luke 11:39-41, page 277)

Their hypocrisy took many forms. Here Jesus is accusing them of 'extortion and intemperance': using their position to extort from the people money and glory, and to enjoy the style of life that went with them. We are reminded of the accusation made by Jesus when he cleared the Temple:

"you are turning it into a robbers' den"

(Matthew 21:13, page 319)

f: MATTHEW 23:27-28 They have no regard for God's Law, and contaminate the people.

27 'Alas for you, scribes and Pharisees, you hypocrites! You who are like whitewashed tombs that look handsome on the outside, but inside are full of dead
28 men's bones and every kind of corruption. •In the same way you appear to people from the outside like good honest men, but inside you are full of hypocrisy and lawlessness.

(Compare Luke 11:44, page 277)

g: MATTHEW 23:29-32 They persecute those who speak God's word

29 'Alas for you, scribes and Pharisees, you hypocrites! You who build the
30 sepulchres of the prophets and decorate the tombs of holy men, •saying, "We

31 would never have joined in shedding the blood of the prophets, had we lived in
32 our fathers' day". •So! Your own evidence tells against you! You are the sons of
those who murdered the prophets! •Very well then, finish off the work that your
fathers began.

(Compare Luke 11:47-48, page 277)

3: **The crimes of the scribes and Pharisees and the resultant destruction of the
city** (Matthew 23:33-39)

a: **MATTHEW 23:33-36**
33   'Serpents, brood of vipers, how can you escape being condemned to hell?
34 This is why, in my turn, I am sending you prophets and wise men and scribes:
some you will slaughter and crucify, some you will scourge in your synagogues
35 and hunt from town to town; •and so you will draw down on yourselves the blood
of every holy man that has been shed on earth, from the blood of Abel the Holy
to the blood of Zechariah son of Barachiah whom you murdered between the
36 sanctuary and the altar. •I tell you solemnly, all of this will recoil on this
generation.

(Compare Luke 11:49-51, page 277)

The story of Abel is found in the Book of Genesis (4:8); that of Zechariah
in the Second Chronicles (24:20-22). These were the first and last books
respectively in the Jewish Canon.

b: **MATTHEW 23:37-39**
37   'Jerusalem, Jerusalem, you that kill the prophets and stone those who are
sent to you! How often have I longed to gather your children, as a hen gathers
38 her chicks under her wings, and you refused! •So be it! Your house will be left
39 to you desolate, •for, I promise, you shall not see me any more until you say:

Blessings on him who comes in the name of the Lord!' [a]

(a: Psalm 118:26)
(Compare Luke 13:34-5 page 284)

The image of a bird is used for God in a number of places in the Old Testament
(cf Deuteronomy 32:11, Isaiah 31:5 and Psalm 36:7).

Jesus' words concerning the city remind us of those of Jeremiah (12:7), and
Ezekiel (8:6, 11:21).

Perhaps the final statement and quotation from the Hallel (Matthew 23:39)
indicate that Matthew shared Paul's hope that one day the Jewish people would
accept Jesus (cf Romans 11:25-32).

* * * * * * * *

In this section Matthew is giving his readers an insight into the broken heart
of Jesus and the reasons for God's judgment upon the religious leaders of the
Jews at the time. Jesus tried to save these men by his love, by his preaching in
parables, by his gentleness and his confrontations; but he seemed to be getting
nowhere and his concern was for the people who were being led astray by their
false teaching. We can't help thinking that what happened to Paul, the Pharisee

(cf Philippians 3:5-16) could have happened to these men if they had only listened and heeded what Jesus was saying to them. We can also hope that words such as the above did reach through to some of them and occasion their conversion.

Matthew is, of course, writing for his own community which had to examine its life in the light of Jesus' words. So must we.

*   *   *   *   *   *   *

k: The essence of discipleship is seen in the offering of a widow:

MARK 12:41-44 (Compare Luke 21:1-4)

41   He sat down opposite the treasury and watched the people putting money
42 into the treasury, and many of the rich put in a great deal. •A poor widow came
43 and put in two small coins, the equivalent of a penny. •Then he called
his disciples and said to them, 'I tell you solemnly, this poor widow has
44 put more in than all who have contributed to the treasury; •for they have all put
in money they had over, but she from the little she had has put in everything
she possessed, all she had to live on'.

The widow stands in sharp contrast to the Pharisees. They epitomise all that is wrong in man's false religious attitudes; she sums up all that is right. Mark has chosen this as the final scene in Jesus' public ministry, followed only by the standard conclusion (an Eschatological Discourse), and the account of Jesus' Passion and Resurrection (which pre-dated Mark). By this fact alone we should realise the importance Mark wanted to give this scene. It sums up all that he has been saying about discipleship.

The anecdote appears simple: a widow with only two of the smallest coins in the currency ('lepta') gives both of them (this is important: she gives both coins, not one!) to the Temple treasury. To all appearances her gift is insignificant, but Jesus says:

'I tell you solemnly, this poor widow has put more in than all who have contributed to the treasury' (12:43)

Jesus also gives the reason, and in doing so, emphasises the essence of discipleship:

'she, from the little she had, has put in everything she possessed, all she had to live on.'
(12:44)

The essence of discipleship is found in giving all in the service of others. Was not this the moral of the story about the loaves and fishes? These seemed totally inadequate to the task of feeding the crowd. Jesus demonstrated what could happen when we give all we have into his hands. God can work wonders through us when we are totally open to him.

We, foolishly, measure everything; we compare; we assess possibilities by our own resources. The Gospel is the Good News that God is a Father; that each of us can live and live to the full; that the secret of life is to listen to the word of God, his creative word of love, and live accordingly. The secret of life is to give all we have, however little it may appear, in the service of others. That is the way Jesus lived; that is the way we can be open, moment by moment, to God's love, and can be, moment by moment, instruments of his love to others.

Anyone can be a disciple of Jesus. A man does not need a lot of resources; he does not need ten talents. He needs only what he has, now; so long as he gives all he has.

The poor widow is the perfect symbol of the disciple.

* * * * * * * *

II: JOHN 12:12-50

John like the Synoptics, concludes his account of Jesus' ministry on the theme of Judgment.

1: Jesus' entry into Jerusalem

JOHN 12:12-19
12   The next day the crowds who had come up for the festival heard that Jesus
13 was on his way to Jerusalem. •They took branches of palm and went out to
    meet him, shouting, '*Hosanna! Blessings on* the King of Israel, *who comes in the*
14 *name of the Lord.'ᵃ* •Jesus found a young donkey and mounted it—as scripture
15 says: • *Do not be afraid, daughter of Zion; see, your king is coming, mounted on*
16 *the colt of a donkey.*ᵇ •At the time his disciples did not understand this, but later,
    after Jesus had been glorified, they remembered that this had been written
17 about him and that this was in fact how they had received him. •All who had
    been with him when he called Lazarus out of the tomb and raised him from the
18 dead were telling how they had witnessed it; •it was because of this, too, that
    the crowd came out to meet him: they had heard that he had given this sign.
19 Then the Pharisees said to one another, 'You see, there is nothing you can do;
    look, the whole world is running after him!'

(a: Psalm 118:26
b: Zechariah 9:9-10
Compare Mark 11:1-11 page 315)

John places this event after the anointing at Bethany (John 12:1-11), an event we shall study later in the context selected by the Synoptics (cf Mark 14:3-9). John also places the entry in the context of the Jewish Passover (cf John 11:55). It is obvious in John's account that Jesus is entering the city for his own Passover when he will be 'glorified' (12:16).

* * * * * * * *

2: The discourse (John 12:20-50)

The Synoptics follow the entry with the clearing of the Temple, the withering of the fig-tree and the scenes in which Jesus passes judgment on the Pharisees, the Sadducees and the lawyers, John has already narrated the clearing of the Temple (John 2:13-25). He replaces it and the other scenes here with the following discourse.

JOHN 12:20-22
20   Among those who went up to worship at the festival were some Greeks.
21 These approached Philip, who came from Bethsaida in Galilee, and put this

22 request to him, 'Sir, we should like to see Jesus'. •Philip went to tell Andrew, and Andrew and Philip together went to tell Jesus.

John commented earlier that Jesus' glorification would be:

'to gather together in unity the scattered children of God'

(John 11:52)

Already he is drawing all men to himself (cf John 12:32). Their desire is the same as that of Jesus' first disciples: they want to see Jesus (John 1:39). They are taken to Jesus, as were the Gentiles in the early church, through the ministry of Jesus' disciples (John 12:21-22). What they saw is expressed poetically in the discourse which follows.

JOHN 12:23-33
23   Jesus replied to them:

'Now the hour has come
for the Son of Man to be glorified.

24   I tell you, most solemnly,
unless a wheat grain falls on the ground and dies,
it remains only a single grain;
but if it dies,
it yields a rich harvest.

25   Anyone who loves his life loses it;
anyone who hates his life in this world
will keep it for the eternal life.

26   If a man serves me, he must follow me,
wherever I am, my servant will be there too.
If anyone serves me, my Father will honour him.

27   Now my soul is troubled.
What shall I say:
Father, save me from this hour?
But it was for this very reason that I have come to this hour.

28   Father, glorify your name!'

A voice came from heaven, 'I have glorified it, and I will glorify it again'.

29   People standing by, who heard this, said it was a clap of thunder; others
30 said, 'It was an angel speaking to him'. •Jesus answered, 'It was not for my sake that this voice came, but for yours.

31   'Now sentence is being passed on this world;
now the prince of this world is to be overthrown.

32   And when I am lifted up from the earth,
I shall draw all men to myself.'

33   By these words he indicated the kind of death he would die.

The opening words 'Now the hour has come' (12:23) must have a powerful impact on John's readers. John has been building up to this point. Three times he has mentioned that this 'hour' 'has not yet come' (John 2:4, 7:30, 8:20). Two other times he has spoken of it in rather unusual terms. To the Samaritan woman Jesus says:

'the hour will come — in fact it is here already — when true worshippers will worship the Father in spirit and in truth.'

(John 4:23)

And to the religious leaders he says:

> 'the hour will come — in fact it is here already — when the dead will hear the voice of the Son of God, and all who hear it will live.'
>
> *(John 5:25, cf 5:28)*

The raising of Lazarus is the sign that this hour is already present. We are about to witness the glorification of the Son.

John highlights the 'now' (12:23, 12:27, 12:31). Luke does the same thing in his Last Supper account (cf Luke 22:36). In fact there are a number of parallels between the above passage and the Last Supper account as found in the Synoptics. John's words about service (John 12:26) remind us of Jesus' words at the Last Supper (cf Luke 22:26-27). John's words about Jesus being troubled (12:27) remind us of Jesus' prayer in the Agony that:

> 'this hour might pass him by'
>
> *(Mark 14:35, cf 14:41)*

The Greeks expressed the desire to see Jesus. John is telling his readers what they should expect to see. They will see a 'Son of Man' (John 12:23). They will see a man whose soul was 'troubled' (12:27), who, like a wheat grain, fell onto the ground and died (12:24). They will see a man who lost his life (12:25) and who asked his followers to do the same:

> 'Anyone who loves his life loses it;
> anyone who hates his life in this world will keep it for the eternal life.'
>
> *(John 12:25)*

These words remind us of similar ones recorded by the Synoptics just after Jesus' first prediction of his coming death:

> 'If anyone wants to be a follower of mine, let him renounce himself and take up his cross every day and follow me.
> For anyone who wants to save his life will lose it, but anyone who loses his life for my sake, that man will find it.'
>
> *(Luke 9:23-24)*

The dead grain yields a 'rich harvest' (John 12:24); so will Jesus and so will his disciple. The Son of Man is to be 'glorified' (12:23):

> 'When I am lifted up from the earth,
> I shall draw all men to myself.' (12:32)

This is the hour of judgment, the hour of the Eschaton:

> 'Now sentence is being passed on this world;
> now the prince of this world is being overthrown' (12:31)

JOHN 12:34-36

•The crowd [34] answered, 'The Law has taught us that the Christ will remain for ever. How can you say, "The Son of Man must be lifted up"? Who is this Son of Man?' •Jesus [35] then said:

> 'The light will be with you only a little longer now.
> Walk while you have the light,
> or the dark will overtake you;
> he who walks in the dark does not know where he is going.
> While you still have the light, [36]

believe in the light
and you will become sons of light.'

Having said this, Jesus left them and kept himself hidden.

The crowd has been following the Law as interpreted by its religious leaders. Jesus, as John pointed out in his Prologue:

'was the true light that enlightens all men'

(John 1:9)

The people are given a final warning, which they fail to take, for:

'Jesus left them and kept himself hidden' (12:36)

Darkness overtook them!

JOHN 12:37-43

Though they had been present when he gave so many signs, they did not 37 believe in him; •this was to fulfil the words of the prophet Isaiah: *Lord, who* 38 *could believe what we have heard said, and to whom has the power of the Lord been revealed?* *a* •Indeed, they were unable to believe because, as Isaiah says 39 again: • *He has blinded their eyes, he has hardened their heart, for fear they should* 40 *see with their eyes and understand with their heart, and turn to me for healing.* *b*
Isaiah said this when he saw his glory, and his words referred to Jesus. 41
And yet there were many who did believe in him, even among the leading 42 men, but they did not admit it, through fear of the Pharisees and fear of being expelled from the synagogue: •they put honour from men before the honour 43 that comes from God.

(a: Isaiah 53:1 b:Isaiah 6:9)

Isaiah saw the glory of God, a glory revealed in the Temple, but a glory which filled the whole earth (cf Isaiah 6:1-5). John refers this glory to Jesus (12:41) because he is the one in whom God's glory is finally manifest.

Isaiah, too, lived to see the tragedy of his people refusing to see the glory of God, and the consequent blindness and hardness of heart that bound them (Isaiah 6:9-10). It was the same for the contemporaries of Jesus. (compare also Deuteronomy 29:1-4):

'They put honour from men before the honour that comes from God.'

(John 12:43)

JOHN 12:44-50

Jesus declared publicly: 44

'Whoever believes in me
believes not in me
but in the one who sent me,
and whoever sees me, 45
sees the one who sent me.
I, the light, have come into the world, 46
so that whoever believes in me
need not stay in the dark any more.
If anyone hears my words and does not keep them faithfully, 47
it is not I who shall condemn him,
since I have come not to condemn the world,
but to save the world:

he who rejects me and refuses my words   48
has his judge already:
the word itself that I have spoken
will be his judge on the last day.
For what I have spoken does not come from myself;   49
no, what I was to say, what I had to speak,
was commanded by the Father who sent me,
and I know that his commands mean eternal life.   50
And therefore what the Father has told me
is what I speak.'

The reader's attention is focused, not on Jesus, but on God, his Father. To believe in Jesus is to believe in the Father (12:44); to see Jesus is to see the Father (12:45); to listen to Jesus is to listen to the Father (12:49). Concentration is upon Jesus as the word of God. Everything Jesus has done and everything Jesus has said was to draw men to share his intimacy with his Father (cf commentary on John 10:14). His desire was to draw men out of darkness into the light (12:46 cf 8:12). He came to save men (12:47 cf John 3:17). He came to give eternal life (12:50 cf John 3:15, 5:24, 8:51).

All of this was under command from his Father (12:49-50, cf John 5:30 and 10:18) who:

'loved the world so much
that he gave his only Son,
so that everyone who believes in him
may not be lost
but may have eternal life.'

(John 3:16)

Those who stand condemned (12:47), those who stand judged on the last day (12:48) are those who do not faithfully keep the word of God (cf John 3:16-21 and 5:19-30). Had they kept his word they would never have seen death (cf John 8:51). But they did not keep his word, and it is this word that is their judge (12:48). The word can be summarised, as it is later by John, with the command:

'love one another
just as I have loved you'

(John 13:34)

'God is love' (1 John 4:8). God is the God who works for the liberation of the oppressed (cf Exodus 3:7-8 and Psalm 82). Jesus is the word of God made flesh. He calls men to work for justice. He calls men to love. This is the only way to freedom (John 8:32, 8:36) and to life. If a man refuses to listen, if he:

'puts honour from men
before the honour that comes from God'

(John 12:43. 'Honour' should read 'glory')

he has chosen slavery in place of freedom; death in place of life. This is not because God has condemned him; it is not because Jesus has condemned him. It is because he has freely chosen to ignore the challenge summoning him to work for justice. He has refused the Word (compare John 3:19 and 7:7).

*   *   *   *   *   *   *   *

Chapter 2
The eschatological discourse

A: INTRODUCTION

1: Old Testament Eschatological Literature

The Jews looked back to the Exodus as the time when they began as a nation, and as the critical event which formed both their basic concept of God and their self-consciousness as a people. The Exodus was a mighty act of God, or, as they prefered to call it, a mighty 'Day of the Lord'. On that Day — so they believed — God appeared to Moses, revealed to him his name ('Yahweh') and revealed himself as a God who hears the cry of the poor and oppressed and delivers them from bondage:

'I have seen the miserable state of my people in Egypt,
I have heard their plea to be free of their slave-drivers.
Yes, I am well aware of their sufferings.
I mean to deliver them out of the hands of the Egyptians
and bring them out of that land to a land rich and broad,
a land where milk and honey flow.'

(Exodus 3:7-8)

On that Day, Yahweh, the God of mercy and compassion, liberated his people through Moses, gave them his Law on Mount Sinai, and led them to the Promised Land.

Again and again in the history of the Jewish people, God acted mightily and delivered them from the powers of darkness; again and again God intervened — such was their belief — to deliver them from oppression and assert his own justice. Two notable 'Days of the Lord' were the liberation of Jerusalem at the time of the fall of Samaria (705 B.C.), and God's delivering his people, through Cyrus of Persia, from exile in Babylon (538 B.C.).

However, in spite of these mighty acts of God, the forces of evil still exercised their power. The untimely death of King Josiah in the battle of Megiddo (609 B.C.) and the destruction of Jerusalem by the Babylonian army (587 B.C.) stand out as symbols of the powers of chaos. The Jews interpreted these events as punishments inflicted on them by God because of their infidelity to the Covenant. At the same time they earnestly looked forward to a 'Day' that they thought of as the 'Last Day' — a Day when God would finally vindicate his justice and utterly destroy all who opposed his will.

The Greek word for the 'Last Things' is 'Eschaton'; hence the literature concerned with this 'Last Day' is called 'Eschatological'.

Most of the prophets indulged in imaginative projections about this Last Day. It was the Last Day that gave meaning and direction to history. As we shall shortly see, the language in which they couched their reflections was drawn, for the most part, from the battlefield. They imagined that on that Day there would occur a final clash of cosmic proportions between the forces of Good and the forces of Evil. At first the work of creation would appear to be reversed and the world to be falling back into primitive chaos. But then God would intervene and rout the forces of evil, establishing his justice and creating, from the chaos, a new heaven and a new earth.

One of the earliest prophets to concern himself with the Last Times ('Eschatology') was the prophet Ezekiel. He was in the first group deported to Babylon in 597 B.C. From there he learned of the destruction of the city of Jerusalem and the temple (587 B.C.). He had a vivid and eccentric imagination and in his Eschatological writings developed a device which was to become very popular: the device of the dream or vision. His dreams of the future were couched in terms of visions in which God revealed to him the mysteries of his will and the manner in which God would finally overthrow his enemies.

The Greek word for 'Revelation' is 'Apocalypse'; hence the literature written in this visionary style is called 'Apocalyptic'.

When the Apocalyptic style is used in passages referring to the Last Day (the 'Eschaton') there is no limit to the fantastic imagery available. Literature concerning the Last Day appealed to a people's yearning for the ultimate victory of their hopes. The Apocalyptic style opened up for them the language of the dream, the language of symbols.

There are many examples of this style of writing in the prophecies of Ezekiel. Let us take one example from Chapters 38-39. Gog, the incarnation of evil, attacks God's own people, Israel. At first Gog is triumphant and chaos appears to reign over the land. But then Yahweh himself enters the field of battle.

> 'On the day Gog attacks the land of Israel — it is the Lord Yahweh who speaks — I shall grow angry. In my anger, my jealousy and the heat of my fury I say it: I swear that on that day there will be a fearful quaking in the land of Israel. At my presence the fish in the sea and the birds of heaven, the wild beasts and all the reptiles that crawl along the ground, and all men on earth will quake. Mountains will fall, cliffs crumble, walls collapse, and I will confront him with every sort of terror — it is the Lord Yahweh who speaks. His men will turn their swords on each other, I will punish him with plague and bloodshed and send torrential rain, hailstones, fire and brimstone against him and his hordes and against the many nations with him. I mean to display my greatness and holiness and to compel the many nations to acknowledge me; this is how they will learn that I am Yahweh'.   *(Ezekiel 38:18-23)*

The people who read this witnessed the destruction of Babylon by the Persians under Cyrus, and one can imagine their exhilaration when they were allowed by Cyrus to return to Jerusalem and rebuild the Temple. This 'Day of the Lord' encouraged them to look forward to the 'Last Day', and they continued to write, for the most part, in the Apocalyptic style. To add to the effect they developed another device: they would write about events occuring in their own day as though God had revealed these events, years before, to one of his prophets. It became popular to add apocalyptic passages to the ancient prophets, especially

Isaiah. The effect of this device was to underline for the reader the truth that God was in control of history; that whatever happened to them, God would finally triumph; that nothing happened without the will of God whose justice would finally prevail. Such writings encouraged the Jews to hold on to their faith in difficult times.

Let us now examine some examples of Eschatological writings from the period after the exile (538 B.C.). The reader may not wish to read all the examples that follow. The material is presented in the hope that it will familiarise the reader with the kind of language that he will find not only in the Eschatological Discourse we are about to study, but throughout the New Testament. Without this familiarity it is all too easy to completely misunderstand the intention of the New Testament authors in writing in this style.

ISAIAH 13:6-10

In this passage the destruction of Babylon is seen as a 'Day of the Lord', a prelude to the Last Day;

'Howl for the Day of Yahweh is near,
bringing devastation from Shaddai.
At this, every arm falls limp . . .
The heart of each man fails him,
they are terrified,
pangs and pains seize them,
they writhe like a woman in labour.
They look at one another with feverish faces.
The Day of Yahweh is coming, merciless,
with wrath and fierce anger,
to reduce the earth to desert
and root out the sinners from it.
For the stars of the sky and Orion
shall not let their light shine;
the sun shall be dark when it rises,
and the moon not shed her light . . .'

The collapse of the city affects the whole of the created universe.

ISAIAH 24:18-23

From an apocalypse revealing events of the Last Day:

'. . . the sluicegates above will open,
and the foundations of the earth will rock.
The earth will split into fragments,
the earth will be riven and rent.
The earth will shiver and shake,
the earth will stagger like a drunkard,
sway like a shanty;
so heavy will be its sin on it, it will fall
never to rise again.

That day, Yahweh will punish
above, the armies of the sky,
below, the kings of the earth;
they will be herded together,

shut up in a dungeon,
confined in a prison
and, after long years, punished.
The moon will hide her face, the sun be ashamed,
for Yahweh Sabaoth will be king
on Mount Zion, in Jerusalem,
and his glory will shine in the presence of his elders.'

ISAIAH 26:16-19

From the same apocalypse:

'Distressed, we search for you, Yahweh;
the misery of oppression was your punishment for us.
As a woman with child near her time
writhes and cries out in her pangs,

so are we, Yahweh, in your presence:
we have conceived, we writhe
as if we were giving birth;
we have not given the spirit of salvation to the earth,
no more inhabitants of the world are born.

Your dead will come to life,
their corpses will rise;
awake, exult,
all you who lie in the dust,
for your dew is a radiant dew
and the land of ghosts will give birth.'

(Isaiah 26:16-19)

Notice especially the theme of birth-pangs — a theme that is popular in New Testament Apocalyptic writing.

JOEL 2:1-14

'Sound the trumpet in Zion,
give the alarm on my holy mountain!
Let all the inhabitants of the country tremble,
for the Day of Yahweh is coming,
yes, it is near.

Day of darkness and gloom,
day of cloud and blackness.
Like the dawn there spreads across the mountains
a vast and mighty host,
such as has never been before,
such as will never be again
to the remotest ages.

In their van the fire devours,
in their rear a flame consumes.
The country is like a garden of Eden ahead of them
and a desert waste behind them.
Nothing escapes them.
They look like horses,
like chargers they gallop on,

with a racket like the clatter of chariots
they hurtle over the mountain tops,
with a crackling like a blazing fire
devouring the stubble,
a mighty army in battle array.

At the sight of them the peoples are appalled
and every face grows pale.
Like fighting men they press forward,
like warriors scale the walls,
each marching straight ahead,
not turning from his path;
they never jostle each other,
each marches straight ahead:
arrows fly, they still press forward,
without breaking ranks.
They hurl themselves at the city,
they leap on to its walls,
climb to the housetops,
and make their way through the windows,
like marauders.

As they come on, the earth quakes,
the skies tremble,
sun and moon grow dark,
the stars lose their brilliance.
Yahweh makes his voice heard
at the head of his army,
and indeed his regiments are innumerable,
all-powerful is the one who carries out his orders,
for great is the day of Yahweh,
and very terrible — who can face it?

"But now, now — it is Yahweh who speaks —
come back to me with all your heart,
fasting, weeping, mourning."
Let your hearts be broken, not your garments torn,
turn to Yahweh your God again,
for he is all tenderness and compassion,
slow to anger, rich in graciousness,
and ready to relent.
Who knows if he will not turn again, will not relent,
will not leave a blessing as he passes,
oblation and libation
for Yahweh your God?'

(Joel 2:1-14)

Joel is describing a locust plague which devastated the countryside. In typical prophetic fashion, he sees it as an image of the great Eschatological battle. He urges his readers to repentance and to hope.

JOEL 3:1-5

'After this
I will pour out my spirit on all mankind.
Your sons and daughters will prophesy,

your old men shall dream dreams,
and your young men see visions.
Even on the slaves, men and women,
will I pour out my spirit in those days.
I will display portents in heaven and on earth,
blood and fire and columns of smoke.

The sun will be turned into darkness,
and the moon into blood,
before the day of Yahweh dawns,
that great and terrible day.
All who call on the name of Yahweh will be saved,
for on Mount Zion there will be some who have escaped,
as Yahweh has said,
and in Jerusalem some survivors whom Yahweh will call'.

(Joel 3:1-5)

Luke quotes this passage as part of Peter's address to the crowd on the day of Pentecost (cf Acts 2:17-21).

ZECHARIAH 12:9-11

'When that day comes, I shall set myself to destroy all the nations who advance against Jerusalem. But over the House of David and the citizens of Jerusalem I will pour out a spirit of kindness and prayer. They will look on the one whom they have pierced; they will mourn for him as for an only son, and weep for him as people weep for a first-born child. When that day comes, there will be great mourning in Judah, like the mourning of Hadad-rimmon in the plain of Megiddo.'

The prophet looks forward to the Day when God will avenge the death of king Josiah in the plain of Megiddo.

*   *   *   *   *   *   *   *

Frequently, writing in this style concludes with a vision of peace when a new heaven and a new earth emerge from the cosmic battle.

ISAIAH 65:17-18

'Now I create new heavens and a new earth, and the past will not be remembered, and will come no more to men's minds. Be glad and rejoice for ever and ever for what I am creating...'

ISAIAH 66:22-24

The final section of Isaiah:

'For as the new heavens
and the new earth I shall make
will endure before me — it is Yahweh who speaks —
so will your race and your name endure.

From New Moon to New Moon,
from sabbath to sabbath,
all mankind will come to bow down
in my presence, says Yahweh.

And on their way out they will see
the corpses of men
who have rebelled against me.
Their worm will not die
nor their fire go out;
they will be loathsome to all mankind.'

JOEL 4:18-21

The final section of Joel:

'When that day comes,
the mountains will run with new wine
and the hills flow with milk,
and all the river beds of Judah
will run with water.
A fountain will spring from the house of Yahweh
to water the wadi of Acacias.
Egypt will become a desolation,
Edom a desert waste
on account of the violence done to the sons of Judah
whose innocent blood they shed in their country.
But Judah will be inhabited for ever,
Jerusalem from age to age.
"I will avenge their blood and let none go unpunished", and Yahweh shall make his
home in Zion.'

* * * * * * * *

Apocalyptic writing found its classical expression in a work written at the time of the Maccabean revolt — an uprising occasioned by the invasion of Judah by the Syrian, Antiochus Epiphanes IV in 168 B.C.

The author is writing about events of his own time. He uses the device of the vision, and writes as though the prophet Daniel had foreseen these events centuries before. He draws his imagery from the classical accounts of the plagues of Egypt and from Ezekiel. He writes of the war, the initial apparent victory of the forces of evil and the final liberation of Judah. He sees these as a further promise of the final Day of the Lord.

Of all the Apocalyptic writings of the Old Testament, it is this book which has the most profound influence on New Testament Apocalyptic writings.

DANIEL 7:9-14

'As I watched:

Thrones were set in place
and one of great age took his seat.
His robe was white as snow,
the hair of his head as pure as wool.
His throne was a blaze of flames,
its wheels were a burning fire.
A stream of fire poured out,
issuing from his presence.

A thousand thousand waited on him,
ten thousand times ten thousand stood before him.
A court was held and the books were opened.

The great things the horn was saying were still ringing in my ears, and as I watched, the beast was killed, and its body destroyed and committed to the flames. The other beasts were deprived of their power, but received a lease of life for a season and a time.

I gazed into the visions of the night.
And I saw, coming on the clouds of heaven,
one like a son of man.
He came to the one of great age
and was led into his presence.
On him was conferred sovereignty,
glory and kingship,
and men of all peoples, nations and languages became his servant.
His sovereignty is an eternal sovereignty
which shall never pass away,
nor will his empire ever be destroyed.'

Mark quotes from this passage in the discourse we are about to study (Mark 13:26 = Daniel 7:13-14) and the Book of Revelation quotes from it at least seven times.

DANIEL 11:31-33

'Forces of his (= Antiochus) will come and profane the sanctuary citadel; they will abolish the perpetual sacrifice and install the disastrous abomination there. Those who break the covenant he will corrupt by his flatteries, but the people who know their God will stand firm and take action. Those of the people who are learned will instruct many; for some days, however, they will be brought down by sword and flame, by captivity and plundering'

DANIEL 12:1-4

'At that time Michael will stand up, the great prince who mounts guard over your people. There is going to be a time of great distress, unparalleled since nations first came into existence. When that time comes, your own people will be spared, all those whose names are found written in the Book. Of those who lie sleeping in the dust of the earth many will awake, some to everlasting life, some to shame and everlasting disgrace. The learned will shine as brightly as the vault of heaven, and those who have instructed many in virtue, as bright as stars for all eternity.

But you, Daniel, must keep these words secret and the book sealed until the time of the end (= "Eschaton").'

* * * * * * * *

We have selected the above passages because they exemplify the kind of highly imaginative language that occurs frequently in writings about the Eschaton. There is one other characteristic of the Eschaton that is important for our present study: the Eschaton is Messianic. The Jews expected God to bring about the Eschaton through the action of a kingly figure of the line of David. This king would be the Messiah, that is, the 'anointed one' (Greek: 'Christ').

2: Eschatology in the writings of the New Testament:

When we come to the writings of the New Testament an immediate problem arises. On the one hand there is faith in Jesus as the Christ and so in the present reality of the Eschaton — the powerful presence of the kingdom of God on earth; on the other hand there is the obvious fact that the universal joy and peace and love associated with the Eschaton has not yet been achieved. The new heaven and new earth promised in Messianic times was still something to come.

Paul addresses himself to this problem in his earliest extant letter. The Christians in Thessalonika had placed their hopes in the Gospel and were distressed when their first members began to die without experiencing the promised Messianic peace (1 Thessalonians 4:13). Paul tries to console them with the thought that Jesus himself died; but he rose again (4:14). He goes on to speak of the 'Day of the Lord' (5:1) in terms drawn from classical biblical literature; and he speaks of it as something that is 'going to come' (5:2). He insists that they should not concern themselves about 'times and seasons' (5:1) but should concentrate on living 'united to Jesus' (5:10) by lives of faith, hope and love (5:8). At the same time his letter opens with a prayer that they enjoy the 'peace' of Christ (1:1), and he means the peace of the Messianic age.

In his second letter to the same community he speaks even more clearly of the Day of the Lord as something that has not yet arrived (2 Thessalonians 2:1-12). In spite of the fact that Jesus is the Christ, something has still to happen before the full realisation of the Eschaton can be manifest. Paul speaks of something — and he does not specify what — that is 'holding back' this manifestation (2 Thessalonians 2:7). He perhaps gives us a hint of what it is that is holding back the complete realisation of the Eschaton when he writes to the community in Rome:

'Glory to him who is able to give you the strength to live according to the Good News I preach, and in which I proclaim Jesus Christ, the revelation of a mystery kept secret for endless ages, but now so clear that it must be broadcast to pagans everywhere to bring them to the obedience of faith.'

(Romans 16:26)

The mystery 'must be broadcast everywhere'. The Eschaton will not be manifest till all men learn 'the obedience of faith'. Then, and only then, can there be a new heaven and a new earth. Then, and only then, can the glory of the Risen Christ be apparent.

Luke has much the same approach in his Acts. There, too, the disciples are concerned to know times and dates (1:7). Jesus tells them not to be distracted with such questions, but rather to set about the task of preaching the Gospel 'to the ends of the earth' (1:8). The disciples are not to spend their time 'standing looking into the sky' (1:11), waiting for God to act. God has acted. The Eschaton is present. God has acted in our world with the power of the Spirit. What is holding back the final manifestation and realisation of the Eschaton is man's failure to repent.

Luke has Peter say to the crowd:

'You must repent and turn to God, so that your sins may be wiped out, and so that the Lord may send the time of comfort.'

(Acts 3:20)

We find the same message in the Second Letter of Peter:

'Since everything is coming to an end like this,
you should be living holy and saintly lives,
while you wait for and hasten the Day of the Lord.'

(2 Peter 3:11)

John too, as we have seen, speaks of the fact that Jesus is the Christ and has already inaugurated the Eschaton (4:25-26). Jesus has already given eternal life, already judged the world (5:21-30; 9:35-37; 11:23-26). At the same time, he too recognises that there is something yet to happen: men have yet to believe in Jesus, men have yet to accept the power of God into their lives, men have yet to work for justice and to love as Jesus loved. As John writes in his First Letter:

'What is being carried out in your lives
as it was in his,
is a new commandment,
because the night is over
and the real light is *already* shining.'

(1 John 2:8)

The constant message of the new Testament writings is that Jesus is the Christ; that the Eschaton has come (cf 1 Cor 10:11, Hebrews 1:2, 1 Peter 1:20, 1 John 2:18), but that man has still to believe in the Gospel for the effects of Jesus' life to become universally apparent. Now, because of Jesus, the full realisation of the Eschaton is possible, 'the night is over and the real light is already shining'. The task of the disciple is to bring about the new heaven and the new earth by believing in Jesus, that is, by carrying out in his life the 'new commandment', the commandment of love. When men learn from Jesus to love each other, when men learn to believe that they too can do what Jesus did, when men believe in the Father's love for them and give their lives in turn in the cause of justice and peace, then, and only then, will everything be brought together under Christ (cf Ephesians 1:10).

3: **The Eschatological theme in the sections of the Synoptic Gospels we have already studied**

In his opening sentence, **Mark** speaks of Jesus as the 'Christ' (1:1). He immediately introduces John the Baptist as an Elijah figure sent to prepare the way for the Christ (1:1-8 and 9:9-13). He writes of Jesus' first appearance in public — his baptism in the Jordan — in terms that remind his readers of the ancient promise that God would intervene in history and bring about a new creation (1:9-11). Immediately, Jesus is engaged in a battle with the powers of evil. This is the great Eschatological battle (1:12-13).

The opening words of the Gospel have a powerful message for anyone familiar with Eschatological writings:

'The time has come and the kingdom of God is close at hand. Repent and believe the Good News.' (1:15)

That this is the end-time (the 'Eschaton') is demonstrated again and again by Mark as he presents Jesus as victorious over the forces of evil. One thinks of the Capernaum demoniac (1:21-28), the Gerasene demoniac (5:1-20), the epileptic demoniac (9:14-29) as well as the many occasions on which Mark reminds his readers that Jesus cast out demons (1:26, 1:34, 1:39, 3:11, 7:30). This power he shared with his disciples (3:15 and 6:13).

Jesus' first parable is about his victory over the prince of demons, Satan (3:22-27). Mark also demonstrates Jesus' victory over the powers of chaos in the anecdote about the calming of the storm (4:35-41) and the anecdote about Jesus walking on the water (6:45-52).

Once Peter acknowledges that Jesus is 'the Christ' (8:30), Jesus sets about instructing his disciples on the urgency of their joining him in his fight against evil. The task is urgent because, in the words of Jesus:

'I tell you solemnly there are some standing here who will not taste death before they see the kingdom of God coming with power.' (9:1)

The same urgency is conveyed by the accounts of Jesus' entry into Jerusalem, his clearing of the temple and his cursing of the fig-tree (11:1-22). We saw that Mark, in recounting these anecdotes, explicitly alludes to the Apocalyptic Eschatological writings of the prophet Zechariah.

Clearly, Mark sees Jesus as the 'Christ', the one who brings history to its close by inaugurating the Eschaton.

Matthew has the same message. Each of the texts just quoted for Mark has a parallel text in Matthew. In terms reminiscent of Daniel (7:13-14), Matthew sees Jesus as bringing about, in his own day, the Final Judgment looked forward to for so long:

'I tell you solemnly, you will not have gone the round of the towns of Israel before the Son of Man comes.'

(Matthew 10:23)

Luke, the historian, is even more explicit. He chooses to write the Prologue to his Gospel in the Apocalyptic Eschatological style precisely because he wants to state that in Jesus history has reached its climax. Jesus brings to this world the peace and joy of the last times. Yahweh, who revealed himself to Moses as the liberator of the oppressed, has finally revealed himself in Jesus, and powerfully, and once for all, overthrown the forces of darkness.

In his opening scene, Luke applies this statement from Isaiah to Jesus:

'The spirit of the Lord has been given to me,
for he has anointed me.
He has sent me to bring the good news to the poor,
to proclaim liberty to captives
and to the blind new sight,
to set the downtrodden free,
to proclaim the Lord's year of favour.'

(Luke 4:18-19)

Luke insists on the fact that God is now reigning, the Eschaton has come:

'There is no need to be afraid, little flock, for it has pleased your Father to give you the kingdom.'

God has intervened in history, by-passed all the ways man tried to limit him, and is powerfully drawing men into the kingdom of his love:

'Go to the open roads and the hedgerows and force people to come in to make sure my house is full.' (14:23)

'Up to the time of John it was the Law and the Prophets;
since then, the kingdom of God has been preached, and by violence everyone is getting in.' (16:16)

Finally, Luke records that the Pharisees asked Jesus 'when the kingdom of God was to come' (17:20) and Jesus answered them:

'you must know the kingdom of God is among you.' (17:21)

Jesus goes on to speak of a 'Day of the Son of Man' that is yet to come. He uses language taken from classical Eschatological texts such as we have just studied. But what he insists on is:

'Anyone who tries to preserve his life will lose it;
and anyone who loses it will keep it safe.' (17:33)

Always the attention of the disciples is being directed away from the 'when' (17:20) and the 'where' (17:37) of this final manifestation of the Eschaton, towards the practical task of living the Gospel.

*　*　*　*　*　*　*　*

In the Gospels, two events stand out as indications of the presence of the Eschaton. Jesus' resurrection is seen as God's ultimate vindication of the 'poor man'; and the destruction of Jerusalem is seen as the punishment received by the city for its rejection of Jesus. In both these events, God's ultimate judgment of history is typified. The synoptics concentrate their attention at this point on the second of these, the destruction of Jerusalem; and they draw from it lessons about the way men should live in the light of God's judgment. This is the subject matter for Eschatology; hence the name given to the following discourse.

B: THE ESCHATOLOGICAL DISCOURSE:

a: Introduction: Jesus foretells the coming destruction of Jerusalem

MARK 13:1-4 (Compare Matthew 24:1-3 and Luke 21:5-7)

13 ¹ As he was leaving the Temple one of his disciples said to him, 'Look at the ² size of those stones, Master! Look at the size of those buildings!' •And Jesus said to him, 'You see these great buildings? Not a single stone will be left on another: everything will be destroyed.'
³   And while he was sitting facing the Temple, on the Mount of Olives, Peter,
⁴ James, John and Andrew questioned him privately, •'Tell us, when is this going to happen, and what sign will there be that all this is about to be fulfilled?'

*　*　*　*　*　*　*　*

Matthew phrases the question in a more explicitly Eschatological way:
'Tell us when this is going to happen
and what will be the sign of your coming
and of the end of the world.'

(Matthew 24:3)

The destruction of the city is a type of the judgment that faces every city, every culture, every people.

*　*　*　*　*　*　*　*

b: **The disciples must expect persecution**

MARK 13:5-13 (Compare Luke 21:8-19)

$\frac{5}{6}$ Then Jesus began to tell them, 'Take care that no one deceives you. •Many will
7 come using my name and saying, "I am he", and they will deceive many. •When
you hear of wars and rumours of wars, do not be alarmed, this is something that
8 must happen, but the end will not be yet. •For nation will fight against nation,
and kingdom against kingdom. There will be earthquakes here and there; there
will be famines. This is the beginning of the birthpangs.
9   'Be on your guard: they will hand you over to sanhedrins; you will be beaten
in synagogues; and you will stand before governors and kings for my sake,
10 to bear witness before them, •since the Good News must first be proclaimed
to all the nations.
11   'And when they lead you away to hand you over, do not worry beforehand
about what to say; no, say whatever is given to you when the time comes, because
12 it is not you who will be speaking: it will be the Holy Spirit. •Brother will betray
brother to death, and the father his child; children will rise against their parents
13 and have them put to death. •You will be hated by all men on account of my
name; but the man who stands firm to the end will be saved.

(13:11-13 compare Matthew 10:17-22 page 116)
(13:11 compare Luke 12:11-12 page 278)

The language of this passage is the language of Old Testament Eschatology:
The language of warfare (13:7-8), of earthquakes (13:8 cf Ezekiel 38:21, Isaiah
24:19, Joel 2:10), of famine (13:8, cf Joel), of persecution and division (13:9-12, cf
Ezekiel 38:21). The words take on powerful significance when we remember that
Mark is writing in Rome in the wake of Nero's persecution and during the build
up of the Roman-Jewish war, while Luke is writing after the desctruction of
Jerusalem.

Luke speaks of 'fearful sights and great signs from heaven' (21:11 cf Isaiah
13:10 and Joel 3:3-4).

While the disciples must expect persecution, they are to remember that their
sufferings are 'birthpangs' (Mark 13:8. cf Isaiah 13:8, 26:17; Romans 8:18).
They will issue in life. Jesus warns them against being deceived (13:5-6); he
tells them not to be frightened (13:7), and to stand firm (13:9).

The disciples are encouraged with the reassurance that the 'Holy Spirit'
(13:11) will be with them. That this is the Spirit of the risen Jesus is made clear by
Luke who has:
"I myself shall give you an eloquence and a wisdom..." (21:15).
Supported by the Spirit they are to boldly carry out their mission of proclaiming
the Good News to all the nations (13:10).

Finally, the message is that of all Eschatological writings:
"The man who stands firm to the end will be saved." (13:13).

*   *   *   *   *   *   *   *

Matthew omits in this context any reference to the 'Holy Spirit' (but cf
Matthew 10:17-22). He also adds some details in 24:12.

He is sufficiently different to warrant reproducing the whole text:

MATTHEW 24:4-14

And Jesus answered them, 'Take care that no one deceives you; •because ⁴₅
many will come using my name and saying, "I am the Christ", and they will
deceive many. •You will hear of wars and rumours of wars; do not be 6
alarmed, for this is something that must happen, but the end will not be yet.
For nation will fight against nation, and kingdom against kingdom. There will 7
be famines and earthquakes here and there. •All this is only the beginning of 8
the birthpangs.

'Then they will hand you over to be tortured and put to death; and you will 9
be hated by all the nations on account of my name. •And then many will fall 10
away; men will betray one another and hate one another. •Many false prophets 11
will arise; they will deceive many, •and with the increase of lawlessness, love in 12
most men will grow cold; •but the man who stands firm to the end will be saved. 13

'This Good News of the kingdom will be proclaimed to the whole world as 14
a witness to all the nations. And then the end will come.

(Matthew 24:10-12, compare Daniel 12:4)

* * * * * * * *

c: **The Jewish-Roman war (66-73 A.D.) as a type, demonstrating God's judgment in man's history.**

MARK 13:14-20 (Compare Matthew 24:15-22)

'When you see *the disastrous abomination* set up where it ought not to be 14
(let the reader understand), then those in Judaea must escape to the mountains;
if a man is on the housetop, he must not come down to go into the house to 15
collect any of his belongings; •if a man is in the fields, he must not turn back 16
to fetch his cloak. •Alas for those with child, or with babies at the breast, when 17
those days come! •Pray that this may not be in winter. •For in those days there ¹⁸₁₉
will be *such distress as, until now, has not been* equalled since the beginning when
God created the world, nor ever will be again. •And if the Lord had not shortened 20
that time, no one would have survived; but he did shorten the time, for the sake
of the elect whom he chose.

(Mark 13:14-15 compare Luke 17:31 page 293)

The 'disastrous abomination', as Matthew explicitly points out (Matthew
24:15), is an expression taken from Daniel, the classical reference book of
Apocalyptic writings

As we saw earlier, Daniel was written during the persecution of the Jews by
the Syrian, Antiochus Epiphanes IV. Daniel writes:

'Forces of his will come and profane the sanctuary citadel; they will abolish the
perpetual sacrifice and install the disastrous abomination there.'

(Daniel 11:31 cf also Daniel 9:27 and 1 Maccabees 1:57)

He is referring to the erection of the statue of Baal Shamem (=Zeus) on the
Temple altar. This action became a classical symbol for any act of profanation
effected by the powers of darkness against God's people.

We know that in 40 A.D. the Emperor Caligula ordered his own statue to be
erected in the Temple. Perhaps Mark is referring to this, or perhaps he is referring

to the many acts of violence perpetrated in the period leading up to the final conflagration of the Jewish-Roman war (66-73 A.D.).

The main point of the passage is that the sufferings of the poor fugitive who has not time even to collect his few belongings (13:14-17) are part of the sufferings of the Eschaton. The reader is being encouraged to persevere in his faith. God is in control; he did 'shorten the time' (13:20). His faithful love for those who have chosen to follow Jesus will not be found wanting (13:20).

At this point **Luke** refers more explicitly to the siege of Jerusalem:

LUKE 21:20-24

20 'When you see Jerusalem surrounded by armies, you must realise that she will
21 soon be laid desolate. •Then those in Judaea must escape to the mountains, those inside the city must leave it, and those in country districts must not take refuge
22 in it. •For this is the time of vengeance when all that scripture says must be
23 fulfilled. •Alas for those with child, or with babies at the breast, when those days come!
24 'For great misery will descend on the land and wrath on this people. •They will fall by the edge of the sword and be led captive to every pagan country; and Jerusalem will be trampled down by the pagans until the age of the pagans is completely over.

We are reminded of the lament for Jerusalem uttered by Jesus on his entry (Luke 19:41-44). Like the above passage, the lament is found only in Luke. Luke sees the destruction of Jerusalem as the end of history as man has known it. It is a powerful statement of the fact that in Jesus a new era has dawned — the era of the Eschaton. In that destruction 'all that scripture says' (21:22), all that has ever been written about the last days and the final Eschatological battle and the powerful action of God judging the world — all this is being fulfilled.

Luke shares Paul's hope, expressed in his Letter to the Romans:

'One section of Israel has become blind, but this will last only until the whole pagan world has entered, and then, after this, the rest of Israel will be saved as well.'

(Romans 11:25 cf Luke 21:24)

d: **Further warnings**

MARK 13:21-23 (Compare Matthew 24:23-25)

21 'And if anyone says to you then, "Look, here is the Christ" or, "Look, he
22 is there", do not believe it; •for false Christs and false prophets will arise and
23 produce signs and portents to deceive the elect, if that were possible. •You therefore must be on your guard. I have forewarned you of everything.

The Gospels are not alone in warning the Christian community against false prophets and false Christs (cf 2 Thessalonians 2:3 — 4:9; 2 Peter 2:1-3; 1 John 4:1 and Revelations 31).

Matthew adds the following verses assuring his readers that they will not need to depend on others to identify the Eschaton. It will obvious — as obvious as lightning.

MATTHEW 24:26-28

26 'If, then, they say to you, "Look, he is in the desert", do not go there;
27 "Look, he is in some hiding place", do not believe it· •because the coming of the

Son of Man will be like lightning striking in the east and flashing far into the
28 west. •Wherever the corpse is, there will the vultures gather.

(Compare Luke 17:22-24, 37, page 293-294)

e: The final judgment

MARK 13:24-27 (Compare Matthew 24:29-31)
24   'But in those days, after that time of distress, the sun will be darkened, the
25 moon will lose its brightness, •the stars will come falling from heaven and the
26 powers in the heavens will be shaken. •And then they will see the Son of Man
27 coming in the clouds with great power and glory; •then too he will send the angels
    to gather his chosen from the four winds, from the ends of the world to the ends
    of heaven.

The Apocalypic style is obvious, though restrained(cf especially Isaiah 13:10,
24:21: Joel 2:10). The 'Son of Man' is a reference to Daniel 7:13. The final
gathering of God's elect is a common prophetic theme (cf Deuteronomy 30:4-5;
Isaiah 60:4-5; Micah 4:1). The poor will be vindicated (cf 'Son of Man', page 77)
and evil will have worked its way to its own destruction.

Mark reassures his readers that the Last Day is not a Day to fear, because the
final struggle and the chaos and the collapse of the universe (all typical
Apocalyptic themes) will inevitably open the way for the victory of God. Men will
all be judged by their relationship to Jesus whom God has appointed judge.

Paul concludes his argument in his Letter to the Thessalonians in much the
same way. Evil, incarnate in the 'Rebel' will do its worst, but:

'The Lord will annihilate him with his glorious appearance at his coming.'

(2 Thessalonians 2:8)

* * * * * * * *

Luke prefers more flamboyant language to describe the Last Day:

LUKE 21:25-28
25   'There will be signs in the sun and moon and stars; on earth nations in agony,
26 bewildered by the clamour of the ocean and its waves; •men dying of fear as they
27 await what menaces the world, for the powers of heaven will be shaken. •And
    then they will see the Son of Man coming in a cloud with power and great glory.
28 When these things begin to take place, stand erect, hold your heads high, because
    your liberation is near at hand.'

It is typical of Luke that he sees the final mainfestation of the Eschaton in
terms of 'liberation' (21:28). The word is the same word frequently used by Paul
and translated 'redemption' (cf, for example Romans 3:24). God is still the God
of the Exodus. His action is still the action of one who redeems from slavery,
liberates from oppression.

**f: Jesus' world and that of his contemporaries is soon to come to an end. Only
God knows when the final end will come.**

MARK 13:28-32 (Compare Matthew 24:32-36 and Luke 21:29-32)
28   'Take the fig tree as a parable: as soon as its twigs grow supple and its leaves
29 come out, you know that summer is near. •So with you when you see these things

30 happening: know that he is near, at the very gates. •I tell you solemnly,
before this generation has passed away all these things will have taken
31 place. •Heaven and earth will pass away, but my words will not pass away.
32   'But as for that day or hour, nobody knows it, neither the angels of heaven,
nor the Son; no one but the Father.

(Luke omits verse 32)

We are reminded of an earlier statement in Mark:

'I tell you solemnly, there are some standing here who will not taste death before they
see the kingdom of God come with power.'

At the beginning of the discourse, the disciples asked Jesus about the
destruction of the city. He tells them it will be soon. So will his vindication in the
resurrection. He does not known when the final end will be.

g: The end must come for each person, each generation. All must face judgment

MARK 13:33-37

33   'Be on your guard, stay awake, because you never know when the time will
34 come. •It is like a man travelling abroad: he has gone from home, and left his
servants in charge, each with his own task; and he has told the doorkeeper to
35 stay awake. •So stay awake, because you do not know when the master of the
36 house is coming, evening, midnight, cockcrow, dawn; •if he comes unexpectedly,
37 he must not find you asleep. •And what I say to you I say to all: Stay awake!'

This is the conclusion to Mark's discourse, and the practical lesson to be
learned from what has gone before. Three times he uses the expression 'Stay
awake' (13:33, 35, 37). The disciple's task is to live the good news; to be a servant,
listening for his master's call; to live as a disciple of Jesus, proclaiming the Good
News by his life.

*   *   *   *   *   *   *   *

Matthew makes the same point:

MATTHEW 24:37-44

37
38   'As it was in Noah's day, so will it be when the Son of Man comes. •For in
those days before the Flood people were eating, drinking, taking wives, taking
39 husbands, right up to the day Noah went into the ark, •and they suspected nothing
till the Flood came and swept all away. It will be like this when the Son of Man
40
41 comes. •Then of two men in the fields one is taken, one left; •of two women at
the millstone grinding, one is taken, one left.

42   'So stay awake, because you do not know the day when your master is coming.
43 You may be quite sure of this that if the householder had known at what time
of the night the burglar would come, he would have stayed awake and would
44 not have allowed anyone to break through the wall of his house. •Therefore, you
too must stand ready because the Son of Man is coming at an hour you do not
expect.

(24:37-41 compare Luke 17:26-7, 35 page 293
24:42-44 compare Luke 12:39-40 page 281)

*   *   *   *   *   *   *   *

LUKE 21:34-38

34 'Watch yourselves, or your hearts will be coarsened with debauchery and drunkenness and the cares of life, and that day will be sprung on you suddenly,
35 like a trap. For it will come down on every living man on the face of the earth.
36 Stay awake, praying at all times for the strength to survive all that is going to happen, and to stand with confidence before the Son of Man.'
37 In the daytime he would be in the Temple teaching, but would spend the night
38 on the hill called the Mount of Olives. •And from early morning the people would gather round him in the Temple to listen to him.

This is Luke's conclusion to the discourse. He, too, stresses the need for alertness and care in living the Gospel day by day. Notice his mention of prayer (21:36). His final two verses act as a link bringing the reader back to Jerusalem and the last days of Jesus' life.

* * * * * * * *

Matthew adds a number of parables to bring out more clearly the necessity for responsible discipleship.

a: The leaders in the community must serve

MATTHEW 24:45-51

45 'What sort of servant, then, is faithful and wise enough for the master to place him over his household to give them their food at the proper time?
46
47 Happy that servant if his master's arrival finds him at this employment. •I tell
48 you solemnly, he will place him over everything he owns. •But as for the
49 dishonest servant who says to himself, "My master is taking his time", •and sets
50 about beating his fellow servants and eating and drinking with drunkards, •his master will come on a day he does not expect and at an hour he does not know.
51 The master will cut him off and send him to the same fate as the hypocrites, where there will be weeping and grinding of teeth.

(Compare Luke 12:42-46 page 281)

Matthew's concern is a practical one. The disciple is not to be concerned with the timing of the final revelation of Jesus. Rather, he should concentrate on living the life of a servant. On this he will be judged. Like Luke (cf Luke 12:42-46), Matthew seems to be especially concerned with those in the Christian community who exercise positions of leadership (24:45). They have a special obligation to carry out their ministry of service in the manner taught them by Jesus (cf Matthew 20:24-28 page 310).

b: The religious leaders are responsible for the church, the bride of Christ

MATTHEW 25:1-13

1 **25** 'Then the kingdom of heaven will be like this: Ten bridesmaids took their
2 lamps and went to meet the bridegroom. •Five of them were foolish and five
3 were sensible: •the foolish ones did take their lamps, but they brought no oil,
4
5 whereas the sensible ones took flasks of oil as well as their lamps. •The bride-
6 groom was late, and they all grew drowsy and fell asleep. •But at midnight there
7 was a cry, "The bridegroom is here! Go out and meet him." •At this, all those
8 bridesmaids woke up and trimmed their lamps, •and the foolish ones said to

the sensible ones, "Give us some of your oil: our lamps are going out". •But 9
they replied, " There may not be enough for us and for you; you had better go
to those who sell it and buy some for yourselves". •They had gone off to buy 10
it when the bridegroom arrived. Those who were ready went in with him to the
wedding hall and the door was closed. •The other bridesmaids arrived later. 11
"Lord, Lord," they said "open the door for us." •But he replied, "I tell you 12
solemnly, I do not know you". •So stay awake, because you do not know either 13
the day or the hour.

(Compare Luke 12:35-38 page 281)

This parable, too, is addressed especially to those responsible for leadership,
whether in the Jewish community or the early Christian community for which
Matthew was writing. It is addressed to those responsible for attending the bride.
It repeats an earlier message: the bridesmaids must be alert to their
responsibilities; they must 'stay awake' (25:13).

c: Our responsibility

MATTHEW 25:14-30

'It is like a man on his way abroad who summoned his servants and entrusted 14
his property to them. •To one he gave five talents, to another two, to a third 15
one; each in proportion to his ability. Then he set out. •The man who had received 16
the five talents promptly went and traded with them and made five more. •The 17
man who had received two made two more in the same way. •But the man who 18
had received one went off and dug a hole in the ground and hid his master's
money. •Now a long time after, the master of those servants came back and went 19
through his accounts with them. •The man who had received the five talents came 20
forward bringing five more. "Sir," he said "you entrusted me with five talents;
here are five more that I have made." •His master said to him, "Well done, good 21
and faithful servant; you have shown you can be faithful in small things, I will
trust you with greater; come and join in your master's happiness". •Next the man 22
with the two talents came forward. " Sir," he said "you entrusted me with two
talents; here are two more that I have made." •His master said to him, "Well 23
done, good and faithful servant; you have shown you can be faithful in small
things, I will trust you with greater; come and join in your master's happiness".
Last came forward the man who had the one talent. "Sir," said he "I had heard 24
you were a hard man, reaping where you have not sown and gathering where
you have not scattered; •so I was afraid, and I went off and hid your talent in 25
the ground. Here it is; it was yours, you have it back." •But his master answered 26
him, "You wicked and lazy servant! So you knew that I reap where I have not sown
and gather where I have not scattered? •Well then, you should have deposited 27
my money with the bankers, and on my return I would have recovered my capital
with interest. •So now, take the talent from him and give it to the man who has 28
the five talents. •For to everyone who has will be given more, and he will have more 29
than enough; but from the man who has not, even what he has will be taken away.
As for this good-for-nothing servant, throw him out into the dark, where there 30
will be weeping and grinding of teeth."

(Compare Mark 13:34 page 357 and Luke 19:11-27 page 312)

There are many similarities between this parable and the parable of the
pounds recorded by Luke (19:11-27). Luke uses the parable of the pounds to
conclude his long section on the journey to Jerusalem. It stresses the urgency of

discipleship and the responsibility of the disciples to live a life that is a close following of Jesus. The primary accent must always be on God and on the gratuitous nature of God's faithful love. But this cannot be understood in a way that enables a disciple to sit back and wait on God.

The basic point of Matthew's parable of the talents is the same. The Eschaton is God's work. The Last Day, the Last Judgment, the Parousia — all expressions for the final manifestation in history of what has already happened in the resurrection of Jesus — is in God's hands, and it is not for us to waste time wondering about the time and place. It is up to us to set about the task of discipleship. For the Parousia is dependent on that:

> 'This Good News of the kingdom will be proclaimed to the whole world as a witness to all the nations. And then the end will come.'   *(Matthew 24:14)*

In case the reader is still not clear on the essential task of discipleship; in case the reader is still not clear on what it means to 'proclaim the Good News of the kingdom', Matthew concludes his treatment of the Eschaton with a statement on the essence of discipleship. The 'Last Judgment' is not something we have to wait for. It is something that has already been made. It is up to the disciple to carry it out.

d: The last judgment

MATTHEW 25:31-46

31   'When the Son of Man comes in his glory, escorted by all the angels, then
32   he will take his seat on his throne of glory. •All the nations will be assembled
      before him and he will separate men one from another as the shepherd separates
33   sheep from goats. •He will place the sheep on his right hand and the goats
34   on his left. •Then the King will say to those on his right hand, "Come, you whom
      my Father has blessed, take for your heritage the kingdom prepared for you
35   since the foundation of the world. •For I was hungry and you gave me food;
      I was thirsty and you gave me drink; I was a stranger and you made me welcome;
36   naked and you clothed me, sick and you visited me, in prison and you came to
37   see me." •Then the virtuous will say to him in reply, "Lord, when did we see
38   you hungry and feed you; or thirsty and give you drink? •When did we see you
39   a stranger and make you welcome; naked and clothe you; •sick or in prison and
40   go to see you?" •And the King will answer, "I tell you solemnly, in so far
      as you did this to one of the least of these brothers of mine, you did it to me".
41   Next he will say to those on his left hand, "Go away from me, with your curse
42   upon you, to the eternal fire prepared for the devil and his angels. •For I was
      hungry and you never gave me food; I was thirsty and you never gave me anything
43   to drink; •I was a stranger and you never made me welcome, naked and you
44   never clothed me, sick and in prison and you never visited me." •Then it will be
      their turn to ask, "Lord, when did we see you hungry or thirsty, a stranger. or
45   naked, sick or in prison, and did not come to your help?" •Then he will answer,
      "I tell you solemnly, in so far as you neglected to do this to one of the least
46   of these, you neglected to do it to me". •And they will go away to eternal punish-
      ment, and the virtuous to eternal life.'

This forms not only the conclusion to Matthew's Eschatological Discourse, but also a culmination of an argument that has been central to his Gospel: the Law has found its fulfilment in Jesus (cf Matthew 5:17).

Jesus showed us that perfection does not come from what we do, from our meticulous observance of an external law. Perfection is a gift from God.

'Come, you whom my Father has blessed,
take for your heritage the kingdom prepared for
since the foundation of the world.'

(Matthew 25:34)

Our response to this gift of God is not making sure we belong to a certain group, or fulfil certain external requirements: it is doing the will of God:

'It is not those who say to me, "Lord, Lord", who will enter the kingdom of heaven, but the person who does the will of my Father in heaven. When the day comes many will say to me, "Lord, Lord, did we not prophesy in your name, cast out demons in your name, work many miracles in your name?" Then I shall tell them to their faces: I have never known you; away from me, you evil men!'

(Matthew 7:21-23)

Jesus showed us what God's will is: to love, to serve, to show humble and prayerful respect to the outsider, the oppressed, the sinner, the outcast. Those who are blessed on the last day were not aware that they were serving Jesus (one gets the impression they may not even have known him). But they did love; they did do what Jesus did; they did do God's will, however unconsciously. And for this they are welcomed.

The Last Judgment — the judgment that was to come with the Eschaton — has already come. We do not have to wait for it. As John writes:

'he who rejects me (=Jesus) and refuses my words
has his judge already:
the word itself that I have spoken
will be his judge on the last day.'

(John 12:48)

Matthew is asking his readers to avoid silly and distracting speculations about the timing of the final manifestation of the Eschaton. Rather, they should set about the task of loving as Jesus loved, of caring for the oppressed as Jesus did, of serving all men, and giving their time and care to meet the needs of their fellow man. This is the meaning of life and the more man lives this way the sooner will be the establishment of the new heaven and the new earth.

There will be sufferings in our life, but, like those of Jesus which we are about to contemplate, they will end in glory if we persevere to the end in our faith in the Lord of history and in loving as Jesus loved.

*   *   *   *   *   *   *

Chapter 3
Jesus' last days

Mark 14:1-42
Matthew 26:1-46
Luke 22:1-46

a: **The final conspiracy to arrest Jesus**

MARK 14:1-2 (Compare Matthew 26:1-5 and Luke 22:1-2)
14 It was two days before the Passover and the feast of Unleavened Bread, and 1 the chief priests and the scribes were looking for a way to arrest Jesus by some trick and have him put to death. •For they said, 'It must not be during 2 the festivities, or there will be a disturbance among the people'.

Jesus died at the time of the celebration of the feast of the Passover, and the events of the last days of his life are placed by the Gospel-writers within the context of the themes and motifs of this feast. We refer the reader to the commentary on page 210 for a treatment of these. We are being prepared for another Exodus, another mighty intervention of God to redeem his people and establish a new covenant.

The Feast of Unleavened Bread (Mazzoth) was originally an agricultural feast celebrating the beginning of the grain harvest. It, too, was a spring festival (celebrated at the first full moon after the spring equinox) and ran for a week. It was combined with the feast of Passover and ran from the fifteenth day of the month, Nisan, to the twenty second day (cf Exodus 12:15-18).

The religious leaders were determined to have Jesus put to death before the feasts because they were afraid that he could be a rallying point for the pilgrims.

* * * * * * * *

Matthew 1 as Jesus speaking of his coming crucifixion (26:2 cf Matthew 20·19). The conspiracy takes place in the palace of the High Priest, Caiaphas (26:3).

* * * * * * * *

JOHN 11:55-57
The Jewish Passover drew near, and many of the country people who had 55 gone up to Jerusalem to purify themselves •looked out for Jesus, saying to one 56

another as they stood about in the Temple, 'What do you think? Will he come
57 to the festival or not?' •The chief priests and Pharisees had by now given their
orders: anyone who knew where he was must inform them so that they could
arrest him.

John records the meeting at which the Sanhedrin decided to kill Jesus (cf
•John 11:45-54, page 253).

* * * * * * * *

b: Jesus is anointed in preparation for his approaching death

MARK 14:3-9 (Compare Matthew 26:6-13)
3   Jesus was at Bethany in the house of Simon the leper; he was at dinner when
a woman came in with an alabaster jar of very costly ointment, pure nard. She
4 broke the jar and poured the ointment on his head. •Some who were there said
5 to one another indignantly, 'Why this waste of ointment? •Ointment like this
could have been sold for over three hundred denarii and the money given to the
6 poor'; and they were angry with her. •But Jesus said, 'Leave her alone. Why
are you upsetting her? What she has done for me is one of the good works.
7 You have the poor with you always, and you can be kind to them whenever you
8 wish, but you will not always have me. •She has done what was in her power to
9 do: she has anointed my body beforehand for its burial. •I tell you solemnly,
wherever throughout all the world the Good News is proclaimed, what she has
done will be told also, in remembrance of her.'

The contrast between this and the preceding scene is striking. While the
leaders are plotting to kill Jesus, a simple woman performs a strange service of
love. In the light of Jesus' death two days later this action was seen as prophetic,
and as indicating God's care for his Son. The woman, without realising it, was
preparing his body for burial (Mark 14:8).

The indignation of the by-standers (Matthew mentions that they were
'disciples' 26:8) is understandable. Jesus warns them that their criteria for judging
waste are inadequate. They judged her action solely from an economic point of
view; Jesus, as usual, saw her love and recognised in her action the presence of his
Father's will.

* * * * * * * *

The fact that Luke omits this episode, but has a very similar one occuring in
the house of another 'Simon' (Luke 7:36-50 compare Mark 14:3) leads some
scholars to suspect that we are dealing with the same event, and that Luke has
made use of a variant tradition.

* * * * * * * *

John, too, has a slightly different version:

JOHN 12:1-11
1 **12** Six days before the Passover, Jesus went to Bethany, where Lazarus
2   was, whom he had raised from the dead. •They gave a dinner for him
3 there; Martha waited on them and Lazarus was among those at table. •Mary

brought in a pound of very costly ointment, pure nard, and with it anointed the feet of Jesus, wiping them with her hair; the house was full of the scent of the ointment. •Then Judas Iscariot—one of his disciples, the man who was to betray 4 him—said, •'Why wasn't this ointment sold for three hundred denarii, and the 5 money given to the poor?' •He said this, not because he cared about the poor, 6 but because he was a thief; he was in charge of the common fund and used to help himself to the contributions. •So Jesus said, 'Leave her alone; she had to 7 keep this scent for the day of my burial. •You have the poor with you always, 8 you will not always have me.'

Meanwhile a large number of Jews heard that he was there and came not 9 only on account of Jesus but also to see Lazarus whom he had raised from the dead. •Then the chief priests decided to kill Lazarus as well, •since it was on his 10 11 account that many of the Jews were leaving them and believing in Jesus.

The basic elements are as in Mark and Matthew: the 'pure nard' (12:3 = Mark 14:5) the 'three hundred denarii' (12:5 = Mark 14:5), the objection and Jesus reply (12:5, 7-8 = Mark 14:5-8).

John links this story, as he linked the mention of the conspiracy (cf John 11:45), with the raising of Lazarus (12:2-3, 9-11). He has the woman 'anointing the feet of Jesus and wiping them with her hair' (12:3), which reminds us of Luke's episode (cf Luke 7:38). He also heightens the tension by mentioning Judas Iscariot and the imminent betrayal (12:4). He places the event prior to the entry into Jerusalem ('six days before the Passover' 12:1 as against Mark's 'two days' 14:1). Perhaps John wishes to use this scene to create a unit of the last week ('six days') of Jesus' life. The mood is one of betrayal, theft, political intrigue and death. It is also one of gentle love and gratitude. In spite of the gathering of the forces of evil:

'the house was full of the scent of the ointment.' (12:3)

The Father is present, and, through this woman, is caring for his Son.

c: **Judas betrays Jesus**

MARK 14:10-11 (Compare Matthew 26:14-16 and Luke 22:3-6)
Judas Iscariot, one of the Twelve, approached the chief priests with an offer 10 to hand Jesus over to them. •They were delighted to hear it, and promised to 11 give him money; and he looked for a way of betraying him when the opportunity should occur.

We can only speculate on the possible motives Judas had for betraying Jesus. John has hinted at the motive of greed by telling us that Judas was a thief (John 12:6); but Judas' treatment of the money he obtained for betraying Jesus (cf Matthew 27:3-10) indicates that we have to look for another motive. Perhaps Judas was hoping to force Jesus' hand and was expecting that Jesus, the Messiah, would be victorious and lead a successful uprising against the Romans. Whatever his reasons for betraying Jesus, Matthew indicates that he was bitterly disappointed at the outcome (cf 27:3-10 cf also Acts 1:16-20 for a variant tradition).

Mark's attention is not centred on Judas, but on Jesus whose bitter fate it was to be betrayed by one of his closest companions.

*   *   *   *   *   *   *   *

Matthew mentions that the chief priests paid Judas 'thirty silver pieces' (Matthew 26:16). This is an allusion to Exodus 21:32 where thirty silver pieces was laid down as the fixed price for the life of a slave. We are reminded of Jesus' own words:

> 'Anyone who wants to be first among you must be your slave, just as the Son of Man came, not to be served but to serve, and to give his life as a ransom for many.'
>
> *(Matthew 20:27-28)*

* * * * * * * *

LUKE prepares his readers for the imminent coming of the great Eschatological battle between Good and Evil. After the temptation in the desert Luke stated that 'the devil left him, to return at the appointed time' (Luke 4:13).

Now the appointed time has come, and:

'Satan entered into Judas' (Luke 22:3).

* * * * * * * *

d: The preparations for the paschal meal

MARK 14:12-16 (Compare Matthew 26:17-19 and Luke 22:7-13)

12   On the first day of Unleavened Bread, when the Passover lamb was sacrificed, his disciples said to him, 'Where do you want us to go and make the preparations
13   for you to eat the passover?' •So he sent two of his disciples, saying to them, 'Go into the city and you will meet a man carrying a pitcher of water. Follow him,
14   and say to the owner of the house which he enters, "The Master says: Where
15   is my dining room in which I can eat the passover with my disciples?" •He will show you a large upper room furnished with couches, all prepared. Make the
16   preparations for us there.' •The disciples set out and went to the city and found everything as he had told them, and prepared the Passover.

The episode with the man carrying a pitcher of water (Mark 14:13-16) is reminiscent of the earlier scene with the man and the donkeys at the time of Jesus' entry into Jerusalem (cf Mark 11:2-6). The dramatic impact is the same: we are reminded that, while Jesus may appear to be the victim of circumstances, God is in fact in command of the situation. It is God's will that is being effected in the events of Jesus' passion.

Mark is obviously determined that his readers see the following meal in the light of the Passover (14:12, 14:16). He is preparing us for the 'sacrifice' of the new Passover lamb.

e: Jesus identifies his betrayer

MARK 14:17-21 (Compare Matthew 26:20-25 and Luke 22:21-23)

17
18   When evening came he arrived with the Twelve. •And while they were at table eating, Jesus said, 'I tell you solemnly, one of you is about to betray
19   me, one of you eating with me'. •They were distressed and asked him, one after
20   another, 'Not I, surely?' •He said to them, 'It is one of the Twelve, one who is

21 dipping into the same dish with me. •Yes, the Son of Man is going to his fate, as the scriptures say he will, but alas for that man by whom the Son of Man is betrayed! Better for that man if he had never been born!'

Judas was first introduced by Mark as 'the man who was to betray him' (Mark 3:19), and Mark has just told us of the arrangement between Judas and the chief priests (Mark 14:10-11). Here he highlights the bitter fate of Jesus: the betrayal is occasioned by a meal that should have been a most intimate sharing between friends. We are reminded of the psalm:

'Even my closest and most trusted friend who shared my table rebels against me.'
(Psalm 41:9 also 55:12-14)

* * * * * * * *

f: **The new Passover. The celebration of the new Covenant, sealed by the blood of the new Passover Lamb.**

We shall break here with our usual practice and attend first to **Luke's** account. Mark and Matthew follow (pages 371-2).

LUKE 22:14-18
14   When the hour came he took his place at table, and the apostles with him.
15 And he said to them, 'I have longed to eat this passover with you before I suffer;
16 because, I tell you, I shall not eat it again until it is fulfilled in the kingdom of God'.
17   Then, taking a cup, he gave thanks and said, 'Take this and share it among
18 you, •because from now on, I tell you, I shall not drink wine until the kingdom of God comes'.

There is a finality about his meal. It is a Passover meal, a meal remembering God's redeeming act when he led his people from slavery in Egypt to the freedom of the Promised Land. It is also the last meal Jesus will have with his 'apostles' until the Passover is:

'fulfilled in the kingdom of God' (22:16)

Luke has been preparing us for the coming of the kingdom all through his Gospel. It is now imminent. The new Passover Lamb is about to be slain. God is about to intervene and liberate his people. He is about to establish the Messianic kingdom.

Having stated that the next meal Jesus has with his friends will be in the kingdom, and the next wine he shares will be in the kingdom, Luke immediately adds:

LUKE 22:19-20
19   Then he took some bread, and when he had given thanks, broke it and gave it to them, saying, 'This is my body which will be given for you; do this as a memorial
20 of me'. •He did the same with the cup after supper, and said, 'This cup is the new covenant in my blood which will be poured out for you.

This is the new meal, the meal shared by Jesus with his disciples 'in the kingdom'. Like the Passover meal it is held this night in anticipation of the morrow when God will redeem his people. Like the Passover meal it is to be repeated 'as a memorial of me' (22:19). It is the new Passover meal; it is also the new meal of the Covenant.

The first Covenant of Sinai was sealed, symbolically, with the blood of sacrificed animals and celebrated in a meal. As we read the account from the Book of Exodus, notice the parallels with this new sacrifice and new Covenant meal.

'Moses went and told the people all the commands of Yahweh and all the ordinances. In answer, all the people said with one voice, "We shall observe all the commands that Yahweh has decreed". Moses put all the commands of Yahweh into writing, and early next morning he built an altar at the foot of the mountain, with twelve standing-stones for the twelve tribes of Israel. Then he directed certain young Israelites to offer holocausts and to immolate bullocks to Yahweh as communion sacrifices. Half of the blood Moses took up and put into basins, the other half he cast on the altar. And taking the Book of the Covenant he read it to the listening people and they said, "We will observe all that Yahweh has decreed; we will obey". Then Moses took the blood and cast it towards the people. "This", he said, "is the blood of the Covenant that Yahweh has made with you, containing all these rules".

Moses went up with Aaron, Nadab and Abihu and seventy elders of Israel. They saw the God of Israel, beneath whose feet there was, it seemed, a sapphire pavement pure as the heavens themselves. He laid no hand on these notables of the sons of Israel: they gazed on God. They ate and they drank.'

(Exodus 24:3-11)

The author of the Letter to the Hebrews recalls this ritual celebration (Hebrews 9:18-21). He also states that the old Covenant was imperfect, and quotes Jeremiah who looked forward to the establishment of a new Covenant (Hebrews 8:8-12 = Jeremiah 31:31-34). This new Covenant was sealed by Jesus in his blood:

'He has made his appearance once and for all, now at the end of the last age, to do away with sin by sacrificing himself.'

(Hebrews 9:26)

The Last Supper anticipates this sacrifice. It is a ritual meal held in anticipation of God's redeeming act. It is a meal celebrating the 'new Covenant in my blood' (Luke 22:20). In this meal the apostles:

'gazed on God. They ate and they drank'.

(Exodus 24:11)

The earliest extant account we have of the Last Supper is in Paul's First Letter to the Corinthians, written from Ephesus in about 54 A.D. Paul writes:

'For this is what I received from the Lord, and in turn passed on to you: that on the same night that he was betrayed, the Lord Jesus took some bread, and thanked God for it and broke it, and he said, "This is my body which is for you; do this as a memorial of me". In the same way he took the cup after supper and said, "This cup is the new convenant in my blood. Whenever you drink it, do this as a memorial of me! Until the Lord comes, therefore, every time you eat this bread and drink this cup, you are proclaiming his death." '

(1 Corinthians 11:23-26)

The meal is a meal held in anticipation: anticipation of the morrow when Jesus, the Passover Lamb, will give his life for men; and anticipation of the final manifestation of the Eschaton, when the kingdom of God will be manifest. The meal is a meal that proclaims the death of Jesus, 'until the Lord comes' (Corinthians 11:26).

This meal is the Messianic banquet to which the prophets looked forward:

'On this mountain,
Yahweh Sabaoth will prepare for all peoples
a banquet of rich food, a banquet of fine wines,
of food rich and juicy, of fine strained wines.'

(Isaiah 25:6)

The nourishment of this meal is the nourishment of the 'body and blood of the Lord' (1 Corinthians 11:27).

It is a meal held in anticipation. It is a meal held in memory. It is, above all, a meal that celebrates the real presence of Jesus with his people. It is a meal shared by Jesus' disciples *with Jesus*.

It is a ritual celebration, in symbol, of what John writes:

'I tell you most solemnly,
if you do not eat the flesh of the Son of Man
and drink his blood,
you will not have life in you.
Anyone who does eat my flesh and drink my blood
has eternal life.'

(John 6:53-54)

As Wisdom says:

'Come and eat my bread,
drink the wine I have prepared.'

(Proverbs 9:5)

Jesus is inviting his friends, on the last night of his life, to share this meal with him, and to continue to share it after his death, as a statement of their commitment to him and their faith that he is still with them. This is no ordinary meal. This is no man-made wishful-thinking dramatic play. When we eat this bread and drink this cup, says Paul,we must be careful to:

'recognise the Body'

(1 Corinthians 11:29)

In fact the early church was faithful to Jesus' request and celebrated this memorial meal on the first day of the week, in memory of the resurrection of Jesus and as a statement of belief in his continued presence nourishing his community (cf Acts 2:42, 2:46, 20:7, 20:11, 27:35; Luke 24:30, 24:35; 1 Corinthians 10:16-22, 11:17-34). It is still celebrated in the Church as the great 'Eucharist' (= 'Thanksgiving') Prayer.

Luke follows his account of the meal with this statement:

LUKE 22:24-30

A dispute arose also between them about which should be reckoned the 24 greatest, •but he said to them, 'Among pagans it is the kings who lord it over them, 25 and those who have authority over them are given the title Benefactor. •This must 26 not happen with you. No; the greatest among you must behave as if he were the youngest, the leader as if he were the one who serves. •For who is the greater: 27 the one at table or the one who serves? The one at table, surely? Yet here am I among you as one who serves!

'You are the men who have stood by me faithfully in my trials; •and now 28 29 I confer a kingdom on you, just as my Father conferred one on me: •you will 30 eat and drink at my table in my kingdom, and you will sit on thrones to judge the twelve tribes of Israel.

(Luke 22:30 compare Matthew 19:28 page 306
Luke 22:24-27 compare Mark 10:42-45 and Matthew 20:24-28 page 310)

Luke has transferred this dispute from an earlier context (cf Mark 10:35-45). He inserts it here because it emphasizes Jesus' isolation, and the failure, even to the end, of his closest friends to understand his basic message. It also demonstrates the essential nature of the sacrifice of Jesus. He is the servant who is giving his life for his brothers.

Luke adds:

'**Now** I confer a kingdom on you' (22:29). The time of the Eschaton has come. This meal, held in anticipation, is the Messianic Banquet, to be eaten in the kingdom. The last judgment is about to occur and they will be with Jesus, judging the world (cf Matthew 19:28).

LUKE 22:31-39

'Simon, Simon! Satan, you must know, has got his wish to sift you all like 31 wheat; •but I have prayed for you, Simon, that your faith may not fail, and once 32 you have recovered, you in your turn must strengthen your brothers.' •'Lord,' 33 he answered 'I would be ready to go to prison with you, and to death.' •Jesus 34 replied, 'I tell you, Peter, by the time the cock crows today you will have denied three times that you know me'.

He said to them, 'When I sent you out without purse or haversack or sandals, 35 were you short of anything? •'No' they said. He said to them, 'But now if you have 36 a purse, take it; if you have a haversack, do the same; if you have no sword, sell your cloak and buy one, •because I tell you these words of scripture have to 37 be fulfilled in me: *He let himself be taken for a criminal.*"Yes, what scripture says about me is even now reaching its fulfilment.' •'Lord,' they said 'there are two 38 swords here now.' He said to them, 'That is enough!'

He then left to make his way as usual to the Mount of Olives, with the 39 disciples following.

(a: Isaiah 53:12)

The meal ends on a tragic note. Jesus is about to face the Eschatological battle. This is the point of the '**now**' (22:36). They will need every resource they have to face the powers of darkness. Jesus is the Suffering Servant, going to his death. Luke quotes one verse from the fourth song of the Servant of Yahweh (Luke 22:37). He wants the reader to meditate on the whole of the song at this stage. The song can be found in Isaiah 52:13 — 53:12. The New Testament frequently uses this song to highlight the meaning of the death and resurrection of Jesus.

'What scripture says of me is even **now** reaching its fulfilment.'

(Luke 22:37)

The disciples, typically, fail to understand Jesus (Luke 22:38). Moreover, Luke prepares his reader for the fact that, in this battle, Jesus is to be alone. Not even his closest friends will stand by him. At the same time there is already the promise of forgiveness and the faithful trust of Jesus who prays for Peter and, even in the face of imminent denial, says to him:

'once you have recovered, you in your turn must strengthen your brothers.' (22:32)

* * * * * * * *

Mark and **Matthew** give a much briefer account of the last Supper.

The Supper:

MARK 14:22-25 (Compare Matthew 26:26-29)
22   And as they were eating he took some bread, and when he had said the blessing
23   he broke it and gave it to them. 'Take it,' he said 'this is my body.' •Then he took
     a cup, and when he had returned thanks he gave it to them, and all drank from
24   it, •and he said to them, 'This is my blood, the blood of the covenant, which is
25   to be poured out for many. •I tell you solemnly, I shall not drink any more wine
     until the day I drink the new wine in the kingdom of God.'

For commentary we refer the reader to Luke 22:19-20, pages 367-369.

g: The blindness of the disciples. Jesus promises to call them again after his Resurrection

MARK 14:26-31 (Compare Matthew 26:30-35)
26
27   After psalms had been sung they left for the Mount of Olives. •And Jesus
     said to them, 'You will all lose faith, for the scripture says: *I shall strike*
28   *the shepherd and the sheep will be scattered,*[a] •however after my resurrection I shall
29
30   go before you to Galilee'. •Peter said, 'Even if all lose faith, I will not'. •And
     Jesus said to him, 'I tell you solemnly, this day, this very night, before
31   the cock crows twice, you will have disowned me three times'. •But he repeated
     still more earnestly, 'If I have to die with you, I will never disown you'. And
     they all said the same.

(a: Zechariah 13:7)

The disciples concluded their meal in the traditional way, by chanting the Hallel (Psalms 113-118, cf Mark 14:26).

Jesus refers to Zechariah (Mark 14:27 = Zechariah 13:7). We quoted at length from this prophet when we were commenting on the entry of Jesus into Jerusalem and his clearing of the Temple (cf Mark 11:1-19). Zechariah speaks of the final ordeal which must precede the dawning of the Messianic Age and the inauguration of the new Covenant. This ordeal will begin when God's representative, the one whom God has appointed as shepherd and leader of his people, will be struck. Jesus is telling his disciples that the ordeal is imminent. At the same time he leaves them in no doubt as to the outcome, by immediately referring to his resurrection (14:28).

It was in Galilee that Jesus first called his disciples (cf Mark 1:16). Frequently throughout the Gospel Mark has shown us that the disciples failed to understand Jesus and lacked faith in him. But each time, Jesus renewed his call, thus demonstrating the faithful and constant love of God. We might recall Mark 4:13 in relation to the parables, or Mark 4:40 and the calming of the storm; also Mark

7:52 where the disciples failed to grasp the message of the miracle of the loaves, and Mark 8:18-21 where Mark expresses the exasperation Jesus felt at the blindness of his friends. The healing of the deaf man (Mark 7:31-37) and the blind man of Bethsaida (Mark 8:22-26) demonstrate the power of God to renew life in men, in spite of their inability to hear and to see him.

Each time Jesus touches on the subject of his own Passion, his disciples fail to understand him (cf Mark 8:33, 9:33-40, 10:35-45). The curing of the blind man of Jericho dramatises again the renewal of the call, for the man does 'follow him along the way' (Mark 10:51).

The final hour is imminent. The disciples, once again, fail to understand Jesus; they fail to believe in him. But he cannot fail, and, after his Resurrection, he promises to go ahead of them into Galilee where he will call them as he called them before (Mark 14:28).

h: **Jesus faces his bitter struggle alone:**

MARK 14:32-42 (Compare Matthew 26:36-46 and Luke 22:40-46)

They came to a small estate called Gethsemane, and Jesus said to his disciples, 32 'Stay here while I pray'. •Then he took Peter and James and John with him. 33 And a sudden fear came over him, and great distress. •And he said to them, 'My 34 soul is sorrowful to the point of death. Wait here, and keep awake.' •And going 35 on a little further he threw himself on the ground and prayed that, if it were possible, this hour might pass him by. •'Abba (Father)!' he said 'Everything 36 is possible for you. Take this cup away from me. But let it be as you, not I, would have it.' •He came back and found them sleeping, and he said to Peter, 'Simon, 37 are you asleep? Had you not the strength to keep awake one hour? •You should 38 be awake, and praying not to be put to the test. The spirit is willing, but the flesh is weak.' •Again he went away and prayed, saying the same words. •And $\frac{39}{40}$ once more he came back and found them sleeping, their eyes were so heavy; and they could find no answer for him. •He came back a third time and said to them, 41 'You can sleep on now and take your rest. It is all over. The hour has come. Now the Son of Man is to be betrayed into the hands of sinners. •Get up! Let us go! 42 My betrayer is close at hand already.'

'Gethsemane' (14:32) means 'oil-press'. The estate lay in the Kedron Valley on the lower slopes of the Mount of Olives, facing Jerusalem. (Luke, preferring the association of Jesus' prayer with the mountain itself, omits mention of the estate.)

'Peter and James and John' (14:33) were chosen to be with Jesus when he raised the daughter of Jairus to life (cf Mark 5:37) and when he was on the mountain of Transfiguration (cf Mark 9:2).

Mark uses an extremely powerful word for what happened to Jesus: the Greek word 'ekthambeisthai', translated here 'a sudden fear came over him' (14:33). The word indicates a profound and sudden shock experienced by a person when events take a sudden turn for the worse, a turn that is not expected or prepared for. Jesus is portrayed as experiencing confusion and restlessness. He desperately needs his friends. Three times (the number expressing perseverance) he prays and three times he comes back to his disciples. But they cannot cope, and he is utterly alone.

We are reminded of the comments made by the author of the Letter to the Hebrews:

> 'It is not as if we had a high priest who was incapable of feeling our weaknesses with us; but we have one who has been tempted in every way that we are, though he is without sin.'
>
> *(Hebrews 4:15)*

> 'During his life on earth, he offered up prayer and entreaty, aloud and in silent tears, to the one who had the power to save him out of death, and he submitted so humbly that his prayer was heard. Although he was Son, he learned to obey through suffering'.
>
> *(Hebrews 5:7-8)*

Luke adds a detail of his own, the better to bring out the parallel between this scene and the one in which Jesus was transfigured on the mountain of prayer (cf Luke 9:28-38):

> 'Then an angel appeared to him, coming from heaven to give him strength. In his anguish he prayed even more earnestly, and his sweat fell to the ground like great drops of blood.'
>
> *(Luke 22:43-44)*

Jesus was not utterly alone, even in this agony: his Father never abandoned him. His flesh was weak, but the spirit of his Father was with him, and as he said to the disciples: 'the spirit is willing' (Mark 14:38). God was there for him, and would have been there for the disciples had they prayed:

> 'God, create a clean heart in me,
> put into me a new and constant spirit,
> do not banish me from your presence,
> do not deprive me of your holy spirit.'
>
> *(Psalm 51:11)*

The agony scene ends on a note of peace. The conflict is resolved and Jesus goes to meet his betrayer as the master of the situation.

* * * * * * * *

The third and final stage of Jesus' ministry ends in the agony. Jesus is alone with his Father in prayer. Our brother, he knows our weakness; but he is faithful in his trust of his Father and determined to do his Father's will. He is determined to continue to give his 'flesh, for the life of the world' (John 6:51) whatever the cost to himself.

John sums up Jesus' attitude beautifully when he has Jesus say:

> 'Now my soul is troubled.
> What shall I say: Father, save me from this hour?
> But it was for this very reason that I have come to this hour.
> Father, glorify your name! '
>
> *(John 12:27)*

Jesus did not want to die (Mark 14:36), but he was able to see, even in his death, a statement of the faithful love of his Father. It was this love that Jesus wanted so much to show. This is what he meant by glorifying the name of his Father.

* * * * * * * *

BOOK 6

Fidelity to Love

FOREWORD

This Book is devoted entirely to John.

In the first half of his Gospel (Chapter 1-12), sometimes called the 'Book of Signs', John selects a scene from the tradition and then proceeds to draw out, in a lengthy discourse, its significance for the life of the Christian. In the second half (Chapter 13-21), sometimes called the 'Book of Glory', he reverses this process. He relates the scenes of the suffering, death and resurrection of Jesus only after he has first meditated on their significance. He wants to prepare the reader to approach the sacred mysteries in the proper manner.

It is this meditation that makes up the matter of this Book. We have presented the whole Book in one single chapter, for it all occurs at the last supper, the Eucharistic meal that is the ritual expression of the mystery of Jesus' death and resurrection. We have divided the chapter into four sub-sections according to John's own division. First there is the supper itself; then follow two discourses; finally there is Jesus' priestly prayer.

Chapter 1
The last supper

John Chapters 13-17

1: **The Last Supper** — John Chapter 13

a: JOHN 13:1-20

1 **13** It was before the festival of the Passover, and Jesus knew that the hour had come for him to pass from this world to the Father. He had always loved those who were his in the world, but now he showed how perfect his love was.

2 They were at supper, and the devil had already put it into the mind of
3 Judas Iscariot son of Simon, to betray him. •Jesus knew that the Father had put everything into his hands, and that he had come from God and was returning
4 to God, •and he got up from table, removed his outer garment and, taking a
5 towel, wrapped it round his waist; •he then poured water into a basin and began to wash the disciples' feet and to wipe them with the towel he was wearing.

6 He came to Simon Peter, who said to him, 'Lord, are you going to wash my
7 feet?' •Jesus answered, 'At the moment you do not know what I am doing, but
8 later you will understand'. •'Never!' said Peter 'You shall never wash my feet.' Jesus replied, 'If I do not wash you, you can have nothing in common with me'.
9 'Then, Lord,' said Simon Peter 'not only my feet, but my hands and my head
10 as well!' •Jesus said, 'No one who has taken a bath needs washing, he is clean
11 all over. You too are clean, though not all of you are.' •He knew who was going to betray him, that was why he said, 'though not all of you are'.

12 When he had washed their feet and put on his clothes again he went back
13 to the table. 'Do you understand' he said 'what I have done to you? •You call
14 me Master and Lord, and rightly; so I am. •If I, then, the Lord and Master,
15 have washed your feet, you should wash each other's feet. •I have given you an example so that you may copy what I have done to you.

16 'I tell you most solemnly,
no servant is greater than his master,
no messenger is greater than the man who sent him.

17 'Now that you know this, happiness will be yours if you behave accordingly.
18 I am not speaking about all of you: I know the ones I have chosen; but what scripture says must be fulfilled: *Someone who shares my table rebels against me.*[a]

19 'I tell you this now, before it happens,
so that when it does happen

you may believe that I am He.
20 I tell you most solemnly,
whoever welcomes the one I send welcomes me,
and whoever welcomes me welcomes the one who sent me.'*(a: Psalm 41:9)*

Once again, John reminds his readers of the approach of the Passover (cf John 11:55 and 12:1). Jesus' hour — the hour we have been awaiting (cf John 2:4, 7:30, 8:20, 12:23, 12:27) — has at last come. It is the:

'hour for him to pass from this world to the Father' (13:1).

Jesus is the new Passover Lamb (cf John 1:29, 1:36, 19:36) who is about to shed his blood so that men might pass over from slavery to freedom, from darkness to light, from death to life.

From the beginning, the reader is prepared for Jesus' approaching death. Three times Jesus' imminent betrayal by Judas is mentioned (13:2, 13:10-11, 13:18). In betraying Jesus, Judas is the instrument of the 'devil' (13:2, cf John 6:70-71). The devil, the 'prince of this world' (John 12:31) is about to unleash all the powers of darkness against the Lord's anointed one (compare Luke 22:3).

Jesus performs a simple ritual: the washing of his disciple's feet. Peter misunderstands him, thinking this is just another ritual purification (John 13:8-10). Jesus explains the real meaning of his action (John 13:13-15). Dressed like a slave (John 13:4), Jesus is serving his disciples. John wants his readers to see the death of Jesus in this light. It is primarily an act of love (John 13:1). Jesus was 'sent' (John 13:20) to manifest the love of God by giving his life in service of men. He washes their feet to illustrate this and to give them an example (John 13:15). They too are to love one another; they too are to give their lives in service of each other. He is commissioning them to carry on his work (John 13:16 and 13:20, compare Luke 22:24-27 page 369).

Once again John uses the mysterious phrase 'I am He' (John 13:19, cf John 8:24, 8:28, 8:58). He wants us to hear the word of God when we listen to the word of Jesus; he wants us to see God when we watch Jesus. In washing the feet of his disciples Jesus is showing us the nature of the true, living God.

b: JOHN 13:21-30

21 Having said this, Jesus was troubled in spirit and declared, 'I tell you most **22** solemnly, one of you will betray me'. •The disciples looked at one another, **23** wondering which he meant. •The disciple Jesus loved was reclining next **24** **25** to Jesus; •Simon Peter signed to him and said, 'Ask who it is he means', •so **26** leaning back on Jesus' breast he said, 'Who is it, Lord?' •'It is the one' replied Jesus 'to whom I give the piece of bread that I shall dip in the dish.' He dipped **27** the piece of bread and gave it to Judas son of Simon Iscariot. •At that instant, after Judas had taken the bread, Satan entered him. Jesus then said, 'What you **28** are going to do, do quickly'. •None of the others at table understood the reason **29** he said this. •Since Judas had charge of the common fund, some of them thought Jesus was telling him, 'Buy what we need for the festival', or telling him to give **30** something to the poor. •As soon as Judas had taken the piece of bread he went out. Night had fallen.

This is the 'night' (John 13:30) that Jesus had spoken of earlier:

'the night will soon be here when no one can work'. *(John 9:4)*

It is the night of the Eschatological battle, the night when the powers of darkness ('Satan' John 13:27) will try to overpower the light (cf John 1:5).

John speaks here of the 'disciple Jesus loved' (13:23). This expression will occur again: John uses it of the disciple who was standing beside the cross (John 19:26), of the disciple who went with Peter to the tomb (John 20:2), and of the disciple who recognised the risen Jesus by the lakeside (21:7, 21:20).

The disciple Jesus loved is responsible for the Gospel (John 21:24) which we know as the 'Gospel according to John'. He seems to have been the leading figure in the community within which the Gospel and the Letters emerged (cf pages 46-47).

c: JOHN 13:31-38
31   When he had gone Jesus said:

> 'Now has the Son of Man been glorified,
> and in him God has been glorified.
32   If God has been glorified in him,
> God will in turn glorify him in himself,
> and will glorify him very soon.
33   'My little children,
> I shall not be with you much longer.
> You will look for me,
> and, as I told the Jews,
> where I am going,
> you cannot come.
34   I give you a new commandment:
> love one another;
> just as I have loved you,
> you also must love one another.
35   By this love you have for one another,
> everyone will know that you are my disciples.'

36   Simon Peter said, 'Lord, where are you going?' Jesus replied, 'Where I am
37 going you cannot follow me now; you will follow me later'. •Peter said to him,
38 'Why can't I follow you now? I will lay down my life for you.' •'Lay down your life for me?' answered Jesus. 'I tell you most solemnly, before the cock crows you will have disowned me three times.

Judas may betray him; Peter may deny him; Jesus may be left alone to face the powers of hell. But:

> 'he who sent me is with me,
> he has not left me to myself,
> for I always do what pleases him.'
> *(John 8:29)*

The hour of darkness is the hour of Jesus' glorification (John 13:31-32), and it is imminent (13:32).

In his account of the Last Supper, John, like the Synoptics has spoken of Judas and Peter. He has not gone into the Passover symbolism of the meal, as do the Synoptics. Rather he has concentrated on Jesus' action of washing the disciples' feet and on the commandment of love (John 13:34-35).

In his First Letter, John explains in what sense the commandment is new:

'My dear people,
this is not a new commandment that I am writing to you,
but an old commandment
that you were given from the beginning,
the original commandment which was the message brought to you.
Yet, in another way, what I am writing to you,
and what is being carried out in your lives as it was in his,
is a new commandment;
because the night is over
and the real light is already shining.'

(1 John 2:7-8)

The commandment to love is the word of God that summoned man from the beginning:

'Something which has existed since the beginning,
that we have heard,
and we have seen with our own eyes;
that we have watched and touched with our hands:
the Word who is life —
this is our subject.'

(1 John 1:1)

When God revealed himself to Moses, he did so as a God of compassion and love. His word was a challenge to Moses to love his brothers and deliver them from bondage. God's word was always like this. The commandment is 'new' because the word has now become flesh (John 1:14). John and the others have heard the word with their own ears. They have seen it with their own eyes. They have watched the word and touched it with their hands. What is new is that the word of God has now been answered by man — by the man Jesus — in a complete response that has released in the world the power of God, that has demonstrated to man the possibility of responding to God's call. The commandment is new because now man has seen that it can be answered. Now the night is over and the real light is already shining.

It is love that is to be the sign of the disciple (John 13:35). As Jesus said:

'If you make my word your home
you will indeed be my disciples,
and you will learn the truth
and the truth will make you free.'

(John 8:31)

In the Last Supper, Jesus is commissioning his disciples to make his word their home; that is, to love one another as he has loved them.

John's account of the Last Supper, like that of the Synoptics, leaves the reader with Jesus facing the bitter struggle against evil, and facing it alone. Before taking us with Jesus on his journey to the cross, John gives us the fruit of his meditation on its meaning. He tries to penetrate into the heart of Jesus and the heart of his mission. He does this in two separate discourses (Chapter 14 and Chapters 15 to 16) and in a prayer (Chapter 17).

2: **The First Supper Discourse** — (John Chapter 14)

JOHN 14:1-4

14 'Do not let your hearts be troubled.   1
Trust in God still, and trust in me.
There are many rooms in my Father's house;   2
if there were not, I should have told you.
I am going now to prepare a place for you,
and after I have gone and prepared you a place,   3
I shall return to take you with me;
so that where I am
you may be too.
You know the way to the place where I am going.'   4

John remembered how troubled their hearts were that night. He remembered, too, the strength communicated to them by Jesus, because he never lost trust in the Father who sustained him. The most profound source of fear is the thought that, however great may be the love of God, it is not for me. To cope with this fear men invent all kinds of false securities: if you belong to a certain race you will be saved; if you belong to a certain religious group you will be saved.

The New Testament insists on the universal nature of God's love:

'God wants everyone to be saved and reach full knowledge of the truth.'
(1 Timothy 2:4)

'It is never the will of your Father in heaven that one of these little ones should be lost.'
(Matthew 18:14)

God's love is not for a select few; it is for the world (John 4:42, 3:16, 6:51). So there are:

'many rooms in my Father's house.'
(John 14:2)

God's love does not force man. It calls him, challenges him, summons him to respond as a free person. Jesus has shown him how to respond (John 14:4), but man can choose to respond or not to respond. The word challenges him to love. If he chooses to listen to the word he will enjoy the same intimacy with God that Jesus enjoyed; he will be where Jesus is:

'*everyone* who believes may have eternal life'
(John 3:15)

'*whoever* listens to my words,
and believes in the one who sent me,
has eternal life.'
(John 5:24)

'*whoever* comes to me,
I shall not turn him away.'
(John 6:37)

'*whoever* keeps my word
will never see death'
(John 8:51)

'*anyone* who enters through me will be safe'
(John 10:9)

'If *anyone* believes in me, even though he dies he will live'
(John 11:25)

The disciples are not to be afraid; they are to keep their trust in God and in Jesus. He promised:

'When I am lifted up from the earth,
I shall draw all men to myself.'

(John 12:32)

He is now going to do this (John 14:2); he is going to his Father. He will return (John 14:3). His Spirit will be with them, drawing them into intimate union with his Father, making it possible for them to love each other as Jesus loved them — making it possible for them to believe in him and to answer the word of God.

The place Jesus is preparing is a place with God. He is not primarily referring to a place beyond death, a place we might call 'heaven'. That is part of the mystery (cf John 11:25). He is referring primarily to this world. Jesus had a place in this world: he was the saviour of the world, the place where God's love was manifest. He is about to pass over from this world to the Father (cf John 13:1); but he is coming back so that his disciples can share his life, his mission, his work; so that they in their turn can be saviours of the world. It is this kind of love that will be the sign that they are truly his disciples (John 13:35). It is this kind of love that will be the sign that Jesus is still living in them.

JOHN 14:5-6

Thomas said, 'Lord, we do not know where you are going, so how can we know the way?' •Jesus said:

'I am the Way, the Truth and the Life.
No one can come to the Father except through me.

Jesus is the Way. We will be united to the Father if we follow Jesus in prayerful obedience to the will of God, carried out in humble service of our fellow man. Jesus is about to demonstrate this way by giving his life for them.

Jesus is the Truth. He is God's fidelity to his promises (cf John 1:14). Jesus demonstrates the fact that God is faithful.

Jesus is the Life. Jesus is the 'Word who is life' (1 John 1:1). He demonstrates what it is like to 'live to the full' (John 10:10). He shows us how to live in intimate union with the living God and in intimate union with our fellow man.

The only way to the Father is the way Jesus showed: the way of love. Moreover he made of this old commandment a new commandment, because he demonstrated that it is possible for us to listen to God and to unite ourselves to God's liberating action in the world.

Let us not distract ourselves by trying to work out the implications of this for those who have never known Jesus. It is not up to us to place limits on God's love or on the ways in which the glorified Jesus draws all men to himself. The fact is that for those of us who have known Jesus there is no other way to God than the way of self-giving, life-giving service, and it is Jesus who has shown us how to live this way. Our task is to be grateful for the privilege and to answer the summons to love one another as Jesus loved us. This is his mission to us.

JOHN 14:7-11

If you know me, you know my Father too.
From this moment you know him and have seen him.'

Philip said, 'Lord, let us see the Father and then we shall be satisfied'. 8
'Have I been with you all this time, Philip,' said Jesus to him 'and you still do 9
not know me?

> 'To have seen me is to have seen the Father,
> so how can you say, "Let us see the Father"?
> Do you not believe   10
> that I am in the Father and the Father is in me?
> The words I say to you I do not speak as from myself:
> it is the Father, living in me, who is doing this work.
> You must believe me when I say   11
> that I am in the Father and the Father is in me;
> believe it on the evidence of this work, if for no other reason.

We should never get used to the amazing claim that John is making here. To
see God is the ultimate aim of every man. It is voiced beautifully by the Psalmist:

'I will sing, I will play for Yahweh!
Yahweh, hear my voice as I cry!
Pity me! Answer me!
My heart has said of you, "Seek his face".
Yahweh, I do seek your face; do not hide your face from me.'   *(Psalm 27:7-8)*

Moses wanted so much to see the face of God, but it was not possible:

'Moses said to Yahweh, "See, you yourself say to me, 'Make the people go on', but
you do not let me know who it is you will send with me. Yet you yourself have said, 'I
know you by name and you have won my favour'. If indeed I have won your favour,
please show me your ways, so that I can understand you and win your favour.
Remember, too, that this nation is your own people."
   Yahweh replied, "I myself will go with you and I will give you rest".
   Moses said, "If you are not going with us yourself, do not make us leave this
place. By what means can it be known that I, I and my people, have won your favour,
if not by your going with us? By this we shall be marked out, I and my people, from all
the people on the face of the earth".
   Yahweh said to Moses, "Again I will do what you have asked, because you have
won my favour and because I know you by name".
   Moses said, "Show me your glory, I beg you". And he said, "I will let all my
splendour pass in front of you, and I will pronounce before you the name Yahweh. I
have compassion on whom I will, and I show pity to whom I please. You cannot see
my face", he said, "for man cannot see me and live". And Yahweh said, "Here is a
place beside me. You must stand on the rock, and when my glory passes by, I will put
you in a cleft of the rock and shield you with my hand while I pass by. Then I will take
my hand away and you shall see the back of me; but my face is not to be seen".'
                                                                    (Exodus 33:12-23)

Elijah, too, the greatest of the prophets, wanted to see God and he journeyed
forty days and forty nights through the desert to come to the mountain where
God appeared to Moses. But he too was unable to see God face to face.

'Elijah was told, "Go out and stand on the mountain before Yahweh". Then Yahweh
himself went by. There came a mighty wind, so strong it tore the mountains and
shattered the rocks before Yahweh. But Yahweh was not in the wind. After the wind
came an earthquake. But Yahweh was not in the earthquake. After the earthquake
came a fire. But Yahweh was not in the fire. And after the fire came the sound
of a gentle breeze. And when Elijah heard this, he covered his face with his cloak and
went out and stood at the entrance of the cave.'   *(1 Kings 19:11-13)*

We are reminded of the scene of the Transfiguration as recorded by the Synoptics. Once again we are on a mountain. Moses and Elijah are both there. This time they are looking on the face of God as they speak with Jesus who is resplendent with God's glory (cf Mark 9:2-8). John is making the same claim in the present text: 'to have seen me is to have seen the Father' (14:9 cf John 12:45). This was the claim he made in the Prologue:

'We saw his glory,
the glory that is his as the only Son of the Father,
full of faithful love.' (1:14)

'No one has ever seen God;
it is the only Son, who is nearest to the Father's heart,
who has made him known'. (1:18)

Paul makes the same claim when he writes:

'It is the same God that said, "Let there be light shining out of darkness", who has shone in our minds to radiate the light of the knowledge of God's glory, the glory on the face of Christ'.

(2 Corinthians 4:6)

The disciple 'knows' the Father by knowing the Son (cf John 10:14). He 'sees' the Father by seeing the Son.

The proof of this is in Jesus' work (John 14:10-11):

'these same works of mine
testify that the Father has sent me'

(John 5:36)

'the works I do in my Father's name are my witness'

(John 10:25)

'If I am not doing my Father's work,
there is no need to believe me;
but if I am doing it,
then even if you refuse to believe in me,
at least believe in the work I do;
then you will know for sure
that the Father is in me and I am in the Father.'

(John 10:37-38)

When Yahweh passed before Moses, he revealed himself as:

'a God of tenderness and compassion, slow to anger,
rich in kindness and faithfulness'

(Exodus 34:6)

Jesus, by his actions, revealed himself as full of this same enduring love (John 1:14, 1:17). Especially in his life-giving act on the cross does Jesus reveal the face of God.

JOHN 14:12-14

I tell you most solemnly, 12
whoever believes in me
will perform the same works as I do myself,
he will perform even greater works,
because I am going to the Father.
Whatever you ask for in my name I will do, 13

> so that the Father may be glorified in the Son.
>
> 14   If you ask for anything in my name,
>
> I will do it.

Once again John is speaking not from theory but from experience. Measured by human standards, many of Jesus' disciples did in fact achieve more than Jesus achieved. What he did he did because of the intimate union he had with his Father:

> 'The Son can do nothing by himself;
> he can do only what he sees the Father doing:
> and whatever the Father does, the Son does too.
> For the Father loves the Son
> and he shows him everything he does himself,
> and he will show him even greater things than these,
> works that will astonish you.'
>
> *(John 5:20)*

The disciples will do even greater works than Jesus because they will share in this same intimacy. In fact it will be Jesus living in them through his Spirit who will achieve these works through them. John will develop this theme in his parable of the vine and the branches (15:1-9).

Paul witnesses to the same faith when he writes:

> 'We, with our unveiled faces reflecting like mirrors the brightness of the Lord, all grow brighter and brighter as we are turned into the image that we reflect; this is the work of the Lord who is Spirit.'
>
> *(2 Corinthians 3:18,*

And again to the Galatians:

> 'I have been crucified with Christ and I live now not with my own life but with the life of Christ who lives in me.'
>
> *(Galatians 2:20)*

The fact that Jesus goes to the Father (14:12) means that he can send his Spirit from the Father and draw us into close intimacy with God. This will make it possible for the disciples to be instruments of God's love and peace to others, and so carry on the mission of Jesus.

Hence the statement on prayer (John 14:13-14). The world is to be transformed by their response to God's word. It is the love of the disciples that is to bring about the new heaven and the new earth. Jesus has shown that it can be done. He, the living and risen Jesus, will do it through them by the power of his Spirit (compare Matthew 21:21).

JOHN 14:15-21

> 15   If you love me you will keep my commandments.
>
> 16   I shall ask the Father,
> and he will give you another Advocate
> to be with you for ever,
>
> 17   that Spirit of truth
> whom the world can never receive
> since it neither sees nor knows him;
> but you know him,
> because he is with you, he is in you.

18   I will not leave you orphans;
        I will come back to you.
19   In a short time the world will no longer see me;
        but you will see me,
        because I live and you will live.
20   On that day
        you will understand that I am in my Father
        and you in me and I in you.
21   Anybody who receives my commandments and keeps them
        will be one who loves me;
        and anybody who loves me will be loved by my Father,
        and I shall love him and show myself to him.'

We have been prepared for the coming of the Spirit from the beginning of John's Gospel. The Baptist introduced Jesus as the one 'who is going to baptise with the Holy Spirit' (John 1:33). Jesus spoke to Nicodemus about being 'born of the Spirit' (John 3:8). Speaking of his going back to his Father, Jesus said: 'It is the spirit that gives life' (John 6:63).

'On the last and greatest day of the festival, Jesus stood there and cried out:
    "If any man is thirsty, let him come to me!
    Let the man come and drink who believes in me!"
As scripture says: From his breast shall flow fountains of living water.
He was speaking of the Spirit which those who believed in him were to receive; for there was no Spirit as yet because Jesus had not yet been glorified.'

(John 7:37-39)

The 'hour' has now come for Jesus to be glorified. It is the hour for the gift of the promised Spirit.

It is clear from the parallelism between 14:15-17 and 14:18-21 that John wants the reader to identify the Spirit and the presence of the risen Jesus (compare Mark 13:11 and Luke 21:15).

After the Resurrection, John and the others experienced the renewed presence of Jesus among them. They experienced the active power of his Spirit. After the initial despondency that weighed down their hearts at the time of the crucifixion, they experienced a recovery of hope, of joy, of courage, of peace. They experienced a renewal of life.

They knew that Jesus was risen and was still with them, because they experienced the presence and power of his Spirit among them:

'You will see me,
because I live and you will live.'

(John 14:19)

As John writes in his First Letter:

'We can know that we are living in him
and he is living in us
because he lets us share his Spirit'

(1 John 4:13)

Paul speaks frequently of this same Spirit:

'Your body, you know, is the temple of the Holy Spirit
who is in you since you received him from God'

(1 Corinthians 6:19)

'The proof that you are sons is that God has sent the Spirit of his Son into our hearts: the Spirit that cries "Abba, Father," and it is this that makes you a son'

(Galatians 4:6-7)

'The love of God has been poured into our hearts by the Holy Spirit which has been given us.'

(Romans 5:5)

'If Christ is in you then your spirit is life itself because you have been made one with God (= "justified"); and if the Spirit of him who raised Jesus from the dead is living in you, then he who raised Jesus from the dead will give life to your own mortal bodies through his Spirit living in you'

(Romans 8:10-11)

'You have been stamped with the seal of the Holy Spirit of the Promise, the pledge of our inheritance, which brings freedom for those whom God has taken for his own, to make his glory praised'.

(Ephesians 1:13-14)

The Spirit is Jesus' new way of being with them after his glorification. Up to this time Jesus has been with his disciples and they could call on him and be sure he would respond with love. After his glorification they can still call on him. (This is the meaning of Advocate = Paraclete John 14:16). Jesus has spoken of himself as the 'Truth' (John 14:6). His Spirit will be the Spirit of Truth (14:17 cf also John 15:26, 16:13 and 1 John 4:6), because, experiencing the presence and power of the Spirit, the disciples will know the enduring love of the faithful God.

John uses expressions that convey the intimacy of this experience. They will 'know' the Spirit (John 14:17). The Spirit will be 'with' them and 'in' them (John 14:17). Jesus will 'come back' to them (John 14:18). They will be 'in' Jesus and he will be 'in' them (John 14:20). They will be 'loved' by his Father (John 14:21). Finally:

'I shall love him and show myself to him'

(John 14:21)

All of this is dependent on one thing: they must keep his commandments (John 14:15 and 14:21). John has already explained what this entails:

'I give you a new commandment:
love one another;
just as I have loved you,
you also must love one another.'

(John 13:34)

He will repeat the same thing later:

'This is my commandment:
love one another as I have loved you.'

(John 15:12)

God is love. It is only when we love and are loved that we can experience God. To hear the word of God, to believe in Jesus, to be a child of God, to be born of God — these are all ways of saying the same thing: to love as Jesus loved.

To link 'love' with a 'commandment' can confuse us. This is because we have lost the sense of our own language. In fact the word is related to our word 'commend'. Basically, a 'command' is something 'commended' by one person to another. It is something 'entrusted' by one person to another. John is giving us

Jesus' last will and testament. He is about to die and he is entrusting to his disciples the mission he was given by his Father. He is trusting them to carry on his work. He is promising them his continued presence and the same experience of intimacy with God that he himself enjoyed, so that they may be able to carry on his work.

JOHN 14:22-26

22   Judas —this was not Judas Iscariot—said to him, 'Lord, what is all this
23   about? Do you intend to show yourself to us and not to the world?' •Jesus
      replied:

> 'If anyone loves me he will keep my word,
> and my Father will love him,
> and we shall come to him
> and make our home with him.

24   Those who do not love me do not keep my words.
      And my word   is not my own:
      it is the word of the one who sent me.

25   I have said these things to you
      while still with you;

26   but the Advocate, the Holy Spirit,
      whom the Father will send in my name,
      will teach you everything
      and remind you of all I have said to you.

Notice, once again, the parallelism between 14:23-24 and 14:25-26. The Spirit is the presence of the risen Jesus.

The answer to Judas' question is in Judas' hands. If Judas and the others keep Jesus' word, and to the extent that they do, Jesus will show himself to the world. A comparison of verse 23 with verse 15 shows that John identifies 'word' and 'command' (compare Deuteronomy 4:12-13). The word they are to keep is the command of love. If they love one another as Jesus loved them, if they obey God's word the way Jesus obeyed it, the whole world will come to see the glory of God.

John began this discourse by speaking of Jesus going to prepare many dwelling places (John 14:1). Here Jesus says:

> 'my Father will love him
> and we shall come to him
> and make our home with him.'

(John 14:23)

Jesus is about to offer his body in sacrifice. He is approaching his Passover. He is asking his disciples, as Paul asks them:

> 'offer your living bodies as a holy sacrifice'

(Romans 12:1)

The body of the disciple will be a sacred place, where God dwells and where God's love is powerfully manifest. If the disciples are faithful, the whole world that God loved so much (John 3:16) will show forth the glory of God.

JOHN 14:27-31

27   Peace I bequeath to you,
                my own peace I give you,

a peace the world cannot give, this is my gift to you.
Do not let your hearts be troubled or afraid.

28 You heard me say:
I am going away, and shall return.
If you loved me you would have been glad to know that I am
     going to the Father,
for the Father is greater than I.

29 I have told you this now before it happens,
so that when it does happen you may believe.

30 I shall not talk with you any longer,
because the prince of this world is on his way.
He has no power over me,

31 but the world must be brought to know that I love the Father
and that I am doing exactly what the Father told me.
Come now, let us go.

The 'peace' (John 14:27) spoken of by Jesus is the Eschatological peace promised by the prophets (cf Isaiah 54:13, 57:19 and Ezekiel 37:26). It is the peace of the last age, the gift of the Messianic times.

The joy of 'gladness' (John 14:28) is the joy experienced by the Baptist at the approach of the bridegroom (cf John 3:29). It is the joy promised by Jesus to those who are to share his mission (cf John 4:36, see also John 15:11 and 16:22).

Peace and joy are among the gifts of the Spirit (cf Galatians 5:22 and John 20:20-21).

It will appear that Jesus is the victim and that he is being crushed by the powers of darkness and death. John wants his readers to remember, as they follow the story of the Passion, that what Jesus is doing he is doing freely (cf John 10:17-18) and in response to the word of his Father. (John 14:29-31).

It is very likely that chapter 14 was followed immediately by chapter 18. The text would then have gone:

'Come now, let us go. After he had said all this Jesus left
with his disciples.'

(John 14:31 and 18:1)

We are reminded of the progression in Mark. Jesus says:

'Get up! Let us go! My betrayer is close at hand already'.

(Mark 14:42)

In both John and Mark, these words are followed by the account of the arrest.

It seems that chapter 15-16 and chapter 17 have been inserted as further reflections on the significance of Jesus' 'hour'.

* * * * * * * *

3: **The Second Supper Discourse:** (John Chapters 15-16)

JOHN 15:1-3

1 **15** 'I am the true vine,
and my Father is the vinedresser.

2 Every branch in me that bears no fruit

> he cuts away,
> and every branch that does bear fruit he prunes
> to make it bear even more.
> You are pruned already,   3
> by means of the word that I have spoken to you.

One of the blessing prayers of the Passover meal was a blessing over the cup, the fruit of the vine. The one who pronounced the blessing lived in hope of the day when he and his family would:

> 'drink the new wine in the kingdom of God'
>
> *(Mark 14:25)*

That would be the Messianic Banquet when:

> 'Yahweh Sabaoth will prepare for all the people a banquet of rich food, a banquet of fine wines, of food rich and juicy, of fine strained wines.'
>
> *(Isaiah 25:6)*

When studying Luke's account of the first Eucharistic meal, we noticed that he spoke of it in terms of this Messianic Banquet (cf Luke 22:19-20). John draws on the same theme for this discourse. If it is true that this discourse is actually a Eucharistic Discourse of John's, the symbolism of the vine takes on an even richer power.

Wine, too, is linked with the gift of the Spirit, as we saw when examining the anecdote of the marriage-feast of Cana (cf John 2:1-10). The hour of the Messianic Banquet has come. The hour has come for the Spirit to be given.

John obviously has in mind his own Christian community. The discourse is addressed to the branches that are in Jesus (John 15:2). Some of them are not bearing fruit; others are bearing fruit, and these are pruned by Jesus' word. The author of the Letter to the Hebrews speaks in similar terms of the word:

> 'The word of God is something alive and active: it cuts like any double-edged sword but more finely: it can slip through the place where the soul is divided from the spirit, or joints from the marrow; it can judge the secret emotions and thoughts. No created thing can hide from him; everything is uncovered and open to the eyes of the one to whom we must give account of ourselves.'
>
> *(Hebrews 4:12-13)*

The constant challenge of the command to love, the constant summons to respond to God's word calling the disciple to give himself for others as Jesus did, acts as a knife, pruning the disciple to bear even more fruit.

JOHN 15:4-8

> Make your home in me, as I make mine in you.   4
> As a branch cannot bear fruit all by itself,
> but must remain part of the vine,
> neither can you unless you remain in me.
> I am the vine,   5
> you are the branches.
> Whoever remains in me, with me in him,
> bears fruit in plenty;
> for cut off from me you can do nothing.
> Anyone who does not remain in me   6

is like a branch that has been thrown away
—he withers;
these branches are collected and thrown on the fire,
and they are burnt.
If you remain in me   7
and my words remain in you,
you may ask what you will
and you shall get it.
It is to the glory of my Father that you should bear much fruit,   8
and then you will be my disciples.

Being a disciple of Jesus is a matter of bearing much fruit (John 15:8). It is
this fruit that gives glory to God (John 15:8). The fruit comes from the vine,
through the branch. But the branch must remain in the vine. The disciple must
keep Jesus' word (John 15:7). If he does he can call upon the power of God and it
will be there for the asking (John 15:7), for it is God's will that all men be saved. It
is God's will that man live to the full (John 10:10). It is God's will that the whole
world be transformed by love.

JOHN 15:9-11
As the Father has loved me,   9
so I have loved you.
Remain in my love.
If you keep my commandments   10
you will remain in my love,
just as I have kept my Father's commandments
and remain in his love.
I have told you this   11
so that my own joy may be in you
and your joy be complete.

This is the explanation of the analogy: it is a meditation on the
commandment of love, on the gift of the Spirit of love. The last verse (15:11) gives
us an insight into the heart of Jesus. Loving called on all his energy; it finally
demanded that he give his life. But it never took from him the 'joy' (John 15:11)
that came from his intimate union with God and with men. This is the joy, the
'blessedness' of which the beatitudes speak (cf Matthew 5:1-12).

JOHN 15:12-17
This is my commandment: 12
love one another,
as I have loved you.
A man can have no greater love   13
than to lay down his life for his friends.
You are my friends,   14
if you do what I command you.
I shall not call you servants any more,   15
because a servant does not know
his master's business;
I call you friends,
because I have made known to you

everything I have learnt from my Father.
16   You did not choose me,
no, I chose you;
and I commissioned you
to go out and to bear fruit,
fruit that will last;
and then the Father will give you
anything you ask him in my name.
17   What I command you
is to love one another.

John is concentrating on the responsibility of the disciple to do what Jesus commanded (John 15:14), to go out and bear fruit (John 15:16), to love as Jesus loved (John 15:12 and 15:17). This is the commission given to the disciple by Jesus himself (John 15:16). This was the meaning of the washing of feet (John 13:1-20), as John pointed out in his account of the Last Supper (John 13:34-35).

At the same time, he is reminding his readers that this love is a love that comes from the vine: it is God's love. He is the one who chose the disciples (John 15:16); He is the one who gives his Spirit. The disciple is able to love as Jesus loved because he is drawn into the embrace of God's love for his Son. It is because the Passover Lamb laid down his life (John 15:13, cf John 6:51 and 10:11-18) that the disciple, in his turn, is able to lay down his life for his friends. It is the enduring love of God that sustains and nourishes and inspires the disciple. It is God's love that makes it possible for the disciple to be a channel of love to others and to draw others to the joy and peace and life that he enjoys. In this mission the disciple can call upon the liberating presence and power of the God who promised:

'I will betroth you to myself for ever,
betroth you with integrity and justice,
with tenderness and love;
I will betroth you to myself with faithfulness,
and you will come to know Yahweh.'

(Hosea 2:22)

JOHN 15:18-25
18   'If the world hates you,
remember that it hated me before you.
19   If you belonged to the world,
the world would love you as its own;
but because you do not belong to the world,
because my choice withdrew you from the world,
therefore the world hates you.
20   Remember the words I said to you:
A servant is not greater than his master.
If they persecuted me,
they will persecute you too;
if they kept my word,
they will keep yours as well.
21   But it will be on my account that they will do all this,
because they do not know the one who sent me.
22   If I had not come,

if I had not spoken to them,
they would have been blameless;
but as it is they have no excuse for their sin.

23   Anyone who hates me hates my Father.
24   If I had not performed such works among them
as no one else has ever done,
they would be blameless;
but as it is, they have seen all this,
and still they hate both me and my Father.

25   But all this was only to fulfil the words written in their Law:
They hated me for no reason.[a]

(a: Psalm 35:19)

When John looks at the world, he is usually moved by the love that God has
for it. He sent his word into the world (John 1:9, 8:26, 10:36); He sent his light
into the world (John 3:19, 8:12, 9:5, 12:46); He:

'loved the world so much
that he gave his only Son'

(John 3:16)

In his love he wanted to 'save the world' (cf John 3:17, 4:42, 12:47); He wanted to
'give life to the world' (John 6:33, 6.51).

Yet, in spite of this, the world did not accept the word (John (1:10); the world
'can never receive the Spirit of truth' (John 14:17); the world cannot give peace
(John 14:27). In spite of God's love, the world hated Jesus (John 7:7). Because of
the world's rejection of Jesus, his death and glorification are seen as a sentence
passed on the world (John 12:31) and a defeat for Satan, the 'prince of this world'
(John 12:31, 14:30).

It is this 'world' (15:18-19) that John is referring to in the above passage: the
world that does not want to see the light or hear the word; the 'world' that hated
Jesus (John 15:18) and persecuted him (John 18:20).

Right from the Prologue, John warned his readers that darkness would try to
overpower Jesus (cf John 1:15). The first indication came when Jesus healed the
sick man at the pool of Bethzatha. He healed him on the sabbath and the religious
authorities began to persecute him (cf John 5:18). John frequently mentions that
they tried to arrest Jesus (John 7:30, 7:44, 10:39) and wanted to kill him (John
8:37, 11:53).

While John uses a number of expressions to describe those who hated Jesus,
the reason for their hatred comes down to one thing. He speaks of them as
refusing to believe in Jesus (John 3:12, 3:36, 5:37-38, 6:36, 6:64, 7:5, 8:45, 10:25-
26, 10:37-38, 12:37). They refuse to listen (John 8:47), they refuse to let his word
penetrate into them (John 8:37, 12:47-48, 17:14), they refuse to keep his word
(John 14:24). These are various ways of saying the same thing:

'The world hates me because I give evidence
that its ways are evil'

(John 7:7)

'On these grounds is sentence pronounced:
that though the light has come into the world
men have shown they prefer darkness to light

because their deeds were evil.
And, indeed, everybody who does wrong
hates the light and avoids it,
for fear his actions should be exposed.'

(John 3:19-20, cf 5:29)

Jesus' word was a command to love (John 13:34-35, 15:12, 15:17) and they refused to listen:

'If I had not come,
if I had not spoken to them,
they would have been blameless.'

(John 15:22)

Jesus' actions (his 'works') were actions of love and they refused to see:

'If I had not performed such works among them
as no one else has ever done,
they would be blameless.'

(John 15:24)

Those who hate Jesus are, by that very fact, hating God (John 15:23, 15:24). Jesus' word is God's word (John 1:1, 1:14, 3:34, 7:16-17) Jesus' actions are 'signs' (John 2:11, 2:23, 4:48, 4:54, 11:15, 11:42, 11:48, 12:37): signs that he is sent by God (John 5:36, 10:25, 10:37); signs that the Father is with him (John 8:29, 10:30, 10:38, 14:9-10, 17:11, 17:21). It is the glory of God that is revealed in Jesus' actions (John 1:14, 2:11, 11:40, 17:5), and Jesus' works are the Father's works (John 5:17, 5:36, 10:38, 14:10).

For this reason, their refusal to believe in Jesus and their persecution and hatred of him, is proof of the fact that they do not know God (John 1:10, 7:28, 8:19, 8:54, 15:21, 16:3 and 1 John 3:1, 5:21). A life of love is the only proof that a person knows God (1 John 4:7-8). Those who hated Jesus, for all their religious posturing, were not living lives of love; their deeds were evil.

In the passage upon which we are reflecting, Jesus is telling his disciples to expect the same treatment (John 15:20 = John 13:16, cf also Matthew 10:24, in the same context). The persecution and hatred they experience comes from the same source as that experienced by Jesus and is for the same reasons. If they love as he has commanded them to love (John 15:17), they will be hated as he was hated (John 15:18). This is made even more clear in John's First Letter:

'You must not be surprised, brothers,
when the world hates you;
we have passed out of death and into life,
and of this we can be sure
because we love our brothers.'

(1 John 3:14)

Matthew makes the same point in his Sermon on the Mount. The final beatitude reads:

'Happy are those who are persecuted in the cause of right:
theirs is the kingdom of heaven.
Happy are you when people abuse you and persecute you
and speak all kinds of calumny against you on my account.
Rejoice and be glad, for your reward will be great in heaven;
this is how they persecuted the prophets before you.'

(Matthew 5:10-12)

According to Matthew, too, those who hated Jesus, and those who hate his disciples, are those who do not know God. They do not know the God of mercy and compassion (Matthew 9:13, 12:7, 23:23); they refuse to do God's will (Matthew 7:15-23) and blaspheme against the Holy Spirit (Matthew 12:31).

Mark, too, links persecution with the proclamation of the Good News (Mark 13:10); in other words, persecution follows on love.

JOHN 15:26 — 16:4

26   When the Advocate comes,
    whom I shall send to you from the Father,
    the Spirit of truth who issues from the Father,
    he will be my witness.
27   And you too will be witnesses,
    because you have been with me from the outset.

1 **16**   'I have told you all this
    so that your faith may not be shaken.
2   They will expel you from the synagogues,
    and indeed the hour is coming
    when anyone who kills you will think he is doing a holy duty for God.
3   They will do these things
    because they have never known either the Father or myself.
4   But I have told you all this,
    so that when the time for it comes
    you may remember that I told you.

The disciples will suffer persecution, but they are not to lose heart. They will be witnessing to Jesus by their word and action, and his Spirit will sustain them (compare Mark 13:11, Matthew 10:20, Luke 12:11-12, 21:15).

JOHN 16:4-11

    'I did not tell you this from the outset,
    because I was with you;
5   but now I am going to the one who sent me.
    Not one of you has asked, "Where are you going?"
6   Yet you are sad at heart because I have told you this.
7   Still, I must tell you the truth:
    it is for your own good that I am going
    because unless I go,
    the Advocate will not come to you;
    but if I do go,
    I will send him to you.
8   And when he comes,
    he will show the world how wrong it was,
    about sin,
    and about who was in the right,
    and about judgement:
9   about sin:
    proved by their refusal to believe in me;
10   about who was in the right:

proved by my going to the Father
and your seeing me no more;
about judgement: 11
proved by the prince of this world being already condemned.

After Jesus' death and resurrection, his disciples experienced his continued
presence among them, sustaining them and driving them to carry out the mission
of love entrusted to them. They missed him because he was no longer among
them 'in the flesh'. But, at the same time, they experienced an energy they had not
known before, because he was with them 'in the Spirit'.

It was indeed for their own good that Jesus went to his Father (cf John 16:7).
It was no longer possible for them to look to Jesus to do the loving, to look to
Jesus for the answers and the example. After his death they had to assume
responsibility themselves, they had to take the cross on their own shoulders. It
was only after Jesus' death that, sustained always by his Spirit, they came to
believe that they could perform even greater works than Jesus did (cf John
14:12). What Jesus did he could do only for a few; his disciples could carry his
mission to the ends of the earth (cf Acts 1:8). Jesus showed that it was possible for
a man to be free, that it was possible for a man to love, that it was possible for a
man to enjoy intimacy with God. Jesus showed the way (John 14:4). After his
glorification he will be with his Father; he will also be with his disciples 'in Spirit':

'You will see me,
because I live and you will live'

(John 14:19)

After his glorification his disciples will learn what Jesus has done for them; they
will learn that they too can be free, they too can love, they too can be intimate
with God, they too can overcome the world. John goes so far as to conclude his
Gospel with the words:

'Happy are those who have not seen and yet believe'

(John 20:29)

Jesus was condemned as a 'sinner' (John 9:24). His accusers saw him as one
who broke the sabbath (cf John 5:18). In disregarding the Law, Jesus, in their
judgment, showed himself to be a blasphemer (cf John 10:33). For Jesus, sin was
something different. Sin was refusing to believe in God's word (cf John 16:9);
refusing, that is, to believe in a God of compassion and to live a life hungering and
thirsting for justice (cf Matthew 5:6). A sinner is one who will not let the word of
God penetrate into his mind and heart; one who will not accept the challenge
given him by God to love as Jesus loved. Once Jesus has died and gone to the
Father, the world will come to see this through the mission of his disciples,
sustained always by the Spirit of Jesus.

Jesus' enemies gave lip service to God's justice: it was, in their opinion,
demonstrated by God's punishment on those who disregarded the Law and failed
to submit to the religious authority of the scribes and Pharisees, and the Temple
cult. Jesus, on the other hand, saw God's justice in the terms of Deuteronomy:

'Circumcise your heart then and be obstinate no longer;
for Yahweh your God is God of gods and Lord of lords,
the great God, triumphant and terrible, never partial,
never to be bribed. It is He who sees justice done for

the orphan and the widow, who loves the stranger and
gives him food and clothing. Love the stranger then, for you
were strangers in the land of Egypt. It is Yahweh your
God whom you must fear and serve; you must cling to
Him; in his name take your oaths'.

(Deuteronomy 10:16-20)

God is just because he liberates the oppressed and sets the captive free. Jesus demonstrated this in his healing and in his teaching. His death and resurrection would prove it to the world. (John 16:10) His disciples, sustained by his Spirit were to carry this Good News everywhere.

Jesus was condemned to death by his enemies. His resurrection and the life experienced by his disciples would demonstrate that it was his enemies who were convicted, not Jesus.

The disciples will suffer persecution. Their persecuters will accuse them of being sinners, will claim to be acting on behalf of a just God and will condemn them. Jesus is telling them to persevere, because he is about to prove the world wrong on all these counts. It is their enemies who will stand condemned because they failed to listen to God's word, to accept the challenge of being instruments of God's justice (cf John 3:19-20).

JOHN 16:12-15

I still have many things to say to you   12
but they would be too much for you now.
But when the Spirit of truth comes   13
he will lead you to the complete truth,
since he will not be speaking as from himself
but will say only what he has learnt;
and he will tell you of the things to come.
He will glorify me,   14
since all he tells you
will be taken from what is mine.
Everything the Father has is mine;   15
that is why I said:
All he tells you
will be taken from what is mine.

After the Resurrection of Jesus, the disciples experienced two things: things that Jesus had said and done while with them gradually became clear to them; and they were able to see the various events in their life in the light of Jesus' words and life. John reflects both of these experiences in the present passage. The truth comes from God. The truth is that God is faithful in his love. This truth was revealed fully by Jesus as he gave his life in love for his friends. But the significance of this act, indeed the significance of all that Jesus said and did could only dawn gradually on his disciples and has to be re-learnt, and seen again by each generation of Christians. This is possible because the Spirit of Jesus, the Spirit of love that unites him to the Father, and by which he lives and in which he spoke, is his gift to the Church.

This is the essential meaning of the technical word 'Tradition'. Tradition is that living presence of Jesus in the community which is the source of the living unity of the church's faith. The written scriptures are themselves a special product of this tradition, expressing the living faith of the first generations of Christians, inspired by the Spirit of Jesus leading them to the complete truth and assisting them to understand their lives in the light of the Gospel. The Spirit did not leave the church after the first century, and the work of enlightening is still going on. The living tradition of the church will never contradict the scriptures for it comes from the same source. The scriptures remain a norm of faith and confirm the movement of the Spirit in our times. But our listening is not only to the Scriptures; it is to the living God, to the Risen Christ whose Spirit is alive in our midst. We are part of a living vine, bringing forth fruit that is to draw people today to the living God.

JOHN 16:16-24

'In a short time you will no longer see me,   16
and then a short time later you will see me again.'

Then some of his disciples said to one another, 'What does he mean, "In a 17 short time you will no longer see me, and then a short time later you will see me again" and, "I am going to the Father"? •What is this "short time"? We don't 18 know what he means.' •Jesus knew that they wanted to question him, so he 19 said, 'You are asking one another what I meant by saying: In a short time you will no longer see me, and then a short time later you will see me again.

'I tell you most solemnly,   20
you will be weeping and wailing
while the world will rejoice;
you will be sorrowful,
but your sorrow will turn to joy.
A woman in childbirth suffers,   21
because her time has come;
but when she has given birth to the child she forgets the suffering
in her joy that a man has been born into the world.
So it is with you: you are sad now,   22
but I shall see you again, and your hearts will be full of joy,
and that joy no one shall take from you.
When that day comes,   23
you will not ask me any questions.
I tell you most solemnly,
anything you ask for from the Father
he will grant in my name.
Until now you have not asked for anything in my name.   24
Ask and you will receive,
and so your joy will be complete.

1: John gives expression here to the traditional Biblical understanding of suffering. Granted belief in God, suffering remains a mystery, but there is always the sense that it is not a meaningless suffering, nor is it a suffering that leads to destruction. It is a suffering which, if accepted in the right spirit, and by one who perseveres in hope, will lead to something beautiful. A constantly recurring image in Biblical literature is the image of birth-pangs (cf Mark 13:8). John uses it here (16:21). Paul also uses this image in one of the finest statements of hope found in the New Testament:

'I think that what we suffer in this life can never be compared to the glory, as yet unrevealed, which is waiting for us. The whole creation is eagerly waiting for God to reveal his sons. It was not for any fault on the part of creation that it was made unable to attain its purpose, it was made so by God; but creation still retains the hope of being freed, like us, from its slavery to decadence, to enjoy the same freedom and glory as the children of God. From the beginning till now the entire creation, as we know, has been groaning in one great act of giving birth; and not only creation, but all of us who possess the first-fruits of the Spirit, we too groan inwardly as we wait for our bodies to be set free.'   *(Romans 8:18-23)*

In the passage before us, John is reminding his readers that the time of the Eschatological battle is imminent, as is the victory of God (16:16-19).

2: John's statement on the efficacy of prayer (16:23) repeats a theme that has occurred again and again in the Supper Discourses (cf 14:13-14; 15:7; 15:16). Prayer is the experience the branch has of openness to the vine; it is the listening that enables Jesus to speak his words through us; it is the breathing in of the Spirit of Jesus that makes it possible to breathe the same Spirit out to others and bear fruits of love. It produces 'joy' (16:24).

JOHN 16:25-28

25   I have been telling you all this in metaphors,
      the hour is coming
      when I shall no longer speak to you in metaphors;
      but tell you about the Father in plain words.
26   When that day comes
      you will ask in my name;
      and I do not say that I shall pray to the Father for you,
27   because the Father himself loves you
      for loving me
      and believing that I came from God.
28   I came from the Father and have come into the world
      and now I leave the world to go to the Father.'

In many ways the final statement in this passage is a summary of the whole of John's Gospel. The movement of the Gospel is from the Father to men and back to the Father. This is also the movement of the Prologue. John sees Jesus as bringing God to man, and lifting man to God. The plain words which Jesus is about to use of his Father are not words that flow from his mouth, but love that flows from his heart. John will dramatise this in his scene of the piercing of the side of Jesus on the cross. From his heart flows his life-blood and the Spirit of God. In the hour of his dying, we see, plainly, that God is self-giving love, that there are no limits to God's faithfulness to the Covenant of love he has made with man, that he empties himself for us, sinners.

This was Paul's experience:

'The life I now live in this body I live in faith: faith in the Son of God who loved me and who sacrificed himself for my sake. I cannot bring myself to give up God's gift.'
                                                      (Galatians 2:20)

JOHN 16:29-33

29   His disciples said, 'Now you are speaking plainly and not using metaphors!
30   Now we see that you know everything, and do not have to wait for questions to

31 be put into words; because of this we believe that you came from God.' •Jesus answered them:

'Do you believe at last?
32   Listen; the time will come—in fact it has come already—
when you will be scattered, each going his own way
and leaving me alone.
And yet I am not alone,
because the Father is with me.
33   I have told you all this
so that you may find peace in me.
In the world you will have trouble,
but be brave:
I have conquered the world.'

The disciples might think they understand. The fact that they do not will be proved by their fleeing in the face of Jesus' Passion (cf Mark 14:27, 14:50).

The fact that the disciples are to be scattered is mentioned here by John to highlight the isolation of Jesus. Isolated, but not alone, Jesus is able to conquer the world (16:33), not through his own power, not because of his friends, but because 'the Father is with me' (16:32). Jesus is about to face his agony alone, but he will triumph, and his triumph will prove that God is with him. It will thus give glory to God and should take away all fear from man because Jesus will reveal unmistakably that God is love and that not even death can come between man and the love of a faithful God.

The final words of this second discourse ring out a hymn of triumph.

4: The Prayer of Jesus (John Chapter 17)

There are no new themes introduced in this final chapter. The reader is advised simply to read it very slowly and reflectively. John gathers his major themes together and brings them to a peaceful resolution. His aim is to penetrate as deeply as he can into the heart of Jesus as he gave his life on the cross. The reader is taken gently into the intimacy of Jesus' relationship with his Father and invited to share that intimacy, before going with John on the journey to the cross (John Chapter 18).

JOHN 17:1-5

17 After saying this, Jesus raised his eyes to heaven and said:

1   'Father, the hour has come:
glorify your Son
so that your Son may glorify you;
2   and, through the power over all mankind that you have given him,
let him give eternal life to all those you have entrusted to him.
3   And eternal life is this:
to know you,
the only true God,
and Jesus Christ whom you have sent.
4   I have glorified you on earth
and finished the work

that you gave me to do.
Now, Father, it is time for you to glorify me   5
with that glory I had with you
before ever the world was.

The hour has come (cf John 12:23 and 13:1). Jesus prays that his Father may draw him to Himself so that, in his dying, he may reveal to all mankind (17:2) the inner reality of God's love. John takes his readers back to the mystery that he developed in his Prologue. Jesus is the word made flesh (John 1:14) who reveals God's glory (John 1:18). Jesus prays that the word that was since the beginning may be now, at last, and finally, manifested in his own dying. Those who hear this word will have the eternal life he came to share (17:2 cf John 10:10); for eternal life is a matter of knowing the only true God as he is revealed in his Christ (17:3). The only true God is the God of justice, the God who liberates the oppressed, who heals the sick, the God of love (cf Psalm 82 and John 10:34-38). It is this God that Jesus revealed through his words and his actions. And now his work is finished (17:4). It is time for the world to know (cf John 10:14) intimately, the power of God's redeeming action.

JOHN 17:6-10

I have made your name known   6
to the men you took from the world to give me.
They were yours and you gave them to me,
and they have kept your word.
Now at last they know   7
that all you have given me comes indeed from you;
for I have given them   8
the teaching you gave to me,
and they have truly accepted this, that I came from you,
and have believed that it was you who sent me.
I pray for them;   9
I am not praying for the world
but for those you have given me,
because they belong to you:
all I have is yours   10
and all you have is mine,
and in them I am glorified.

Jesus' mind goes towards his close disciples, those who have kept the word of God (17:6) and believed that it was God whom Jesus was revealing though his life (17:8). Jesus knows that it is only through these disciples that the world will come to know him (17:10) and so come to know his Father and enjoy eternal life. So he prays for them (17:9).

JOHN 17:11-19

I am not in the world any longer,   11
but they are in the world,
and I am coming to you.
Holy Father,
keep those you have given me true to your name,
so that they may be one like us.
While I was with them,   12

I kept those you had given me true to your name.
I have watched over them and not one is lost
except the one who chose to be lost,
and this was to fulfil the scriptures.
But now I am coming to you   13
and while still in the world I say these things
to share my joy with them to the full.
I passed your word on to them,   14
and the world hated them,
because they belong to the world
no more than I belong to the world.
I am not asking you to remove them from the world,   15
but to protect them from the evil one.
They do not belong to the world   16
any more than I belong to the world.
Consecrate them in the truth;   17
your word is truth.
As you sent me into the world,   18
I have sent them into the world,
and for their sake I consecrate myself   19
so that they too may be consecrated in truth.

Jesus' prayer is that the disciples be drawn into the intimate embrace of the all-holy God. Ever since the inaugural vision of Isaiah (Isaiah 6:1-4), the word 'holiness' was reserved for the majesty and transcendence and power of the God whose:

'glory fills the whole earth.'

(Isaiah 6:3)

Jesus addresses his Father as 'Holy Father' (John 17:11). He himself was filled with the Holy Spirit of God (cf John 1:33, 14:26, 20:22) without reserve (cf John 3:34). He was the 'Holy One of God' (John 6:69), consecrated to God in intimate love (cf 10:36, 17:19). Note that the Greek word for consecrate comes from the word 'holy'; it means to 'make holy'. In this prayer he prays that his disciples will share this intimacy. He wants them, too, to be 'consecrated' (John 17:17, 17:19). He wants them to be 'consecrated in truth' (John 17:17, 17:19).

Something is 'true' insofar as it is real, dependable, trustworthy, faithful. John has spoken of true light (1:9), of the true prophet (6:14), of true bread (6:32), of true food and true drink (6:55), of true judgment (8:16), of the true vine (15:1). John has spoken of the true God (3:33, 8:26, 17:3), the God, that is, who is faithful to his word, in whom we can place our trust. John has spoken of Jesus as the one whose word is true (8:40, 8:45, 8:46, 16:7), who is the true saviour of the world (4:42), who is full of truth (1:14, 1:17 cf 7:18, 14:6). John has spoken of the Spirit of truth (14:17, 15:26, 16:13). Jesus and his Spirit present among his disciples after his death can be relied on to draw men to the Father and reveal the true God, the God of faithfulness.

John has defined a true disciple as the one who makes the word of God his home (8:31). Such a person will worship God in truth (4:23, 4:34); he will come out into the light (3:21); he will find freedom (8:32).

God's fidelity ('truth') is fidelity to love. God's word is a word of love. A disciple of Jesus is one who keeps this word; he is one who loves as Jesus loved. To be 'consecrated in truth', therefore, is to be drawn into the inner life of God, to know the love of God and to live this love faithfully in relation to one's fellow man. Jesus is praying that his disciples may:

'love one another;
just as I have loved you,
you also must love one another.'

(John 13:34)

JOHN 17:20-23

I pray not only for these,	20
but for those also	
who through their words will believe in me.	
May they all be one.	21
Father, may they be one in us,	
as you are in me and I am in you,	
so that the world may believe it was you who sent me.	
I have given them the glory you gave to me,	22
that they may be one as we are one.	
With me in them and you in me,	23
may they be so completely one	
that the world will realise that it was you who sent me	
and that I have loved them as much as you loved me.	

The heart of Jesus reaches out beyond his immediate disciples to the world that God loved so much (John 3:16). He is the Paschal Lamb about to be sacrificed, the 'lamb of God that takes away the sin of the world' (John 1:29). He is the saviour 'of the world' (John 4:42). His life, his love, his flesh he gives 'for the life of the world' (John 6:51). Here his heart goes out to this world. He wants the world to believe (17:21). He wants the world, in spite of the hatred he met and the death he is about to undergo, to come to believe in the God of love who sent him and whom he reveals (17:21). He wants the world to know love, to know that Jesus loved the world as much as his Father loved him (John 17:23).

He prays that the world will know the same kind of unity that he experiences with his Father. He knows God (8:55). He remains in his Father's love because he keeps his Father's word (John 15:10). He experiences a complete unity with his Father (John 10:20, 10:38), a unity that flows from a complete intimacy of love. He knows and lives out in his every action the compassion and fidelity of love (John 1:14, 1:17). It is this same unity, this same glory, this same intimacy that he prays for when he thinks of those who through the word of his disciples will learn to believe in him (John 17:20). Only if they live the love he and his immediate disciples lived will the world come to know God.

JOHN 17:24-26

Father,	24
I want those you have given me	
to be with me where I am,	
so that they may always see the glory	
you have given me	

> because you loved me
> before the foundation of the world.
> 25 Father, Righteous One,
> the world has not known you,
> but I have known you,
> and these have known
> that you have sent me.
> 26 I have made your name known to them
> and will continue to make it known,
> so that the love with which you loved me may be in them,
> and so that I may be in them.'

With these words, John concludes Jesus' prayer and his reflection on Jesus death and resurrection. He began his reflections on the theme of love (John 13:1). The dominant theme throughout has been the command of love, the mission of love which he shared as a last will and testament with his disciples. It is fitting that John ends on the same theme.

He prays that his disciples will be where he is (John 17:24); he speaks of continuing to make God's name known (John 17:26). We are listening to someone who is about to die; but someone who knows that he is to live on, and to be present and active in our world. He wants his disciples to be in the world where Jesus is (John 17:15). He wants them to love as he loved, to be a light as he was a light, to save the world as he saved it. He wants them, through their obedience to his command, to see God's love revealed in the world, to know the Spirit of love that united Jesus to his Father (John 17:24). Jesus prays that his disciples may know the love he and his Father share, so that he will be able to live on in them (John 17:26).

BOOK 7

Jesus' Death and Resurrection

FOREWORD

Book 7 brings us to the climax of the Gospel. First there is the stark account of Jesus' sufferings and death on the cross. This is followed by a creedal statement of the faith of the early church in Jesus' resurrection: a statement associated with the empty tomb. Finally, we are presented with statements forged out of the faith-experience of Jesus' followers, illustrating the many ways in which Jesus demonstrated that he was still alive, with God in glory, and actively present among his followers.

Chapter 1
Jesus' passion and death

Mark 14:43 — 15:47
Matthew 26:46 — 27:61
Luke 22:47 — 23:56
John 18:1 — 19:42

1: Jesus' arrest

MARK 14:43-52 (Compare Matthew 26:47-52, 55-56; Luke 22:47-53)

Even while he was still speaking, Judas, one of the Twelve, came up with 43 a number of men armed with swords and clubs, sent by the chief priests and the scribes and the elders. •Now the traitor had arranged a signal with them. 44 'The one I kiss,' he had said 'he is the man. Take him in charge, and see he is well guarded when you lead him away.' •So when the traitor came, he went 45 straight up to Jesus and said, 'Rabbi!' and kissed him. •The others seized him 46 and took him in charge. •Then one of the bystanders drew his sword and struck 47 out at the high priest's servant, and cut off his ear.

Then Jesus spoke. 'Am I a brigand' he said 'that you had to set out to 48 capture me with swords and clubs? •I was among you teaching in the Temple day 49 after day and you never laid hands on me. But this is to fulfil the scriptures.' And they all deserted him and ran away. •A young man who followed him had 50 51 nothing on but a linen cloth. They caught hold of him, •but he left the cloth 52 in their hands and ran away naked.

The betrayal of Jesus by one of the Twelve (14:45), the clumsy action of one of the bystanders (14:47) and the fact that they 'all deserted him and ran away' (14:50), throw into powerful relief the lone figure of Jesus facing the violence of armed men (14:43).

By refering to the scriptures (14:49), Mark reminds his readers that all is under the control of God.

* * * * * * * *

Matthew mentions that it was one of the 'followers of Jesus' who drew the sword (Matthew 26:51 compare Mark 14:47 'bystander'). Matthew adds:

MATTHEW 26:53-54

•Jesus then said, 'Put your
53 sword back, for all who draw the sword will die by the sword. •Or do you think
that I canno' appeal to my Father who would promptly send more than twelve
54 legions of angels to my defence? •But then, how would the scriptures be fulfilled
55 that say this is the way it must be?'

Matthew is alluding to a threat contained in the covenant made by God with
Noah. According to the Genesis myth the murder of Abel by his brother Cain led
to a situation in which:

'the earth grew corrupt in God's sight, and filled with violence'

(Genesis 6:11)

The Flood came as a punishment, but the just man, Noah, was saved from the
deluge. God made a Covenant with him; but it contained the following threat:

'He who sheds man's blood,
shall have his blood shed by man,
for in the image of God
man was made.'

(Genesis 9:6)

The power of Jesus is the power of the just man, a power that is from God. He
refuses to be part of the corrupting violence around him.

*   *   *   *   *   *   *   *

Luke adds a further detail to the episode of the sword, mentioning that it was
the man's 'right' ear that was cut off. He also mentions that Jesus healed it (Luke
22:50-51). This is in line with a recurrent theme in Luke's Passion account: Jesus'
concern for others amidst his own suffering (cf the women of Jerusalem, Luke
23:28; his prayer for his executioners, Luke 23:34; his forgiveness of the good
thief, Luke 23:43).

Luke concludes his account with the dramatic words:

'But this is the hour; this is the reign of darkness.'

(Luke 22:53)

*   *   *   *   *   *   *   *

JOHN 18:1-11

1 **18** After he had said all this Jesus left with his disciples and crossed the
Kedron valley. There was a garden there, and he went into it with his
2 disciples. •Judas the traitor knew the place well, since Jesus had often met his
3 disciples there, •and he brought the cohort to this place together with a detachment of guards sent by the chief priests and the Pharisees, all with lanterns and
4 torches and weapons. •Knowing everything that was going to happen to him,
5 Jesus then came forward and said, 'Who are you looking for?' •They answered,
'Jesus the Nazarene'. He said, 'I am he'. Now Judas the traitor was standing
6 among them. •When Jesus said, 'I am he', they moved back and fell to the ground.
7 He asked them a second time, 'Who are you looking for?' They said, 'Jesus the

8 Nazarene'. •'I have told you that I am he' replied Jesus. 'If I am the one you
9 are looking for, let these others go.' •This was to fulfil the words he had spoken,
   'Not one of those you gave me have I lost'.
10   Simon Peter, who carried a sword, drew it and wounded the high priest's ser-
11 vant, cutting off his right ear. The servant's name was Malchus. •Jesus said to
   Peter, 'Put your sword back in its scabbard; am I not to drink the cup that the
   Father has given me?'

King David crossed the Kedron valley when he was forced by his son
Absolom to leave Jerusalem (cf 2 Samuel 15:23). John concentrates on the
kingship of Jesus all through his account of the Passion. It is possible that his
mention of the Kedron here (18:1) is an allusion to King David.

In their account of the agony — a scene omitted by John — Mark (14:32) and
Matthew (26:36) speak of a 'small estate called Gethsemane'. John, alone, speaks
of 'a garden' (18:1). Perhaps he wishes us to think of Adam and the first garden.
Jesus is the new Adam who is to triumph over temptation and reverse what
Adam did. As Paul writes:

'Adam prefigured the One to come, but the gift itself considerably outweighed the
fall. If it is certain that through one man's fall so many died, it is even more certain
that divine grace, coming through the one man, Jesus Christ, came to so many as an
abundant free gift. The results of the gift also outweigh the results of one man's sin:
for after one single fall came judgment with a verdict of condemnation, now after
many falls comes grace with its verdict of acquittal. If it is certain that death reigned
over everyone as the consequence of one man's fall, it is even more certain that one
man, Jesus Christ, will cause everyone to reign in life who receives the free gift that he
does not deserve, of being made righteous. Again, as one man's fall brought
condemnation on everyone, so the good act of one man brings everyone life and
makes them justified. As by one man's disobedience many were made sinners, so by
one man's obedience many will be made righteous.'

(Romans 5:15-19)

The Synoptics mention the detachment of guards sent by the Sanhedrin.
John adds the Roman cohort (John 18:3). It is hardly likely that Pilate could
have spared 600 men to arrest Jesus. This is more likely a dramatic detail added
by John to highlight the significance of what is happening. Jesus, alone, is
confronted by the powers of darkness, both Jew and Gentile. Jesus does not need
a lantern, for he is the light of the world. The powers of darkness need substitute
lights. But these do not prevent them from stumbling and falling to the ground
(18:6, compare John 12:35).

The response of Jesus 'I am he!' (18:5) has a divine ring about it and the effect
on the soldiers is described in terms of a theophany (cf Daniel 10:9; Acts 9:4 and
Revelations 1:17).

We are reminded of the words of the Psalmist:

'When evil men advance against me
to devour my flesh,
they, my opponents, my enemies,
are the ones who stumble and fall.'

(Psalm 27:2)

In this arrest scene it is Jesus who is master, even to commanding that his
disciples go free (18:8-9). John reminds the reader of his earlier statements:

'The will of him who sent me
is that I should lose nothing
of all that he has given to me'

(John 6:39)

and again:

'The sheep that belong to me listen to my voice;
I know them and they follow me.
I give them eternal life;
they will never be lost
and no one will ever steal them from me.
The Father who gave them to me is greater than anyone,
and no one can steal from the Father.
The Father and I are one.'

(John 10:27-30)

We have seen a gradual progression in the details of the anecdote about the cutting of the ear. John adds the final touch, giving us the names of those involved: Malchus and Peter (18:10-11). Jesus' statement to Peter (18:11) reminds us of the remark Jesus made to James and John:

'Can you drink the cup that I must drink?'

(Mark 10:38)

Also the prayer of Jesus in the Agony:

'Abba (Father). Everything is possible for you. Take this cup away from me. But let it be as you, not I, would have it.'

(Mark 8:33)

We are reminded also of an earlier rebuke given by Jesus to Peter:

'Get behind me, Satan! Because the way you think is not God's
way but man's.'

(Mark 14:36,)

*   *   *   *   *   *   *   *

2: Jesus' testimony before the Jewish authorities, and Peter's denial

MARK 14:53-72 (Compare Matthew 26:57-75 and Luke 22:54-71)

They led Jesus off to the high priest; and all the chief priests and the elders 53 and the scribes assembled there. •Peter had followed him at a distance, right 54 into the high priest's palace, and was sitting with the attendants warming himself at the fire.

The chief priests and the whole Sanhedrin were looking for evidence against 55 Jesus on which they might pass the death-sentence. But they could not find any. Several, indeed, brought false evidence against him, but their evidence was 56 conflicting. •Some stood up and submitted this false evidence against him, 57 'We heard him say, "I am going to destroy this Temple made by human hands, 58 and in three days build another, not made by human hands" '. •But even on 59 this point their evidence was conflicting. •The high priest then stood up before 60 the whole assembly and put this question to Jesus, 'Have you no answer to that? What is this evidence these men are bringing against you?' •But he was silent 61 and made no answer at all. The high priest put a second question to him, 'Are you the Christ,' he said 'the Son of the Blessed One?' •'I am,' said Jesus 'and 62

you will see *the Son of Man seated at the right hand of the Power* and *coming with*
63 *the clouds of heaven.'* *ᵃ* •The high priest tore his robes, 'What need of witnesses have
64 we now?' he said. •'You heard the blasphemy. What is your finding?' And they
all gave their verdict: he deserved to die.

65   Some of them started spitting at him and, blindfolding him, began hitting
him with their fists and shouting, 'Play the prophet!' And the attendants rained
blows on him.

66   While Peter was down below in the courtyard, one of the high priest's
67 servant-girls came up. •She saw Peter warming himself there, stared at him and
68 said, 'You too were with Jesus, the man from Nazareth'. •But he denied it.
'I do not know, I do not understand, what you are talking about' he said. And
69 he went out into the forecourt. •The servant-girl saw him and again started
70 telling the bystanders, 'This fellow is one of them'. •But again he denied it.
A little later the bystanders themselves said to Peter, 'You are one of them for
71 sure! Why, you are a Galilean.' •But he started calling down curses on himself
72 and swearing, 'I do not know the man you speak of'. •At that moment the
cock crew for the second time, and Peter recalled how Jesus had said to him,.
'Before the cock crows twice, you will have disowned me three times'. And
he burst into tears.

(a: Daniel 7:13)

Mark begins with Peter and ends with him, thus effectively highlighting the
centre-piece: the witness of Jesus.

The scene is a court-room with the high court of offical Judaism condemning
Jesus to death. Mark is careful to stress that they could find no evidence on which
to base their judgment (14:59). At the same time he hints at the real reason for
their determination to get rid of Jesus: he had spoken against the Law and the
Temple (14:58). The conflict between Jesus and the official interpreters of the
Law has been one of the main themes in Mark's Gospel, climaxing in the clearing
of the Temple and the cursing of the fig tree (cf Mark 11:1-25). Jesus challenged
the vested interests of those who used religion for their own power, and it was for
this that they killed him. The same accusation will be hurled at Jesus while he is
hanging on the cross:

'Aha! So you would destroy the Temple and rebuild it in three days!'

(Mark 15:29)

Jesus is silent before this accusation (14:61). They appear to be judging him, but
in fact are being judged by what they are doing to him.

Not only did Jesus challenge their interpretation of the Law, he also was
claiming, by everything he said and did, to be the Christ. Hence the second
question asked by the high priest (14:61).

The reply of Jesus is couched in terms taken from the Book of Daniel (14:62 =
Daniel 7:13). Mark has already referred to this in his Eschatological Discourse
(cf Mark 13:26 page 356). Jesus is condemned as a false prophet (cf Deuteronomy
13:5, 18:20).

The treatment given Jesus (14:65) recalls the words from the third servant
song of Isaiah:

'For my part, I made no resistance,
neither did I turn away.

I offered my back to those who struck me,
my cheeks to those who tore at my beard;
I did not cover my face
against insult and spittle.'

(Isaiah 50:6)

Peter's three-fold denial indicates persistent refusal to acknowledge Jesus.

The isolation of Jesus is complete. Mark recalls the prediction made by Jesus at the Supper (14:72 cf 14:30) to remind the reader that, in spite of appearances, God is controlling events.

* * * * * * * *

Luke has Peter's denial before the trial, to highlight the fact that Peter's failure was a failure of courage, not of faith (cf Luke 22:32, page 370). He avoids the possibility of the reader thinking that Peter denied what was affirmed at the trial — namely that Jesus is the Christ. He also includes the following moving words:

'and the Lord turned and looked straight at Peter, and
Peter remembered ... and he went outside and wept bitterly'

(Luke 22:61-62)

There is no mention, in Luke, of a death sentence passed by the court.

* * * * * * * *

JOHN 18:12-27

12   The cohort and its captain and the Jewish guards seized Jesus and bound
13 him. •They took him first to Annas, because Annas was the father-in-law of
14 Caiaphas, who was high priest that year. •It was Caiaphas who had suggested
    to the Jews, 'It is better for one man to die for the people'.
15   Simon Peter, with another disciple, followed Jesus. This disciple, who was
16 known to the high priest, went with Jesus into the high priest's palace, •but
    Peter stayed outside the door. So the other disciple, the one known to the high
    priest, went out, spoke to the woman who was keeping the door and brought
17 Peter in. •The maid on duty at the door said to Peter, 'Aren't you another of
18 that man's disciples?' He answered, 'I am not'. •Now it was cold, and the servants
    and guards had lit a charcoal fire and were standing there warming themselves;
    so Peter stood there too, warming himself with the others.
19
20   The high priest questioned Jesus about his disciples and his teaching. •Jesus
    answered, 'I have spoken openly for all the world to hear; I have always taught
    in the synagogue and in the Temple where all the Jews meet together: I have said
21 nothing in secret. •But why ask me? Ask my hearers what I taught: they know
22 what I said.' •At these words, one of the guards standing by gave Jesus a slap
23 in the face, saying, 'Is that the way to answer the high priest?' •Jesus replied, 'If
    there is something wrong in what I said, point it out; but if there is no offence
24 in it, why do you strike me?' •Then Annas sent him, still bound, to Caiaphas
    the high priest.
25   As Simon Peter stood there warming himself, someone said to him, 'Aren't
26 you another of his disciples?' He denied it saying, 'I am not'. •One of the high

priest's servants, a relation of the man whose ear Peter had cut off, said, 'Didn't
27 I see you in the garden with him?' •Again Peter denied it; and at once a cock
crew.

John does not mention, in this context, the trial before the Sanhedrin,
though he does refer (18:14) to an earlier meeting (cf John 11:46-52). Nor does he
mention here any formal charge laid against Jesus. (For the accusation of
blasphemy cf John 10:33 and 19:7).

Like Mark, he has the denial by Peter acting as a setting, bringing out by
contrast the witness of Jesus. Jesus' witness is not before the Sanhedrin (compare
Mark 14:55-64) but before Annas, the father-in-law of the high priest, Caiaphas
(18:13).

**3: Jesus is handed over to the Roman governor, condemned to death and
ridiculed.**

MARK 15:1-20 (Compare Matthew 27:1-2, 11-18, 20-23, 26-31)
1   **15** First thing in the morning, the chief priests together with the elders and
scribes, in short the whole Sanhedrin, had their plan ready. They had
Jesus bound and took him away and handed him over to Pilate.
2   Pilate questioned him, 'Are you the king of the Jews?' 'It is you who say it'
3 he answered. •And the chief priests brought many accusations against him.
4 Pilate questioned him again, 'Have you no reply at all? See how many accusations
5 they are bringing against you!' •But, to Pilate's amazement, Jesus made no
further reply.
6   At festival time Pilate used to release a prisoner for them, anyone they asked
7 for. •Now a man called Barabbas was then in prison with the rioters who had
8 committed murder during the uprising. •When the crowd went up and began to
9 ask Pilate the customary favour, •Pilate answered them, 'Do you want me to
10 release for you the king of the Jews?' •For he realised it was out of jealousy that
11 the chief priests had handed Jesus over. •The chief priests, however, had incited
12 the crowd to demand that he should release Barabbas for them instead. •Then
Pilate spoke again. 'But in that case,' he said to them 'what am I to do with the
13
14 man you call king of the Jews?' •They shouted back, 'Crucify him!' •'Why?'Pilate
asked them 'What harm has he done?' But they shouted all the louder, 'Crucify
15 him!' •So Pilate, anxious to placate the crowd, released Barabbas for them and,
having ordered Jesus to be scourged, handed him over to be crucified.
16   The soldiers led him away to the inner part of the palace, that is, the Prae-
17 torium, and called the whole cohort together. •They dressed him up in purple,
18 twisted some thorns into a crown and put it on him. •And they began saluting
19 him, 'Hail, king of the Jews!' •They struck his head with a reed and spat on him;
20 and they went down on their knees to do him homage. •And when they had
finished making fun of him, they took off the purple and dressed him in his own
clothes.

The scene moves from the court-room of the Jews to the judgment seat of the
Romans. Jesus is condemned before both. The Jews condemned him because, in
claiming to be the Messiah, he threatened the basis of their religion as
propounded by the religious authorities of the time. But the Jewish authorities
had no power, under Roman Law, to execute Jesus. They had to appeal to the
Roman governor and had to convince him that Jesus was a threat to the peace.

The drama is superb. Centre-stage stands Jesus — silent (Mark 15:15). All around him can be heard the accusations of the chief priests, the questioning of Pilate and the shouts of the crowd. Centre-stage stands Jesus — a free man in spite of his bonds (Mark 15:1). Opposite him is Pilate — to all appearances in charge of the situation, yet a prisoner of the whims of a fickle crowd.

Mark mentions that Pilate had the custom of releasing a prisoner on the occasion of the festival (Mark 15:6 cf also Matthew 27:15). This may have been the case, though we have no evidence of such a practice in any documents of the time. It may have been that Pilate had already arranged an execution of three leaders of the uprising (cf Mark 15:7) and used the inconvenience of a fourth man as an excuse to try to avoid condemning Jesus whose innocence he suspected (Mark 15:10). The crowd were demanding instant action. Pilate offered to pardon one of the criminals. They demanded the release of a man called 'Barabbas' (= 'son of the Father'). Mark wants his readers to see Barabbas as a symbol of all men. He, the 'son of the Father', the son of Adam, a guilty man like us all, is released. Another man takes his place, the Son of the Father, an innocent man who gives his life in his stead (cf Galations 2:20).

The condemnation of Jesus by the Roman authority is followed by a scene of ridicule and mockery (Mark 15:16-20). Pilate had asked Jesus: 'Are you the king of the Jews?' (Mark 15:2). The mock court-scene put on by the Roman soldiers provides the ironic answer. Yes, Jesus is a king, but not one that fits into the expectations of the Romans or the Jews. His kingship is divine. The kingdom he brings about is the kingdom of God. It is a kingdom ruled by the poor in spirit, the gentle, those who mourn, those who hunger and thirst for justice, the merciful, the pure in heart, the peacemakers (cf the Beatitudes, Matthew 5:1-10).

The mockery is a powerful statement of man's perversity, a powerful symbol of sin:

'Without beauty, without majesty (we saw him),
no looks to attract our eyes;
a thing despised and rejected by men,
a man of sorrows and familiar with suffering,
a man to make people screen their faces;
he was despised and we took no account of him.'

(Isaiah 53:2-3)

* * * * * * * *

After mentioning that Jesus was being led away to be handed over to Pilate, and before the account of the trial, Matthew recounts the death of Judas.

MATTHEW 27:3-10
When he found that Jesus had been condemned, Judas his betrayer was filled 3 with remorse and took the thirty silver pieces back to the chief priests and elders. 'I have sinned;' he said 'I have betrayed innocent blood.' 'What is that to us?' 4 they replied 'That is your concern.' •And flinging down the silver pieces in the 5 sanctuary he made off, and went and hanged himself. •The chief priests picked 6 up the silver pieces and said, 'It is against the Law to put this into the treasury;

it is blood-money' •So they discussed the matter and bought the potter's field 7
with it as a graveyard for foreigners, •and this is why the field is called the Field 8
of Blood today. •The words of the prophet Jeremiah[a] were then fulfilled: *And* 9
they took the thirty silver pieces, the sum at which the precious One was priced
by children of Israel, •*and they gave them for the potter's field, just as the Lord* 10
directed me.
(a: Actually a free rendition of Zechariah 11:12-13, combined
with ideas drawn from Jeremiah 18:2f, 19:1f, 32:6-15)

Luke gives quite a different account of Judas' death (cf Acts 1:16-19). According
to Luke's account, Judas bought a small farm with the money. Then:

> 'He fell headlong and burst open, and all his entrails poured out. Everybody in
> Jerusalem heard about it and the field came to be called the Bloody Acre, in their
> language Hakeldama.'
> (Acts 1:18-19)

Jeremiah (Matthew 27:9) was instructed by God to buy a field at the time of
the destruction of Jerusalem (cf Jeremiah 32:6-15). This was to be a sign to the
people that God would ensure that Jerusalem would one day be prosperous
again. Matthew seems to want to remind his readers of the fact that, in spite of the
rejection of Jesus by the religious leaders and his betrayal by one of his intimate
friends, God is in control of events and His will would prevail.

Zechariah was speaking of the treachery of those who were supposed to be
the shepherds of the people, but refused to listen to God's prophet. They insulted
God by offering his prophet the price of a slave (i.e., 'thirty shekels') for wages.
Matthew has just recounted the rejection of the prophet Jesus by the Sanhedrin.
His reference to the words of Zechariah act as a condemnation of the religious
leaders who are repeating the sin of their forebears. Their acceptance of the
money (27:6) is equivalent to an admission of Jesus' innocence.

Matthew's account of Judas' death recalls the death of Ahithophel. He
betrayed King David and tried, treacherously, to bring about his death. Then:

> 'he saddled his donkey and set off and went home to his own town. Then, having set
> his house in order, he strangled himself and so died.'
> (2 Samuel 17:23)

It would appear that Jesus is the victim and the religious leaders the victors.
Jesus has been condemned in the name of God as a blasphemer and has been
handed over to the Romans for execution. By placing the account of Judas' death
here, Matthew is making a comment on those responsible for condemning Jesus.
The religious authorities are false shepherds; Jesus' betrayer gains nothing from
his act, but remorse and despair and a violent self-inflicted death.

Matthew adds two details to Jesus' trial under Pilate.

MATTHEW 27:19
Now as he was seated in the chair of judgement, his wife sent him a message, 19
'Have nothing to do with that man; I have been upset all day by a dream I had
about him'.

Matthew once again uses the dream as a vehicle for revealing the mysterious
presence and power of God (cf Matthew 1:20-23 and 2:13).

MATTHEW 27:24-25
Then Pilate saw that he was making no impression, that in fact a riot was 24
imminent. So he took some water, washed his hands in front of the crowd and

said, 'I am innocent of this man's blood. It is your concern.' •And the people, 25
to a man, shouted back, 'His blood be on us and on our children!'

Pilate's gesture is an empty one. His action is an action of self-interest, an act
of weakness. At the same time, the 'greater guilt' (John 19:11) lies with those who,
not knowing God, nevertheless in God's name, but for their own interest, handed
Jesus over for judgment. The blood of Jesus did come down on the Jews.
Understandably, Matthew and his contemporaries would have seen the
destruction of Jerusalem, just as it was seen earlier by Jeremiah, as a punishment
of God for their refusal to accept Jesus (cf Matthew 23:37-39 page 334).

At the same time, there is irony in the shout of the crowd. Matthew's hope,
like Paul's (cf Romans 11:26), is that the blood of the Messiah will come down on
the chosen race, to bring them forgiveness and life.

*   *   *   *   *   *   *   *

LUKE 23:1-25

23 The whole assembly then rose, and they brought him before Pilate. 1
They began their accusation by saying, 'We found this man inciting our 2
people to revolt, opposing payment of the tribute to Caesar, and claiming to be
Christ, a king'. •Pilate put to him this question, 'Are you the king of the Jews?' 3
'It is you who say it' he replied. •Pilate then said to the chief priests and the crowd, 4
'I find no case against this man'. •But they persisted, 'He is inflaming the people 5
with his teaching all over Judaea; it has come all the way from Galilee, where he
started, down to here'. •When Pilate heard this, he asked if the man were a 6
Galilean; •and finding that he came under Herod's jurisdiction he passed him 7
over to Herod who was also in Jerusalem at that time.

Herod was delighted to see Jesus; he had heard about him and had 8
been wanting for a long time to set eyes on him; moreover, he was hoping to see
some miracle worked by him. •So he questioned him at some length; but without 9
getting any reply. •Meanwhile the chief priests and the scribes were there, violently 10
pressing their accusations. •Then Herod, together with his guards, treated him 11
with contempt and made fun of him; he put a rich cloak on him and sent him
back to Pilate. •And though Herod and Pilate had been enemies before, they 12
were reconciled that same day.

Pilate then summoned the chief priests and the leading men and the people. 13
'You brought this man before me' he said 'as a political agitator. Now I have 14
gone into the matter myself in your presence and found no case against the man
in respect of all the charges you bring against him. •Nor has Herod either, since 15
he has sent him back to us. As you can see, the man has done nothing that
deserves death, •so I shall have him flogged and then let him go.' •But as one $^{16}_{18}$
man they howled, 'Away with him! Give us Barabbas!' •(This man had been 19
thrown into prison for causing a riot in the city and for murder.)

Pilate was anxious to set Jesus free and addressed them again, •but they $^{20}_{21}$
shouted back, 'Crucify him! Crucify him!' •And for the third time he spoke 22
to them, 'Why? What harm has this man done? I have found no case against
him that deserves death, so I shall have him punished and then let him go.' •But 23
they kept on shouting at the top of their voices, demanding that he should be
crucified. And their shouts were growing louder.

Pilate then gave his verdict: their demand was to be granted. •He released ²⁴₂₅ the man they asked for, who had been imprisoned for rioting and murder, and handed Jesus over to them to deal with as they pleased.

Luke adds to Mark's account the actual accusations brought by the Sanhedrin against Jesus (Luke 23:2, 23:5). He also omits the scene of mockery instigated by the Roman soldiers and the scourging ordered by Pilate, and inserts, in their place, the scene with Herod. He also has the Roman judge pronounce Jesus' innocence three times (Luke 23:5, 23:14, 23:22).

A study of the second part of Luke's work, the Acts of the Apostles, makes it clear that one of Luke's aims in writing his Gospel for the Gentile communities in the Roman Empire, was to demonstrate that Christianity, in itself, did not pose a threat to the Empire. In this present scene, besides the statements of Jesus' innocence, Luke seems to want to underplay anything that could be interpreted as Roman-Christian antagonism.

* * * * * * * *

JOHN 18:28 — 19:16

They then led Jesus from the house of Caiaphas to the Praetorium. It was now morning. They did not go into the Praetorium themselves or they would be defiled and unable to eat the passover. •So Pilate came outside to them and said, 'What charge do you bring against this man?' They replied, •'If he were not a criminal, we should not be handing him over to you'. •Pilate said, 'Take him yourselves, and try him by your own Law'. The Jews answered, 'We are not allowed to put a man to death'. •This was to fulfil the words Jesus had spoken indicating the way he was going to die.

So Pilate went back into the Praetorium and called Jesus to him, 'Are you the king of the Jews?' he asked. •Jesus replied, 'Do you ask this of your own accord, or have others spoken to you about me?' •Pilate answered, 'Am I a Jew? It is your own people and the chief priests who have handed you over to me: what have you done?' •Jesus replied, 'Mine is not a kingdom of this world; if my kingdom were of this world, my men would have fought to prevent my being surrendered to the Jews. But my kingdom is not of this kind.' •'So you are a king then?' said Pilate. 'It is you who say it' answered Jesus. 'Yes, I am a king. I was born for this, I came into the world for this: to bear witness to the truth; and all who are on the side of truth listen to my voice.' •'Truth?' said Pilate 'What is that?'; and with that he went out again to the Jews and said, 'I find no case against him. •But according to a custom of yours I should release one prisoner at the Passover; would you like me, then, to release the king of the Jews?' •At this they shouted: 'Not this man,' they said 'but Barabbas'. Barabbas was a brigand.

19 Pilate then had Jesus taken away and scourged; •and after this, the soldiers ¹₂ twisted some thorns into a crown and put it on his head, and dressed him in a purple robe. •They kept coming up to him and saying, 'Hail, king of the Jews!'; and they slapped him in the face.

Pilate came outside again and said to them, 'Look, I am going to bring him out to you to let you see that I find no case'. •Jesus then came out wearing the crown of thorns and the purple robe. Pilate said, 'Here is the man'. •When they saw him the chief priests and the guards shouted, 'Crucify him! Crucify him!' Pilate said, 'Take him yourselves and crucify him: I can find no case against him'.

7 'We have a Law,' the Jews replied 'and according to that Law he ought to die, because he has claimed to be the Son of God.'

8
9   When Pilate heard them say this his fears increased. •Re-entering the Praetorium, he said to Jesus, 'Where do you come from?' But Jesus made no answer.

10 Pilate then said to him, 'Are you refusing to speak to me? Surely you know I
11 have power to release you and I have power to crucify you?' •'You would have no power over me' replied Jesus 'if it had not been given you from above; that is why the one who handed me over to you has the greater guilt.'

12   From that moment Pilate was anxious to set him free, but the Jews shouted, 'If you set him free you are no friend of Caesar's; anyone who makes himself
13 king is defying Caesar'. •Hearing these words, Pilate had Jesus brought out, and seated himself on the chair of judgement at a place called the Pavement, in
14 Hebrew Gabbatha. •It was Passover Preparation Day, about the sixth hour.
15 'Here is your king' said Pilate to the Jews. •'Take him away, take him away!' they said. 'Crucify him!' 'Do you want me to crucify your king?' said Pilate.
16 The chief priests answered, 'We have no king except Caesar'. •So in the end Pilate handed him over to them to be crucified.

John emphasises the kingship of Jesus. This is typical of the whole of his Passion account: Jesus is glorified on the cross. It is on the cross that he draws all men to himself. There we see the reign of God's love. There the kingdom of God is established.

From a structural point of view, the crowning with thorns (John 19:1-3) forms the centre-piece of John's Passion story: even by their mockery, the soldiers highlight the meaning of Jesus death. Jesus is the king of the Jews; indeed, of the whole world.

The judgment scene dramatises the confrontation between Jesus and the world. Jesus is establishing the reign of God's love in the world; he is bearing witness to God's faithfulness (John 18:37). The world cannot convict him; in fact, three times (compare Luke) Jesus' innocence is pronounced (cf John 18:38, 19:4, 19:6)

The second appearance of Jesus before Pilate, after the mockery (John 19:4-7) is staged after the fashion of the ceremony of presentation of the Emperor. Jesus is presented to the crowd for their acclamation.

The irony is masterful. Pilate appears to be the powerful one (John 19:10), but it is the silent Jesus who is master of the situation. Jesus appears to be the one being condemned (John 19:6, 19:16), but it is those who condemn him who are pronounced guilty (John 19:11).

The real reason for the Jews handing Jesus over to Pilate is made clear when they say:

'We have a Law and according to that Law he ought to die, because he has claimed to be the Son of God.'

(John 19:7)

This was made clear by the Synoptics in their account of the trial before the Sanhedrin (cf Mark 14:61, Matthew 26:63 and Luke 22:70). Jesus was condemned because he claimed to be the Messiah.

The title 'Son of God' while primarily a Messianic title, does carry with it mysterious overtones of divinity. Pilate is moved to ask Jesus a question that has been asked so often before in John's Gospel:

'Where do you come from?'

(John 19:9)

Those present at the wedding-feast where Jesus performed his first sign, were faced with the mystery of Jesus (cf John 2:9); so was the Samaritan woman (cf John 4:11). The Jewish leaders were continually confronted by this question (cf John 7:27-28; 8:14; 9:29-30). Like them, Pilate lacked the courage to walk by the light of the 'truth', and 'in the end' (John 19:16) cared more for the approval that comes from men, and condemned Jesus.

Another irony in John's account is the fact that the chief priests rejected the Covenant ('We have no king except Caesar' John 19:16), just as they were about to celebrate it.

John has demonstrated that the world has no power over Jesus (cf John 14:30), and that, in spite of appearances, Jesus has 'conquered the world' (John 16:33).

* * * * * * *

4: The crucifixion

MARK 15:21-32 (Compare Matthew 27:32-44; Luke 23:26, 32-38)

They led him out to crucify him. •They enlisted a passer-by, Simon of Cyrene, 21 father of Alexander and Rufus, who was coming in from the country, to carry his cross. •They brought Jesus to the place called Golgotha, which means the 22 place of the skull.

They offered him wine mixed with myrrh, but he refused it. •Then they $\frac{23}{24}$ crucified him, and shared out his clothing, casting lots to decide what each should get. •It was the third hour when they crucified him. •The inscription giving the $\frac{25}{26}$ charge against him read: 'The King of the Jews'. •And they crucified two robbers 27 with him, one on his right and one on his left.

The passers-by jeered at him; they shook their heads and said, 'Aha! So you 29 would destroy the Temple and rebuild it in three days! •Then save yourself: 30 come down from the cross!' •The chief priests and the scribes mocked him among 31 themselves in the same way. 'He saved others,' they said 'he cannot save himself. •Let the Christ, the king of Israel, come down from the cross now, for 32 us to see it and believe.' Even those who were crucified with him taunted him.

Mark alone mentions that Simon was the 'father of Alexander and Rufus' (15:21). Perhaps these two men were known to the Roman community for whom Mark was writing. (It is interesting to note that Paul refers to a certain 'Rufus' in his Letter to the Roman church: Romans 16:13).

In the Book of Proverbs we read:

'Procure strong drink for a man about to perish,
wine for the heart that is full of bitterness:
let him drink and forget his misfortune,
and remember his misery no more.'

(Proverbs 31:6)

Jesus refuses the drink (15:23). His heart is not full of bitterness; he is not about to perish!

Mark recalls also the Psalmist:

'There they glare at me, gloating;
they divide my garments among them
and cast lots for my clothing.'

(Psalm 22:18)

Mark tells us that Jesus was crucified at the 'third hour' (15:25); that is, somewhere between 9:00 a.m. and midday. (Contrast John 19:14, where Jesus is condemned by Pilate 'about the sixth hour' = noon).

The mockery is ironical: it goes to the heart of the Gospel message. Jesus had said:

'If anyone wants to be a follower of mine,
let him renounce himself and take up his cross and follow me.
For anyone who wants to save his life will lose it;
but anyone who loses his life for my sake, and for the sake
of the Gospel, will save it.'

(Mark 8:34-35)

Jesus is saving himself, but not in the way they expect. He is saving himself in the only way possible — by giving himself for others, for that is the very nature of God's love and the only way to life. The sign they ask for is the very contradiction of the God whom Jesus is revealing.

Matthew adds the following words to their taunt:

'He put his trust in God;
now let God rescue him if he wants him.
For he did say, "I am the Son of God."'

*(Matthew 27:43
Compare Psalm 22:8 and Wisdom 2:18-20)*

This, too, is ironical, for the Resurrection will show just how effectively God did rescue Jesus. Not only do the taunters fail to understand what it means to save oneself, they have no understanding of what it means to be a 'Son of God'. In his account of the temptations in the desert, Matthew established that sonship is a matter of complete trust in the Father and so of wanting the will of God. God's will was that Jesus continue to love. It was his love that brought him into conflict with the civil and church leaders. Jesus trusted, as a Son should, that even though his love seemed to be bringing about his death, if he kept loving, his Father would rescue him in his own way. His trust was not misplaced.

*   *   *   *   *   *   *   *

Luke adds the following passage:

LUKE 23:27-31
•Large numbers of people followed him, and of women
28 too, who mourned and lamented for him. •But Jesus turned to them and said,
'Daughters of Jerusalem, do not weep for me; weep rather for yourselves and for
29 your children. •For the days will surely come when people will say, "Happy are

those who are barren, the wombs that have never borne, the breasts that have
30 never suckled!" •Then they will begin to *say to the mountains,"Fall on us !"*; *to the*
31 *hills, "Cover us !"* ᵃ•For if men use the green wood like this, what will happen
32 when it is dry?'

(a: Hosea 10:8)

Luke refers to the prophecy of Hosea (Luke 23:30 = Hosea 10:8). Hosea is
warning his contemporaries of the coming of the Assyrian armies as instruments
of the punishment of God. Luke, remembering the destruction of Jerusalem in 70
A.D. makes an obvious parallel. Jesus is not to be pitied. He is doing his Father's
will and he will be saved. The real ones who deserve pity are those who in
rejecting Jesus are rejecting God's saving love.

LUKE 23:34
• Jesus said, 'Father, forgive them; they do not know what they are doing'.

This is an allusion to the Fourth Servant Song of Isaiah:

'I will grant whole hordes for his tribute,
he shall divide the spoil with the mighty,
for surrendering himself to death
and letting himself be taken for a sinner (cf Luke 22:37),
while he was bearing the faults of many
and *praying all the time for sinners.'*

(Isaiah 53:12)

LUKE 23:39-43
39 One of the criminals hanging there abused him. 'Are you not the Christ?'
40 he said. 'Save yourself and us as well.' •But the other spoke up and rebuked him.
'Have you no fear of God at all?' he said. 'You got the same sentence as he did,
41 but in our case we deserved it: we are paying for what we did. But this man has
42 done nothing wrong. •Jesus,' he said 'remember me when you come into your
43 kingdom.' •'Indeed, I promise you,' he replied 'today you will be with me in
paradise.'

Throughout his Gospel Luke has taken every opportunity to dwell on Jesus
reaching out to the outcasts and sinners. This forms a beautiful climax just before
Jesus' death. His last relationship is with one who is being killed as a criminal.
Jesus welcomes him with love.

* * * * * * * *

JOHN 19:17-24
17 They then took charge of Jesus, •and carrying his own cross he went out
of the city to the place of the skull or, as it was called in Hebrew, Golgotha
18 where they crucified him with two others, one on either side with Jesus in the
19 middle. •Pilate wrote out a notice and had it fixed to the cross; it ran: 'Jesus
20 the Nazarene, King of the Jews'. •This notice was read by many of the Jews,
because the place where Jesus was crucified was not far from the city, and the
21 writing was in Hebrew, Latin and Greek. •So the Jewish chief priests said to
Pilate, 'You should not write "King of the Jews", but "This man said: I am King
22 of the Jews" '. •Pilate answered, 'What I have written, I have written'.
23 When the soldiers had finished crucifying Jesus they took his clothing and
divided it into four shares, one for each soldier. His undergarment was seamless,

woven in one piece from neck to hem; •so they said to one another, 'Instead of   24
tearing it, let's throw dice to decide who is to have it'. In this way the words
of scripture were fulfilled:

> They shared out my clothing among them.
> They cast lots for my clothes. ^a

This is exactly what the soldiers did.

(a: Psalm 22:18)

John avoids anything that might distract the attention of his readers from
Jesus. For this reason he writes that Jesus was 'carrying his own cross' (John
19:17), and he omits any reference to Simon (compare Mark 15:21). He also
omits any reference to the jeers and scoffing of the passers-by (compare Mark
15:29-32). There is no mention of the 'wine mixed with myrrh' (Mark 15:23), but
all the other features of Mark's account can be found in John's. He dwells on the
inscription (John 19:19-22) because it highlights the central theme of John's
Passion account: the kingship of Jesus.

* * * * * * * *

5: The death of Jesus

MARK 15:33-41 (Compare Matthew 27:45-51a, 54-56 and Luke 23:44-49)

When the sixth hour came there was darkness over the whole land until the 33
ninth hour. •And at the ninth hour Jesus cried out in a loud voice, 'Eloi, Eloi, 34
lama sabachthani?' which means, '*My God, my God, why have you deserted me?*'^a
When some of those who stood by heard this, they said, 'Listen, he is calling on 35
Elijah'. •Someone ran and soaked a sponge in vinegar and, putting it on a reed, 36
gave it him to drink saying, 'Wait and see if Elijah will come to take him down'.
But Jesus gave a loud cry and breathed his last. •And the veil of the Temple was 37 38
torn in two from top to bottom. •The centurion, who was standing in front of 39
him, had seen how he had died, and he said, 'In truth this man was a son of
God'.

There were some women watching from a distance. Among them were Mary 40
of Magdala, Mary who was the mother of James the younger and Joset, and
Salome. •These used to follow him and look after him when he was in Galilee. 41
And there were many other women there who had come up to Jerusalem with
him.

(a: Psalm 22:1)

The darkness over the whole land (Mark 15:33) was the darkness that was to
accompany the Day of Judgment:

> 'Day of dark and gloom,
> day of cloud and blackness.'

(Joel 2:2)

Jesus died with the name of God on his lips (Hebrew 'el'). Both Mark and
Matthew associate his cry with the opening words of Psalm 22. It is the prayer of
a man in the depths of suffering, a man who feels abandoned by God, and yet retains
his trust in God and his belief that his cry will be heard. Let us read the whole
psalm reflectively as Mark wants us to do.

'My God, my God, why have you deserted me?
How far from saving me, the words I groan!
I call all day, my God, but you never answer,
all night long I call and cannot rest.
Yet, Holy One, you
who make your home in the praises of Israel,
in you our fathers put their trust,
they trusted and you rescued them;
they called to you for help and they were saved,
they never trusted you in vain.

Yet, here am I, now more worm than man,
scorn of mankind, jest of the people,
all who see me jeer at me,
they toss their heads and sneer,
"He relied on Yahweh, let Yahweh save him!
If Yahweh is his friend, let him rescue him!"

Yet you drew me out of the womb,
you entrusted me to my mother's breasts;
placed on your lap from my birth,
from my mother's womb you have been my God.
Do not stand aside: trouble is near,
I have no one to help me!

A herd of bulls surround me,
strong bulls of Bashan close in on me;
their jaws are agape for me,
like lions tearing and roaring.

I am like water draining away,
my bones are all disjointed,
my heart is like wax,
melting inside me;
my palate is drier than a potsherd
and my tongue is stuck to my jaw.

A pack of dogs surround me,
a gang of villains close me in;
they tie me hand and foot
and leave me lying in the dust of death.

I can count every one of my bones,
and there they glare at me, gloating;
they divide my garments among them
and cast lots for my clothes.

Do not stand aside, Yahweh.
O my strength, come to my help;
rescue my soul from the sword,
my dear life from the paw of the dog,
save me from the lion's mouth,
my poor soul from the wild bull's horns!

Then I shall proclaim your name to my brothers,
praise you in full assembly:
you who fear Yahweh, praise him!
Entire race of Jacob, glorify him!
Entire race of Israel, revere him!

For he has not despised
or disdained the poor man in his poverty,
has not hidden his face from him,
but has answered him when he called.'

(Psalm 22:1-24)

Jesus' cry does come from the depths. It begins from the pain and sense of being alone and abandoned. But it issues in a cry of confidence and comes from a heart that never lost trust. Jesus, according to Mark and Matthew, did cry to his God from the depths of his pain. But in that cry of trust he saw the face of God and heard God's answer. The God in whom Jesus had always placed his trust:

'has not hidden his face from him, but has answered him when he called'

(Psalm 22:24)

To the end, Jesus revealed God as faithful to his covenant with his people. God proved himself faithful to Jesus. This is the spirit of Jesus' last cry.

Luke omits the reference of Psalm 22. In its place he has:

'When Jesus had cried out with a loud voice, he said, "Father, into your hands I commit my spirit". With these words he breathed his last.'

(Luke 23:46)

These were the last words of the customary night prayers of a devout Jew. With them a man entrusted his spirit to God in sleep, confident that God would give him back his spirit on the morrow. The prayer ends with the words 'el 'emet'. Luke chooses to associate Jesus' last cry ('el') with this Psalm rather than with Psalm 22.

'In you, Yahweh, I take shelter;
never let me be disgraced.
In your righteousness deliver me, rescue me,
turn your ear to me, make haste!

Be a sheltering rock for me,
a walled fortress to save me!
For you are my rock, my fortress;
for the sake of your name, guide me, lead me!

Pull me out of the net they have spread for me,
for you are my refuge;
into your hands I commit my spirit (cf Luke 23:46),
you have redeemed me, Yahweh, God of truth' ('el 'emet').

(Psalm 31:1-5)

Both psalms are, ultimately, psalms of complete trust and abandonment to God.

Jesus had often spoken of death simply as 'sleep' (Matthew 9:24, 27:52 and John 11:11-12). Now he accepts his own death in the same simple trust:

'The Father loves me,
because I lay down my life
in order to take it up again.
No one takes it from me;
I lay it down of my own free will,
and as it is in my power to lay it down,
so it is in my power to take it up again;
and this is the command I have been given by my Father'

(John 10:17-18)

Jesus' cry is misunderstood by the by-standers. Their complete lack of sensitivity to what is going on in the heart of Jesus, their distracted hope for some wonderful happening associated with the return of the prophet Elijah, and the sympathetic (or mocking?) action in offering him some of their sour drink — all dramatises the isolation of Jesus in his last moments.

'Jesus gave a loud cry and breathed his last'

(Mark 15:37 and Luke 23:46 Matthew uses the expression: 'yielded up his spirit 27:50)

* * * * * * * *

At last God is revealed. Or as the Synoptics express it, dramatically:

'The veil of the Temple was torn in two from top to bottom'

(Mark 15:38)

Man can now look on the face of God! No longer is there a veil separating men from the Holy of Holies. As the author of the Letter to the Hebrews puts it:

'He has entered the Holy of Holies once for all'

(Hebrews 9:12)

'Brothers, through the blood of Jesus,
we have the right to enter the sanctuary.'

(Hebrews 10:19)

The revelation of God is seen by the centurion standing by the cross (Mark 15:39). The Old Covenant is ended. There are no longer any barriers holding men back from God. God's love, unveiled in the death of Jesus, is there calling all men to faith and life. Mankind is redeemed!

* * * * * * * *

Mark concludes his account by mentioning the women who witnessed Jesus' death (Mark 15:40-41; also Matthew 27:55-56; Luke 23:49 mentions the fact without mentioning the names of the women). These women will be the ones who observe the burial and discover the empty tomb.

* * * * * * * *

Matthew adds some Apocalyptic scenes to his account of Jesus' death:

MATTHEW 27:51-53

the earth
52 quaked; the rocks were split; •the tombs opened and the bodies of many holy men
53 rose from the dead, •and these, after his resurrection, came out of the tombs,
54 entered the Holy City and appeared to a number of people.

The reader should be familiar with this kind of literature from our introduction to the Eschatological Discourse. Matthew is underlining the truth that the death of Jesus is God's final saving act. In witnessing it we are witnessing the Eschaton.

JOHN 19:25-30

25 Near the cross of Jesus stood his mother and his mother's sister, Mary the
26 wife of Clopas, and Mary of Magdala. •Seeing his mother and the disciple
he loved standing near her, Jesus said to his mother, 'Woman, this is your son'.
27 Then to the disciple he said, 'This is your mother'. And from that moment the
disciple made a place for her in his home.
28 After this, Jesus knew that everything had now been completed, and to
fulfil the scripture perfectly he said:

'*I am thirsty*'.*ᵃ*

29 A jar full of vinegar stood there, so putting a sponge soaked in the vinegar on
30 a hyssop stick they held it up to his mouth. •After Jesus had taken the vinegar
he said, 'It is accomplished'; and bowing his head he gave up his spirit.

(a: Psalm 69:21)

It is not clear whether John is referring to three or four different women. If
his 'mother's sister' is to be identified with 'Mary, the wife of Clopas' this could
well be the same woman that Mark refers to as 'Mary who was the mother of
James the younger and Joset' (Mark 15:40). These latter are spoken of as
brothers of Jesus (cf Mark 6:3). On the other hand if his 'mother's sister' is a
different woman from 'Mary, the wife of Clopas', she may be the woman referred
to by Mark as 'Salome' (Mark 15:40), or by Matthew as 'the mother of Zebedee's
sons' (Matthew 27:56).

More to the point is the fact that John alone mentions the presence at the
cross of Jesus' mother (John 19:25). She was present when Jesus performed his
first sign, at Cana in Galilee (cf John 2:1). It was at her instigation that he set out
on the road that was to lead to this hour (cf John 2:4). In the Cana scene she was a
symbol of the people of the old Covenant, the mother of the Messiah, asking for
the new wine of the Spirit.

In the scene before us, the 'hour' has come. She is present again, this time as
the mother of the people of the new Covenant (symbolised by the 'disciple he
loved' John 19:26 cf John 13:22-23 and commentary). In both scenes Mary is
addressed as 'Woman' (John 2:4 and 19:26). As Jesus is the new Adam, so Mary
is the new Eve, bringing forth children for God in pain (cf Genesis 3:15-16 and
Revelation 12:1-5). We are reminded of a statement in John's second supper
discourse in which John referred to the suffering that was to usher in the
Messianic kingdom:

'I tell you most solemnly,
you will be weeping and wailing
while the world will rejoice;
you will be sorrowful,
but your sorrow will turn to joy.
A woman in childbirth suffers,
because her time has come;
but when she has given birth to the child she forgets her suffering
in her joy that a man has been born into the world.
So it is with you: you are sad now,
but I shall see you again, and your hearts will be full of joy,
and that joy no one shall take from you.'

(John 16:20-22)

Jesus' death is the final act of suffering that is to bring to birth a new and redeemed people (cf Isaiah 49:20-22). Mary stands as a symbol of this fact.

John mentions the offering of vinegar (John 19:29 compare Mark 15:36); it reminds him of Psalm 69:21:

'When I was thirsty, they gave me vinegar to drink'.

Like Psalm 22 (cf Mark and Matthew), Psalm 69 is a prayer of a man in distress; a prayer, nevertheless, that includes these words:

'For myself, wounded wretch that I am,
by your saving power, God, *lift me up.*
I will praise the name of God with a song,
I will extol him with my thanksgiving'

(Psalm 69:29-30)

Instead of a 'reed' (cf Mark 15:36), John mentions a 'hyssop stick' (John 19:29). He wants to remind his readers of the hyssop stick that was used to place the blood of the Paschal Lamb on the door-posts of those whom God was to redeem (cf Exodus 12:22). Jesus is the new Passover lamb 'that takes away the sin of the world' (John 1:29 cf John 13:1).

The loud cry of the Synoptics is interpreted by John as a final and powerful statement of victory and accomplishment (John 19:30). With that cry:

'He gave up his Spirit'

(John 19:30)

We are reminded of John's words earlier:

'He was speaking of the Spirit which those who believe in him were to receive; for there was no Spirit as yet because Jesus had not yet been glorified.'

(John 7:39)

JOHN 19:31-37

It was Preparation Day, and to prevent the bodies remaining on the cross 31 during the sabbath—since that sabbath was a day of special solemnity—the Jews asked Pilate to have the legs broken and the bodies taken away. •Consequently 32 the soldiers came and broke the legs of the first man who had been crucified with him and then of the other. •When they came to Jesus, they found he was already 33 dead, and so instead of breaking his legs •one of the soldiers pierced his side 34 with a lance; and immediately there came out blood and water. •This is the 35 evidence of one who saw it —trustworthy evidence, and he knows he speaks the truth—and he gives it so that you may believe as well. •Because all this happened 36 to fulfil the words of scripture:

Not one bone of his will be broken,[a]

and again, in another place scripture says: 37

They will look on the one whom they have pierced.[b]

(a: Exodus 12:46 and Psalm 34:20; b: Zechariah 12:10)

The final text quoted by John is taken from the prophet Zechariah. Zechariah is speaking of the coming of the Messianic age. It will, according to the prophet, flow from the suffering and mysterious death of the one who captains the forces of good against the forces of evil.

428 THE DEATH AND RESURRECTION OF JESUS

'Over the House of David and the citizens of Jerusalem
I will pour out a spirit of kindness and prayer.
They will look on the one whom they have pierced;
they will mourn for him as for an only son, and
weep for him as people weep for a first-born child.
When that day comes there will be a great mourning in Judah,
like the mourning of Hadad-rimmon in the plain of Megiddo.
And the country will mourn clan by clan; the clan of the
House of David apart, with their wives by themselves;
the clan of the House of Nathan apart, with their wives by
themselves, the clan of the House of Levi apart, with their
wives by themselves. All the clans that remain, clan by clan,
with their wives by themselves.
When that Day comes, a fountain will be opened for the House
of David and the citizens of Jerusalem, for sin and impurity.'

(Zechariah 12:10 — 13:1)

The same allusion is present in the Book of Revelation:

'It is he who is coming on the clouds;
everyone will see him, even those who pierced him,
and all the races of the earth will mourn over him.'

(Revelation 1:7)

All men mourn at the death of Jesus. From his pierced heart, water flows. This is the fountain of which Zechariah spoke (Zechariah 13:1). We are reminded of the water that flowed from the rock struck by Moses (Exodus 17:6). We are reminded of the fountains of wisdom that God pours out over his people (cf Proverbs 13:14, Sirach 15:3, 24:25-29, Baruch 3:15). We are reminded of the water of the Spirit poured out by God (cf Psalm 36:9-10, Isaiah 12:3, 55:1, Ezekiel 47:1-2). This is the Spirit promised by the Baptist (John 1:33); the Spirit promised by Jesus (John 6:63, 7:38-39).

Jesus has just died. John refers to a ritual practice concerning the sacrifice of the Paschal Lamb (John 19:16 = Exodus 12:46), to remind the reader that he is the new Paschal Lamb who is dying to take away the sin of the world (John 1:29). The Psalmist uses the same statement to speak of God's care for the virtuous man who suffers but continues to place his trust in God (cf Psalm 34:20). Jesus has just died, and the world mourns for him. But the mourning is not without hope, for in his death God is victorious and man has been redeemed from slavery. We are invited, in the words of Isaiah, to draw water with joy from the springs of the Saviour (cf Isaiah 12:3).

'Anyone who drinks the water that I shall give him
will never be thirsty again:
the water that I shall give
will turn into a spring inside him,
welling up to eternal life.'

(John 4:14)

6: The burial of Jesus

MARK 15:42-47 (Compare Matthew 27:57-61, Luke 23:50-56 and John 19:38,41-42)

It was now evening, and since it was Preparation Day (that is, the vigil of the 42
sabbath), •there came Joseph of Arimathaea, a prominent member of the •43

Council, who himself lived in the hope of seeing the kingdom of God, and he boldly went to Pilate and asked for the body of Jesus. •Pilate, astonished that 44 he should have died so soon, summoned the centurion and enquired if he was already dead. •Having been assured of this by the centurion, he granted the 45 corpse to Joseph •who bought a shroud, took Jesus down from the cross, 46 wrapped him in the shroud and laid him in a tomb which had been hewn out of the rock. He then rolled a stone against the entrance to the tomb. •Mary of 47 Magdala and Mary the mother of Joset were watching and took note of where he was laid.

It was in accordance with Roman custom to allow relatives and friends to dispose of the body of a criminal. Mark tells us that Joseph of Arimathaea (a 'disciple of Jesus' according to Matthew 27:57) took charge of burying Jesus. Mark also mentions the women as they are to be important witnesses of the resurrection (15:47).

* * * * * * * *

Luke mentions that the 'sabbath was imminent' (23:54); hence the burial was done in haste and the women:

'returned and prepared spices and ointments'. (23:56)

* * * * * * * *

John adds the following details:

JOHN 19:39-40
Nicodemus came as well—the same one who had first come to Jesus at night-time 39 —and he brought a mixture of myrrh and aloes, weighing about a hundred pounds. •They took the body of Jesus and wrapped it with the spices in linen 40 cloths, following the Jewish burial custom.

A hurried burial it was, but a kingly one, all the same.

* * * * * * * *

Chapter 2
The empty tomb

Mark 16:1-8
Matthew 27:62-28:15
Luke 24:1-12
John 20:1-18

The material concerning Jesus' resurrection can be divided neatly into two sections. The first concerns the empty tomb, and expresses what Jesus' early disciples believed it to signify. It has been suggested that we are dealing with a ritual text used by devout Christians as they visited the empty tomb. It is a creedal statement expressing what they believed. Why they believed, the grounds for their faith in the resurrection, form the material of the second section, the 'appearances' of Jesus.

1: The empty tomb

MARK 16:1-8

16 When the sabbath was over, Mary of Magdala, Mary the mother of James, 1 and Salome, bought spices with which to go and anoint him. •And very early 2 in the morning on the first day of the week they went to the tomb, just as the sun was rising.

They had been saying to one another, 'Who will roll away the stone for us 3 from the entrance to the tomb?' •But when they looked they could see that the 4 stone—which was very big—had already been rolled back. •On entering the 5 tomb they saw a young man in a white robe seated on the right-hand side, and they were struck with amazement. •But he said to them, 'There is no need for 6 alarm. You are looking for Jesus of Nazareth, who was crucified: he has risen, he is not here. See, here is the place where they laid him. •But you must go and 7 tell his disciples and Peter, "He is going before you to Galilee; it is there you will see him, just as he told you".' •And the women came out and ran away 8 from the tomb because they were frightened out of their wits; and they said nothing to a soul, for they were afraid...

The women (16:1) are the same ones who witnessed the crucifixion (Mark 15:40) and the burial (Mark 15:47).

It seems that we are meant to imagine this scene occuring in darkness. The expression translated here 'very early' (16:2) has a more precise meaning in Greek, referring to the hour between three and four a.m. This makes the expression 'just as the sun was rising' (16:2) a dramatic statement, preparing us for the news of the angel.

There is no mention of any reaction to the sight of the stone rolled away from the tomb; the amazement (16:5) of the women is a reaction to the manifestation of God's presence in the form of an angel.

The women do not witness the Resurrection; they are told of it by God. It is revealed to them that the Jesus they knew 'Jesus of Nazareth':

'has risen, he is not here'. (16:6)

The expression conveys, very succinctly, the paradox and mystery of the Resurrection as believed in by the early church.

a: **'He has risen'** (or, perhaps better: 'He was raised' Greek 'egeiro')

The imagery is simple. Mark uses the same word for the raising up of a sick person from bed (Mark 1:31), for raising a person from sleep (Mark 4:38). He also uses it for raising a person from death back to this present life (Mark 5:41). When it comes to the mystery of life-beyond-death, we do not have language that is adequate for it lies beyond our everyday experience. At the same time we have to use words, by analogy, and Mark uses the same expression 'was raised' of this mystery (Mark 12:26 and 14:28). A person is lying in death and God is imagined as raising that person up to himself, as you would raise a sick person from bed. Obviously this raising implies a profound transformation, the elements of which are beyond our fathoming (cf 1 Corinthians 15:35ff).

A similar expression is used for the same mystery when Mark speaks of 'rising' or 'standing up' (Greek: anastasis). This is the expression employed when Jesus foretells his resurrection (Mark 8:31, 9:31 and 10:34).

Neither of these words comprehend the mystery of the resurrection, so the New Testament authors sought other words to give expression to their faith. They speak of Jesus 'going up' or 'ascending' (Greek: anabaino). Mark uses the word for Jesus going up to Jerusalem (Mark 10:32 and 51:41) and for going up to the hills (Mark 3:13). John likes to use it of Jesus going up to his Father (John 3:13, 6:62, 6:62, 20:17) Paul, too, uses it to express one aspect of the resurrection (Ephesians 4:8-10). John and Paul use another expression to get at the same mystery: they speak of Jesus being 'lifted up', 'exalted' (Greek: hypsoo). (John 3:14, 8:28, 12:32, 12:34; Philippians 2:9, Hebrews 7:26, cf also Acts 2:33 and 5:31).

Another approach to the same reality is found in the use of the word 'glorified' (Greek: doxein). Mark uses this expression of the Son of Man (Mark 8:36 and 13:26). It is a favorite expression of John (cf John 7:39). The risen Jesus is seen as being caught up in the glory of God. The New Testament likes to use this same expression of our own risen bodies, seeing them as sharing in this same glory (cf 1 Corinthians 15:34, Philippians 3:21 and 2 Thessalonians 2:14).

Perhaps the simplest expression that sums up what the above expressions are reaching for is the statement that Jesus of Nazareth, who was crucified, died and was buried, is now *alive* with God (cf Mark 16:11). When the subject of the resurrection from the dead came up earlier, Jesus expressed his confident hope by saying that:

'He is God, not of the dead, but of the living'

(Mark 12:27)

The New Testament authors frequently use this simple but profound word to express the mystery of the resurrection (cf Luke 24:5, 24:23; Acts 1:3, 25:19; John 5:21, 5:25; Romans 6:10; 2 Corinthians 13:4; Revelations 1:18).

When Mark has the revelation expressed in the words 'He is risen', it is this faith of the early church that he is expressing.

b: 'He is not here'

It was obvious to the early church, as it is obvious to us, that Jesus of Nazareth is no longer with us. The New Testament writers speak of 'waiting for him' (cf 1 Thessalonians 1:10, Philippians 3:20). Once again we have no words to express accurately something that is a matter of hope and something that lies beyond our empirical experience. The early church used expressions like the following to give words to the faith they shared.

They spoke of waiting for Jesus to 'come' (1 Corinthians 11:26). Mark applies the word to the coming of the Son of Man (Mark 8:38, 13:26, 14:62; cf also John 14:3, 14:18, 14:23, 14:28; Revelations 22:17, 22:20 and Acts 1:11).

They spoke of waiting for him to 'be revealed' (Greek: 'apocalypse'). They saw themselves, that is, as waiting for the veil that hid him from them to be taken away (cf 2 Thessalonians 1:7).

They spoke of awaiting his 'presence' (Greek: parousia; cf Matthew 24:39, 1 Thessalonians 2:19, 3:13, 2 Peter 3:12).

At the same time the early church believed that the risen Jesus while 'not here' was present to them in many ways. Hence Mark has the angel say:

c: 'you will see him'

The word 'see' is inadequate, of course, as a word to communicate the experience of the presence of the risen Jesus, just as it is inadequate when used of the experience of God that lies in wait for us. (John speaks of us 'seeing' God as he really is, 1 John 3:2; and 'seeing' him face to face, Revelations 22:4). Our direct sensory experience is limited to the world we know, between birth and death; we must use words analogously when we endeavour to express experiences that go beyond this world.

What the actual experience was is not told us by Mark. He has the women being told to 'go and tell the disciples' (Mark 16:7), and opens the way for some experience they were to have in 'Galilee' (Mark 16:7).

This tells us something about the fidelity of Jesus. Again and again, as we have seen, the disciples fail to understand Jesus; again and again, Jesus calls them and shares the Good News with them. At the end, at the last supper he was to have with them, Jesus promised them that, in spite of their desertion of him, in spite of Peter's forthcoming denial and Judas's betrayal, he, Jesus, would come back to them and call them again. Whatever their infidelity to him, he would not abandon them:

'You will all lose faith, for the scripture says: I shall strike the shepherd and the sheep will be scattered; however, after my resurrection, I shall go before you into Galilee'

(Mark 14:27-28)

Mark reminds his readers of this promise.

Presumably the disciples fled at the time of Jesus' arrest. They were not there when he was crucified. Possibly already they were making their way home to the relative safety of Galilee. And it was there, where Jesus had first met them and called them, that the risen Jesus called them again. It was there that they experienced, once again, his presence as a power in their lives. It was there that they re-grouped in the power of his Spirit and the phenomenon of the Church began.

Mark implies all this. His Gospel ends on a realistic and strange note: the women are bewildered and afraid to speak. They had come, in the dark, searching for the dead body of Jesus to perform the anointing which they had been unable to do on the Friday because of the hasty burial. They find only an empty tomb. Jesus is absent. But part of that experience — and Mark does not attempt to analyse this — is an experience of faith and a promise. The Jesus they knew is still alive and he will encounter them, back in Galilee. When, where, how, is not explained. But the promise is there and hope has dawned.

Mark's Gospel was written for the Church in Rome. It was a community that had just undergone violent persecution under Nero (64 A.D.). It was a church that was in a helpless and apparently hopeless position. It was a church that was 'frightened out of their wits ... afraid' (Mark 16:8). For them, too, Jesus was largely experienced as the absent one. But for them too the promise was there. They had to wait on God; they had to wait, like the deaf man and the blind man of Mark's Gospel, for the divine miracle. The Jesus of Mark's Gospel is a Jesus with whom they could identify. He too was faced with weakness. But he relied on God and God delivered him. God will do no less for the community which believes in him.

The empty tomb does not prove anything. It does, however, raise a question. It reminded the women of what Jesus himself had hoped for, and it prepared the women for an encounter in faith with the living, risen, Jesus. Mark leaves his readers there. We, too, can only wait in hope for him to touch our lives. If and when he does we will recognise him.

* * * * * * * *

Matthew enlarges Mark's account. He has six scenes in all. Three describe the attempts by the enemies of God to thwart God's plan; we will designate these three scenes as X, X1 and X2. The other three scenes (Y, Y1, Y2) describe God's victory. The first five scenes relate to the empty tomb; we shall examine them here. The final climax scene is Matthew's way of describing the experience of the early church of the presence of the risen Jesus; we shall leave it till the next section.

Scene 1: (X): The tomb is sealed and guarded

MATTHEW 27:62-66

Next day, that is, when Preparation Day was over, the chief priests and the 62
Pharisees went in a body to Pilate •and said to him, 'Your Excellency, we 63
recall that this impostor said, while he was still alive, "After three days I shall

rise again". •Therefore give the order to have the sepulchre kept secure until the 64
third day, for fear his disciples come and steal him away and tell the people,
"He has risen from the dead". This last piece of fraud would be worse than what
went before.' •'You may have your guard' said Pilate to them. 'Go and make 65
all as secure as you know how.' •So they went and made the sepulchre secure, 66
putting seals on the stone and mounting a guard.

The enemies of God seem to be the only ones who know clearly what to
expect. They are acting in the day, but their actions are those of the night. In their
effort to secure the death of Jesus, they seal his tomb and mount a guard. The
tomb, hewn out of rock, was, for the Jews, a symbol of Sheol — the underworld,
where the shades of dead men eked out their shadowy existence. Jesus was dead,
and now the sealing of the rock-tomb and the mounting of a guard stands as a
powerful symbol of the efforts of the power of darkness to ensure that he will stay
dead. Evil has seemingly triumphed on the Friday. Now, on the sabbath, it is
consolidating its victory.

Scene 2: (Y): The women go to the tomb

MATTHEW 28:1

'After the sabbath, and towards dawn on the first day of the week, Mary of Magdala
and the other Mary went to visit the sepulchre.'

The expression translated here 'towards dawn' is more accurately translated
'just at the rising of the day'. When it is remembered that the Jewish day began at
6 p.m. and that the women would have been anxious to visit the tomb as early as
possible on the conclusion of the sabbath, we realise that Matthew is more
probably referring to a time just after 6 p.m. rather than to our 'dawn'.

In other words the scene is set in darkness and stands out in stark contrast to
the previous one. There the powers of darkness were working in the day; here the
powers of light are working in the night. There the powers of darkness thought
they knew what to expect; here the powers of light are expecting nothing — they
do not expect a resurrection, but are simply going to visit the tomb.

Scene 3: (X1): The resurrection: light overpowers darkness

MATTHEW 28:2-4

•And all at once 2
there was a violent earthquake, for the angel of the Lord, descending from
heaven, came and rolled away the stone and sat on it. •His face was like lightning, 3
his robe white as snow. •The guards were so shaken, so frightened of him, that 4
they were like dead men.

Matthew turns his attention, once again, to the enemies of God. In highly
dramatic terms he describes God himself ('the angel of the Lord' cf Genesis 16:7,
22:11 and Exodus 3:2) exercising his power and thwarting the plans of his
enemies. One moment the tomb is sealed and guarded in darkness by the powers
of evil. Then all is light and the tomb bursts asunder. Death is robbed of its prey
and God's enemies are 'like dead men'.

Scene 4: (Y1): The women are told of the resurrection

MATTHEW 28:5-10

•But the angel spoke; and he said to the women, 5 'There is no need for you to be afraid. I know you are looking for Jesus, who was crucified. •He is not here, for he has risen, as he said he would. Come and see 6 the place where he lay, •then go quickly and tell his disciples, "He has risen 7 from the dead and now he is going before you to Galilee; it is there you will see him". Now I have told you.' •Filled with awe and great joy the women came 8 quickly away from the tomb and ran to tell the disciples.

And there, coming to meet them, was Jesus. 'Greetings' he said. And the 9 women came up to him and, falling down before him, clasped his feet. •Then 10 Jesus said to them, 'Do not be afraid; go and tell my brothers that they must leave for Galilee; they will see me there'.

We refer the reader to the commentary on Mark (pages 431-4). It is interesting to note the different reaction of the women. Besides the awe and amazement, there is 'joy' (28:8). Whereas Mark tells us that:

'They said nothing to a soul'

(Mark 16:8)

Matthew gives us the impression that they actually carried out their mission.

The main addition is an encounter with the risen Jesus himself. Little more is involved that a personal confirmation of the word spoken to them by God, and our concentration is still directed to an experience that is yet to come in Galilee. But already Matthew speaks, however mysteriously, of Jesus himself touching the lives of these women.

Scene 5: (X2): The authorities try to cover up the resurrection

MATTHEW 28:11-15

While they were on their way, some of the guard went off into the city to tell 11 the chief priests all that had happened. •These held a meeting with the elders 12 and, after some discussion, handed a considerable sum of money to the soldiers with these instructions, 'This is what you must say, "His disciples came during 13 the night and stole him away while we were asleep". •And should the governor 14 come to hear of this, we undertake to put things right with him ourselves and to see that you do not get into trouble.' •The soldiers took the money and carried 15 out their instructions, and to this day that is the story among the Jews.

The powers of evil have, in fact, been defeated. Their only hope now is to conceal the facts. Matthew presents us with a scene of bribery and lies and conscious deceit. How feeble this is will be demonstrated in Matthew's final scene in which he describes how, by the power of God, not only is the presence of the risen Jesus not hushed up, it is proclaimed to the ends of the earth. We shall leave this final climax scene till we have looked at Luke's and John's account of the empty tomb.

* * * * * * * *

LUKE 24:1-12

24 On the first day of the week, at the first sign of dawn, they went to the 1
tomb with the spices they had prepared. •They found that the stone had 2
been rolled away from the tomb, •but on entering discovered that the body of the 3
Lord Jesus was not there. •As they stood there not knowing what to think, two 4
men in brilliant clothes suddenly appeared at their side. •Terrified, the women 5
lowered their eyes. But the two men said to them, 'Why look among the dead
for someone who is alive? •He is not here; he has risen. Remember what he told 6
you when he was still in Galilee: •that the Son of Man had to be handed over 7
into the power of sinful men and be crucified, and rise again on the third day
And they remembered his words.   8
When the women returned from the tomb they told all this to the Eleven and 9
to all the others. •The women were Mary of Magdala, Joanna, and Mary the 10
mother of James. The other women with them also told the apostles, •but this 11
story of theirs seemed pure nonsense, and they did not believe them.

Peter, however, went running to the tomb. He bent down and saw the binding 12
cloths but nothing else; he then went back home, amazed at what had happened.

We refer the reader to the commentary on Mark (pages 431-4). Luke has 'two men' appearing to the women. He identifies them later (Luke 24:23) as 'angels'. The 'two' is perhaps an allusion to the Old Testament requirement of two witnesses to attest to something in a court of Law (cf Deuteronomy 17:6).

We can see already a tendency to underplay the importance of the empty tomb. The reaction of the women was not faith, it was simply:

'they stood there not knowing what to think' (24:4)

At the sight of the angels — that is, at the approach of God — the women 'lowered their eyes' (24:5). This is perhaps in contrast to the statement of Jesus earlier:

'When these things begin to take place, stand erect, hold your heads high, because your liberation is close at hand'

(Luke 21:28)

Obviously, the women are not expecting liberation.

The central message of the angels is:

'Why look among the dead for someone who is alive' (24:5)

Luke seems to prefer the expression 'the living one' to 'the resurrected one' (cf Luke 24:23 and Acts 1:3 and 25:19). This is perhaps because the word 'resurrected' could cause the Greek mind to think of the soul as once again giving life to *the same* physical body. The mystery is obviously more profound than that. Paul tries to come to grips with it in his First Letter to the Corinthians (Chapter 15). The risen body is not the same body we know now. The risen person is the same person, but the body, the living flesh, has a special relationship to the Spirit of God. In some way it is an 'embodiment of the Spirit' (1 Corinthians 15:44).

Paul had some trouble with the Greeks of Athens over this very point (cf Acts 17:31). Luke, anticipating similar misunderstandings, prefers the vaguer term 'living'. The central point is that Jesus who died *is alive.*

There is another interesting difference in Luke's account. Mark and Matthew both refer to Galilee; so does Luke. They, however, refer to it as the place where the disciples are to meet Jesus. Luke refers to it only as a point of reference in the past (Luke 9:22, 12:50, 17.25, 18:31, 34. See also 26:44). For reasons we have discussed earlier, Luke wishes to have Jerusalem, not Galilee, as the place where the encounters with the risen Jesus are made (compare the accent on 'Jerusalem' in Luke 24:13, 33 and 52; also Acts 1:8).

The account by the women of their experience is quite obviously not a source for the faith of the early church in the Resurrection ('they did not believe them' 24:11). Some credence is given the account by introducing Peter; but even then the effect is simply 'amazement' not 'faith'. Luke will make this point again when he has the men on the road to Emmaus say:

'Some of our friends went to the tomb and found everything exactly as the women had reported, but of him they saw nothing.'

(Luke 24:24)

* * * * * * *

JOHN 20:1-18

20 It was very early on the first day of the week and still dark, when Mary 1 of Magdala came to the tomb. She saw that the stone had been moved away from the tomb •and came running to Simon Peter and the other disciple, 2 the one Jesus loved. 'They have taken the Lord out of the tomb' she said 'and we don't know where they have put him.'

So Peter set out with the other disciple to go to the tomb. •They ran together, 3 4 but the other disciple, running faster than Peter, reached the tomb first; •he bent 5 down and saw the linen cloths lying on the ground, but did not go in. •Simon 6 Peter who was following now came up, went right into the tomb, saw the linen cloths on the ground, •and also the cloth that had been over his head; this was 7 not with the linen cloths but rolled up in a place by itself. •Then the other disciple 8 who had reached the tomb first also went in; he saw and he believed. •Till this 9 moment they had failed to understand the teaching of scripture, that he must rise from the dead. •The disciples then went home again. 10

Meanwhile Mary stayed outside near the tomb, weeping. Then, still weeping, 11 she stooped to look inside, •and saw two angels in white sitting where the body 12 of Jesus had been, one at the head, the other at the feet. •They said, 'Woman, 13 why are you weeping?' 'They have taken my Lord away' she replied 'and I don't know where they have put him.' •As she said this she turned round and 14 saw Jesus standing there, though she did not recognise him. •Jesus said, 'Woman, 15 why are you weeping? Who are you looking for?' Supposing him to be the gardener, she said, 'Sir, if you have taken him away, tell me where you have put him, and I will go and remove him'. •Jesus said, 'Mary!' She knew him then 16 and said to him in Hebrew, 'Rabbuni!'—which means Master. •Jesus said to 17 her; 'Do not cling to me, because I have not yet ascended to the Father. But go and find the brothers, and tell them: I am ascending to my Father and your Father, to my God and your God.' •So Mary of Magdala went and told the 18 disciples that she had seen the Lord and that he had said these things to her.

(Compare Mark 16:9-11)

The fact of the empty tomb is reiterated here by John, but it is certainly not a basis for belief in the Resurrection. In fact Mary of Magdala is dramatised as drawing the conclusion that:

'They have taken the Lord out of the tomb,
and we don't know where they have put him' (20:2)

Like Luke (cf Luke 24:12) John concentrates on the visit of Peter to the tomb. With him is 'the other disciple, the one Jesus loved' (20:2). It is said of this disciple that:

'he saw and he believed'. (20:8)

Perhaps what John is saying is that the empty tomb can be a sign that leads to faith, but only for one whose understanding comes from love.

Like Luke (24:12), John mentions the linen cloths. It is a simple and effective way of saying that the body was not stolen and that here we have a resurrection that is quite different from the resurrection experienced by Lazarus (confer John 11:44).

Matthew mentioned briefly the meeting between the risen Jesus and the women (Matthew 28:9-10). John concentrates on Mary of Magdala and builds a scene in which we see an example of how faith in the risen Jesus grows. As in Matthew's account the risen Jesus takes the initiative and simply repeats the words spoken by the angels (20:15=20:13). Mary sees a gardener, she does not see Jesus.

Then Jesus calls her by her name. We recall the statement in Isaiah:

'Do not be afraid for I have redeemed you;
I have called you by your name, you are mine'.

(Isaiah 43:1)

The risen Jesus makes known his presence to Mary in the same way he had always done. In this experience she recognises him.

John had written earlier in his supper discourse:

'Now I am going to the one who sent me . . .
and you are sad because I have told you this'

(John 16:6-7)

'You will be weeping and wailing
while the world will rejoice;
you will be sorrowful
but your sorrow will turn into joy'

(John 16:20)

John dramatises this scene, and Mary is the symbol of the Christian. Jesus had said:

'In a short time the world will no longer see me;
but you will see me,
because I live and you will live.'

(John 14:19)

In a way that John does not (cannot) describe, Mary experiences a renewed presence and love of the one who loves her so much. This was her experience of the resurrection. She 'saw' him with the eyes of love, the eyes of faith.

This experience is not to be received in isolation; it is to be taken to the community. It is in view of an experience of the risen Jesus in community. The intimacy of this community is stressed by the use of the word 'brothers' (20:17) and by the identification of Jesus' Father with the Father of his brothers (20:17).

There is no need to cling to Jesus (20:17). As he had said earlier:

'I am going away and shall return'

(John 14:28)

Though he is going away , though he is not seen, though they cannot cling to him the way they used to, he is still present to them because his Spirit is with them:

'After I have gone and prepared you a place,
I shall return to take you with me;
so that where I am
you may be too.'

(John 14:3)

'Anybody who loves me will be loved by my Father,
and I shall love him and show myself to him' *(14:21)*

Mary loved Jesus. Jesus is with his Father. Mary too is with God and therefore Jesus is present to Mary, sharing his Father with her, sharing his Spirit with her. The same can be for all his brothers.

* * * * * * * *

The text of Mark's Gospel as we now have it includes a section, Mark 16:9-20, which is absent from many manuscripts. It seems to be an addition by a later editor. The first few verses are a condensed account of Jesus' meeting with Mary of Magdala. The author stresses the fact that Jesus' companions did not believe Mary (16:11, compare 16:13, 16:14).

MARCAN CONCLUSION 16:9-11

9   Having risen in the morning on the first day of the week, he appeared first to
10   Mary of Magdala from whom he had cast out seven devils. •She then went to those
     who had been his companions, and who were mourning and in tears, and told
11   them. •But they did not believe her when they heard her say that he was alive
     and that she had seen him.

* * * * * * * *

Chapter 3
The Resurrection appearances

Matthew 26:16-20
Luke 24:13-53
John 20:19-21:25
Marcan Conclusion 16:9-20

Before examining the Gospel texts, let us attempt some review of the ways in which the early church experienced the continued presence of the risen Jesus among them.

a: Jesus' living and powerful word present with them in their mission

The whole tenor of the Gospels indicates that Jesus' words were understood, by his disciples, to be God's words to them (see, for example, the Transfiguration account, 'This is my Son, the Beloved. Listen to him' (Mark 9:7) and Luke 5:1: 'the crowd pressing around Jesus listening to the word of God.' John speaks of Jesus as God's word made flesh (John 1:1, 14: also 1 John 1:1, John 14:10, 24; 17:8, 14).

After his death on the cross, Jesus' followers experienced his word staying with them (John 15:7, 20), still coming to them (Acts 1:3, 9:4, 18:9, 2 Cor 12:9, also John's account of Jesus and Mary of Magdala, 20:16, page 438). It was the word of Jesus that they preached (Luke 1:2; Acts 4:29-31, 6:7; 10:44, 14:3; Ephesians 6:17, Philippians 2:16). When they preached his word, the effect was the same as when he was living with them: it healed, and liberated and gave life. It was a living word (Acts 4:30, 10:44, 14:3; Romans 10:17, 15:18; Colossians 3:16; 1 Corinthians 2:13, 12:8, 1 Tim 6:3, 1 Thess 1:5). They experienced being called again by the one they knew, being sent by him, and being accompanied by him on their mission.

All these experiences meant, for them, that he was still alive and active among them.

b: Jesus' Spirit present with them in their lives

The New Testament writings witness to the fact that Jesus' disciples, after his death, experienced the presence in their midst of the Spirit of God that they had experienced in Jesus (Luke 12:12, compare Luke 21:15; Acts 2:4, 4:8, 10:44, 16:7; Romans 8:9-11, 1 Corinthians 6:19, 2 Corinthians 1:22, 3:17; Galatians 4:6, 5:22, 5:25; Philippians 1:19, Titus 3:5, John 3:34, 7:39, 14:17, 26, 15:26, 16:13).

The presence of the living Spirit of Jesus could only mean that Jesus himself was still alive and active among them.

c: The community of Christians formed a living body united to the risen Jesus

Jesus' followers experienced themselves continuing his life and his mission. Because it was the living Spirit of God in Jesus that gave life to the community, they saw themselves, by analogy, as the 'Body of Christ', the place where his living Spirit was active (Romans 12:4-5, 1 Corinthians 10:16-17, Ephesians 1:23, 2:16, 3:6, 4:4,12,16; 5:23,30; Colossians 1:18,24; 3:15).

The many experiences they had, as a community, could only mean that Jesus himself was still alive and active among them.

d: The 'Breaking of Bread': The Eucharist

It was especially when Jesus' disciples came together to remember him at the 'Breaking of Bread', that they experienced his living presence among them. It was at the 'Breaking of Bread' that they remembered him; it was there that they heard his word; it was there that they experienced the presence of his Spirit; it was there that they experienced their unity as his body, and the real presence of the living Jesus in their midst, nurturing them as he had nurtured them before his death, inspiring them, forgiving them, calling them and sending them to continue his mission.

The experience of the Eucharist is central to the 'Resurrection appearances'.

*   *   *   *   *   *   *   *

Before examining the texts, it may be well to draw attention to the use of the word 'see' in these texts.

We are, of course, aware of Paul's statement that:

"flesh and blood cannot inherit the kingdom of God"

(1 Corinthians 15:50)

We are also familiar with Paul's words concerning the risen body:

"Someone may ask, 'How are dead people raised, and what sort of body do they have when they come back?' They are stupid questions".

(1 Corinthians 15:35)

At the same time we cannot imagine a risen person, a risen 'body' except after the manner of the body we now experience.

Likewise, we are accustomed to use the word 'see' for enlightenment at all different levels of consciousness, from the sensation that occurs when the optic nerve is stimulated to the most profound 'seeing' associated with mystical prayer. Yet, when it comes to the beautiful texts in which the early church expresses her experiences of the risen Jesus, we forget this and, in spite of what is revealed by a close examination of these same texts, we tend to hold strongly to the word 'see', as though the authors are referring to an ocular sensation, and as though the object 'seen' could have been photographed were that possible.

An examination of the actual Greek words used in the texts alerts us to the fact that all these words are used at all different levels of enlightenment, and so we should approach the texts without ready-made assumptions. The word 'ophthalmos' (Greek: 'eye') is found in Luke's account of the disciples on the road to Emmaus (24:16,31) and of the ascension (Acts 1:9). But note Luke's use of the word in Acts 26:18 and 28:27 for a 'seeing' that transcends the experience of the physical eye. Likewise, Luke uses the Greek word 'blepo' ('to see') in his account of the ascension (Acts 1:9); but note his use in Acts 2:33. 'Theaomia' (Greek: 'to gaze at with wonder') is found in the following texts (Luke 24:39; Acts 1:11; John 20:14; Marcan conclusion 16:11). But note Luke's use in regard to the vision of Stephen where it refers to an experience that transcends that of the eye (Acts 7:56). Similarly with the Greek word 'phaino' (to bring to light, to show, to appear: Luke 24:31; Acts 10:40; John 21:1,14; Marcan conclusion 16:9,12,14; Colossians 3:4; 2 Corinthians 4:10).

Finally, the most common word for 'see' used in the texts relating to the 'appearances' of the risen Jesus is the word 'horao', from which derives our English word 'aware'. This word is used regularly for to 'perceive', to 'become aware of' (Luke 21:27, 24:34,39; Acts 4:20,9:17,10:27; 13:31; 22:14,15,18; 26:13,16; John 16:16, 20:18,20,25,27). See also John's use in John 14:9: 'to have seen me is to have seen the Father', and 1 John 3:2: 'we shall be like him because we shall see him as he really is'; and Matthew 5:8 'Blessed are the pure in heart; they shall see God'.

This digression has simply been to warn the reader not to approach the following texts with misconceptions or assumptions based on a simplistic reading. They are profound texts, attempting to describe the indescribable. They are texts born of prayer and of real experience, and they express in powerful symbolic language the most meaningful experiences that formed the early church, and founded their faith in the presence of the risen Jesus in their midst. They must be read from within the same prayer, and while reflecting on our own experiences of the risen Jesus.

1: Galilee

When Jesus was killed, his friends dispersed, back to their own territory, Galilee. And it was there that they saw him. This tradition is preserved by Mark and Matthew in their account of the Last Supper:

"after my resurrection I shall go before you to Galilee"

(Mark 14:29, Matthew 26:32 page 371)

Both writers include it in their accounts of the empty tomb:

"He is going before you to Galilee; it is there you will see him, just as he told you."

(Mark 16:7 page 431, Matthew 28:7 page 435)

Mark ends his Gospel leaving the reader to find the risen Jesus for himself. Matthew however concludes with the following scene:

MATTHEW 28:16-20.

Meanwhile the eleven disciples set out for Galilee, to the mountain where 16 Jesus had arranged to meet them. •When they saw him they fell down before 17 him, though some hesitated. •Jesus came up and spoke to them. He said, 'All 18 authority in heaven and on earth has been given to me. •Go, therefore, make 19 disciples of all the nations; baptise them in the name of the Father and of the Son and of the Holy Spirit, •and teach them to observe all the commands I 20 gave you. And know that I am with you always; yes, to the end of time.'

444   THE DEATH AND RESURRECTION OF JESUS

If we were to go back and read the account of the appearance of God to Moses in the burning bush (cf Exodus 3:6-12) we would find there the same sense of majesty and power; we would find the same hesitation and feeling of awe; we would find a smiliar mission and the same assurance: 'I shall be with you'. Likewise if we read the account of the appearance of God to Jeremiah (cf Jeremiah 1:5-8). In other words, Matthew has constructed this scene along traditional lines. We are witnessing an epiphany — an appearance of God. This time, God is present in the presence of his living Son, commissioning his disciples to continue his work.

Mountains have featured at important junctures of Matthew's Gospel. There was the mountain where the devil offered Jesus "all the kingdoms of the world and their splendour" (Matthew 4:8). Jesus was faithful to his Father, and now, at the end, has far more than the devil could have offered him. Now he is given "all authority in heaven and on earth" (28:18). There was the mountain from which Jesus proclaimed the new Law (Matthew 5:1, cf 8:1). Matthew refers to these same 'commands' here (28:20). There was the mount of transfiguration (Matthew 17:1-8) and the mount of prayer (Matthew 14:23). Jesus had challenged his disciples to be like a city on a mountain (Matthew 5:14). In this final scene, the disciples go to that mountain of prayer, and from that mountain, with the risen Jesus present among them, they go forth to build the new heaven and the new earth; to proclaim the kingdom of God.

Matthew mentions that 'some hesitated' (28:17), assuring us, thereby, that seeing the risen Jesus is something beyond the eye of man. What is needed is faith and the obedience of carrying out his commission. It is in the mission that we will know his presence.

Finally, Matthew ends his Gospel where he began it. Jesus was to be called 'Emmanuel, a name which means 'God-is-with-us' (Matthew 1:23). Jesus had been God for them all through his public ministry; especially did he show them the face of God by the manner of his life-giving on the cross. Now, the risen Jesus promises:

"know that I am with you always; yes, to the end of time"

(Matthew 28:20)

When the disciples fled back to Galilee, he was there for them, calling them, strengthening them, commissioning them. Matthew is telling his community that the risen Jesus will be there for them too, if they climb the mountain of prayer. Our faith in the fact that it is the risen Jesus that comes to us on the mountain is founded firmly on the experience had by the disciples of Jesus. For it is they who *recognised* him as the same Jesus of Nazareth that they had known and loved.

At the Exodus, God had asked Moses to trust him. 'I will be who I will be for y.ou' (= Yahweh). We are being asked to trust that the risen Jesus is in our midst, and, as we carry out his commission, we will find him there, always, and always **for us.** Such is the covenant love of God; such is his fidelity. The experience of it is the liberation ('redemption') effected by Jesus.

*   *   *   *   *   *   *   *

The appendix to John's Gospel also records a Galilean experience:

JOHN 21:1-25

21 Later on, Jesus showed himself again to the disciples. It was by the Sea 1 of Tiberias, and it happened like this: •Simon Peter, Thomas called the 2 Twin, Nathanael from Cana in Galilee, the sons of Zebedee and two more of his disciples were together. •Simon Peter said, 'I'm going fishing'. They replied, 3 'We'll come with you'. They went out and got into the boat but caught nothing that night.

It was light by now and there stood Jesus on the shore, though the disciples 4 did not realise that it was Jesus. •Jesus called out, 'Have you caught anything, 5 friends?' And when they answered, 'No', •he said, 'Throw the net out to starboard 6 and you'll find something'. So they dropped the net, and there were so many fish that they could not haul it in. •The disciple Jesus loved said to Peter, 'It is 7 the Lord'. At these words 'It is the Lord', Simon Peter, who had practically nothing on, wrapped his cloak round him and jumped into the water. •The 8 other disciples came on in the boat, towing the net and the fish; they were only about a hundred yards from land.

As soon as they came ashore they saw that there was some bread there, and 9 a charcoal fire with fish cooking on it. •Jesus said, 'Bring some of the fish you 10 have just caught'. •Simon Peter went aboard and dragged the net to the shore, 11 full of big fish, one hundred and fifty-three of them; and in spite of there being so many the net was not broken. •Jesus said to them, 'Come and have breakfast'. 12 None of the disciples was bold enough to ask, 'Who are you?'; they knew quite well it was the Lord. •Jesus then stepped forward, took the bread and gave it 13 to them, and the same with the fish. •This was the third time that Jesus showed 14 himself to the disciples after rising from the dead.

After the meal Jesus said to Simon Peter, 'Simon son of John, do you love 15 me more than these others do?' He answered, 'Yes Lord, you know I love you'. Jesus said to him, 'Feed my lambs'. •A second time he said to him, 'Simon son 16 of John, do you love me?' He replied, 'Yes, Lord, you know I love you'. Jesus said to him, 'Look after my sheep'. •Then he said to him a third time, 'Simon 17 son of John, do you love me?' Peter was upset that he asked him the third time, 'Do you love me?' and said, 'Lord, you know everything; you know I love you'. Jesus said to him, 'Feed my sheep.

'I tell you most solemnly,   18
when you were young
you put on your own belt
and walked where you liked;
but when you grow old
you will stretch out your hands,
and somebody else will put a belt round you
and take you where you would rather not go.'

In these words he indicated the kind of death by which Peter would give glory 19 to God. After this he said, 'Follow me'.

Peter turned and saw the disciple Jesus loved following them—the one who 20 had leaned on his breast at the supper and had said to him, 'Lord, who is it that will betray you?' •Seeing him, Peter said to Jesus, 'What about him, Lord?' 21 Jesus answered, 'If I want him to stay behind till I come, what does it matter 22 to you? You are to follow me.' •The rumour then went out among the brothers 23 that this disciple would not die. Yet Jesus had not said to Peter, 'He will not die', but, 'If I want him to stay behind till I come'.

This disciple is the one who vouches for these things and has written them 24 down, and we know that his testimony is true.

There were many other things that Jesus did; if all were written down, the 25 world itself, I suppose, would not hold all the books that would have to be written.

This anecdote locates the meeting between Jesus and his disciples in Galilee, where, according to both Mark and Matthew, the disciples first experienced the renewed presence in their midst of the risen Jesus.

The disciples, as was most probably the case, had fled Jerusalem when Jesus was captured and had returned to their old haunts and their old occupation. But things were not the same. Jesus had made a lasting impression on them. Their own human weakness is dramatised in their failure to catch any fish. But someone was present in their lives who gave them a power that was not their own. We remember that Luke took basically the same story and used it for the very first calling of the disciples (cf Luke 5:1-11). There it demonstrated the mission that these men would experience because of the call of Jesus. Wonder was something they experienced in a special way only after the death of Jesus and so the present appendix places the anecdote in a more logical place. The essence of the story is that, in some way, the disciples of Jesus, back in Galilee, experienced the presence of the power of Jesus in their lives.

It is the 'disciple Jesus loved' (21:7) who is the one who recognised it as the presence of Jesus, and the rest of the story centres on Peter and this disciple.

It is a meal scene (a 'communion breakfast'). Again it is stated that the risen Jesus is not seen with the eyes of the flesh (21:12). It is a much deeper experience, an experience of faith.

In a scene reminiscent of the three-fold denial of Jesus by Peter, Peter is forgiven and makes a three-fold confession of faith. As in the other Resurrection scenes, forgiveness and faith come with mission. It is in the experience of 'feeding my sheep' that the disciple knows he is loved and sustained by the living presence of his Lord.

The appendix incorporates the earliest written record of Peter's martyrdom (in Rome about 64 A.D.; 21:18-19). Jesus concludes with the very first words he addressed to his disciples: 'follow me' (21:19). This is the call promised by Jesus at the Last Supper and by the angel at the tomb. Back in Galilee, Jesus came to them and called them again by name. What a beautiful symbol of the faithful love of God. His disciples scattered and Peter denied him, but Jesus calls them again to be his disciples. The call is always there to be answered, and it is in answering that call that the disciple will experience the presence of the living Jesus:

'You will see me because I live and you will live.'   *(John 14:19)*

2: Jerusalem

Luke, in his Last Supper scene, omits any reference to Galilee (Luke 22:31-34 compare Mark 14:29). In his exposition of the empty tomb, he mentions Galilee, but as the place where Jesus spoke of his resurrection, not as the place where they would see him (Luke 24:6 compare Mark 16:7). The resurrection 'appearances' in Luke are located in Jerusalem (cf commentary page 34).

a: The road to Emmaus: Jesus is recognised in the breaking of bread

LUKE 24:13-35

That very same day, two of them were on their way to a village called Emmaus, 13 seven miles from Jerusalem, •and they were talking together about all that had 14 happened. •Now as they talked this over, Jesus himself came up and walked by 15 their side; •but something prevented them from recognising him. •He said to 16 17 them, 'What matters are you discussing as you walk along?' They stopped short, their faces downcast.

Then one of them, called Cleopas, answered him, 'You must be the only 18 person staying in Jerusalem who does not know the things that have been happening there these last few days'. •'What things?' he asked. 'All about Jesus 19 of Nazareth' they answered 'who proved he was a great prophet by the things he said and did in the sight of God and of the whole people; •and how our chief 20 priests and our leaders handed him over to be sentenced to death, and had him crucified. •Our own hope had been that he would be the one to set Israel free. 21 And this is not all: two whole days have gone by since it all happened; •and some 22 women from our group have astounded us: they went to the tomb in the early morning, •and when they did not find the body, they came back to tell us they 23 had seen a vision of angels who declared he was alive. •Some of our friends 24 went to the tomb and found everything exactly as the women had reported, but of him they saw nothing.'

Then he said to them, 'You foolish men! So slow to believe the full message 25 of the prophets! •Was it not ordained that the Christ should suffer and so enter 26 into his glory?' •Then, starting with Moses and going through all the prophets, 27 he explained to them the passages throughout the scriptures that were about himself.

When they drew near to the village to which they were going, he made as if 28 to go on; •but they pressed him to stay with them. 'It is nearly evening' they said 29 'and the day is almost over.' So he went in to stay with them. •Now while he was 30 with them at table, he took the bread and said the blessing; then he broke it and handed it to them. •And their eyes were opened and they recognised him; but he 31 had vanished from their sight. •Then they said to each other, 'Did not our hearts 32 burn within us as he talked to us on the road and explained the scriptures to us?'

They set out that instant and returned to Jerusalem. There they found the 33 Eleven assembled together with their companions, •who said to them, 'Yes, it is 34 true. The Lord has risen and has appeared to Simon.' •Then they told their 35 story of what had happened on the road and how they had recognised him at the breaking of bread.

They are walking away from Jerusalem, away from their hopes and dreams; they are walking back, back to the empty lives they lived before they walked with Jesus.

But the risen Jesus is present to them, and walks with them (24:15). Our translation reads 'something prevented them from recognising him' (24:16). The Greek text has: 'their eyes were held'. Luke is telling us that you do not see the risen Jesus with the eyes of the body. Later, at the breaking of bread, we are told that 'their eyes were opened and they recognised him: but he had vanished from their sight' (24:31). It is the eyes of faith, enlightened by the scriptures ('He explained the scriptures' 24:32, should read 'he **opened** the scriptures'), that recognise the risen Jesus.

Hearing about the resurrection from others (24:22-24) is not enough. The disciple needs personal companionship with Jesus. He needs Jesus to walk with him and to open the scriptures for him. Finally, it is in the experience of the Eucharist that the scriptures reveal their fullest meaning.

Luke also insists that a private 'revelation' must be taken to the church to be authenticated. These men experienced the presence of the risen Jesus, walking with them in their journey of life. But they took this experience to the 'Eleven assembled together' (24:33); and it was the community that said, "Yes, it is true" (24:34).

* * * * * * * *

MARCAN CONCLUSION 16:12-13

12   After this, he showed himself under another form to two of them as they
13 were on their way into the country. •These went back and told the others, who did not believe them either.

Note the editor's stress on the failure of the disciples to believe.

* * * * * * * *

b: The assembled, Eucharistic, community

The central, critical, and normative experience of the risen Jesus is the experience of the community assembled at the 'breaking of bread'. Luke, the editor who wrote the conclusion to Mark's Gospel, and John, all conclude their Gospels with it.

LUKE 24:36-53

36   They were still talking about all this when he himself stood among them
37 and said to them, 'Peace be with you!' •In a state of alarm and fright, they thought
38 they were seeing a ghost. •But he said, 'Why are you so agitated, and why are
39 these doubts rising in your hearts? •Look at my hands and feet; yes, it is I indeed. Touch me and see for yourselves; a ghost has no flesh and bones as you can see
40
41 I have.' •And as he said this he showed them his hands and feet. •Their joy was so great that they still could not believe it, and they stood there dumbfounded;
42 so he said to them, 'Have you anything here to eat?' •And they offered him a piece
43 of grilled fish, •which he took and ate before their eyes.
44   Then he told them, 'This is what I meant when I said, while I was still with you, that everything written about me in the Law of Moses, in the Prophets and
45 in the Psalms, has to be fulfilled'. •He then opened their minds to understand the
46 scriptures, •and he said to them, 'So you see how it is written that the Christ would
47 suffer and on the third day rise from the dead, •and that, in his name, repentance for the forgiveness of sins would be preached to all the nations, beginning
48 from Jerusalem. •You are witnesses to this.
49   'And now I am sending down to you what the Father has promised. Stay in the city then, until you are clothed with the power from on high.'
50   Then he took them out as far as the outskirts of Bethany, and lifting up his
51 hands he blessed them. •Now as he blessed them, he withdrew from them and
52 was carried up to heaven. •They worshipped him and then went back to
53 Jerusalem full of joy; •and they were continually in the Temple praising God.

We are still on the first day of the week (Luke 24:1,13,33,36): the day of the Resurrection, and the day of the Eucharist celebrations that re-lived it. The church is assembled, and a meal is being shared. Jesus does not come in and join them. Luke tells us that 'he himself stood among them' (24:36). The point is that he is always among them, but in glory. The veil that hides him is being lifted, as he eats with them. We are reminded of the statement in the Book of Revelations:

> "Look, I am standing at the door, knocking. If one of your hears me calling and opens the door, I will come in to share his meal, side by side with him".
>
> *(Revelations 3:20)*

Luke is writing in the Roman world. He had to convince them that he was not speaking of a 'ghost' (24:37). The risen Jesus is fully alive; he is a living person, with a glorified 'body'. We must be careful when reading his powerful, dramatic, statement of this not to draw conclusions about the properties of the glorified 'body' in relation to physical digestion. Jesus is truly alive, and not a shade returning from the underworld. As a vital living person, though in a way far transcending anything we can imagine, he continues table-fellowship with them, in the Eucharist (cf Acts 10:41). That it is Jesus of Nazareth is proved by the 'hands and feet' (24:40), bearing the wounds suffered in love for them.

The disciples are told to 'remember'. He opens their minds to understand what he had said, and he opens their minds to understand the pattern of history as outlined in God's faithful dealings with his people (24:44-47).

They know he is alive, not only through reflection of the word; not only through their experiences of his real presence in the Eucharist; but also through their experience of continual liberation ("the forgiveness of sins"), and on their mission (24:48). They, like Jesus, are to preach 'repentance' (24:47 — cf Acts 2:38, 3:19, 5:31, 10:43, 13:38-41), so that the world will experience God's love and liberating power.

Jesus' mission flowed from his experience of being baptised by the Holy Spirit in the Jordan (Luke 3:21-22). They are to expect the same grace (24:49).

Luke concludes his Gospel with an ascension. 'He is not here' (Luke 24:6). He is with his father in glory. He blesses them with the blessing Zechariah was unable to give (Luke 1:22, page 34-35), and the Gospel ends where it began. The Gospel opened with the old people of God praying for the promised one (Luke 1:10). It ends in the same Temple with the new people of God praying for the coming of the Spirit of Jesus.

Luke will return to this at the beginning of the second part of his work (the 'Acts of the Apostles'), where he speaks of Jesus being taken into the glory-cloud, and the Spirit of Jesus being poured out on the community, filling them with power to begin the mission that we call church.

Here, in the conclusion of his Gospel, Luke has demonstrated the faith of the community in the experience of the risen Jesus in their midst as they ponder the word and celebrate the Eucharist. He promises to be with them as they preach the Good News to the nations. He blesses them with the blessing of God and then withdraws from their sight, leaving them, and us, to a life of faith, waiting for the coming of his Spirit, and waiting till we see him, with his Father, face to face.

Mark's Conclusion

MARK 16:14-20

14   Lastly, he showed himself to the Eleven themselves while they were at table. He reproached them for their incredulity and obstinacy, because they had refused
15   to believe those who had seen him after he had risen. •And he said to them,
16   'Go out to the whole world; proclaim the Good News to all creation. •He who believes and is baptised will be saved; he who does not believe will be condemned.
17   These are the signs that will be associated with believers: in my name they will cast
18   out devils; they will have the gift of tongues; •they will pick up snakes in their hands, and be unharmed should they drink deadly poison; they will lay their hands on the sick, who will recover.'
19   And so the Lord Jesus, after he had spoken to them, was taken up into heaven:
20   there at the right hand of God he took his place, •while they, going out, preached everywhere, the Lord working with them and confirming the word by the signs that accompanied it.

The stress on the incredulity and obstinacy (16:14) of the disciples is typical of the 'Marcan conclusions' (cf also 16:9-11, 12-13).

The 'signs' are found only here. Casting out devils and healing the sick have been basic to Jesus' work. The disciples are to carry on his mission. The gift of tongues was a phenomenon experienced in the early church and associated with a special gift of prayer in the Spirit. Picking up snakes without being harmed has an apocalyptic ring about it. The snake was a classical biblical image for evil. What in effect is being said is that the powers of evil will not be able to stand against the community (compare Luke 10:19-20 and Revelations 12:7-9).

Finally, the author sees the triumphant progress of the Gospel throughout the Gentile world as a proof of the presence and power of the risen Jesus.

* * * * * * * *

JOHN 20:19-31

19   In the evening of that same day, the first day of the week, the doors were closed in the room where the disciples were, for fear of the Jews. Jesus came
20   and stood among them. He said to them, 'Peace be with you', •and showed them his hands and his side. The disciples were filled with joy when they saw
21   the Lord, •and he said to them again, 'Peace be with you.

'As the Father sent me,
so am I sending you.'

22   After saying this he breathed on them and said:

'Receive the Holy Spirit.
23   For those whose sins you forgive,
they are forgiven;
for those whose sins you retain,
they are retained.'

24   Thomas, called the Twin, who was one of the Twelve, was not with them
25   when Jesus came. •When the disciples said, 'We have seen the Lord', he answered, 'Unless I see the holes that the nails made in his hands and can put my finger into the holes they made, and unless I can put my hand into his side,
26   I refuse to believe'. •Eight days later the disciples were in the house again and

Thomas was with them. The doors were closed, but Jesus came in and stood
27 among them. 'Peace be with you' he said. •Then he spoke to Thomas, 'Put
your finger here; look, here are my hands. Give me your hand; put it into my
28 side. Doubt no longer but believe.' •Thomas replied, 'My Lord and my God!'
29 Jesus said to him:
'You believe because you can see me.
Happy are those who have not seen and yet believe.'
30   There were many other signs that Jesus worked and the disciples saw, but
31 they are not recorded in this book. •These are recorded so that you may believe
that Jesus is the Christ, the Son of God, and that believing this you may have life
through his name.

John concludes his Gospel with the same scene as Luke: on the first day of
the week (the day of the Eucharistic celebration) the community is assembled and
experiences the presence in its midst of the risen Jesus.

In Luke, Jesus shows them his 'hands and his feet' (24:40). Here, for reasons
that we discussed when examining John 19:34 (page 427) Jesus:
'showed them his hands and his side'. (20:20)
The pierced side reminds us of his suffering and glorification and the gift of the
Spirit which poured from his heart on the cross. In fact the final words of the
crucifixion scene: 'They will look on the one whom they have pierced' (John
19:37) make a fine summary of the main theme of John's Resurrection scenes.
scenes.

As with both Matthew and Luke, John goes on immediately to speak of
mission: the community will experience the joy of the presence of the risen Jesus
when it carries on his mission of redeeming love. The Spirit that poured from his
side on the cross, the Spirit that he breathed forth as he died, is here breathed over
his disciples. A new creation has begun, and the Christian community shares in
the power of Jesus to pour God's healing power out for the forgiveness of sins and
the reconciliation of man with his God.

In Luke the reaction of the disciples to the presence of Jesus was one of joy.
But:
'their joy was so great that they still could not believe it, and they stood there
dumbfounded.'
(Luke 24:41)
John, too, speaks of 'joy' (20:20). He reserves the doubt for a special scene.
Thinking no doubt of 'those who have not seen and yet believe' (20:29), John
creates a further scene. It is a later Eucharist ('eight days later' 20:26). It is all the
Eucharists shared by the early communities down to John's time. And Thomas is
the symbol of the disciple (for earlier mentions of Thomas in this role cf John
11:16 and 14:5). Thomas refuses to believe on the word of others. He demands his
own personal experience of what they claim. Such is the fidelity of Jesus to
Thomas, that his demand is met, and Jesus manifests his presence to him also.

In an earlier scene, Thomas had asked the way (John 14:5); here he is shown
it. The way to come to faith in the risen Jesus is to be involved in practical love
with the wounded ones of this world with whom Jesus had always identified.
Their wounds are the wounds of Jesus. Compassionate love is the way to come to

faith. It is important also that the disciple maintain union with the assembled community of believers, remembering Jesus and celebrating his death and resurrection in the Eucharist. It is there that Thomas is led, through contemplation of the Passion, to the heart of Jesus and the fountain of God's healing spirit.

John concludes his Gospel with a statement that comes as no surprise. Throughout his whole work he has been striving to penetrate the mystery of Jesus' words and actions to the heart of the one he had known, to show that special relationship that existed between the Father and his Son, and so to lead his readers on the way of life.

It is here, too, that we leave the reader. There is a lot of Thomas, thank God, in all of us. We hunger for life, and we are not content to learn from others and conform to their pattern of behaviour or expressions of wisdom. We sense that we have a right to experience life for ourselves; we sense that the ultimate journey, the religious journey, undertaken in response to a deep call within us all, is a personal journey, shared with others, but challenging each person to free, responsible decisions.

Jesus assures us that this is right, and he shows us the way: the way of fidelity in loving, the way of compassion. For that is what God is really like, and we, like Thomas, will come to know we are in the presence of the sacred, when our whole being is moved to love in a creative, compassionate and faithful way. It is a life-long journey. May we dare to undertake it, and one day be able to say in recognition:

"My Lord and my God".

*   *   *   *   *   *   *   *

APPENDIX

APPENDIX A:
The structure of the Gospel according to Mark

SECTION ONE:
INTRODUCING JESUS *(1:1-13)*   *page*
1: The beginning: John the Baptist heralds the coming of One who is
   to fulfil the Messianic hopes of Israel *(1:1-8)*   9-12
2: The Baptism of Jesus: Jesus is the Son of God *(1:9-11)*   57-8
3: The Temptations: Jesus is our brother *(1:12-13)*   61-3

SECTION TWO:
JESUS' MINISTRY PRIOR TO CAESAREA PHILIPPI

PART ONE:
THE GOOD NEWS: GOD'S HEALING AND LIBERATING
WORD
1: Summary of the Good News *(1:14-15)*   71
2: Jesus invites others to spread the Good News with him *(1:16-20)*   74
3: Jesus' healing word *(1:21-45)*
   a: The healing effect of Jesus' teaching *(1:21-28)*   78-9
   b: Healing is in view of service *(1:29-31)*   80
   c: Healing is a demonstration of the activity of God *(1:32-39)*   80
   d: Jesus heals because he shares the condition of the sick *(1:40-45)* 81-2
4: Jesus' liberating word *(2:1-28)*
   a: Jesus liberates from sin *(2:1-17)*   102-5
   b: Jesus liberates from conformity to religious ritual *(2:18-22)* 105-6
   c: Jesus liberates from the Law *(2:23-28)*   107
5: The upholders of the Law conspire to destroy Jesus *(3:1-6)*   109-10

PART TWO:
THE GOOD NEWS: GOD'S POWERFUL WORD
1: God's word is for all men *(3:7-19)*   151-2
2: The power of God's word illustrated in parables *(3:20 - 4:34)*   169-78
3: No circumstances can withstand the powerful word of God
   (4:35 - 5:43)
   a: No environment can withstand the powerful word of God
   (4:35-41)   181-2
   b: No 'spiritual' powers can withstand the powerful word of God
   (5:1-20)   182-4
   c: Sickness and death cannot withstand the powerful word of God
   (5:21-42)   184-5
4: Lack of faith is the only barrier to God's powerful word *(6:1-6)*   185-6

PART THREE:
THE GOOD NEWS: BY A MIRACLE OF GRACE MAN IS ABLE
TO HEAR AND PERCEIVE THE WORD
1: The word of God continues to spread in spite of growing opposition
   (6:6-31)
   a: The mission of the Twelve *(6:6-13)*   187-8
   b: The death of the Baptist *(6:14-29)*   188-9
   c: The return of the Twelve *(6:30-31)*   189
2: Only a miracle of grace can bring men to hear and understand the
   word of God *(6:32 - 7:37)*
   a: The miracle of the loaves (first account) *(6:32-44)*   191-3
   b: The disciples fail to understand the miracle *(6:45-52)*   193-5
   c: The crowds fail to understand Jesus *(6:53-56)*   196
   d: The Pharisees fail to understand Jesus *(7:1-23)*   196-8
   e: A stranger, a Gentile woman, understands Jesus *(7:24-30)*   199
   f: Hearing comes through a miracle of grace *(7:31-37)*   200
3: Only a miracle of grace can bring men to see and understand the
   word of God *(8:1-26)*
   a: The miracle of the loaves (second account) *(8:1-10)*   201
   b: The Pharisees are obstinate in their refusal to 'see' Jesus *(8:11-13)* 201-2
   c: The disciples still fail to understand *(8:14-21)*   202
   d: Perception comes only through a miracle of grace *(8:22-26)*   203
4: Caesarea Philippi: Jesus is acknowledged as the Messiah *(8:27-30)*   203-4

SECTION THREE:
JESUS' MINISTRY FROM CAESAREA PHILIPPI TO
JERUSALEM (The 'Journey to Jerusalem')
1: A disciple is to follow Jesus on the road to the cross and the
   resurrection *(8:31 - 9:40)*

a: Jesus speaks for the first time of his suffering, death and resurrection *(8:31-32a)* ... 257
b: The disciple Peter fails to understand *(8:32b-33)* ... 257-8
c: The disciple will find life by following Jesus *(8:34 - 9:1)* ... 258
d: God's response to Jesus and his disciples *(9:2-8)* ... 258-60
e: The fate of the Baptist is prophetic of the fate of Jesus *(9:9-13)* ... 260-1
f: Jesus' union with his Father's will is the source of his healing *(9:14-29)* ... 261-2
g: Jesus speaks for the second time of his suffering, death and resurrection *(9:30-32)* ... 262
h: The disciples fail to understand *(9:33-40)* ... 263-4
2: Instructions for disciples *(9:41 - 10:31)*
a: General *(9:41-50)* ... 265-6
b: Marriage is a commitment to a special love *(10:1-12)* ... 296-9
c: Childlike faith *(10:13-16)* ... 303
d: Reliance on God, not on possessions *(10:17-27)* ... 304-5
e: The disciple's reward *(10:28-31)* ... 305
3: Discipleship is possible only because of a miracle of grace *(10:32-52)*
a: Jesus speaks for the third time of his suffering, death and resurrection *(10:32-34)* ... 309
b: The disciples fail to understand *(10:35-45)* ... 309-10
c: Jesus gives sight to a blind man *(10:46-52)* ... 310-11

SECTION FOUR:
JESUS MINISTRY IN JERUSALEM
1: The final confrontation between Jesus and his opponents *(11:1 - 12:44)*
a: Jesus enters Jerusalem *(11:1-11a)* ... 315-7
b: The judgment of God on Israel *(11:11b-22)* ... 317-9
c: The necessity of faith *(11:23-25)* ... 319-20
d: Where does religious authority lie? *(11:27-33)* ... 320-1
e: God will sentence the religious authorities; He will vindicate His Son *(12:1-12)* ... 321-2
f: Jesus exposes the hypocrisy of the Pharisees and Herodians *(12:13-17)* ... 324-6
g: Jesus exposes the errors of the Sadducees *(12:18-27)* ... 326-9
h: The central place of love *(12:28-34)* ... 329-30
i: Jesus makes a final attempt to open the minds of his adversaries *(12:35-37)* ... 330
j: Jesus' final judgment on the hypocrisy of the religious leaders *(12:38-40)* ... 331
k: The essence of discipleship is seen in the offering of a widow *(12:41-44)* ... 333-4
2: The 'Eschatological Discourse' *(13:1-37)* ... 341-357
a: Introduction *(13:1-4)* ... 352
b: The disciples must expect persecution *(13:5-13)* ... 353
c: The Jewish-Roman war as a type, demonstrating God's judgment in man's history *(13:14-20)* ... 354-5 / 355
d: Further warnings *(13:21-23)* ... 356
e: The final judgment *(13:24-27)*
f: Jesus' world and that of his contemporaries is soon to come to an end. Only God knows when the final end will come *(13:28-32)* ... 356-7
g: The end must come for each person, each generation. All must face judgment *(13:33-37)* ... 357
3: Jesus' last days *(14:1-42)*
a: The final conspiracy to arrest Jesus *(14:1-2)* ... 363
b: Jesus is anointed in preparation for his approaching death *(14:3-9)* ... 364
c: Judas betrays Jesus *(14:10-11)* ... 365
d: The preparations for the paschal meal *(14:12-16)* ... 366
e: Jesus identifies his betrayer *(14:17-21)* ... 366-7
f: The supper *(14:22-25)* ... 371
g: The blindness of the disciples. Jesus promises to call them again after his resurrection *(14:26-31)* ... 371-2
h: Jesus faces his bitter struggle alone *(14:32-42)* ... 372-3

SECTION FIVE:
THE DEATH AND RESURRECTION OF JESUS

PART ONE:
JESUS' PASSION AND DEATH
1 Jesus' arrest *(14:43-52)* ... 407

2 Jesus' testimony before the Jewish authorities and Peter's denial
   (14:53-72)   410-2
3: Jesus is handed over to the Roman governor, condemned to death
   and ridiculed *(15:1-20)*   413-4
4: The crucifixion *(15:21-32)*   419-20
5: The death of Jesus *(15:33-41)*   422-5
6: The burial of Jesus *(15:42-47)*   428-9

PART TWO:
JESUS' RESURRECTION
1: The empty tomb *(16:1-8)*   431-4
2: Conclusion added to Mark's Gospel *(16:9-20)*
   a: Mary of Magdala *(16:9-11, cf John 20:1-18)*   440
   b: The two disciples *(16:12-3, cf Luke 24:13-35)*   448
   c: Conclusion: The assembled, eucharistic, community *(16:14-20, cf*   450
      Luke 24:36-53)

APPENDIX B:
The structure of the Gospel according to Matthew

	Studied under study of Mark	Special study of Matthew
	pages	*pages*
SECTION ONE:		
INTRODUCING JESUS *(1:1 - 4:11)*		
The Prologue *(1:1 - 2:23)*		19-29
1: John the Baptist heralds the coming of One who is to fulfil the messianic hopes of Israel *(3:1-12)*	9-12	12-3
2: The baptism of Jesus: Jesus is the Son of God *(3:13-17)*	57-8	58-9
3: The temptations: Jesus is our brother *(4:1-11)*	61-3	63-6
SECTION TWO:		
JESUS' MINISTRY PRIOR TO CAESAREA PHILIPPI *(4:12- 16:20)*		
PART ONE:		
THE GOOD NEWS: GOD'S HEALING, CHALLENGING AND LIBERATING WORD *(4:12 - 12:14)*		
1: Summary of the Good News *(4:12-17)*	71	72
2: Jesus invites others to spread the Good News with him *(4:18-22)*	74	
3: Jesus' Word: 4:23-25 and 7:28-29		79
5:1 - 7:27		86-99
4: Jesus' healing word *(8:1-17)*		
a: Jesus heals the leper *(8:1-4)*	81-2	
b: Jesus' healing is in response to faith; it extends to the Gentiles *(8:5-13)*		82-3
c: Healing is for service *(8:14-15)*	80	
d: Jesus heals because he shares the condition of the sick *(8:16-17)*		82
5: Jesus' challenging word *(8:18-22)*		101
6: Jesus' liberating word *(8:23 - 12:8)*		
a: Jesus liberates from fear of a hostile environment *(8:23-27)*	181-2	101-2
b: Jesus liberates from fear of hostile 'spiritual' powers *(8:28-34)*	182-4	102
c: Jesus liberates from sin *(9:1-13)*	102-5	105
d: Jesus liberates from conformity to religious ritual *(9:14-17)*	105-6	
e: Jesus liberates from the Law *(9:18 - 12:8)*		
i) The foundation of the new covenant is faith *(9:18-34)*		113-4
ii) Faith is experienced in the church, the community of the new covenant. *(9:35 - 11:1)*		115-9
iii) Jesus fulfils the Law: the nature of his messiahship *(11:2-30)*		119-23
iv) Jesus liberates from the Law as imposed by the Pharisees *(12:1-8)*	107-9	107-8
7: The upholders of the Law conspire to destroy Jesus *(12:9-14)*	109-10	
PART TWO:		
THE GOOD NEWS: GOD'S POWERFUL WORD *(12:15 - 13:58)*		
1: God's word is for all men *(12:15-21)*		151-2

458

2: The power of God's word illustrated in parables *(12:22 - 13:52)*   169-79
    12:22-24, 30-32, 33-45   170-2
    13:10-17   173-4
    13:24-30, 33-52   177-9
3: Lack of faith is the only barrier to God's powerful word *(13:53-58)*   185-6

PART THREE:
THE GOOD NEWS: THE DISCIPLES COME TO
ACKNOWLEDGE GOD'S WORD
1: The power of Jesus' opponents illustrated in the murder of the
Baptist *(14:1-12)*   188-9   189

2: Jesus continues to live the Good News in spite of opposition and the
failure of others to understand him *(14:13 - 15:31)*
    a: The miracle of the loaves (first account) *(14:13-21)*   191-3
    b: The disciples fail to understand the miracle *(14:22-33)*   193-5   195-6
    c: The crowds fail to understand Jesus *(14:34-36)*   196
    d: The Pharisees fail to understand Jesus *(15:1-20)*   196-8   198-9
    e: A stranger, a Gentile woman, understands *(15:21-28)*   199
    f: Jesus lives the Good News *(15:29-31)*   200
3: The disciples come to understand *(15:32 - 16:12)*
    a: The miracle of the loaves (second account) *(15:32-39)*   201
    b: The Pharisees are obstinate in their refusal to 'see' Jesus *(16:1-4)*   201-2
    c: The disciples come to understand Jesus *(16:5-12)*   202   202-3
4: Caesarea Philippi: Jesus is acknowledged as the Messiah *(16:13-20)*   203-4   204-5

SECTION THREE:
JESUS' MINISTRY FROM CAESAREA PHILIPPI TO
JERUSALEM (The 'Journey to Jerusalem') *(16:21 - 20:34)*
1: A disciple is to follow Jesus on the road to the cross and the
resurrection *(16:21 - 18:5)*
    a: Jesus speaks for the first time of his suffering, death and
resurrection *(16:21)*   257
    b: The disciple Peter fails to understand *(16:22-23)*   257-8
    c: The disciple will find life by following Jesus *(16:24-28)*   258
    d: God's response to Jesus and his disciples *(17:1-8)*   258-9
    e: The fate of the Baptist is prophetic of the fate of Jesus *(17:9-13)*   260-1
    f: Jesus' union with his Father's will is the source of his healing
power *(17:14-20)*   261-2   262
    g: Jesus speaks for the second time of his suffering, death and
resurrection *(17:22-23)*   262
    h: Jesus and his disciples are sons of God *(17:24-27)*   262-3
    i: The disciples are to be as little children *(18:1-5)*   263
2: Instructions for disciples *(18:6 - 20:16)*
    a: General *(18:6-10)*   265-6   266
    b: Forgiveness *(18:12-35)*   266-8
    c: Marriage is a commitment to a special love *(19:1-11)*   299-302
    d: Celibacy for the kingdom *(19:12)*   302-3
    e: Childlike faith *(19:13-15)*   303
    f: Reliance on God, not on possessions *(19:16-26)*   304-5
    g: The disciple's reward *(19:27 - 20:16)*   305   305-7
3: Discipleship is possible only because of a miracle of grace *(20:17-34)*
    a: Jesus speaks for the third time of his suffering, death and
resurrection *(20:17-19)*   309
    b: The disciples fail to understand *(20:20-28)*   309-10
    c: Jesus gives sight to two blind men *(20:29-34)*   310-1   311

SECTION FOUR:
JESUS' MINISTRY IN JERUSALEM *(21:1 - 26:46)*
1: The final confrontation between Jesus and his opponents *(21:1 - 23:39)*
    a: Jesus enters Jerusalem *(21:1-11)*   315-7
    b: The judgment of God on Israel *(21:12-20)*   317-9   320
    c: The necessity of faith *(21:21-22)*   319-20
    d: Where does religious authority lie? *(21:23-32)*   320-1   321
    e: God will sentence the religious authorities; he will vindicate his
Son *(21:33 - 22:14)*   321-2   322-3
    f: Jesus exposes the hypocrisy of the Pharisees and Herodians
(22:15-22)   324-6
    g: Jesus exposes the errors of the Sadducees *(22:23-33)*   326-9
    h: The central place of love *(22:34-40)*   329-30

i: Jesus makes a final attempt to open the minds of his adversaries
  (22:41-46)   330-1
j: Jesus' final judgment on the hypocrisy of the religious leaders
  (23:1-39)
                                                                            331-4
2: The 'Eschatological Discourse' *(24:1 - 25:46)*   341-61
  a: Introduction *(24:1-3)*   352
  b: The disciples must expect persecution *(24:4-14)*
                                                                            353-4
  c: The Jewish-Roman war as a type, demonstrating God's judgment in
     man's history *(24:15-22)*   354-5
  d: Further warnings *(24:23-28)*   355-6
  e: The final judgement *(24:29-31)*   356
  f: Jesus' world and that of his contemporaries is soon to come to an
     end. Only God knows when the final end will come. *(24:32-36)*   356-7
  g: The end must come for each person, each generation. All must face
     judgement. *(24:37-44)*   357
  h: The leaders in the community must serve *(24:45-51)*   358
  i: The religious leaders are responsible for the church, the bride of
     Christ *(25:1-13)*   358-9
  j: Our responsibility *(25:14-30)*   359-60
  k: The last judgement *(25:1-13)*   360-1
3: Jesus' last days *(26:1-46)*
  a: The final conspiracy to arrest Jesus *(26:1-5)*   363
  b: Jesus is anointed in preparation for his approaching death
     (26:6-13)   364
  c: Judas betrays Jesus *(26:14-16)*   365   366
  d: The preparations for the paschal meal *(26:17-19)*   366-7
  e: Jesus identifies his betrayer *(26:20-25)*   366-7
  f: The supper *(26:26-29)*   371
  g: The blindness of the disciples. Jesus promises to call them again
     after his resurrection *(26:30-35)*   371-2
  h: Jesus faces his bitter struggle alone *(26:36-46)*   372-3

SECTION FIVE:
THE DEATH AND RESURRECTION OF JESUS

PART ONE:
JESUS' PASSION AND DEATH
1: Jesus' arrest *(26:47-56)*   407
2: Jesus' testimony before the Jewish authorities, and Peter's denial
   (26:57-75)   410-2
3: Jesus is handed over to the Roman governor, condemned to
   death and ridiculed *(27:1-31)*   413-4   415-6
   : the death of Judas *(27:3-10)*   414-5
4: The crucifixion *(27:32-44)*   419-20   420
5: The death of Jesus *(27:45-56)*   422-25   425
6: The burial of Jesus *(27:57-61)*   428-9

PART TWO:
JESUS' RESURRECTION *(27:62 - 28:20)*
1: The empty tomb *(27:62 - 28:15)*
  a: The tomb is sealed and guarded *(27:62-66)*   434-5
  b: The women go to the tomb *(28:1)*   435
  c: The resurrection: light overpowers darkness *(28:2-4)*   435
  d: The women are told of the resurrection *(28:5-10)*   435
  e: The authorities try to cover up the resurrection *(28:11-15)*   435
2: The appearance of the risen Jesus in Galilee *(28:16-20)*   443-4

APPENDIX C:
The structure of the Gospel according to Luke

	Studied under Mark	Special study of Luke
	pages	*pages*
SECTION ONE:		
INTRODUCING JESUS *(1:1 - 4:13)*		
General introduction *(1:1-4)*		13
Prologue *(1:5 - 2:52)*		30–45
1: John the Baptist heralds the coming of Jesus *(3:1-20)*	9-12	13-4
2: The Baptism of Jesus: Jesus is the Son of God *(3:21-22)*	57-8	58
3: Jesus is our brother:		
a: Jesus' ancestry: He is the son of man *(3:23-38)*		59-60
b: The temptations *(4:1-13)*	61-6	66-7
SECTION TWO:		
JESUS' GALILEAN MINISTRY		
Introduction: Jesus announces the Good News and is rejected by his own people *(4:14-30)*		72-3
PART ONE:		
JESUS' HEALING AND LIBERATING WORD *(4:31 - 5:16)*		
1: Jesus' healing word *(4:31 - 5:16)*		
a: The healing effect of Jesus' teaching *(4:31-37)*	78-9	
b: Healing is for service *(4:38-39)*	80	
c: Healing is a demonstration of the activity of God *(4:40-44)*	80	
d: Jesus invites others to join him *(5:1-11)*		74-5
e: Jesus heals the leper *(5:12-14)*	81-2	
f: conclusion *(5:15-16)*		83
2: Jesus' liberating word *(5:17 - 6:5)*		
a: Jesus liberates from sin *(5:17-32)*	102-5	
b: Jesus liberates from conformity to religious ritual *(5:33-39)*	105-7	
c: Jesus liberates from the Law *(6:1-5)*	107-9	
3: The upholders of the Law conspire to destroy Jesus *(6:6-11)*	109-10	
PART TWO:		
JESUS' WORD IS FOR ALL MEN *(6:12 - 8:3)*		
1: Jesus chooses the Twelve *(6:12-16)*		152-3
2: The 'Sermon on the Plain' *(6:17-49)*		155-61
3: The essence of Jesus' mission *(7:1 - 8:3)*		162-7
PART THREE:		
JESUS' POWERFUL WORD *(8:4 - 9:17)*		
1: The power of God's word illustrated in parables *(8:4-21)*	172-6	
2: No circumstances can withstand the powerful word of God *(8:22-56)*	181-5	
3: The word of God continues to spread in spite of growing opposition *(9:1-10)*	187-9	
4: The miracle of the loaves *(9:10-17)*	191-3	193
PART FOUR:		
JESUS IS THE CHRIST, THE SUFFERING SERVANT *(9:18-50)*		
1: Caesarea Philippi: Jesus is acknowledged as the Messiah *(9:18-21)*	203-4	205
2: Jesus is the Suffering Servant. He invites his disciples to follow him, but they fail to understand *(9:22-50)*		
a: Jesus speaks for the first time of his suffering, death and resurrection *(9:22)*	257	
b: The disciple will find life by following Jesus *(9:23-27)*	258	
c: God's response to Jesus and his disciples *(9:28-36)*	258-60	260
d: Jesus' union with his Father's will is the source of his healing power *(9:37-43)*	261-2	
e: Jesus speaks for the second time of his suffering, death and resurrection *(9:44-45)*	262	
f: His disciples fail to understand Jesus *(9:46-50)*	263-4	

SECTION THREE:
JESUS' JOURNEY TO JERUSALEM *(9:51 - 19:40)*
A: Luke has a section proper to his Gospel *(9:51 - 18:14)*   268-296
   (- for set out of this insert see page 270-1)
B: Further instructions for disciples *(18:15 - 19:27)*
  1: Jesus asks of his followers a childlike faith *(18:15-17)*   303
  2: Jesus asks of his followers that they rely on God, not on their
    possessions *(18:18-27)*   304-5
  3: The reward offered by Jesus to his followers *(18:28-30)*   305
  4: Jesus speaks for the third time of his suffering, death and
    resurrection *(18:31-34)*   309
  5: Following Jesus is made possible by a miracle of grace *(18:35-43)*   310-11
  6: The Son of Man has come to seek out and to save what was lost
    (19:1-10)   311-2
  7: The responsibility inherent in being a disciple *(19:11-27)*
C: Jesus enters Jerusalem *(19:28-40)*   315-7   312

SECTION FOUR:
JESUS' JERUSALEM MINISTRY *(19:41 - 22:46)*
1: The final confrontation between Jesus and his opponents *(19:41 - 21:4)*
  a: Jesus laments over his rejection by Jerusalem *(19:41-44)*   320
  b: The judgment of God on Israel *(19:45-48)*   317-9   320
  c: Where does religious authority lie? *(20:1-8)*   320-1
  d: God will sentence the religious authorities. He will vindicate his
    Son *(20:9-19)*   321-2
  e: Jesus exposes the hypocrisy of the religious leaders *(20:20-26)*   324-6
  f: Jesus exposes the errors of the Sadducees *(20:27-40)*   326-9
  g: Jesus makes a final effort to open the minds of his adversaries
    (20:41-44)   330-1
  h: Jesus' final judgment on the hypocrisy of the religious leaders
    (20:45-47)   331
  i: The essence of discipleship is seen in the offering of a widow
    (21:1-4)   335-6
2: The 'Eschatological Discourse' *(21:5-38)*   341-58
  a: Introduction *(21:5-7)*   352
  b: The disciples must expect persecution *(21:8-19)*   353
  c: The Jewish-Roman war as a type, demonstrating God's judgement
    in man's history *(21:20-24)*   355
  d: The final judgment *(21:25-28)*   356
  e: Jesus' world and that of his contemporaries is soon to come to an end
    (21:29-33)   356-7
  f: The end must come for each person, each generation. All must face
    judgement *(21:34-6)*   358
  g: Conclusion *(21:37-8)*   358
3: Jesus' last days *(22:1-46)*
  a: The final conspiracy to arrest Jesus *(22:1-2)*   363
  b: Judas betrays Jesus *(22:3-6)*   365-6
  c: The preparations for the paschal meal *(22:7-13)*   366
  d: The new Passover. The celebration of the new covenant, sealed
    by the blood of the new Passover lamb *(22:14-20)*   367-9
  e: Jesus identifies his betrayer *(22:21-23)*   366-7
  f: The greatness and the weakness of Jesus' disciples *(22:24-39)*   369-71
  g: Jesus faces his bitter struggle alone *(22:40-46)*   372-4

SECTION FIVE:
THE DEATH AND RESURRECTION OF JESUS

PART ONE:
JESUS' PASSION AND DEATH *(22:47 - 23:56)*
1: Jesus' arrest *(22:47-53)*   407   408
2: Jesus' testimony before the Jewish authorities, and Peter's denial
  (22:54-71)   410-2
3: Jesus is handed over to the Roman governor, ridiculed by Herod,
  and condemned to death *(23:1-25)*   413-5   416-7
4: The crucifixion *(23:26-43)*   419-20   420-1
5: The death of Jesus *(23:44-49)*   422-5   424
6: The burial of Jesus *(23:50-56)*   428-9   429

PART TWO:
JESUS' RESURRECTION *(24:1-53)*
1: The empty tomb *(24:1-12)*   431-4   437-8
2: The appearances of the risen Jesus
  a: Jesus is recognised in the breaking of bread *(24:13-35)*   447-8
  b: Jesus appears to his disciples gathered at table *(24:36-53)*   448-9

APPENDIX D:
The structure of the Gospel according to John

SECTION ONE:
INTRODUCING JESUS *(1:1-51)*
The Prologue *(1:1-18)*   46-56
    (1:6-8, 15)   15
1: John the Baptist heralds the coming of One who is to fulfil the
   Messianic hopes of Israel *(1:19-28)*   •   15-6
2: The Baptism of Jesus: Jesus is the Son of God *(1:29-34)*   60-1
3: Jesus calls his disciples *(1:35-51)*   75-8

SECTION TWO:
THE NEW COVENANT *(2:1 - 5:47)*
1: Jesus inaugurates a new covenant *(2:1-25)*
  a: Cana *(2:1-12)*   126-7
  b: Jesus clears the Temple *(2:13-25)*   127-9
2: The implications of the new covenant
  a: for a Jew *(3:1-21)*   129-33
  b: for a follower of the Baptist *(3:22-36)*   133-4
  c: for a non-Jew *(4:1-42)*   134-9
  d: The new covenant is offered to all *(4:43-54)*   139-40
3: The religious leaders reject the new covenant *(5:1-47)*   140-6

SECTION THREE:
THE PERSON OF JESUS *(6:1 - 11:54)*
1: Jesus is the 'Holy One of God' who gives the 'living bread' *(6:1-71)*   209-17
2: Jesus gives 'living water'. He is the 'Son' who is the 'light of the
   world' *(7:1 - 8:59)*   219-34
3: Jesus is 'one with the Father'. Man is judged by the stand he takes
   towards Jesus who gives 'light' and 'life'. *(9:1-10:42)*   235-47
4: Jesus gives 'eternal life' *(11:1-54)*   249-54

SECTION FOUR:
JESUS PREPARES FOR HIS PASSION *(11:55 - 12:50)*
1: The final conspiracy to arrest Jesus *(11:55-57)*   363-4
2: Jesus is anointed in preparation for his approaching death *(12:1-11)*   364-5
3: Jesus' entry into Jerusalem and judgment of the religious
   authorities who reject him *(12:12-50)*   336-40

SECTION FIVE:
JOHN'S REFLECTIONS ON THE MEANING OF JESUS'
DEATH AND RESURRECTION *(Chapters 13-17)*
1: The last supper *(13:1-38)*   377-80
2: The first Supper discourse *(14:1-31)*   381-9
3: The second Supper discourse *(15:1 - 16:33)*   389-400
4: The prayer of Jesus *(17:1-26)*   400-4

SECTION SIX:
THE DEATH AND RESURRECTION OF JESUS

PART ONE:
JESUS' PASSION AND DEATH
1: Jesus' arrest *(18:1-11)*   408-10
2: Jesus' testimony before the Jewish authorities and Peter's denial
   (18:12-27)   412-3
3: Jesus is handed over to the Roman governor, ridiculed and
   condemned to death *(18:28 - 19:16)*   417-9
4: The crucifixion *(19:17-24)*   421-2

5: The death of Jesus *(19:25-37)*   426-8
6: The burial of Jesus *(19:38-42)*   428-9

PART TWO:
JESUS' RESURRECTION
1: The empty tomb *(20:1-18)*   438-40
2: The appearances of the risen Jesus to his disciples gathered at the table *(20:19-31)*   450-2
3: Appendix to John's Gospel *(21:1-25)*   444-6

APPENDIX E:

The readings cited below are from the Roman Catholic lectionary. Occasionally a particular reading in the lectionary of another denomination differs from the listing below.

1: Season of Advent (preparing for Christmas)

SUNDAY 1   Year A: Matthew 24:37-44 page 357 (+p.341-52)
Year B: Mark 13:33-37 page 357 (+p.341-52)
Year C: Luke 21:25-28, 34-36 page 356-8 (+p.341-52)

Monday: Matthew 8:5-11 p.82-3   Tuesday: Luke 10:21-24 p.273
Wednesday: Matthew 15:29-37 p.200   Thursday: Matthew 7:21-27 p.98-9
Friday: Matthew 9:27-31 p.114   Saturday: Matthew 9:35-10:1, 6-8 p.115-6

SUNDAY 2   Year A: Matthew 3:1-12 page 9-13
Year B: Mark 1:1-8 page 9-12
Year C: Luke 3:1-6 page 9-12, 13-4

Monday: Luke 5:17-26 p.102-4   Tuesday: Matthew 18:12-14 p.266
Wednesday: Matthew 11:28-30 p.122-3   Thursday: Matthew 11:11-15 p.120-1
Friday: Matthew 11:16-19 p.121   Saturday: Matthew 17:10-13 p.260-1

SUNDAY 3   Year A: Matthew 11:2-11 page 119-21
Year B: John 1:6-8, 19-28 page 14-6
Year C: Luke 3:10-18 page 9-12, 14

Monday: Matthew 21:23-27 p.320-1   Tuesday: Matthew 21:28-32 p.321
Wednesday: Luke 7:19-23 p.164   Thursday: Luke 7:24-30 p.164
Friday: John 5:33-36 p.144-6
(The eight days prior to Christmas have special Masses)

Dec 17: Matthew 1:1-17 p.19-22   Dec 18: Matthew 1:18-24 p.23-4
Dec 19: Luke 1:5-25 p.30-5   Dec 20: Luke 1:26-38 p.35-6
Dec 21: Luke 1:39-45 p.36-8   Dec 22: Luke 1:46-56 p.36-8
Dec 23: Luke 1:57-66 p.38-9   Dec 24: Luke 1:67-79 p.38-9
    Matthew 1:1-25 p.19-24 (vigil)

SUNDAY 4   Year A: Matthew 1:18-24 page 23-4
Year B: Luke 1:26-38 page 35-6
Year C: Luke 1:39-45 page 36-8

2: Season of Christmas

CHRISTMAS   Midnight: Luke 2:1-14 page 39-42
Dawn: Luke 2:15-20 page 39-42
Day: John 1:1-18 page 14-15, 46-56

HOLY FAMILY   Year A: Matthew 2:13-15, 19-23 page 26-9
Year B: Luke 2:22-40 page 42-3
Year C: Luke 2:41-52 page 44

Dec 29: Luke 2:22-35 p.42-3   Dec 30: Luke 2:36-40 p.42-3
Dec 31: John 1:1-18 p.46-56

MARY, MOTHER OF GOD   Luke 2:16-21 page 39-42
(January 1)

Jan 2: John 1: 19-28 p.15-6   Jan 3: John 1:29-34 p.60-1
Jan 4: John 1:35-42 p.75-8   Jan 5: John 1:43-51 p.75-8
Jan 6: Mark 1:6b-11 p.9-12, 57-58 Jan 7: John 2:1-12 p.125-7

EPIPHANY   Matthew 2:1-12 page 24-6

Monday: Matthew 4:12-17, 23-25 p.72,79   Tuesday: Mark 6:34-44 p.191-3
Wednesday: Mark 6:45-52 p.193-5   Thursday: Luke 4:14-22 p.72-3
Friday: Luke 5:12-16 p.81-3   Saturday: John 3:22-30 p.133-4

3:   The First Season of Ordinary Time
(The length of this season varies with the time of Easter. We shall include here the first 9 weeks).

SUNDAY 1   Year A: Matthew 2 '3-17 page 57-9
(BAPTISM)   Year B: Mark 1:6b-11 page 9-12, 57-8
             Year C: Luke 3:15-16, 21-22 page 9-12, 57-8

Monday: Mark 1:14-20 p.71-4   Tuesday: Mark 1:21-28 p.78-9
Wednesday: Mark 1:29-39 p.80   Thursday: Mark 1:40-45 p.81-2
Friday: Mark 2:1-12 p.102-4   Saturday: Mark 2:13-17 p.104-5

SUNDAY 2   Year A: John 1:29-34 page 60-1
             Year B: John 1:35-42 page 75-8
             Year C: John 2:1-12 page 125-7

Monday: Mark 2:18-22 p.105-7   Tuesday: Mark 2:23-28 p.107
Wednesday: Mark 3:1-6 p.109-10   Thursday: Mark 3:7-12 p.151
Friday: Mark 3:13-19 p.152   Saturday: Mark 3:20-21 p.169-70

SUNDAY 3   Year A: Matthew 4:12-23 page 72-4
             Year B: Mark 1:14-20 page 71-4
             Year C: Luke 1:1-4, 14-21 page 13, 72-3

Monday: Mark 3:22-30 p.169-71   Tuesday: Mark 3:31-35 p.172
Wednesday: Mark 4:1-20 p.172-5   Thursday: Mark 4:21-25 p.175-6
Friday: Mark 4:26-34 p.176-8   Saturday: Mark 4:35-41 p.181-2

SUNDAY 4   Year A: Matthew 5:1-12 page 85-9
             Year B: Mark 1:21-28 page 78-9
             Year C: Luke 4:21-30 page 72-3

Monday: Mark 5:1-20 p.182-4   Tuesday: Mark 5:21-43 p.184-5
Wednesday: Mark 6:1-6 p.185-6   Thursday: Mark 6:7-13 p.187-8
Friday: Mark 6:14-29 p.188-9   Saturday: Mark 6:30-34 p.189

SUNDAY 5   Year A: Matthew 5:13-16 page 89-90
             Year B: Mark 1:29-39 page 80
             Year C: Luke 5:1-11 page 74-5

Monday: Mark 6:53-56 p.196-7   Tuesday: Mark 7:1-13 p.196-8
Wednesday: Mark 7:14-23 p.196-8 Thursday: Mark 7:24-30 p.199
Friday: Mark 7:31-37 p.200   Saturday: Mark 8:1-10 p.201

SUNDAY 6   Year A: Matthew 5:17-37 page 90-3
             Year B: Mark 1:40-45 page 81-2
             Year C: Luke 6:17, 20-26 page 155-9

Monday: Mark 8:11-13 p.201-2   Tuesday: Mark 8:14-21 p.202
Wednesday: Mark 8:22-26 p.203   Thursday: Mark 8:27-33 p.203-4, 257
Friday: Mark 8:34-9:1 p.258   Saturday: Mark 9:2-13 p.258-61

SUNDAY 7   Year A: Matthew 5:38-48 page 93
             Year B: Mark 2:1-12 page 102-4
             Year C: Luke 6:27-38 page 159-61

Monday: Mark 9:14-29 p.261-2   Tuesday: Mark 9:30-37 p.262-3
Wednesday: Mark 9:38-40 p.263-4 Thursday: Mark 9:41-50 p.265-6
Friday: Mark 10:1-12 p.296-9   Saturday: Mark 10:13-16 p.303

SUNDAY 8   Year A: Matthew 6:24-34 page 95-6
             Year B: Mark 2:18-22 page 105-7
             Year C: Luke 6:39-45 page 161

Monday: Mark 10:17-27 p.304-5
Wednesday: Mark 10:32-45 p.309-10
Friday: Mark 11:11-26 p.317-20

Tuesday: Mark 10:28-31 p.305
Thursday: Mark 10:46-52 p.310-1
Saturday: Mark 11:27-33 p.320-1

SUNDAY 9   Year A: Matthew 7:21-27 page 98-9
Year B: Mark 2:23-3:6 page 107-10
Year C: Luke 7:1-10 page 162

Monday: Mark 12:1-12 p.321-2
Wednesday: Mark 12:18-27 p.326-9
Friday: Mark 12:35-37 p.330-1

Tuesday: Mark 12:13-17 p.324-6
Thursday: Mark 12:28-34 p.329-30
Saturday: Mark 12:38-44 p.331-5

4:   Season of Lent (preparation for Easter)
ASH WEDNESDAY   Matthew 6:1-6, 16-18 page 94-5

Thursday: Luke 9:22-25 p.257-8
Friday: Matthew 9:14-15 p.105-6   Saturday: Luke 5:27-32 p.104-5

SUNDAY 1   Year A: Matthew 4:1-11 page 63-6
Year B: Mark 1:12-15 page 61-3, 71-2
Year C: Luke 4:1-13 page 63-7

Monday: Matthew 25:31-46 p.360-1
Wednesday: Luke 11:29-32 p.276-7
Friday: Matthew 5:20-26 p.91-2

Tuesday: Matthew 6:7-15 p.94-5
Thursday: Matthew 7:7-12 p.97
Saturday: Matthew 5:43-48 p.93

SUNDAY 2   Year A: Matthew 17:1-9 page 258-60
Year B: Mark 9:1-9 page 258-60
Year C: Luke 9:28-36 page 258-60

Monday: Luke 6:36-38 p.159-61
Wednesday: Matthew 20:17-28 p.309-10
Friday: Matthew 21:33-46 p.321-2

Tuesday: Matthew 23:1-12 p.331-2
Thursday: Luke 16:19-31 p.291-2
Saturday: Luke 15:1-3, 11-32 p.287-9

SUNDAY 3   Year A: John 4:5-42 page 134-9
Year B: John 2:13-25 page 127-9
Year C: Luke 13:1-9 page 381-2

Monday: Luke 4:24-30 p.72-3
Wednesday: Matthew 5:17-19 p.90
Friday: Mark 12:28-34 p.329-30

Tuesday: Matthew 18:21-35 p.267-8
Thursday: Luke 11:14-23 p.276-7
Saturday: Luke 18:9-14 p.295-6

SUNDAY 4   Year A: John 9:1-42 page 235-8
Year B: John 3:14-21 page 129-33
Year C: Luke 15:1-3, 11-32 page 287-9

Monday: John 4:43-54 p.139-40
Wednesday: John 5:17-30 p.140-4
Friday: John 7:1-2, 10, 25-30 p.219-24

Tuesday: John 5:1-16 p.140-6
Thursday: John 5:31-47 p.144-6
Saturday: John 7:40-53 p.224-7

SUNDAY 5   Year A: John 11:1-45 page 249-53
Year B: John 12:20-33 page 336-8
Year C: John 8:1-11 page 227-8

Monday: John 8:1-11, 11:1-45
p.227-8/249-53
Wednesday: John 8:31-42 p.230-2
Friday: John 10:31-42 p.245-7

Tuesday: John 8:21-30 p.228-30
Thursday: John 8:51-59 p.232-4
Saturday: John 11:45-56 p.253-4

PALM SUNDAY Procession   Year A: Matthew 21:1-11 page 315-7
Year B: Mark 11:1-10 page 315-7/John 12:12-16
page 334-6
Year C: Luke 19:28-40 page 315-7

Mass: Year A: Matthew 26:14-27:66 page 265-74, 407-34
Year B: Mark 14:1-15:47 page 363-365, 407-29
Year C: Luke 22:14-23:56 page 367-374, 407-29

Monday: John 12:1-11 p.364-5
Wednesday: Matthew 26:14-25 p.365-7

Tuesday: John 13:21-38 p.378-80

HOLY THURSDAY: **Mass of Chrism:** Luke 4:16-21 page 72-3
The Lord's Supper: John 13:1-15 page 377-8

GOOD FRIDAY John 18:1-19:42 page 408-29
5. Season of Easter

466

EASTER SUNDAY (Vigil)   Year A: Matthew 28:1-10 page 435-6
Year B: Mark 16:1-8 page 431-4
Year C: Luke 24:1-12 page 436-8
Day: John 20:1-9 page 438-40

Monday: Matthew 28:8-15 p.436
Wednesday: Luke 24:13-35 p.447-8
Friday: John 21:1-14 p.444-6
Tuesday: John 20:11-18 p.438-40
Thursday: Luke 24:35-48 p.448-9
Saturday: Mark 16:9-15 p.449-50

SUNDAY 2   Year A: John 20:19-31 page 450-2
Year B: John 20:19-31 page 450-2
Year C: John 20:19-31 page 450-2

Monday: John 3:1-8 p.129-30
Wednesday: John 3:16-21 p.132-3
Friday: John 6:1-15 p.209-10
Tuesday: John 3:7-15 p.130-2
Thursday: John 3:31-36 p.133-4
Saturday: John 6:16-21 p.210-11

SUNDAY 3   Year A: Luke 24:13-35 page 447-8
Year B: Luke 24:35-48 page 448-9
Year C: John 21:1-19 page 444-6

Monday: John 6:22-29 p.211-2
Wednesday: John 6:35-40 p.212-4
Friday: John 6:52-59 p.215-6
Tuesday: John 6:30-35 p.211-4
Thursday: John 6:44-51 p.214-5
Saturday: John 6:60-69 p.216-7

SUNDAY 4   Year A: John 10:1-10 page 238-41
Year B: John 10:11-18 page 241-4
Year C: John 10:27-30 page 245

Monday: John 10:1-10 p.238-41
Wednesday: John 12:44-50 p.338-9
Friday: John 14:1-6 p.381-2
Tuesday: John 10:22-30 p.245
Thursday: John 13:16-20 p.377-8
Saturday: John 14:7-14 p.382-5

SUNDAY 5   Year A: John 14:1-12 page 381-5
Year B: John 15:1-8 page 389-91
Year C: John 13:31-35 page 379-80

Monday: John 14:21-26 p.385-8
Wednesday: John 15:1-8 p.389-91
Friday: John 15:12-17 p.391-2
Tuesday: John 14:27-31 p.388-9
Thursday: John 15:9-11 p.391
Saturday: John 15:18-21 p.392-5

SUNDAY 6   Year A: John 14:15-21 page 385-8
Year B: John 15:9-17 page 391-2
Year C: John 14:23-29 page 388-9

Monday: John 15:26-16:4 p.395
Wednesday: John 16:12-15 p.397-8
Tuesday: John 16:5-11 **p.395-7**

ASCENSION THURSDAY: Year A: Matthew 28:16-20 page 443-4
Year B: Mark 16:15-20 page 450
Year C: Luke 24:46-53 page 447-8

Friday: John 16:20-23 p.398-9
Saturday: John 16:23-28 p.398-9

SUNDAY 7   Year A: John 17:1-11a page 400-2
Year B: John 17:11b-19 page 402-3
Year C: John 17:20-26 page 403-4

Monday: John 16:29-33 p.399-400
Wednesday: John 17:11b-19 p.401-3
Friday: John 21:15-19 p.445-6
Tuesday: John 17:1-11a p.400-1
Thursday: John 17:20-26 p.403-4
Saturday: John 21:20-25 p.445-6
(vigil: John 7:37-39 p.224-6)

PENTECOST SUNDAY: John 20:19-23 page 450-2

6:   The Second Season of Ordinary Time
(This begins at a different week each year, depending on the date of Easter. We begin here with week 10)

SUNDAY 10   Year A: Matthew 9:9-13 page 102-5
Year B: Mark 3:20-35 page 169-72
Year C: Luke 7:11-17 page 162-3

Monday: Matthew 5:1-12 p.85-9
Tuesday: Matthew 5:13-16 p.89-90

Wednesday: Matthew 5:17-19 p.90   Thursday: Matthew 5:20-26 p.91-2
Friday: Matthew 5:27-32 p.92   Saturday: Matthew 5:33-37 p.92-3

SUNDAY 11   Year A: Matthew 9:36-10:8 page 115-6
           Year B: Mark 4:26-34 page 176-8
           Year C: Luke 7:36-8:3 page 165-7

Monday: Matthew 5:38-42 p.93   Tuesday: Matthew 5:43-48 p.93
Wednesday: Matthew 6:1-6,16-18 p.94-5 Thursday: Matthew 6:7-15 p.94-5
Friday: Matthew 6:19-23 p.95-6   Saturday: Matthew 6:24-34 p.95-6

SUNDAY 12   Year A: Matthew 10:26-33 page 117-8
           Year B: Mark 4:35-40 page 181-2
           Year C: Luke 9:18-24 page 203-5, 257-8

Monday: Matthew 7:1-5 p.96-7   Tuesday: Matthew 7:6, 12-14 p.96-8
Wednesday: Matthew 7:15-20 p.98-9 Thursday: Matthew 7:21-29 p.98-9, 79
Friday: Matthew 8:1-4 p.81-2   Saturday: Matthew 8:5-17 p.80-3

SUNDAY 13   Year A: Matthew 10:37-42 page 118-9
           Year B: Mark 5:21-43 page 184-5
           Year C: Luke 9:51-62 page 268-72

Monday: Matthew 8:18-22 p.101   Tuesday: Matthew 8:23-27 p.101-2
Wednesday: Matthew 8:28-34 p.102 Thursday: Matthew 9:1-8 p.102-4
Friday: Matthew 9:9-13 p.104-5   Saturday: Matthew 9:14-17 p.105-6

SUNDAY 14   Year A: Matthew 11:25-30 page 122-3
           Year B: Mark 6:1-6 page 185-6
           Year C: Luke 10:1-9 page 172-3

Monday: Matthew 9:18-26 p.113-4   Tuesday: Matthew 9:32-38 p.114-5
Wednesday: Matthew 10:1-7 p.115-6 Thursday: Matthew 10:7-15 p.115-6
Friday: Matthew 10:16-23 p.116-7   Saturday: Matthew 10:24-33 p.117-8

SUNDAY 15   Year A: Matthew 13:1-23 page 172-5
           Year B: Mark 6:7-13 page 187-8
           Year C: Luke 10:25-37 page 274-5

Monday: Matthew 10:34-11:1 p.118-9 Tuesday: Matthew 11:20-24 p.121-2
Wednesday: Matthew 11:25-27 p.122 Thursday: Matthew 11:28-30 p.122-3
Friday: Matthew 12:1-8 p.107-8   Saturday: Matthew 12:14-21 p.151-2

SUNDAY 16   Year A: Matthew 13:24-43 page 177-8
           Year B: Mark 6:30-34 page 189-92
           Year C: Luke 10:38-42 page 274-5

Monday: Matthew 12:38-42 p.171-2 Tuesday: Matthew 12:46-50 p.172
Wednesday: Matthew 13:1-9 p.172-3 Thursday: Matthew 13:10-17 p.173-4
Friday: Matthew 13:18-23 p.174-5 Saturday: Matthew 13:24-30 p.177

SUNDAY 17   Year A: Matthew 13:44-52 page 178-9
           Year B: John 6:1-15 page 209-10
           Year C: Luke 11:1-13 page 275

Monday: Matthew 13:31-35 p.177-8 Tuesday: Matthew 13:36-43 p.178-9
Wednesday: Matthew 13:44-46 p.178-9 Thursday: Matthew 13:47-53 p.179
Friday: Matthew 13:54-58 p.185-6 Saturday: Matthew 14:1-12 p.188-9

SUNDAY 18   Year A: Matthew 14:13-21 page 191-3
           Year B: John 6:24-35 page 211-4
           Year C: Luke 12:13-31 page 279-80

Monday: Matthew 14:22-36 p.195-6 Tuesday: Matthew 15:1-2, 10-14 p.196-9
Wednesday: Matthew 15:21-28 p.199 Thursday: Matthew 16:13-23 p.203-5, 257
Friday: Matthew 16:24-28 p.258 Saturday: Matthew 17:14-20 p.261-2

SUNDAY 19   Year A: Matthew 14:22-33 page 193-5
           Year B: John 6:41-52 page 214-5
           Year C: Luke 12:32-48 p.279-81

Monday: Matthew 17:22-27 p.262-3 Tuesday:Matthew 18:1-5, 10-14 p.263-6
Wednesday: Matthew 18:15-20 p.267 Thursday: Matthew 18:21-19:1 p.267-8
Friday: Matthew 19:3-12 p.299-303 Saturday: Matthew 19:13-15 p.303

SUNDAY 20   Year A: Matthew 15:21-28 page 199
           Year B: John 6:51-59 page 214-6
           Year C: Luke 12:49-53 page 282

Monday: Matthew 19:16-22 p.304-5

Tuesday: Matthew 19:23-30 p.304-5

Wednesday: Matthew 20:1-16 p.306-7

Thursday: Matthew 22:1-14 p.322-3

Friday: Matthew 22:34-40 p.329-30

Saturday: Matthew 23:1-12 p.331-3

SUNDAY 21   Year A: Matthew 16:13-20 p.203-5
Year B: John 6:61-70 page 216-7
Year C: Luke 13:22-30 page 283-4

Monday: Matthew 23:13-22 p.332-3

Tuesday: Matthew 23:23-26 p.333

Wednesday: Matthew 23:27-32 p.333-4

Thursday: Matthew 24:42-51 p.357-8

Friday: Matthew 25:1-13 p.358-9

Saturday: Matthew 25:14-30 p.359-60

SUNDAY 22   Year A: Matthew 16:21-27 page 257-8
Year B: Mark 7:1-8, 14-15, 21-23 page 196-9
Year C: Luke 14:1, 7-14 page 285-6

Monday: Luke 4:16-30 p.72-3

Tuesday: Luke 4:31-37 p.78-9

Wednesday: Luke 4:38-44 p.80

Thursday: Luke 5:1-11 p.74-5

Friday: Luke 5:33-39 p.105-7

Saturday: Luke 6:1-5 p.107

SUNDAY 23   Year A: Matthew 18:15-20 page 267
Year B: Mark 7:31-37 page 200
Year C: Luke 14:25-33 page 286-7

Monday: Luke 6:6-11 p.109-10

Tuesday: Luke 6:12-19 p.152-5

Wednesday: Luke 6:20-26 p.156-7

Thursday: Luke 6:27-38 p.159-61

Friday: Luke 6:39-42 p.161

Saturday: Luke 6:43-49 p.161

SUNDAY 24   Year A: Matthew 18:21-35 page 267-8
Year B: Mark 8:27-35 page 203-4, 257-8
Year C: Luke 15:1-32 page 287-9

Monday: Luke 7:1-10 p.162

Tuesday: Luke 7:11-17 p.162-3

Wednesday: Luke 7:31-35 p.164-5

Thursday: Luke 7:36-50 p.167-8

Friday: Luke 8:1-3 p.167-8

Saturday: Luke 8:4-15 p.172-5

SUNDAY 25   Year A: Matthew 20:1-16 page 306-7
Year B: Mark 9:29-36 page 261-3
Year C: Luke 16:1-13 page 289-90

Monday: Luke 8:16-18 p.175-6

Tuesday: Luke 8:19-21 p.172

Wednesday: Luke 9:1-6 p.187-8

Thursday: Luke 9:7-9 p.188-9

Friday: Luke 9:18-22 p.203-4, 205

Saturday: Luke 9:43-45 p.261-2

SUNDAY 26   Year A: Matthew 21:28-32 page 321
Year B: Mark 9:37-47 page 263-6
Year C: Luke 16:19-31 page 292-3

Monday: Luke 9:46-50 p.263-4

Tuesday: Luke 9:51-56 p.268-72

Wednesday: Luke 9:57-62 p.272

Thursday: Luke 10:1-12 p.272-3

Friday: Luke 10:13-16 p.272-3

Saturday: Luke 10:17-24 p.273-4

SUNDAY 27   Year A: Matthew 21:33-43 page 321-2
Year B: Mark 10:2-16 page 296-300, 303
Year C: Luke 17:5-10 page 293

Monday: Luke 10:25-37 p.274-5

Tuesday: Luke 10:38-42 p.274-5

Wednesday: Luke 11:1-4 p.275

Thursday: Luke 11:5-13 p.275

Friday: Luke 11:15-26 p.276-7

Saturday: Luke 11:27-28 p.276-7

SUNDAY 28   Year A: Matthew 22:1-14 page 322-3
Year B: Mark 10:17-30 p.304-6
Year C: Luke 17:11-19 p.293

Monday: Luke 11:29-32 p.276-7

Tuesday: Luke 11:37-41 p.277-8

Wednesday: Luke 11:42-46 p.277-8

Thursday: Luke 11:47-54 p.277-8

Friday: Luke 12:1-7 p.278

Saturday: Luke 12:8-12 p.278

SUNDAY 29   Year A: Matthew 22:15-21 page 324-6
Year B: Mark 10:35-45 page 309-10
Year C: Luke 18:1-8 page 294-5

Monday: Luke 12:13-21 p.279-80

Tuesday: Luke 12:35-38 p.281

Wednesday: Luke 12:39-48 p.281

Thursday: Luke 12:49-53 p.281-2

Friday: Luke 12:54-59 p.281-2

Saturday: Luke 13:1-9 p.282-3

SUNDAY 30   Year A: Matthew 22:34-40 page 329-31
Year B: Mark 10:46-52 page 310-1
Year C: Luke 18:9-14 page 295-6

Monday: Luke 13:10-17 p.282-3
Wednesday: Luke 13:22-30 p.283-4
Friday: Luke 14:1-6 p.285-6

Tuesday: Luke 13:18-21 p.283
Thursday: Luke 13:31-35 p.283-4
Saturday: Luke 14:1, 7-11 p.285-6

SUNDAY 31   Year A: Matthew 23:1-12 page 331-2
Year B: Mark 12:28-34 page 329-30
Year C: Luke 19:1-10 page 311-2

Monday: Luke 14:12-14 p.285-6
Wednesday: Luke 14:25-33 p.286-7
Friday: Luke 16:1-8 p.289-90

Tuesday: Luke 14:15-24 p.385-6
Thursday: Luke 15:1-10 p.287-9
Saturday: Luke 16:9-15 p.290

SUNDAY 32   Year A: Matthew 25:1-13 page 358-9
Year B: Mark 12:38-44 page 331-4
Year C: Luke 20:27-38 page 326-9

Monday: Luke 17:1-6 p.292
Wednesday: Luke 17:11-19 p.293
Friday: Luke 17:26-37 p.293-4

Tuesday: Luke 17:7-10 p.293
Thursday: Luke 17:20-25 p.293-4
Saturday: Luke 18:1-8 p.294-5

SUNDAY 33   Year A: Matthew 25:14-30 page 359-60
Year B: Mark 13:24-32 page 341-52, 355-7
Year C: Luke 21:5-19 page 341-54

Monday: Luke 18:35-43 p.310-11
Wednesday: Luke 19:11-28 p.312
Friday: Luke 19:45-48 p.317-20

Tuesday: Luke 19:1-10 p.311-2
Thursday: Luke 19:41-44 p.320
Saturday: Luke 20:27-40 p.326-9

SUNDAY 34   Year A: Matthew 25:31-46 page 360-1
Year B: John 18:33-37 page 417-9
Year C: Luke 23:35-43 page 419-21

(CHRIST THE KING)

Monday: Luke 21:1-4 p.335-6
Wednesday: Luke 21:12-19 p.353-4
Friday: Luke 21:29-33 p.356-7

Tuesday: Luke 21:5-11 p.341-54
Thursday: Luke 21:20-28 p.355, 356
Saturday: Luke 21:34-36 p.358

Other Books from Winston Press

Bright Intervals
by James Bitney

Experiencing God All Ways and Every Day
by J. Norman King

God Present
by Georges Lefebvre

Faith in Jesus Christ
by John Coventry

Gospel Journey
by Ernest Ferlita

Kept Moments
by Gerhard E. Frost

Pilgrimage to Renewal
by Herb Brokering

Praying
by Robert Faricy

Our Story According to St. Mark
by William H. Barnwell

Songs of Suffering
by Nathan R. Kollar

The Breath of Life
by Ron DelBene

The Joy of the Psalms
by Herb and Mary Montgomery

Toward the Heart of God
by John Dalrymple

What Christians Believe
by Richard Harries